EX REME

For Roy

On living in the
intensity of the moment

Stephen L. Arrington

Extreme is a completely updated and fully expanded autobiography originally released as *Journey Into Darkness* (1992) by Huntington House Publishers. Those who have read that book will quickly realize that this is an entirely new work that goes far beyond the original text in both scope and definition. There are some excerpts from Stephen Arrington's youth series, *High on Adventure (I, II & III)*, which contribute to the book's message regarding the importance of right choices in life. A docu-drama based on *Journey into Darkness, "Out of the Night,"* won three first place awards, including a Gold Medal in two separate categories at Worldfest, a Gold Medal at the Christian Covenant Awards for Best Non-broadcast Christian Video of the Year, and a Silver Telly Award for filming and editing excellence. The DVD, *Journey Into Darkness*, a public broadcasting documentary on this story has aired in seventeen countries. Currently, Steve and Cindy Arrington have their own weekly television show *"High on Adventure,"* that airs worldwide on satellite and cable to one hundred and ten countries on Loma Linda Broadcasting Network, which is also available on the internet at www.llbn.tv.

These videos as well as Stephen Arrington's other documentaries and books are available through www.drugsbite.com. Note: *Journey Into Darkness*, after seven reprintings, is no longer available, as Huntington House Publishers has ceased doing business.

Many thanks to Walt and Ruth Barber and to Dr. Tim Elloway for reviewing the manuscript. Special appreciation to Kari Lambert, who though not an editor did an excellent job of catching many of my errors. If you find any that got past her careful eye, please so advise me.

Copyright © 2008 Stephen Arrington
Published by Drugs Bite, PO Box 3234, Paradise, CA 95967

Cover Design and text layout by Jonathan Gullery
Cover art by Andy Charles
Illustrations by Andy Charles,
visit www.andycharles.com regarding availability of his art
Illustrations by Margery Spielman, you can cmail hcr at spiclmanrccf@sbc.nct

Library of Congress Card Catalog Number
ISBN: 978-0-9799575-0-5

Dedicated to all those who think themselves lost. There is hope in knowing that shadows are defined by light—and that light is there for all of us.

Especially for my wife and lifelong companion, Cynthia Elizabeth Arrington. I could not have written this work without her love, support and adventurous spirit that daily teaches me about life, wonder and the magnificence of a shared existence.

EPIGRAPH

WARNING: THIS work is written in the intensity of the moment and contains true depictions of the criminal underworld and of life inside prison that may be disconcerting to some, but are necessary if I am to convey the magnitude of where bad choices can lead those who would dance the criminal waltz. Realizing that this work is designed to capture the attention of youths and young adults, as well as families, I have made every effort not to be too shocking, nor to use inappropriate language, while writing about the appalling and deplorable behavior where illegal drug use leads the reckless and the naive. Currently in the United States, the fastest growing rate of incarceration, per capita for a single group of people, is teenage girls. The USA has the world's largest prison system (per capita) in the industrialized world. This work is meant to reduce the flow of our youths and young adults into the prison system and for those already incarcerated to give them hope for the future.

Some names have been changed to protect the innocent. To effectively portray the essence of this true story some minor events have been moved within the timeline to prevent undo confusion for the reader. In addition, after twenty-five years, I cannot claim to remember the exact words in some conversations; however, the manuscript remains true to the character's intent and attitude at the time. This work is written from the mature perspective of the author who has grown as a person since the events that so shaped my life. I truly hope that none of my friends that appear in this work is offended by what they read, which is why most of their names have been changed. Instructor McNair is a real person (name-changed) who is sometimes given credit for statements and actions of other bomb disposal instructors. The intense and complex training program at Naval School Explosive Ordnance Disposal requires a battery of motivated instructors most of whom are colorful characters.

DANGEROUS REEF, SOUTH AUSTRALIA

*I need a volunteer to jump inside an experimental, completely trans-
parent Lexan shark cage. We are amongst the Great White Shark. Stephen
Arrington is an instant volunteer, just like he was with munitions in
Vietnam when deactivation was required.*

*As you read Steve's book, you will discover his sense of courage even as
it gets confused with a blind acceptance of orders—perhaps submission due
to an "overdose" of confidence. It is easy to abuse such people and Stephen
Arrington was taken advantage of and misguided. Imagine if I had asked
Steve to jump into a shark cage that did not work.*

*I feel good to have contributed to the recovery and success of this kind
human being. People should receive a second change when they have been
abused.* Jean-Michel Cousteau

In memory of Captain Jacques Yves Cousteau, June 11, 1910 –
June 25, 1997. When I was a child, he was my boyhood hero and
my role model. Later, he became my friend and employer. He, and
his son Jean-Michel, opened my world to incredible adventures
and made my youthful dreams an adult reality. The world will miss
Captain Cousteau, but it is a better place because of him.

FOREWORD

By James Walsh, Jr., Federal Prosecutor

M Y JOB is the prosecution of serious federal crimes—for the most part, narcotics crimes—and it brings me into contact with a broad cross-section of humanity. Most of those contacts are in court and very few of them are pleasant. So why am I writing introductory remarks for a book written by Stephen Arrington?

I first met Stephen in my professional capacity, as a narcotics prosecutor. He was there in court, in handcuffs, wearing a prison jumpsuit, looking somewhat dazed. Well he might, since he had been arrested by federal drug agents as part of one of the most celebrated narcotics undercover investigations of the past decade—the DeLorean Case, as it came to be known to most of the civilized world. Stephen Arrington's role in the events of that case was minor; he was the side-kick of Morgan Hetrick, the man who supplied the cocaine that John DeLorean bounced on his knee in the famous video tape.

Steve was processed in the usual way in the case. His lawyer made efforts on his behalf and eventually negotiated a plea agreement for him. He was convicted on his guilty plea and received a five-year term of imprisonment. He went off to prison and I continued with the prosecution of the case, never expecting to hear from him again.

It is one of the strange aspects of my job that I almost never see or hear again from people upon whom I have an impact. This is not surprising, for although the interaction that I have with them is a very memorable event in their lives, it is also usually the worst thing that has happened to them, and they don't want to relive it, and I don't either. When I do hear from one of "my people," it is usually because they have gotten out of jail and back into trouble—they are going around for another cycle of arrest, trial and prison.

You can easily imagine, then, how surprised and pleased I was to receive a telephone call from Steve one day several years later. He told me that he had done his time in prison and been released, and he was calling to invite me to attend an award ceremony being given by the Red Cross to recognize his successful effort to save a person from drowning in Long Beach. You see, Steve had been a diver in the Navy and had done several tours of duty in Vietnam. He told me that he had landed a job with the Cousteau Society as a diver and , wanted to have the Government's permission to travel with the Cousteau Society. Since he was still on parole, the government's agreement was necessary. It was one of the easier things that I have been asked to do in my job.

I went to the ceremony and was impressed with the friends of "Steve's who were there to help him celebrate the occasion. It is an unusual pleasure to be able to see tangible proof that someone who has descended into the underworld of drugs and danger can resurface, with his character intact, and make his way to a successful and fulfilling career. It is even more of a pleasure to see such a person be willing to share his experience with others in an effort to ensure that they won't have to make that full journey themselves.

A few years after Steve invited me to share in his award from the Red Cross he called again, this time to offer his services as a lecturer to civic groups and schools on the perils of the drug culture, gangs and prison. He knew that I was involved in a Boy Scout troop in the Long Beach area and asked if he could come and speak to the troop about his experiences. Now, anyone who has ever been involved in Boy Scouts can tell you how difficult it is to hold their attention for even a few minutes. Steve came to the meeting and held them spellbound for the better part of an hour as he described his own experiences, in prison and out. The message—that drugs and gangs lead to jail and perhaps even worse—is a message that can bear frequent retelling, but it comes most convincingly form someone who has "been there. It will never be told more convincingly to that audience of Boy Scouts.

So, while I can claim no credit for the resurrection of Stephen Arrington, I am pleased and flattered to have been a part of the publication of that project. The raw material was sound, and so the job was perhaps deceptively easy. Nevertheless, his story is an important example to make the point that you can go home again, if you really want to. He did, and we are richer for it.

> *"Human beings, by changing the inner attitudes of their*
> *minds, can change the outer aspects of their live, "*
> William James (1842-1910)

CONTENTS

*"Do not then train youth to learning by force or harshness,
but direct them to it by what amazes their minds so that you
may be better able to discover with accuracy the particular
beat of the genius of each,"* Plato 427-347 BC

INTRODUCTION

IN OCTOBER of 1982, I was abruptly thrown into a unique period of deep self-evaluation. There were few demands upon my time. I did not drive a car, own a telephone, pay bills, cook food, do laundry, visit friends or go anywhere at all. I was in a jail cell at Terminal Island Federal Prison. At the time, I was facing up to forty-five years behind bars for flying a quarter of a billion dollars worth of cocaine into the United States from Columbia. James Walsh, the Federal Prosecutor, in the John Z. DeLorean drug trial of 1982, determined that value. I was the pilot in what has been called the drug trial of the century. At the time, it was the largest known drug haul in American history. My only previous involvement in drug trafficking was four ounces of marijuana worth a couple of hundred dollars while I was in the Navy serving in Hawaii.

I never thought that I would wind up on the wrong side of crime. As a youth, I wanted to do good things with my life. I volunteered for military service right out of high school during the Vietnam Conflict and served four tours helping to rescue downed pilots off

15

the north coast of that war torn country. As a Navy Bomb Disposal Frogman, I had worked with the Secret Service, the CIA and with the ATF (Department of Alcohol, Tobacco and Firearms). When I started using marijuana, I misguidedly thought it a rather harmless drug, a weed. Yet this *harmless weed* hurled me into the dark under belly of the drug world. The criminal whirlwind that nearly destroyed my life is told in the intensity of the moment within these pages.

My involvement was forced, under the threat of a gun, but this is not offered as an excuse. Flaws in my character and moral fiber led me into that horrific situation. I deserved my punishment and determined during my sojourn in prison to make something good come out of my incredibly foolish criminal blunder.

Extreme is a journey of self-discovery. In this book, I will share what I have learned, both the good and the bad, from a full and adventurous life. Living on the edge even for the briefest moment captures the intensity of our existence and for an instant, it can be held in perfect suspension like peering into a revolving prism with thousands of facets each with a single meaningful reflection.

> *"The soul is dyed the color of its thoughts. Think only on those things that are in line with your principles and can bear the full light of day. The content of your character is your choice. Day by day, what you think, and what you do is who you become. Your integrity is your destiny…it is the light that guides your way,"* Heraclitus 535-475 BC

The path of the righteous is like the first gleam of dawn,
shining ever brighter till the full light of day. But the way of
the wicked is like deep darkness; they do not know what makes
them stumble. Proverbs 4:18-19

JUNGLES OF COLUMBIA, JUNE 1982

THE TWIN-ENGINE aircraft shutters in a hot downdraft as we fly over another jungle covered ridge at low altitude. We are below two thousand feet looking for a concealed runway. It is sweltering, hot and humid inside the narrow cockpit. The fuel gauges are bouncing on empty and we are lost. Stretch stares at a stained map then wiping sweat from his brow looks anxiously for a landmark and sees none that he recognizes. I thin the fuel mixture a tad more, which is causing the engines to run dangerously hot. Beneath us, the tropical rainforest offers no place to land. There are small farms hacked out of the dense jungle, but nothing resembling a clandestine airstrip.

Suddenly a weak whistle blares from the near continuous static of the radio, two long warbling highs followed by a short descending note.

Stretch grabs the microphone and whistles back, two long one short. They have seen us from the ground. "Del Norte, amigo, via Norte," urges a coarse Colombian voice. Stretch turns the wheel towards the north and quickly lowers the nose of the aircraft. We begin losing altitude as the small plane bucks into the wind surge coming over a sharp-edged ridge. Then crossing over a broad valley, I abruptly see patches of jungle in motion. Three trucks laced with foliage slowly move revealing a short dirt strip. We line up on the tiny strip. Stretch cuts power and pulls back on the stick as the twin engine Aztec slows and then quickly settles to the ground. Feeling the jar of solid earth beneath the wheels is a huge relief, but the emotion lasts only for a few moments. That touchdown alters my life forever. It is in that instant of time that I truly have become a criminal. Up until this moment, I have been somewhat able to deny the criminal bent my life has taken, but now it is a certain reality.

The Twin slows rapidly as the dirt and gravel drags at the plane's wheels. At the end of the runway stands a stout man with a large black moustache. He is wearing a New York Yankees' ball cap, a sweat stained khaki shirt, a bandolier of red shotgun cartridges draped over his shoulder and greasy jeans. He uses the double barrel shotgun in his hairy hand to wave us under a large Banyan-like tree. The engines rev loudly as we taxi beneath the broad green canopy and then we shut down the engines; after many hours of listening to the continuous roar of the propellers, it is startlingly quiet. I hear the creak of the engines dissipating heat, the squeak of the door as I open it, the screech of a tropical bird in the tree, and the stout man say, "You're late Gringos," then I step out into a world that has suddenly become very frightening and is forever altered.

The hot tropical air swelters with humidity as I feel rivulets of sweat running down my back. Armed men are gathering about the aircraft. A pick-up truck skids to a stop twenty feet away in a cloud of dust as several men jump down from the back bed. Everywhere there are guns, but the men are in a buoyant mood. They laugh, exchange words in Spanish and smile at us. Yet the smiles do not extend to their cold hard eyes. They are hardened criminals, robbers, smugglers and murderers. The worst of it all is that they consider me to be on their side. They call me amigo, hombre and hey gringo mixed with many Spanish words I do not know. I have never felt so lost or alone in my entire life, suddenly, without a doubt; I know that a prison cell is lurking in my future. My next thought startles me in its intensity. It is a silent plea, "*Please let the jail cell be in America, not down here in this crude and horrible place.*"

"Character is like a tree and reputation like its shadow. The shadow is what we think of it; the tree is the real thing,"
Abraham Lincoln 1809-1865

Adversity introduces a man to himself. Anonymous

Chapter 1

MAUI, HAWAII, JANUARY 1988

THE ORB of the sun rises slowly above the ocean's horizon in a blue sky chased with bulbous clouds. The radiant sunlight shimmers softly on the shifting surface of the deep blue water. A light trade wind blows from the Hawaiian Island of Maui carrying a delicate scent of tropical flowers as its passage gently ripples the ocean's surface. The sunlight plays on the restless water casting a soft sheen of metallic colors: radiant yellows and fiery reds. I am drifting on the water in a black rubber-hulled Zodiac preparing for another glorious day of diving with Humpback whales. My job as a chief diver and expedition leader for The Cousteau Society has taken me to many exotic places. For three incredible weeks, we have been filming the giant Humpbacks during their breeding season.

Whales are the largest creatures on our planet, yet we know so little about them. They are highly intelligent mammals, yet whale thoughts are a mystery to us. Their communication covers a complex range of intricate squeaks, massive grunts and deep bellows that blend into a cascade of submarine music. During the breeding season bulls vocalize to charm and captivate the cows and possibly to claim submerged territory. Whale melodies are mournful songs that dance at each end of the musical scale with prolonged, penetrating squeaks and squeals that descend into deep rumbling lows. Sometimes the songs echo with a twittering, throat-clearing resonance like a massive cat purring with the intensity of a giant foghorn.

Unexpectedly the Zodiac's rubber pontoon upon which I am sitting begins to pulsate softly echoing the first notes of a Humpback's song. Water has a density that transmits subsurface sound waves with far more speed and intensity than sounds generated in a less dense air atmosphere.

Quickly donning a dive mask, I peer eagerly over the side. Deep below the rubber boat, I see the enormous hulking silhouette of a bull whale. He is hovering in a head downward position. The leviathan's dynamic energy is fully concentrated on singing his passionate love song.

Grabbing fins and a snorkel, I quietly slip over the side. The cool water resonates with alien, untamed music. Taking three quick breathes to purge off excess carbon dioxide, I then take a final deep inhalation; packing my lungs with oxygen. Jackknifing downward to aid my vertical descent, I begin swimming silently down into the deep blue water. My heart thuds with eager anticipation. I, a small human, am descending towards a ninety-thousand-pound bull whale during the lust of the breeding season...sweet!

Plunging downward with vigorous strokes of my fins the Humpback looms majestically within the narrow confines of my dive mask. The whale's song is a commanding, all surrounding, living presence. I feel the music washing over and through my body penetrating even into my bones. The effect is like holding a giant throbbing tuning fork in both hands in an atmosphere where gravity does not exist. Nothing distorts or hinders each perfect tone as I feel my skeleton softly vibrating in accord with the bull's musical serenade. One of the wonders of whale harmonics is that their songs are a true physical force. Submerged, I can feel the leviathan melodies as soft, tickling vibrations that play against, and inside, my entire torso. The deep notes echo powerfully through my lungs and sinuses, the high-pitched squeaks and squeals send long quivering vibrations the length of my bones, while the softer gurgling notes bounce against my skin in a trembling cadence that feels like a body-hugging tickle involving thousands of non-existent bubbles. Swimming downward into an ocean suddenly alive with dynamic sounds and rhythmic vibrations is like descending inside one of the larger pipes of a giant cathedral organ.

Kicking harder I sink impatiently deeper. The whale's head-down position allows me to approach unseen. For an instant, I wonder if the whale is bouncing its song off the ocean floor to enhance its reverberation and range. The majestic tail hovers forty feet beneath the shimmering surface. Rays of slanting sunlight filtering down into the depths are bent into long waving beams that flicker in harmony with the undulating surface water. The sea-softened light washes across the giant Humpback painting its body in the gently glimmering colors of the atmospheric sunrise unfolding above us.

I yearn to reach out and touch the giant mammal. I am like a mouse in tall grass wondering at the massive passage of an elephant only a few feet away. One does not purposefully startle a creature that weighs over five hundred times more than you do. Swimming just yards away from the giant bull, I wonder what it would be like to lay a hand on a singing whale. In awe, I can only imagine the incredible power behind each perfect note as it causes this submarine section of the vast ocean to dance in harmony with its song.

Abruptly the giant bull becomes aware of my presence. I am descending past its pectoral fin when I see the whale's huge eye rotating in my direction. The pupil is the size of a softball. Seeing my tiny reflection in its dark surface, I marvel at the wild intelligence that is regarding me... unexpectedly the whale's song ends on a deep rumbling low. It is an ominous sound that seems to hover somewhere between majestic disappointment at my interruption and royal anger that I, such a tiny creature, would dare to intrude. The sudden silence and lingering glare causes me to shudder and for a moment, fear freezes my fins into immobility. I feel so very tiny and vulnerable in the whale's massive presence.

The whale's gigantic tail begins to move ponderously. It passes just mere feet away, large and majestic. With graceful, yet powerfully increasing beats of its fluke, the huge leviathan descends trailing a rising steam of bubbles that glitter softly as they pass through a wandering ray of soft sunlight in the dark gloom of deep water. A wake of depth-chilled water rushes upward from the passage of the whale. The cold water is like a gusting winter wind that washes over me instantly sweeping away the magic of the moment. Then, as if in passage with the Humpback, a cloud passes in front of the morning sun. In the cloud's footsteps walks a long, lingering shadow that casts the chilled depths into gloomy twilight. Abruptly alone, low on air, I look up to the darkening surface and realize I am deep–much deeper than I thought! Caught up in the magic of the moment, I forgot to pay attention to my depth. The surface is seventy feet away and I feel a thudding panic as my heart races in sudden fear. I begin swimming urgently upwards, but the world of light seems so far away. I am cold and abruptly so very afraid.

Unexpectedly from the dim corridors of my memory, stalks another instant of near absolute panic. It comes with a chilling feeling of that initial remembered moment when I first woke up inside a federal prison. It was that instant of time, passing from deep sleep to a brisk awakening in the damp darkness of a jail cell. In wild panic, I had hoped with all my might that it was all just a bad dream—that the guns and the handcuffs of the night before were just imaginings of a bad night's tossing and turning. Then a cell door slams and from down the corridor, I hear an inmate cursing and know that the nightmare I so feared is a living reality and I am caught within its icy grasp. My usually hopeful and buoyant spirit collapses into a dark hole of knowing that my mistakes were real. There would be no escaping the dungeon-like certainty of concrete walls, steel bars and inmate brutality that was now to be my world into the distant foreseeable future.

Swimming vigorously upwards, momentarily caught between two worlds, one of shadow and the other of light, I remember the dark gloom of that prison cell. I think how it was such a lonely place where there was little music and no laughter without an underlying shadow of cruel intent. To be in prison is to give up so many things. I did not see a sunrise or a sunset for almost a year. Immersion in water was something I could just daydream about and showers were a place of fear where primal cruelty preyed upon the naked weak. There were no long walks amongst trees or happy times with friends and family. At first, I was completely lost and alone. Then I realized it did not have to be that way. At three o'clock in the morning, four months after my incarceration, I got down on my knees and gave what I thought was now an all but wasted life to Jesus Christ. In the darkness of a jail cell, I took my first step back into the world of light. In the confinement of a prison, I found my first real hope of freedom. My expectations for the future were not bright. The prosecutor was threatening a hope-dashing sentence of forty-five years to life, yet somehow I just knew that if I trusted in the Lord, things would work out according to His will because I was no longer just a wasted soul in a prison cell.

Twenty feet from the surface, I suddenly know that I will make it. It is also when the cloud's shadow passes from the sun. Ascending into dazzling morning light, I inhale deeply the fragrant tropical air. For a full minute, I lay on the surface breathing deeply and basking in the morning sun. Climbing into the rubber Zodiac, I take off my fins and mask then look towards our charter boat named *Kai Kekoa* (Hawaiian for Ocean Warrior). The cabin cruiser flying a green Cousteau Society flag is underway and motoring towards a rainbow trailing a rainsquall off Maui. I think about the odyssey of adventure that is now my life. As a chief diver for The Cousteau Society, I am one of the leaders of a ten-year round-the-world expedition of discovery. I am a free man basking under a warm tropical sun in an island paradise and deeply in love with a woman that I will soon marry.

The dark times are now just a memory though they still occasionally shadow my sleep. It is almost unimaginable that only five short years earlier my life had hit rock bottom. Then a judge seeing a changed man in manacles and chains standing before him graciously gave me a shortened sentence of only five years. Later as I strived to be a model inmate, he would reduce my sentence to three years. Good behavior and a right focus in prison encouraged the authorities to release me five months early.

Back in society, I was a wounded person, determined to do right and eager to help others. I took a path that led to an incredible offer by Captain Jacques and Jean-Michel Cousteau to join their team despite my being an ex-felon who did not even speak French. My probation officer cut my special probation from three years to time served so I could freely leave the country with the Cousteau's expedition teams.

In prison my awareness of who I was and who I wanted to be had changed. My Christian focus while incarcerated led first to a modest series of wonders, then to true life-saving miracles. I remembered the awe I felt at becoming the chief engineer of an inmate fire crew. Leaving the prison in a fire truck with the siren wailing, the red lights blazing and the guards rushing to raise the barrier as I hurled down the road in the driver's seat. We saved lives on the desert highways and in the process, our own lives were forever changed and again given meaning and purpose. It is a rare gift to be an inmate entrusted with life-saving responsibilities. My Christian awareness tied to a sincere trust in the Lord's love opened these incredible opportunities to a once wounded and tortured soul.

Sitting in the Zodiac on the threshold of five more years of incredible adventure with The Cousteau Society, I have no idea that even greater Christian adventures are rushing at me from the near future. I pause to send up a prayer of thanks then hear the crackle of radio static. Cindy is calling on the walkie-talkie. "Where have you been?" She asks. "Jean-Michel is eager to find whales."

It pleases me greatly that Cindy is here to share in this adventure with the Cousteau Society. She would be my partner in many more adventures to come, but I did not know that yet as I reached for the radio to answer. Suddenly I feel the rubber pontoon vibrating again. The whale song begins on a high note as I respond to Cindy's call, "Tell Jean-Michel he does not have to go far. There's a big guy looking for love under my rubber boat."

"There is only one admirable form of the imagination; the imagination that is so intense that it creates a new reality, that it makes things happen," Sean O'Faolain 1900-1991

Photo Arrington, Pipeline
Note surfboard and barely visible head of surfer being "sucked over the falls!"

*Life sometimes gives you the test before you've
had a chance to study the lesson.* Anonymous

Chapter 2

OAHU, HAWAII, JANUARY 1979

S URPRISINGLY THE day my life shifted in a truly negative way would begin on another beautiful morning in Hawaii on the North Shore
of Oahu. I am with three new friends on a surf safari. Bill's battered
black Volkswagen bus lumbers out of a light rain on the two-lane
road to the North Shore. Through the beat of the windshield wip-
ers, I see the morning sun painting brilliant shafts of light across the
tropical hillsides. About us, lush sugarcane fields stretch for miles.
The trade winds are blowing amongst the sugarcane stocks rippling
the tall grassy fields like an undulating green sea. The cane's spindly white tops bend to the insistent winds resembling ocean spray
on restless green waters.

The interior of the Volkswagen bus is crammed with four surfers,
breakfast debris from a Taco Bell, an assortment of towels (in various
states of cleanliness) and a very excited large black mongrel dog
named Boats. The dog's face is jammed ear-deep inside an empty,
salsa-stained, burrito bag. "Hey Boats," I get his attention with a
tortilla chip, "want this boy?"

He sniffs and then chomps in what appears to be a single motion.

I wipe a smear of dog saliva off my hand and on to Bill's towel while he stares intently out the front windshield. For Bill driving is a challenging experience. He takes a wet corner too fast putting a serious tilt on the minibus as the blown shock absorbers bottom out. Everyone inside leans hard right, particularly Boats who is actually attempting to get closer to Greg's soft taco.

"Get off me you big lug," complains Greg. He tries to push the over-sized dog away foolishly allowing the taco to come within muzzle range.

"Hey Bill, your clod dog just ate my taco." He stares at the tiny wedge of shredded taco left in his hand, and then takes a closer look at his wet fingers. "Is that drool? Oh wow, I just got dog-slimed."

I pass him Bill's towel.

As the Volkswagen tops a rise between two sprawling sugarcane fields, we get our first view of the distant coastline. There is a major swell pounding the North Shore. Everyone leans forward for a better view, including Boats, who snuffs at the front seat for any more unguarded treats.

"Looks big," Bill, states the obvious downshifting into second gear, saving the razor thin brakes for accident avoidance; a shutter vibrates the length of the Volkswagen as it decelerates. The front tires have been out of alignment ever since he tried taking the VW bus up a homemade wooden skateboard ramp.

Staring out the cracked windshield from the backseat, while avoiding the dog's wagging tail, I see large rolling waves and lots of windblown white water. "It's too big," I offer nervously from the back seat.

"Scary," says Greg voicing my fears. "I'm in," he adds enthusiastically.

"*Woof*," Boats joins our conversation. I hear him snuffing about the front seat followed by a wet chewing sound.

"I think your dog is eating something," Greg says suspiciously.

"Nothing up here to eat," replies Bill, "Keno already wasted all our groceries."

Keno, a large Hawaiian sitting in the passenger seat pretends to be offended, but then belches contentedly and shakes taco crumbs from his Local Motion T-shirt.

Greg attempts to take a closer look inside Boat's mouth just as the dog chokes and coughs wetly. A heavy, moist cloud of white bits sprays his face from just inches away. Yuck," he complains loudly then quickly scrubs at his face with Bill's towel.

Sniffing at one of the white bits, I solve the chewing mystery, "It's Keno's surfboard wax."

"Oh man!" Keno is upset, "that was a brand new bar."

I rub Boat's ears then use Bill's towel to wipe the rest of the wax and drool debris off his broad muzzle then flick the towel into the back of the VW.

Ten minutes later, we arrive at Laniakia Beach Park and everyone unloads out onto the dirt parking lot. The surf is a lot bigger than we hoped as we stare in awkward silence. None of us wants to admit that the big surf is truly terrifying. The waves are over two stories tall and crashing down beyond the barrier reef with the distant sound of rolling thunder.

"I think I am going to need a bigger board," quips Bill.

"What do you think," I ask Keno, "is it too big?" I am having serious reservations about paddling out.

"You guys just need some artificial courage," guffaws the big Hawaiian. He lights up a marijuana joint, and after a massive drag, passes it to Bill.

I first tried marijuana during the Vietnam Conflict. I did not like its mind numbing effect in a war environment and made a positive decision to avoid other service members that were using the drug. Later, back in the states, I experimented on occasion usually when I was already under the influence of beer or wine. Now my military career as a bomb disposal frogman was far too important to me. I did not want to do anything foolish that might jeopardize what I had worked so hard to achieve. I enjoyed my assignment to EODMUONE (Explosive Ordnance Disposal Mobile Unit One), out of West Loch, Hawaii. Being a water-oriented person, living on an island paradise, I naturally took up surfing. Now I am surprised to discover that my three new surfer friends use marijuana. Bill is a support diver with our command and Greg is a bomb disposal technician just like me.

Greg chokes on the harsh smoke then offers the joint to me. "Go ahead," he mumbles. Seeing my hesitation, he adds, with smoke leaking from his lips, "It is okay, over half of the command smokes weed."

"Hurry up," Bill complains, "the roach is going to go out, man."

Taking the joint, I notice that the tip is brown and wet with saliva from two other people. Keno strikes a match touching the flame to the end of the blackened joint. "Do it brah," he urges.

The joint touches my lips and I take a pull. The acid smoke immediately burns my throat and lungs. I quickly exhale the harsh fumes as Bill snatches the joint from my hand and takes a drag.

The joint passes from hand-to-hand, then back to me. It is now barely half-an-inch in length. My reaction is to throw it away, but Keno stops me.

"Don't waste it, dude," the Hawaiian has his big hand on mine, "take another drag only this time hold the smoke in."

As I begin to inhale the flame abruptly runs down the rolling paper burning my lip and then a smoking ember flies into my mouth.

"Ouch!" I shout pawing at my singed lips.

"What a light-weight," laughs Keno knuckling me in the chest. Then he and Greg grab their surfboards and run down to the water.

"Better hurry," urges Bill wiping his hands on the towel. Then he sniffs suspiciously at his fingers, "Wow, hope that wasn't something I ate." He runs down and plunges into the swirling water. Feeling clumsy and uncoordinated, I nervously follow. He dunks his board under the first oncoming wave of white water then porpoises out the backside. Because of my muddled mental condition, I have forgotten to wax-up my surfboard. Without the traction of a fresh coat of wax, the white water immediately washes me off the slick board. By the time I recover, my friends are fifty yards ahead of me.

Alone I paddle hard to catch up. The surf looks even bigger from the flat perspective of lying on a surfboard. As I get further out the surf gets larger and louder.

In my pot-fogged brain, alarms are going off. An oncoming wave breaks with a thunderous sound as it cascades into a mass of turbulent white water. Thrashing my way into the on-rushing wall of water, it instantly flushes me from my board. I surface choking and spitting salt water to see the other guys paddling frantically up the face of a two-story wave. Urgently wiping salt water from my eyes, I begin paddling furiously. Reaching the wall of water just before it pitches, I wildly paddle up the face and then plunge down the backside. A spray of saltwater clouds my vision. Then I see another huge wave rushing toward shore. Already it is beginning to pitch as my friends reach the top and disappear over the back. The big breaker is pulling the surface water into itself increasing the size and velocity of the wave. Aided by the on-rushing surface current feeding the massive wave I sprint up the turbulent nearly vertical face. The thick lip throws outwards as I fight my way up and see the tip of my board almost punching through the crest. I feel the thick breaker pitching as it pulls the surrounding water and its small human cargo irresistibly backwards. I struggle against the wave's sucking pull thrusting my arms deep as I paddle with all my might then just barely break free. Out of breath, exhausted, I slide rubber-armed down the backside of the breaker and that is when I see that there is yet another wave coming. It is only a few feet taller than the last one, but it is much thicker and it is already breaking. I watch a building-sized wall of white water swallow my friends. Taking a deep breath, I push my board away and frantically dive for the bottom, but do not get very far.

Because of the marijuana stupor, I have now forgotten to remove the leash from my leg. The surfboard floating on the surface is keeping me from getting very deep. I turn to free the Velcro tab from my ankle just as the wall of water crashes down. It is like being slugged with a giant hydraulic sledgehammer. The sharp impact pounds the air from my lungs. The surfboard leash snaps taunt as it drags my body wildly spinning in its wake like a lost kite in a gale. Soberly I realize I could drown in the next minute or two. Instantly I wish with all my might that I had not gotten stoned. My tortured lungs are carrying the burden of that damaging smoke. Bubbles swirl about me, as I am drug violently through the raging submarine turbulence. I am out of air and beginning to panic when the rubber surfboard leash breaks slowing my horizontal underwater journey. Struggling upwards, I barely make it back to the surface. In the frothy water, I inhale deeply then wiping stinging saltwater from my eyes, I see another huge wave descending upon me.

I must have taken four or five trips on the underwater subway that morning. Finally, completely exhausted, I made it back to the beach after catching my surfboard going back out through the surf in a rip current. Standing in the shallow water with the surge sucking around my ankles I thought it the most foolish day of my life—actually, it was just the beginning of a series of stupid mistakes.

The most important thing I remember about that day is not the size of the surf, but rather that I had stood on the threshold of two possible futures...and made the wrong choice. I allowed peer pressure to push me onto a different path in life. I would eventually become a hostage to marijuana. Over the next two years, I was a first-hand witness to the corruption of Stephen Arrington, yet argued against my obvious downward slide because my ego shielded me from truly recognizing that I had just taken a huge step towards becoming a loser. Marijuana would corrupt my values and make it a lot easier for me to deceive myself. Later in a federal prison, I would learn one of the biggest lessons of my life. The first person a liar must try to deceive is himself. The liar has to justify living the lie.

Buy the truth and do not sell it; get wisdom, discipline and understanding.   Proverbs 23:23

Photo Arrington
Revelstoke with a curling wave painted on hood.

"Everything that deceives may be said to enchant," Plato

Chapter 3

OAHU, HAWAII, JANUARY 1979

A MARINE GUARD waves the black VW bus through the gate at Barbers
Point Naval Air Station on the southwest shore of Oahu. A few
minutes later, we arrive at the Officers Beach, which is where I had
left my Chevy truck for the day. I fetch my surfboard from the top
of the Volkswagen, rub Boats' ears and am about to say goodbye to
the guys when Bill casually reaches his hand out the driver's window and slips something into my T-shirt pocket.

"What's that?" I ask dipping my fingers into the pocket to discover
a fat joint.

"A present," laughs Bill, "something to play with tonight."

"Wait," I instantly panic, "I don't want to get busted with this on
base."

"Don't worry about it," Bill grins, "this is Hawaii man. There are
more people smoking dope here than anywhere else in the whole
United States. The cops hardly even bother to write a ticket for it.
The stuff is just a misdemeanor…it's nothing, man."

"But we're on base," I lament.

He pats my shirt pocket, "Know where I got the bag that joint
came from?" Bill leers as he answers his own question, "Mr. Gonzales,
our Executive Officer."

"The Command X.O?" I am shocked!

"He's a Vietnam vet. All the guys who served in "The Nam" smoke weed, excepting maybe for Red Charlie who's too straight for anything like that. Heck, you did time in Vietnam didn't you?"

"It's where I first tried pot," I admit.

"Well you're living in Hawaii now, the pot capital of the world. Trust me, no one's going to get excited about a little bit of weed." I hear the Volkswagen's transmission grind as Bill shifts into first, pops the clutch and then the black van lurches away.

I watch the battered mini-bus accelerate out of the parking lot trailing a thin wake of blue exhaust from its rusted muffler. My mind is rampant with conflicting thoughts and one very big temptation. Digging keys from the front pocket of my jeans, I walk up to the truck, unlock the backdoor and step inside.

Revelstoke is a one-of-a-kind truck. It is a high cub van. The front looks like a typical Chevy van, but the back is a box, six feet four inches tall, eight feet wide, and twelve feet long. The box part is my home and I am living a rather unique mobile lifestyle. Revelstoke is the name of the small Canadian railroad town where my grandfather was born. I liked the word, which for me meant *Revel* or revelry, which equates to a celebration of fun and *stoke* or stoked, surfer slang for something very pleasing or way cool.

I bungee the surfboard to the ceiling over the bed, which makes it the first thing I see in the morning when I wake up making it easier to plan my day's activities. The wooden interior of Revelstoke resembles the captain's cabin on an old sailing ship. The polished floor is dowelled and pegged oak plank. The walls are varnished mahogany and the ceiling is covered with a multi-shaded red cedar. The wood insulates the interior from outside sounds and helps to keep the inside cooler on hot days. The dresser and kitchen counter top are fine-grained teak hand-oiled and rubbed smooth. The bathroom has a small one-person hot tub (a large converted laundry sink), true luxury for a nomadic surfer. Clear aromatic cedar lines the walls of the bathroom and closet. The inside of Revelstoke smells like a rain forest, particularly on rainy days when the moist air brings out the fragrant scent of the exotic woods. There is a lot of shiny brass about including a porthole that looks out over the cab of the van. In various niches there are a variety of green houseplants, mostly hanging ferns, creeping ivy, delicate mosses and a couple of stunted bonsai maple trees about a decade old. In the cedar ceiling, two stained glass skylights wash the interior with warm color-tinted sunlight. I lay down on the couch, which folds out into a large comfortable bed and hit two switches turning on the stereo and pre-amp. Hawaiian slack-key music begins to play softly from fourteen independent speakers recessed into the varnished wooden walls and ceiling.

I pull the joint from my pocket, sniff at its putrid odor and then lay there staring at it.

I built Revelstoke while attending the U.S. Navy's Bomb Disposal School in Indian Head, Maryland. The memory of the truck's long conversion into a custom mobile home takes me back to one of the most important and trying periods of my life. It is August 1975, I am attempting to fulfill a childhood dream. I am a recent arrival at the Naval Explosive Ordnance Disposal (EOD) School with the very big hope of becoming a bomb disposal frogman. It is the first day of pool training and I am swimming frantically.

Taking a desperate breath of air, I quickly peer underwater and see that Hank is a good two body-lengths ahead of me. Not surprising, Hank, a Navy SEAL attempting to convert over to Explosive Ordnance Disposal, is in superb physical condition. I lunge upwards for another urgent gulp of air, but then the twenty-pound weight belt strapped firmly around my waist drags me immediately back underwater.

The pool is one hundred-twenty feet long, sixty feet wide and twenty-four feet deep. At the wall, Hank does a quick flip turn despite his twenty pounds of lead baggage and then shoots past me underwater going the other way. I hit the wall and awkwardly push off. Surfacing for another breath I hear my team cheering me on and then I am back underwater all too aware of the wild thumping of my heart and of the pain inside my chest from not enough oxygen. Hank touches the distant pool edge as his teammate dives over him into the water. Too many seconds later I touch the pool's edge and hear one of my teammates scream as he launches over me with his own twenty-pound cargo of lead ballast. The instructors have divided our class of thirty bomb disposal candidates into two relay teams and thanks to me; my side is already falling behind. The losers get to do fifty push-ups before the whole class goes on a three mile run through the forest.

Exhausted, I watch Hank propel himself up and out of the pool with a single push of his brawny arms. I settle for a one legged lift-up as I struggle to get out of the water, then pass off my heavy weight belt to the next frog candidate in line. Water flows from my nose to the wet cement deck as I watch the lead-laden swimmers laboring across the pool, then I feel the subtle probing of a worrisome thought. It is my lifeguard training asserting itself. All of us are standing at one end of a very long pool and the lead weighted swimmers are lumbering towards the other end. The pool is twenty-four feet deep for serious diver training. I decide to voice my concern to our instructor. "Excuse me, Instructor McNair."

Master Chief Gunner's Mate McNair glares in my direction then looks up my name on his clipboard, "What do you want Candidate Arrington?"

"Don't you think I should maybe stand at the other end of the pool…just in case someone gets in trouble?" I ask hopefully. Perhaps he will notice that I am thinking ahead by doing a little potential problem prevention. Instructor McNair is from the Deep South and is strongly opinionated. He has not yet allowed that the confederacy may have actually lost the Civil War. He has a lanky build with deceptively strong ropey muscles and quick reflexes. His mind is agile and crafty like a predator. McNair can mentally plunge to the depths of a problem and tackle the solution, which usually involves punishment exercise for one or more of us unfortunate students.

"Are you planning on being the class troublemaker?" The tall instructor glares at me over his clipboard. McNair is wearing mirrored sunglasses and a blue ball cap even though we are inside an indoor training facility. He looks less than friendly...kind of like a rattlesnake eyeing a fat rodent blundering down a path.

"Just trying to help..." my words fade under the reptilian glare behind those reflective sunglasses.

"The purpose of this exercise is to see if you half-witted EOD candidates can swim with lead baggage and hopefully have enough brain activity to drop the weight belt before getting into trouble," Master Chief McNair lowers the clipboard so he can lean right into my face. From just inches away, I get an up-close view of my pale reflection in his aviator sunglasses, "Go to the back of the line and give me fifty pushups, clown." My reflection in his sunglasses gets quickly smaller as I scurry rapidly backwards.

At the rear of the line, Hank watches me drop down on the wet concrete deck for my penalty pushups. "Hooyah," he growls, which is a frogman shout of aggression for participating in physical or combat training. He drops into the prone position alongside me rapidly firing off four-dozen pushups followed by two one-arm ones. Apparently, he does not like to see anyone do punishment exercise alone or maybe it is his SEAL (Sea Air and Land) training asserting itself. SEAL's are into push-ups in a big way.

Wiping both hands on my wet shorts, I peer over the shoulders of my teammates and see that the fourth set of swimmers is now laboring across the water. Suddenly at mid-pool, the trailing swimmer begins to frantically dogpaddle. He squeaks, gurgles loudly then disappears beneath the surface in a froth of wildly waving arms.

I do not remember running past the other guys as I dive headfirst into the pool. Through the blur of looking underwater, I see the potential drownee desperately clawing upwards as he sinks rapidly towards the bottom. I swim frantically to mid-pool, do a jack-knife dive, and plunge downward. I am halfway-down when Hank catches up with me. It is also when I notice that I am winded and desperate for a breath of air. I am about to abort and go back up, figuring that Hank can finish the rescue when the drowning candidate comes clawing upwards minus his weight belt. Hank and I each grab an arm and head upwards with him. On the surface, we assist the coughing man to the side of the pool where Instructor McNair is angrily waiting. "Hey numbskull," he demands of the unfortunate student, "what's with the drowning routine? Why didn't you drop the weight belt sooner?"

"I guess I wasn't thinking," laments the young man choking up a mouthful of chlorinated water; a free-swinging strand of snot hangs from his nose.

McNair glares at the young man then shakes his head. "Frogmen, particularly us bomb disposal types, always think clearly particularly in emergencies or people around us die. Obviously you aren't cut from that kind of fabric young man." McNair consults his clipboard. "You're Hopkins right?" he asks sternly.

"Yes sir," he looks up fearfully and nods; the snot strand commands my attention, as it swings in sync with the motion of his head. He is probably dreading some serious punishment exercise, but McNair shocks us all.

"Do not refer to me as Sir. I am only to be addressed as Instructor McNair or Gunner McNair by my friends and superiors. In any case go clean out your locker."

A look of total shock descends upon the young man's face, "Don't I get a second chance?" he pleads.

"Not possible," McNair states flatly, "this ain't an elementary school recess problem. If that is what they taught you in public school then they did you a disservice. Explosive devices never give bomb disposal men any second chances. You either succeed the first time or fail spectacularly." McNair pauses and then in a low gravelly voice says, "Go on kid, you weren't meant for this job."

From the low perspective of the water at the pool's edge, I stare dumbfoundedly. Gaining acceptance to attend EOD School is a long and arduous path. The sad eyed guy at the side of the pool is already out.

We have been together as a class for just under a month. Our first two weeks of training were at Red Stone Arsenal in Huntsville, Alabama for Chemical Warfare instruction. Then we were transferred to NAVSCH EOD for orientation, advanced physical training and general academic testing. We had already lost two other students from the grueling academics in Core Basics.

McNair's voice pulls me back to the moment as he growls, "What are you waiting for, Hopkins?"

Hopkins is a shattered man. He climbs out of the pool and with his feet slapping wetly on the concrete floor walks dejectedly through the locker-room double doors. I watch the twin doors swing back and forth several times in a squeaking diminishing arc and then they are still. It is silent on the pool deck except for the gentle slap of the water against the side of the pool.

I look from the doors to see that Instructor McNair is glaring at me, "Arrington, who told you and your water rodent buddy that you could get into my pool?"

Hank and I glance at each other, but neither of us is willing to voice an answer. The locker room doors are looming very large behind Instructor McNair.

"Never mind," orders McNair, "you two can fetch my weight belt."

After the morning's pool training and a full load of punishment push-ups, sit-ups and pull-ups, Instructor McNair takes the class out for our three mile run through a forest alongside the Potomac River. Jogging through the trees three abreast on a dirt road, I continue to ponder my recent rescue fiasco. Very few of us frogman candidates can expect to graduate. The dropout/failure rate usually takes about seventy to eighty percent of the class. The few remaining graduates will get to join the Navy's elite Explosive Ordnance Disposal Teams and be able to participate in extraordinarily challenging adventures. When not involved as part of America's frontline of defense, bomb disposal frogmen work with NASA's space program recovering re-entry vehicles, deploy with Secret Service teams to protect domestic and foreign Heads of State, participate in super-secret CIA operations and are involved in leading-edge marine research programs. A frog's normal work week can include mini-adventures such as sky diving from very high or very low altitudes, locking-out (to exit through an airlock) of submarines underwater, scuba diving to survey sunken wrecks, blowing up various objects in creative ways and touring the world in conjunction with high-tech military operations. All of these mission profiles can be life threatening, which is why the command structure at the Explosive Ordnance Disposal School is going to make sure that no one graduates from our class who cannot be absolutely depended upon to think clearly in an emergency. It is startling for me to realize that I have just dramatically revealed I am capable of failing that trust.

As I listen to the cadence of our boots pounding along the dusty road, I think about another pair of boots. The ones attached to the feet of Hopkins who has just washed out of our class on the very first day of pool training. He is probably waiting in the administration department for orders back to the fleet. Hopkin's blunder involved overlooking the obvious...not an optimistic statement regarding someone attempting to defuse high explosives. My failure was more subtle...half way down in the pool, I was ready to abort the rescue. In the clear water of the swimming pool, I would have had a second chance to swim down and get my teammate. In the open ocean, I probably would not get a second chance. A poorly conceived first effort on my part in the open ocean or in a dark river could lead to a terminal teammate.

In the rescue attempt, I failed because I had gotten mind-locked. Running along the pool's side deck would have been much faster than my frantic out-of-breath swim. From the height advantage of the side deck, I could have seen Hopkin's exact location beneath the water, and been able to take a deep breath before diving in thus reaching him much faster. This would have given me more time underwater if needed to release his weight belt and help him to the surface.

What was I thinking just before I dove into the water? I wonder.

The answer hits me with the mental impact of a speeding freight train. My last thought just before the big plunge was that this is my chance to look good over the rest of the class. I even recall that I wanted to make sure my racing dive was impressive for McNair. It is such a startling thought that I do not immediately know what to with it. Am I that shallow? I mentally cringe as I realize that McNair probably saw right through my little drama.

We are nearing the end of the run as I cautiously glance over at McNair noting he is not even breaking a sweat or breathing faster than normal.

"You eyeballing me, Arrington?" he snarls edging closer to me.

I know there is not any point in denying the obvious, "Yes sir, Instructor McNair."

"What's going on in that hard little head of yours, Numbskull?"

"That I really screwed up, Instructor McNair," the answer comes without thought, but there is still more truth to it than I am currently willing to admit to myself.

"Really?"

Am I imagining it or is McNair almost cracking a smile?

"Running kind of airs out the old brain pan doesn't it?"

"Yes sir, Instructor McNair," I grin in a friendly way with my liking for the man growing by the second.

"Do you think I dropped Hopkins because he tried to drown on me?"

Yes, I think to myself letting my grin get hesitantly a little bigger.

"Nope, I dropped Hopkins because that boy is an accident looking for a place to happen. He is the kind of guy who always gets someone else hurt. The drowning bit just saved him the anguish of suffering through any more of my training than was necessary. I knew he was going to be history just by the way he reluctantly got into the water. Amazing, squeamish around water and he thinks he wants to be a frogman."

McNair leans a little closer and taps my chest with a leathery, boney finger, "Want to know a secret? I am going to be darn surprised if you make it through this class, Arrington."

"Not make it?" I echo fearfully, my recent grin hanging in a shambles.

"Yeah, that's what I said. In EOD, we are team players. Everything is a combined effort. We work together." McNair's sunglasses are doing that reflective thing again, "I think your favorite team is you and your stupid ego. That's not going to last long around here."

I could not think of an answer to such a cutting question. We are approaching the chow hall and McNair is about to call an end to the run.

"Arrington," he growls, "when the class falls out for chow, why don't you take that ego of yours around the forest loop again and try to wear it down some."

"Yes sir...I mean yes, Instructor McNair." The added punishment feels almost welcome. While the rest of the class falls into line at the chow hall, I take off for a second loop. I do not miss the sound of a pair of boots running behind me. There is no way that I am going to turn around and let Instructor McNair catch me *eyeballing* him a second time. The sound of the running boots keep gaining on me and finally pull alongside. I glance over to see the radiance of Hank's beacon-like grin.

"Mind if I tag along?" he asks sunlight flashing off his massive front teeth. Staring at Hank, I instantly feel the warm glow of his friendly way and am very pleased to have him running alongside. Because he honestly cares about others, I know that Hank would always be the most popular guy in our class. It is a pleasing realization that this capable and caring man simply wants to be my friend and is even an eager participant in the punishment part of my reprimand.

"A friend is a present you give yourself," Robert Lewis Stevenson

Lying on the bed inside of Revelstoke, I momentarily wonder why my thoughts had drifted to Instructor McNair, Hank and my first days at Naval Explosive Ordnance Disposal School. I roll the joint between my fingers, hesitate and then begin to rummage in a drawer for matches.

The light shines in the darkness, but the darkness has not understood it. John 1:5

A few years later, inside a prison cell, I would remember that moment and instantly know its meaning. I was troubled and on the wrong side of a bad decision that involved my new friends. People are social creatures; we like to do things with others. If someone is doing something good, that person naturally wants to involve his or her friends. Conversely when someone is doing something wrong, he or she will try to involve his or her friends or family members. Hank, however, was the kind of friend one could count on during times of adversity. His friendship was built on strength of character and on powerful moral values. My new surfer friends had a drug problem and were eager to share it with me. True friendship is not built on a foundation of bad judgment and corruption. I could not imagine them offering marijuana to Hank or to McNair, but they did offer it me. Apparently, I was radiating the type of character that they recognized because it was like their own—lacking a moral compass.

Note: to see color pictures of Revelstoke, visit www.drugsbite.com and look under "Cool Links".

Photo Arrington
Interior of Revelstoke; front to back

For what son is not disciplined by his father? Hebrews 12:7

Chapter 4

OAHU, HAWAII, JANUARY 1979

FROM A drawer I take a book of matches and strike one, touching the flame to the tip of the joint. *Two hits,* I tell myself, *I will only do two hits.*

A drug-induced fog descends upon my consciousness. I wander about the small interior of Revelstoke, content to do absolutely nothing at all. I paw through a few of my possessions, amongst them a small photo album taken from the same drawer as the matches. I stare at a faded picture of myself at a YMCA camp. In it, I am a lanky fourteen year-old standing in front of a straw archery target with a bow and arrow in my hands. In the background, there are pine trees. It is one of my happiest childhood memories.

After a week of youthful adventures at the camp in the mountains above San Bernardino, I was reluctant to return home. My parents had never sent me to a youth camp before let alone one that taught Christian values. My parents were not big on church, though out of obligation we might visit one on Easter or during the Christmas holidays. Anyway, I thrived in the atmosphere of youthful fellowship, which was more about being friends than competitors. Because my father kept changing jobs, we moved almost on a yearly basis. Always the new kid on the block my interaction with other boys had been more about competition and distrust than actual friendship.

At the camp, I had come away with a deep respect for one counselor in particular. I thought it amazing that he actually thought me interesting and found time just to talk with me. We had some long thought-provoking discussions. Questions rambled around in my mind as our bus pulled into a church parking lot where laughing parents were waiting to retrieve their children and their bags of dirty laundry.

My mother, was late again picking me up. Most of the parents and other children were long gone when she pulled into the mostly vacant parking lot. On the ride home, I wanted to talk about questions regarding her beliefs. Instead, she quietly said, "Steve, your father will not be coming home anymore." Completely stunned, I only half listened as she talked about his infidelities to her. I thought about my feelings regarding my father. I did not admit it to her, but I was secretly very glad that he would not be coming home anymore.

My father was an alcoholic who regularly took out his problems on my big brother Jim and me. The golden rule in the Arrington household when Father came home was to go completely silent and at the first opportunity to slip back to our room or sneak outside so as not to attract his attention. I was very much afraid of him. Interestingly he interpreted my fear as an indication of youthful respect, which it certainly was not. I was often terrified in his presence. It was an attitude he re-enforced by being unapproachable except to assign us work or to deliver physical discipline.

In school, I was a straight D & C student. I just did not much care about grades, nor did my parents; neither of them completed the tenth grade. After the divorce my mother had to find employment; something completely new to her and suddenly she was rarely home. In the early evening, she often visited friends or dated. My older brother Jim, a senior in high school, saw no reason to hang around. He seldom came home until late at night. After school, I worked at a commercial laundry stuffing large industrial washing machines with big bags of hospital laundry. Sometimes I found extremely disgusting things wrapped in the surgical towels and bed sheets. I regularly returned home in the evening to an empty house. The age of fourteen is when my family life, such as it was, ended.

My most prevalent childhood memory is something I do not fully recall. I was twelve years old, working at a rest home as a dishwasher. The cook told me to take out the trash. It was dark in the back parking lot that winter night. I remember that there was a cold wind rustling amongst the trees and that their limbs creaked and groaned in the darkness. I hurried to an uneven row of battered trashcans and lifted off a dented lid. Glancing inside I saw a fairly new blanket on a bed of debris. By the shape I knew there was something hidden inside its folds. It is in the unwrapping of the blanket that my memory fails me. The police must have asked me questions, but I do not remember any of it. What I did remember is that my parents were vacationing in Hawaii and that my dad called my brother to say that coming home early was not an option. When they returned a week later, my dad asked me if I was okay with having found a dead baby in the trash. I remember this because I always listened to what my father said, as it tended to be painful if I did not. I found out very early in life that it was always best to tell my dad whatever he wanted to hear. So, I told him that I was okay, though I was definitely anything but okay.

By the age of twelve, I had grown used to being left home alone. When I was ten my father surprised the family with a brand new travel trailer. After a first glance at the interior, my brother Jim and I were not allowed in it anymore because my father worried that we would just get it dirty. Often, both my parents would disappear with it for four or five days at a time while Jim and I fended at home for ourselves. They claimed they were going off for business trips, yet returned with mementos from Yosemite National Park, Palm Springs and Las Vegas. It was from my parents that I learned it was okay to lie.

> *Hear ye children, the instruction of a father, and attend to*
> *understanding.* Proverbs 4:1 KJV

When I turned sixteen, I bought a car with my savings from working regular after school jobs. With it came freedom. It is also when I regularly began ditching school. I went to the beach a lot to hang out and amassed a great deal of excused absents because I had been writing my own notes since my freshman year. Mine was the only copy the school had of my mom's signature. I guess it was just one of the byproducts of learning at an early age that lies were acceptable so long as I was not caught. My parents did not really care what I did as long as it did not involve them.

It is a wonder that I actually stayed with my mother long enough to graduate from high school. After receiving my diploma, I paused to watch a friend in his cap and gown surrounded by an adoring family. Alone, I got into my car and drove home. At the apartment complex, a neighbor saw me carrying my cap and gown and insisted on getting a picture. I intended to mail it to my father, but never did.

A couple of weeks later, my mother got up early to drive me to the Naval Induction Center in Los Angeles. Because I was under-aged, she had had to sign my enlistment papers. I determined it was the last favor I would ever ask of her. I figured that the U.S. Navy would be my family now. The year was 1966 and I was following my brother's lead. He had joined the Army a year earlier and was serving in Vietnam. Over the next five years, I would serve four tours off the coast of North Vietnam helping to rescue downed pilots. It was in the Navy that I discovered that I had value. However, even that issue was in question when the forward engine room was short a man. To fill the vacancy, they traded a bail of rags and half a case of motor oil for me.

Back in Revelstoke, I look at the last picture in the photo album. It shows a skinny seventeen-year-old kid in a cap and gown holding a high school diploma in an empty apartment. Picking up the matches, I re-lit the joint.

"Even a minor event in the life of a child is an event of that child's world and thus a world event," Gaston Bachelard

Later, I would be proven wrong about not asking my mother for any more favors. When she came to visit me at Terminal Island Federal Correctional Facility she would bring a roll of quarters at my request so I could buy cookies and processed food from the candy machines in the prison visiting room.

As of the writing of this book, over forty percent of the children in the United States live in a single parent household. Because of divorce and separation up to four out of five children in America will at some point live in a single parent residence... notice I did not say home, which would imply that that there is a normal family life going on inside. Currently over three million children are being raised by their grandparents.

I personally believe that less father (and mother) time directly equals more prison time for a child. As of the new millennium, the fastest growing part of California's inmate population per capita is teenage girls going into lock-up facilities. Many of the youth detention programs in California are co-ed facilities as are the schools for students at risk (children in crisis). California spends over $80,000 per year for each youth in lock-up; this excessive amount of money has little or no impact on preventing re-incar-ceration. I have seen ten-year old girls and eight-year old boys in detention centers where I have spoken as part of my Drugs Bite Program and these pre-adolescent children are clueless on how to behave in such a lonely and terrifying environment. They quickly become victims of the rage of the older boys and girls who are furious to have been rejected by their families and by society.

Youth lock-ups are the fast track to becoming a troubled adult at a very early age. The girl's lock up also has the highest per capita ratio of acts of physical violence of any California correctional facility. In the foster care program, highly troubled youth command a greater sponsorship fee for their foster parents. These children already in crisis quickly equate that the more trouble they get into the more money they are worth. It is a very articulate and persuasive argument for determining self-value in a young troubled mind searching for answers.

"Love will enter cloaked in friendship's name,"
Ovid, 43 BC – 17AD

Chapter 5

MAUI, HAWAII, JANUARY 1998

I, AND my sunflower, arrive early at the airport. It is a particularly large sunflower and it is commanding a lot of attention. I am wearing a radiant smile; it is the second thing people notice, right after the gargantuan blossom. I stand at the arrival gate in happy anticipation. Finally, the plane arrives and people begin walking down the ramp. I am watching for a tall, athletic brunette with hazel eyes. It is not just Cindy's height that makes her stand out in a crowd, it is her cheerful gregarious way. Complete strangers quickly bond with her happy outlook about life in general. When she sees the flower, happily waving above the heads of the waiting crowd, Cindy instantly knows I am close by.

A moment later, she is in my arms. "Welcome to Hawaii," I grin handing her the huge flower

"In Hawaii you are suppose to meet ladies with a flower lei." Cindy is most happy when she is giving me a hard time.

"But this is such a nice sunflower," I say in the gigantic blossom's defense. "It really wanted to come to the airport, and it is very pleased that you are here."

This is our third date. I have asked her to join our Cousteau expedition after getting permission from Jean-Michel. An hour later, she and I walk together down a wooden pier at the Lahaina Yacht Harbor. For this expedition, I have chartered a thirty-two foot, twin-screwed, cabin cruiser, the *Kai Kekoa.* Jean-Michel Cousteau and Michel DeLoire (our cinematographer), are on deck prepping an underwater cinema camera.

Cindy is very nervous about joining the Cousteau expedition. "Steve," she takes my arm, "I really want to be a part of the team, so don't hesitate to put me to work. I can cook, wash dishes and help with the diving gear...anything."

"I already have a job for you," I smile mischievously.

"Chief deck scrubber?" asks Cindy throwing a snappy salute.

"No," I deadpan, "actually I thought you might drive the boat."

"What?" Cindy sputters.

As a student missionary in the South Pacific, Cindy spent a lot of time operating small craft. She also worked in a marina for several years while attending college so I know she is well qualified for the assignment. By having her run our support craft, it will free up an extra diver for underwater operations.

"Which would you rather be," I ask playfully, "the skipper or chief dishwasher?"

Cindy grabs a handful of my T-shirt and drags me closer, "Treat your skipper with more respect or I will have you scrubbing the bilges, sailor." Cindy then punches me lightly in the chest re-enforcing her statement. I like being punched by Cindy; it means she is in a playful mood.

"Yes ma'am, Captain Bligh." I answer, pleasantly surprised at how quickly Cindy adapts to new situations.

For the next week, Cindy's job is to keep the charter boat in the general vicinity of our dive operations as a support vessel. From it we reload the cameras, charge our scuba tanks and prepare the rubber Zodiacs for approaching the whales. Unfortunately, this means Cindy is always a good distance from the main whale activity—that is until that one glorious day.

It is a blustery, stormy morning. The gusting wind is whipping the restless ocean into a froth of white caps. Sea spray drenches my skin, but it feels good in the tropical heat. I am riding in a Zodiac on sharp lookout for whales, yet it is Jean-Michel Cousteau who sees them first. It is a fast-moving pod of many whales not far from Cindy's boat. Jean-Michel, who is operating our Zodiac's outboard, quickly grabs a walkie-talkie.

"Cindy, this is Jean-Michel," he calls urgently.

"Cindy here," she replies.

"Shut down your engines, the whales are heading straight for you," Jean-Michel urges.

"Roger, going dead in the water," Cindy answers, then hoots loudly.

Hearing her eager enthusiasm over the radio, I look in the distance to see Cindy prancing down from the flying bridge for a close-up view of the oncoming Humpbacks. I did not know it at the time, but the whale pod consists of a single cow and the rest are all large overly excited bulls. It is the end of the breeding season and the cow is running from fourteen hefty admirers; each of whom weighs up to forty-five tons. The cow is tiring from the lustful pursuit and apparently looking for shelter when she sees Cindy's boat.

Onboard the *Kai Kekoa*, Cindy has no idea why fifteen whales are heading straight for her small craft. She is just ecstatic to be in their path...not realizing that her little boat is actually their intended destination in a close and personal way. The Humpback whales are coming at full-stampede speed. Cindy could not be happier as she sees the charging cow surface forty feet away spewing a column of water high into the air as she takes a rapid breath. The massive Humpback is torpedoing straight for her as it submerges passing mere feet beneath the boat's keel. Cindy rushes to the other side, expecting to see the huge whale swimming away; instead she is about to get the whale watching experience of a lifetime.

The cow has gone from racing speed to full stop as she tries to hide underneath the small cabin cruiser. The thirty-two-foot-long boat only shelters the front half of the massive whale. Cindy's shriek of surprise is drowned-out by the boisterous arrival of the fourteen charging bulls. A couple of them propel their ninety-thousand pound bodies high out of the water in dual flanking breeches as they slam back into the ocean with tremendous force. White water from whale-induced belly whoppers explodes into the air. The strong trade winds send a deluge of seawater cascading across the boat's deck soaking Cindy, much to her delight.

The bulls are fighting amongst themselves as they try to get next to the cow. They ram each other littering the water with floating pieces of whale skin and blubber from the violence. A couple of the bulls attempt to nudge the cow; their massive bodies are so close to Cindy that she could touch their slick black skin as they descend on either side of the hull of *Kai Kekoa*. The wild excitement increases as one of the inflamed bulls swings its mammoth tail high into the air. The whale's fluke hangs suspended two stories above the water, higher than the *Kai Kekoa's* bridge and then the tail slams down with tremendous force. The sharp impact echoes across the water like a cannon shot. Cindy's boat is rocking wildly from side-to-side. I can just barely hear her yelps of ecstatic excitement above the thrashing tempest of the whales.

The cow, probably realizing that her sanctuary is not so safe, abruptly makes a run for it. She surfaces next to *Kai Kekoa* for a quick breath and then flees with powerful strokes of her tail. The bulls charge in pursuit. Many of them pass under Cindy's boat with currents from their wakes beating against the boat's hull sending it spinning first in one direction and then the other.

The whales are now heading directly toward us in the Zodiacs. Jean-Michel cuts the engine and yells, "Quick, everyone into the water!" Michel DeLoire, our cameraman, snatches a mask and rolls over the side. Grabbing an underwater still camera, I quickly slip in after him. Clay, a tall athletic American, is acting as the safety diver for Michel. They take several deep breaths, and then descend beneath the frothy water. I will observe the pair from a shallower depth to keep from accidently getting in the way of Michel's cinema camera, yet hope to capture some still photographs of the whales.

Beneath the surface, the water is deceptively calm, then I see the whales hurling at the divers. They are right in the path of the huge charging animals each the size of an eighteen-wheeler truck. It is an underwater stampede with the whales racing ten times faster than human swimming speed. It is one of the risks of working with large wild animals. Yet, even in their excitement, the whales are graceful swimmers. Long pectoral fins extend from their bodies like wings of giant birds in flight. Incredibly, each of the racing whales slightly alters its course upwards to keep from running over the two tiny creatures hovering right in the path of the lustful rampage.

The cow passes just fifteen feet from Michel DeLoire, but then, perhaps wondering what are these little silver creatures she rolls on to her back carving a sharp descending vertical U-turn for a second look. With her long pectoral fins extended like wings, the massive whale reminds me of a B24 flying fortress pulling out of a steep dive. As the cow comes level with Michel DeLoire's camera, she abruptly accelerates with strong beats of her tail. The trailing bulls quicken their pace, each jostling to get closer to her. The lead bull nudges her underbelly, which prompts her into overdrive. The rest of the mammoth bulls charge in pursuit each executing sharp cornering U-turns in our tiny segment of ocean. For thirty-long seconds we are in the midst of the vast stampeding pod. The enormous bodies gliding by seem almost surrealistic because all of this mammoth activity is taking place in the total silence of the submarine world.

As I swim furiously taking pictures of the nimble Humpbacks, I think how amazing life is when one pursues wonder and adventure. It is not just by chance that I am here. Previously, I spent years perfecting my diving skills and purposefully took courses to enhance my qualifications. I also worked on my physical abilities, practicing long-distance swimming and breath-hold diving. As a U.S. Navy frogman, I spent years leading military dive operations into remote and dangerous locations. I took every possible opportunity to learn more about my chosen trade as a diver. If it can be dreamed then it is within the realm of the possible.

"Opportunity favors the prepared mind," Louis Pasteur

To realize dreams and exploit opportunities it is necessary to be completely reliable. When people depend upon us, we should never disappoint them. Many times when the alarm clock rang at 2:00 or 4:00 a.m., I did not want to get up, let alone arrive enthusiastic and good-natured, yet these are the type of characteristics that team expeditions demand.

At a depth of twenty feet, I aim my camera at the last bull whale, which is passing ten feet beneath my flippers and shoot the final frame in the camera. Out of film, I capture the climax of the whale's passage in the theater of my mind. The rapidly swimming whale, forty-five feet long, takes only three seconds to hurl underneath me, then it passes from my field of vision into the gloom of deep water. I feel a wisp of remaining current from its passage, and then the three of us divers are alone in the vast and suddenly empty ocean.

Surfacing, out of breath, I see the whales, again arriving at Cindy's boat. Their spouts of water and mist surround her small craft in an aquatic celebration of life. Cindy is running from rail to rail hollering happily at the whales. That is one of the wonderful benefits of pursuing and achieving your dreams, it means you can take the ones you love with you. A dream shared is the best kind of living fantasy, and, just like in a fairy tale, it leads to a purer, happier, and deeper love of one's companion.

Half an hour later, as I climb back onto the gently rolling deck of the *Kai Kekoa*, Cindy hugs me. Her Hazel eyes glow with excitement. It is one of the happiest moments of my life. I remember the golden key to dreams and opportunity that landed me this incredible job with the Cousteau Society. It was a direct result of what I did after my release from prison in 1985. In a jail cell awaiting my trial and sentencing I gave what I thought was a now worthless life to Jesus Christ and made a promise to try to do good for the rest of my life. After thirty-one long months, I was released from prison and started speaking at public schools and at churches to youth about the importance of choices. I encouraged them to pursue their dreams through discipline and positive commitment. In the process, I discovered the reality of my own childhood dream coming true when I was hired by Jean-Michel Cousteau as a chief diver and expedition leader just two short years out of prison...and I did not even speak French—and still do not.

"When you're good to others you're best to yourself,"
Benjamin Franklin

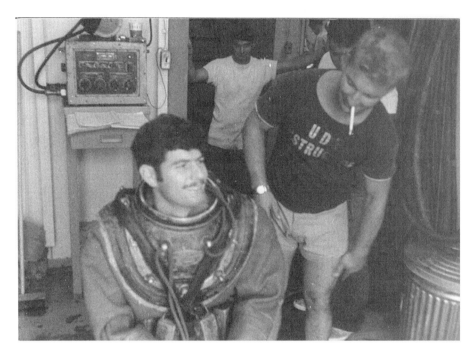

The author at Navy Deep Sea Diving School 1971

"Life has more imagination than we carry in our dream,"
Christopher Columbus

Chapter 6

INDIANHEAD, MARYLAND, SEPTEMBER 1975

◀◀ THE BRASS needs to be brighter," orders Instructor McNair dropping a polishing rag into my lap, "I want to be able to pick my teeth in its reflection." The brass he is talking about is the viewing ports on an old diving helmet. Pouring a touch of polishing compound onto the rag, I begin the laborious task of rubbing away a stubborn coat of tarnish from the dented spun nickel and copper helmet.

"Nineteen forty-four," Hank is reading the manufacturer's nameplate while he polishes the helmet's breastplate. "This helmet was made a decade before I was even born." As usual, Hank is wearing his chipmunk grin beneath which lurks his ever-positive attitude about life in general. His continuous high spirits can be rather irritating, particularly when we are doing something lousy such as punishment exercise at *dark-thirty* (any hour of darkness after midnight and prior to dawn). However, right now I happen to agree with his buoyant mood. I like the USN Mark V deep-sea diving rig. I made my very first dive in a Navy Mark V that was actually older and in far worse condition than this one. Turning the old helmet on the workbench to get at a patch of tarnish under the faceplate, I regard the Mark V kind of like an old friend. Enjoying watching the brass slowly brighten I slip back in time to my very first underwater adventure.

My journey towards becoming a Navy diver began in an old hardhat diving suit. It is a pre-World War II relic made for when divers used to stomp around on the ocean floor. The antique diving rig is lying on the stern deck of a worn-out tugboat in Los Angeles Harbor. Standing before me is a seasoned diving veteran wearing a sock cap and frayed sweatshirt. Willie is old enough to be my grandfather's father. He fits right in with the dilapidated tugboat and antiquated suit.

The U.S. Navy sent me here for what they call an orientation dive. I have applied for diving school. It is the late 1960's and before the Navy is willing to waste any time or money training a rookie diver, they want to see how the recruit takes to being underwater.

I am sitting on a diving stool wearing a pair of Willie's threadbare long underwear to insulate me from the cold water. The shabby wool material itches and there are a few suspicious stains, but Willie has assured me that these are his lucky long underwear. Apparently, all the recruits who wore these shabby drawers made it through diving school. Scratching my chest, I nervously watch him greasing the leather seals on the old helmet.

"So you want to be a diver, huh boy?" Willie has a beard full of gray stubble, skin that looks like creased leather and a chipped gold front tooth.

"Yes sir," I answer, eyeing the debilitated diving suit warily.

"Handsome peace of gear ain't it?" Willie lays a prideful hand on the old dented helmet.

"Isn't that faceplate cracked?" I ask suspiciously. There is a crack running in three directions across the glass port.

"Ain't no big deal," Willie shrugs, "suit's got a few holes in it too, but you won't be down that long, nor deep enough for it to manner none."

"Holes, what kind of holes?" I'm not finding this reassuring at all, as I try to examine the old canvas and rubber suit lying beside a rusting anchor windlass.

"Look," Willie appears to be getting a mite upset, "don't worry about what don't concern you. If too much water gets in your suit, I'll just pull you up."

"Ah, Willie," I know I'm asking too many questions, but can't stop myself, "just what constitutes too much water?"

"Let me know if the suit fills much above your waist," Willie is dragging over the frayed canvas and rubber suit in question, "otherwise you might be a bit too heavy for me to get off the bottom."

"That suit looks like a pair of old frayed sneakers," I know I shouldn't be complaining.

"It should," Willie's laugh has a sinister ring to it, "Converse, the people who manufacture high-top sneakers use to make these rubberized-canvas suits too. Only they closed the plant about thirty years ago. This suit is practically one of a kind so don't be putting any new rips or tears in it."

I decide it might be better not to ask any more questions. If Willie reports that I seem too nervous about the dive, it could kill my chances of getting into diving school, and I want to be a Navy diver more than anything. I jam both feet into the canvas suit, which is soaking wet on the inside and smells rather strongly of old mold and mildew.

With the suit around my waist, Willie reaches over and grabs a tub of grease. "Here boy, stick your hands in here," he says with a reassuring grin.

"What?" I can't hide my shock, "That's motor grease."

"Course it's grease, I just put new wrist seals on the suit and don't want you ripping them with your paws," Willie is definitely upset.

I put both hands into the cold grease then shake off the excess. Willie doesn't notice that a glob of the grease lands in his beard, nor do I tell him.

"Now you just sit there and let old Willie dress you out," Willie is glaring just daring me to say something. I silently watch him scratch his beard, unknowingly spreading the grease across his chin and onto his nose.

Lifting a brass breastplate, he places it around my neck, then bolts it to a rubber gasket on the suit. Next, comes the brass and leather boots that weigh eighteen pounds apiece, followed by a seventy-pound leather and lead belt. I am trying to adjust to all the weight, when I see Willie beating on a valve with a hammer.

"What are you banging on?" the question just kind of slips out accidentally.

"Your air valve is a mite stuck," Willie says hitting it a final wallop. "That should do it." He picks up the helmet and plops it over my head before I can raise any complaints. After locking it in place, he opens the face port with the spider-web cracks in the glass. "Now you just stand up and I'll walk you over to the ladder. Be careful the rig weighs almost two hundred pounds so you might be a bit awkward."

As he closes the faceplate, the helmet feels immediately confining, though it is rather fun to look out through the portholes. I clomp over to the ladder, then begin climbing awkwardly down into the harbor.

"When the water reaches your helmet grab a hold of the descent line and let go of the ladder," Willie is talking to me through the helmet's speaker. "Be sure to let yourself down slowly," he cautions, "you don't want to go and burst an eardrum or collapse a lung on me."

As the water covers my helmet, I nervously reach for the rope, and saying a silent prayer, release my grip on the ladder. Instantly, I am plunging straight down. The grease on my hands is keeping me from getting a grip on the rope. I slide rapidly downwards and slam into the bottom hard. The impact drives my heavy boots several feet into the harbor muck.

"Man you sure must have been excited to get down," Willie's voice echoes through the helmet, "I got you at thirty-three feet already."

Abruptly, I can hardly believe that I'm really underwater. I start to take a step, then quickly realize that I am stuck in the thick harbor mud. It is also when I first notice the cold water seeping into my suit.

"Go ahead," says Willie, "walk around a bit."

It is very dark on the bottom of the harbor. There is almost no light penetrating the muddy water. Holding my hand up to the faceplate, I can barely see my fingers as I wiggle them. Then, I realize that if I can see my hand, so can a shark. I quickly tuck both hands firmly out of sight under my armpits. That is exactly how I stay for the next fifteen minutes with cold water quietly creeping into my suit and images of sharks slipping through my imagination.

"You having fun down there, boy?" Willie sounds curious as to what I'm doing.

"Yeah, this is great," I know Willie will report my performance to the diver recruiting officer.

"So you about ready to come up?" he asks.

The cold water inside my suit is already above my knees, so *coming up* is the best news I could have heard. "I guess so," I respond trying to sound slightly reluctant to leave the seabed.

The umbilical goes very taunt, I have to work at freeing my boots but they finally pull out of the soft mud with a loud squishy-sucking sound. Looking upwards through the murky water as I ascend, I see it is slowly getting lighter above me. For the last few fathoms, I briefly wonder what aquatic adventures the future holds, in any case I hope it gets much better from here.

Two hours later the dive locker and all its equipment is shinning about as much as the antique banged-up and student abused gear is ever going to get. Not that McNair displays any satisfaction in our work as Hank and I offer the burnished helmet and breastplate for his inspection. "What? Fishing for compliments just for doing your job?" he growls. "Get this gear out to the swimming pool before I get the urge to hurt one of you."

During the past week, we have lost five more EOD candidates reducing the class to twenty-four. Three of the unfortunates were dropped during drown-proof training. The goal of this *character-building* drill was to teach us that drowning is not an acceptable option for a frogman. To convince us, McNair and his fellow instructors had us lie face down at the edge of the pool. Using stout rope, they bound our ankles together and tied our hands behind our backs. With a carelessly applied foot, McNair shoved us unceremoniously into the water where we were expected to be extremely active for the next forty minutes. The key is to take an extra deep breath as you roll into the water, which allows you to hang with your head suspended just beneath the surface with the buoyancy from your lungs. McNair had already shared that our heads are the most negatively buoyant part of our bodies and are about the size and weight of a bowling ball, which according to him unlike our heads at least had a functional purpose. To get another breath we had to dolphin kick back to the surface, then hurriedly exhale and inhale just like a dolphin. To be a bit slow in the rapid breath sequencing resulted in an express trip to the bottom of the pool. This meant one of the instructors would have to dive down to the bottom to recover the unfortunate candidate before he did something else stupid such as dying. Just before the drown-proofing exercise, McNair warned us, "If any of you dummies go into a drowning mode on me I will throw you out of the program like a stomped on toad being thrown like a Frisbee. However, just to show that I am a good sport I am willing to give you up to two successive drowning attempts."

One of the assistant instructors voiced his surprise, "You never give second chances McNair, what gives?"

All of us rope-bound EOD candidates laying face down on the wet cement eagerly awaited the answer as McNair offered a toothy grin, "Fun factor," he leaned down so we could better appreciate his predatory smirk, "some of these little fish aren't going to survive my little exercise. It'll be fun watching them thrashing around down there wondering how long I will let them do their drowning routine."

"Yeah, we should do a betting pool," answered one instructor, "think anyone will beat the two minute record?"

"The longer we let them thrash about down there…the less they seem to mind being dropped from my class."

Five minutes into the drown-proofing exercise, we lost our first candidate. I watched him rapidly sinking towards the bottom both times. It felt weird watching a friend in full drowning frenzy, while

I a trained lifeguard could not do anything about it. After forty minutes, our class was two candidates smaller, but before McNair would consent to haul us out of the pool, he wanted his dive mask fetched. It was hanging from a rope at a depth of twelve feet. Each of us had to dolphin kick down to the mask, grab it with our teeth, then dolphin kick back to the surface and show it to McNair while grunting like a seal. The trick to this exercise is a finely balanced amount of air in your lungs. Too much air made it difficult to get in a head down position, then you wasted your breath trying to dolphin kick down; however not enough air might mean an unintended continuing descent to the bottom and an express trip out of EOD School.

"Time," yelled McNair from the pool's edge, "You guys go ahead and untie yourselves."

"How?" Gurgled one of the guys...dolphin breathing only allowed one-word conversations on our part.

"With your teeth dummy," McNair yelled as he held open one of the double doors for the other instructors to pass through. "So where do you guys want to do lunch?" We heard him ask though the closing doors.

I quickly dolphin kicked over to Hank and looked affectionately at his rodent-like smile, "Hi Bucky," I burbled. Hank did not get to test his beaver abilities that morning as two of the assistant instructors returned to haul us out of the water. Later, at the chow hall, I stated my relief that the dreaded drown-proofing test was behind us. I was in a celebratory mood as I added a squirt of ketchup onto my mash potatoes. Being a vegetarian in a Navy chow hall required a certain sense of imagination.

"Had to do drown proofing training at BUDS (*Basic Underwater Demolition School, i.e. SEAL training*) in Coronado," quipped Hank, "but having to swim down to fetch a dive mask with my teeth was a new twist."

"Yeah, what was with that?" asked a classmate at our long table. "You guys ever wonder why McNair always makes everything extra hard just for our class? I mean is it something personal to all of us or has he got one of us in particular in his sights?"

Glancing up from my pink mashed potatoes, I noticed most of my classmates looking in my direction. "What?" I exclaimed.

"Well he does seem to single you out."

"No he doesn't..." I was pleased to hear Hank argue in my defense.

"Thank you Hank," I smiled.

"Steve attracts negative attention from all of the staff," Hank finished his statement with a hand flourish.

"No I don't," I argued.

"It's true," echoed the first guy, "Steve's always in trouble and then we get drug into it."

"Does make the class a bit more interesting," added another.

"Yeah, we always know he is going to take most of the heat," snickers Charlie.

They were now talking as if I wasn't even there.

"So who wants to be his buddy during the practical explosive exercises?

"Man that would be a real drag. We should have to pick straws... short one loses."

"Hey," chimed in Charlie, our California surfer, "who wants him for your pool harassment swim partner?"

"Oh, that would be the worst," laughed Mickie Doke, the guy who brought the subject up in the first place, "You know that is the only time that McNair actually gets into the pool with the class?"

"That is a privilege I could do without," said a husky Montana candidate we nicknamed Cowboy.

"McNair wouldn't miss it," exclaimed Charlie, "that is his opportunity to physically abuse us with his own bare hands. Hey Arrington, you better start practicing your breath-holding abilities...you're going to need it."

"I'll swim buddy with Arrington," Hank offered, "McNair is really going to go after him and I want to be where the action is."

After cleaning and polishing the WWII vintage diving equipment, we again find ourselves standing at the side of the pool while the instructors split us into four six-man teams. Hank volunteers to be first into the water for our team, which as usual involves a rather distinctive race. A two-inch thick rope runs the length of the pool. At the rope's center hangs a fifty-pound lead weight, which puts a deep V into the taunt line. The object of the hardhat race is to tug our way arm-over-arm down that rope in our heavy gear to the lead weight hanging at a depth of eighteen feet. Then we must pull ourselves up the other side of the rope until we reach the far side of the pool, where another rope plunges straight down. The heavy gear diver must grab that rope and then rapidly descend to the pool bottom. Each candidate will be timed from the moment he lets go of one side of the pool until he reaches the bottom at the other side. The team's combined race time will determine the winners. The first place team only has to run two miles before lunch. The losers get to run an additional mile for each successive position after first place with possible distance enhancements for additional minutes lost. Losing took on a completely new perspective at EOD School. As McNair liked to remind us, "Sportsmanship is not factored into your overall grade, nor is it a desirable quality for a SPEC WAR candidate."

Earlier in the program, one of the candidates wanted to know why McNair was so down on sportsmanship. "Frogmen are combat swimmers. Combat infers that you will be industriously trying to kill people who aren't on your side. Murdering the other team in a brutal and efficient manner isn't normally considered sportsman like conduct."

"Okay slime balls listen to me," yells McNair. "The idea of this exercise is to teach you how to control the buoyancy of the hardhat rig. Inflating the deep-sea diving suit with air makes it buoyant. Dumping out the air turns it into sixty pounds of negative buoyancy, which means an express trip to the bottom of my pool. "Any questions?" McNair glares expecting none, and then orders, "Good, let's get the first divers into the water."

While suiting up Hank, I convince the rest of the team to let me be the anchorman. "Why do you want to be last?" I smile at Hank's question as I lower the breastplate onto his broad shoulders.

"I am going to be our secret weapon," I whisper. "I spent three months training in this rig at the Navy's Deep-sea Diving School in Washington D.C. in 1969." It is pleasing to see the envious smiles on my classmates' faces. "The other teams are going to be toast," I boast.

The race begins pretty much as expected. Having never dove heavy gear the guys are awkward in their movements as they first try to muscle themselves down the rope to the fifty-pound lead clump, then even more awkwardly pull themselves up towards the other end of the pool. Keeping a proper balance of air in the rig is a challenging task. It requires the constant use of one or the other hand to open and close both the air inlet and exhaust valves. The air exhaust valve is on the lower left side of the helmet, while the air inlet value is located at the lower right side of the chest harness.

The four teams are in a close draw. While my classmates are suiting me up, I mentally go over my plan and see no obvious flaws. Unfortunately there is one huge flaw dangling right in front of my face, but I am so caught up in trying to win the race I do not notice it. The problem is I am again leading with my ego and it almost costs me my dream of becoming a bomb disposal frogman.

Sitting on the dressing stool, I eagerly tug on the heavy rubber and canvas diving suit, which by itself weighs almost twenty pounds. Two teammates buckle brass and lead boots weighing eighteen pounds apiece onto my feet. To make sure they do not pull off on a mud bottom the boots are also laced with stout rope. To lose a weighed boot underwater could mean being flipped upside down. Any water in the suit (all canvas diving suits leak) would flood down into the helmet drowning the diver. Next, a brass breastplate is screwed with hand wrenches onto a thick rubberneck grommet attached to the canvas suit. They sling a seventy-pound weight belt from my shoulders and buckle it snugly at my waist. Then they pass a crotch strap between my legs and snug it as tight as a strong man can make it. This pulls the breastplate down firmly onto the shoulders and causes serious discomfort in and around the crotch. When

compressed air flows into the suit underwater this jocking technique prevents the helmet and breastplate from rising up too high
when the suit is inflated. A poorly *jocked* diver cannot see out of
his faceplate, nor could he properly control the clumsy rig. Finally,
the dented helmet is lowered onto my head rounding out the full
one hundred and ninety-eight pounds of deep-sea diving dress.
Inside the rig, I jack my shoulders to settle the breastplate, shoulder
harness and weight belt; I feel like a mule in a wagon harness. Yet
I am relatively comfortable being familiar with the pressing weight
of the rig and am quite eager to race. Cracking open the air inlet
valve at my chest I inhale the air rushing into the helmet. Diver's
compressed air has a unique smell that instantly reminds me of past
underwater adventures.

When Hank thumps the top of my helmet twice, the signal to
stand, I practically leap to my feet. I am anxious to get into the
water, yet the ponderous weight of the deep-sea rig limits me to short
shambling steps. Shuffling quickly to the ladder, I descend into the
cool water, instantly feeling the rig's massive weight beginning to
fall away as the water rises above my chest, its buoyancy displacing
gravity. The water covers my faceplate. About me, I watch a mass
of bubbles breaking on the surface that are floating free from my
canvas suit. It is an amazing visual transition slipping beneath the
pool's surface looking through a World War II era diving helmet. I
hear the helmet mounted exhaust valve beginning to bubble madly
as water covers its exhaust port. A couple of inches beneath the
surface I stop to do another shoulder shrug to settle the rig and
loop my left arm over the downward slanting rope.

I did not grab the rope with one hand like the other guys. I do
not intend to tug my way along the rope at all. Looping an arm over
and around the rope allows that hand to operate the air inlet valve
at my chest. This frees my other hand to work the exhaust valve on
the side of helmet.

Stepping off the last rung of the ladder, I take a deep breath
while quickly shutting off my air supply and rapidly spin the exhaust
valve wide open. Immediately the hardhat rig loses its buoyancy as

air from the suit rushes up into the helmet, and then bubbles freely out of the exhaust valve. The face port becomes awash with a cloud of ascending bubbles as I feel myself sliding speedily downward at a sharp angle. The rubberized canvas suit clamps wetly against my skin from the increasing water pressure forcing the last pockets of air from my canvas suit. The only remaining air is a cubic foot or so inside the helmet surrounding my head.

I rapidly, but effortlessly, slip down the rope to the fifty-pound clump. Just before reaching the lead weight, I spin the exhaust valve shut and twirl the air inlet valve open. Immediately the suit begins to expand creating enormous buoyancy that shoves me up the rope on the other side like an ascending cork. My speed and buoyancy are so great my heavy boots are actually beginning to lift upwards. I see the shimmering underside of the surface water while sliding briskly up the rope, in a boots first almost horizontal position. I arrive abruptly at the other end of the pool and quickly reach out to grab the descent line. Again, I hurriedly shut off the air supply valve dumping air from the suit as I begin to descend like a plummeting rock. My lead and brass boots hit the pool bottom so hard my legs almost buckle. The crash of my impact echoes across the bottom of the pool like a modest tsunami-like sound wave. The pool's sides and bottom are constructed of thick steel.

I check for spinal damage as I attempt to stand upright at the bottom of the pool. Convinced that I am okay I hurriedly stride across the bottom of the pool to the ascent line that hangs beside the pool's ladder. My tenders immediately begin pulling me upward and I am quick to assist rapidly climbing the rope. Looking upwards at the underside of the shimmering surface, I am eager to hear my well earned praise from Instructor McNair. I just know that the old school record for the hardhat race is toast. *Arrington the Speedster* is very buoyant inside his World War II era diving rig. Climbing up the ladder, I shuffle quickly toward the dressing chair while barely resisting a temptation to do a little shuffle step like the football receivers do in the end-zone after a dramatic touchdown.

Not doing a shuffle boogie to the dressing stool turns out to be my only good decision of the morning. Had I attempted a victory rumba in the old dive suit, McNair would have tackled me and hammered my body with his fists he is so furious. I hear his loud angry voice blaring from the helmet's small speaker about two inches from my ear puncturing my buoyant mood like an exploded balloon. "Get his helmet off," Gunner McNair rages, "Get it off, I am going to strangle him!"

As Hank lifts the heavy helmet off my head, McNair shoulders his way in, "Just what do you think you were doing down there, idiot?"

"Racing," I answer meekly.

"This is not about a race, squid brain," he growls, "it's about learning how to control the buoyancy of the rig. You were hamming it up. You want people to notice you? Well you got my full attention. How would you feel about clearing out your locker? I bet that is an attention getter. The whole class will notice that!"

I am hunkering down inside the old diving dress.

"Arrington, what you did was not just stupid it was foolishly dangerous! Nah, it was imbecilic. What do you think would've happened if your balloon stunt ruptured the canvas suit? Any idea how fast seventy pounds of lead ballast sinks?"

I hunker deeper into the clammy old suit.

Sit up straight fool," he knuckles me in the chest, "you're making my suit look bad!"

I feel like a turtle lifting its head out of its protective shell with a predator in close attendance. I am ready to duck, but too late, as McNair's calloused palm slams into my forehead.

"Get those shoulders back. Try to look like a man when I am talking to you." McNair's sunglasses are inches from my face, "Now tell me again what you were doing in my pool?"

McNair is cocked, loaded and sporting a hair-trigger; the wrong answer and I am meat. Not a good time for me to get mad, but I cannot help myself, the pent up words just coming tumbling out, "I wanted to prove to you that I can be the best student you've ever had."

McNair grabs the two ropes at the front of my chest, which secures the air hose to my breastplate, and hauls me to my feet. The closest classmates take a step backwards not sure what is about to happen next. I am instantly regretting my anger and reflectively try to pull back.

"Don't you dare back down from me," he spits. "You just stood up for yourself. Now, why would you do a fool stunt like that?"

"Because it's the truth," I growl.

"You're damn right it is boy," McNair is smiling…it is a real smile…lots of teeth. "Being the best is a worthwhile goal, you're just going about it all wrong, clown."

Stunned, I am at a loss what to say in response.

"Talk to me boy, don't just sit there. Exactly what is it that you want from me?"

"Respect," the word just leaps out, a hidden inner thought suddenly expressing itself publicly. I so desperately crave the respect of a father, but do not openly admit it…not even to myself and certainly not to a grown man that I look up to with a feverish desire to please.

"Yeah?" McNair tugs sharply on the breastplate ropes again, "what about them?" McNair's sunglasses sweep over the rest of the class."

"Yeah, them too." I nod.

"You guys respect this piece of meat?" McNair is staring at me again, gauging my reaction as he waits for an answer.

The silence is stunning. My heart pounds beneath the damp sweatshirt I am wearing underneath the rubberized canvas deep-sea suit. I feel my toes cramping inside the brass, lead and leather boots. Then I hear Hank's voice loud and clear breaking the silence, "I'd go into combat with him."

McNair turns on Hank, "Why?"

"Because he's a survivor and he'd never leave a friend in a hard spot."

"But has he earned your respect?" McNair and my eyes lock again.

Hank exhales, "Yeah, sort of...well mostly...look he is working through some issues but so am I. The bottom line is he tries hard and he is dependable...well, mostly."

My eyes have drifted to Hank; my emotions are raging.

McNair jerks the breastplate ropes recapturing my full attention. "You just got to share in something special, Arrington. Hank's is the only opinion in this class that matters to me. He is a SEAL, a bona fide member of my aqua fraternity of underwater warriors. In our community, respect is everything."

Suddenly, I realize that Hank and McNair have been treating each other more like respected companions than the student instructor relationship the rest of us have to suffer through.

"Arrington, the only reason you are still in my class is that you might...just might...have the kind of character that we are looking for; but the problem is that you've got it buried under a trash heap of emotional and immature hang ups. You are going to have to empty that dumpster of emotional trash you're carrying around and get with the team concept. This is not all about you; just get over it."

I am so worked up I don't know how to react. I want to say something positive, but am truly at a loss for words. Abruptly, McNair' expression hardens. I know something tough to hear is coming, but instead of hunkering down, I sit up straighter ready to take whatever is coming...knowing that I deserve the verbal punishment and am determined to take it.

"As a Navy hardhat diver you might have shared a few things to help your classmates to get a better team time. I am not going to drop you from this class," McNair leans forward his cologne mingles with the marine smell of my hardhat dress. "Instead I am going to do you a favor." He is doing his jerking on my chest ropes thing again. "From now on, your only focus at this school is to help your classmates in every way possible. And if you're luckier than I think you are, maybe...just maybe...you'll still be with them on graduation day."

"Aye aye, Instructor McNair." I am fully committed.

"Just so we really understand each other." He is very grim. "If you don't graduate from this program, I do not think you'll be able to handle just fading back into the fleet. You either excel as a team member in this class or you get out of my Navy."

McNair turns to the rest of the class, "Put his helmet back on, I want to see him do the hardhat race again the right way." McNair looks over his shoulder and leers at me, "Hank, throw another weight belt on him. That should slow this rabbit down."

Hank is back to his huge beaver grin mode as he slings the second seventy pounds of lead and leather from my breastplate. "Try not to make the rig look bad," he murmurs softly. While his strong hands thread the thick leather strap through the oversized brass buckle I whisper in his ear, "Thank you."

He then lowers the heavy helmet over my head, double taps the top of it and leans back on my air hose to give me extra support, as I slowly stand upright under the pressing weight of 268 pounds of copper, lead, leather and wet canvas. Shuffling carefully toward the descent ladder, I hear McNair bark out, "Stand up straight Arrington, you're making my suit look bad."

An hour later, after storing the heavy gear, McNair decided that the whole class needed another mood adjustment. So he took us out for a little five mile run through the woods courtesy of yours truly again. Running with my classmates was quickly turning into my main opportunity for the serious pondering of my faults. Running at my side Hank flashed me his perpetual smile and a big wink. A major clue about success and happiness in life was materializing in my mind and like a drowning man being thrown a buoy I desperately clutched at it.

What I really wanted in life was for people to like me. Trying to look good in front of my classmates was not the way to win them over as friends. We care about our friends, are sensitive to their needs and feelings, and we should be eager to help them. I had unfortunately been more concerned about myself. The word *selfish* materialized in my mind and stuck hard like a chunk of chewed gum on the bottom of my boot.

I snuck a glance at Instructor McNair and then quickly looked away. This man was a lot deeper than I thought. The punishment he had assigned me was his way of teaching a very big lesson about who I was and how others saw me.

Next I hazarded a quick glance at Hank and began to understand that he too had been teaching me this lesson but in a much more subtle way. Looking at Hank, I knew that in any situation he could be relied upon to help his friends and classmates first before attending to his own needs. I doubted that anyone would be quick to think of me in those terms. My supposed punishment was to help my classmates, but Instructor McNair was actually coaching me to help myself. If left to my old ways I would industriously continue to alienate most of my teammates. Instead, McNair was showing me how to be a real member of the class. He was attempting to instill in me the value of being a true friend. Something I had not fully learned because we moved so often in my youth, which is why I had had so very few childhood friendships, none of them long lasting.

That is when I was broadsided by a thought that soared right up out of my childhood memories like a circling buzzard discovering something stumbling lost in the desert. Maybe our moving so often was not the real reason why I had so few childhood friends. In my adolescent years, I hungered for attention and approval from my father, which was a lost cause. My father, who was seldom around, did not care about anyone but himself. He never wanted a family. I once heard my mother confiding to a friend that they got married at the age of sixteen because she was pregnant with Jim. They both dropped out of high school in the tenth grade, dad to find a job and my mother to become a parent. For the first time, I realized that that was when they forfeited their own childhood. Having to grow up so abruptly must have ravaged their youthful dreams. Maybe the reason our parents left Jim and I alone so often was because they were trying to recapture something they had lost too early in their young lives. In the end, it didn't work as proved by their divorce.

The wreckage of my family cast Jim and I adrift in a storm of emotions with no easy solutions. Our parents went their way and

Jim and I went off each in our own direction. From the age of fourteen, I had to work a fulltime job after school to help make ends meet. My joining the Navy was an escape attempt at finding a better life. Yet here I was still dragging along emotional baggage from my damaged childhood and it was continuing to influence all that I said and did as a young adult. It was an untrusting inner presence pawing at life, but not letting anything touch it.

McNair was currently the main authority figure in my life. I was unconsciously, yet desperately, trying to win his approval. I was emotionally starving for a father figure…actually, I was instinctively dependent upon it. This abrupt insight brought to sudden attention that there was a massive void within me that I knew nothing about. An emotional hollowness was dictating my behavior and I had not even realized it was there…lurking, defining my behavior and tainting all of my relationships and intercourse with others. My father's rejection made me distrustful and unable to give true value to acceptance by others. There was an emotional abyss inside of me that would never be satisfied as I was now living my life. To fill that emptiness I did not need to seek attention, rather I should be giving it. McNair's punishment was to force me in the direction of giving instead of taking.

By not having a true caring father at home, I had missed that mature male guidance that teaches boys how to become men with masculine grace and paternal love. It had left me emotionally flawed and wanting. To mature as a man meant putting childhood emotions and cravings into the past, and assuming the moral responsibilities of being an adult. Yet, my emotional cravings had me stuck still trying to satisfy my boyhood needs. This was so deep I almost did not overhear Charlie's comment to Cowboy, "See, just like I said, Arrington always takes the heat."

"You'd think he'd get it after awhile," drawls Cowboy.

"Na, he's a sponge for attention; can't help himself."

He who spares his rod hates his son. But he who loves him disciplines him diligently. Proverbs 13:24

This is one of the most difficult times ever in America for young people growing up. The core family unit in America is often a disaster in progress. Because of divorce, separation, suicide, drug use and incarceration (one out of every twenty American men go to prison) the extended family is falling apart on a large scale..and growing. The children suffer the most. With the turn of the millennium, suicide has become the number two killer of teenagers in America. Currently the fastest growing rate of suicide per capita is children between the age of ten and fourteen. This is an age group that has been determined to be most dependent upon a close relationship with their father. Children who lack that fraternal bond are pre-disposed to the burden of emotionally damaged lives. This often dictates that at a young age many of their most critical life decisions will be determined by emotional needs rather than by sound logical determination. It means choosing from the flawed advice of emotional dependence and a lack of confidence instead of from the strong foundation of self worth.

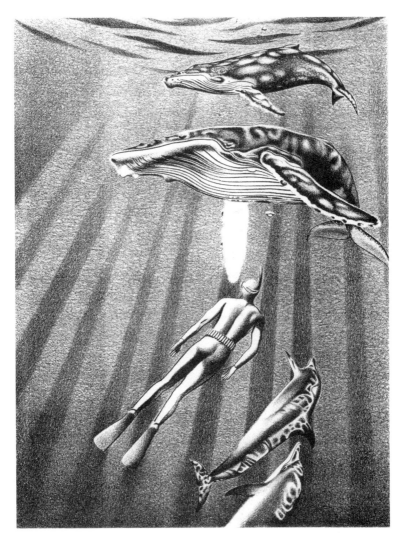

Illustration by Andy Charles
Dolphins attending Humpback whale with calf

"Living moments do not come from committees,"
John Henry Newman

Chapter 7

MAUI, HAWAII, JANUARY 1988

A SIXTEEN-FOOT LONG rubber boat is not very big. Considering that there are only three of us in the Zodiac, one would not expect it to be a logical place for a mutiny. What I am not getting is cooperation. Thierry has shut down the outboard and neither he, nor Michel DeLoire will let me near it.

"It is not fair," I complain.

"We don't care," the mutineers reply in unison, their French accents fit the moment of their frustrating behavior.

After spending all morning chasing whales, we have returned to the *Kai Kekoa* for more film and fresh camera batteries. Cindy has thoughtfully made me a peanut butter and jelly sandwich. Only after loading the other equipment, Thierry has motored twenty feet away so I could not have my lunch.

"But I am hungry," I throw myself on their mercy. It does not work. "Typical French non-cooperative attitude," I mumble half to myself.

"This boat is on a diet," responds Michel DeLoire.

"The boat is not on a diet, you guys are," I am getting desperate.

Yesterday, I had located a Hawaiian health food store with all kinds of specialty treats. I personally ground a variety of fresh roasted nuts (macadamias, cashews, peanuts and almonds) into thick nut butter. I also picked up a heavy loaf of seven-grain wheat bread and an assortment of tropical jellies and jams and other Hawaiian culinary delights. I really want this sandwich.

Cindy joins in the teasing by dangling the brown paper sack provocatively over the railing. "Don't you want your lunch, Steve?" she teases, "I put a special surprise in here."

I look hopefully at my friends in the boat, but see I am getting nowhere.

"Shouldn't we be getting back to the whales?" Thierry asks Michel as he cold-heartedly starts the outboard and shifts into reverse.

Michel glances at his watch. "Don't worry Mr. Steve," he says patting me on the back, "we will return promptly for your sandwich in a couple of hours."

In a moment, it will be too late. The gap between Cindy's vessel and our Zodiac begins to widen. As my panic builds I know there is only one other option. "Cindy, throw the bag," I shout.

Without hesitation, she hurls the brown sack in a high arc. Thierry jams the engine in full reverse. Leaning desperately outwards, I claw at the falling paper bag and just as I barely catch it...Michel DeLoire pushes me over the side of the rubber boat.

Surfacing, I frantically lift the wet paper bag out of the water. Taking a deep breath, I float on my back then carefully set the soggy sack on my chest and peer optimistically inside. Secretly I am enjoying the attention from my friends, then with a joyous shout, I pull out my sandwich inside a plastic baggy and hold it up triumphantly...the bag is a waterproof zip-lock. Still floating, like an otter, I happily open the plastic baggy to find not only a peanut butter and jelly sandwich, there is a surprise wrapped in shiny aluminum foil. I set the aluminum surprise package on my stomach for later consideration. It is in plain view of the mutineers and must be some kind of fattening dessert.

Knowing the guys will not leave me because I am Michel DeLoire's safety diver; I leisurely take a big bite of the sandwich. "Hmmm," I announce loudly, "Arrington bionic nut butter, sliced banana and guava jelly with a hint of fresh passion fruit."

Michel, who loves guavas, snorts his dissatisfaction, "Only an American barbarian would smear peanut butter on fresh passion fruit and then eat the mess floating in seawater."

Thierry is staring curiously at the shiny foil package resting on my tummy. "Aren't you going to open it?" he finally asks.

The foil glistens in the bright sunlight as I purposefully take my time unwrapping it. "Wow, chocolate-covered Maui potato chips!"

"Chocolate what?" Thierry maneuvers the rubber Zodiac closer as Michel leans outward for a better look. With obvious irritation, the two dieters unhappily watch me dramatically holding up a large chocolate-covered chip (Maui potato chips are huge). With great relish, I eat each chip and then slowly lick my fingers and the foil carefully. Before it could turn into an ugly situation, Cindy saves the day. "Anyone care for a chocolate fudge donut?" she asks innocently.

Motoring back out to the whales, I grin at my friends, who are gobbling a half-dozen chocolate, fudge-covered, with nut sprinkles, donuts. "I thought you guys were on diets?" I chuckle.

"Donuts are okay for dieters," mumbles Thierry, crumbs falling out of his mouth.

"Donuts are loaded with white flour, sugar and butter then they are deep fried in saturated oil," I reply.

"But you haven't considered the hole in the donut," Michel deadpans, "imagine how many calories we are not eating."

"The hole in the donut is an elegant idea," adds Thierry, "which is why it was invented by the French."

I am preparing to explore that statement when a breaching whale interrupts us. A forty-five ton whale can reach breaching speed with only three strokes of its powerful tail. What makes this breech particularly captivating is it is happening only twenty feet away and it is a whale calf doing the breaching. The little whale circles our rubber boat, throwing its tiny body out of the water seven times in rapid succession. The calf is the size of a very small school bus and this breaching business must be a lot of fun. Maybe it thinks our inflatable is a whale calf too and it is trying to encouraging it to play.

Donuts forgotten in favor of cameras Michel and I hurl ourselves into the water. He leads the descent. On Cousteau filming expeditions, the cinematographer has priority over still photographers. It means I always get the second-place position. It does not help that Michel is able to dive deeper and stay down longer, but he is cheating to do it. Michel has taken to wearing a pony tank, which is a very little scuba cylinder about the size of a loaf of bread. He figures that with the reduced air supply he will take fewer breathes and thus be less disturbing to the whales. I think his idea is in the same category as his donut hole theory. Holding my breath, I follow his small trail of bubbles downward.

The calf is slightly below and ahead of us as it swims back to its mother. I recognize the cow and am instantly pleased. She is a particularly human-friendly whale, affectionately known as Daisy (because of her spotted tail and tranquil disposition). Both whales turn in our direction and slowly swim over for a better look. I watch their eyes tracking Michel DeLoire and then I too come under the whales' scrutiny. The cow's huge eye has a friendly unconcerned look to it. I imagine I see a touch of pride for the playful calf swimming at her side. I watch the giant eye rotate to check the calf's position as it swims just above her right pectoral fin. It is amazing to look so closely into such a large intelligent eyeball. As the giant orb revolves back towards me, I wonder at the mysterious thoughts whirling behind that giant pupil. What is she thinking? Does she know we are only visitors to this underwater world? The thought gives me pause.

Whales live both above and below the water. When swimming on the surface they see us aboard gigantic ships or in small boats. Do they know these floating machines are lifeless, but for us? What must they think of our coastal cities? When swimming close to the Hawaiian Islands at night do they wonder at the mysterious lights glittering on the shore? Then again, maybe small shrimp and fish are of a far greater concern to them and we are just tiny, inconsequential creatures of little interest.

My thoughts about whale perception take off in a new direction with the arrival of the calf. It is swimming almost straight toward us. Its eyes wild with curiosity flicker from Michel to me, then back to Michel. *"What are these strange creatures?"* It must be wondering, *"Do they play?"* Possibly putting these thoughts to action, the baby whale moves hesitantly closer veering slightly away from its protective mother.

Without warning, the peaceful beauty of the moment is shattered by a large column of rising bubbles. There are thousands of them in a huge shimmering curtain that rises out of the depths completely engulfing Michel and me. The startled calf flees in panic back to its mother. Beneath us, a giant bull whale continues to express its concern by exhaling another long stream of air bubbles. It is a warning, not to be taken lightly. The massive bull weighs ninety thousand pounds and he is upset at us!

Bull whales leave bubble wakes as a warning, or as a challenge, to other creatures. The huge eye regarding us looks hostile and angry. His deep, penetrating glare sends a shutter racing down my spine. I look in alarm from the angry bull, to Michel, who is emitting a small bubble wake of his own from the pony tank. Could the bull be misinterpreting Michel's tiny bubbles as a challenge? We do not wait to find out as Michel and I torpedo for the surface.

Back in the Zodiac, Michel strips off the pony tank. "I don't think the bull likes my bubbles."

"No kidding," I answer.

We are telling Thierry about the encounter with the bull, when we see the whales returning toward the Zodiac. Instantly, Michel and I hurl ourselves back into the water; less his little bubble machine. We descend rapidly; the whales are deeper than before. Daisy and her calf attempt to approach us, but the bull herds them away. Again, the upset bull passes beneath us, only this time the gigantic mammal comes closer than before. The threat is very real as he voices his irritation by releasing a dense stream of large bubbles in an ascending curtain that all but obscures Michel DeLoire from my sight. My alarm is somewhat lessened by the impact of the giant air bubbles, which tickle as they bounce against my bare skin. Unable to hold our breath any longer, we nervously swim back towards the surface; surrounded by buoyant bubbles bouncing and glittering gaily in the submarine light.

Over the next fifteen minutes Daisy and her calf make four more friendly attempts to swim by us, but each time the bull drives them off...and he seems to be getting angrier with each encounter. Michel and I are near exhaustion from the repeated breath-hold dives. The calf announces it presence with a tiny spout of water a hundred feet away, a second closer spout indicates that it is heading in our direction. I quickly pull on my fins, but Michel is winded, probably from too many chocolate donut holes. "Go Stephen," he gasps, "they are your whales."

"My whales?" I am ecstatic...yet instantly uneasy. Slipping into the now chilly water, without the security of a friend, the depths seem darker and more foreboding. I swim apprehensively on the surface towards the approaching calf. Looking right, left, and down-ward repeatedly, I fretfully wonder where the bull might be, when a giant tail suddenly erupts from the water in front of me. The bull is only forty feet away. In stunned amazement, I see the massive fluke rising higher and higher, water coursing down its sides, until it towers two stories above me. Then the giant tail slams down in a mighty concussion of water and sound. Frozen in terror, I watch the huge flukes strike the water repeatedly. Each thunderous impact creates dual sound waves; one underwater that hammers against my body in a powerful shock wave, and the other an above water sound wave that echoes with heavy concussions, hammering against my eardrums and half blinding me with a deluge of flung of water.

Abruptly the tail descends then the enormous whale surfaces and blows mightily. The bull lies motionless in the water—waiting. It is a huge mobile roadblock awaiting my next move. Like an angry hippopotamus preparing to pounce on a mouse. Beneath the surface I nervously peer at the huge eye, and without hesitation, flee back towards the rubber boat. The whale blows one last time then slips below the water.

Returning to the Zodiac, I climb into the rubber boat without any assistance from Michel and Thierry, who are both laughing hysterically. Simmering with water dripping from my nose, I glare at my happy companions, and then I also begin to laugh. Life is more pleasurable when we do not take ourselves too seriously. The laughter spills out of the Zodiac and drifts on the wind to the *Kai Kekoa*; hearing it Cindy waves a greeting; sharing in our pleasure without knowing why.

"A light heart lives long," William Shakespeare

Goals are the bridges that span our dreams. Anonymous

Chapter 8

INDIANHEAD, MARYLAND, OCTOBER 1975

BENDING DOWN I shove my arms through the scuba pack webbing then lift the twin ninety cubic foot scuba cylinders over my head and slide them down my back. The key to cleanly lifting a scuba pack over your head is to keep pushing the pack away from you throughout the lift, then let them settle onto your back. This technique also works for heavy backpacks, etc. I automatically do a shoulder shrug settling the ninety-pound air cylinders into place then put the mouthpiece of the double hose regulator into my mouth. A quick exhalation ensures that there is nothing lurking inside the inch-and-a-half thick hoses. Earlier in the week, Charlie inhaled a large cockroach probably put there by Mickey Doke, the class practical joker. I take a short breath to make sure the regulator is delivering air. I pick up my dive mask, spit into it and then glance about as I unconsciously begin rubbing the saliva onto the faceplate to keep it from fogging up. There are only eighteen of us standing at the side of the pool and we are all extremely nervous…except for Hank who is thrilled that the dreaded pool harassment test is finally upon us.

"Look at Hank," grumbles Cowboy, "he is so energized you'd think he was a kid standing in line for the submarine ride at Disneyland."

Hank acknowledges the comment with his ubiquitous smile, "Oh, this is going to be way more fun than any old Disney ride."

"Fun," exclaims Charlie strapping on a weight belt, "McNair and his cronies are going to spend the next hour endeavoring to drown us and you think it is going to be fun?"

"Sure, the pool harassment exercise is a major confidence builder." Hank is buoyant, "After passing this there is not much of anything underwater we can't handle."

"Yeah? Well I could take a pass on this," laments Charlie adjusting a fin strap.

"No you couldn't," Hank, for once, is not smiling, "you want to be a Navy combat diver, you gotta get through pool harassment first. This is not just a test...it's a rite of passage. All combat frogs know that every member of their team has been through this and passed with flying colors. It means you can be depended upon when everything else is going wrong. It means when your dive buddy's life is at stake you'll be there no matter what is coming at you." Hank stalks away from Charlie, then turns and snarls, "No matter what you don't leave your swim partner!"

Watching Hank laying it out for Charlie, I realize I am seeing Hank's true character. Sure, he smiles a lot and has a buoyant personality, but inside Hank is a very serious and dedicated warrior. It would be an honor to serve on his team. I glance at Charlie and realize I could not say the same about him and then secretly wondered what the guys would think of serving with me? Maybe that question will be partially answered here at the school. I might even get a piece of the answer in the next few minutes. *No,* I promise myself, *failure is not an option.*

I dip my mask into the pool and slosh the water around washing out the saliva. There is a flock of butterflies fluttering around in my stomach. Everyone knows that I am going to be McNair's prime underwater target. I look down at the water slapping gently at the side of the pool. The bottom looks deeper than twenty-four feet. The pool shimmers underneath the ceiling floodlights. Then I see a glimmering reflection of a diver stepping up to stand beside me.

Hank looks at the water then nudges me, "Hey Arrington, want to be my dive buddy?"

I look sideways at my closest friend here at the school, "You bet, Hank."

"Mind if we're the last ones off the bottom?" he asks. "It's kind of important to me."

"Wouldn't have expected anything else," I say with more bravado than I am feeling. Glancing at the pool bottom again, somehow it just does not seem quite as deep or as threatening with Hank standing at my side.

"How much air you got in your tanks Candidate Arrington?" Instructor McNair's voice causes my heart to leap. How long has he been standing behind us I wonder?

"Three thousand pounds Instructor McNair."

"Good, you're going to need every square inch of it." McNair is carrying a mask, fins and a snorkel. He has a large sheath knife (K-Bar) strapped to his narrow waste. I am wondering about the knife; it is not something one normally takes into a swimming pool.

"Okay girls," states McNair setting down his snorkel gear and rubbing his big hands together in eager anticipation, "here's the pool harassment rules...there are none. Just go to the bottom of the pool, do not lose your swim buddy and if anyone breaks the surface before their cylinders are completely empty automatically gets to be a fleet sailor again with all the boring assets of extended time at sea in cramped smelly compartments doing mind-numbing routine jobs. Pass this test and you just might get a shot at working with the space program recovering astronauts, get to jump out of perfectly good airplanes, lockout of submerged submarines and my personal favorite, blowing things up in a big way. There is more underwater adventure waiting in your future than any of you idiots can imagine. All you got to do is get past me and that ain't going to be easy at all."

Of course, we already know that the only rule is that if you surface or abandon your dive buddy, you are out of the class, but what we are really wondering about is that knife McNair is wearing. Charlie takes the plunge. "What's the knife for?" he asks nervously.

"In case I get inspired." McNair glances at his watch, "You girls got five seconds to get out of my sight."

Eighteen bodies create a pressure wave that sloshes over the concrete deck. Underwater Hank gives me the thumbs up then we begin swimming rapidly downward. *Failure is not an option*, I whisper to myself. I am not going to fail Hank, myself or McNair. I want to be a Navy frogman more than anything else in the world. It is just an issue of holding your breath…while getting beat up by extremely motivated instructors who do not intend to share their unique underwater fraternity with any men of lesser caliber.

McNair arrives in a flash of fins. In a couple of vicious seconds he tears my mask away, rips the mouthpiece roughly from my clenched teeth and snatches the fins from my feet. First, the air supply I tell myself reaching over one shoulder to grab the thick rubber air hose right where it comes out of the regulator. I stretch out the corrugated hoses until I find the mouthpiece and then quickly plug it into my mouth. I cautiously exhale into the mouthpiece to clear out the water and try to take a shallow breath. It is not a surprise to discover that my air is off. Okay, I hit the quick release at my waist and the one on my left shoulder. This allows me to pull the bulky double tanks around in front of me. I crank the air valve back on and am rewarded with a surge of bubbles. I grab a deep breath then notice through the blur of the water, I am still mask-less, that Hank is giving me the hand signal that he wants to buddy breath.

One of the interesting aspects of buddy breathing with a double hose regulator is that you must give up the mouthpiece without any assurance that the person receiving it is going to give it back in a timely way. This is where trust becomes a major issue. I would trust Hank with my life , I quickly push the mouthpiece towards his beaver teeth. He takes two quick breathes to purge his lungs, and then the mouthpiece is mine again. I grab two short breathes, pass the mouthpiece back and while Hank takes his breaths, I put my mask back on, clear it and glance about the bottom of the massive almost three stories-deep pool.

All about us, it is an underwater war zone. Students are scattered the length of the hundred twenty foot pool with their dive gear drifting about them like debris from detonations or strewn in heaps much like road kill on the pool bottom. At mid-pool, a set of twin tanks thuds into the cement floor amidst an explosion of bubbles. McNair and his fellow assailants are hitting each buddy team like a coordinated shark attack in a panicked school of minnows. While we are recovering the rest of our gear I notice why Hank has to buddy breathe with me. The twin tanks on his back are missing their regulator; McNair has it attached to his knife belt. McNair and his band of pirates are free diving, which makes them quick and agile. Gunner McNair is elegant as he free dives downward two and one half stories to attack a dive team from behind. He strips them of their gear then uses the tank straps to rapidly tie the regulator hoses, fins, and dive masks into a large bulky knot. Then he hovers like a lurking predator to see if he can cause any more mischief before heading to the surface for another quick breath.

After organizing our equipment, Hank and I begin swimming a circuit of the pool. We are staying about three feet off the bottom, which somewhat limits the direction of McNair's next attack. Since we are still buddy breathing, Hank is riding on my tanks. I take two breaths, then pass the regulator upwards to Hank. I feel a tap on my shoulder as the mouthpiece comes back to me. I begin to take a breath while looking for McNair, when suddenly I know exactly where he is creeping about. Not only is there no air flowing from the mouthpiece, it is not attached to my tanks anymore as the empty yoke drifts in front of my faceplate. How did McNair do that I wonder without my feeling it? While McNair is ripping the mask from my face, I realize that it had to have happened when Hank was supposed to be getting his two breaths. Okay, I could really use a breath of air, but Hank must be getting desperate. I re-attach the regulator yoke to the cylinder, spin open the air value then push the tanks toward Hank who is a blurred figure three feet away. Hank does a quick double breath then jams the mouthpiece into my mouth. While I do my breaths, he slides the scuba pack over my shoulders and settles them onto my back. A few seconds later we are swimming our circuit again only be to attacked a minute or two later.

About fifteen minutes into pool harassment, I notice the first set of fins at the surface. Wait…make that two sets of fins. A buddy team is hugging the side of the pool. Sixteen I think to myself. I have no idea who they are because Hank and I am again mask-less and back under attack. This time McNair has added an interesting twist. He has stretched the corrugated double hoses the length of the tanks and wedged the mouthpiece between the bottoms of the twin ninety cylinders. Hank flips the tanks upside down, pulls the regulator out and snatches a breath from the free flowing mouthpiece, then he passes it to me…and he is laughing! A gurgle of bubbles ascends from his lips in a buoyant cascade. *Wow, Hank is actually enjoying this.* Taking the regulator from my mouth, I take the time to leisurely blow an air ring and watch it ascending towards the surface. Blowing air rings underwater is easy. Simply lean back so your face is horizontal and then blow a short puff of air out while holding your tongue centered in your mouth. I watch the air ring expanding, a silvery shimmering wheel of air holding its shape for about ten feet before collapsing into a shower of bubbles that rushes upwards in a sparkling cloud that dissipates into thousands of tinier bubbles as they break against the underside of the pool's surface.

Too cool! I shout wordlessly. My fear of pool harassment dissipates like the bubble ring. Hank is right. If we can handle this then we can handle anything. Immediately, I correct my thoughts. It does not mean we can handle anything because nature can be brutal, particularly underwater, but we are as prepared as the best combat diver-training program in the world permits.

Over Hank's shoulder, I see McNair and his crew of brigands descending on another buddy team. Stripped of all their equipment they begin to buddy breath, then one of them begins to lose it. It is Charlie. He looks upwards. "No Charlie," I shout into my regulator, but underwater I am the only one who hears the sound-less warning. Cowboy is on the bottom looking forlornly upward as his dive partner heads for the surface. A great sadness washes over me as I watch Charlie struggling upwards. I am losing a friend. I am a silent observer incapable of sharing any words of encourage-ment. All I can do is watch him go and deep down inside of me something shudders. It is a compelling feeling of real loss. I realize I have never had friends like this before. Our friendship has been tempered in the kiln of many hardships shared. It is not just the tragedy of losing a friend; it is that this friendship has helped to define my own self-worth. Facing real challenges with the rest of the class has established a true feeling of military camaraderie amongst us. Forging a fighting force out of untrained strangers has been the mission of military trainers since the beginning of recorded human history. My intense feelings of loss are interrupted by the enthusiastic arrival of McNair and company flush with the success of culling our class of another candidate.

Hank and I wait a few patient seconds while violence is rendered upon us. As the bubbles clear, it is apparent that something major is wrong. We no longer have a regulator. I am wondering if we are supposed to swim down to another team for a foursome of buddy breathing, when I notice that Hank has cupped his hands over the open tank valve. An upward rush of bubbles funnels through his hands from which he is sipping a breath of air. He pauses and nods downward encouraging me to breathe from his cupped hands. I swallow a fair share of water filtering bubbles between my teeth, but get just enough air to stay down. To make this awkward way of breathing underwater work requires that one hold their tongue vertical in their mouth with the tip of the tongue touching the roof of the mouth. The bit of water that accompanies the air strikes the bottom of the tongue keeping it from choking you. The air easily flows around the tongue.

McNair swims over to stare at us. He looks amused as he hands back over our regulator. Hank reaches out to take the regulator, but then he purposefully grabs McNair' hand. I am wondering what he is up to when I see Hank's other hand reach for something at the back of his swimsuit and places it firmly in the surprised instructor's hand. It is McNair's knife. Apparently, he stole it, while McNair was removing my regulator.

McNair' faceplate rotates towards the knife as he stares. The big blade reflects boldly against the plate glass. He brings the knife closer until it is inches from his mask. His eyes seem to glitter behind the plate glass, then he purposefully grabs my regulator's mouthpiece and with two slashes cuts away the hoses before swimming away.

Hank and I re-attach the regulator and crack open the air valve. Air bubbles froth from the cut hose making it is a lot easier to breathe than snatching bubbles from our cupped hands. True to my promise to Hank, I close down the valve between breaths to conserve air. We are going to stay down as long as possible to be the last buddy team off the bottom.

"Destiny is not a matter of chance, it is a matter of choice; it is not a thing to be waited for, it is a thing to be achieved,"
William Jennings Bryan

"A good conscience is a continual Christmas,"
Benjamin Franklin

Chapter 9

MAUI, HAWAII, JANUARY 1988

IT IS 2:00 a.m. and I am unable to sleep. Cindy left on the sunset flight back to California. She could only join the whale expedition during the ten days of spring break. Tomorrow, Cindy will be back in her college classroom, studying her lessons, but no doubt thinking about whales...and, maybe, if I'm lucky, about me.

Lying in bed, I wonder about our future. I already know that I will ask Cindy to marry me; the big question is when? This is not an easy thing for a man to ask. Curled on the nightstand lies the flower lei she wore to the airport. In the morning, I will cast the lei into the ocean. It is an ancient Hawaiian custom, a physical promise to return to these tropical islands one day. Lifting the tealeaf wrapped lei, I inhale the fragrant flowers' delicate bouquet. Dropping it onto my bare chest, I ponder the wonder of an adventurous life with someone who is as much fun and courageous as Cindy.

Outside I hear the rustle of palm trees swaying in the island trade winds. Several of the long fronds are lightly brushing against the window's wooden shutters. The soft scraping sound blends with the deep-toned chunking chorus of a stand of bamboo trees clunking against each other. The tall, hollow trees are thick and old, the bamboo stand echoes with deep reverberations like a forest of wooden wind chimes. Beneath the music of the wind, there is the deeper rumble of pounding surf. I lean out the open window and see shimmering waves bathed in moonlight.

My bungalow is nestled amongst the trees, a mere hundred feet from the shore. A few minutes later, I step out its front door. In one hand, I carry Cindy's flower lei, in the other hand are my swim fins and mask. Walking across the white sand beach, I see an almost full moon sailing in a cloudless sky. Its lunar light glistens on the restless ocean; closer to shore the surf is emitting a faint neon glow of its own. The tumbling action of the wave is exciting the phytoplankton in the water. These tiny life forms, also known as Dinoflagellates, become bioluminescent through a molecular process known as luciferase. They emit a soft blue glow just like fire flies. The cadence of the waves creates a rippling, luminescence that pales and fades with each passing breaker.

Walking out into the warm tropical water, I don my mask and fins then begin to swim out. Placing the lei around my neck, I am planning on releasing it out beyond the surf zone. Diving into the white water from the first oncoming wave, I abruptly feel the surge ripping Cindy's lei to shreds. Turning to look through my mask behind me underwater, I see the spinning flowers washing away, leaving tiny florescent wakes in their passage. So I immediately move to part two of my plan—night bodysurfing!

When swimming out through surf, it is easier to go under the waves. Taking a deep breath, I dunk under the next breaker. The surf is running three to four feet; challenging, but fun-sized waves. Underwater the bottom is shadowed in darkness, above me the waves ripple with soft light from their florescent glow. It is here that I begin to hear the whales singing. The Humpback sounds are at first faint, but the whale music intensifies and fades as I reach deeper water. Immersed in the songs of the Humpbacks that fade and swell with the ocean's surge, I surface just beyond the surf zone, looking to catch my first wave.

In the near darkness, depth perception is difficult to judge. Yet, as the wave before me builds, I see moonlight radiating through the gleaming wall of water. Using the moon as a floating reference, I begin kicking vigorously with both fins as the rising swell of water sweeps me upwards. Just before the leading edge of the wave begins to throw-out, I launch face-first down the tumbling wall of cascading water. For an instant, I am almost in full freefall then my chest plows into the vertical moving surface. Arching my back and reaching out with my right arm creates controlled lift as I begin skimming rapidly across the upward rushing water. My right arm acts as a rudder, pointing upwards it carries me higher into the racing breaker. Passing over a submerged reef, the wave becomes critical then the lip before me pitches outward into a perfect revolving cylinder of spinning water. Momentarily caught inside a hydraulic rotary vortex, I watch glowing swirls of luminescence play across the fast-moving liquid surface. My outstretched hand knifes into the smooth water leaving a comet-like wake of soft neon blue florescent fire. Through the shadowy sheen of the wave's surface, I see the glowing orb of the moon shimmering in the satin black water. Then the wave abruptly collapses upon itself sending me spinning along the bottom.

The underwater surge weaves a luminescent glow around each object it washes over. The bottom is alive with swirling trails of florescent light from the phytoplankton. Swimming back to the surface, I shake the water from my hair and eyes, and abruptly see something I did not even know existed. Just before each wave breaks, the night wind lifts a fine mist of water from the feathery leading edge of the breakers. Caught within the mist, as it fleetingly hangs suspended in the wind, is a pale moon bow. The ghostly colors, softly radiant in the mist, evaporate in hardly more than an instant, like fairy dust only imagined.

For a couple of hours I play in the surf zone. This is the first and only time I have witnessed plankton luminescence in Hawaii and I am determined to stay immersed in it as long as possible. I watch the moon set and the night parade of the stars. The whale music swells and fades with its own secret rhythm. Finally, exhausted and cold, I ride a breaker back to the shore. On the beach, I see one of Cindy's flowers resting on the white sand. Picking it up I wish with all my might that Cindy could have shared this magic night with me. One of the truths I have learned about life is that happiness, challenge and adventure are all enhanced by being shared with a companion.

> *"Marriage is an adventure in cooperation. The more we share the richer we will be; and the less we share the poorer we will be,"* Harold B. Walker

Setting the flower back into the water, I watch it swirling back out to sea. In the quiet of the night, I make Cindy a silent promise, *"Though you may become my wife, I promise that you will first always be my best friend."*

When we treat family as friends and friends as family, we are sharing the best qualities of these relationships with the people we care about the most. Friendships are life's treasures; they define the quality of our existence amongst other human beings.

A man of many companions may come to ruin, but there is a friend who sticks closer than a brother. Proverbs 18:2

Graduating class July 6, 1976; Hank is 2nd from left, author 3rd from left.

Leadership is action, not position. Anonymous

Chapter 10

INDIANHEAD, MARYLAND, NOVEMBER 1975

WEARING BATTLE dress utilities (BDU's), jungle boots, a slouch hat and with a sheathed K-Bar knife hanging from a web belt, I stand on the edge of a forest beside a slow flowing river. Draped over one shoulder is my bomb disposal tool pouch. A light breeze drifting from the forest carries the fresh scent of pine needles. Nervously I wonder what awaits me inside the dense and almost haunting woods.

The forest lies alongside the Potomac River and is located at the Explosive Ordnance Disposal School in Indian Head, Maryland. Forty acres of wild woodlands hide a broad assortment of practical ordnance problems. Our class of a dozen remaining EOD candidates is working in teams of three. For the day's exercises, each of the team members is tasked with a single practical problem to solve. This morning it is my turn.

Instructor McNair looks at me and grins, "Hey meat," he laughs, "bet you're gonna smell like burnt hamburger oozing ketchup in the next couple of minutes." With those reassuring words, he starts his stopwatch and gives me a shove down a dirt path. I walk slowly following the narrow trail as it goes around a bend disappearing into the dense forest with all my senses keenly alert for trip wires and other booby traps. In my back pocket, I carry a three-by-five-inch situation card.

My card reads, Da Nang, Vietnam, 1968, Tet Offensive. Your bomb disposal team has been dispatched to an oil storage yard where three Viet Cong sappers have penetrated the base defenses. You have two hours to inspect the site rendering safe any explosive devices encountered. Because of the strategic need of this facility, BIP procedures are not authorized. *Author's note: BIP means blow in place, which is the easiest and safest way to dispose of an IED (Improvised Explosive Device; i.e. homemade bomb); it is a technique favored by bomb disposal men worldwide and is almost never authorized.*

Creeping cautiously down the narrow path I listen to the crunch of Instructor McNair's boots walking on the trail in my wake. In his hands, he carries a clipboard to grade my performance. It is very disorienting to try to sneak with an instructor in tow that behaves a lot like Rambo on steroids. Having to split my attention between the ordnance problems that lay ahead of me and the man with the explosive personality stalking me from behind is daunting. In a real unexploded bomb situation the disposal man would walk in alone…it is known as the longest walk in the world. This being my very first practical ordnance exercise I particularly want to do well. Somewhere in my immediate future lurks a half-pound block of TNT attached to a booby trap device. If I do anything wrong the device will trigger an explosion just far enough away to be a total shock, but not damaging to my body…or so I have been told.

Around another bend in the trail, beyond a clump of old trees, I see the dull sheen of a steel oil tank. Resisting the urge to hurry I glance at my wristwatch. I have used fifteen minutes of my precious time to cover barely seventy-five yards of trail. Taking a deep breath does not steady my frayed nerves. With each step, I pause to peer carefully about looking for bent branches, damaged leaves or freshly turned soil. The hard-packed dirt of the trail seems undisturbed—or did it? Something just does not feel right as I face a narrow point in the trial. Crouching down for a more careful look,

I see something more noticeable from this lower perspective. The dirt line on a sharp-faced rock is a half-inch higher than the ground surrounding it. I look suspiciously at the loosely packed dirt trail. To one side there are a few crumbs of disturbed dirt half-hidden by a ground-hugging leafy branch and a couple of dead leaves. The pieces of dirt are half-damp...someone has been digging. The placement of the sharp rock and leafy branch ensure that anyone coming down the trail will place a foot right on top of the barely disturbed patch of dirt.

Earlier Instructor McNair confided that each situation could have up to three explosive hazards. Slowly I sink down onto my knees and suppressing a surge of excitement I turn and grin at Instructor McNair, who looks away pretending not to notice that I am onto his first booby-trap. It is another positive clue.

Unsheathing my K-Bar knife, I gently probe the ground. The blade tip sinks easily downward through two inches of loose packed soil and then it grates against something solid. With great care I slowly scrape away the crumbly dirt gradually revealing a hand-made Vietnamese anti-personnel mine. It is a simple matter to pull a pin from my pocket and slip it into the plunger. The device is now rendered safe and I am about to lift it out...when I hear McNair take a single step closer to look over my shoulder. What was he trying to see? He knows what is here since he is the one who probably did the digging. Suspicious, I wonder if another surprise lurks beneath the first device. Gently scooping the dirt out from under the anti-personnel mine my index finger encounters a taunt wire attached to the bottom of the mine.

"*Oh man,*" I think to myself, "*he booby trapped the booby trap.*"

Holding my breath, I unearth a second mine. It is a Bouncing Betty. This is an American device. When triggered a small explosive charge bounces the mine four to six feet into the air before going off ensuring maximum personnel damage. The top mine had a plunger for a trigger, this one has a pull mechanism to function the device. Any disturbance of the top mine would trigger the second booby trap. Using another pin, I render safe the pull mechanism, then brushing dirt from my hands, I grin again at Instructor McNair. He grins back, which does nothing to steady my frayed nerves. Usually when Instructor McNair grins, it means I am in, or about to be in, trouble. Setting the two mines to one side for later disposal, I stand just beyond the hole and peer down the trail. I could not help feeling the warm flush of success; two down and only one more to go...and I already know right where the third device could be found.

Obviously, the goal of the sappers was to blow the oil tank. Problem number three is undoubtedly attached somewhere to that tank. So I head at a faster pace directly for it. I do not intend just to beat the practical problems. I want a good total problem time too. I am completely unaware that my ego has just weighed in as a negative dimension to solving this practical problem. Instead, I am eager for McNair to notice my deductive reasoning that is leading me to the obvious location of the last device. I move forward at a rather reckless pace for someone playing hide-and-seek with explosive devices. Five minutes later, I am rewarded with the sight of an IED attached to the metal cylinder near one of the tank's lower welds. There are six sticks of dynamite taped to the steel plate with a simple chemical pencil fuse. After a short inspection, I confidently render the device safe by merely jerking out the chemical fuse, and then jam its explosive tip downward into the dirt. I may have done the jerking out and jamming into the dirt with rather more flourish than necessary, but I was in a buoyant mood and wanted to make a bit of a statement.

"Done," I announce proudly.

Instructor McNair smiles at me, which I should have recognized as not being a good sign, but I am flushed with an overwhelming feeling of accomplishment. He glances at his watch, "Only an hour and fifteen minutes. That is a pretty good time for this problem."

I grin at the compliment knowing I earned it.

"Usually students use the whole two hours just to make sure they have not missed anything." He is rubbing his hands together like a person anticipating something pleasurable. "Sure you're done?"

"Three problems," I answer confidently, "three solutions."

"Then call in your team," smiles McNair.

There is that McNair smile softly warning me again. Abruptly, I feel a lot less confident. "No more than three devices per problem. That is what you said, right?" I ask feeling a sudden need for reassurance.

"Yep," McNair has the toothy grin of a hungry lion leering at its lunch. A human lunch that is stupid enough to stand within striking distance with his hands in his pockets trying to look confident.

"Hank, Mickie, you can come in," I yell no longer fully convinced that they should at all.

McNair has me take the other team members to the land mines and the IED to show them how I found each device and explain what I did to render them safe. My self-assurance has returned and I am feeling quite proud of myself. I can tell the other two guys are a bit envious of my hundred-percent grade on the first problem with forty-five minutes to spare. McNair glances at his digital watch, and then leads us over to a gnarled old oak tree.

"There's one more point I would like to cover about this problem," he says merrily as he pauses to look at his watch again. "Here," he motions with his hands, "I want you guys to stand right about here." He places us just beyond the old oak, then quickly steps back and leans against the tree's broad trunk. His posture is of someone trying to avoid being hit by something.

"Uh oh," Hank utters under his breath, "I have a really bad feeling about this." I see him sniffing at the air. "Smells like burnt gun powder."

Burnt gunpowder? My mind echoes realizing that this is the problem's blasting site. I glance nervously at McNair, who appears to be counting silently on his fingers, then he looks up from his watch, flashes us his broad student-eating smile and jams his index fingers into both ears.

"Hit the deck," I yell too late.

Though expected, the shock of the blast hits us with complete surprise. Twenty-five-yards away a half-pound of TNT explodes in a shallow pool dug out specifically for this purpose. A thirty-foot-tall eruption of mud, dirty water and shredded leaves rains down on us.

"Four! There were four!" I yell urgently over the ringing in my ears, "You said that there would only be three."

"Dumb idiot," mumbles McNair shaking his head, "there were only three problems. The first two mines were connected so they only count as one device."

"But that's not fair," I start to argue.

"Excuse me, Bird Brain, fair is not even a factor in this equation. You just blew a war problem. Anyone smell steaming roast American meat in an Asian jungle?"

I jam my hands in my pocket and kick at a clump of smoking leaves.

"Come on," leers McNair, "want to see what killed you?"

Walking doggedly in McNair' footsteps, I am not at all in the mood to see *what killed me.* Ten feet from the oil tank McNair points to a simulated explosive charge hidden in a bush beneath a transfer valve. "It's okay, Arrington," McNair offers, with a crocodile grin, "a lot of overconfident candidates fail this exercise."

"Fail," I echo, "but I found and safed the first two problems. Don't they count?"

"Get over it Arrington," scolds McNair, "If this was real you'd be shredded meat basted in jungle muck and served up in a black ziplock body bag for shipment home to your mother."

"Oh yeah, I forgot about that," I answer lamely as I quietly hear Mickey Doke trying to suppress a snicker.

"Look at the bright side," McNair continues cheerfully, "you've got nine more practical problems to try to pull your grade back up. Only from now on, I want you to be a little more focused on what your main commitment in life is supposed to be."

"I am committed," *Did that just sound like a whine?*

McNair steps right up to my chest as he flatly snarls, "You are attempting to become a bomb disposal frogman in my world. In this profession we tend to realize that when someone plants a bomb they are usually interested in blowing something or someone up," McNair sounds like he is lecturing a five-year-old. "That could be you...or more importantly me. That is if you make it through my school, which does not appear to be very promising right now. Your stupid mistake can get your whole team killed, which might incidentally include me because we could wind up one day working together, which again is rather doubtful at this moment. In the real world, there are only two types of bomb disposal frogmen: live ones and dead or maimed ones. When it comes to bombs and booby-traps you learn to anticipate the unexpected. This means not ever taking anything for granted. A bomb disposal man has to be completely aware, totally alert and constantly exploring everything around him with all of his senses all the time."

"I was alert," I start to argue.

"Na Arrington," McNair shakes his head and knuckles my chest with his fist to punctuate his words. "You were being dense as usual and completely inattentive. Thinking you could second guess the sappers you hurried down a trail you were told was booby-trapped."

"But I was right," I interrupt, "there weren't any more mines on the trial."

McNair glares at me, "So what? You just had a lucky guess. Now tell me how many mistakes a bomb disposal man can make?" He is mimicking an explosion motion with his hands.

"None," I hazard meekly.

McNair continues to trash my procedure with great satisfaction. "If you were even remotely alert simple logic would have told you that there was another device."

I want to say something in my defense. Instead, I carefully think through each of the problems, but nothing comes to mind. "I missed something?" I finally ask feebly.

"Yeah, sometimes the answer is found in what is not there," confides McNair urging me on hopefully, but I am confused and feeling rather dense, not that I was about to admit it to McNair.

"Use your eyeballs dummy." McNair grabs my head with his

two big hands and forces me to look at the wire with the digital timer leading from the last bobby trap. "This is the only device with an electrical wire leading from it to trigger the half pound block of TNT in the waterhole. The other devices did not have a wire running from them."

"Oh," I whisper weakly.

"That is a really big hint, Rocks For Brains. How could you miss the fact that one of the problems has to be rigged to live explosives? We are working with real ordnance. That is why this is called a practical explosive problem. So, what did it gain you to hurry?"

I am really wishing I could be anywhere else, but McNair is waiting for a straight answer. "A better grade?" I hazard.

"When are you going to understand this is not about grades? It is about learning what it takes to be a bomb disposal frogman in the real world."

"I am not taking this seriously enough?"

"Darn right you're not! Think about it," McNair lays a hand on my shoulder, "you overlooked the obvious, made lousy suicidal assumptions, and you're an idiot liable to wipe-out your whole team."

"I am?"

"Sure. You just admitted it, didn't you?" McNair has that sparkle in his eyes that all teachers get when they think a student may actually be getting close to the point. "Remember," cautions McNair, "in real life you'd be worm food in that black plastic zip-lock waiting to be FedExed home to mom."

"I'm the idiot who just blew up his team," this is not something easy to admit, particularly in front of Hank and Doke.

"Good, now that you're ready to begin learning for real," McNair hoists up on his belt. His posture is that of a person about to say something important. "I am going to tell you a great secret of mine. It is better to appear ignorant than to be stupid."

"Huh?" Is he purposefully trying to confuse me again?

"It's simple. Prideful people are reluctant to ask questions because they don't want to reveal that they don't know all the answers. Instead they blunder around unaided when a simple question can immediately focus them in the right direction."

"I see," I answer, yet I am still not real sure about anything just yet.

"No you don't see it at all," McNair, sighs wearily, "you don't ask many questions because you're always trying to pretend that you have all of the answers."

Well that laid it out pretty straightforwardly...I'm the prideful person McNair is referring to in his explanation. I nod slowly encouraging McNair to continue though I am not real happy about it.

"Now if we are in agreement about you being rather dense and slow we might have a starting point to begin your real education." McNair kneels down on one knee and motions for us to join him. "My job is to weed out all the hot shots that are too stupid..." McNair glances at me and smiles, "or too vain, to realize they are actually here to learn something. If you think you're smart, then you're not." McNair is again punctuating his words by jabbing me in the chest with his blunt finger. "Real intelligence is an open self-admission that learning is a never ending process." Finger poke. "Knowledge always breeds more questions." Finger poke. "Learning does not end until the biological life form is terminated."

Biological life form terminated? Is McNair a *Star Trek fan?* I wonder to myself.

Suddenly McNair smiles; it is the first openly friendly smile he has offered us and it looks completely out of place on his rugged face. "As a bomb disposal frogman you get only one chance in an explosive situation. Make one mistake and you, I or someone else is going to exit this life in a very dramatic way." McNair stands and brushes off his pants. "You guys are on the threshold of a very challenging and adventurous life, but that is only if you prove to be truly alert and aware. Let me introduce you to a new term: global awareness."

"Like the environment?" asks Mickey.

"Want me to hurt you?" replies McNair. "I'm not talking about being a Tree Hugger. This is about being in a continuous state of heightened awareness. As a bomb disposal frog, you need to make a major shift in the way you think. Your brain has to be in tune with your immediate global world. This way if something is out of place you notice it right away. This is a skill that will serve you well no matter where you are at or what you are doing; doesn't matter if you're in a war zone or in your mom's backyard eating barbeque. This is not just about being a warrior; it is about being an aware and alert human being. It means being the one to notice the accident that is about to happen and getting out of its way. It is about perceiving the dark shape shadowing you in the darkness and knowing how to escape...or kill it. It is about caring to learn new skills that will enhance your ability to solve problems. It is about being more than just another common moron crawling about on this fascinating planet."

McNair stands up and asks, "Do I look threatening?"

"Always," quips Mickey Doke.

McNair whips out his K-Bar knife testing the razor-sharp point with his thumb, "How about now?"

"Much more threatening," Mickey Doke says nervously.

"Don't move; not an inch," cautions McNair as he slowly reaches out with the knife and flicks a button off Mickey Doke's shirt. "How's your state of awareness working right now?"

"Real good." He is sweating and closely eyeballing the knife.

"In Vietnam, most soldiers didn't get the mind set until they had been in country for awhile. Some of them didn't live long enough to develop their warrior consciousness at all. The point is that a true warrior doesn't wait until he gets into combat to start thinking like a fighter."

McNair sheaths his knife and all of us visibly relax. "The point is you don't wait until you graduate from this school to start thinking like a bomb disposal man. You graduate from this school and you'll never be the same person again."

"Education is the best provision for the journey to old age,"
Aristotle

Illustration by Marjory Spielman
How I imagined my childhood in the foothills behind my house.

"Childhood is frequently a solemn business for those inside it," Gore Vidal

Chapter 11

HANA, BIG ISLAND OF HAWAII, JAN/FEB 1988

$\int$ WITCHING OFF the light in my hotel room, I wonder if I will be able to sleep. Tomorrow promises to be one of the scariest and most challenging days of my life. I am taking a team of friends into extreme danger. As the expedition leader, they rely on me to take charge of the situation. This means extensive planning and research on my part. I must be aware of everything that can possibly go wrong and take steps to prevent any potential disasters. A simple mistake can cost someone his life...or even endanger the entire team. For a moment, I consider how this mission began, in Jean-Michel Cousteau's office in West Hollywood on a late Friday afternoon.

Like most divers, Jean-Michel Cousteau collects stuff from his life as a diver. Considering that Captain and Jean-Michel Cousteau are the premier divers in the world, their offices are full of really interesting diver stuff. On a side table is one of the first double hose regulators ever built, but the one piece that totally captures my attention is an old wood and glass underwater camera housing. It housed the camera that filmed the underwater scenes from Jules

Verne's, *Twenty Thousand Leagues Under the Sea.* The workmanship is exquisite, made by a master carpenter. Made in 1954 this is not leading edge technology, but rather sound workmanship by a true craftsman. The housing is made out of varnished wood. There are black metal gears and levers to operate the camera, hand-cut horsehide gaskets to keep the water out and a flat plane of glass for the camera lens to capture the underwater scenes. Running my hands over the smooth wood casing the inquisitive boy inside me is thrilled to touch something that so impacted my childhood and therefore my adult future.

As a young boy growing up in Southern California I loved watching movies like *Swiss Family Robinson, Twenty Thousand Leagues Under the Sea* and *Robinson Crusoe.* My quest for adventure in life began through a hole in our backyard fence. Normally, I would get down on my knees and wiggle though it. Today, it basically being the last day of my true childhood as I am starting high school tomorrow, I decide to climb over the fence and rip my jeans in the process. Mouser, my-love-to-explore-but-not-too-far-from-the-house cat, opts for the convenience of the hole, but then she abandons me fifty yards up the trail. The fat cat pretends an interest in a singing bird in a tree, but she does not like being this far from her food dish.

Jumping over a narrow brook, I pause on the far side to stare at minnows swimming in the clear water, and then spend five more minutes looking for a bullfrog croaking under a broad-leaf fern. On a mossy rock, I leave three pieces of bread. I am hoping the raccoons that live in the hollow of a brook-side tree will not try washing the bread in the slow flowing water again. Last time the wet bread fell apart, which turned out to be good news for the minnows.

It takes me a good hour of hiking and climbing to reach the secret spot. It is high up on the south side of the tallest foothill. The narrow dirt trail leading to it seems to end at a cliff where a house-size boulder tilts outward over a box canyon. I quickly scramble over the top of the boulder, and then drop down onto a small slab shelf.

An outcropping of rocks shades the ledge and provides shelter for a little brown mouse that lives in a deep crack in the stone wall. Actually, there are now two mice, but I do not know that until I open my lunch sack. Sitting down on the warm rock, I take out a peanut butter and jelly sandwich wrapped in wax paper. Breaking off a tiny piece, I set it on the toe of my sneaker. The mouse I know, and who is very familiar with my lunch sack, is quickly out of his burrow to investigate the morsel. He leaps on the delectable crumb, scurries into a shaded spot and stuffs all of it into his mouth with his tiny paws. The other mouse is not so sure about this giant intruder on her front porch. She eyes me suspiciously from the safety of her burrow. I see her tiny nose industriously working the delectable scent of peanut butter and strawberry jam.

I continue placing sandwich crumbs here and there, and one large one on my jeans. She anxiously watches her mate greedily cramming crumbs into his face. She waits until I pretend to glance the other way, then pounces on the big crumb near my knee and drags it closer to her burrow. Our new friendship ends at about the same time that I run out of sandwich.

While the bolder mouse investigates the empty brown paper sack, I lean back against the warm coarse stone and dangle my feet over the shear face of the cliff. Happily, I stare at puffy white clouds floating in a pale blue sky. I watch a hawk soaring upward on a wind shear. Its shadow passes over the ledge sending both of the mice scurrying in alarm back into their crevice.

Way below my sneakers, I gaze out at my little town of Monrovia and in the distance at the broad Los Angeles basin. On the horizon, a mixture of sea haze and smog obscures the Pacific coastline. On clearer days, I can see the ocean from my rocky crow's nest. When the hot Santa Ana winds blow in from the high desert, it sweeps away all the dust and smog. On those incredibly clear days, I sometimes think I can see distant Catalina Island riding low on the sea blue horizon; probably I am just giving weight to cloud shadows on the water.

I have already determined that the ocean is where I am going to work when I grow-up. I will probably become a sailor, like my uncle who is a boson's mate with the Navy's Seventh Fleet in Asia. I briefly wonder what it would be like to stand at the helm of an enormous battleship. Yet, what I really hope to be is a scuba diver. I love watching television programs about divers and their underwater adventures. Sometimes I wear fins and a dive mask while watching Cousteau documentaries so I can pretend I am underwater too. My biggest hero in the whole world is Captain Jacques Yves Cousteau.

High above my ledge I see a large bird soaring near a windswept cloud. In my imagination, I pretend that the cloud is a huge whale, and like the bird, I could fly alongside the whale cloud. That is what I think diving underwater must be like...flying in slow motion with no gravity to weigh me down. Staring at the dense smog that hides the distant coastline, I secretly hope this part of the ocean is concealing a sunken Spanish galleon. In my mind I can see the wreck resting on the ocean bottom not that far from the view of my secret spot. I vividly imagine the treasure in her hold...probably protected by a giant octopus lurking in the darker corners of the captain's cabin. With my eyes closed, I can visualize the wreck's moss-covered decks with rusted cannons pointed outwards into the gloom of deep water, and in the tangle of her seaweed-laced rigging, I imagine large sinister sharks patrolling endlessly.

"Get your paws off my camera housing," Jean-Michel's voice startles me from my childhood memories.

He has been on the telephone with Captain Cousteau, but since they were speaking in French, I had no idea what they were discussing so I allowed myself to get distracted. I have been studying French for over a year, but the romantic-sounding language remains a mystery to me. Jean-Michel hangs up the telephone, and turns in his chair to face me. "So Stephen, are you ready for a little adventure?" he asks innocently.

I grin, it is my favorite kind of question.

"I need for you to take a small flying team to Hawaii to film Humpback whales," he says casually.

My grin gets bigger. I like this conversation more and more.

"Then, I need for you to fly over to the Big Island of Hawaii. The Kilauea volcano is erupting, and I want you to film the lava flow."

My grin is now out-of-control, it happily slops across most of my face.

Jean-Michel grins back at me. He is talking so matter-of-factly, it should have been a clue that my boss is setting me up. Jean-Michel loves to tease...so he drops his bombshell, offhandedly...like it was no big deal, "The lava is flowing into the ocean and we want some underwater footage."

My grin collapses into itself. "What?"

Jean-Michel smiles mischievously, "Captain Cousteau particularly wants you to get close-up footage of the lava flowing underwater."

"Close-up footage...of lava flowing underwater?" I echo weakly.

"Yes, preferably from underneath with it flowing down toward you," nods Jean-Michel, "something close-up, you know dramatic." He turns in his chair to gloat over his antique wooden camera housing. "The bigger the lava flow the better. Lots of molten red rock streaming underwater right at the camera."

"How do you film lava flowing underwater?" I blurt.

Jean Michel boyishly swings his feet up onto the desk, "Well, you begin by going downstairs and getting some of the guys to help you pack up the equipment." Jean-Michel is really enjoying this. "Then all of you get onto an airplane. When you get to Hawaii, get off the plane and look for an erupting volcano then follow the lava flow to where the ocean is smoking..."

"Jean-Michel!" I interrupt him.

He smiles and stands happily placing an arm over my shoulder. "Stephen, it is for me to think up the ideas, it is up to you to carry them out. We both know you're going to figure out how to do it. Just be careful."

As I head for the door, my thoughts in turmoil, Jean-Michel throws a last piece of advice at me. "Diving with lava is going to be scary, but if you plan well, it can be a lot of fun too."

"Thanks," I answer soberly.

"Oh," Jean-Michel pretends to remember something. I know he

is still setting me up as he reaches into his pocket, takes out a business card and stuffs it into my pocket.

"What's this?" I ask reading the front of the card.

"That's the card of the volcanologist that told me about the lava flowing into the ocean. Call him up, he's full of good advice. He's dove with the lava more times than anyone else in the world."

"Really."

"Only don't call the number on the front of the card."

"No?"

"Look on the back."

I flip the card over and read the handwriting, "Wheeler hospital?"

"Yeah, he's going to be released soon so call him right away."

"What's he doing in the hospital?"

"Got caught in an underwater avalanche; sucked him down to a depth of almost three hundred feet. Wound up with a case of CNS bends (bends involving the central nervous system…the worst kind, which can leave a diver paralyzed for life.).

In my hotel room in Hawaii, I glance over at the clock. It is 11:00 p.m. and I must be up before dawn. *"Lots of fun, right,* I think to myself remembering Jean-Michel's words and then I consider just some of the hazards lurking beyond the sunrise.

All of the diving activities will be in a completely exposed surf zone where big breakers will be regularly pounding the shoreline. That means we will be swimming in strong underwater currents, probably in limited visibility water, while playing hide-and-seek with two thousand degree Fahrenheit rock in motion. The lava flow itself is very unpredictable, like a shifting ocean tide, the flowing lava can abruptly surge creating flash floods of racing molten rock. The volcano's outflow is between three hundred-fifty thousand to half-a-million cubic yards a day. Every day there are multiple minor earthquakes occasionally punctuated by a real earthmover. The shoreline where the lava spills into the ocean is extremely unstable. According to the unfortunate volcanologist, landslides are a regular event. After spending a month recovering in the hospital, he now refuses to go anywhere near the lava flow.

"*So much for the hazards,*" I think to myself, "*now, what about my plans for preventing them?*"

My first consideration had been to find the right kind of boat and captain for going into harm's way. This required a special blend of man and machine because each is only as good as the other's weakest qualities. Usually the condition and layout of the boat is a reflection of the character of the skipper. After some serious searching, I found exactly the right combination of boat and captain.

I chartered a Force 30, which is built locally and therefore better designed for Hawaii's turbulent waters and heavy surf. *Tsunami* (means tidal wave in Japanese), is an aluminum-hulled, thirty-foot-long, lightweight boat. She has a half-covered steering station with an open back beneath which are dual V-8 engines. She will be quick and agile, a boat that can move aggressively in the face of danger. The owner, a barrel-chested Hawaiian named Russell, is a professional fisherman. He often fishes with his boat in big surf conditions off this coast so he knows the wave and current patterns around the lava flow.

I also hire an underwater lava guide, the owner of a dive shop in the town of Hilo. Harry has logged over a dozen dives on the lava flow. He is actually an ex-student of mine, which is a pleasant surprise. We met at the College of Oceaneering where I taught commercial deep-sea diving. I knew him to be competent and dependable, which turns out to be very important. This is because Harry is now handicapped. An automobile accident several years ago left him with three-fused vertebra in his neck. He is unable to turn his head without rotating his entire upper body. It makes his more animated conversations with two or more people visually distracting. It pleases me greatly to ask this physically challenged person to join our team.

I have also had extensive discussions with the local volcanologist. I know the underwater topography of the lava flow, have driven to the Hilo hospital (so I know the way), and I have the radio frequencies for calling in the Coast Guard, should we need emergency evacuation or hyperbaric services (a recompression chamber for treating the bends). More importantly, my dive team members are all professionals. We are also close friends, which is a critical key to our safety. As adventurers, we rely on each other to look out for the safety of the entire team. Ours is the close bond of friends who have faced danger together. It is a unique camaraderie built on trust, loyalty to each other and on hardships overcome through team effort.

Lying in my bed, I snuggle down into the covers confident that we are ready for tomorrow's challenges. Taking a deep relaxing breath, I am unprepared for the abrupt arrival of an earthquake.

The bed begins to shake lightly and I see the clock's red glow vibrating on the nightstand. After a few seconds, the minor earth shaker fades away leaving me wide-eyed, visualizing underwater earthquakes and landslides.

At first light, we trailer *Tsunami* behind a big black pickup truck with huge knobby wheels to a little used boat ramp on the South Shore. Most boaters avoid using this ramp because getting out into open water is a boat threatening experience. A small cement pier and tiny rock jetty provide little protection even when the surf is small. Today, of course, large breakers are pounding the south shore. Standing nervously in the parking lot I watch every third or fourth wave wash over the jetty and smash into the small but sturdy wooden wharf.

"What do you think Russell?" I ask the big Hawaiian.

"Can do, brah," Russell's short answer is not so easy to understand. Many Hawaiians favor speaking in Pidgin, a local blend of English and Hawaiian that uses as few adjectives, adverbs and modifiers as possible. Russell's speech is even harder to grasp because he is shoveling a jelly donut into his mouth. He glances out at the pounding surf; the waves are cresting at heights of eight to ten feet. "More better come back lunch time," he mumbles cramming another half donut into his face. As Russell bites down, a blob of red jelly squirts out of the donut sprinkling his T-shirt with red droplets.

"Why do we have to be back by lunch time?" I repeat his statement for Michel DeLoire's sake. Michel is listening closely, but the
Frenchman is totally lost in this strange Hawaiian accent.

"Tide be high brah, surf bigger," replies Russell wiping at the
jelly globs effectively spreading them across his white T-shirt.

Russell's plan is simple. He has all of us get into the boat while it
is still on the trailer. Standing at the helm Russell carefully watches
the rhythm of the waves, and then abruptly yells at his cousin, who is
behind the wheel of the pickup. The cousin revs the engine, slams
the big truck into reverse, and quickly shoves the boat trailer down
the ramp, then stands on the brakes. The Force 30 slides off the
trailer and crashes into the water as Russell fires up both engines,
spins the wheel and throws the dual throttles forward to the stops.
The stern of the powerful boat digs-in, turns one hundred-eighty
degrees and launches forward. The whole process takes about fifteen
seconds before we are plowing into the first oncoming wave.

Russell takes the waves at an angle to better slice through the
powerful surf, yet the hydraulic force is so great it drives our sturdy
vessel nearly vertical with each wave face. The most interesting
aspect of his crashing through the breakers is that there are surfers
riding some of the waves. Russell sets his course and leaves it up to
the surfers to get out of his way. A couple of them shout and wave as
we pass, but by the clenched fists, I do not think it is friendly greetings we are getting.

As we begin our high-speed run toward the lava flow, I ask Russell
an important question. "If the surf is going to be bigger when we
return, won't it be trickier bringing the boat back in?" I ask.

Russell grins, "Yeah, more hard than getting out."

"So what's your plan?"

"Same plan," laughs Russell, "only go faster."

At 9:00 a.m., we reach our destination and begin motoring just
beyond the turbulent water of the lava flow. The boat engines'
water inlet temperature is ninety degrees Fahrenheit and we are
still two hundred yards from shore. The dark water is varying shades
of dirty brown with occasional large blotches of black soot. The

surface looks like a giant bubbling mud puddle with floating black shadows of dense debris. The bubbles are rising from the depths from volcanic activity below and the result of ocean water spontaneously meeting molten rock at the shoreline.

For safety sake Michel, Harry, and I will make the first reconnaissance dive. The other two members of the team will stay on the boat. Thierry does not seem to mind that he is not yet going into the dangerous water. The inlet temperature is now one hundred and five degrees. Russell carefully maneuvers the boat closer to shore.

Yesterday when I surveyed the lava flow from a helicopter, the lava spilling into the ocean looked very scary, but it could be dove.

This morning, from the up-close perspective of a small boat, the lava flow is downright terrifying—it looks like a futuristic war zone. I am watching a half-mile wide wall of molten rock and fire spilling into the ocean. In a few places, the lava weeps slowly into the bubbling water, but mostly the fiery rock is gushing forth in thick globs or in fast flowing streams. A billowing wall of sizzling steam laced with sulfur rolls off the turbulent water. At the heavy flow points, the liquid rock is so hot that the ocean water instantly flashes into super-heated vapor. I watch a wave break off a large chunk of steaming lava that falls hissing loudly into the water. Then it explodes hurling long liquid tracers of lava through the air. One of the tracers fall back into the water only fifty feet from the boat, it momentarily spins about spewing out spits of steam like an errant firework.

Russell reverses the engines and motors back out looking for cooler water.

"It's really out-of-control today," offers Harry, echoing my thoughts exactly.

"Think it is safe enough to dive?" I ask seriously.

"Na," he shrugs, awkwardly turning his whole body from the shoreline towards me, "it's never safe. That's why so few people have tried to dive the lava flow."

"This is going to be more fun than diving with saltwater

crocodiles," laughs Michel as he begins suiting up.

"Is he kidding? No one dives with crocodiles."

"Last year in an Australian river," I answer, "he filmed a twelve-foot-long salt water crocodile from only two feet away."

"From inside a sturdy steel cage no doubt," Harry says in sudden awe of Michel.

"Actually," replies Michel nonchalantly, "I did not like how the cage bars restricted my filming and I had no mobility. So I went into the water without it."

"Wow," Harry is impressed, "would you do it again?"

"No, crocodiles have very large teeth and move fast, I was not being very smart." Michel picks up the underwater cinema camera. "Are we ready?" he asks calmly.

I glance at the engine's water inlet thermometer; it is back down to one hundred-and-one degrees. "Let's rock and roll," I say with more enthusiasm than I am feeling.

Stepping to the side of the boat, I glance at the black frothy water and leap overboard. The water is hot and dirty, like someone dumped a big bag of charcoal into a hot bubbling Jacuzzi. The hot liquid rushes through the openings in my wetsuit rapidly running up my legs and arms and down round my neck. Hot yellowish water half-floods my dive mask sloshing up my nose. The mask reeks of sulfur and charcoal, my nose tickles outlandishly, but I do not pause to clear the mask, instead we urgently swim straight down. The water is hottest near the surface. Quickly submerging to a depth of thirty feet, we level off in the cooler, yet still sweltering water. My wrist-mounted thermometer is indicating eight-five degrees. The water feels muggy like wading through a hot swamp. Checking my compass and the direction of the sun, I orient us towards the shore-line as we begin our approach.

In the dark depths, it is very murky; we pass through black under-water clouds of soot and drifting ash. Closer to shore the sunlight dims to a dull red glow that waivers and fades to darkness with each passing soot cloud. I keep glancing at the compass, yet hardly need it. The lava flow is producing a pounding cascade of underwater explosions. The liquid atmosphere about us pulsates with loud crackling shock waves. This is raw physical energy announcing its presence with the terrible sound of rock ripping, tearing and being blowing apart. As we get closer, the crackling, tearing reverberations intensifies. I can feel the abrupt passage of each shock wave as it strikes the rubber hood covering my head and ears.

I am doing continuous buddy checks. Michel is swimming strongly with his camera to my left. I see Michel's faceplate sweeping side-to-side as he eagerly looks for the first sign of liquid lava. I am used to seeing light reflected off a diver's faceplate, but Michel's is a black unreflective orb, a dark mirror in an underwater hell. On my right, Harry swims oddly because of his fused neck. He is doing extraordinarily exaggerated kicks with his fins. Each of the extra long strokes causes his body to roll off keel. He does this purposefully to create the rolling effect that permits him to look to each side with a passing downward glance. During one of his partial revolutions our eyes briefly lock...he smiles grimly around his mouthpiece, and then rotates away from me. My compass needle swings wildly. The liquid metals ores in the underwater lava flow are making the sensitive instrument useless. I look for the sun to check my direction, but in the shadowed twilight of the underwater soot clouds it is completely hidden. I try determining our heading by listening to the concussion of sound...and that is when I realize the bulk of the terrible noise is now coming from directly beneath us. We are passing straight over the main part of the lava flow. The water becomes hotter and more active. There are abrupt heated currents swirling up from the depths that lick at us like a hot wet tongue. We swim onwards through dark bubble clouds and are assaulted by sudden liquid concussions. I am sweating inside my wetsuit; it is a strange sensation underwater. Swimming more slowly, peering fearfully into the dark water below, my mind paints its own terrifying images of the inferno that is happening beneath us.

Looking forward I see a looming wall of darkness. This soot cloud is terrifyingly vast in its dimensions. It is a vertical black wall with no bottom, sides or ceiling; it pulsates like a beast breathing...I am extremely reluctant to swim into it. We have become slightly separated; the other two divers swim at the edge of the water's visibility, yet they are only a dozen feet away as we slowly enter the dark cloud. I watch Harry as his body rotates away; for a moment it is lost in shadow, almost disappearing, then he rotates back toward me, but his form is waif-like in an emersion of drifting shadows. Abruptly, I have the most unsettling feeling that we could completely lose each other inside this shifting darkness. Holding up my fist, I signal the other divers to stop. The situation is just too dangerous to continue. I look at Michel and shake my head side-to-side, then jerk my thumb back in the general direction of the boat. He reluctantly shrugs, an adventurous spirit being pulled back from the edge of an alluring quest.

As we are gratefully swimming back out I hear a deep rumble, then a far-off submarine sound of deep rolling thunder and grinding rock. Somewhere behind, or deep below us, a major avalanche is occurring. I am thankful not to be near it as the water around us slowly brightens. Seeing faint sunlight glimmering through the water, I slightly alter our course towards it. I inhale deeply through my regulator; life feels so good. In the distance, we hear a metallic clanging sound. It is Thierry beating two metal pipes together from the back of the boat. The ringing noise is like a bell calling us home as we swim eagerly towards it.

We spent an entire month trying to film the lava flow underwater without success. The situation was just too dangerous.

In life, we cannot always accomplish everything we seek to do. Yet, the most important thing about reaching for dreams or goals is the journey on which they take us. It is what we learn along the way. We weave our experiences, whether they are accomplishments or failures, into a tapestry upon which we formulate our integrity and build our character. This becomes the fabric of our strengths and of our weaknesses and the cloth of our resolve.

To be truly happy, we need to live according to a code of right and wrong. This is part of the wonder of a Christian commitment. Our focus is towards what is good and loving. From goodness and love comes the strength of truth and right living. These are good foundations upon which to build an adventurous and satisfying life.

When a person is about to die, some will wonder...did my life have meaning or purpose? Others may regret the things they did not do. I expect that I will wonder at the many adventures that have crossed my path, be thankful that my years in prison weren't decades instead and fully appreciate that my life has been blessed— though I certainly did not deserve it.

Instead of returning to the mainland, Jean-Michel orders our team back to Maui to get more Humpback whale footage. On the trials of being a Cousteau diver.

The next morning the trade winds are blowing the ocean into a froth of colliding waves and white water. Too rough to film I have given the team the day off. Carrying a towel I step through a gate at our hotel leading to an exotic swimming pool. Lava rocks and tropical landscaping surround a waterfall that spills over a ledge into the pool. Normally we could not afford such luxury, but the management likes having the Cousteau team staying at its hotel. Therefore, we are enjoying a four-star hotel at economy rates. It is a common occurrence for Cousteau expedition teams; a re-enforcement that doing good things leads to good things coming back at you. Reaching under a broadleaf fern, I pick up a large smooth-sided rock that I hid there several days ago. This is a rather special rock. A ten-pound black stone I carried here from the beach. The dark smooth surface is warm from lying in the sun as I hug it to my bare stomach. Carrying the rock towards the swimming pool, I am about to do what Cindy calls my *rock thing*.

A few moments later, I am standing at the edge of the pool with my rock. I notice a young woman sitting beside the pool in a bikini working on her tan. Though her eyes are hidden behind sunglasses, I can tell that she is watching me. She is probably wondering what I am going to do with this rock. For a moment, I consider warning her. My *rock thing* can be a bit startling for strangers. Instead, I decide it will be more amusing to wait and see how she reacts. With that cheerful thought, I smile at her, take a deep breath, note the time on my watch, and jump into the deep-end of the pool.

Swiftly arriving at the bottom, I settle myself in a comfortable cross-legged sitting position with the rock tucked into my lap. Looking upwards, I can see the woman; she is standing now peering uneasily down into the rippling water. She is probably thinking that I am some kind of suicidal nut or maybe just another Southern California idiot. Actually, I am working at my breath-holding ability. This is one of those professional diver skills that need constant honing.

The woman, she appears quite attractive despite the shimmering distortion of the water, is now at the edge of the pool apparently trying to decide if she should dive in to rescue the idiot sitting on the pool's bottom or go call security to have this nut hauled away. I wave to reassure her that all is well. Actually, I am pleased that she is standing there giving me something to look at instead of empty pool walls. I see her glance at her watch so I look at mine. Slowly the seconds tick away. My watch is a digital timepiece. The sequential march of the dimly lit numbers is blurry from the water's distortion. I am staring at the cadence of each digital second when an unbidden memory swims up into my consciousness from the depths of my past. Knowing that the distraction will help the time to pass I allow myself to slip into the visual memory of another digital clock. Only this one is on a wall.

The clock rapidly emerging from my memory has large bright red numbers that momentarily blur from sweat dripping into my eyes. Quickly wiping the sweat away, I calculate my remaining time. Fifty-seven more minutes, enough time to take the extra precautions that might prevent a mistake or a reduced grade. The wall clock is in the Nuclear Weapons Training Bay at the Naval Bomb Disposal School. There are only seven of us left in our class and this is my last pre-graduation problem. If I get a passing grade on this practical situation, I will finally become a bomb disposal frogman.

A situation card is lying on a tray inside my toolbox. It is not a normal toolbox. This set of tools is designed specifically for disarming the nuclear warhead of an American ballistic missile. These are very complex tools made out of special inert metals to reduce the hazard of a spark or disruption of a magnetic field detector. The non-magnetic nature of our tools is important for working on magnetically activated explosive devices. I often hear jokes about the government buying six hundred dollar hammers. Three of them of various sizes are in my toolbox. Other tools are far more expensive with specific functions that I cannot write about because of The Secrecy Act associated with national security. The situation card reads, *a nuclear weapons accident/incident occurred in the weapons bay at a missile base. An unsecured weapon was damaged by a blunt impact with a forklift blade. The weapon must be disassembled and rendered safe. Allotted problem time is two hours.*

Over half of my allotted problem time is gone. I am kneeling beside a simulated nuclear warhead from a ballistic missile. The warhead is painted blue, which indicates that it is an inert training device and not a real nuclear weapon. Actually, the only difference between this training device and a real nuclear warhead is the lack of genuine explosives and a functional physics package. Otherwise, this device is an exact copy of an actual atomic weapon. Even the cost is realistic of an actual nuclear theater weapon. This training device costs millions of dollars and I am industriously attacking it with a $900 hacksaw with a non-sparking, depth-limiting, non-magnetic, easily dulled, super-expensive beryllium blade. It seems odd to use such a primitive tool on something as sophisticated as a nuclear weapon...but that is exactly how it must be done. In a real nuclear weapon rendering-safe situation, a power tool would convey heat and the possibility of an electrical charge into the bomb's sensitive devices that could instantly change a human body with power tool into subatomic vapor. The aerodynamics of a ballistic warhead combined with the critical machining tolerances of a nuclear weapon makes it extremely difficult to open one up correctly. It is a long laborious process. I am beginning to wonder why we could not just simulate the sawing process. Couldn't they design a training device with a self-opening seam like a bag of potato chips? The casing I am sawing on is interchangeable with a real weapon. It costs the government almost $10,000 for this chunk of metal so I can whack away at it with my overly expensive hacksaw. Noting that the sawing is going slower, I see that the hacksaw blade needs replacing again. There goes another $175 as I am beginning to have a bit of an attitude about the need for me to be doing all this stupid sawing.

The procedure for rendering safe a nuclear weapon is not something I can put in this book. However, there is one interesting aspect of a nuclear weapon that is not general knowledge. In every film that involves an atomic weapon there is a digital clock counting down the seconds before the dreaded explosion. Usually the hero disarms the bomb with just mere seconds left. Yet, I have never seen a real nuclear weapon with a digital clock. Hollywood installs the clock for our observation to add drama to their film. Without the digital clock, the filmed moment would be less immediate.

Still sawing, I begin to imagine what it would feel like to render safe a real nuclear weapon. I mentally put in a crowded city to destroy if I do not succeed. Next, I probably would have to add some terrorists and maybe a good-looking female hostage or two—but for the mind-jarring event, that abruptly wastes my daydream. What I am pretending at could potentially become a real event in my future. This world has been getting crazier by the decade. Terrorist are actively seeking nuclear toys and have already deployed chemical and biological weapons with limited success. The United States Government takes this threat seriously enough to invest a lot of money and effort in my education. The school staff makes these training situations as realistic as possible to prepare us for confronting the real thing. Obviously, they believe this exercise important enough to require me to wield a pricey hacksaw on a very expensive hunk of metal.

My attitude changes in a heartbeat. I forget about sawing for a timed grade and instead concentrate on the precision of each saw cut. Ten minutes later the two pieces of the weapon's casing finally come apart and I carefully begin a very complicated process of rendering safe each of the multiple stages of the nuclear device.

Though the problem is a clocked event, I completely lose track of time. Finally removing the last of the simulated formed-explosive blocks from around the physics package, I glance at the clock on the wall and say, "Done."

"You just passed," says Instructor McNair, whom I have forgotten is hovering over my shoulder.

"I know," I reply, "there's three minutes left."

"I am not referring to the clock," McNair kneels down to my level and picks up the physics package (something one would never do with a real nuclear device). The shiny silver globe rests very heavy in his hand like a size junior high-tech bowling ball. He slowly turns it as both of us gaze at the silvered mirrored surface. "I just saw you become a real bomb disposal technician," McNair is not smiling. He is dead serious.

"I...I am?" *Did I actually just stutter?* "I mean I did?"

"Something changed, "McNair is staring at me intently. "It happened when you were halfway through with the sawing. Want to tell me about it?"

I forget for the moment that the rest of the class is standing in the background listening. Breaking eye contact with Instructor McNair, I stare at the shiny physics package in his hand. Looking at the mirrored metal, it is startling to see the reflection of the both of us standing together. A momentary thought flickers through my mind; McNair and I are on the same team. We are working together towards a common goal; defending America. Delving back into my thoughts of the previous hour, something begins to emerge but I cannot quite get a handle on it...and then I do. "It became real," I say softly. It is almost as if I am speaking to the simulated atomic egg in his hand.

"It is real," echoes McNair, "take it."

The metal globe passes from his hand to mine. It is very heavy for its size. "Nothing was going to actually blow up, but the problem you just defeated is as real as it gets in training. If you failed this one you would not graduate from this school." McNair grooms his moustache with a thumb and finger.

"Steve," McNair had never called me by my Christian name before. The effect is startling. "I am not asking you about the problem, I want to know what just changed in you."

"Me?" My first reaction is to say I have not changed, yet I have, "I took the problem seriously?"

"That is a little truth," smiles McNair, "the big truth is that your perception about yourself just changed."

"What?"

"Per...cep...tion," he says each syllable slowly. Perception is how we see the world and our place in it. Little children learn about their small world mostly from their parents and siblings and through games and at play. As we mature, we become more aware of the complex world around us. Yet our perceptions about life mostly remain tailored to our established beliefs, which formed when we were still living in our child's smaller world, which is always all about ourselves." McNair looks at each of us to emphasize his point, "Most people think of themselves as independently thinking individuals. Yet much of who we are and how we think is mostly a creation of mass-induction by our family, school and society. Childhood and adolescent conditioning is a powerful implement. Both Hitler and Stalin knew the value of conditioning to control the masses. We are all deliberately trying to live our lives within certain preconceived notions. Perception is a mental tool that we unconsciously use to gauge events around us. When we recalibrate our perception, new opportunities begin to open to us. Instead of just reacting to events, we can create them and develop prospects that lead in totally unique and vastly independent directions."

McNair frowns at me, "You don't understand any of this do you?"

"No, not exactly..." I am trying not to scratch my head.

"I got an idea. Get into the leaning rest and start doing push-ups until I order you to quit," he commands.

"I am being punished for not understanding?"

"I am not punishing you," McNair effortlessly drops into the leaning rest and begins doing push-ups alongside me. "Look I will even do them with you."

Hank quickly drops down for push-ups on the other side of me. Soon the whole class, well, all seven of us counting McNair, is doing push-ups in cadence.

"Is this difficult?" inquires McNair of the class in general.

"No Instructor McNair," we answer together.

"Are we having fun, gentlemen?

"Yes, Instructor McNair."

"Why are we having fun guys?" To hear Instructor McNair call us gentlemen and guys as if we were real people is a little unnerving. So is his question, which he repeats, "I said why is this fun?"

Hank verbally leaps into the conversation, "Because it is something we have learned to do together and because we do it so often we are comfortable with it."

"Only partially right, I want all of it," urges McNair.

"You have changed our perception about push-ups Instructor McNair," offers Mickey Doke.

"Not good enough," barks McNair, "I am looking for a precision thought."

"Our perception about ourselves has changed," corrects Hank.

"There it is," laughs McNair, who begins doing one-arm push-ups for his own amusement. "Steve, your perception about the value of the practical problem changed. You considered the sawing to be a worthless exercise until you realized its importance; which by the way is a type of conditioning."

"Uh huh," I grunt, trying a one arm push-up and losing my balance almost smash my face into the shiny tile floor.

McNair switches from his left to his right arm as he continues to lead us in push-ups at a much slower pace. "In this class we have muscled-up your bodies and packed your brains with facts and procedures," McNair slows the push-up pace even more as my arms begin to wobble. "But what we have really tested is your strength of character. Character determines how a person will react in a stressful or dangerous situation. Perception both inwardly and outwardly focused is the key that leads to strength of character. By the way it also unlocks most of the mysteries of life."

Back at the bottom of the pool at our hotel in Maui, I am becoming somewhat frantic for a breath of air. Carefully setting my rock down I resist the urge to shoot upwards, instead I slowly float to the surface. The woman is waiting. "What are you doing?" she half-screams.

Between gasps for air I answer, "Training...I am a professional diver."

"You're a professional idiot is what you are!" In a huff, she returns to her lounge chair. I shrug off her words, take a couple of deep breaths, and swim back down to my rock.

Back at the bottom of the pool, I reconsidered McNair's arguments about perception from a different viewpoint. Interestingly enough these thoughts lead me back to where my *rock thing* actually began...at the bottom of the Boron Prison Camp pool. In prison, there is no such thing as privacy. Naturally, prison guards watch their charges very carefully. Yet, it is the constant prying eyes of other inmates that strip away any concept of ever being alone. Mostly the ever-curious inmates are looking for opportunities that they can exploit for personal gain. Even the simple act of un-wrapping a candy bar gathers the attention of would-be moochers. Imagine a career bank robber or even a serial murderer asking to share a piece of your candy bar. Therefore, in prison candy bars are eaten clandestinely. I liked to eat mine at the bottom of the Boron Prison swimming pool. Prisons do not normally have a swimming pool, but this one was a left over from when the camp was a military facility during World War II.

None of the inmates would have imagined that someone would eat a candy bar underwater. Actually I became quite good at it. I could only take one bite per breath, but the chocolate bar lasted much longer. The bottom of the inmate pool became my refuge. Submerged in the silent solitude of being underwater I found momentary freedom from the convict world in which I lived. In prison, I never lost tract of the realization that my incarceration was my own fault. This self-perception allowed me to accept my fate and even to embrace my punishment. I was carrying a heavy load of guilt for my mistakes. Doing prison time was an opportunity to begin paying off that debt.

"Education is not preparation for life; education is life itself,"
John Dewey

Illustration by Marjory Spielman
Author ascending from underwater avalanche while diving with lava.

"The secret of all victory lies in the organization of the non-obvious," Oswald Spengler

Chapter 12

LOS ANGELES, CALIFORNIA/HILO, HAWAII MARCH 1988

BARELY A month later, I am sitting at my desk in the basement of the Cousteau Society office in Hollywood. It is late in the afternoon, and I am looking forward to picking up Cindy at the airport. I am in a bit of a mood, as I have not yet worked up the courage to ask her to marry me. I am pondering this problem when the telephone rings.

"Steve, this is Doctor Clague, the volcanologist at the Hawaiian Volcano Observatory," he is bubbling with enthusiasm. "We have a new eruption. A fresh lava flow is heading for the ocean. If you can get out here right away you might have ideal diving conditions for the next couple of days."

Excited for another opportunity to capture the underwater lava footage, yet with a sinking heart about the prospects for Cindy's and my date, I carry the news upstairs to Jean-Michel Cousteau.

"Wonderful," exclaims Jean-Michel eagerly, "how fast can you reassemble the team?"

Thinking about my date with Cindy, I try to sound disappointed as I say, "Well, everyone's still on vacation from the Papua New

Guinea expedition. It will take at least a few days to pull a four-man team together."

Jean-Michel leans back in his chair and lightly tugs at his beard.. this is not a good sign. He is thinking of alternatives. Grabbing his notebook, he makes a quick telephone call to Bob Talbot, a famed whale cinematographer.

"Hello, Bob," Jean-Michel gets right to the point, "how would you like to film lava flowing underwater in Hawaii?" I see my boss beaming as he gets an affirmative answer. "Good, look I don't have time right now for details; just get your equipment together. You'll leave with Steve tomorrow from LAX. Steve will get back to you with details."

Hanging up the telephone, Jean-Michel grins triumphantly at me. "Bob is bringing his assistance, so now you only need one more person to act as a safety diver." At that moment, David Brown walks nonchalantly into the office. He is a lecturer for The Cousteau Society. He has a simple question about a speaking date, but Jean-Michel interrupts him. "David," Jean-Michel leers at his victim, "how would you like to go diving in Hawaii with Steve?"

David is ecstatic. "When are we leaving?" he asks enthusiastically.

"Tomorrow," answers Jean-Michel, who is picking up the telephone again, already moving on to other problems. "Steve will give you the details."

As I head unhappily for the door, I try my last hope for Cindy's and my evaporating date. "Uh, Jean-Michel," I say weakly, "Cindy's arriving tonight."

Jean-Michel looks up and chuckles, "Good, she can help you pack."

I nod, "That's what I thought you'd say."

Jean-Michel happily acknowledges my statement, his mood improved by my discomfort, "Must be good advice."

Closing the door behind me, David fires his first question, "Are we going to dive with Humpback whales?"

"How do you feel about underwater volcanoes and swimming

with lava?" I answer leaving a stunned David Brown standing in my wake.

David is busy in the basement packing up equipment with several other helpers as I head off to meet Cindy with the bad news.

When she steps off the airplane, I am waiting with a bouquet of roses. She is wearing my favorite outfit, snug jeans, tan buttoned shirt and red converse sneakers. I buy jeans with a 32-inch inseam; Cindy's are 36-inches and a still a little short. She gives me a quick hug then buries her face in the red velvety flowers inhaling deeply. "Is this because you love me?" she asks, hazel eyes sparkling happily.

"Well..." I pause, "Yes and no."

Cindy lowers the flowers, her eyes taking on a fiery quality. I wonder if she is freeing up her slugging hand. "You're leaving on another adventure aren't you?"

"Hawaii to dive with the lava again," I answer meekly.

"And you didn't call to tell me to cancel my flight...why?"

Flowers transfer to her left hand, she is definitely freeing up that right slugger I have been warned about. I take a cautious step backwards; Cindy has a four-inch reach on me, which is one of the reasons she is such a good competitive climber. "I just found out two hours ago," I say a bit lamely.

"Tell me you're flying out tomorrow morning." Cindy's voice is less than friendly.

"Well actually, I don't have to leave until the early afternoon," I offer lamely as I retreat another half-a-step out of slugging range.

Cindy notices my slightly defensive posture. "It's okay," she says soberly, "I never hit a date who brings me roses."

"We will have to change your return flight," I say wanting to get all of the bad news out of the way up front. I know that this date is not going well.

Cindy shrugs, "I'll just tell them that my fiancée got hurt and I have to fly home unexpectedly.

"Got hurt? How did he get hurt?" I ask warily.

"Don't know, this date isn't over yet." Cindy turns and begins walking away. Those long legs are carrying her rapidly along as a sudden realization hits me. Cindy clearly said the word, fiancée. Was that an accidental Freudian slip or is she dropping a hint the size of an elephant? My heart surges...she loves me!

I move quickly, well actually I run, to catch up. As I take her elbow Cindy quips, "You know Steve, if this was our first date it would be our last date."

Driving from the airport, Cindy is in a dangerous mood; claws extended, like a cat daring someone to try to pet it. Her temper makes her incredibly attractive. I imagine the excitement of what it would be like to be married to such a fiery woman. *Should I pop the question?* I see her nails tapping and imagine a sassy cat, its long tail squishing as it sizes up a cornered mouse. *Dare I?*

We arrive at my apartment complex where I need to pick up some dive gear for the trip, then we are supposed to go directly to the Cousteau Expedition Office to help pack.

Pulling into the underground parking facility, I glance over at Cindy sitting in the low light with her roses. She is so beautiful and I am such a lucky man to be her boyfriend. Dare I risk that now? Cindy looks at me and our eyes lock. I almost blurt something that should not be said in an underground parking facility. I shove open my door and hustle over to her side of the car. A true gentleman, I open her door as she smiles at me...then abruptly my mouth makes a life-changing decision all on its own, "Cindy, will you marry me?"

Cindy's eyes go wide in shock then they harden into a squinty Clint Eastwood stare. "Don't you dare ask me a question like that in an underground parking lot!"

I take a defensive step backwards.

"Look," Cindy is pointing at my feet. "You're standing in a puddle of oil."

"So?"

"Every girl dreams about their proposal of marriage and not once does it ever involve an underground parking lot with some fool standing in a dirty puddle of oil."

"Oh." I quickly close her door and hurry back to the driver's door, get back inside and start the engine.

"Where are we going now?" asks my thoroughly perturbed bride to be.

"The Los Angeles Observatory," I answer attempting to sound calm yet all jittery inside.

"Why?" Cindy's curiosity is kicking into high gear.

"I want to show you something before I leave," I am being purposefully evasive.

Cindy's look is deep and penetrating, I can see she wants to ask more questions; instead, she places her hand on mine and simply says, "Okay."

Less than an hour later, we arrive at the observatory. Getting out of the car, I take Cindy down a wooded trail. She is still carrying her flowers, which have gained a ladybug stowaway. Cindy is enjoying the short walk. She grew up in the mountains of Northern California and enjoys long hikes on wooded paths; however, she far more loves running along mountain ridgelines; the steeper the better. I have a serious fear of falling and tend to avoid steep rocky edges, which are a powerful lure to Cindy. She sees my fear of falling as a definite fault and has often speculated that this could be an unforgivable liability in our relationship.

Hand in hand, we arrive five minutes later at a promontory over-looking Los Angeles. Beneath us, the twinkling lights of the vast city sprawl as far as the eye can see. The broad freeways pulsate with swiftly moving ribbons of red and white light, while vibrant neon signs define the borders of the darker suburban streets. At the center of the huge metropolis, as if rising above a shimmering ocean of light, stands the glass-walled skyscrapers. The towering buildings glisten with inner and reflected radiance, like windows into a futuristic world, which is what I am doing right now… reaching into the future.

"It's beautiful!" exclaims Cindy. Effortlessly she steps over the protective railing to peer downward then glances back at me. Her look is an unspoken challenge as I too step over the railing, a hint more awkwardly and with a bit of concealed reluctance.

She places her hand in mine as I stare at the animation and happiness shining in her eyes. Holding the roses in one hand, she tilts her head up. I am slightly less an inch taller than Cindy; an inch that she vigorously contests as a mere figment of my imagination. I know she wants me to kiss her instead, I again ask Cindy to marry me.

"You're not going to let this go are you?" demands Cindy.

"I said, will you marry me?" The suspense is more nerve wracking than diving with sharks.

"Of course, I will marry you, Stephen," Cindy punctuates her statement with a light kiss, "but this doesn't get you off the hook for leaving me behind when you're going off on another way-cool adventure."

"That's why I brought you up here," I nod at the glowing metropolis beneath us. "Life is a great big adventure full of mystery and wonder. I want to explore these wonders and to chase after dreams, but more importantly, I want to do all these things with you. All of my escapades are only half the fun when you aren't there to be a part of them."

Cindy steps closer and whispers into my ear, her breath fluttering against my neck, "I want that written into a prenuptial agreement, cowboy."

Despite the urgency to pack, we instead sit on the promontory with stars above us and the city lights at our feet, making plans for a future where dreams, adventures and happiness are equally shared.

Forty-eight hours later, the small Cousteau flying team stands nervously at the stern of the *Tsunami*. We are at the eastern edge of the lava flow. West of us, it looks just as out of control as it did before. However, at this location, the lava is flowing into the ocean at a single point. It means our approach will be a little bit less hazardous.

Leaping into the hot water, we quickly swim downwards and level off at thirty feet. The water is slightly cooler than before, around eighty-three degrees Fahrenheit. Again, there is a continuous bombardment of underwater concussions and explosions punctuated by the deep rumblings of submarine landslides. Huddled in a tight group, we swim towards the loudest of the sounds. The water darkens as we near the shoreline then abruptly we see a faint red glow radiating up from the darkness below us. Triggering his cinema camera, Bob Talbot leads the way with me hovering at his side. Like a black curtain opening, the surging water abruptly clears before us revealing a thick lava tube weaving its way down the steep shelf like a giant angry red worm.

While Bob films, intently focused on the slowly moving lava in front of him, I watch other lava worms weaving their way towards us. Gently taking Bob's elbow, I squeeze a warning when one gets too close. Reacting instantly, Bob shifts the camera lens to capture the questing tube as it drops over a shelf slowly spilling tons of molten rock. In amazement, I realize that unlike a waterfall, water spilling over rock, I am looking at liquid rock spilling over water. It is an incredible sight seen by few people and instantly I regret that Cindy is not at my side.

Twenty minutes later, the camera empty, we beat a hasty retreat back to the *Tsunami*. Heading back to the boat launch, everyone is in high spirits. Our excitement lasts all the way back to the hotel, right up until the moment Bob opens the underwater cinema camera, and instead of film on rollers—discovers plastic confetti. The complex threading system inside the high-speed thirty-five millimeter camera slipped a cog. Immediately, the sharp-edged gears began chewing all our prize footage to shreds.

The following morning, we again prepare to jump into the frothy water from the stern of *Tsunami*. Staring at the shoreline, I nervously see that the lava flow has increased dramatically. What was a stream of flowing lava yesterday is now a river of cascading molten rock. It is pouring into the water in broad fiery sheets, a liquid avalanche of red-hot gushing stone. Jumping into the stifling water, and swimming quickly downwards, we discover that the water is much hotter than before at the thirty-foot level.

Determined to recapture the lost footage, we swim vigorously towards the shoreline. The barrage of underwater sound and shock waves intensifies. Then we see the steep slope of the very unstable bottom through parting clouds of swirling debris. I turn and signal Bob's assistant and David Brown to maintain a position well above us. Splitting the team into buddy pairs gives us a safety backup should anything go dramatically wrong.

Swimming in towards the steep rocky shelf, we begin filming unstable lava rubble upon which a fresh lava worm is rapidly descending. The shelf has a forty-five degree downward incline and lava boulders are tumbling down each side of the pillowing lava worm, which is about two feet in diameter. Abruptly, a large area of lava debris begins to slide quickly becoming a minor avalanche that plunges, rumbling loudly, into the dark depths below. I am not at all used to such tremendous amounts of noise underwater. Carefully moving in closer to capture the dramatic footage, a huge smoking boulder narrowly misses Bob and I. It tumbles down from above us without warning, fully two-yards in diameter. Weeping jets of steam and laced with red fiery cracks, it looks like a falling meteorite burning its way through a fluid atmosphere. It bounces between us, then somersaults over the shelf disappearing into the deep blackness below. Wisps of debris floating in the water slowly dissipate in the wake of its angry passage.

The water visibility keeps changing, going from six to twenty feet, then back to six feet or less. It is very disorienting with the surging water sweeping us back and forth from the surf above us. Then we see a faint glimmer of red glowing at a depth of sixty feet. Swimming cautiously downward, we discover a large lava tube, more than a yard in diameter. It momentarily, stops its downward plunge, a black crust begins to form and then the leading edge of the tube bulges outward. The crust cracks and splits open like an alien egg hatching, then a cascade of molten rock spews forth in a glorious fountain of thick liquid fire like hot mucus from a fire-breathing dragon.

Following the weaving tube downwards at the rate of a half-foot every second, we stop our descent at ninety feet. The seawater making sudden contact with the super hot lava worm causes implosions and explosions that shoot out bone-rattling shock waves. Because we are so close to the lava tube, the concussions visibly move the dive masks against our faces. The increased water pressure at this depth magnifies the shock waves to a painful level. As the camera empties its film load, we beat a fast retreat back to *Tsunami*.

Returning to the hotel, we are ecstatic to discover the film intact inside the camera. Our celebration is somewhat dampened by the intense sinus headaches we are suffering caused by the violent underwater shock waves.

Over the next couple of weeks, we have many spectacular days of diving with the molten lava. However, our final dive proves to be almost fatal; it is my closest brush with death while with the Cousteau's. Bob and I are filming a pair of lava tubes at a depth of eighty feet, when a massive shock wave erupts out of the vast darkness below slamming into our bodies. The lava debris before us begins to tumble ripping apart the twin lava tubes in a jumbled cascade of black rock and red molten lava. Then, from beneath us comes the heavy rolling thunder of an enormous avalanche. A deep black thunderhead of debris rushes upward from the depths engulfing us in shifting darkness mixed with sweltering heat. Bob and I reach out and clutch the precious movie camera between us. I see the whole wall of rock before us begin to slide and tumble as a tremendous undertow caused by the landslide engulfs us. The plunging current hurls us tumbling and spinning in complete darkness down into the foreboding depths below.

After many terrifying seconds, hearing rocks colliding with head-crushing force, the turbulence begins to subside. Swimming against the still powerful downward pull, we finally break free of the down current; only to find ourselves lost in deep darkness, not knowing up from down. Sensing the changing water pressure against our dive masks as our only guide, it takes three long minutes to struggle back to clearer water. Thankfully re-uniting with the other diver pair, I check my depth gauge and am astounded to discover that the undertow pulled us down to a depth of one hundred and thirty-five feet. After allowing extra minutes in the shallow water for decompression, we retreat to Russell's boat.

Pulling off my steaming wetsuit, I look towards the fiery tempest raging at the shoreline. The massive lava flow continues to grow more dangerous on a daily basis. I realize it is time to end this expedition. With thoughts of Cindy filling my mind, I turn to the divers and thankfully say, "Pack up, we are going home."

> *"The grand essentials to happiness in this life are something*
> *to do, something to love, and something to hope for."*
> Joseph Addison

"It is all one to me if a man comes from Sing Sing Prison or Harvard. We hire a man, not his history," Malcolm Forbes

Chapter 13

WEST HOLLYWOOD, CALIFORNIA, APRIL 1988

I AM AGAIN sitting in Jean-Michel's office. Outside his window, a night-time rain beats against the glass. Rivulets of water cascade down its slick wetness, refracting multi-colored neon lights shimmering in an envelope of black wetness. The headlights of passing cars on Santa Monica Boulevard are rimmed in sparkling halos of misty white brightness. Just back from Hawaii, I am remembering my assignment there after completing EOD School. Graduation day was on July 6, 1976. Only half listening to Jean-Michel speaking French, I let my mind slip backwards.

The late morning sunlight glistens on the parade ground. I am the last of seven sailors standing in a short row wearing dress white uniforms with medals. We are all that remains of the thirty-two original candidates of class 76B. I think about all the men that are not standing here. I remember their high hopes when they were successful and the pride-shattering finality of their failure when they were dropped from the class. There were no opportunities for debate or hopeful argument; second chances were non-existent. To stand in this line meant you earned the absolute right to be here.

The brotherhood of being an Explosive Ordnance Disposal frogman would follow each of us for the rest of our lives.

The combat swimmer program began with the Underwater Demolition Teams (UDT) and Explosive Ordnance Disposal Technicians of World War II. During the Vietnam War SEALS (Sea, Air and Land) evolved from the best of the UDT ranks. The Naval Special Warfare Command is a highly elite aqua-fraternity that will be an important part of me until the day I die.

Taking a couple of deep breaths to settle my nerves, I glance at McNair standing at attention with knife-edge creases in his crisp uniform and multiple rows of medals on his ample chest. When a professional service person wears that many medals and awards, it is proper military slang to refer to the colorful rows as "fruit salad." McNair could open up a fruit stand. There is no military band, no bunting flying from the bleachers. On the small parade ground, there are just a few instructors, the School's Commanding Officer, 2 wives, 4 children and the 6 of us about to be frogs.

I am enjoying that this is such a private ceremony. It makes it far more personal, witnessed only by the Navy's best of the best and our classmates' families. We are graduating just two days after the bicentennial celebration of our nation's Declaration of Independence. I had spent the weekend in Washington DC watching all of the elaborate ceremonies with massive barrages of fireworks, marching military bands and parading rifle corps. The fact that our nation was founded so nearby, and the memories of all the Americans who had lost so many battles on the ground upon which we stand, and yet went on to win in the end is a powerful statement of the commitment we are making towards insuring our nation's freedom for the future.

The CO begins at the other end of our short row as he pins the EOD insignia, the coveted EOD silver crab, to the proud chest of Mickey Doke. When he finally gets to me, he pauses and smiles, "Master Gunners Mate McNair, front and center," he orders.

McNair marches to his side and salutes, "Sir."

"Perhaps you would enjoy the honors," he offers McNair my silver crab.

As he pins the device to my chest, he holds my gaze, then growls, "Make me proud Arrington."

Normally enlisted men do not salute each other. My right hand snaps to my temple and McNair returns it before about-facing and returning to his original position. An orderly approaches him and hands over a stack of manila envelopes. "This completes the graduation ceremony. All of you are immediately detached to temporary assigned duty at Lake Hurst, New Jersey, for basic jump training (parachutist school). Afterwards you will report to your new command. When I say your name step forward to receive your orders," he barks.

The EOD Command is split into two groups, one out of Norfolk, Virginia and the other in West Loch, Hawaii. Each group is responsible for all military and terrorist operations within their respective half of the world. This means fielding rapid response teams to incidents of war, regional conflicts, explosive situations and to NBC accidents/incidents (Nuclear, Biological and Chemical warfare situations).

I am, of course, hoping for Hawaii. In my mind are promising visions of South Pacific Islands, white sand beaches and sunken wrecks loaded with unexploded ordnance. The Pacific Command is also involved in the recovery of space vehicles and in cutting-edge war technology. What is there not to like as an adventurous young man?

McNair calls out Hank and my name together, "Hate to split you two up, but Hank you're going to Virginia and Arrington, time to learn to say Aloha."

"Are you listening to me?"

Cousteau's voice snaps my attention back to him. "Yes, Jean-Michel," I reply, sitting up more attentively in my chair.

Jean-Michel impatiently taps a pencil on his desk, "What was I saying then?"

"That Michel DeLoire forgot something," I reply, pleased to know the answer. Yesterday, Michel DeLoire flew directly from Hawaii to Papua New Guinea to join *Alcyone*, the Cousteau Society's newest research vessel; nicked named the wind ship by the crew

"Would you like to know what Michel forgot?" Jean-Michel asks quietly.

Alarm bells are suddenly ringing in my head. Am I the one responsible for the forgotten item? "What did he forget?" I nervously inquire.

Jean-Michel consults his notebook. I watch his index finger going down a brief list, which is not only upside down from my perspective, but it is also in French. Lacking any visible hints, I anxiously await my fate.

Jean-Michel's finger pounces on the missing item. "You!" He exclaims with great drama.

"Me? What?" I ask imploringly.

"You," Jean-Michel points an accusing finger at my chest, "you are what he forgot."

"He forgot me?" I want to feel relieved, instead I am feeling confused.

"Yep!" Jean-Michel grins, and then slides an airline ticket across the desk. "You're leaving for Papua New Guinea, tomorrow at 8:00 p.m."

"But, but..." I sputter hopelessly, "Cindy's arriving tonight."

"Good, you're going to need her help."

"I am?" In my mind, all the fun and adventurous activities I have planned to share with Cindy over the weekend are fading abruptly.

Jean-Michel hands me a lengthy telex. "It seems *Alcyone* needs a few things."

I quickly scan the telex, which begins with this sentence, "Dear Stephen, you will be welcome aboard *Alcyone*, if you bring..." What follows is a date-ending three-page shopping list.

Four days later, I am again looking out a window at a nighttime rain. A bright stab of lightning re-enforces that this is not a gentle California rain shower. This is a tropical thunderstorm eight thousand miles away from the comfort of Jean-Michel's office and the rather upset girl I left behind. I am aboard the research vessel *Alcyone* and sailing straight into a massive thunderhead. Glancing at the revolving light bar on the radarscope, I see the towering clouds painted in angry shades of red, orange and yellow luminous light. The wind ship is sailing straight into the heart of the storm. Fortunately, at the ten-mile range on the scope, I can see we should hit clear water in another hour or so.

It is my very first watch aboard the wind ship and other than being slightly seasick life is terrific. At the helm of a world famous research vessel, with a course set for adventure, I am living out my childhood dream. Watching heavy raindrops pelting the wind ship's plate glass windows, I turn up the music on the stereo. The Beach Boys are singing California Girls, which sets me to thinking about Cindy.

My big weekend date with Cindy lasted less than eighteen hours. We spent the entire time packing twenty-two boxes of supplies. Then we went to the airport together in the Cousteau truck, she with her light carry-on bag for her return trip home, and I with my mountain of luggage in back heading for the South Pacific. Crammed in the front seat with the driver and I, Cindy was not in the best of moods.

"You know this weekend is right down there at the bottom of the dating chart," she says regretfully.

"Because we spent the entire time packing supplies?" I ask unhappily.

"No, because you're going off on another fun adventure and I am going back to school." Cindy punches my arm to add impact to her words.

"Hey, school can be exciting too," I offer defensively.

"You want another punch?" Cindy playfully draws back her fist, but instead of hitting, she leans her head against my chest and fakes a sniffle. It is amazing how well Cindy works my emotions. Before I know it, I am apologizing for unfairly going off on another adventure.

"I will do better next time," I promise trying to snuggle a little closer.

Dropping her off at the domestic terminal, I collect a hug and a wise crack.

On the *Alcyone's* bridge, the Beach Boy's song ends, but my thoughts about Cindy continue well into the night. Her comments about adventure have set me to thinking. In a quality relationship both people must share equally. Since Cindy and I are both adventure hounds it is only fair if I ensure she gets her quota of excitement too. One of the challenges of love is always to share…particularly the best in favor of the other. Sharing improves everything it touches.

A thick bolt of lightning strikes the ocean off to the starboard side. Seconds later, the vibrato of deep rolling thunder walks upon the Beach Boy's song *Good Vibrations.* The powerful uplifting beat fits my mood perfectly as I increase the volume to compete with the drumming of heavy rain on the metal overhead. Humming along with the music, I step to the chart table to check our position. Our destination is the Bismarck Archipelago, a long chain of lush tropical islands in the northern waters of Papua New Guinea. Staring at the chart under my hands as I prepare to plot *Alcyone's* course, I realize that our lives are also like a charted course. On life's journey, we are always coming from one point in our existence and en route to somewhere else. Realizing that this is a never-ending journey, then it is not the single destination that counts as much as the quality of the passage.

As a Christian, I have strong motivations to live each day with a right focus. My daily goal is to make positive uplifting choices and to do good work. The chart in my hands, points out the various marine hazards, such as shallows, underwater reefs, etc. With this map, I can navigate *Alcyone* past the obstacles…as long as I know where I am at in the first place. Being a Christian gives me my daily starting point. The chart I use for plotting my life's course is written in the Bible, Mark 12:30-31. It is here that Jesus is asked, "Of all the commandments which is the most important?" He replied, "Love the Lord your God with all your heart and with all your soul and with all your mind and with all your strength. The second is this: Love your neighbor as yourself. There is no commandment greater than these."

By following these two simple laws, we automatically set off on the right course. We always know exactly where we are…or should be…and theoretically, where we are going…or suppose to be going. Any decision in life can be weighed against these two laws making the correct answer easier to choose. Our fault is that we do not always do what is best for us, our fellowman or for our walk with Christ...even though we know better.

Later that night, Thierry, our navigator, relieves me at the helm. Going below, I silently step into the Captain's cabin. Mine is the upper bunk, a lingering habit from prison. Quietly slipping under the covers, I let the rolling motion of the ship lull me to sleep with thoughts of Cindy slipping lightly through my mind.

Two days later, I am lounging in the shade of a coconut tree watching island children playing in the sun. Actually many of them are involved in work, yet from their happy attitudes one wouldn't know that this is youthful labor. The boys, most accompanied by their fathers, are fishing from canoes, mending nets or tending tiny patches of garden. The girls, depending upon their age, are either helping their mothers make meals or are weaving baskets from coconut fronds. The younger children are at play in the water or chasing each other about the beach and amongst the coconut trees.

This village is located on one of Papua New Guinea's smaller islands called Tench (which means rock). It is a tiny, only a half-square-mile in area, isolated outpost in the Indian Ocean. Flying above the island's fringe are Red-footed Bobbys, Brown and Black Noddies and higher up, gliding on the air currents, the graceful Greater Frigate Bird. The villagers (there are less than sixty of them) live simply in wooden huts with bamboo-frond thatched roofs. Because of the island's very low elevation the houses are built on wooden stilts to keep storm waters from washing through them. The highest point on the island is less than six feet above sea level. They are a happy people who take great pride in their family history and generational traditions. They regularly sweep the island's dirt paths and like to encourage flowering plants to grow around their thatched huts. Their needs are not complex. There is no electricity, nor radios or telephones in the village. Kerosene lamps or small open fires provide a soft evening glow for reading and the flame's light smoke helps to keep the mosquitoes away. Money is mostly non-existent in this quiet island society, except for the necklaces. The village's money necklaces are made from tiny seashells, about the size of a small child's little finger nail. It takes the entire village a full day's labor to make a money necklace. Only special shells of the right size and color will do, the children and adults comb the beaches and hunt underwater for them. Each shell is laboriously hand-sanded to a tiny flat oval, the size of a BB, then a hole is carefully bored into them with a primitive bow-like awl. In the evening, the women weave strands of their hair into fine cords on which they string the precious shells.

The resulting necklace has such great value it is given a name. When chiefs from other islands meet in traditional ceremonies, they exchange money necklaces to the honor of each village. The necklaces are also one of the ways that the island adults show the children how important they are to them. When a young couple is to wed, the whole village contributes to their bridal dowry...usually thirty money necklaces or more. A single necklace can be traded for a small pig. With thirty necklaces they can have a hut built, purchase a hollowed-out canoe along with a fishing net, acquire baskets for storage, a cast iron pot for cooking and tools for gardening. In other words, the money necklaces provide all that the young couple will need to start a life together in their little island community.

In the evening, the people gather wherever there is light from a kerosene lantern or the inviting glow of a small fire. They share family stories and village lore with modest outbreaks of laughter and soft whispers. They are truly a small crowd of cheerful people living a simple, yet rewarding existence with little or no intrusion from the rest of the world.

A week later, after some incredible diving, we anchor at Wuvulu Island, the last and one of the most isolated islands of the Bismarck Archipelago. There are two villages, Aunna and Onne, on this, larger than Tench, but still rather small island that encompasses less than five square miles of land mass. It has some of the best diving I have ever encountered. The islanders have underwater farms where they raise giant clams, some of them weigh upwards of three hundred pounds. Each family will lay out an underwater plot on a patch of sand that they surround with coral rocks. They search the surrounding reef for small clams that they move to their farm where these mollusks will spend many years growing until they are harvested for holidays or during times of food shortages.

I could not help but notice that there was a subtle difference between the quiet villagers of Tench and the busier people of Wuvulu. These islanders were more often dressed in western clothes, seemed a bit more stressed and the children were not quite as free and happy. On this remote beautiful island, I discover a device that is changing these simple island people from their peaceful ways. The instrument of their change comes out only at night. Several men carry it into the middle of the village like a hoarded, almost sacred, treasure. The islanders hurry to get the best places to pay homage to this new alluring wonder.

In stunned fascination, I watch the impact of television on simple island people unprepared for the high-tech invasion of twentieth century entertainment. The television arrived several months ago, along with a gasoline generator for power and a VCR to feed it. Every ten days an island trading boat arrives. Besides bringing essential supplies, the boat also serves as a video rental store.

The village chief, standing beside me, proudly confides the wisdom of his decision to purchase the television equipment with community funds. "It is like we have joined the rest of the world," he whispers, eyes fixed on the captivating television monitor. "The movies unlock the mysteries of real life beyond our island," he says caught up in cinematic awe.

The movie the villagers are watching is "Scar Face," with Al Pacino. This is an extremely violent movie about the cocaine trade in Florida. On the glaring orb of the television screen, we see a man from a rural Cuban background, immigrating into the United States with nothing to his name. He is a criminal type being purged from Cuba by dumping he and his felonious companions on a Florida beach. Through the drug trade, he rapidly acquires money, power, fast cars, a beautiful wife and an expensive home. He also happens to kill people, lots of people.

As I look at the villagers, all but hypnotized by the crime drama, I wonder if they realize that the only time Scar Face smiles is when he is hurting, or about to be hurting, someone. Do they see the evil that the drug trade represents? Since drugs are not yet found in this remote community, I doubt they understand the horror lurking behind the Hollywood magic of bright city lights, drama, sex and intrigue. The movie is about violence, raw emotions and visual impact and it is making a huge impression upon these simple, very traditional people.

When the movie ends, the young boys run out into the night amongst the palm trees pretending to shoot one another with machine pistols. By an open fire, the men are talking excitedly about a scene where a person is murdered with a chain saw. A couple of the smaller kids are rapidly pushing toy wooden canoes through the sand and making racecar noises.

The chief looks at all the activity and grins proudly. "Next week the boat is bringing us Rambo," he says with a broad smile. "The movie is hard to get. I have to pay double."

Walking down to the beach, I shove our rubber Zodiac out into the dark water. Taking a last look back at the village, I see three boys silhouetted before a fire. Two older boys are holding down a toddler and pretending to chain saw off his limbs. The little boy is crying at the harsh treatment—the older boys are laughing maliciously.

Motoring back out to *Alcyone*, listening to the slap of water against the hollow rubber pontoons, I think about the tremendous impact television is having on these aboriginal people. I do not doubt that the youths will want to move to the bigger towns and small cities of Papua New Guinea, where they can hope to experience what they have seen. They are probably thinking of trading their hollowed-out canoes for motorcycles and their bamboo huts with star-filled nights for apartments in neon-lit cities. In my hand, I am holding a money necklace that I am planning to give to Cindy. This small string of primitive beads has defined the intensity of the bond between these remote island families for many generations far into the past. Yet now I do not doubt the precious love and human significance woven into these small necklaces is beginning to fade for the children and adults of Wuvulu. In the near future, the primitive social fabric of this tightly knit island society is going to unravel—forever.

That night in my cabin aboard the wind ship, I ponder the impact television is having on American youths. We tend to judge ourselves by those we see around us. Television programming adds a new dimension or standard to these vital key values. In television dramas and in music videos, we often see attractive people exploring the dark edges of what is not acceptable behavior. Television is more than just a window into a fantasy world where real life merges with creative imagination. It allows people in the movie trade to present their own perspectives, morals, judgments and values as extremely persuasive arguments...they control the lighting, sound, image and cadence while commanding basically the complete attention of their audience. Though their teachings may be distorted, or even malicious, the message will be presented in an alluring and attractive way. Deception is most effective when it pretends to be something that is supposedly good.

With the new millennium, every day more than a thousand teenagers attempt suicide in the United States; approximately two dozen are successful. It is the number two killer of teenagers in America. Per capita the fastest growing rate of suicide is amongst children only ten to fourteen years old. Television values weigh heavily upon all of us. The average North American youth sits idly watching television for an average of six to six-and-one-half hours a day. Such a loss, when real life adventure is always waiting just outside the front or back door. The short time of our youth is when we are the most creative, imaginative and energetic. How horrible to waste all that youthful wonder, curiosity and energy...just sitting or lying idly in front of an electrical box. An unmonitored television is a lot like inviting a stranger into your home and letting them baby-sit your children.

The next morning, what begins as a regular day of Cousteau

underwater adventure, suddenly becomes an event of a lifetime. We encounter three Orcas hunting amongst the reefs of Wuvulu Island. For eight incredible hours, the Cousteau crew splits into twin teams taking two-hour shifts to dive with the killer whales. My team is just exiting the water as Jean-Michel's team takes over for the last dive rotation of the day. The sun will be going down soon so my team decides to drift alongside Jean-Michel's empty Zodiac. I am relaxing, leaning comfortably against the inflatable's warm rubber pontoon, when Jean-Michel, erupts from the water shouting excitedly, "The orcas, they are eating sharks!"

Three sets of hands lunge for dive masks as we rush to peer eagerly over the side. Beneath us, we see a twenty-eight-foot-long orca swimming towards the other team with an eight-foot long reef shark dangling in its massive jaws. The divers closest to the orcas hear cartilage crunching as the killer whale consumes the whole shark in three gigantic bites. Quietly, so as not to disturb the incredible action below, I take a breath and slip into the warm water.

I cannot approach the action for fear of accidentally getting into the frame of the other team's cameras. As the surrounding water grows darker with the setting sun, we watch the orcas eat three more sharks. We do not see them catching the sharks. The killer whales hang vertically suspended just beneath the surface. Facing downward, they wait patiently, without movement. It is the classic posture of a hunter waiting in ambush. I believe they are echo locating to sense where the sharks are trying to hide. Then without warning, they torpedo downwards. A minute or two later, they ascend with the sharks draped lifelessly in their powerful jaws.

It is amazing that the whales are purposefully returning to us to eat their prey. Is this like a cat who proudly displays a caught mouse or are we a source of entertainment while they eat their meal? Watching small clouds of shark blood drifting in the wake of the killer whales feeding, I cannot help wondering why this super predator does not eat people.

Earlier in the day, I had found myself alone in the water with a large Orca cow. She seemed to be resting, just floating below the surface slowly drifting with the tide. I was idling about thirty feet away having shot my last still picture. Holding my breath a dozen feet beneath the surface I was taking a moment just to stare at this magnificent creature. She was at an angle to me, when I noticed that she was slowly turning in my direction. Her eyes were looking right at me with such primal intelligence—suddenly, I felt threatened. My heartbeat surged. Instantly, I realized that she was probably aware of my rapidly thumping heart. Orcas are incredibly sensitive to the tiniest of sound vibrations. My heart was beginning to beat out a cadence of fear. For a marine predator, this had to be like ringing the chow bell. From a head on perspective, I saw her tail slowly go up and then down. The killer whale was coming toward me and I was not sure what to do, nor her intent. I quickly glanced about, but there was no Zodiac or other person in sight from my limited underwater perspective. There was nowhere to flee. The surface beckoned, particularly since I desperately needed a breath of air, but I could not tear my eyes from the oncoming Orca. I watched the head growing rapidly in size as she closed on me. I became completely aware of her predatory attributes, the huge mouth filled with sturdy teeth, her broad girth and the muscled hump of her massive back. My heart was now jack hammering. She approached to about eight feet and then did something quite amazing. She turned slowly sideways. For a few seconds that seemed an eternity, I looked at the length and girth of this magnificent predator, and then I looked back to her head and our eyes locked. I was stunned. I have never so deeply communicated with a wild animal in such a brief moment. I had no idea what she was thinking or what the moment might have meant to her. My heartbeat slowed as I stared into that wild intelligence lurking behind her eye, which for humans is so often the window to what we are thinking. I intrinsically felt that she had purposefully turned sideways to appear less threatening. Then, unable to resist the overpowering demand for air, I shot to the surface in a wash of fluttering fins. When I looked back under the water, she was gone.

I was surprised that an animal of such size and mass could move so quickly in absolute silence. I spun in a rapid circle looking all about and for a heart-stopping moment stared directly beneath me, but the water below was suspiciously empty. Completely unnerved, I quickly swam over to the Zodiac, which was floating empty fifty feet away. Climbing aboard, I could feel my heart pounding inside my chest. I peered back over the side, but the water below was still oddly empty. My thoughts were rampant, what had just happened? Floating alone beneath the hot tropical sun, I pondered the whale's actions. Was she just curious or did her lingering look imply more?

Now, floating on the surface I see the whales descending after consuming their prey, probably going after another shark to feast on. As the sun drops behind the cloudless horizon, the light fades casting the depths into shadowed darkness. Jean-Michel signals for the team to return to the surface. They are unable to film in the submarine twilight and maybe there is a hint of fear for what lurks below that helps propel the divers back to their Zodiac.

Instead of rushing back to *Alcyone*, with dusk quickly turning to night, we drift under the evening sky as it fills with stars. Eager hands hold the twin Zodiacs together as we relive the incredible experience. Everyone bubbles with excitement as we share the wonder of seeing the killer whales hunting sharks. Twenty yards away, a black orca fin rises almost five feet out of the dark water. Starlight glistens on the wet black fin as it cuts through the smooth glassy surface, then the whale exhales a cloud of mist into the air and disappears with a powerful flick of its tail.

> *"The most beautiful thing we can experience is the mysterious.*
> *It is the source of all true art and science,"* Albert Einstein

"A man cannot be comfortable without his own approval,"
Mark Twain

Chapter 14

OAHU, HAWAII, MAY 1977

THE TRAVEL alarm chimes softly in the darkness. It is 4:00 a.m. as my eyes snap open and the first thing I see is my surfboard bungeed to the cedar ceiling. The night before I parked Revelstoke at my favorite surf spot on the southwest shore of Oahu. I am out of bed in a heartbeat, a skill vigorously instilled at EOD School. Outside I hear breaking surf while rummaging in a drawer for a quarter bar of pineapple-scented surfboard wax. Five minutes later, I swing open the back door and in mere seconds, am running across soft white sand before plunging into the ocean. What a wake-up call feeling the rush of cool salt water flushing over my body. Paddling quickly, I pass through the surf zone and am shortly sitting on my board waiting for the first wave of the day in the nautical twilight an hour before sunrise.

Millions of stars glisten brilliantly in the night sky with no artificial light to spoil their heavenly pageant. The moon is a gleaming crescent low on the ocean's horizon suspended like a shining jewel over a rumpled black satin blanket. A sliver of lunar light glistens softly on the shadowy water as it undulates with each passing swell.

It is difficult to judge the waves, which are dim hulking shadows rushing shoreward in a continuous parade of untapped hydraulic energy. The surf is running four to five feet, a measurement taken from the back of the wave. When the swell begins to pass over the reef beneath my board, it will slow the wave's foot producing a face several feet overhead to a standing surfer. Carefully judging the set pattern I maneuver for a fast moving five footer. Turning the back of my board into the sucking surge of the oncoming wave, I begin paddling furiously and then thrusting my chest forward use gravity to help propel the board down the wave's rushing crest. Feeling the sudden downward surge, I leap to my feet and angle the surfboard down the right-side face of the wave's peak. Pumping with my knees to generate more speed I reach out with my right hand and touch the glassy surface. My fingertips leave a frothy wake in the smooth liquid facade. The vertical wall of upward swirling water is only inches from my eyes. The flowing dark liquid shimmers under the starlight and in its sheen are faint lines of ascending brush strokes of sea foam that define the inward curving face. In the moving depths of the vertical wall of water, there is a subtle florescent glow of the crescent moon. The submerged pool of refracted lunar light rushes with my passage down the wave face, like a rainbow parading with a wandering rainsquall, that for an instant silhouettes a small fish pursued by a somewhat larger one.

Shifting pressure to my right rear foot and digging my toes into the inside rail I feel the board's tail bite into the wave. It launches me up the traveling perpendicular face, then leaning forward and putting downward pressure with my right heel frees the inner rail. The board accelerates as it carves across the crest of the wave sending a slash of water spraying across the top of the wave in an iridescent fan that lightly sparkles for an instant before sweeping away into the enveloping darkness. With a shout of joy, I plunge back down toward the base of the wave. A deeper shade of darkness envelopes me as the wave again shadows the crescent moon. The foot of the breaker begins to drag across a sharp-edged inner reef hidden in the murky shallow water. Sensing the reef's presence by the sudden steepness of the wave face, and an abrupt hydraulic surge of energy, I know it is time to bail. Stepping down hard on the board's tail forces its nose vertical as it launches through the wave's pitching crest. The surf board spins into the night sky shedding water droplets like flung diamonds as I plunge screaming happily back into the dark ocean.

At 7:00 a.m., I am at Lualualei Weapons Station in West Loch, Hawaii standing on the exercise lawn in a big circle with the rest of the command. There are thirty-six of us frogmen preparing for morning calisthenics. What a way to start the day; a couple of hours of surfing in Hawaii and now two hours of physical training with a enthusiastic group of extremely fit men. Each morning we select a frogman at random to lead the physical exercise. It is an unspoken challenge to see who can command the most exhausting regimen of exercise. Push-ups and sit-ups are done in sets of fifty or more. We do our pull-ups slowly in sets of fifteen or twenty with one-armed-pull-up challenges enthusiastically offered and accepted. We end the exercise period with a three to five mile run followed by a quick shower.

By 9:00 a.m., I am at my workstation in the Operations Department. My clerical ability gained from a couple of typing classes in high school has gained me this coveted position. I check on the status of our various teams in remote parts of the Pacific and Indian Oceans. On the operations board I am reminded that my team, EODMUONE TM11 (Explosive Ordnance Disposal Mobile Unit One Team 11) is slated this evening for a nighttime water insertion jump. Picking up the telephone, I call the flight line at Barbers Point Naval Air Station to make sure that two helicopters will be ready for this evening's parachuting operations. At 11:00 a.m., the executive officer passes through the department collecting bodies for a game of jungle rules volleyball. An operational requirement of being a combat frogman is to maintain a suntan. The command allows us a two-hour lunch break during which we must exercise in the sunlight. Special Warfare Operatives have to keep themselves well bronzed because you never know where your military commitments might take you. One sunburned person can affect the operational readiness of an entire team.

At 7:00 p.m., the sun is low on the horizon as the helicopters settle onto the black tarmac at Barbers Point Naval Air Station. We mount up two men per chopper. Each frog team consists of four members, an officer, a chief petty officer and two enlisted men. Several months after arriving in Hawaii my advancement to chief petty officer (CPO), came through. Though a brand new EOD Tech, I have the good fortune of being the enlisted team leader. Tom Dye and I are in the lead chopper, Mike Mullen (a Hawaiian) and Gunner Molley (our very Italian Warrant Officer) will make the second jump. We sit on the helicopters vibrating metal deck with our rubber booted feet dangling out the open door way; the copter's starboard back door has been removed for freer access. Web waist belts snapped to D-rings in the deck keep us in place as the helicopter slowly rises to the deep thwacking sound of the spinning rotors, then lowering its nose accelerates over the dark tarmac. We fly north over a vertical black lava ridge, part of the Waianae Mountain Range climbing rapidly into a darkening sky. When I estimate that we are over a thousand feet up, I unsnap the safety belt. It makes flying in the chopper with your feet hanging over empty air a lot more exciting and if anything should go suddenly wrong, I can hurl myself clear and go for canopy.

At the ocean-side town of Waianae, we angle west out across a white sand beach towards the dark ocean. A bonfire is burning in one of the fire rings. I see from a vertical perspective people moving around the tall dancing flames. Someone aims the bright beam of a flashlight at us waving it back and forth. Our pilot waggles his rotors in reply as we pass over the post-jump party crew. Frogs do not need much of an excuse to stage a beach party. Watching comrades parachuting into the ocean at night is the perfect party excuse and reason for some to invite their wives and girlfriends.

Tom nudges me with his shoulder then shouts into my helmet to be heard over the heavy thump of the rotor blades and the piercing whine of the turbo engines. "Gail is down there, I saw her car in the parking lot." Gail is Tom's newest squeeze. His relationships tend to be short lived because he cannot resist pulling pranks on his unsuspecting girlfriends.

I watch the waves rushing towards the beach as we go *feet wet*, which meaning we are now flying over water. It is an eerie feeling being on the verge of jumping from a secure platform into a dark sky thousands of feet above a vast empty ocean. I glance over at Tom, who is chuckling cheerfully.

"What are you so happy about?" I ask, shouting to be heard over the noisy helicopter.

"I am going to mess with my girlfriend's mind," he laughs, "I told her that I would be the one falling with just one strobe light so she would know it is me." Tom is leering through his goggles as he rips away a strobe light that is taped to his ankle. "When we jump I am going to turn this on and toss it. I will not activate the one on my helmet until I am just above the water. Gail's going to go nuts when she sees the light cream into the water at full velocity."

"You sure you want to do this? You two have only been dating a couple of days."

"Sure, it'll get her all fired up; better than paying for a date at the stock car races back home."

The air crew chief taps me on the shoulder and points. Three thousand feet beneath us, I see the twin wakes of our Zodiac pick up boats. The pilot adjusts our course to pass over the speeding boats about a mile offshore. I activate both of my strobe lights and, true to his promise, Tom only switches on the one he is holding in his hand. I shake my helmet to let him know he is blowing it before throwing my body out the door. I go into a head's up arch as the choppers skids pass inches from my face so I can watch Tom's exit. He is a rapidly moving black shadow against the faint red outline of the chopper's open hatch. I can see the soft glow of the instrument lights that are momentarily blotted out by his shadowy passage. Then the helicopter is gone from my sight. Instantly I feel the jarring at the shoulders and crotch from the parachute harness as my canopy slams open. Completing my first swing, I glance upward to see Tom's parachute drifting a hundred feet above me. Looking down and right into the empty night sky, I see Tom's strobe falling at over one hundred-twenty miles per hour flashing its lonely beacon. It splashes into the water not far from one of the Zodiacs, which is rushing towards it. From the beach Tom's girlfriend would have seen one set of lights falling slowing under canopy, that being me, and a single light strobing on a vertical sprint to the ocean, that supposedly being Tom hurling towards a major accident. At one hundred-twenty miles-per-hour, the ocean surface is about as forgiving to a live falling object as a cement sidewalk.

Glancing upward, I see the helicopter about a thousand feet above me and turning back towards shore as I descend slowly under canopy through the dark column of tropical air. Below the shadowed surface of the Pacific Ocean ripples. All is quiet, but for the rustle of wind rushing through the cloth canopy as I slowly drift across the star-filled sky.

Looking back down towards the water, I see the twin wakes of the two black Zodiacs speeding in my direction. This nighttime parachuting operation is a standard part of our ongoing frogman training. Every three months we are required to make a night jump into the ocean. Maintaining our jump qualifications is one of the more enjoyable aspects of this exciting job and we draw an extra fifty-five dollars a month of hazardous duty pay for it. I am in quite the chipper mood until I suddenly notice that there is something not quite right about the pickup boats. I can tell that they are speeding in my direction, but they seem to be falling slowly behind. Which is very surprising considering these boats are extremely fast for rubber inflatables. Looking more closely at the ocean surface, I realize I am not looking at starlight dancing on the water, but wind froth from white caps. There is a strong wind blowing and it is hurling Tom and I straight out to sea.

For a heart stopping moment, I consider the possibility of being lost in a vast ocean at night. The word *shark* even flutters through my thoughts an instant before my feet hit the water. A half-second later, I am jerked back out of the water as my parachute, which is still full of wind, continues to race straight out to sea. I am skimming across the surface, splashing from white cap to white cap, face down. Salt water is shoveling up my nose at an appalling rate. Am I in threat of drowning from nasal ingestion I wonder in sudden panic? Reaching quickly for a shoulder cape-well, I trigger its release mechanism freeing one set of shroud lines. The wind spills from the parachute and the canopy collapses, which is good until it drapes over my head. It is not easy breathing under wet nylon as I urgently work my way towards the edge of the parachute following one of its sewn ribs. I pull the wet nylon sheeting from my helmet just in time to see a speeding Zodiac narrowly miss running me over. A loud splash dozens of feet away announces Tom's arrival just before he begins his own horizontal sprint across the windblown ocean.

Strong hands pull me into the inflatable. "Has the other half of the team jumped yet?" I ask urgently.

"Not yet," says the boat captain. I hold out my hand for his walky-talky, "Helo 2, this is Zodiac 1, abort abort. I say again abort abort. Excessive surface winds gusting to twenty knots."

"Roger Zodiac One, Helo Two aborting."

Tom's parachute collapses as he releases one of his cap wells and we pull alongside to pick him up.

"How do you know it is gusting to twenty knots," inquires the boat captain, we don't have a wind gauge."

"Don't need a gauge to know that white caps begin to form when the wind exceeds seventeen knots," I answer, "basic seamanship."

The boat captain apparently does not like the way I framed my answer as he takes it out on Tom. "What happened to your lights man?

"Couldn't get the helmet light to work," Tom complains.

"Yeah, well what happened to the one on your ankle?"

"I tossed it."

"You what?"

"I tossed it, wanted to give my girlfriend a fright."

"Are you nuts? I could have lost you or even run you over in the dark."

"Like you almost did me?" I laugh as I join the conversation trying to get him to lighten up. It works.

"Na just didn't want you wet too long Chief," he laughs. Then he slaps Tom's shoulder, "that stunt is going to cost you back at headquarters and I bet your girlfriend is not too thrilled when we get to the beach."

The boat captain swings the bow of the Zodiac back towards the shore and opens up the throttle. In a few minutes, we will be joining the party crew on the beach and Tom will find out his uncertain fate with his new girlfriend. On the short ride, I am pondering my mistakes.

When Tom told me about the stupid stunt he wanted to pull, I should have shut it down immediately. As the chief of the team, it is my obligation to insure operational safety. Because of the party atmosphere on the beach, Tom and I had treated this training evolution far too casually. The aircrew and the boat crew were in radio contact, yet no one mentioned the strong surface winds and I had not even thought to ask. I had overlooked an important factor. By not paying attention to my environment, I could have made a potentially fatal mistake. I pause to remember a high school friend who took a dare to jump off a cliff into a swimming hole. The other kids incorrectly assumed he knew about the underwater rock that they naturally avoided. That one foolish mistake, a brief moment of inattention and bad judgment, placed him in a wheelchair for life.

The boat captain hauls up the outboard as the Zodiac surfs the white wash onto the beach. We quickly unload the wet parachutes, strip off the engine and carry the Zodiac to a trailer as Tom glances eagerly around for his new girlfriend. "Anyone seen Gail?" he asks hopefully.

"She left a few minutes ago," laughs one of the wives.

"Left?" groans Tom unhappily.

"Yep," laughs the woman, "she didn't think much of your little stunt. You know Tom, you can be such a clod."

Chuckling I head for Revelstoke which is parked in the beach lot. I collect the keys from a friend who offered to drive it up. "Aren't you going to stay for the party?" He asks.

"Na, there's a swell heading for the North Shore, think I'll go camp there and score some early morning surf," I reply.

Standing at the backdoor, I unlock a small, chest-high compartment and pull out a flexible metal hose. Turning on the water valves, I wash the sand off my wetsuit and rinse my hair with the warm water. Opening the backdoor, I step inside and light a candle instead of turning on a light. I strip off my wetsuit and hang it in the small bathroom to drip while I dry off with a towel then use it to wipe up the small puddle of water I have left on the oak floor. Pulling on a pair of jeans and a T-shirt I head up to the driver's compartment and start the engine. Tuning in a local Hawaiian station, I turn on the headlights, blow out the candle and drive out of the beach lot.

Building Revelstoke was one of my best ideas ever. It so fit in with my Hawaiian roving lifestyle. I could take my traveling house anywhere on Oahu, in a sense making the whole island my home. My mood determined by destination. When the surf was running on one side of the island, I would drive there to spend the night. Arriving at Pipeline, Sunset Beach, Waikiki or Makapuu, I would camp at the beach parking lot listening to the sound of pounding waves and anticipating an early morning paddle out. By being there so early, I usually had the pick of the waves to myself. When the surf was down, I would head for the solitude of the island's mountains. I might camp by a waterfall, beside a flowing stream or near a babbling brook. On stormy nights, I liked to park high up on the Pali Pass at the top of its sheer cliff walls. The blustery winds racing up out of Kaneohe through the steep valleys would buffet and rock Revelstoke while pounding rain drummed a primal beat upon its metal roof. Warm and dry inside I would listen to the cadence of the storm, light half a dozen candles and wrap myself around a good adventure book that usually had my mind traveling to exotic far-off places, many of which I planned to visit someday in the future.

When the trade winds blew, I had a secret place high up on Tantalus Drive above Makiki Heights overlooking Waikiki. I had

discovered a campsite inside a miniature tropical rain forest thick
with Elephant bamboo. Nestled amongst the thick smooth bamboo
shafts was like being inside a giant wind chime. The swift currents
of air wove themselves amongst the tall hollow trunks driving them
against each other in a thundering reverberation of sound that
ebbed and flowed to the beat of the gusting winds. I was living a life
of total nomadic freedom in an island paradise and imagination
was my guide and friend.

Driving away from the beach party, I think about the wisdom
of my decision. The rest of the guys will drink far too much and
stay up excessively late. In an hour, I will be passing through
Haleiwa to park just off the Kamehameha Highway at Laniakia
Beach Park. Tomorrow I will wake up refreshed for some magnificent early morning surfing. Glancing about the interior cockpit of
Revelstoke, I take one hand off the steering wheel and run it over
the leather dash, which was a gift from a friend who crafted hand-
tooled leather for a hobby. She had worked in a colorful tropical
scene reflective of island life with huts, coconut trees, a sandy beach
and tubular waves. Driving into the warm Hawaiian night, inhaling
the rich smell of oiled leather, I mentally shuffle backwards in
time sorting through a caravan of distinctive memories revolving
around my many adventures in Revelstoke. I am heading back to
the very beginning of my nomadic lifestyle; it is when my life shifted
dramatically from the norms of daily life to the unique challenges
of becoming a road wanderer.

It all began on a very special fall day in coastal Maryland where
my mind captures an image of dense woods with tall trees swaying
in a blustery fall wind. The leaves on the trees are changing colors
as winter approaches. Nature has been busy with broad strokes of
her brush painting the lush forest in a swarm of brilliant fall colors.
Each tree is a biological masterpiece of tint and shading with flaming
reds, vibrant oranges and soft canary yellows. Many of the leaves
are beginning to curl with tips stained a brittle earthy brown. It is
mostly these leaves that the gusting wind is striping in clusters from
the swaying branches, gathering them like flocks of colorful birds,

before sending them swirling in an airborne dance of changing hues and shifting aerial patterns. A ground hugging breeze scoops up a thick blanket of mostly brown leaves then hurls them across a black tarmac highway where they are abruptly scattered by the passage of a large brown speeding van. The leaves swirl in the wake of the vehicle and then the wind carries them swiftly away as the van slows to drive through a security gate at the Explosive Ordnance Disposal School's blasting range.

Pulling into an empty parking place, I shut off the truck's engine, then settle back to wait for the rest of my class that will soon break for dinner. Sitting proudly in the driver's seat I breathe in the clean leather-like smell of the brand-new vehicle. I have missed the opportunity to blow up several pounds of TNT while picking up the van at the Chevy dealership where I custom ordered it several weeks earlier. There is a final rolling explosion from the range beyond a protective berm and then I see my classmates spilling out of a concrete bunker. Quickly they head for the parking lot where an old gray Navy bus waits to take them to the cafeteria. Seeing me, I hear Hank yell to the rest of the class, "Hey, forget the bus, Steve's van is big enough to haul all of us to the chow hall."

The double backdoors are thrown open as eighteen men clamber inside jousting each other for a place to sit on the empty floor. Hank plops down in the passenger seat and cheerfully knuckles my arm. "So you're going mobile on us?" he quips. "This is such a cool idea. Wish I had thought of it."

"You can share in the experience if you want," I offer, "might even be a few bucks in it for you."

"Sure, what do I get to do?" Hank is sporting his eager beaver ready-to-help smile.

"Well," I grin, "you could begin by helping to me cut a few holes in the metal siding."

"What?" he laughs. "You just picked up a new van and you want me to cut holes in it? And I get paid to do this?" he asks innocuously.

At the chow hall, a couple of cooks in the parking lot are surprised to see so many men piling out of the back of the van.

Hank and I quickly wolf down a pile of groceries each. Frogman training requires huge amounts of calories. Flipping our empty metal trays into soapy tubs of water, we rush outside and drive over to the dormitory where I have been stockpiling tools and motor home parts. I am eager to get to work because winter is coming and I want to be into my mobile home before the ice and snow hits.

While Hank runs an extension cord, I grab a heavy-duty drill motor, lock in a shiny new bit, and then step inside the back of the van. Revving the motor, I pause to look at the truck's shiny fresh paint.

"So what are you waiting for? Having second thoughts about drilling holes in your new ride?"

"Na," I laugh, "just savoring the moment." Without breaking eye contact with Hank, I blindly stick my arm straight out at my side and quickly push the spinning drill bit through the unblemished metal. I am about to cut a two-foot-square hole so I do not have to be very precise where I actually drill the first hole. I have been planning this conversion in detail for a long time and know exactly where to install each window. After chalking a quick outline I grab a power jigsaw insert the blade into the still warm hole and rapidly cut out a large chunk of metal then watch it drop to the ground. Through the square opening, I see a couple of my classmates watching the process in a state of modest surprise. "Now that is what I call instant depreciation," quips Mickey Doke,

A minute later, a like chunk of metal hits the ground from the other side. "Hey, this is fun," Hank revs the saber saw and grins. At the open backdoor Mickey Doke steps in, "Hey, if you need any more holes cut can I do it?"

"Sure," I pass him the power drill and jig saw, "I need a couple of holes cut in the roof." With templates for the roof vents, I rapidly chalk their exact pre-chosen location then turn him loose with the jigsaw. Soon there are half a dozen guys involved in a diversity of projects. We install sliding side windows that are too high on the outside for people to see inside, which later would prove to be an extraordinarily important choice. We mount roof vents and, over my yet-to-be-built bed, I carefully fit a stained glass skylight made by an artist friend in California.

The weeks pass quickly as I busily put all my spare time into creating Revelstoke. Many of my classmates could not resist offering advice on its construction. For me it was an opportunity to hand them a couple of tools and say, "Okay, go ahead and show me." I felt like a modern day Huckleberry Fin and was thoroughly enjoying myself. Work shared with friends is not labor, but constructive fun and active companionship. The guys were sharing in a dream becoming reality and like me were reveling in the childlike qualities of the fantasy from which it was being born. It was like the youthful enthusiasm of children building a tree fort only we were grown men and our tree fort had wheels and a big engine. We framed the interior with exotic woods; fragrant cedars, multi-colored redwoods and soft-grained mahogany planks that I had salvaged from packing crates containing equipment being shipped back to the USA from Vietnam. Surprisingly some of the guys would bring personal treasures that they wanted to contribute or had just happened to find at a swap meet or antique store. One classmate brought twin brass lanterns that cast a candle's soft glow to the fresh cut wood interior. Another gave a ship's clock that he found at a garage sale. Every half-hour it would chime softly.

On Christmas Eve, Revelstoke was finally ready for me to move in though the work would continue to be a never-ending project for the next decade. Over time Revelstoke would develop into far more than a mobile home; it grew to be a living art project in an incessant state of transition. In a sense, the unique motor home was a physical reflection of who I was on the inside and a tribute to the generosity of my friends. Over the next ten years, Revelstoke would play an almost magical role in my life. Inspiration could quickly become physical reality within the childhood fantasy that I was living. This uniqueness of the life-changing path I was about to launch myself into was confirmed on that first day that I moved into Revelstoke.

Carrying the last of my possessions, a cardboard box full of dirty laundry, out of my room I pass through the dormitory's dayroom.

It being Christmas Eve many of the guys are on holiday leave with their families. With the growing expenses of building Revelstoke, I could not afford a plane ticket home, nor apparently could the half-dozen young men sitting in front of the dayroom's television. They are involved in a friendly argument over what to watch as I quietly slip out the door.

In the parking lot, I open one of Revelstoke's twin back doors and step inside. *With that step I am a nomad now,* I think merrily to myself. In that instant, I find myself considering a very interesting decision of where should I spend the night this evening? With a week's leave and a full fuel tank all the directions of the compass are open to me. Mountains or ocean is an intriguing question that instantly comes to mind. The decision process does not take very long as I drive out the base gate and head for the Atlantic Coast. A few hours later, the sunset finds me walking on a windswept beach on the Maryland seashore. There is no one else in sight. Day vacationers have fled the windblown beach as I shuffle across the sand watching waves with my thoughts swirling in a whirlwind of activity. A new sense of inner freedom is spreading its wings. I realize that being mobile expands my prospects for adventure, challenge and mystery. Instead of eventually needing to go home for the night, I have brought my home with me. Truthfully, I have grabbed more time out of the typical twenty-four hour day. This evening I own a larger chunk of the night. The constraints of time's constant demands just relaxed. I am free to explore the beach or just wander under the stars. Picking up a rock, I hurl it into the restless ocean, and then inhale the cold brisk air feeling vitally alive with a growing excitement about my expanding horizons. Back at the dormitory, I imagine the guys in the dayroom synchronizing their activities to television programming, commercial breaks and tightly scheduled cafeteria meals. Idly they sit in chairs or lay upon the floor staring into an electric glaring orb that encourages immobility and deadens intellectual thought.

Often we make our daily choices unconsciously. It is easy to become a creature of habit. Repeated behavior becomes static conditioning like being caught in a hard-sided mold, imagination becomes restrained and decisions self-limiting. Timing one's schedule to make it home in time for a favorite television program should make a person wonder if their priorities are in proper order. Watching television is to see actors pretending at life while the viewer is forfeiting valuable moments from the living reality that is their existence—and it plays out only once. For each of us our life's clock is ticking and every lost minute is gone forever. Throwing away youthful moments is to cast off the very best of what life has to offer. We only get the one life…it is real, it is here, and we are living it now. To waste even a bit of our lives is a private tragedy, particularly the days of our childhood, which should be filled with youthful adventures, wonder and daydreams yearning to become tied to adult realities and meaningful memories.

My choice to become a road traveler was to accept a new independence that would enhance my life and broaden my awareness. Yet, there are many paths that contribute to personal freedom. Getting a quality education opens up avenues to prosperity, understanding and to challenge. Learning a trade and deciding to do your best at it means having greater opportunities. A commitment to good health leads to physical adventure and to a robust lifestyle. Accepting Jesus Christ as a best friend opens us to the gifts of truth, love and forgiveness. By forgiving others, we set ourselves free from self-made bonds that chain our spirit. It means not being a slave to the burden of negative emotions. Through devotion to law, we gain freedom. I think of the Ten Commandments as laws of liberty that set us free. All of these are lessons I would learn later in life when I discovered light and freedom through Jesus Christ in the darkness and confinement of a prison cell.

True autonomy in life is only found through commitment to what is right and good. Without commitment to doing good work there can be no real self-determination and unsaddled freedom. To be willing to stand for what is right, to have the courage to challenge the unknown, to reach further than we thought ourselves capable of is to know the true wonder of being a fully dynamic and aware human being. We are the only one of God's creations that is blessed with the inconceivable gift of complete self-awareness and the determination to do something about it.

"...unlike the mediocre, intrepid spirits seek victory over those things that seem impossible..."
Ferdinand Magellan, Explorer 1520

When Jesus spoke again to the people, he said, "I am the light of the world. Whoever follows me will never walk in darkness, but will have the light of life." John 8:12

Chapter 15

PAPUA NEW GUINEA, APRIL 1998

STANDING AT the plunging bow of the Alcyone, I listen to the whispery sound of water-rushing pass the wind ship's hull as she races into the warm tropical night. The rest of the crew is sleeping soundly below. I am standing the midnight watch. I am supposed to be in the bridge, which is just forward of the stern, monitoring the radar, gauges and ship's computer. Yet there is something magical standing all the way forward at the pitching bow. My knees flex automatically as the deck rises on the back of an ocean swell, then plunges downward several feet as the ship accelerates into the roller's trough. Looking upwards, the heavens are a vast unending radiance against the blackness of deep space. At sea, there are no city lights to dim the nighttime majesty of the stars and planets. A couple of points off the bow lay the Southern Cross. The shield-like configuration of four stars rides high on the horizon like a beacon pointing the way to unknown adventures.

When I was a youth growing up in Southern California, on summer nights I often camped in my backyard. Under the mysterious glow of a flashlight's beam, I enjoyed reading adventure stories, mostly about sailors of the past and their tall sailing ships. My heroes were real life explorers discovering the wonders of distant oceans and exotic far off lands. Then, turning off my flashlight, and staring into the night sky, I would look for the Big Dipper and pretend it was the Southern Cross. In the mental stage of my youthful mind, I would become one of those globetrotting explorers.

Now as I feel the powerful hum of *Alcyone's* engines vibrating up through the soles of my sneakers, I ponder the wonder of childhood dreams that actually come true. For a moment, I think about that little boy growing up in a crowded California suburbia. Though much older now, that youth is still very much a part of who I am today. I chuckle realizing that in my jeans, T-shirt and white high-top Converse sneakers, I still dress like him. There is even a flashlight in my hand and on the wind ship's deck lays my old flannel sleeping bag. I could not resist bringing it along when Jean-Michel Cousteau asked me to join *Alcyone's* crew. Under the bright beam of the flashlight, I can still barely read the faded Coleman label where my mother stenciled my name to keep me from losing it at YMCA camp. After my watch, I am planning to sleep out under the stars just like when I was a kid. Tonight the explorer will try to remember the child and recapture his youthful dreams. Turning off the flashlight, I return to the bridge.

Sitting down in the Captain's chair, I first check the radar screen. Its soft green glow paints a mostly clear horizon. There are no other vessels within its ten-mile range setting. Since we are crossing deep water in an open ocean, this should be a relaxing watch. I do a quick sweep of the various gauges to make sure that all is well with the engines and then check the compass to ensure the wind ship is on course. Secure and confident, I open my Bible to the book of Proverbs and begin to read.

The proverbs of Solomon son of David, king of Israel: for attaining wisdom and discipline; for understanding words of insight; for acquiring a disciplined and prudent life, doing what is right and just and fair; for giving prudence to the simple,   knowledge and discretion to the young—let the wise listen and add to their learning, and let the discerning get guidance. Proverbs 1:1-5

"*Wow,*" I think to myself, "*can there ever be an introduction to a book more powerful than that?*" King Solomon, a man who had all that a kingdom could provide, a king of great knowledge, with vast wealth and having lived an incredible diversity of worldly experiences. The Lord favored King Solomon, because he asked for so little, God blessed him with great wisdom and incredible fortune. From the distant past, his words, inspired by God's hand, span time to reach out and touch each of us with wisdom and with guidance. As a Christian, I can claim this incredible gift of knowledge so that I too can live a fruitful life full of meaning and purpose.

I close the Bible, but do not set it down as I think about what I have just read. All of us want to live happy, satisfying lives and that one simple paragraph sets us firmly upon the path to knowledge, understanding and purpose.

A gentle chiming from the ship's chronometer announces the top of the hour. It is two o'clock in the morning and time for me to plot our location. At the chart table, I draw intersecting lines on an Indian Ocean map. We are exactly three hundred miles southeast of Indonesia, and a quarter of a mile off course. At the helm, I turn a small black knob two clicks to port. The autopilot instantly responds as *Alcyone* turns slightly into the wind.

For a moment, I think how the Bible is very much like my map and autopilot. As we plot our life's journeys, we sometimes get a little off course. The winds of the world often try to blow us in wrong directions or into troubled waters. Yet, by regularly reading the Bible, we can more easily find our way back to the right path, the path that leads to simple happiness, self-satisfaction and a closer relationship with our creator.

Opening the Bible again, I turn to a proverb that greatly influenced me as a child and is now an adult foundation for my life's quest. "Buy the truth and do not sell it; get wisdom, discipline and understanding," Proverbs 23:23

When I was a youth, growing up in a busy Los Angeles suburb, I knew that with discipline and focus, I could realize my dreams. One day I would see the Southern Cross for real. Proverbs 23:23 was now my adult passport for getting me there. The Book of Proverbs is my guide for appreciating all that life offers.

Sitting at the helm of the wind ship, I again check the radar then quietly continue to read The Bible and think about a man named King Solomon.

"I will study and prepare myself and then someday my chance will come," Abraham Lincoln.

"Courage is being scared to death—but saddling up anyway," John Wayne

Chapter 16

SAN DIEGO, CALIFORNIA, JUNE 1978

A FTER MY assignment to Hawaii, the next few years pass quickly with many head-to-tail military operations. Sometimes they were flying team assignments, which involved transport in aircraft or naval vessels to remote destinations. I worked with NASA recovering an ultra-secret re-entry vehicle from space that splashed down into the ocean off Vandenberg, California, participated in a super-secret mission for the CIA, dove all about the South Pacific and Mid-Pacific Ocean, conducted jungle-training operations and got to blow things up on a fairly regular basis. EOD Teams tend to become specialized in their skills with a tendency towards picking up specific assignments particular to their skills. Team 11's operational area of expertise was nuclear powered aircraft carriers. We served aboard the USS Ranger (CVA 61), USS ENTERPRISE (CVA 65) and the USS CONSTELLATION (CVA 64). It was aboard the USS CONSTELLATION that I would discover an important insight into my own character.

It is early in the morning, pre-dawn, as I watch a gray sea mist drifting across the restless water of the inner harbor at San Diego

Naval Station. The mist ebbs through the darkness, swirling just above the water to the pace and whim of a light gusting wind. A security light spills a pool of bright radiance upon the black water as I watch the mist momentarily sparkling as it passes through this small oasis of luminosity, then the wind lifts the miniature cloud of misty particles and sends them twirling through the open window of my grey military pickup truck. Warm and snug with the heater on high to take away the early morning chill, I rub condensation from the inside of the windshield and peer through the wet sheen. Through the misted glass, I stare spellbound at the twinkling lights of a massive aircraft carrier shrouded in wisps of fog and drifting steam. Its ponderous bulk fills the dark horizon; its twinkling lights haloed like Christmas ornaments by the condensation on the glass. Through two very large openings in the hull, I can see into the huge plane-handling bay that is larger than two football fields laid end to end. Inside I see shadows within shadows defined by red and yellow lights shining softly in the darkness of the pre-dawn morning. There are silhouettes of sailors walking the multiple decks extending seventeen stories into the ink black sky. My pickup truck is dwarfed by the majestic presence of one of the largest and most fearsome fighting machines of the modern world, the nuclear-powered aircraft carrier *USS CONSTELLATION* (CV 64). Virtually it is a never-sleeping floating city with a crew of over five thousand men. In just a few hours, with the fast approaching dawn, it will become home for EODMUONE TM 11 (Explosive Ordnance Disposal Mobile Unite One Team 11). As the chief petty officer in-charge of the team, it is with high expectations that I mentally begin readying myself for this sea deployment as a bomb disposal frogman. I take my leadership responsibilities extremely seriously. One tends to be rather alert when working on a flight deck crowded with screaming jet engines, warplanes landing and taking off at over a hundred knots and with the added excitement of high explosive bombs, rockets, large caliber guns and the occasional nuclear weapon.

Two hours later a bright Southern California sun is climbing the horizon against a pale gunmetal blue winter sky as I shoulder my heavy sea bag, begin my own ascent up a steel staircase and walk across a narrow gangway. Flipping a jaunty salute to the ship's flag, then another to the Officer of the Deck, I stride forth into what will become a twenty-thousand-mile journey across two oceans to eight Asian countries and another adventure of a lifetime.

My berthing assignment is in the chief's quarters a couple of levels below the flight deck. Regularly from my bunk, day and night, rain or shine, I hear the rumbling whoosh and running vibration of the steam catapults launching heavy aircraft into the sky. Over the next couple of months, I thoroughly enjoy how the massive ship barely rolls even in a stormy sea.

I had no idea that I was so prone to getting seasick when I joined the Navy. It was a very unpleasant discovery the first time I found myself leaning over the rail *feeding the fish*. Over the years, the fairly regular physical act of heaving my guts out had become just one of those little sacrifices I had to pay for adventure on the high seas. My how I hated getting seasick.

My favorite place aboard ship was the flight deck, particularly at night with the darkness slashed by the roaring red and yellow blowtorch flame of jet engines in full afterburner. It was thrilling weaving a careful course between closely packed aircraft with their jet engines growling aggressively as they shot out rolling waves of blistering heat. My job as a bomb disposal frogman was to ensure that the missiles and bombs aboard the fighters and attack bombers were in a proper state of readiness. Primarily my charge was to be prepared to react instantly to any weapons accidents or better yet, prevent them from ever happening. Since an aircraft is best launched into a thirty-knot wind, I liked to position myself forward and amidships between the number one and two cats (catapults). In an emergency, it is easier to move aft with a wind at your back than it is to struggle forward against a stiff wind that might inciden-tally be carrying a deadly cargo of sharp-edged metal debris and liquid, body-toasting, flames. When recovering aircraft, I shift my position to just forward of the aircraft carrier's island superstruc-ture to stand alongside a yellow crash truck. On a flight deck, the fire truck offers a ready shelter in the event of a crashing tumbling aircraft shedding saw-toothed, red-hot metal Frisbees.

It pays in dangerous environments to be extra vigilant. I found that determining potential escape routes before an emergency occurred was a common sense approach to ensuring continued personal survival with all limbs intact. There was a very good reason why flight deck operations are considered hazardous duty. On extended cruises, an aircraft carrier usually loses an individual or two…or more…to fatal accidents. On this cruise, five people would die from preventable accidents. One of the accidents involved eating too much high fat, sugarcoated foods. An overdose of gut bombs (donuts) ended a life that should have still been in its prime. Anyway, the best way not to be on the receiving end of a life-threatening accident was to anticipate the best courses of action before one occurred. I had mixed feelings depending on the various types of potential high-speed airplane calamities that might occur on the flight deck. If a plane crashes in a big way, I was going to head in the opposite direction as rapidly as possible. Having the island superstructure only five running paces from my current position would protect me from flying debris and the body-roasting effect of a high-octane fuel fire fanned by thirty-knot winds. However, if the accident was manageable, then I was expected to go dashing in to render safe any explosives involved, which is where it tended to get rather interesting. It was also my prime reason for standing next to the crash truck. If a plane creamed-in on a flight deck the best protection for the aircraft carrier was an aggressive fire fighting response. That meant the crash truck was going to attack the fire. Since I would also have to go in the direction of the accident, it might make sense to latch onto the back of the crash truck and ride it in. The bulk of the fire truck would protect me from the flames and by standing on the rear bumper; my feet would not be in contact with a possibly burning flight deck longer than necessary.

Flight deck operations are noisy affairs. The roar of thirty or more jet engines within the confines of little more than four acres of flight deck can be deafening. To protect their ears flight deck personnel wear oversized earmuffs affectionately called mouse ears. My mouse ears also contained a two-way radio for instant communication with the various controlling departments; air boss, catapult officer, weapons officer, safety officer, etc. Earmuffs make an already dangerous flight deck an even more hazardous place. Not being able to hear surrounding sounds means an accident can sneak up on a less than alert potential victim. Therefore, you learn to look around a lot, called rubbernecking, and your visual memory improves significantly. You tend to remember where planes and weapons are staged and when something mechanical might be moving in your general direction. Small tractors dart about between the airplanes towing bombs, oxygen cylinders and other heavy things that gives them instant right-of-weight as far as we pedestrians are concerned. Jet engines require particularly close attention. Walking too close to the business end of a jet engine can turn the unwary into an instant crispy critter or send the unfortunate person bouncing down the deck towards all kinds of waiting sharp or blunt obstacles. The front end of a jet engine is the most feared danger from carrier aircraft. Jet engines under full military power have an awesome suction ability that can, and has, slurped people in from a number of feet away, from human being to sprayed charred-graffiti in a body-grinding couple of microseconds. You have to watch out for tie-down chains, fuel hoses, electrical cables and other obstacles that can trip the inattentive. Sometimes newer individuals get so caught-up in watching the planes they forget to notice what is under...or not under...their feet as they unintentionally walk right off the edge of the flight deck. They next discover the interesting sensation of unexpected free fall as they plunge a hundred feet down to the ocean soon to be followed by the hamburger-making properties of the ship's four house-sized propellers. That is how we lost one of our people. A young man in eager pursuit of a slightly higher than expected flying Frisbee. Flight decks are a great place for forcibly enhancing a person's perception of global awareness.

Four months into the cruise, I am casually standing between the number one and two catapults facing aft somewhere in the Indian

Ocean. It is late at night in the middle of a rainstorm so I am not exactly feeling very casual, nor particularly comfortable. Actually, I am wet and looking forward to my nice warm bunk below deck. Standing there with cold water dripping off my nose I am not expecting the life-endangering incident that is hurling at me. Well hurling may not be the best term. The airplane in question is actually standing still—in fact, it is standing in the wrong place. It is in the wrong place by all of six inches.

Aligning an aircraft with a catapult sled takes extreme precision. The plane is about to be hurled from a standstill to over one-hundred-forty-knots in about two seconds. That short journey has to be a straight shot, but this bird is six inches too far to the left. An interesting fact about jet fighters is that they cannot back up. That means to realign this bird we are going to have to push it back manually. Currently the wings of this F14 Tomcat are swept forward in sub-sonic configuration, which provides for greater lift on take-off. Before we can manually push the aircraft backwards, the pilot has to retract the wings into their supersonic configuration to reduce stress on the wing's joints and locking struts. On a hand signal from the catapult officer, about thirty of us run to the leading edge of the Tomcat's wings and push the aircraft backwards ten feet. As we quickly re-take our positions, the pilot slowly taxis forward and this time winds up six inches too far to the right. The catapult officer walks right up to the nose gear and stares at it just to assure himself that the plane really is too far to the right then signals us forward to repeat the push back process.

Over my headphones the voice of the air boss crackles angrily, "Quit messing around and launch that bird. I have got aircraft to recover."

Glancing about I notice that all the other launch aircraft are gone. A precision operation is rapidly falling behind schedule. The pilot retracts the wings and we push the aircraft back ten feet. The plane taxis forward again and the pilot advances the wings back to subsonic configuration only to discover that he is now six inches too far to the left again.

The air boss is furious. "Launch that aircraft or strike it below decks,"

I hear the catapult officer's hurried reply, "Yes sir. Just one more try, Sir."

The retract-the-wings-push-back-taxi-forward process is hurriedly repeated. The rain is coming down harder as the catapult officer quickly examines the alignment, which is finally dead on.

"Launch that bird now," rages the air boss over the mouse ears.

The catapult officer quickly scans the deck for readiness, then jabs two fingers at the fighter pilot in a dramatic hand gesture that signals him to go to full afterburner. The pilot slams the throttles forward to full military power. Twin cones of bright orange/red inferno tipped in brilliant white heat, each over thirty-feet-long, leap from the back of the sleek jet fighter. The Tomcat's nose lowers under the massive thrust like a crouching predatory cat about to leap. I feel the tremendous power of the jet engines vibrating across the deck and radiating up through the soles of my boots. Between the twin cats, we crouch down on one knee so the wing of the about to be launched fighter will pass over us should we be a step or two too close. It is then, with the twin jet engines roaring their fury and the deck vibrating madly, that I notice something is wrong. At least I am pretty sure that something is wrong. There is no threat of the wing passing over us because the pilot has forgotten to advance the plane's wings back into subsonic configuration. Quickly glancing left and right I anticipate that someone else will catch this. I am here for weapons safety, not aircraft flight configuration. Supersonic configuration will not provide enough lift for takeoff. The wild thought that *this is not my call...*that I am doing something wrong and about to get into really big trouble is echoing through my mind as I stand up.

I did not consciously make the decision to take action. Though it had not yet happened, in my imagination I see the fighter launch...see it stall...see it tumble into the ocean. Even if the pilot and gunner/navigator react quickly enough to eject they and their aircraft would probably still be run over by the ponderous passage of the massive aircraft carrier.

Abruptly the world seems to be moving in slow motion. I see the catapult officer's helmeted head swing towards the bow to take a last quick check of the launch path. I find myself purposefully striding towards the front of the fighter where I will be more visible with my arms crossed over my head signaling *fouled deck, do not launch*, another completely unconscious choice. It will do little good trying to shout a warning over the roar of the jet engines. All my senses focus on the sudden and urgent presence of the fighter hovering over my shoulder. The roar of its straining engines fills my ears. The shuddering deck beneath my boots sets my body to trembling. In the fear of the moment, I wonder if I am about to be run over by a forty-thousand-pound aircraft or be sucked up into a jet engine at full military power if the bird launches. About me, I am conscious of other men suddenly standing and swinging their arms up in the fouled-deck signal or waving them vigorously to capture the attention of the launch officer. Anxiously I watch the catapult officer's helmeted head rotating back toward the aircraft, his right hand already raised for the downward motion that will signal the launch, then his black reflective goggles shift to me and he stares.

The catapult officer slowly raises his left arm and crosses it over his right mimicking my fouled deck signal. The high-pitch scream of the war bird hovering over me throttles back to a low mind-numbing rumbling roar. The vibrating deck stills. Suddenly, I feel my heart thudding loudly in my chest. Realizing that I am holding my breath, I exhale in relief. A vapor cloud from my exhalation fogs my goggles. Through the misted lenses, I see a distorted image of the catapult officer, steam from the catapult slot drifts around his boots as he opens his arms palms upward in the classic wordless expression—why?

Pointing towards the retracted wings of the fighter, I stick both of my both arms out and then lower them to my sides mimicking the fighter's supersonic flight configuration several times; surely, I look like a flightless chicken.

"Strike that aircraft below deck!" the air bosses' voice roars over the address system. "Secure from launch operations. Prepare to recover aircraft." Instantly there is frenzied activity as men rush to their recovery assignments. For a moment, I watch the swirl of activity. A plane director motions me to one side so he can take charge of the fighter, which still is in super-sonic configuration for easier taxiing in close quarters. The catapult officer is still watching me, but I cannot read his expression through the twin black orbs of his goggles. As I begin to walk away, I glance up at the cockpit of the fighter, which is just beginning to taxi away. The pilot's helmeted head turns, I see the dark faceplate following me then very slowly he raises his right hand in a lingering salute. With a grin, I snap back a salute and with a new spring to my step head for the crash truck and my own recovery station.

Five minutes later I am watching as the four-inch-thick arresting cable snags the first landing Tom Cat bringing it from one-hundred-fifty-knots to a full stop in less than two seconds. While the planes continue to land, one right after the other I think about the precision of the high-speed operation and compare it to the warp speed thinking process of the human mind. Part of the human brain reacts instinctively to emergencies; it propels us to action while the rational section of our brain is still considering its safest options. Our survival mechanism takes charge in a crisis; it super-charges our bodies for ultra-high-performance action (fight or flight syndrome). It is not something we consciously decide on doing. The process does not seem to require, nor desire, conscious thought on our part. The choice to take action occurs somewhere outside the normal decision process. I believe the switch that activates our behavior in an emergency lies in, or is controlled by, the part of our brains where our character resides. Our character traits determine how we will behave in a life-threatening emergency. In the fury of combat, the hero who runs towards the battle or the coward who flees is usually not determined by a decision of the moment. Rather the life-long character building process initiates the unconscious choices each individual makes in an emergency. Fear is not the main determining factor because fear motivates and influences both the hero and the coward. The integrity of the human spirit is determined when an individual's moral character takes charge and leads forth into a life-changing event. Love is the most powerful human motivator in propelling a person purposefully into danger's path.

Be on your guard; stand firm in the faith; be men of courage;
be strong. Do everything in love. 1 Corinthians 16:13

I remember an event I read about at a National Park. A black bear was dragging a child in a sleeping bag into the bushes. The little girl could not get out of the bag and was screaming for help. Men were running alongside yelling at the bear to get the big predator to let go, but fear of the bear kept them just beyond the reach of fangs and claws. Grandma had the only workable solution. She grabbed a hot iron skillet off a campfire and ran right in close banging the beast repeatedly on the head with the smoking skillet until it let go of the child and fled into the woods. Afterwards, grandma, in a state of shock, had to sit down completely amazed at what she had just done. Grandma's courage to save a child was defined and motivated by the strength of her character and the instinctive womanly imperative to protect her child or grandchild.

"Life shrinks or expands in proportion to one's courage,"
Anais Nin

Courage to do what is right is the defining edge of a person's moral character. It is that inner strength of integrity that encourages us to stand up for what we believe in despite the physical risk, social and financial hardship or mortal danger. Obviously, I am pleased that I automatically moved to stop the launch of the fighter. However, the defining moment is not my standing up and walking into a dangerous situation. What is important is while my conscious mind was speculating that this was not my job and while it desperately sought excuses for non-action, my character flipped the action switch.

As a Christian, I realize that the Lord has given us a wonderful gift. It is an everlasting covenant. When the Lord uses the words *everlasting covenant,* it means we are about to hear something critically important to our relationship with God. "I will give them singleness of heart and action, so that they will always fear me for their own good and the good of their children after them." Jeremiah 32:39

That is a straightforward solution...divinely given...to all of life's problems. Christians are motivated, "singleness of heart and action," by love of God and love for our fellow man. This is the anchor for our character, strength, focus and commitment in life. It encompasses all the values I will try to instill into my own children; that God's compass always points towards eternal love and forgiveness.

As I stand on the flight deck watching the landing aircraft, I do not understand the motivating Biblical principles that I am now writing about because at the time, I was unfortunately not a practicing Christian.

A month later, the USS *CONSTELLATION* arrives at the mouth of Pearl Harbor Naval Station at 8:00 a.m. I am standing on the flight deck, manning the rail, with a couple of thousand other sailors wearing dress whites. Colorful signal flags flap in the breeze in celebration of our return from extended operations in the Pacific and Indian Oceans. While the ship's band plays, I look to the north at the distinctive shape of the extinct volcano Diamond Head, at its base lays Waikiki, famous for white sand beaches and bikini-clad tanned bodies. It is such a pleasure to be returning to Hawaii. In a couple of hours, I will be back at Lualualei Naval Weapons Station where Revelstoke waits inside a large World War II era Quonset hut. Team members store their vehicles in the domed-shaped sheet metal building while on deployment. It will take only a brief amount of time to wash and clean my motor home, then a short stop at the grocery store, and I will be heading for a late afternoon surf session on the North Shore.

On the flight deck, we are a hundred feet above the waterline, which gives us a panoramic view of the massive naval base. Slowly we sail past black-hulled nuclear submarines, grey ships of the line and the Ford Island facility just to the south. The piers are crowded with destroyers, frigates, cruisers and ammunition ships. During World War II, the piers at Ford Island were known as Battleship Row. This is where the Japanese surprise attack on December 7, 1941 caught the pride of the Pacific Fleet resting in peacetime conditions. Just beyond Ford Island, I see the American Flag waving proudly over the Arizona Memorial. The world famous battleship took a direct hit in its magazine. The resulting massive explosion took the ship down rapidly killing over a thousand men in just a few short minutes. Staring at the rippling stars and stripes of the flag that I so proudly serve, basking in the pride of a successful deployment, I am without a clue that I am looking at the exact location where my military career will come completely undone-the Arizona Memorial. That moment is just a year away.

"Ignorant men don't know what good they hold in their hands until they've flung it away,"
Sophocles 496 - 406 BC

With permission David Sullivan
German heavy battle cruise Prinz Eugen

"Men occasionally stumble over the truth, but most of them pick themselves up and hurry off as if nothing ever happened," Sir Winston Churchill

Chapter 17

TRUK ATOLL, MARCH 1979

WHEN ONE has it all, adventure, challenge, happiness and foreign travel while living in an island paradise how do you explain throwing it all away? After many years of contemplation, I finally understand it...mostly. The course I took towards destroying my naval career involved many manipulating influences, but the prime incentive simply involved lying to myself.

Deceit is a powerful motivating force. With it, one can be convinced that wrong is not so bad and may even be somewhat okay. I need to define a very simple concept. When we do good things, we feel good about it. Conversely, when we choose to participate in wrong or bad behavior, we always wind up feeling wrong or bad about it. If someone believes that doing something wrong is okay, they need to do a reality check of their moral compass because something...or someone...is out of whack. Doing good things leads to all that is right or positive about life; happiness, love, wonders, forgiveness, challenges, adventures and dream realizations. Please notice I am writing these positive adjectives mostly in the plural form because life is a long journey where there are many opportunities for God to bless us with multiple wonders and miracles. Life excels when we focus towards what is right, good and uplifting. To do wrong leads to unhappiness, lack of self-respect, hate, tragedy and sometimes to living nightmares; I know I've been there.

> *"When I do good, I feel good; when I do bad, I feel bad, and that is my religion,"* Abraham Lincoln

Human beings are social creatures; we like to do things together. When someone is doing something good, he or she will always try to involve his or her friends. Conversely, when someone is doing something wrong that person is usually not content to do it alone; they also want to involve their friends and yes sometimes a member or two of their family.

My new surfer friend Bill liked to smoke marijuana. He preferred not to smoke it alone. He had another reason for involving his friends in the habit. He sold marijuana for profit. It was interesting that Bill did not consider himself a drug dealer. In his words, "A drug dealer is someone on the street selling drugs to strangers," he said seriously. "I don't do that. I only sell marijuana and just to my friends." I remember he took a deep inhalation off a fat joint. "What I'm doing," he said exhaling a thick cloud of putrid smoke, "is helping my friends."

A liar first has to lie to his or her self, yet drugs make the lies much more convincing in the mind of the liar.

I do not hold Bill responsible for what happened to me…it was totally my own fault. Bill did not introduce me to marijuana. That had happened slowly over a number of years. First in Vietnam, when I was exposed to it by some sailors, then in California by a girlfriend. Then again at a friend's party where the beer was flowing a little too freely. All of these people were friends of mine and all of them had a casual attitude about marijuana use. I simply parroted what I learned from them; that they undoubtedly learned from their supposed friends or drug-corrupted family members. A recent study found that twenty-percent of the children doing drugs in public schools were first introduced to those drugs by their parents. It was with my father and stepmother that I first tried hash. Fortunately, I did not like it. My father also began buying me six packs of beer when I was sixteen. He was convinced that learning to handle your alcohol was something every young man should be able to do. I did so want him to be proud of me as a child.

After my marijuana episode in Hawaii on the surf trip with Bill, it became a much more regular event. Soon I was buying a quarter ounce every week, which later became a half-ounce or more. My new friends were telling me that it was relatively harmless, "Just weed man, not a big deal." Yet I knew I was becoming dependent upon its instant attitude altering capacity. Being the slightest bit bored was an instant excuse to light up. Oh, foolishness of foolishness, I threw so very much away...and I did it willingly—I chose to walk down that corrupt path. My trail guides were my father and my supposed friends, but I walked that path alone.

"It is curious that physical courage should be so common in the world and moral courage so rare," Mark Twain

Team 11 has deployed with Team 4 to check the various sunken Japanese ships in Truk Atoll for hazardous ordnance. These shoal-sheltered waters were a major stronghold and harbor for Japan's war effort during WWII. American air might turned it into Japan's version of Pearl Harbor with the Japanese on the receiving end of a massive military fist. Almost a hundred of their ships lie on the bottom and we are going to check all the ones that lie in depths accessible to sports divers.

This dive is going to be deep. The vessel is lying at a depth of one hundred and fifty feet; normally considered beyond the range of sports divers, yet the lure to dive this wreck is irresistible. The vessel will not even be visible until we are well into the descent. Because of the great depth our bottom time will be extremely limited, no more than ten minutes from when we leave the surface to when we must leave the bottom; kind of an extended bounce dive. We do not intend to try to enter the wreck; we just want to see it. The vessel is an intact Japanese submarine.

We descend one team at a time. Ours is first as we swim rapidly downward with the nitrogen clock ticking. The deeper a diver goes and the longer they are there causes the body to absorb nitrogen gas from their lungs. The blood carries the dissolved gas in solution to the various body tissues. The high ambient pressure of depth is the driving mechanism that forces the nitrogen into the body's blood and tissues. When the diver ascends, he or she has to do so slowly allowing the inert gas to exit the body. If the partial pressure of the gas changes too quickly it comes out of solution while still in the joints, tissues or blood stream causing physical trauma and blockage of blood vessels; aka the dreaded bends, which can leave a diver paralyzed for life.

Japanese submarines tended to be larger than the American boats (submarines are always referred to as boats). This one was a WWII classic without a hint of damage to her hull or superstructure. According to the Japanese records, she had crash-dived with her engine room hatch wide open when surprised by an American dive-bomber. The huge weight of the ocean water pouring into a hole fully two foot across took her straight to the bottom. Inside the doomed submarine, the sailors quickly closed the interior hatches sealing off the engine room. Japanese divers had reported hearing pounding sounds from the forward part of the submarine. The few survivors lived until the oxygen ran out then the sounds died.

We are about a third of the way down when the boat slowly comes into view. She is resting upright on a white sand bottom. Sea faded sunlight dapples the ocean floor. The sand bottom is rippled, but featureless, like an underwater desert. I see shifting shadows from the weak light penetrating the restless surface and washing across the submarine. Passing a hundred feet of depth, I begin to feel the first hint of nitrogen narcosis. At these depths and greater, nitrogen takes on a narcotic-like effect known as rapture of the depths. Under its influence, divers have totally disregarded their personal safety, depth limitations and bottom-time considerations. The result has often been fatal.

I notice that the engine room hatch is closed to prevent intrusion as this is considered a burial site and a war memorial. The great depth compresses my rubber wetsuit decreasing its buoyancy accelerating my free fall towards the submarine. I drift rapidly downward then flare my arms to slow the descent as I pass slowly over the conning tower. The periscope stands in perfect condition adjacent to the radio mast. I see no marine growth on the hull, which surprises me. It is like finding an intact WWII aircraft in the desert. From all appearances, the boat could have recently settled here.

I kick along the forward deck passing the deck gun. Continuing forward I roll onto my back to look at the conning tower, then roll face down and descend toward the forward torpedo tubes. The outer torpedo hatches are closed. Swimming just a few feet above the sand bottom, I follow the dark hull back toward the stern. Passing the conning tower again, I look upward impressed by the size of the vessel. I fully intend to swim back to the aft screws, but have to settle for a lingering look at the engine room hatch. I am almost out of time as I pause to consider the fate of the Japanese sailors. Every single one of them drowns or suffocates from lack of oxygen in a submarine tomb where there was no realistic chance of rescue.

Out of time, I signal the team to ascend to our first safety stop thirty feet from the surface. We follow it with two decompression stops at twenty and ten feet respectively.

That evening I walk out to a deserted piece of beach and stare out over the moonlit ocean. Glancing about to make sure that no one is about I reach into my pocket and take out a joint. I have not admitted it to myself yet, but I am now addicted to marijuana. Some argue that pot is not addictive, yet I am obsessed with its use. After a couple of hits I tuck the roach carefully into a plastic bag, rinse my hands and mouth with seawater, then quietly return to my room. My secretive behavior and stupid drug habit is beginning to affect my work, but again I have chosen to overlook it in favor of my regular need for *instant attitude adjustment.*

The next morning one of the divers from Team 4 approaches me. He has a reputation as a party animal and I have pretty much avoided associating with him. "Hey Steve," he whispers clandestinely, "Loan me a joint, man."

"What!" I am stunned. How does he know I have pot?

"You know dude," he whispers louder, "what you've got hidden in that regulator."

Whoa, how does he know I smuggled a dozen joints on this mission. I had hidden them inside the one-way valve of a double-hose diving regulator. Then it hit me, I rolled them while high with Bill. He must have told this character and now I was in a panic. My secret was out!

"I threw them away," I quickly lied, "lost my nerve just before we left Hawaii."

"Yeah, right," he does not believe me.

In alarm, I go straight to my room, remove the hidden joints from my regulator and flush everyone of them down the toilet. Several times that day I promise myself that my pot smoking days are history. It was an easy promise to keep simply because I did not have any more dope.

> *"We can easily forgive a child who is afraid of the dark; the real tragedy of life is when men are afraid of the light,"* Plato

Two months later, we have moved our operations to Kwajalein Atoll. I am walking barefoot across the white sand beach down to the little sailing catamaran drawn up on the shore, I think how fortunate I am to be living such an adventurous life. At work or play my daily activities usually involve tropical beaches, rainforests and ocean adventures. The Pacific Ocean is a big part of my life; surfing its waves, scuba diving in its depths on reefs and wrecks, or riding on a ship upon it to some point of interest to do something exciting. My life is filled with intense adventure such as the one I am embarking upon. After shoving the light sailing boat into the water, I tow it over to a wooden pier where I have stacked my dive gear and an underwater scooter. It is where two members of my team, Mike Mullins and Tommy Dye, are standing. Mike is a large tough-looking Hawaiian with a deceptively sensitive nature; Tommy Dye is a serious weight lifter who loves pulling practical jokes.

"Sure you guys don't want to come?" I ask hopefully. Diving alone is not the best of ideas, but there is no way I am going to pass up an incredible wreck diving opportunity like this one. Truly this is an extraordinary dive that will probably only be offered once in a lifetime; I could hardly imagine that any diver worth their fins and snorkel would pass up a chance to dive on one of the most famous World War II shipwrecks.

"Come on Chief," laughs Mike, "We have been diving on sunken ships practically every day for the past three months. It is our first Sunday off and you want us to go dive on another wreck?"

"But it is the Prinz Eugen," I urge enthusiastically, "How many chances does a guy get to dive on a famous heavy German battle cruiser?"

"Hey," chimes in Tommy, "how many times does a guy get to get totally drunk on a Sunday afternoon and there's no one to give him grief about it?"

"The Prinz Eugen was the only war ship to sail with the Pocket Battleship Bismarck. When the British fleet pounced on Bismarck, she sent the Battleship HMS Hood straight to the bottom. Prinz Eugen fought in one of the most famous sea battles of all time," I urge hopefully. "We are talking serious World War II history here and almost no one is diving on it."

"Well I am talking about serious drinking," leers Tommy, "no responsibilities, nowhere to go, just walk from our room to the bar...get plastered and pass out on the beach later."

"You're really going to spend your afternoon getting drunk?"

"No, we are going to party."

"It's not like there's anything else to do on this rock," adds Mike, "maybe we should check the flick at the base theater before hitting the bar."

"Na," laughs Tommy, "let's hit the movie in between bar episodes. This is going to be an epic drunk."

"You already saw the flick in Guam," I argue, "a stupid re-run instead of diving on a heavy German battle cruiser? "Look," I point out toward the far side of the lagoon, "it's right out there, a heavy battle cruiser and almost no one is diving it."

"Actually we are going to get so stupefying drunk that it will not matter that we have already seen the movie; besides the theater's air conditioned."

"Let's shove him off," encourages Tom, "he is just going to just keep harping on us."

"And I thought I left my old lady at home, he sounds just like her," Mike unties the bowline from the pier's cleat and shoves the sailboat's bow out with his big brown foot.

"Your old lady is only twenty-two years old. Keep passing up these adventures for booze and some more audacious person just might run off with her."

"Hey I am audacious," chirps Tom, "maybe she'd like to run off with me."

Mike punches Tom, "You don't even know what audacious means."

"Don't get eaten by a shark," Tommy throws over his shoulder. I watch them walk down the wooden pier and then along a dirt path that leads to a poolside bar.

Hauling in on a rope lanyard I raise the sail, its colorful canvas quickly fills with wind as the little boat scuttles merrily away from the pier. With my hand resting on the wooden tiller, I sail just pass the edge of the pier and set a course that will take me to the opposite side of the broad lagoon. On the new heading, the little catamaran rapidly picks up speed skimming across the smooth water. For a few minutes, a flock of sea birds flies squawking in my wake, but soon abandons the catamaran for a school of fish jumping in the near distance. I imagine the finned predators below, tuna or barracuda, which are herding the smaller fish to the surface where there is nowhere for them to flee. Altering course slightly, I sail through the melee. The air abounds with intense squawking as frantic sea birds, their wings beating loudly, dive bomb the surface on either side of the swift sailing catamaran. A splat against the colorful sail just inches above me shows where an airborne deposit narrowly missed my head. I rinse it off with a couple of handfuls of saltwater then re-correct my heading.

I sail for several miles to the site where the Prinz Eugen went down. The little sailboat is speeding at about fourteen knots with the occasional flying fish leaping out of the water before the swift catamaran. I watch the unique fish gliding rapidly away and wish I had a companion with whom to share this adventure. It is a shame my friends did not want to come along. I think how they are wasting an incredible diving opportunity to get drunk and am instantly thankful that I threw my dope away two months ago. I am thinking clearer, with greater focus and my discipline has improved. When I get back to Hawaii, I make a silent promise not to smoke marijuana again. *Later I would remember that promise made impulsively and would think how much different my life would have been had I honored that pledge. A commitment not honored is a lie fulfilled.*

It is so beautiful in the solitude of the tropical lagoon. I hear only the whisk of the catamaran's twin hulls cutting the water, the ruffle of wind in the sail and the fading sounds of the feeding birds. I gaze at cumulous clouds drifting across the horizon against a cobalt blue sky. Then, in the distance, I see a lush green barrier island. I head for its shore where there is a white coral beach with tall coconut trees leaning over the pale blue sea. The water becomes a darker blue as the white bottom abruptly falls away. It is there, about a hundred yards offshore, that I see sunlight glistening brightly on a huge brass propeller protruding out of the water. Lowering the sail, I arrive with high expectations at my destination.

Beneath the shimmering water, I peer at the massive ship lying on its side. The heavy battle cruiser was damaged during the Bikini Island nuclear tests. A storm drove her onto the beach where she rolled and sank with her stern barely protruding from the surf while the bow lies far below at a depth of 120 feet. One propeller is above the water, the other submerged.

Quickly donning my diving equipment, I plunge into the cool inviting water; then reach up and pull in the underwater scooter. For a moment, I pause to stare through my dive mask at the wreck adventure that awaits me. The water is clear, about a hundred foot of visibility, and full of tropical fish. Below, I stare through my face-plate at the massive dreadnought with its living canopy of colorful corals and sea fans waving back and forth in a light tidal surge. Less than a fifth of the huge ship, its stern, is visible. The rest lays hidden in the dark depths below.

Triggering the scooter, I begin a spiraling descent through the cool water. Riding behind an underwater scooter is like flying in slow motion. Imaging what it must have been like to be a World War II pilot, I do a wing over and go into a nearly vertical dive. I fly over a twelve-inch gun turret that has fallen to the side of the wreck. This is the rear most of her four gun turrets, each named after a major Austrian city, Graz, Braunau, Innsbrook and Wien. The heavy cruiser named for Prince Eugene of Savoy of Austria was commissioned in August 1940. I stare down at the gun turret lying on a bed of sand and soft corals then angle up over the armored side of the battle cruiser and drop down close to the ship's wooden decks. Except for the occasional sheathing of colorful corals there is little damage or rust on the superstructure. She is constructed with the best quality German armored steel plate. Multi-hued schools of fish, their scales glistening in the soft light, swarm the wreck swimming into and out of the durable deck compartments. They flow into and out of oval doors and gush through round portholes like holiday streamers riding a gusting wind. Continuing to play bomber pilot, I wind my way down closely paralleling the ship's looming super-structure. As a nuclear test vessel, the cruiser had no crew when she went down, yet I cheerfully imagine the German gunners manning their stations to blow me out of an imagined flak-filled sky.

The backside of the bridge looms ahead. Like the rest of the ship, it lays 90 degrees onto its side. The muted sunlight strikes

the wreck at an unusual angle because of the 90-degree list gener-
ating deep shadows that beckon me inside. I have to contain my
urge to explore wanting to conduct the deepest part of the dive
first to build a bit of a safety factor for my decompression later. I
have to content my curiosity by sweeping the superstructure with
the scooter's powerful front light. The searching light leads me on
a weaving, spiraling descent as I challenge my steering ability by
heading directly into the narrow dark corridors, then pulling up
at the last second. As the scooter narrowly misses the looming steel
bulkheads, I repeatedly curve and angle my body to avoid touching
the more delicate sea fans and corals that adorn the wreck. Along
a walkway, I skim just inches above the wood planks watching small
tropical fish flee in sudden alarm when the headlight paints them
in their brilliant colors. To the little fish, I and my scooter with its
dazzling headlight must have looked like a locomotive hurling out
of the depth's twilight. I am thoroughly enjoying this until I see one
of the smaller colorful fish, probably blinded by my light, flee right
in front of a larger drab camouflaged fish hiding beneath an old
cleat. In a flash of movement, it sucks the little yellow, blue and black
fish into its jaws. The little fish wiggles frantically then the bigger
fish's jaws flex that the smaller fish disappears down its throat. The
image burns into my mind as I pass and I instantly regret my care-
lessness. Angling upwards, I know that there is nothing I can do
about the little death in my wake and some of the magic of the dive
drains away.

Approaching the bridge, I see a small black-tipped reef shark
cruising one of the open ports. It is not a very big shark, but where
there is one there has got to be more. I keep an eye out for any
of its toothy big brothers while images of the little fish being swallowed echo through my mind. I trim my body behind the scooter
helping it to increase its speed. I fly closely to the bridge door then
drop towards the main deck and pass through a thermo cline. The
abruptly colder water swirling past me flushes through my wetsuit.
The deep-water turns a murky brown as I hurl towards the bow
resting on the reef at a depth of 120 feet. Diving alone can be a

bit unsettling, particularly in dark water. Warily, I glance over my shoulder…not actually expecting to see anything…shockingly there is a huge eye regarding me. It is an enormous fish, a giant grouper over three or four hundred pounds! His big bulging eye glares coldly as he swims just off to my side. Hoping he is just curious and does not have a mean disposition, I reverse direction aiming the scooter right at him. With rapid beats of its gigantic tail the monster fish swiftly disappears downward into the darkness below.

"Wouldn't you know it?" I think to myself, *"just the direction I wanted to go in too."* I am having bothersome thoughts that in waiting darkness below nature may be about to swallow me whole and spit my life right out of existence

My depth gauge reads 104 feet. The gloomy water continues to get colder and darker then finally I see the shadowed form of the bow. I have already determined to limit my bottom time, but knowing that big predatory fish is lurking somewhere in the darkness, I promptly decide to retreat back to clearer and warmer water. Turning around I keep imagining that big fish is skulking just over my shoulder. Big-mouthed groupers inhale their prey whole. I am having troublesome images of my just flippers sticking out from its massive lips. I am now really regretting seeing that little fish swallowed. Knowing that it was my fault gets me to worrying about things like karma.

Reaching the fifty-foot level without seeing a sign of old bug eye, I begin to relax and am eager to explore inside the sunken ship. Tying the scooter off to a handrail, I cautiously swim into a broad open door aft of the bridge. The glow of my dive light plays off pale soft sponges and causes a spider crab to run for cover leaving little clouds of silt that traces his tiny steps across the deck like the impact of tracers. Stacked along the inside bulkhead are a rack of explosive-filled torpedoes. I know they are live weapons because the Navy wanted their nuclear tests to be fully authentic. All of the warships in the test were loaded with a full complement of ordnance to see if they got any secondary explosions. Swimming down a narrow corridor, I slip deeper inside the ship; a coating of silt covers all the exposed surfaces untouched by cleansing ocean currents. The deeper I go a spreading darkness precedes me. I am careful to keep my fin kicks minimal so as not to stir up the visibility. Through an open cabin doorway, I peer into a machine room of some sort. I do not go very far inside because I am only wearing a single scuba tank. Glancing at my air gauge and checking my watch, I know it is time to return to the scooter and continue my ascent.

Twenty feet from the surface I pause for short safety stop to out gas nitrogen, then take another two-minute decompression stop at ten feet. After attaching the scooter to a line hanging from the boat, I amuse myself by trying to make friends with a small fish, which suddenly flees in alarm. Spinning around it is startling to see the big grouper just a couple of feet away. I scream in surprise, which comes out as a blast of bubbles. Bug Eye jets for the bottom as I rocket out of the water scrambling up onto the boat without removing my scuba tank or weight belt.

Quickly peering over the side, I see only empty water and feel the rapid beating of my pounding heart.

A half hour later, I am underway sailing into a light tropical rain. I enjoy the refreshing feeling of the raindrops and heel the catamaran tighter into the gusting trade wind. Entering the little harbor, I quickly tie the small boat to the pier and hurry off to find my friends. I cannot wait to tell them about the giant grouper. They are not at the poolside bar so I head for the enlisted man's club.

Entering the darkened bar, I smell the heavy stench of cigarette smoke that hangs in a lingering cloud. Loud music blasts from the jukebox and then I see my friends at the bar. One of them snores loudly, his head resting near a puddle of spilt beer. The others are completely drunk and arguing some foolish point. Fortunately, they do not see me as I quickly step back outside into the late afternoon sunlight.

Following a jungle path back towards the harbor, I smell the fragrance of tropical flowers and hear a couple of exotic birds singing. Basking in the warm sunlight, I think how my friends have wasted an incredible opportunity while I consider my own life. I am still mad at myself over the marijuana. It has been a couple of months since I threw away the joints. I could not believe how I had so foolishly risked the naval career that I so enjoy. In addition, there is something more that I have foolishly risked something so very important that I have been working diligently towards its realization for the past two years.

The military offers its enlisted men the opportunity to join its officer's ranks through the LDO (Limited Duty Officer) Program. Enlistees who have reached the rank of E-6 or above (I am an E-7) can apply for the program. The selection process will focus on performance and personal achievement. I applied for the program six months ago and am eagerly awaiting the results. I have every reason to be hopeful. Unlike the rest of the Navy, Explosive Ordnance Disposal Teams require a high ratio of officers to enlisted men. An officer leads every four-man EOD team. In the rest of the fleet, there are dozens of enlisted men for each officer. The command has billets to advance four enlisted men this year from EODMUONE and I am determined to be one of them. Lieutenant (junior grade) Stephen Arrington has such a nice ring to it.

I am so glad I had thrown away the marijuana. *How could I have been so foolish?* I wondered. The combined teams are returning to Hawaii in two weeks. I look forward to getting home and silently make another commitment to stay away from marijuana. *If I'm smart, I'll stay away from Bill too,* I think to myself.

> *"Many persons have a wrong idea of what constitutes true happiness. It is not attained through self-gratification but through fidelity to a worthy purpose,"* Helen Keller

"It is better to light one small candle than to curse the darkness," Confucius

Chapter 18

PEARL HARBOR, HAWAII, MAY 1979

I AM WORKING in the Operations Department at Lualualei Naval Weapons Station when the Executive Officer posts a list on the bulletin board. "Case anyone is interested," he states loudly, "this is the promotion list from the LDO (Limited Duty Officer) selection board."

I rush over eagerly to read the list and then with sinking heart see that my name is not on it. Four men are being selected from our command. I believe that two of them certainly deserve the advancement, but question why two of the others are going to be advanced over me. There is a specific reason why I feel this way—I typed their LDO applications.

The LDO application process required that each candidate submit a three to four page typed letter that follows very specific written guidelines on how it must be formatted. Part of the selection process was to ensure that the candidate could originate correspondence that at least minimally meets the literary standards of the United States Navy. It had been noted by one of the other applicants that I had an unfair advantage in this regard. As the CPO

(Chief Petty Officer) in-charge of the Operations Department, I had the use of a magnetic card typewriter. In 1979, the personal computer had not yet been invented. My IBM typewriter had a credit-card-sized slot into which I could insert a memory card. On it, I could type a two-page letter that would then be printed automatically by the typewriter without error. In the 1970's this was momentous event through it would take two memory cards to write my four-page application.

The Executive Officer listened to the other candidates complain about my auto-typing advantage and came up with a simple solution. To eliminate CPO Arrington's unfair advantage, each of the other candidates would originate their own letters with pencil and paper then give them to me to make a perfect copy. The document included all of the applicant's pertinent information including performance evaluations, academic accomplishment, awards, correspondence courses completed, fleet recommendations, etc. Having read the other applications in detail was one of the reasons I was so confident of my selection. It is important to understand that I had spent over two years seriously preparing for my candidacy. I knew that I well exceeded the guidelines for selection and was completely aware that two of the men selected were not only barely marginal in meeting those requirements, but had not even completed any extracurricular accomplishments such as college classes or military correspondence courses.

"No big surprises here," quirks the first class petty officer standing next to me who also was not selected.

I glance at him. I had typed his application and knew that his chances for selection were not very high. His evaluations were consistently average. However, I am curious what he has seen on the list, "What do you mean?"

"Read the names of the officers on the selection board," he states flatly. "They only selected candidates from their own teams. It's not who you are, but who you know."

I am stunned.

I request a meeting with the CO. When I walk into his office at the appointed time he tells me to sit down, then says, "I know why you're here, Chief. It's about the LDO selection list."

"Yes sir," I reply calmly while making a serious effort not to go ballistic. I know he is about to explain to me, in the calmest terms, why my dream of becoming a Naval Officer is not going to happen.

"Look, you weren't selected for two reasons. First you have only been with the command for less than three years; the other men have far more experience than you."

"Excuse me, Sir," I politely, but firmly interrupt, "but time in command is not listed as part of the selection criteria. What is the difference between a new officer fresh from EOD School and me? After all, I have been the leading chief of my team for over two years."

"The need for more experience is the prerogative of the selection board," the CO states categorically. "However, the second reason was the defining consideration in your not being selected."

I lean forward in my chair.

"They thought you were too immature."

"What?"

"Think about it. You live in a truck; a surf mobile I think they called it."

"I am not being selected because of my truck?"

"No, not because of your truck," he is pleased to make the distinction, "it is because you live in it."

"That's ridiculous." I argue feeling insulted.

"Funny, that is exactly what one of the officers on the board said." The CO tepees his hands, "It would be ridiculous to have one of our officers living in a truck pretending he is some kind of surf character."

I am speechless. I am so upset, if I tried to talk, I would just sputter.

"Look," he continues, "submit again next year. I can actually guarantee that you will be accepted, particularly if you get rid of that stupid surf wagon."

I want to say something, but hesitate because whatever I am about to say will be instantly regrettable.

Incredibly, the CO takes my silence as acceptance as he shifts gears, "Look we need to send a new team out to the *USS ENTERPRISE* and I want it to have a chief who has plenty of flight deck experience. Since you have already served aboard the Big E (*USS ENTERPRISE CVA 65*) and two other aircraft carriers I have cut you a set of orders. You will leave in a couple of weeks as soon as the team completes initial workup."

"I don 't think that is a good idea sir," I answer flatly.

"Excuse me?"

"If you send me out, you'll just have to bring me back in four months before the deployment is over."

"What are you talking about?" The man's face is beginning to redden.

"My enlistment is up in four months."

"You're kidding!" the man is taken aback, "you've got over thirteen years in the Navy. You're not going to throw that away."

"Sir, I have served thirteen years believing that I would always be treated fairly by the Navy. I don't believe that anymore. Please be advised that I will not be re-enlisting in four months."

The CO has turned beet red under his tropical suntan, "Very well Arrington, you're excused."

"Thank you, sir." I rise from my chair and walk out of his office. Closing the door, I pause to lean against it. *Did I really just do that?* I think regretfully to myself.

Over the next couple of weeks, my popularity in the Operations Department slips away like an explosion-accelerated landslide. Everyone knows that I am just marking time and it affects everyone's attitude, particularly my own. Every year for the past decade, our command has won the Golden Anchor Award. It is this big bronze plaque for perfect re-enlistment within a single command. It was presently hanging just outside the Commanding Officer's door. *Well, they aren't going to be winning it this year,* I thought with great satisfaction. Yet, in my heart, I knew I was being unreasonable, but my decision seemed irreversible. Therefore, I just accepted it, which did not improve my mood or popularity.

Surprisingly, my pronouncement to leave the Navy also resulted in my selling Revelstoke to Bill who had long coveted it. I was going to need the money as I considered what to do with the rest of my life. I figured I would return to California and finish my BA degree with financial assistance from the G.I. Bill. To save money instead of renting an apartment, I moved in with Bill and his new wife at the enlisted housing complex in Ewa Beach. It was astounding how quickly my life was changing. Suddenly I did not know where I was going, let alone when I was going to get there.

"Nothing in the world is more dangerous than
sincere ignorance and conscientious stupidity, "
Dr. Martin Luther King

A week later, I am in a sixteen foot long Boston Whaler tied up to the Arizona Memorial. The King of Tonga will soon be arriving to lay a flower wreath at the memorial and we are part of his security party making sure that no terrorist has placed any bombs along his intended path. Our job is to check the memorial below the waterline for explosives. Bill is on my team as a support diver for this mission. I glance over the side of the memorial to insure that there is no debris or obstacles floating beneath us then give Bill the thumbs up signal before jumping over the side into the water.

It takes only a few minutes to check around and under the Memorial's platform and stanchions and then we both begin to descend towards the sunken wreck below. The water visibility goes from about a dozen feet, down to six and then down to three. I switch on my powerful dive light, but the beam only moderately penetrates the deep gloom surrounding us. Tidal clouds of sediment drifts in the murky water as I sweep the beam side to side. Then in the wavering funnel of yellow light, I see a metal shape looming out of the surrounding darkness. It is a ship's hatch, a vertical door, now welded shut. During the war, hardhat divers sealed the hatches closed with welding rods making it the world's largest steel coffin for the regiment of tortured souls entombed within.

Swimming the main deck of the ghostly ship, I ponder the last acts of the doomed men who died inside. On an early Sunday morning, the bombs began to rain down unexpectedly. Many men were still sleeping in their bunks when the massive explosions tore through the mighty war vessel. Abruptly plunged into darkness and inhaling superheated smoke, the deck beneath their feet began to leap violently from the thunderous explosions. Placing my hand against a porthole's armored hatch, I mentally glimpse a distinctive image of what it must have been like inside the ill-fated ship in those few brutal minutes. The physical trauma of concussions from huge explosions within confined compartments, the roar of fire and the rushing sound of flooding water…and of men screaming their lives out. Then as the dreadnaught began to settle towards the depths, they would have heard the groaning of steel bulkheads buckling under the massive weight of thousands of tons of water. What a horrible way to die, in the flooded, smoke-filled darkness, listening to the screech of armored steel being ripped apart and the wretched screams of your companions, without even knowing that Japan has thrown down the gauntlet of war.

For a few moments, I consider the fate of the Japanese submarine's crew. At least those men knew that they were at war. They had the vital comfort of knowing why they were risking their lives; they were fighting for their country, their families and loved ones. The peacetime American sailors entombed inside the Arizona only knew that they were dying.

Swimming the main deck of this stricken grey "lady of war," I stick my bare hand through a six-inch thick layer of clinging mud and sediment to touch the wooden deck. The timber feels grimy and rotten. I withdraw my hand and attempt to rinse it clean by shaking it in the murky water. Each kick of my fins lifts a thin veil of brown black silt that rises slowly in a mushrooming cloud. Abruptly it is soul-chilling cold down here. The water seeping through my wetsuit feels like ice creeping down my spine. I aim the muted yellow beam of my light upwards then begin to follow its dim cone back towards the surface. Swimming slowly upwards I peer once more down into the depths at the gray lady that has lost her fleet, I see the silt cloud closing about her like an open grave caving into itself.

On the boat, I cannot get my dive gear and wetsuit off fast enough. I am craving the heat of the tropical sun on my body. The dive was too much like descending into a submarine graveyard, and then I am startled to realize that is exactly from where I have come. My mind still lingers over the shadowy image of that massive submarine tomb.

We load our boat behind a military pick up and take it back to Lualualei Weapons Station. Bill and I rinse the clinging mud from our dive gear, and then we drive together back to his house. Sitting in his front room, I could not shake a feeling of intense dismay. Like most divers, I harbor a secret dread of drowning while being trapped underwater. I am trying to return from the mental holocaust of being immersed with over a thousand drowned souls when I hear Bill say the words that would doom what was left of my military career and alter my future in a horrible unforgiving way.

"Want an instant attitude adjustment?" he asks. I look over at him…Bill is holding up a marijuana cigarette. I instantly think of my commitment not to smoke again. He holds a match to the tip and takes a deep pull then offers the smoking joint to me. As I reach out for it, I do not grasp that that smoldering cylinder of paper and weed was essentially a coffin spike that seals my fate hurling me down a dark path towards corruption and bereavement.

Bill rolls the smoking joint between his fingers, "This stuff is elephant buds from Maui, it's the best man." He leans forward, "I know where I can get four ounces of it pretty cheap."

"So get it, I'll buy some from you," I offer thinking that my Navy career is almost over anyway.

"I can't," laments Bill, "I don't have the dough, but you do. Look if you put up the cash, I will sell three of the four ounces." He passes the joint back to me, "then I will give you back your money and we'll have the remaining ounce and split it. It'll be like smoking for free," he leers.

I put up the money and Bill sold the three ounces that night, which of course led to our buying more dope. Bill began every day with a joint. Once he even referred to marijuana as his best friend. Two months before my enlistment was up Bill and I were busted by the NIS (Naval Investigative Service). I heard them coming through the front door and ran back to flush the evidence…and that is how I was arrested, kneeling in front of a toilet with my arm buried elbow deep into the bowl.

While awaiting my court martial Bill asked me to buy back Revelstoke as he and his new wife desperately need the money.

The Navy extended my enlistment so I could attend my own court martial.

Every man's way is right in his own eyes, but the Lord weighs the hearts. Proverbs 21:2

My military court martial is a moment in time that will haunt me forever. I stand before the court of five naval officers in total disgrace. Ours is an elite command and I have tumbled from its ranks. Once so very proud to be a Navy bomb disposal frogman, I am now an acute embarrassment to the command I so loved and had eagerly served.

In the back of the court are seven men from the teams, five officers and two senior chief petty officers. They have volunteered to make statements regarding my character prior to the advent of my drug problem. However, before they can be called to the stand, the judge asks to talk privately with the prosecuting officer and my defense counsel.

"Bad news," whispers the military lawyer defending me as he returns to our table. "Since you're pleading guilty, they can't call any witnesses against you. However, if any one takes the stand to make positive statements about your character, the prosecution will have the opportunity for rebuttal by calling witnesses against you."

"There are witnesses against me?" I ask quite surprised.

"Your buddy, Bill," he shrugs.

"Bill?"

"They are giving him a deal and he is prepared to testify that you were the one in-charge of the whole marijuana thing...that he worked for you. It won't go well. You outrank him so naturally the board will assume that it's all probably true."

"What should we do?" I am crushed that someone I considered a friend would so wrongfully betrayal me to make things easier on himself.

"I have to ask the judge to excuse the witnesses; that's all we can do."

When the judge dismisses the witnesses, I resist turning around to watch them go. I will now face the court alone; my shame could not have been greater. I put my head down on my hands and close my eyes. I don't want to see them leave...then I abruptly have a deeper thought...I don't want to see the looks on their faces seeing me about to be sentenced for a drug crime. My mind is making a difficult leap or maybe more apt adjusting to a big downward plunge...from a rising star within an elite command to drug felon. No, I truly do not want to witness their departure. Then I hear the sounds of the men standing, there is a brief conversation amongst them and then they begin to walk, but they are not leaving—they are striding in my direction. All seven of them in their dress white uniforms walk in a file to the bench behind mine. They stand there for a moment at rigid attention, then they sit down on the bench.

I turn and stare at the grim faced men sitting at rigid attention. They risk much regarding their careers lending their support to me, a military felon. They are with honor, mine hangs about me in tatters. They deserve the respect their presence commands; I am throwing myself at the mercy of a military court. It is the low point of my life. Then my defense counsel leans close and whispers, "I've never seen anything like this before. This is huge. They could not have made a more important statement regarding clemency. Whatever the judge rules, whatever your sentence, know that these men still believe in you."

I sit up straighter, turn in my chair, look each man in the eye and nod my thanks. Each in his own way reaches out to touch me in an encouraging way, a handshake or a pat on the shoulder.

The court noting the support of these respectable men gives me the absolute minimum sentence allowed by the Uniform Code of Military Justice, reduction in grade from chief petty officer to seaman recruit, a sentence of one month in the brig and a Bad Conduct Discharge. I could have gotten six months in the brig, a major fine and a Dishonorable Discharge. My defense counsel is quite pleased; I sit next to him looking straight ahead with raging thoughts of shame and humiliation. Later I would learn that the court would throw the book at Bill.

The naval brig, Pearl Harbor is an imposing two-story building of a simple cement block design. The exterior walls are a depressing battleship grey. Crossed sledgehammers hang over the metal gate entrance. Inside, a stern-faced marine sergeant waits. He marches me into the guardroom where he orders me to remove all of the insignia from my uniform. From my collar, I take the silver and brass fouled anchors that symbolize my rank as a chief petty officer and place them onto a scarred wooden table. Next to the brass anchors, I lay three bars of Vietnam era ribbons that had been pinned to my chest, followed by my gold jump-wings and the silver insignia that identifies me as a bomb disposal frogman. Memories of McNair pinning that device to my chest try to echo through my mind, but I quickly shut them out. Then, removing my khaki uniform and clad only in my boxer shorts, I sit stooped over on a small wooden stool while the guard roughly shaves my head.

Completely humiliated, I am led down a grey-walled corridor still clad only in my boxer shorts and locked into a cold isolation cell. The days pass slowly while I sit alone in that cell rummaging through my thoughts of personal failure.

"The keenest sorrow is to recognize ourselves as the sole cause of all our adversities," Sophocles 495-406 BC

Make your ear attentive to wisdom. Incline your heart to understanding. Proverb 2:2

Chapter 19

SAN DIEGO, CALIFORNIA, SEPTEMBER 1981

I AM SITTING in botany class at San Diego State University, when the well-dressed young lady sitting next to me sniffs then purposefully moves her chair further away. I know her unvoiced complaint undoubtedly concerns the smell of marijuana that clings to my clothes. It is a rather long bus ride out to the university. To keep from getting too bored along the way I had taken a couple of hits off a bong pipe before leaving Revelstoke. I parked the truck on a corner in La Jolla to catch the city bus. The big truck gets less than ten miles to a gallon so I am saving my limited funds and keeping down wear and tear on Revelstoke, which is now almost six years old. I am beginning my second year at SDSU as a photojournalism major. I have not yet taken any classes in photojournalism so when asked, I tell people I am majoring in prerequisites. According to my counselor, I am in the down side of my junior year.

Stepping off the bus on the return trip back to La Jolla, I hurry over to Revelstoke, which has undergone a few artistic improvements. I have covered the exterior of the back shell with redwood strips. It makes the truck look like a mountain cabin with wheels. She still attracts lots of attention from people, which is not something I can honestly say about myself. It is startling actually, to be surrounded by a host of friendly people at the beach where I hang out, yet I am becoming a bit of a hermit.

Five minutes later, I arrive at work. Walking into La Jolla Surf Systems, I always enjoy the fragrant smell of surfboard wax, which barely masks the smell of freshly silkscreened T-shirts. I glance around to see if there are any new surfboards, then go over to say hello to my boss Jeff Junkins. He is a Vietnam vet, ex-green beret, who earned a silver star along with three purple hearts, which he refers to as Viet Cong Marksmanship Metals. Jeff is a war hero and a very busy drug addict. He does everything to excess marijuana, alcohol, cocaine, pills, etc. I smoke marijuana with an occasional line of coke that Jeff sometimes offers me in the backroom. Earning not much more than minimum wage, I am on a tight budget. I have nothing in savings. Actually, I do not have a savings account, checkbook or credit card. I live paycheck to paycheck. Times are not good.

I go over to a shelf loaded with stacks of T-shirts and begin refolding the ones carelessly dropped by customers. Folding T-shirts is not nearly as much fun as selling surfboards. I often try to convince myself that I am happy, but lately it has been getting harder to make that mental leap. I have always thought I missed something by not attending college before joining the Navy so I mostly tell myself I am making up for what I missed. I am maintaining a three point-five grade point average, but feel a bit odd being thirty-two years old when the bulk of my classmates are teenagers right out of high school. The only other high point in my life is that I am living a surfing lifestyle. I surf a couple of times a day, but when the surf is down, the beach gets boring. I am into jogging in a big way but like most of my activities, I tend to do a hit or two...or three before beginning the run. I am currently in favor of the argument that marijuana is not addictive. Luckily, the mirror inside my truck is rather small; otherwise I might not like what I see reflected in it.

I am re-folding the last of the rumpled T-shirts when a young man walks through the door, does a double take, then says, "Hey Chief, what are you doing here?"

I instantly recognize the clerk from the Weapon's Department during my last tour aboard the aircraft carrier *USS Constellation.* I have not seen him in over thirty months.

"Hey clerk," I could not remember his name, "how ya doing?"

"Great Chief, I made first class petty officer a couple of months ago."

"Terrific, what brings you in here?"

"Just thinking about taking up surfing; thought I would take a look around."

"Want me to show you a couple of boards?" I offer.

"Boards? You mean you work here?" he asks astounded.

"Have you surfed before?" I am trying to ignore his shock that I am an employee of the surf shop. "We have a good selection of long and short boards."

"Chief, what are you doing here?" he asks again.

"I work here."

"Why?"

"I left the Navy a couple of years ago." I am really hoping he will not inquire into the details of my disgrace.

"Why would you leave the Navy?" he asks, sensing that there might be some embarrassment hidden here. "What happened chief?"

I suddenly realize that *chief* is a title that would never again be a part of my life. The regret is overwhelming; so is my sense of extreme loss. This young man once looked up to me. I even remember his praising comments after I helped to prevent the launch of the F14 with the wings locked in supersonic position.

"I made a stupid marijuana mistake," I blurt.

"No, not you chief."

"I'm not a chief anymore," I sigh, "just call me Steve. Want to see a couple of boards?"

"No, sorry," he is unsure what to say or do. He starts to leave, then turns back to me. "I know some other people who got busted for pot," he offers almost as an apology. "I'm sorry...you were a good chief."

"Thanks, I appreciate it," we are both at a loss what to say or do next. "Not interested in a board are you?"

"No, not right now," he tries to grin, then shakes my hand while staring with sorrowful eyes, pauses at the door for a last look before walking out into the sunshine.

I go back to folding T-shirts at another counter. I am not a happy puppy.

> *"Whatever you would make habitual, practice it; and if you would not make a thing habitual, do not practice it, but habituate yourself to something else."* Epictetus (1st Century AD)

A couple of months have passed since the visit of the clerk at the surf shop. If before I was uncomfortable with my marijuana-induced downswing in life, now I was downright dissatisfied. My masquerade as a radical character immersed in the local surf culture had been revealed as a fool's blunder. The words, "What happened to you, chief?" keeps echoing through my mind. Marijuana induced attitude adjustments could not hide that I was going nowhere fast. My dreams of becoming a surf photographer and writer seemed to hold little weight. I had convinced myself that I was living for the moment when actually I had just been living for the next high. It was in fact a low point of my life. College was becoming another shattered dream because I had no social life and no true focus; my homework was too often done under the fog of a marijuana stupor. Though I was actually getting good grades, I was not remembering much of what I learned. Two days later, my world shifted when Morgan called.

I am at La Jolla Surf Systems, folding the never-ending stack of T-shirts, when Jeff calls me over to the register. "Phone call for you," he hands me the receiver with his hand over the mouthpiece, "don't tie up the line too long; I am trying to score some dope."

"Steve, it's Morgan," Morgan Hetrick's commanding voice immediately brings to mind memories of airplanes, yachts and fancy cars. Seven years ago, he sought me out for private scuba instruction. He is a multi-millionaire and the owner of a highly successful aviation business. Though he is twenty years older than I am we had quickly became friends. I have not seen Morgan since I left Point Mugu Naval Air Station as a support diver to attend bomb disposal school.

"So Steve," his sophisticated voice is friendly and eager, "I have been wondering where you'd gotten to after leaving the Navy."

"Just getting in some college time and a bit of surfing," I am trying to sound upbeat and casual like I am a *got the world by the tail kind of guy.* It is an exciting moment having a multimillionaire call when you are just barely on the up side of down and out.

"What are you doing for money?" Morgan asks getting right to the point.

"Oh, a bit of GI Bill for college and I work part time in a surf shop for the fun of it." I answer flippantly.

"How much do you get paid?"

I tell him implying that I am doing this more for recreation than survival.

"Are you kidding? I pay my janitor three times that." Well there is a rewarding thought; it puts my lack of success under a bright mental spot light.

"How about going to work for me?" he asks jauntily.

"Work for you?" I echo stunned. Jeff glances over at me then shrugs like it is nothing. Minimum wage does not instill overwhelming job loyalty. He knows there is a long line of surf rats eager to take my place.

"You're a licensed pilot aren't you?"

"Yeah, but I haven't flown for a couple of years." Actually, I have not flown since starting my marijuana habit. It is a startling realization. I really enjoyed flying; spent a couple of paychecks to learn how. It is a rude awakening to realize my drug highs have stolen something else so important to me…and I did not even notice it was missing! *Marijuana kicks motivation's butt*, I think bluntly.

"Doesn't make any difference, I can get you up to speed in a couple of days. Look, why don't I fly down there so we can talk tête-à-tête?"

"Fly down?"

"Let's do lunch tomorrow. There's an airport just North of La Jolla."

As Morgan gives me directions to the airport and describes his airplane so I will recognize it, I bubble with enthusiasm while Junkins stares at me unhappily taping his wristwatch. He doesn't like not being high. Junkins wants his junkie. It is a sad realization that so did I.

Fortunately, I was not so foolish to break into my stash of marijuana that night.

I arrive early at the small county airport and join a couple of airplane enthusiasts at a waist high chain-link fence. We watch small planes landing and taking off for about half an hour when I hear one of them comment, "Here comes a Mooney 231; now that is one nice airplane."

"A flying Porsche is what it is," adds his friend.

I watch Morgan's plane taxiing to a row of tie-downs. He waves as he shuts down the engine. I walk out and block the main gear as Morgan opens the door and steps out. "Sweet machine eh?" He shakes my hand, "You're looking in good shape."

"Must be the surfing," fortunately I am still a fitness nut.

"Let's eat here at the airport," Morgan throws an arm over my shoulder as we head for the snack bar. "So why are you going to college anyway? I never figured you for the diploma type."

"I'm not planning on graduating, just figured to broaden my education a bit." Surprisingly it is a completely truthful answer. My main interest revolves around English and writing classes. At the age of thirty-two, I am still trying to work out a civilian occupation while taking advantage of the GI Bill.

The snack bar features aviation memorabilia on all the walls with model planes hanging from the ceiling. A large plate glass window faces the runway. The floor is surprisingly clean with alternating black and white tiles. We both order a cup of tea. Morgan opts for a steak sandwich and fries. He is about forty pounds overweight; he should have just ordered a salad hold the dressing. Being a vegetarian, I am considering the salad, but decide I should probably order something more manly, "Grilled cheese on whole wheat, please."

"You want coleslaw or French fries?" asks the attractive young waitress.

Remembering that Morgan went for the full fat hit, I settle for the fries. We both watch her walk away, but Morgan does not turn back to me until the kitchen door swings closed behind her. "Oh my," he says.

Obviously, he has not changed from the man I knew seven years ago. Back then, Morgan was always chasing a skirt.

"Hey, remember how successful Morgan Aviation use to be?" he asks cheerfully.

"Sure, you had quite an operation."

"Well you should see me now," he grins opening his arms and leaning back expansively. "I have got seven domestic corporations and two international companies; got my hanger facility up in Mojave next to Burt Rutan's facility. He's the guy looking to fly around the world non-stop without refueling." Morgan continues to expound about how well he is doing. His voice gets a bit louder as the waitress arrives with our order. "Last year we brought in over three million dollars," he smiles as she sets his plate down in front of him, "now that is pure profit, not gross income."

She gives me a look that says she has heard this kind of stuff before; I however, am impressed. I am pulling down $325 a month in GI Bill benefits and earning about a buck twenty-five an hour over minimum wage at the surf shop. Heck, with her tips the waitress out earns me by far.

I lose Morgan's attention again while she returns to the kitchen.

Knowing he is watching she puts a bit more kick in her swing. I have no doubt that she just earned a major tip as Morgan turns around, places a hand over his heart and sighs. I am waiting for the job offer wondering what Morgan is planning. If he is in character it means this is going to be a lot more about him than about me. Maybe he wants me to help run his yacht; give his guests private scuba lessons. *How much should I ask for?* I am wondering. Steve makes the big move from surf bum to marina handyman.

"I want you to be my right-hand man," he blurts.

I almost choke as I inhale a ketchup-soaked French fry, "Right-hand man?"

"It's better than it sounds," he offers.

I am thinking it is sounding pretty darn terrific, but like everything else in his life, Morgan is just getting started with his unbridled enthusiasm. "I am rich and don't have enough time to enjoy it. I am going to retire in about five years. I want you to start learning the ropes; when I retire, I will make you Executive Vice President."

"Vice President...of Morgan Aviation?" I ask in astonishment.

"No," he laughs, "Executive Vice President of all my companies. I stare at him speechless.

"Look," he confides happily, "we'll start you off low, say $50,000 a year."

I have picked up a French fry, but it hangs forgotten half way to my mouth. Start off low at fifty thousand? I am making barely six hundred a month folding T-shirts and scraping wax off used surfboards to resell.

"Course we are going to have to get you your commercial, multi-engine, instrument license. I know just the place down in Alabama. They've got some great looking lady instructors," he says fondly as if he is remembering something from a pleasant experience. "Of course that means we'll have to get you your own airplane."

"My own plane?" Did I just gasp?

"Of course your own plane," he slugs me happily, "You're in the aviation business now son."

In a celebratory mood, I pick up the plastic ketchup container and squirt a big red blob in the middle of my plate then dunk the grilled cheese into it.

A little later, I watch Morgan taxi out onto the runway and then lift off. I stare after the Mooney as it gets smaller and smaller until it is only a spec in the sky then it disappears over the horizon. I am sincerely hoping he does not crash.

In less than a week, I dropped out of college, quit my job and gleefully said goodbye to my few friends. All of them were smokers and dealing with their own various levels of un-admitted addiction. They were all astounded at my good fortune, though most of them were not quite buying my story. "This guy's hiring you as a commercial pilot and executive vice president...of an aviation company?" I was asked skeptically. My explanations were accepted so doubtfully that after while I just left it alone.

La Jolla Surf Systems did not need two weeks' notice; surf rats swarmed the front door eager to take my place...at a reduced wage, I hoped. My stash of marijuana went out the window along with my old life. I was shedding the old Steve Arrington like a wet dog shaking off a dunking at the beach.

Pulling out of the parking lot at La Jolla Shores, I glance out the window and wave goodbye to a couple of surfer buddies sitting on a low concrete wall that keeps sand out of the parking lot. It is amazing that the parking lot and the curb beside the Surf System has been my home for two years. Most people lay claim to four walls and maybe a lawn. For me it has been six wheels and a chunk of asphalt. Considering that I am living a mobile lifestyle, it is startling that I have not been anywhere outside San Diego County in some time. I watch the ocean until I hit the freeway north. Then I turn up the music and wonder what it is going to be like living in the desert.

I arrive at Morgan Aviation with half a tank of gas, twenty dollars in my pocket and a mostly positive attitude. I am not enthusiastic about being so far from the ocean.

Over the next eight weeks, I discover that my job is mostly about hanging out with Morgan. He likes spending as little time as possible in the Mojave Desert, which suits me just fine, as I am not very fond of the desert either. I am an ocean person; I like being on it in a boat, riding its waves with a surfboard and diving beneath it. All of Morgan's recreation, which he takes seriously, revolves around the pursuit of women. He has a yacht in Florida mostly used for trolling for new girlfriends and his one sport, scuba diving in the Bahamas. He takes me along to mind the dive gear, teach diving when required and operate the boat. It is not the Executive-Vice-President-in-training kind of life that I had anticipated. I could almost hear some of my friends in La Jolla snickering and it bothered me a lot.

> *"The childhood shows the man, as morning shows the day,"*
> Milton; Paradise Lost

Thus says the Lord of Hosts, "Consider your ways!"
Haggai 1:7

Chapter 20

LAS VEGAS, NV/LOS ANGELES, CALIFORNIA, APRIL 1982

STROLL INTO one of the bars at Caesar's Palace wearing 501 jeans, a blue surfer T-shirt and white sneakers. Morgan is upstairs in his room with another so-called girlfriend courting a possibly incurable social disease, while I am enjoying the rare treat of just being alone. The bar is mostly empty as I slide into a table next to a booth where four very attractive ladies are engaged in an animated conversation. The women are dressed to be noticed. I figure they are working, waiting for some mark with more money than sense. Morgan's face leaps instantly to mind. I order a beer from the waitress then notice that one of the women, a particularly pretty brunette, is looking at me. "Hey you," she smiles sweetly, "don't you know you belong over at the Mirage or something a bit more in style with your T-shirt and jeans?"

The women laugh as I look down at my favorite T-shirt; a Surfer Magazine Team Rider T-shirt no less. The jeans are my normal attire, however, Morgan particularly prefers that I wear them for practical reasons. Morgan goes through a lot of cash; lately he has been stuffing my pockets in case he runs short and needs serious spending money. In my left front pocket, there is a stack of one hundred fifty dollar bills; a thicker bundle of hundreds is in my right pocket. I have over fifteen thousand dollars in a pair jeans that I got on sale and surprisingly not a nickel in a bank account. In fact, Morgan has not actually paid me a salary yet. Strangely, it did not seem right to complain about money with my pockets full of cash…yet it is not actually my cash. The demeaning remark by the brunette gives me an audacious idea. I don't laugh often anymore. I find that I have begun to lose respect for Morgan, and in the process respect for myself is now in question. A little practical joke might lift my spirits a little.

The brunette and a blond with too much makeup are still making snide remarks about the hick in the jeans and snickering at their wit when the waitress arrives with my beer. "That'll be four bucks," she states flatly sounding bored and obviously not expecting much of a tip from the guy in jeans and a slightly faded surfer T-shirt.

I stand up, mostly to catch the attention of the amused women, then reach into my left pocket and pull out a half-inch stack of new fifties. I fan the bills with my thumb, which now also has the complete attention of the waitress. "Woops, wrong pocket," I apologize stuffing the fifties back and reach into my right pocket. Out comes the thicker stack of crisp brand new hundred dollar bills. I peel one off and drop it on the waitress's tray, "keep the change," I say casually. Stuffing the wad of bills back into my pocket and turn to leave.

"Hey," the brunette shouts, "where are you going?"

I smile and tip my beer bottle to her, "To the Mirage of course; thanks for the tip."

Walking away, I hear them chattering excitedly. The moment is my highlight of an unexciting two-day trip to Vegas. Mostly I have been hanging out at the pool swimming doing laps wondering if leaving college was such a good idea. The answer to that question comes the very next day.

I am driving Morgan's silver Cadillac Fleetwood down Century Boulevard; Morgan is setting in the passenger seat counting out money…a lot of money. "Know where all this cash comes from?" he asks nonchalantly.

"Your offshore investors?" Morgan has alluded that there are people overseas who send him a lot of money. I knew it was tied into Morgan Aviation, but had not figured out the extent of his business activities.

"Yeah, but do you know why they send me so much money?" he leers. I am half looking at Morgan and half-keeping track of what is going on with the cars in front of me.

"It's because I fly their cocaine."

The statement takes me completely by surprise, "You what?"

Morgan laughs; he is enjoying himself. "I'm a smuggler Steve. I fly coke up from Colombia through the Gulf of Mexico a quarter ton at a time." He reaches into a cash-filled satchel on his lap and stirs the money joyfully; like a toddler with his arms buried to the elbows in a box full of his favorite toys. He giggles lost in the moment.

"No!" I am horrified—not drugs!

Morgan lifts his gaze from the briefcase full of money and turns to glare at me. His thick glasses capture and reflect my image distorting it. The pasty flesh of his nose is riddled with black heads… strange that I never noticed that so intently before. Then I realize that I have avoided looking too closely at the man for whom I work. Maybe by not being too observant I was also overlooking who I was becoming. Subconsciously, I wonder what I would see if I looked too closely at my own face lately.

Dramatically he holds up his hands in which he clasps twin thick bundles of money. "This is fifty thousand dollars," he crows. "It is yours if you will co-pilot one of my planes to Colombia."

Flash memories cycle through my brain of Morgan using his money like a cudgel to beat young women into submission. The corruption of his illicit behavior washes over me as I remember how he pounds feminine protests into submission with fists full of money…and now I realize that it is my turn.

"No Morgan," I growl in sudden anger, "I will not be a part of this."

"But Steve," Morgan says casually, "you already are."

"What do you mean?" I blurt.

"Don't be stupid. You spend my money, drug money and that makes you a part of it." Morgan glares at me, "Look I am not asking anything of you that I haven't already asked of my own sons. It's not fair that they should take their share of the risks while you benefit from their money and do nothing in return."

I actually feel momentarily guilt, but then refuse to accept his fraudulent reasoning. "Morgan, I am not flying to South America," I answer fiercely.

Morgan is furious, disappointment laces his voice, as he grumbles, "Look, just think about it okay?"

We ride in silence. Morgan shovels the money back into the satchel and angrily snaps it closed. In his mind, he is probably thinking "a gift rejected," while I am working on thoughts of corruption avoided. I pretend to be focusing on the traffic. My mind is raging down dark pathways and not seeing the shining light of hope anywhere. He speaks only to give me directions as we pull into the parking lot of the LAX Marriott Hotel. We go into the lobby. Morgan has me carry the money filled satchel...I do not know why. In fact, I do not have a handle on much of anything. My world is upside down and I am working on autopilot.

We ride an elevator up to the fifth floor. Inside the room, Morgan places a black briefcase on top of a dresser, opens it and reaches inside. He turns around abruptly and slaps something metallic into my hand. "I want you to carry this," he orders.

I look at my hand, which is holding a forty-five caliper automatic pistol. It feels inordinately heavy and sinister, something from the dark underside of our social order. Almost by reflex, I drop out the magazine and pull back the slide ejecting a round that flies in a shiny trajectory to land upon the bed. Like an ugly statement, it lies there screaming at me. "What in the hell is going on," I snarl.

Morgan shrugs his shoulders, "We're here to pick up a lot of money...the gun is just to make sure that no one takes it away."

"Forget it," I growl tossing the now empty gun upon the bed.

"Okay, leave the gun," grumbles Morgan, "I just hope you don't have a problem with helping me to carry the money." He steps to the door, opens it and stands there waiting. I reluctantly follow Morgan back out into the corridor. All of this is coming at me so fast I am unsure of what I should do. Running screaming for the elevator would have been a good choice, but I did not take it. Instead, like a stupid puppet, I yield to Morgan's glare as he points with his chin that we should walk deeper into the motel. He stops at a door and knocks once sharply then twice more softly. The door swings silently open.

It is dim in the corridor, but darker inside that room. A large muscular Latin man stands just inside. His face is heavily scarred like someone once ran upon it with spiked shoes. He is all in black including his automatic pistol, a Mack 10 that he uses to wave us into the room. Against the wall are two more men with guns, but the most threatening of all is the unarmed man standing in the room's center...his empty hand extended in greeting.

Morgan quickly grasps the proffered hand, "Hello Max," he grins then turns towards me and says, "This is Steve, the new right-hand man I told you about. I trust him with my life."

The salutation is not lost on Max. I watch his hooded eyes as hand reaches out and takes mine, "Morgan has told me a lot about you." The grip tightens, "He says you could be a real asset to our operations, that you use to be a frogman and that you're an expert with weapons and explosives." Max has still not let go of my hand, it's like he is tugging at my soul. The eyes are so dark and sinister. He is evaluating me, waiting for my reaction. His grip slackens as I quickly withdraw my hand. I want to run. It is a half-dozen long steps to the door, but then I could be gone. Instead, I stand there like a deer in the headlights of speeding truck.

"You do any time in Vietnam?" he asks.

"Four tours," I answer, "mostly helping to rescue downed pilots."

"Kill anyone?" It is a searching question. I am being sized-up; a couple of dogs circling each other only he is a mean junkyard dog and I am more like a pet that has strayed into an alley.

"No, thankfully." I answer feeling sweat gathering at my armpits.

Max snuffs, a predator checking for fear. He nods towards one of the Colombians casually propping up the wall, "He has and so has Juan, who's leaning against the door." Juan, the man in black, grins at me holding up four fingers.

Max's eyes cut back to me, "So you know how this works. All my boys are shooters and they enjoy their work. You understand what I am saying don't you?"

I nod automatically, but my mind is boggling at the death threat so casually thrown.

Max turns to the other man in the room and snaps his fingers. He obediently picks up a heavy suitcase, drops it onto the bed then releases the snaps, opens it and steps away. "It'll take too long to count," says Max, "seven hundred thousand dollars in used bills just like last time."

Morgan greedily runs his hands over the money then closes the lid. "Bring the suitcase," he says to me as he heads for the door. Max moves to one side as I step to the bed and grab the handle of the suitcase. I am surprised at how much it weighs, it matches the heaviness of my heart as I follow him out of the suite with the eyes of Max and Juan following me the whole way. We stop at Morgan's room just long enough to collect the forty-five caliper pistol and his satchel of money. Then we begin the return trip to the Mojave Desert.

The sun is low on the horizon, silhouetting the cactus and other desert shrubbery when Morgan finally turns towards me and says, "Want to know who Max really is?"

I shake my head not wanting to hear any of this.

"His full name is Max Mermelstein," Morgan chuckles, "with that dark skin of his you wouldn't think that he is really a Jew from New York City. Well, old Max is the number one man in the United States for the Medellin drug cartel. His boss is Rafael Cardona Salazar, who is one very bad hombre. You absolutely do not want that man as an enemy. People he doesn't like don't live long. He has a couple of signature ways of doing them in. It's quite unpleasant. Want to hear about it?"

I shake my head preferring to sit in dazed silence, my own thoughts rampant. I have seen plenty of crime movies about drug-crazed villains and am remembering some of the grosser scenes in a very personal way.

Morgan does not seem to mind the one-sided conversation; the words tumble freely from him as he pulls me deeper into a dark abyss from which I do not know how to escape. "Rafa, as he is known by his friends, answers directly to the Ochoa family." Morgan sits back in his seat looking very smug. "You know you're going to have to make that airplane trip don't you?" It is no longer a question.

With a fluttering heart I reply, "Morgan, I don't want to do it." Both of us are aware of the change in my choice of words, "will not," had become "don't want."

Morgan smiles. At that moment, he is closest to the father image he plays so well. Then he says the words that drag me down into the depths of the criminal underworld, "You don't have a choice anymore, Steve. You have to do it to prove yourself to Max…and to the Medellin cartel."

Morgan's side of the car is dark except for the lingering strobe of headlights from passing cars. The light flickers off his glasses magnifying the crystal orbs in an inhuman way. The ugliness of his true nature is seeping out of him much like a demon throwing off its human disguise. It is frightening to realize that he does not feel the need to hide his corrupt criminal bent from me anymore. I know he is trying to remake me. Unable to appeal to my own darker side, something that lurks inside every human being, he is instead beating me down with brute fear. An animal musk radiates from him. Despite regular bathing, Morgan radiates body odor. It rises in a funk from his side of the car sapping at my resistance and pulling me into a sensory nightmare. It is a humid feral smell; much like the muskiness of a furred predator that is old and not right inside.

In a tone of voice that anticipates no argument Morgan orders,

"Pack a bag when we get home, you'll be leaving first thing in the morning."

Home, the word rages through my mind. Morgan maintains a sterile three-bedroom house in the desert. It is nothing but walls wrapped around emptiness. I think of the inside of Revelstoke so full of warmth and life. I look out at the dark desert and wish with all of my might that I was back in La Jolla; parked at the beach listening to the cleansing sound of the ocean's surf. Instead, I hear the heavy rhythmic breathing of Morgan invading my thoughts and know that I am lost in a world without hope.

At first light the runway looks like any other airstrip, but this time the white interrupted line painted down the middle of the black tarmac points toward the corrupt world of criminal enterprise. The pilot, his name is Stretch, checks the gauges as we pause at the end of the runway in the specially modified twin-engine Aztec. With the plane's 8 custom wing tanks and a hundred gallon fuel bladder resting behind our seats, we can stay airborne for almost fourteen hours. I listen to the throaty roar of the engines as Stretch increases the throttle rapidly toward maximum rpm then with a glance towards me; he releases the brakes. The Aztec lurches forward then rapidly begins to accelerate down the runway. At eighty miles an hour, the nose lifts off, followed almost immediately by the main gear. With a gut-wrenching feeling, I watch the ground falling away, knowing that my life has been forever altered in a terrible and unforgiving way. The powerful twin climbs quickly. Looking out the window at the desert terrain below us, I suddenly feel cold inside. Is it because of the chilly high-altitude air or is this icy feeling in my gut because I am doing something criminal and terribly wrong? My fingers tremble slightly as I reach for the switch that activates the heater. Then sitting back in the seat, I close my eyes and while waiting for the heater's warmth, try to understand the events over the last twenty-four hours that have so completely taken control of my life.

Abruptly the volatile smell of gasoline fumes stirs me from my thoughts.

"The heater," yells the pilot urgently. "Shut down the heater! Hurry before this thing blows up!"

I flip the heater switch to *off*; then, thinking that the fuel bladder behind our seats must have sprung a leak, I turn to check it. Surprisingly, the hundred-gallon bladder is full; the black rubber-ized skin reassuringly taut to my touch. I look closely at the cockpit deck; there is no sign of gasoline leaking anywhere.

Stretch, unsure what is wrong, alters course for Blythe, an isolated desert strip, then begins a rapid descent.

Five miles out of Blythe, the starboard (right) engine fails without any warning; it just suddenly sputters and dies. The heavy plane rapidly begins to lose speed. Stretch frantically cranks the idle engine. The propeller turns in short jerks, but the engine refuses to catch. The plane begins to vibrate heavily as the airspeed decreases toward a stall. A violent shudder runs the length of the fuselage. The stall warning horn blares loudly in the small cockpit; then the right wing falls away and the nose drops sickeningly as the plane plunges into a steep dive. Thrown forward against the instru-ment panel, I awkwardly reach between the seats switching the fuel selector from the outer wing to the main tanks.

The desert floor is rushing up at us and I know I am going to die when abruptly the starboard engine coughs once loudly belching a thick cloud of black smoke. The propeller turns once slowly then the engine begins to fire rapidly. Stretch slams the starboard throttle forward to full power. The super-charged engine races to maximum rpm, yet we are rapidly continuing to lose altitude. Stretch fights for control, pulling vainly back on the wheel. Slowly, the nose of the Aztec begins to respond. At two hundred feet, with the desert floor flashing beneath us in a blur, the plane finally levels out. Stretch immediately points the nose back toward the Blythe runway and gains a few hundred feet of altitude.

Stretch's hands shake on final then the wheels hit the runway with a heavy, but reassuring jolt.

We taxi to a vacant side of the small airport before shutting down the engines. The hot desert air reeks of gasoline inside the cramped cockpit. I open the door and jump out onto the runway. Looking beneath the plane, I first hear and then am astounded to see a solid stream of aviation gasoline spilling from the fuselage onto the hot asphalt. I open an access door to find the entire bottom of the forward fuselage awash with high-octane gasoline. Above the heater, a fuel line nut is loose; actually it is almost completely backed-off. The volatile gasoline has been spilling in a steady stream directly onto the heater. Either the heater's metal casing is preventing the fuel from reaching the spark-ignition inducer or the gasoline is drowning the inducer in volatile fuel denying it oxygen. We are extremely fortunate to be alive.

For a pregnant moment, I wonder if this is indeed an accident. Did the nut loosen from vibration or is someone looking for a way to end Morgan's cocaine business? I have an all too vivid vision of the aircraft going down trailing black smoke with the cockpit awash in flames while the two of us scream our lives outs.

We thoroughly check the rest of the plane for other possible "innocent mistakes," then taxi to the fueling station to refill the outer wing tanks. The failure of the starboard engine was a direct result of the right wing-tip tank dumping its twenty gallons of gasoline straight into the forward compartment when I turned on the heater.

Barely an hour after our emergency landing, the plane is once again charging full speed down the runway before lifting off into the clear desert sky. Bewildered, I sit in the copilot's seat wondering why I am so foolishly risking my life. It certainly is not for money. It is fear that is driving me. It just does not make sense. I wonder how many other criminals began their felonious careers because they feared the people who manipulated them. Is Morgan using fear to force his own sons into this too? I think about Max and know that I am right to be scared.

We fly all that day and into the night stopping only to refuel. At dark thirty on the following morning, we taxi out onto a rainy runway at an airport in New Orleans. The long dark runway glistens from a light but steady rain. Through the wet sheen of the cockpit windshield, I watch jagged bolts of lightning strike across a broad weather front masked in thick black clouds that marches against the coastline out of the Gulf of Mexico. The rolling thunder of the electrically charged night all but drowns out the roar of our powerful engines as we race down the slick runway and take off into the dark threatening sky.

At first Stretch likes that the storm shrouds us from coastal radar, but then it gets worse…far worse. Lightning bolts shatter the darkness outside the tiny cockpit; the strobing light paints towering thunderheads advancing before near gale force winds. The Aztec tosses and bucks in the heavy turbulence like an enraged bronco. If we stray too close to the massive thunderheads, the violent shear winds could dismember our plane in a frenzied instant.

Weaving and threading our way between the towering nebulous walls is like flying though the Grand Canyon of the heavens. Thunder crashes and reverberates against the plane's thin skin; lightning bolts split the black sky striking downward from towering thunderheads to the raging ocean below. Violent air pockets rocket us upward or drop us like a stone hundreds of feet in stomach wrenching seconds. A bolt of lightning or a sudden sheer wind could flick us out of existence in an instant. In the dark cockpit, lit only by the dim red glow of the instrument lights, Stretch struggles with the controls as I fight with my own inner consciousness and dread. A sheen of sweat glistens on Stretch's face and the rank odor of fear, laced with the lingering smell of gasoline fumes fill the restricted cockpit.

The storm buffets us throughout the rest of the night and then with the red glow of dawn we pass from its embrace into an open sky filled with puffy white clouds. Stretch, tired and weary, slumps at the controls. He jerks upright then looks at me with red-rimmed eyes. "You better take the stick. I'm going to lie down in back." He rests his head on the black fuel bladder then says wearily, "We're somewhere southeast of Cuba. Just stay on a compass heading of 187 degrees and keep an eye out for Cuban fighters. That storm may have driven us a bit too close to their air defense perimeter."

Soon he begins to snore fitfully as I stare hopelessly at his pencil marks on the stained air chart. I cannot believe I am in a drug plane somewhere over the Gulf of Mexico watching out for Cuban fighters that may force us to land in that communist dictatorship. It is my fear of the Medellin Cartel, coupled with Morgan's manipulations that are hurling me into the belly of the beast. I am lost in a dark world outside my control and have no idea how to rescue myself.

In the early afternoon, the green coastline of Colombia appears low on the horizon. We check our heading by tuning in the Bogotá airport's radio signal then turn southeast towards the deeper jungle. Stretch keeps tapping the fuel gauges, but they stay adamantly in the red. Fighting the storm has cost us our small fuel reserve.

From three thousand feet, the dense jungle canopy seems to stretch forever, its vastness broken only by winding muddy rivers and long mountainous ridges. We are lost and low on fuel when suddenly a weak whistle blares from the near continuous static of the radio, two long warbling highs followed by a short descending note.

Stretch grabs the microphone and whistles back, two long, one short. They have seen us from the ground. "Del Norte, amigo, via Norte," urges a coarse Colombian voice. Stretch turns north while lowering the nose of the aircraft. We begin losing altitude as the small plane bucks into the wind surge coming over a sharp-edged ridge. Then crossing over a broad valley, I abruptly see several patches of jungle in motion. Three trucks laced with foliage slowly move revealing a short dirt strip. Stretch pulls back on the wheel causing the Twin to flare cutting our airspeed and then quickly the plane settles to the ground. Feeling the jar of solid earth beneath the wheels is a huge relief, but the emotion lasts only for a few moments. That touchdown alters my life forever. It is in that instant of time that I truly have become a criminal. Up until this instant, I have been somewhat able to deny the criminal bent my life has taken, but now it is a certain reality.

The Twin slows rapidly as dirt and gravel drag at the plane's wheels.

At the end of the runway stands a stout man with a large black moustache. He is wearing a New York Yankees' ball cap, a sweat stained khaki shirt and greasy jeans. A bandolier of red shotgun cartridges is draped over his shoulder. He uses a double barrel shotgun in his hairy hand to wave us under a large Banyan-like tree. The engines rev loudly as we taxi beneath the broad green canopy, then we shut down the engines; after many hours of listening to the continuous roar of the propellers, it is startlingly quiet inside the cockpit. I hear the creak of the engines dissipating heat, the creak of the door as I open it, the screech of a tropical bird in the tree and then the stout man growl, "You're late Gringos." Reluctantly, with fear riding on my shoulder, I step out into a world that is suddenly extremely frightening and forever altered.

The hot tropical air swelters with humidity as I feel rivulets of sweat running down my back. Armed men gather about the aircraft. A pick-up truck skids to a stop a dozen feet away in a cloud of dust as several men jump down from the back bed. Everywhere there is the threat of guns, yet the men are in a buoyant mood. They laugh, exchange words in Spanish, and smile at us. Yet the smiles do not extend to their eyes. These are hardened criminals, robbers, smugglers and murderers. Worst of it all, they consider me to be on their side. They call me Amigo, Hombre and hey, Gringo mixed with many Spanish words I do not know. I have never felt so lost or alone in my entire life and suddenly, without a doubt, I know that a prison cell is lurking in my future.

Hours later, there are long shadows draped across the plane's hot metal skin as a line of men pass five-gallon jerry cans of gasoline from an old truck to the plane. A cloud of mosquitoes descends upon us with the approaching tropical twilight. Standing on a wooden ladder with the last full jerry can in my hands, I cannot help but think that if we were attacked I would be nothing but a running target, not knowing friend from foe. Looking at the coarse cartel soldiers standing about me, I realize that there are no friends here, I am completely alone and my *stupidity* could cost me my life. No one back home would even know what happened to me. I would just be a pile of meat rotting in the jungle, another unknown corpse in the cocaine wars. I stare at the darkening jungle lost in thought until the man beneath the ladder nudges me irritably commanding that I hurry up, "Oye gringo, apresúrese."

Glancing at the coarse bearded outlaw, it is appalling to realize that I am actually on the side of the bad guys. A memory of when I worked on the right side of the law with police and government agencies as a bomb disposal man pounds at my consciousness. Wearily, I shrug off the thoughts of my once proud past and begin pouring the last of the fuel into the wing tank. I feel the gasoline's icy bite as some of it spills down my bare arm in cold rivulets chasing mosquitoes from the sweat-covered skin.

As the dark of night descends, I despairingly stagger along a jungle path toward a crude cement-walled house with a thatched roof. Through gaps in the weathered wood-plank door, I see a yellow flicker of an open flame. Spanish music weeps gently upon the air to us, along with the smell of roasting meat, eliciting hungry growls from the men as they shove past me.

The door squeaks loudly as the man with the shotgun jerks it open and shouts a greeting at the cook inside. The cook glances over his shoulder and laughs while continuing to turn a charred animal carcass over a raised open fire pit. He is a big man with a huge belly that bulges against a greasy apron. A large butcher knife half hidden by a roll of fat protrudes from his thick leather belt. He says something in Spanish, which sends the men scurrying towards a rough-hewn wooden table.

For a paralyzing moment, I stare at the animal carcass watching thick globs of fat dripping wetly into the fire where they sizzle in a loud searing hiss amongst the bright red flames licking at the black-ened meat. The cook motions with a jerk of his head for me to join the rest of the men who are noisily taking seats around the table. The outlaws lean their rifles and shotguns against the wall, but their pistols they lay within easy reach next to their plates. I take a seat between Stretch and a man with a black and grey beard; he grins at me, exposing yellowed and broken teeth with wide gaps revealing discolored gums. "Mucho Gusto," he nudges me good naturedly, then rubs his hairy hands together in anticipation as he stares at the meat searing over the open flame in the next room.

The cook shoulders past two of the men standing by the door bringing out blackened pots of beans, rice, chorizos (spiced pork sausage), fried chilies and onions along with a pan of cornbread. With a flourish, he returns carrying in the animal carcass on a wood platter and dumps it onto the middle of the table. The men bois-terously attack the charred carcass with gusto, ripping chunks of meat away with their knives and bare hands. Blood and grease leak from the wooden platter onto the table then run across the rough surface to fall in a wet splatter onto the dry dirt floor below.

Though desperately hungry, I stare with reluctance at the half-stripped carcass; its bones half exposed, the crust of the meat blackened and blood streaked. I know it is not a pig. Its size is consistent with a goat or a lamb. I look hopelessly at the pilot who is loading up his plate. "Aren't you going to eat?" he asks.

"I'm a vegetarian," I whisper.

"I wouldn't tell them that," he laughs ripping meat from a bone with his teeth.

The cook not understanding my hesitation leans across the table and knuckles me cheerfully in the chest. He is obviously proud of his cuisine as he plunges his butcher knife shoulder-deep into the half-dismembered animal cutting away an entire limb in a brutal sawing slash. He happily drops a kilo of blood-red meat, bone and charred gristle onto my plate. Leaning close, his handle bar mustache flut-tering in the gruffness of his voice, he rumbles, "Eat gringo," then he piles on scoops of rice, black beans and fried onions in heavy-handed flourishes. Almost as an afterthought, he grabs a hunk of cornbread and drops it onto the plate then lumbers back into the kitchen. His massive body is momentarily silhouetted by the soft red glow from the fire pit as he passes from sight.

I attack the plate mimicking the coarse behavior of the feeding men. The cook returns and is delighted when he sees me gnawing meat directly from the bone. Slapping my back vigorously he proclaims, "Mos macho hombre, eh?"

Looking at his coarse, yet friendly face, I cannot help but wonder if this is how he gets his kids to eat at home. I am almost in a good mood as I look back at my plate then notice a stub nose, thirty-eight revolver casually laid where my napkin would normally go. The lead bullets are plainly visible inside the six-round cylinder. Across the head of each bullet, a deep X has been crudely gouged. The bullets are cut to ensure maximum damage on impact. When an X-scored bullet hits a person, the bullet splits into four or more pieces that wreak havoc with human flesh and bone. The outlaw to my right notices my stare then possessively slides the revolver closer to him. The gun is an instant reminder that this is the depths of the smuggler's world. The realization shatters the momentary easiness I had been having with the cook as I look back at the criminal to my right. Having the gun fully back into his territory he is relaxed again as he snags a bottle of Ron Caldas rum from the table and urges me to drink. I never drink hard liquor, yet my hand takes the proffered bottle and I take a short pull. I feel the Colombian rum burning all the way down as it courses to my stomach where its heat immediately flares upwards numbing my brain. He grunts his approval then raises the bottle to his own lips and drinks thirstily in big gulps. I watch his Adam's apple, grimy with dirt and five days beard growth going up and down with each swallow.

Most of the dishes are carried away as we finish the meal; others are just shoveled into the middle of the table. The cook returns to upend a brown paper sack onto the table. Clods of marijuana spill across the grease-smeared wood planks. The men begin rolling thick joints with yellowed cornhusks. They light them with burning twigs from the fire. The room quickly fills with the pungent marijuana smoke. It rises thickly into the still humid air, curling around the smut stained rafters before drifting out into the night through the thatched roof.

When the fat joint passes to me, I do not hesitate to take a long pull. The cornhusk joint burns fiercely, its harsh smoke irritating my throat and despite the burning in my chest, I hold the smoke in, anxious to get stoned. I hope for the drugged drowsiness that might help me to sleep. I stare at moving shadows of the men cast on the wall by the fire and feel my stomach burning from the rum. I am on the verge of being physically sick; my mental condition is far worse. I close my eyes when the room begins to spin and am only barely able to shuffle to a sleeping mat; hay covered with torn burlap.

Throughout the long night, paranoid and restless, I toss and turn upon my grass mattress. I listen to the guards conversing in soft Spanish outside the window. Finally, I fall into a troubled sleep only to be prey to bizarre dreams.

In the morning, we are out early to load the plastic-wrapped kilo bricks of cocaine. They take the coke blocks from a dirty cement-walled room where there are a couple of thousand bricks of cocaine stacked in rows almost to the ceiling. The headman counts out three hundred bricks that the men stuff into sea bags and then load onto the grossly over-burdened airplane.

While Stretch supervises the loading of the last bag, I look at the plane's bulging tires and note how heavily the plane squats upon the dirt runway. Though it is early morning it is already hot and humid which will significantly reduce lift.

Stretch starts the engines then the men help to push the heavy plane into position. Stretch crosses himself, which startles me—why would he ask for God's blessing for criminal activities? With his feet firmly applied to the brakes, Stretch runs the engines up to full throttle. The Aztec shudders and vibrates as it strains against the brakes then, with a lurch, the plane begins to roll ponderously, slowly building up speed as it plows through the soft dirt and gravel. The airspeed indicator laboriously climbs to sixty mph, as the end of the short runway looms dangerously close. At eighty mph, the waiting trees begin to fill the windshield as the wheels finally leave the ground. I jerk up the lever that retracts the gear just as a tree sweeps beneath the fuselage. At five hundred feet, we begin a slow turn to the north banking the Aztec back towards North America.

Twelve hours later, we are using the New Orleans's Airport

radio locator to vector our heading and altitude. Every couple of minutes, Stretch gets a signal confirming our heading, then he quickly drops the nose of the aircraft lower towards the ocean not that far below us. By flying just under the radio signal, we are also below most shore-based radar. The altimeter is currently reading three hundred feet. The homing device swings five degrees to port. Stretch pushes the twin's nose down and corrects our heading. We level off at two hundred feet, but it sure seems like we are flying much closer to the water.

Five minutes later, I see the first oil platform ahead and slightly to starboard. Stretch pulls back on the stick and reduces power to the engine. As we close on the oilrig, I see another and then a line of them extending off to the West. Stretch makes a thirty degree turn to port. I already know his plan, but Stretch cannot help repeating it. "If we stay low they might call us in to the authorities as a possible drug runner. By climbing above the rigs and angling to fly almost over them I am hoping they'll think we are company executives checking out the platforms."

"What if they still think we are a drug plane?" I voice my obvious concern.

"That is the beauty of my plan," he says pridefully, "they cannot be sure we aren't oil executives. They won't make the call fearing they might upset the boss."

I shrug, it is a good plan, "What about the shore radar? They're going to see us for sure."

"I am planning on it," laughs Stretch, "but notice we aren't flying straight into New Orleans, we are paralleling the coastline. Most drug smugglers go straight in taking the shortest line possible. We are not fitting their drug profile by paralleling the coast. In fact, if we stay over the rigs for awhile they are liable to paint us as a helicopter servicing the oil platforms."

"Sure hope it works."

"It has worked perfectly eleven times in a row."

Make that twelve.

Better is a poor man who walks in his integrity.
Proverb 19:1

Not two weeks later, Morgan found out that he was under investigation by the DEA (Drug Enforcement Agency) for suspicion of transporting and selling cocaine. It seemed he had bragged a little too loudly to one of his girlfriends at a restaurant about how much money he was making with his nonstop airplane trips to Colombia. Someone overheard the conversation and dropped a dime (called it in to the authorities).

"I can't believe it," he shouts in frustration, "I don't sell cocaine. I am not some dirt bag drug dealer."

"Flying it in or selling it. What's the difference?" I ask surprised that he is acting so offended. It is obvious in my mind that Morgan is indeed a drug dealer...unfortunately so am I, yet it secretly pleases me that Morgan is under investigation. He is getting what he deserves, but then again he and I are in the same boat. So why am I feeling an almost pleasant excitement at the news that we are under investigation?

"What's the difference?" he shouts in answer to my question. "I'll tell you the difference, I fly cargo. It may be illegal cargo, but it is still just cargo; like tools or fish."

"It's cocaine, Morgan, you might not be dealing it on the streets, but you're still in the drug dealing business."

"I'm not in the drug business! I am in the aviation business. I fly planes. I don't use drugs, nor do I push them on anyone else. I think anyone who does drugs is stupid, but what they do is their business...not mine!"

"Are you serious?"

"Yes, I'm serious," he rages, "It's just cargo. The stuff's illegal only because some jerk in Washington has decided to make it so. It doesn't mean I have to pattern my life according to someone else's stupid law. Whose side are you on anyway?"

"I am just trying to make sense is all," which seems like a lost cause. How could he be in such denial about something so obvious?

"Look it's as simple as this. Because an idiot government committee made it illegal, I get to charge a thousand dollars per pound to fly it. All I am is the transporter. I move it from point A to point B. I don't force anyone to use it and I do not use it myself. This is an issue of airfreight. No different than cheating on your taxes. But no, they have to send a whole stupid government agency after me."

Whole government agency? I wonder at his words. Morgan is upset, but he also appears to be feeling self important about all the attention. Then it hits me. *I am working for a mad man! I have gone from working on the side of the law as a bomb disposal man, doing positive adventurous things that I believed in with my whole heart and soul to being stuck in Morgan and Max's criminal world with no way to get out without being killed. The real me is thrilled about the investigation. The Steve Arrington I like, desperately wants to be back on the right side again. The problem is how do I get there when I have been swallowed so deeply into the belly of the criminal beast.*

I wisely decide to stop arguing with Morgan as he continues to rant and rave. The one piece of good news is his abrupt proclamation that we are out of the drug business forever. Yet despite his assurances, I am becoming convinced that a prison cell may be waiting for me in the very near future; an assumption that the DEA would prove absolutely correct and in a far more dramatic way than I could have ever imagined. Morgan is also going to get a lot more attention than he would like as we are swept towards an arrest that will be played out on the world stage.

Later, in a jail cell, I would have plenty of time to remember Morgan's arguments that he was not a drug dealer, or even a part of the illegal drug business. I found myself comparing his criminal denials to like arguments I often heard from other supposedly innocent felons. It made me realize that all criminals have to find a way to justify their illegal behavior. The fault, according to them, was rarely their own. Blame is slung off in every direction except towards personal acceptance. The essence of criminal denial can be distilled down to a simple concept. A liar must first tell the lie to himself. He has to be self-convincing enough to justify the telling of the lie. Lies must be rationally justified in the mind of the liar. After awhile the lie takes on its own type of corrupted truth for the pretender, which means the liar will never be convinced that he or she actually did anything wrong and as such will not learn from their mistakes. The lie incarcerates them not just in the present, but well into the future.

When I became a Christian in prison, I realized some forthright truths. A Christian cannot lie to God, which forces the Christian into deep self-evaluation from a truthful perspective. By recognizing that I had sinned, I began to take ownership of that sin. It is then...and only then...after taking true ownership, of accepting that the sin is mine that I can truly ask the Lord to take it away from me. I could not give what I did not own. This realization made my incarceration not just bearable, but it gave me a worthy purpose in prison. The Stephen Arrington that was lured into Morgan's web was a flawed character capable of evil. If I ever hoped to be a happy person again I was going to have to deal with those flaws and accept that I was incapable by myself to purge away my evil side. The only thing that made the re-creation of Stephen Arrington possible is that I did not have to face that daunting task alone.

For a week I have been in Fort Lauderdale, Florida working on Morgan's yacht the *Highland Fling*, which has some serious maintenance issues. He calls while I am switching out the marine radio.

"It isn't good news," Morgan begins anxiously, his panic approaching the frantic level. I smile inwardly. Although I am involved, I would like to see justice reach out and touch Morgan and company...even though I am a part of that company. Practically breathless, Morgan continues, "Just in case things get worse, I want you to ready the Fling for an extended trip out of the country."

"I'm going to need some money for repairs and to buy supplies," I answer.

"I can't risk sending any from here; I know they're watching me. You'll have to get the money from Max."

The thought of seeing Max sends a shiver down my spine, "How do I get a hold of him?"

"You don't, he'll get in touch with you." The phone goes dead in my hand.

The next morning I am returning to the boat with a bag of groceries when I see two Latin men lounging on the stern deck. One of them is Scar Face, the Colombian who was guarding Max's door at the Marriott Hotel. As I board the boat, Scar Face steps between the salon door and me. He peers into the grocery bag then flicks open a butterfly knife and stabs a green apple off the top. I carefully keep both of my hands wrapped around the paper sack in plain sight—non-threatening. Scar Face slices off a piece of the apple and bites into it. A second later, he spits it onto the deck. "These apples are sour!" he scowls.

"I was going to make a pie," I answer without thinking.

Scar Face looks at the other Colombian, who is standing to one side of me and slightly behind. "He was going to make a pie," mocks Scar Face. He turns back to me, "I bet you're an expert with a spatula too."

I say nothing, knowing that the man is in a dangerous mood. He likes baiting me. It is a competitive thing, two alpha dogs sizing each other up. I used to consider myself a rather dangerous person, but now I have to reconsider. Scar Face is a criminal with an aggressive villainous attitude. He wants to prove something with his knife or gun. The threat of a fistfight is the limit of my aggressiveness. Scar Face and I are not even in the same league and we both know it. Not getting the response he hopes for Scar Face closes the knife after wiping the wet blade on the paper sack. "Forget the pie," he snarls, "you're coming with us. Max wants to see you." The ride to Miami in the back of their car is long, hot and sweltering. Being scared does not help matters any.

Max lives in a wealthy neighborhood called Miami Lakes at the end of a plush street. His house is white stucco with a red tile roof. It is a lavish affair with a small man-made lake lapping at the back-door. According to Scar Face, Max owns the houses on either side of his home surrounding himself with the trusted security of his

Colombian family for protection. Scar Face opens the door and pushes me into the shadowed coolness inside.

Max strides purposefully across the front room tile floor to meet me. He is about five-foot, ten-inches tall with a stocky build. He is wearing a loose, white shirt and black chino trousers that gather at the ankles. His eyes still have the flat piercing, reptilian look that so commands my attention. They are of the darkest brown with large black pupils that hint that he may be a bit crazy. He exudes a bestial power that lurks within the realm of the sadistic. Max scares me so much that I have to focus on not letting my hand tremble as he shakes it.

He places his arm over my shoulder and leads me into his private domain. There are two more armed men standing right and left just outside the kitchen door. Max introduces me to his two cousins by marriage to a Colombian woman.

"I only employ family," he states proudly, "who else can I trust?" Then squeezing my shoulder firmly, he adds, "I want you to get acquainted with my men, Steve, so you will truly know they are from me should I ever have to get a hold of you unexpectedly." The reptile eyes blink. My soul shudders under that cold stare. His meaning is incredibly clear; I am again being not so subtly warned.

The money is not here yet, so Max asks me to join him for lunch. He is having some issues that he wants to discuss. Since I am supposedly Morgan's right-hand man, Max feels he can speak frankly. First, he is not happy about Morgan's new banking arrangements. Morgan is currently laundering his money through a San Francisco bank that apparently does not mind accepting large quantities of cash without a paper trail. Max, who does not know about Morgan's current investigation problems, says he thinks it stinks of a DEA sting operation. Later, his suspicions would prove correct.

Max is also having a little trouble with the attitude of one of Morgan's pilots, Stretch, the man I flew with to Colombia. Apparently, Stretch has tried to work out his own deal with Max, who is presently shaking his head in disgust. "The guy's a drunk too. You just can't trust someone like that; he might talk too much with all that booze in him. I think we ought to dump on him, you know what I mean?" Max looks at me with a frank expression.

"You mean fire him?"

"Na," Max laughs, "I mean dump him, you know, something more permanent." Those eyes are watching me. "Nothing very painful," Max smiles slowly, "at least not for very long."

My heart races as I realize that Max is actually talking about killing a person. He says it so casually, with all the emotional feeling of a man swatting a pesky fly.

Memories of Stretch leap to mind. This is someone that I know, someone who has told me about his hopes and aspirations—and Max wants to know whether I think killing him is a good idea? I wonder how Morgan would react to this news. I cannot see him sanctioning the death of a friend. Yet, I do not doubt that Max will do whatever suits him, with or without Morgan's permission.

The whole conversation is getting to be far too much for me, I am not sure what to do. The reptilian eyes are watching, waiting for the proper response. Fortunately, the arrival of the money saves me from answering. The promised twenty-five thousand dollars is in the care of a twelve-year-old boy wearing shorts, a Space Invader T-shirt and white sneakers. His name is Pedro and he is carrying a large black leather satchel.

His father accompanies Pedro; he is Max's number two man, directly under Scar Face. Roberto is a sharp dresser with sophisticated Cuban tastes. He is wearing a white shark skin suit tailored to fit his slim, medium height, frame. He moves with the smooth, effortless, flowing quality of a cat. Roberto exudes barely contained energy just standing in the kitchen doorway, a lethal observer; like a booby trap waiting to be triggered. I have seen his type before in Vietnam. He is the quiet competent killer.

I glance back at the boy who is looking at his father with obviously devotion. Pedro knows exactly what he wants to be when he grows up—a killer just like dad. Standing beside the table, he is apparently at an acceptable age for learning the family trade. *So much for a happy childhood,* I think to myself.

Pedro sets his satchel down on the table and reaches greedily inside. He takes out two black leather cases and carefully opens one. It is startling to see that it contains an Ingram MAC 10 machine pistol. He hands it to Max, who immediately begins checking the piece. He drops out the magazine, checks the load then jams it back into place and works the slide mechanism, which chambers a round and cocks the piece. Max passes the now cocked pistol back to Pedro, who fondles it with a loving caress. The big gun looks ugly in his small hands. I can almost see the bloodthirsty thoughts running through his young mind. Unexpectedly, he looks directly at me. Hostility leaps from those young eyes with such sudden ferocity that the hair on the back of my neck stands on end. I cannot imagine this child playing with other children on a playground; he would more closely resemble a small barracuda amongst a school of minnows.

Max, who has not missed Pedro's look says, "Go ahead, Pedro give it to him." I look from Max back to Pedro to see the gun pointing at my head. His finger is white on the trigger, the barrel is abnormally large; Pedro's eyes are huge.

I react instinctively, reaching out and slapping the barrel down, but not before I hear the machine pistol's hammer hit firing pin! The sound of the pistol's hammer falling on an empty chamber is shockingly loud in the silent room. The twelve-year old boy seems surprised that the piece did not fire then he looks at me and our eyes lock. I see him slowly smile; he is embarrassed. He shrugs his shoulders as if it is all just a joke, but I know what just happened. This is a test for Pedro and a warning for me. He thought his gun was loaded. Pedro glances at Max who is glaring at him. Instant fear flashes from Pedro's eyes, but then Max laughs boisterously, leans over and ruffles Pedro's hair. Max cuts his eyes to me as he says, "This kid is going to be one tough hombre." The praise dissipates the child's fear. Pedro beams at the compliment then he looks to his father in the doorway who nods proudly. I notice that Roberto's right hand casually hangs beside the concealed pistol on his hip. I hear Scar Face snicker to my left and know that at least four other guns are eagerly ready. I am in a pack of predators that have brought live prey to their den for an adolescent killer in training. Pedro's head swivels back to me—the happiness abruptly drains from those young eyes; they become cold and hard. He is remembering that I am not family…I am prey. Deep inside Pedro there is still a child lurking, I got to see him briefly during his moment of embarrassment, but that boy is gone for now. The toughened Pedro is looking at me again and I know he is wishing for his missing bullets from the empty magazine.

Max sits back in his chair and claps his hands ending the tense moment. "Pedro," he orders, "give Steve what you really brought him."

The small outlaw reaches into the satchel and takes out a four-inch bundle of used bills. He can barely grip it with his small hands. He tosses the money onto the middle of the table like it is nothing. He returns his attention to the machine pistol that is far more interesting to his young corrupt mind. Apparently, he has already learned that money is just another tool in the family trade.

Pedro, lost in a fantasy world of ricocheting bullets, spins in his chair and puts an imagined burst into an unknown enemy, "Burp, burp." Pedro's upper torso shakes as he imitates the shudder of the gun on full auto. I too had played with toy guns and imagined enemies as a child, but the Mac-10 in Pedro's hands is no toy and I do not believe his fantasy enemies are the normal villains conjured up by the average twelve-year old child.

Watching the young dark eyes seeking out imagined targets, I think about the childhood happiness that Pedro will never know. The family would require that Pedro grow up far too quickly in the criminal world that eagerly waits to embrace him. I expect that he will live a violent, cruel life, motivated by twisted values and corrupt pleasures tainted with pain and brutality.

Our business finished, Max escorts me to the front door. I realize that we have not actually eaten any lunch. Placing his hand on my back in a friendly way that is very intimidating, he says, "Remember to talk with Morgan and just call if you want me to take care of that little problem with the pilot. My boys are always so anxious to please." The reptilian eyes smile.

It is dark when Scar Face and company return me to the marina. I watch them drive away to be sure that they are truly gone. The night is unsettling with imagined predators lurking in the dark. I rush down the pier ramp and step aboard the *Highland Fling*. Unlocking the door, I walk through the salon glancing at the grocery sack on the kitchen counter. Green apples will never be the same for me again. I rush below to my quarters and open a secret drawer. With shaking hands, I quickly roll a joint. I am again smoking marijuana as I desperately seek to cope with my out-of-control life. I am running scared, lost in a criminal world with no one to turn to and nowhere to go. Fear is my constant companion and paranoia my bedmate.

"Man perfected by society is the best of all animals; he is the most terrible of all when he lives without law, and without justice," Aristotle

"Courage is resistance to fear, mastery of fear—not absence of fear," Mark Twain

Chapter 21

FORT LAUDERDALE, FLORIDA, OCTOBER 1982

THREE MONTHS later, I am still in Fort Lauderdale, Florida at the marina working on Morgan's forty-six foot long yacht. He has me checking electronics, replacing components that may soon wear out and cleaning the hull down to bare wood. Lately, I have been wondering if Morgan is keeping me out of sight to limit his liability in the investigation. There are a lot of other places I would rather be than working on Morgan's tub waiting to be arrested.

I am scraping old paint from a section of the bow when I discover a section of rotting wood.

"Morgan, it is Steve," I am calling his new private cell phone; Morgan is changing cell phones on a weekly basis.

"Don't say your name," he says shrilly, "I know who you are."

"Fine, but you should know that *The Fling* has a big section of wood rot in the bow and there may be some others patches I haven't found yet."

"That is going to throw off our schedule." Morgan wants the yacht moved back to the Bahamas after the repairs to keep the government from possibly seizing it.

"I know that is why I called. It's also going to delay my trip."

"To Australia?"

"I thought we were saying as little as possible on the phone." Did that little slip occur on purpose?

I have been harassing Morgan that I needed to get away for a little while. An idea he did not like one bit at first. Then I mentioned that if I were somewhere in Australia surfing, I would not be available for questioning by certain government authorities. That is when Morgan got somewhat behind my idea. What he did not know is that I was not going to Australia, nor was I coming back. I had been working on this escape plan for a couple of months. There were places in Hawaii and California where I could disappear for a while. Though Hawaii was my preference I figured it would be easier to disappear into California's seven hundred miles of coastline.

"How long to replace the rotten wood?" he asks.

"A week, maybe two depending how much there is and how good of a job you want me to do."

"How about if I ask Sam to come out help?"

"No," I answer quickly, "I can hire someone here."

Sam is my surfer friend in California. He is a very immature twenty-one year old, who lives for surfing. Morgan thinks I am paying his way to go surfing with me to Australia. Actually, I have only told Morgan that so I could get extra funds. Though Morgan still kept a few thousand in my pockets, it was not enough for me to stage a disappearance. He also was not paying me an actual salary, nor had he paid me the fifty grand for the airplane trip. He told me that he was setting up an offshore account in my name. When he found out about the investigation, it gave him a new excuse to delay payment. He thought it would look better if I did not have much in the way of traceable funds so I would look more in character; i.e. the broke Stephen Arrington who arrived at Morgan Aviation with just twenty dollars in his pocket. Great reckoning on Morgan's part, which was another reason why I was going to get every nickel I could and split. Morgan had agreed to give me twenty thousand dollars of my money for the Australia trip. If I had asked for the full fifty grand then he would suspect that I was not coming back and find some way…or someone…to cancel my trip. I doubted that Morgan would imagine that I would walk away from thirty thousand bucks, but that was part of the plan. I would give a few hundred to Sam for his time, which he could turn into a week of surfing. His attendance at the health food market where he worked stuffing groceries into paper sacks solely depended upon the state of the surf and the amount of cash in his pockets. Mine was not the best of plans, but it was all I had…and I was getting desperate.

"I can have Sam on a flight out tomorrow," urges Morgan.

"I don't need him." The last thing I wanted was Sam around Morgan the great corruptor.

"Okay, but get the job done as fast as you can."

After Morgan hung up, I went back to scraping *The Fling's* hull.

The telephone woke me at 6:00 a.m. Sam is calling to say he arrived on the red-eye flight out of Los Angeles and needed a ride.

"What are you doing here," I ask angrily after meeting him curb-side at the airport.

"Morgan said our trip was delayed so he offered me an airline ticket to come out to help." Sam is very thrilled to be in Florida, "Gave me five hundred bucks too; cash money. Want to see it?" I shake my head, "So how's the surf?" he asks.

I glance over at my young friend. For him working on a million-aire's yacht in Fort Lauderdale had to be a lot more interesting than bagging bananas and cold-pressed wheatgrass juice. Got me to thinking about how I felt folding T-shirts when Morgan offered me a job as Executive-Vice-President-in-training. Morgan is such a liar.

"You're not here to surf Sam, you're going to be cutting out rotting wood and scraping paint."

"I know that," he shrugs as the baggage carousel starts up and Sam's luggage arrives, a frayed duffel and a very creatively wrapped surfboard. Multiple layers of cardboard, bubble wrap and duck tape conceal Sam's most treasured possession.

We work at scraping paint until the sun goes down. I fix dinner in the kitchen while Sam unpacks his board and waxes it up. He spends the whole evening talking about surfing with the board in his lap.

The next morning Sam and I are sitting in the lineup at a local surf spot. The waves are Florida small, but it is giving me a little time to think. I watch Sam snag a two-foot wave making the most of its small surging face. He is carefree without a problem in the world.

I have known him since he was a sixteen-year-old surf rat in Hawaii. His father was stationed at Barbers Point Naval Air Station in Hawaii. He arrived in the islands at the age of fourteen discovered surfing and marijuana…hadn't been interested in much of anything else ever since. I had counseled him to take some classes at the local community college in San Diego. The only course he ever talked about was a drama class where he was playing a supporting role to Dracula. Sam was young, foolish and needed to be as far from Morgan's manipulations as possible. Only he was not taking my advice about returning to California.

Two days later, I am fitting a piece of wood into *The Fling's* bow. I pause to wipe sweat from my forehead and glance down at the pier to see Morgan staring up at me. "How would you two like to leave a little early for your surf jaunt to Australia?" he asks unexpectedly.

I am suspicious of Morgan bearing gifts, "What's the catch, Morgan?"

"What catch?" he exclaims. "Actually, I've got a relatively simple job, something I think you will both thoroughly enjoy." Sam steps out from underneath the boat to listen in on our conversation. "I need a new car driven out to California," continues Morgan removing his glasses to wipe sweat from them.

His offer does not seem strange, Morgan has been pricing Rolls Royces in Florida to avoid any California record of the sale. Morgan is quite cheerful as he tells us to pack our bags; that we will be leaving first thing in the morning. I should have known that something was up. Morgan only gets that cheerful when he is about to make a lot of money or in pursuit of a female significantly less than half his age.

Sam and I spent the evening foolishly celebrating. He is particularly excited about tying his surfboard to the top of a Rolls Royce. "Think we could do a little detour down to San Diego?" he asks hopefully. "Imagine the surf pack seeing us roll up in a Rolls Royce with my surfboard tied on top. That would be way too cool, man."

The next morning I am a little late joining Morgan for breakfast. Over the rim of his coffee cup he says, "Look you want to be real careful how you drive this car."

I shrug my shoulders, "Of course we'll be careful. It's not exactly like we are going to be racing about in your Rolls Royce. Can you imagine that Sam wants to tie his surfboard on top of it?"

Looking genuinely surprised Morgan asks, "What?"

"Hey, he's only kidding about tying the surfboard on top."

"The surfboard can go in the trash," rages Morgan, "this trip is far too important to worry about a stupid surfboard."

"Sam will be crushed, he loves that old board."

"Buy him a new one in Australia. He'll get over it."

"So? Is it a Rolls?"

"What's all this about a Rolls Royce?"

"You said you were buying a new car, I just figured it was one those luxury cars you've been pricing."

Slamming his coffee cup down, he answers irritably, "I am not buying a new car; we are just doing a favor for a friend. It is his car, not mine."

Spilt coffee spreads across the white linen as I instantly realize that Morgan is setting me up again. "Morgan," I ask already dreading the answer, "is there anything in particular I should know about this car?"

"Don't ask," he quips, "this way what you and Sam don't know can't hurt you."

"Can't hurt us? Are you out of your mind! I thought you were out of the drugs business. What about the investigation?" Morgan anxiously looks at the other tables while motioning with his hands for me to keep my voice down.

Leaning across the table he whispers, "Everything is cool. Look how would you like to take an extra twenty thousand with you to Australia? Do this one last trip and I will give it to you."

I know instantly that there is no way Morgan is going to let me go unless I do this trip. I so desperately want out. The thought of being free of Morgan and his manipulations quickly over rides any other argument in my mind. The extra twenty grand is also extremely appealing. I see it as an extension of my freedom. My stress level is so high I am incapable of thinking anything through logically. I am completely in over my head and there is no one to help me.

My silence is all the answer Morgan needs.

"Throw the surfboard away," he repeats.

I stare at Morgan wondering whatever happened to the man I thought I knew seven years ago. After going to work for him, Morgan told me he lost his successful aviation company in a nasty divorce and now he is on a major "the world owes me" trip. It is hard to imagine that I ever thought him likeable. "When we get to California, I am immediately getting on an airplane to Australia."

"No problem," Morgan sits back opening his arms expansively, "I will have the money waiting for you."

Walking out of the restaurant into the bright Florida sunshine, I mentally struggle with the fact that I am heading right back into the nightmare of the criminal machine…then again I had not actually left it.

"The greatest penalty of evildoing - namely, to grow into the likeness of bad men," Plato

Morgan wanted me to take his current girlfriend to the airport. I told Sam to come along for the ride. The two of them rode up front with me chatting about suntans, bikinis and other irrelevant nonsense, while I pondered Colombians with guns and dark jail cells.

After dropping her off at the American terminal, I turn to Sam, "You're getting out here too. I want you to take the next flight home and wait for me there. If you fly standby, you can pocket the extra cost of changing your ticket. I'll join you in four or five days."

Sam's shock is obvious, "No way," he answers back firmly, "I'm going with you."

"Sam," I put a comforting hand on his shoulder, "Trust me on this one okay? It will be much better if you go now, then we'll be ready to leave that much sooner."

Sam shoves my hand away, "It's okay Steve, I know there's going to be something in the car. Morgan called from the restaurant, he offered me five thousand bucks just to ride shotgun with you. Pretty neat, huh."

"He what?"

"Five thousand bucks," echoes Sam, "now I can pay my own way to Hawaii."

"Wait, did you tell Morgan we're going to Hawaii?"

"Course I did. The man wanted me to ditch my surfboard. No way, it's a perfect Hawaiian stick. I know it doesn't look too good, but the curve, hard rails and tail lift are perfect for dropping in on a juicy North shore breaker."

"Don't you remember?" I want to knuckle his head, "We are supposed to be going to Australia."

"Yeah, that's what I told my girlfriend."

Logic is a lost cause. I make a mental promise to myself not to tell Sam anything else of importance. Now Morgan is going to be wondering about my conflicting destinations. Sam has put my plan in serious jeopardy.

One of the aspects of being a criminal is all the continuous lying. A criminal way of life demands constant attention to all the different lies one is telling various people. I am deceiving my mother and friends with one set of lies that has me honestly employed by Morgan Aviation, where I am supposedly learning commercial flying. Meanwhile, I am balancing a whole different series of lies for Morgan and company regarding my intentions of running. Then there are the lies I am trying to use on myself to justify what I am doing, but none of it is working.

The biggest lie of all was that throughout all of this, I still believed myself to be a good person. The corruption was swirling all around me, but it did not include me. I was still the good person that I was most comfortable seeing in the mirror. Trying to find a way out was, in my own mind, verification that I was not corrupted. My excuses were huge, almost believable and not true.

I now understand that without a moral compass, we are capable of heading down the wrong path reassuring ourselves with every step that we are actually good people trying to find a bendable solution to a moral problem. It is the rare criminal indeed, who recognizes their own failings and wrongful bent.

Another problem was my relying solely upon myself to find a solution. Yet, it was the way it had always been for me. For most of my childhood, my parents and brother did their own thing. I was usually left to figure out my own particular path in life. I did a lot of playing alone within the scope of my imagination and was an avid reader, losing myself into books and stores. In school, I remained a loner, it was the same with the Navy. Now a hostage of criminal enterprise, I was relying on the only person I truly trusted…me. I did not know how to reach beyond myself and had no compulsion to do so.

I glance over at Sam, who is sulking in the passenger seat. "So where's this perfect board now?" I ask.

"Oh," Sam shrugs, "sold it for forty bucks to a wannabe at the marina. He was pretty hot for it when I told him about all the prime waves it has ridden at The Pipe and at Sunset."

"You've never surfed The Pipe or Sunset." Both waves are for high performance surfers only. Sam and I were not in that class. Going out in those line-ups takes a savvy surfer otherwise you just screw it up for everyone else. Larger Hawaiian surfers can cop a serious attitude about stupid haolies (white people) dropping in on their primo waves. They even have a term for it, *Knock a haolie.*

"I couldn't ruin the dude's dreams," smiles Sam. "Besides it got an extra ten bucks out of him. We can use it for fast-food money."

"Sam, you don't want to do this; there is not anything cool about it. Go get on the airplane."

We argued for about fifteen minutes, but Sam was adamant.

One of his arguments kept marching through my mind; that he could not let me take the risk alone. That sounded too much like Morgan's statement to me about his sons taking all the risk while I did nothing. Yet it was more than just Morgan guilt tripping Sam that was so upsetting. I could not get away from the feeling that Sam was trying to stand by me. He was using my behavior as a benchmark for his own choices. If good old Steve was willing to do this, well why couldn't his buddy Sam? I briefly remember the sixteen-year-old kid, I used to surf with and find myself having to work a little harder than normal to bury my self-incriminating emotions beneath a less than stoic veneer.

Leaving the airport, I tell Sam that he can ride with me on one condition only, if we are busted, he must act as if he did not know about what was hidden in the car.

It's coke isn't it," states Sam excitedly.

I look at my young friend and wonder where his simple innocence has gone. It is not just Morgan's manipulations working here. The other friends Sam smoked marijuana with while he was growing up, all contributed to the immorally susceptible young man sitting next to me foolishly imagining himself to be a sophisticated drug smuggler, the guy who had just snagged an extra ten bucks lying about a dinged-up surfboard to a marina rat.

Back at the Pier 66 Hotel, Sam and I are anxiously waiting for the car to arrive. Half a delivered pizza lies uneaten on a table. A clear clue to how nervous Sam is, normally he can toast a large pizza by himself in four or five minutes. The phone rings…it is Scar Face calling to say he is waiting outside. I go out alone into the dark to meet a man who truly frightens me.

Max is waiting for me at the far edge of the parking lot, where it is the darkest. As I walk out towards him, I note other Colombians lurking in groups of two or three in the shadows. I count eight of them, plus Max. I know there has to be a lot of coke hidden in the car. Max only plays in the big leagues.

Walking across the seemingly long parking lot, I am thinking about my running skills. At the Spec War Command in Hawaii, I was the second fastest long distance runner. I'm slow for a sprint, but once going I can keep the pace up for hours. That's what I wanted to do right now, run as far and as fast my legs would carry me. Instead, I glare narrow-eyed at Scar Face knowing he cannot read my expression with the lights of the motel silhouetting me from behind.

Scar Face is leaning against a Chevy Caprice cleaning his fingernails with his butterfly knife. "Ready for a little ride?" he asks sarcastically. He opens the car door, the interior of which stays dark. "I disconnected the dome light," he states flatly. Using a pen light he points to a button hidden under the dash, then pats the backrest of the rear seat. "Understand?" he asks. "The button is the trigger that releases the backseat. We hid the coke between the backseat and the trunk's forward wall. Don't let anyone sit back here the seat bottom is rock hard."

Scar Face chuckles at his little joke, "Rock hard, you get it?"

"Very funny," I answer abruptly realizing I do not remember his real name.

Still laughing softly he walks around to the back of the car and opens the trunk. Except for the spare tire it is empty but for a large net bag of fancy wrapped pineapples. He cuts the nylon webbing with his knife and picks up two of the large tropical fruits bashing them together several times. He seems amused by the morbid clunking sound, like two heads forcefully colliding. Juice leaks from his fingers as he drops the cracked and bruised fruit onto the trunk's carpet. "Keep a couple of them smashed up and let them roll around. The Pineapples, they mask the smell of the cocaine you know."

Scar Face grabs another pineapple and flicking open his butterfly knife hacks out a piece of the fruit. He points the tip of the fruit-laden knife at my face, "Don't screw up huh? There's a lot more than you think riding on this deal."

"I won't screw up," I growl pushing the knife with the chunk of pineapple away.

Whenever I smell fresh pineapple, echoes of Scar Face frequently drift unbidden through my mind. The tropical scent of the fruit too often stirs the memory of that dark parking lot with the gunmen lurking in the shadows. Our mistakes have a way of haunting us for the long term. Criminals habitually carry a lot of stress-inducing emotional baggage. It keeps us perpetually messed-up in the head, regular walking basket cases incapable of living a semi-normal life and unable to relate with honest people in any meaningful or productive way. Criminals belong in the shadows where we think we can conceal our corruption.

Back in the room, I collect Sam and the half-full pizza box. I know he will be into it once we clear the city. We are walking across the parking lot when he suddenly becomes suspicious of all the Latin men lurking in the shadows. He sidles up to me and whispers, "Hey, see all the Mexicans hanging about?"

"They are Colombians, not Mexicans, Sam," I am trying to be patient.

"Well, don't worry," he whispers in his best macho voice, "anything goes down you can count on me."

"Look, absolutely don't think or do anything at all." I am wondering what he is going to do against eight Colombians armed with automatic weapons and sawed-off shotguns...threaten them with his pocketknife?

"Yeah, but they look like bad guys," he mutters.

"Of course they look like bad guys," I cannot believe what is coming out of his mouth, "they are smugglers and some of them are murderers, Sam."

"Murderers?"

"Sam, the bad guys are on our side."

"They are?" My explanation is outside Sam's simple logic. He is still trying to see himself as a good guy on a rogue adventure and I am trampling all over that assumption.

"Your job is to just get into the passenger seat," I growl. I am not in the best of moods as I open the driver's door.

"They're on our side?" Sam repeats as he climbs in on the other side of the car.

"Yeah, welcome to the wrong side of the criminal world." I look not unkindly at my young friend as I start the engine. "I tried to warn you Sam. You know, it's not too late to drop you off at the airport. You really do not want to be in this car."

"I'm staying with you." Sam is too into the intrigue of the moment and the promise of five thousand dollars to be dissuaded. He shakes his head then stares out the window at the Colombians.

I drive slowly out of the parking lot, make a left turn and with the competing smells of pineapple and cocaine filling the car accelerate into the night.

An hour later on the interstate in the northbound lane, I look for some music on the radio when I come across a news bulletin. President Ronald Reagan is talking about his new War on Drugs policy. In a state of semi-disbelief, I listen to the President of the United States describing a full anti-drug effort, a war against drugs and the criminals that are bringing them into America. The moment is hard for me to comprehend. Ronald Reagan is one of my childhood heroes. As President of the United States, he had been my Commander-in-Chief when I was in the Navy. This is a man, I highly respect and he is declaring war on drug smugglers, while I am driving a car loaded with millions of dollars worth of cocaine.

Sam is finishing off the last of the pizza as he reaches for the radio dial, "You drive; I'll find us some music."

He is oblivious to the President's statements.

"Didn't you hear what the President just said?" I ask.

"Wasn't listening," he pops the last bit of pizza crust into his mouth, "news is too depressing. I'm more into music." Sam tunes in a Cuban music station and turns up the volume, "Hey this is interesting."

With Latin music blaring from the radio, I drive into the night alone with my desperate thoughts and Sam head bopping in the passenger seat to the beat of rumba drums.

I now know that many people, both young and mature, can accidently blunder into the criminal world through a series of stupid choices. No one wakes up one morning and decides to become a felon. The criminal waltz is a dance that pulls you in one step at a time and then suddenly your whole life is swirling down the toilet. The paper the Devil used to wipe away my previous life was a marijuana joint. Drugs have corrupted many young person's values and morals. There is no doubt in my mind that without the corrupting influences of marijuana, I never would have been sucked up the criminal world. Youths and adults who experiment with drugs are flirting with the dangerous fringe of the criminal world. The enticement of a seemingly harmless escapade into forbidden territory is actually an open trap waiting for the foolish to tumble into it. Once someone plunges down that dark hole of addiction, the masquerade of drugs just being a harmless social vice reveals itself as a beast that forever feeds upon the soul, but is never satisfied.

After spending a brief restless night at a small motel, Sam and I are off well before sunrise. I drive all that day and well into the night. Sam is eager to drive, instead I leave him in-charge of the radio. Late that evening we enter east Texas, I am so dog-tired that I finally agree to let Sam drive. Instead of resting, I have to watch Sam carefully, who I am discovering is an inattentive driver. While trying to tune in a fading radio station, he almost sideswipes a pickup truck.

"Get your paws off the radio," I snarl. "Just watch the road and keep your speed down and don't pass anybody."

"But we're only doing sixty-five," he laments.

"That's the speed limit." I glare at him. "What do you want to do? Drag race so you can be the first one into a prison cell?"

Sam's driving is so jerky, I decide to get him off the highway before he has an accident. We get off the interstate at small town where I have seen a flashing motel sign. We stop for a traffic light in the left turn lane then wait for it to turn green. All Sam has to do is make a simple left turn into the motel parking lot. There is a slight complication that the street light is out and the dark motel driveway is at a slight upwards angle to the road. The light turns green and, amazingly, Sam misses the driveway and winds up making an illegal U-turn.

"Sam," I yell, "what are you doing? The last thing we need is a hassle with a small town Texas cop over a U-turn."

Sam shrugs, "Sorry." He drives about three quarters of a mile down the road to where it is safe to turn around. We then proceed back to the light. I look angrily at Sam and snarl, short-tempered, "Now, don't mess up this time."

He does. I couldn't believe it. "Look, idiot, it's not real tricky, just aim the stupid car into the stupid driveway?" I am livid.

A couple of minutes later we return to the signal. It's red, of course. While we wait, I notice that Sam's knuckles are white on the steering wheel. I know I should say something to calm him down, but I am too upset. Instead, I glare at him. When the light finally flashes green, Sam, who has been staring intently at the signal, begins to accelerate into the turn. "Look out!" I scream.

Sam stomps on the brakes stopping the car inches from a hurling eighteen-wheeler that is running a red light. I gape at the huge machine rumbling past mere inches from our front bumper; its tires flinging dirt and gravel against our windshield. As a cloud of dust settles about the car, Sam sits in a state of shock with his mouth hanging open. Behind us other cars begin honking their horns anxious to make the light. "Go!" I yell.

Sam floors it. The car lurches forward almost giving me whiplash. Unbelievably, he is in the process of missing the narrow driveway again. Frantically, I reach across and grab the wheel, fighting him for control. The car bounces over the curb, across a narrow side-walk, and into the motel parking lot before coming to a jerky stop. Sam has stalled the engine and is looking at me in a state of panic. I growl at him, my words unintelligible. I'm ready to drag him from behind the wheel; my fingers flex like claws in eager anticipation. Pulling the keys out of the ignition, I roar, "Wait here!"

I stomp off into the motel foyer. My mood doesn't improve when I discover that the probably flea-infested motel is booked.

Sam doesn't' ask any questions when I get back into the car and drive angrily back toward the interstate. He just sits quietly in the passenger seat, sulking.

> *Woe to those who call evil good and good evil, who put darkness for light and light for darkness, who put bitter for sweet and sweet for bitter.* Isaiah 5:20

Photo Arrington
Sam

*"The world is a dangerous place, not because of those who do
evil, but because of those who look on and do nothing,"*
Albert Einstein

Chapter 22

HIGHWAY 40, ARIZONA, OCTOBER 1982

TWO DAYS later, we are eating lunch in a small two-bit town just off the interstate in Arizona. To keep a low profile, I am only stopping at small, out of the way places. This restaurant certainly qualifies as off the beaten strip. It is a cowboy joint with creaky wooden tables, mismatched chairs, clapboard walls and a single paper menu. The overweight waitress has an attitude problem, which probably extends uninterrupted back a couple of decades. I have kept my order simple, fried eggs, hash browns, toast and coffee. Sam was being more particular.

"This is white toast," he complains, "don't you have any whole wheat?"

"Got no wheat," she snaps, "it all looks the same coming out of the toaster, buster."

"White bread isn't good for you, don't you know that?"

"The store down the street don't sell it so I don't serve it."

"Can't be much of a store if it doesn't sell whole wheat bread," grumbles Sam.

Once Sam locks on to a thought it can be difficult to distract him from it. I kick him under the table and mouth silently, "Shut up."

Four hardy looking men are eyeballing us from the adjoining table. Two of them are wearing coveralls; the other set are dressed in well-worn wrangler jeans and frayed cowboy shirts. These are robust, salt of the earth type of men who work from "can't see to can't see." They are the sort of men who take pride in little things like their town, their own piece of land and their families. I do not doubt that the woman waiting our table is kin to one or more of these men. They are eyeing Sam like a nest of rattlers seeing a fat gopher blundering down a dirt path.

I look at Sam who is dressed for the beach in his red shorts, Mad Max T-shirt and flip-flops. He is going to get us stomped if I don't do something fast. "Sam, forget the bread, just eat. We got to go."

The woman turns to walk away as Sam fires a parting shot. "What about ice cream? You got any ice cream?" *Great,* I think to myself, *the health nut who won't eat white bread now wants ice cream for breakfast. This is too like the overweight person that orders a thin-crust pizza with double cheese and bacon.*

The woman spins around hands on her stout hips. I believe she is ready to take Sam down herself. "It's breakfast time, we don't be serving any ice cream."

Sam is about to retort, two of the men are half out of their chairs, as I grab Sam's arm and snarl at him, "Shut up. Don't say one word."

Sam tries to pull his arm away, I squeeze harder, "Listen to me," I whisper fiercely, "we are leaving now!"

"Please excuse our bad manners," I am shedding bills onto the table, which has not gone unnoticed by either the waitress or the men. Grabbing Sam's upper arm I steer him outside and hustle him over to the car, "Get in now; we're leaving." He is sputtering about wanting his breakfast when I hear the screen door bang shut. Two of the men are standing on the front step. One of them is actually rolling up his sleeves.

The engine kicks on the first try and I spray gravel shooting out of the dirt and rock parking lot.

"What is your problem?" Shouts Sam.

"You were about to get us killed."

"By those old hicks? Are you kidding?"

"Sam, those men aren't as old as you think. They are cowboys weathered by the wind and sun. Did you happen to notice how thick their wrists were? Their prime recreation is probably kicking and stomping a couple of city boys before breakfast."

"We aren't city boys," argues Sam, "we surf."

Like that answers anything? I think to myself, "Sam, what happened to our keeping a low profile?"

Not having an answer, Sam sits back in his seat and broods.

Later in the afternoon, I am driving with the window down. Despite the hot air whipping through the car, I am having trouble keeping awake. Ignoring an inner warning, I decide to let Sam drive for a while. It feels like I have just dropped off, when I hear him wrestling with something in the backseat. I try to ignore the sound, but then the car veers wildly.

"What are you doing?" I growl opening my eyes.

Sam has dragged a brown paper sack into his lap; he reaches in and takes out half of a pineapple.

"Have you been into the pineapples again?" I ask shrilly. Sam has been diligently working his way through the net bag. He is consuming our cover scent, the idiot.

"It's just one."

"One! You've eaten over half of them." I rage.

"So I'm bored."

"We are hauling millions of dollars worth of cocaine and if we get busted you'll be older than your hick friends back there by the time you get out of jail…and you're willing to risk all that because you're bored?"

"Yeah," he shrugs, "I'm bored."

"Just drive and wake me before we get to the California border. There's an agricultural inspection station there."

"So?"

"So I want to do the talking and I'm going to chuck the pine-apples before we get there."

"Why can't I do the talking?"

"Well, what would you tell them if they asked where you are coming from?"

"Fort Lauderdale, why?"

"Because saying we are coming from Florida might get them to thinking about cocaine smugglers. It would be better to just say we are coming back from a weekend in Las Vegas, which is only about a hundred or so miles north of us right now."

"Did we win or lose?"

"Win or Lose?" I shout, "It doesn't matter." I close my eyes and snuggle down in the seat. "Just be sure to wake me before the inspection station."

Sudden voices raised in argument stirs me abruptly from my nap. Opening my eyes, I am blinded by bright light. It is late in the afternoon and the sun is glaring through the windshield. Rubbing my eyes, I look towards the sound of the voices and see the silhouette of a man standing at the driver's window. Something flashes silver upon his chest. As my eyes focus, I see that it is a silver badge against a tan uniform. My heart leaps as I realize that it is a border inspector. Glancing quickly left and right confirms that we are stopped at the California inspection station.

"It is against the law to bring potentially infested fruit into California." The inspector is all but leaning in through the window.

"It's not like I picked it from a tree in South America or anything," Sam is holding the pineapple protectively against his chest, "I bought it in a supermarket in Florida."

"Doesn't matter, it could still be harboring bugs."

"Where?" Sam peers suspiciously at the pineapple, "I don't see any bugs."

"They could be under the leaves."

"The leaves? That's your problem?" Sam rips the green top off the pineapple and hands it to the inspector, "There problem solved."

The man looks at the green leafy top, somewhat surprised it is sitting in his open hand. Then he glances back at Sam; an obvious idiot. "Get out of here," he barks stepping back and waving us angrily through.

Sam hits the window switch, waves through the mirror at the angry inspector and then flips the pineapple into the backseat as he accelerates away from the border station. "Pretty cool, huh," he leers.

"You just risked our being arrested over a pineapple?" I am considering bashing him about the head and shoulders with it.

"You heard him," Sam is giving me a look as if I am not paying attention, "he didn't want the whole pineapple just the top."

I am speechless.

"Got two more hidden in my bag," he snickers.

"With the tops I assume?"

"Oh yeah, forgot about that."

"Did you also forget that we were supposed to be coming from Las Vegas?"

"He didn't ask."

"So why did you feel the need to mention South America and Florida in the same sentence," I am ready to kill, "and pineapples do not grow on trees!"

"Hey, I know that. I lived in Hawaii you know."

"What I know is that your stunt drew attention we didn't need. If he decided to check the backseat and discovered the other pineapples in your bag, then maybe he might have also noticed that the backseat smells a lot like a cocaine factory."

"Sorry."

"If we get arrested, you'll be sorry alright. Pull over, I am driving."

> *"Laws are partly formed for the sake of good men, in order
> to instruct them how they may live on friendly terms with
> one another, and partly for the sake of those who refuse to be
> instructed, whose spirit cannot be subdued, or softened, or
> hindered from plunging into evil, "* Plato

There are moments when something happens and suddenly a decision is made that change a person's life. For me that moment involved a deer, a mule deer to be exact.

Sam and I are driving down a flat straight piece of highway. About us, the empty desert stretches as far as the eye can see. I have the cruise control set two miles per hour under the speed limit. The tarmac is black, the desert shades of brown and the sky darkens as twilight sets the stage for nightfall. As the evening settles upon the desert, I turn on the headlights and sink deeper into the seat relaxing with the knowledge that our trip is almost over.

Suddenly a hefty shape running at the corner of my eye snags my attention. It is a large mule deer, a magnificent buck racing across the highway. I slam on the brakes. The glare of the headlights captures each moment in brief mental snap shots. The mule deer is so close to the windshield that I lose sight of its head and antlers as it attempts to hurtle over the car's hood. I see the haunch muscles clenching beneath its fur, the fore hoofs raising upwards, the ample chest and whitish under belly elevating over the hood and then the trailing rear hoofs come even with the left front fender. There is a noise, not quite a thump or a bang, but the smallest of pops and the slightest of shudders that could be just imagined and then the buck passes into the darkness beyond my range of vision. I slow quickly and pull over to the side of the road.

"Did you hit that deer?" Sam, who had been dozing, is wide-awake.

"I don't know," I answer anxiously opening the door and stepping out of the car. "I felt a slight impact, but we didn't run over anything."

I walk up to peer at the front grill seeing no damage at all. I am about to breathe a sigh of relief then by the surrounding glow of the left headlight, I see a small tuft of brown fur wedged under a chrome strip on the upper side of the fender. There is a slight dent almost un-noticeable. In my mind, I know that the deer cleared the highway, but am uncertain of its condition. I easily imagine a broken rear leg and an animal once magnificent and proud suddenly hobbling and wounded, barely walking prey. More than anything else, I want to go back and check on the deer, but know I cannot. To park on the side of the highway in the middle of the desert at night could attract the attention of a state trooper. It is something I cannot just risk.

In extreme frustration, I kick the front tire. It is completely against my nature to leave a possibly hurt animal without aid, particularly when I am the cause of its suffering. I look back down the highway and see only darkness and an empty road, then turn to look at the vacant road ahead of us and make a decision.

Opening the front door, I get back into the car.

"Did we hit the deer?" asks Sam.

"Yes."

"We have to go back and check on it."

"No."

"What do you mean no?"

"We can't go back. It could attract the attention of a cop."

"What are we going to do?"

"We are going home," I turn to look at Sam as I shift the engine into gear and floor the gas pedal. "Only we are not following Morgan's plan anymore."

"Won't he get mad?"

It is the stupidest question I have ever heard, yet with those four words, my anger evaporates. I look at Sam sitting forlornly in the passenger seat and realize that I absolutely have to save him from this madness. I now understand that Sam has not matured beyond the surfer self-image he so aspired to in Hawaii. He may be twenty-one years old, but mentally he is still a teenager with imma-ture hopes of making it into Surfer magazine. My stress levers are beyond comprehension, while Sam looks for idle distraction from his boredom with an abrupt fetish for pineapples and ice cream for breakfast. I realize that in a unique way Sam is a bit like the mule deer; caught in a blinding light about to be run over by a speeding machine simply for being in the wrong place at the wrong time.

In this case, the wrong place was being beside his friend. I figure that his being in this car is as much my fault as it was Morgan's. I now have the final reason for abandoning Morgan's plan. The only problem is that I do not yet have an alternate plan.

"All things may corrupt when minds are prone to evil,"
Ovid 384-322 BC

Arriving in Los Angeles, we pick up Sam's Baja Bug then I have him follow me to the Valley Hilton. Leaving Sam at the hotel, I drive to the Sky Ways Restaurant at the Van Nuys Airport where I abandon the drug car in the parking lot. I glance at the pineapple laying on the backseat then turn away. It gives me a lot of satisfaction to walk away from that car. In the restaurant, I call for a taxi to take me back to the Hilton.

Walking into the room I am not surprised to see Sam watching television; a 1950's sci-fi flick.

Did you really just abandon the car?"

"Yep."

"What if someone steals it?"

I shrug, trying to imply I have the situation under control. Actually, I am terrified that someone might in fact steal the car. My plan for escaping Morgan is not complicated and obviously, there are some major holes in it.

"Where'd you leave it?"

"Can't tell you that, Sam."

"Does this mean I am not going to get the five thousand dollars?"

I stare at Sam long enough to make him uncomfortable and go back to his movie. Picking up the telephone, I call Morgan in Florida.

"Yeah?" I hear his distinctive voice. It has a nervous quality to it. He has been sweating this call. He is hiding out in a hotel so no one would know where he was if anything went wrong. When I made my airplane trip to Colombia, Morgan fled to his boat in the Bahamas until he knew it was safe to return to the United States. I did not doubt that if anything went wrong Morgan would be gone in an instant, probably abandoning his sons in the process, so much for honor among thieves.

"Morgan," I all but roar over the telephone, "I've had it. You can keep your drug money, but I want out." I'm feeling a bit emotional.

"Hold on, Steve," Morgan cautions, "what's the problem?"

"Your car's the problem," I snarl.

"Calm down," he urges, "Now exactly where is the car?"

"I parked it. You want it. Come get it."

"Where are you?"

"Just tell me where you want me to meet you."

"Call me at the LAX Marriott on Century Boulevard. I'll be there before five PM." I slam down the telephone receiver.

"What if he comes looking for us here?"

"Why do you think I booked us into the Hilton?" I am trying to sound decisive, at least one of us has to think that I know what I am doing. "They have great security here; cameras, guards, the whole bit. No one's going to hit us at the Hilton."

"Cool," Sam goes back to his movie.

The following day, October 18, 1992, began slowly, yet it will be the most eventful day of my life. At 6:30 p.m., I call the Marriott. Morgan keeps it short, probably fearing wiretaps, "Bring the car to the Marriott, I'm in room 501."

"Okay, I will see you in about half-an-hour," then I realize he has already hung up the telephone. I turn to Sam, "Get your keys Sam, we're leaving."

"Did he sound mad?"

"Don't worry Sam, you're not even going to see him."

"I'm not?" he is visibility relieved.

"Nope, you're just my ride."

We are a little late arriving in the parking lot. Sam forgot to tell me that the Baja Bug was running on empty. I splurged and had him fill it up though I was not sure if we would be around long enough to empty it again. At least it made Sam optimistic.

I glanced around the dark parking lot before getting out of the car. I sure was getting tired of hanging out in dark parking lots waiting for bad guys with guns. "Just stay here, Sam. When I come back, I will be alone."

"What if you're not alone?" Sam asks the obvious.

"Then you can assume that my plan is not working so well," I put a reassuring hand on his shoulder. "In that case get out of here as fast as you can."

"Really?" Sam is suddenly scared, "I thought you said Morgan isn't mad."

I keep a sharp eye out crossing the parking lot, but do not see any Colombians lurking in the shadows. Avoiding the front desk, I walk up to a lobby phone and dial five oh one.

I hear Morgan's voice, "Yeah?"

"I'm in the lobby."

"Come on up."

"Nope, you come down."

A minute later an elevator door opens and Morgan comes striding out. He extends his hand to shake, but instead I drop the car keys into it.

"Where's the car? In the parking lot?" he asks hopefully.

"No Morgan," I answer, "the car is in front of the Sky Ways Restaurant at the Van Nuys Airport."

He totally flips out, "You mean the car is just sitting there, unattended? Are you nuts?"

"Remember? I'm quitting," I am in an emotional state.

"Forget quitting," he curses, "this is not a time for games. We are dealing with some very heavy dudes. These guys are mobsters. They're waiting upstairs with the money on the table. They aren't the kind of people to screw around. If we don't hand deliver that cocaine, you and I are going to wind up in a couple of garbage bags." he pauses, "Don't move."

He rushes back into the elevator. In a couple of minutes, he returns flanked by two other men in suits. One is short and dumpy.

He is so fat he waddles as he walks. His name is James Timothy Hoffman, whom I have met before. I remember that Morgan said not to trust him. The other man is lean and mean. His walk is more like a prowl. He has a permanent sneer on his face…probably influenced by the bulge in his coat from the heavy caliber pistol he is packing in a shoulder holster.

"This is Louie," Morgan nods towards the lean man, "and you already know Hoffman."

All I know is that I am not going to like what is coming next. "You have to take them to the car," Morgan frowns at me in a way that allows no argument. At that moment, I am wondering why I did not split as soon as I dropped the keys in Morgan's hand. Maybe I was just being foolishly hopeful that Morgan would let me go once he knew where the car was and that I did not want any money.

"Okay," I concede, "but I have to go outside and get rid of Sam."

Walking rapidly out the door, I notice that Louie is following me, yet he keeps his distance. Then I see why, there are more men lingering in the parking lot. At least I can make sure Sam gets away I counsel myself.

Walking up to the Volkswagen I am amazed to see that Sam has the dome light on and is reading a Surfer Magazine. "What are you doing?" I blurt. He had not noticed me walking up.

"Hey, you gotta see these pictures of Pipeline," he says excitedly.

"Turn off that stupid light," I growl. Now that Morgan knows exactly where the car is there is no assurance that his friends will not knock us off. I feel like I am part of a Mutt and Jeff tag team.

"Okay," Sam actually dog-ears the page before turning off the overhead light.

"What did Morgan say?" he asks.

"He is going to need me for a little while. I want you to go back to the hotel and wait for my call."

"Sure," Sam replies, "there's a movie I want to catch on the television."

I step away from the car so that Louie and friends will know that I am not about to make a fast getaway. Sam starts the souped-up engine, revs it towards redline and then peels out of the parking lot. I watch the Baja Bug cut off a couple of cars and realize that this may have been the last time I will ever see Sam again. I watch his tail lights disappear from sight then reluctantly walk back towards Louie.

"Morgan's called for his car," he states flatly. A few moments later Morgan's silver Cadillac pulls smoothly up in front of the lobby entrance. A young uniformed driver steps out and holds the door open with his hand outstretched for a tip. Reaching into my wallet for a couple of dollar bills, I think how crazy life is, here I am possibly on my way to my own funeral and I am worrying about tipping the parking valet. Hoffman lowers his bulk into the back-seat. I feel his breath on the back of my neck as he leans forward to get settled.

Pulling out onto the busy three-lane street, I momentarily see a Baja Bug exactly like Sam's racing in the opposite direction.

"So," Louie interrupts my thoughts, "when we get to the car are you going to have any friends waiting?"

I glance at his eyes, which glare coldly in the semi-darkness. I am wondering if he has orders to try to kill me once he gets his hands on the cocaine. For all I know Hoffman could have a gun pointed at the back of my head right now. He is so big he could conceal a riot shotgun in his huge suit and I would not know it. Maybe a little insurance would be a good idea. If they think I have men hidden outside the Sky Ways Restaurant they might not be so fast with the guns.

Instead, I answer truthfully, "No, there isn't anyone else...just me." *Wow,* I mentally chastise myself; *Steve, you sure are one lousy criminal!*

What I do not know is that my answer may have just saved my life because Louis is wired for sound and there are four carloads of armed-to-the-teeth Federal Agents hot on our trail. It would not have been a very good idea for me to get them overly excited with rumors of hostile gunmen in a dark parking lot.

The man riding next to me doing a fine job of impersonating Louie, the crazed Italian killer, is actually a DEA (Drug Enforcement Agency) undercover agent named Gerald Scotti. James Hoffman in the backseat is an ex-drug smuggler turned government informant...and me, well I am totally in the dark thinking they are both Mafia bad guys from Chicago.

When I pull into the Sky Ways parking lot, Louie voices his amazement that I actually left the car unattended, "You really left all that cocaine just sitting here?"

It did not seem like a good idea to tell a mafia bad guy that I was just looking for a way out. He might decide to provide a quick one-way solution.

There are no open spaces near the Caprice. So, I park the Caddie then go get the Caprice and park it in an adjoining space.

"Where's the stuff?" Scotti asks anxiously as I step out of the Caprice.

"Stashed behind the backseat," I answer, "there's a trick button under the dash below the light switch."

I push the release then step out of the car, while Scotti attacks the backseat, jerking and pulling on it. With his attention focused on getting at the cocaine, I silently back away moving towards the driver's door of the Cadillac. Carefully I open the door and slide behind the wheel. I glance over at Louie who has a plastic-wrapped brick of cocaine in his hand. I see him plop it down on the roof of the Caprice and stab a knife into it. He jams a finger into the opening and tastes it. Smiling hugely, he sticks his thumb up into the air and pumps his arm excitedly. Abruptly a small army of armed men come running out of the darkness. There are at least a dozen of them converging on the Cadillac from multiple directions. I reach for the ignition, but the keys are not in it. I quickly look down at the floor hoping to see them on the carpet, but am too late. I am convinced that this is a rival gang looking to rip off the cocaine and that I may be about to die.

The driver's door flies open. The dome light seems inordinately bright as I see a man's face lunging towards me. In his right hand there is a huge revolver, at least it looks huge from my close-up perspective. The barrel slams into my temple, the gun sight cuts the skin. I feel a rivulet of blood running down the side of my face as he yells, "Move, scum bag, and I'll blow your head off!"

Instantly the Cadillac's other doors fling open and guns are stuck in from the sides, front and back. Two more men stand at the hood of the car, their pistols aimed at my head through the windshield. I turn my head to the right to stare numbly at the gaping bore of a riot shotgun aimed at my face and side from the passenger side door. In apparent slow motion, I see coarse hands, matted on the backs with black hair, work the pump action sliding a shell into the chamber. The *click-clack* of the mechanism is uncommonly loud in the restricted space of the car. The massive barrel pushes forcefully against my chest. Still convinced that it is a rip-off, I wonder if I will hear the shot that will end my life. "Put your hands up," yells the man with the shotgun. "Move and die," yells the guy with the handgun.

Move and die? Put your hands up? Unsure what to do…I put my hands halfway up. Then the guy with the revolver yells the greatest words I have ever heard, "Federal agents, you're under arrest, dirt bag."

In that instant, I know I am not going to die. I am so relieved I could hug the men, but for all the guns pointed at me. Absolutely I know that I am going to prison. Yet more importantly, I am suddenly free from a life that has been out of control for far too long. My relief is immense; these are the good guys. For seven long months, I have been lost in the dark underworld of organized criminals.

They throw me up against a black-sided van. In the shiny distorted reflection of the dark paint, I see the men gathered about me. There are more guns on me than I can count. They jerk my arms behind my back and cuff them tightly. I feel hands running up and down my body searching for weapons while I stare for a long moment at my own image.

The man with the riot shot gun leans in from my right. "Hey

jerk, you should have seen the look on your face when I worked the action on my shotgun." I smell garlic and onions on his breath. "There was already a load in the chamber so I didn't have to do that. I just like to see you supposed bad guys reacting to the *clacking* sound of a shotgun round being chambered against your chest. Amazing how cooperative you tough guys get."

They hustle me into the back of a black sedan. Louie climbs into the front seat and turns to look at me, "Well, dirt bag, I guess this isn't the best day of your life is it?"

I do not have to force my answer, "Actually, I think it is."

Looking mildly confused Louie turns away to ponder my answer, then he grabs a microphone, "Okay we got the stuff and Arrington in custody. Go ahead and arrest Morgan Hetrick."

> *But they lie in wait for their own blood; they ambush their*
> *own lives. So are the ways of everyone who gains by violence.*
> Proverbs 1:18-19

Illustration by Marjory Spielman
Puu

"To him who is in fear everything rustles,"
Sophocles 496-406 BC

Chapter 23

TERMINAL ISLAND PRISON,

LOS ANGELES HARBOR, CALIFORNIA, OCTOBER 1982

BEGAN MY sojourn in prison in lock step with two other inmates. We are wearing handcuffs and are shackled together at the ankles with chains and leg irons. We walk in short steps. If one man gets out of step, it causes the ankle manacles to gouge the skin of the other two inmates, not the best way to meet an abruptly upset felon. The stainless steel chain lightly drags across the dark parking lot making a merry tinkling sound that is at odds with my depressed state of mind. We are also wearing handcuffs so we move awkwardly with short steps known as the inmate shuffle. We hobble in a short line from a Marshal's van, through a chain link fence topped with razor wire and are about to pass through a second chain link gate, which a prison guard is unlocking. Waiting for the gate to open I shiver in the cold October night air. A sea fog is drifting in from the harbor coating my skin with chilly droplets.

Terminal Island Federal Correctional Facility squats on an

industrial peninsula in Los Angeles Harbor. The prison sprawls across twenty acres in a long desolate rectangle. Before us looms a depressing cement walled building three stories tall with a few dark barred windows on the upper floor. Extending on both sides of the foreboding wall are gun towers that drift in and out of view with the shifting fog. A guard stands outside one tower watching our entry. A riot shot gun casually rides on his shoulder. I am not looking forward to going inside.

The cold fog is appropriate to my mood. The guard opens the gate before us as the Marshal standing beside me lightly raps my arm with his baton, "Move it boy; I don't like getting wet."

"Yes sir," I shuffle forward shoulders slumped still looking upward with dread at those dark walls. The dragging chain begins its merry tinkling cadence while my mind desperately tries to deal with the reality of the prison before me. I am losing control of my life and all I can do is slowly shuffle forward as the prison waits to swallow me. The chain link gate locks behind us with a solid metallic click as another guard opens a steel door at the base of the foreboding building. It is called a sally port and from it there is a dim, not-inviting, dirty yellow glow. All my senses are arguing against my going through that ugly port, which makes the chains, handcuffs and manacles we are wearing understandable. I reluctantly pass from the cold, but refreshing fog into the gloom and musty smell of Federal correctional custody.

We enter into a narrow corridor at the bottom of a rusted steel staircase. The thick cement walls press in upon us. They are damp from the moisture-laden air with patches of peeling pea green paint. My cuffed hand brushes against the damp metal scaffolding and comes away slimed with grime and wet rust. We climb the staircase in cadence, the solid thump of our feet and tinkle of the chains echoing hollowly off the dense concrete walls. I do not make it to the second story without breaking step and hear a deep-chested snarl from the large man behind me. At the top of the staircase, they herd us into a holding cell where they remove the leg irons and handcuffs. I rub my bruised ankle.

The man whose ankle I gouged glares at me then walks over to a toilet with a half-busted away seat. The holding cell smells of tobacco, pungent body odor, and then strongly of urine as the man relieves himself loudly into the toilet bowl. I step to the opposite side of the cell where there is a barred window with small glass panes painted a dark shade of brown. One of the panes has been broken out. I go up on to my tiptoes to peer out. The metal rim still has sharp glass fragments embedded in it. They gleam like tiny teeth as I press my nose into the opening. I am experiencing a sudden drowning feeling like being gulped down by a gigantic reptile. I am inside its constricted throat peering out through the teeth-rimmed mouth. Then abruptly a light breeze wafts through the small opening. Fog fresh air momentarily washes the stench of the cell away. Inhaling deeply though the three by five inch opening I get my first look into the Terminal Island Prison's North Yard. The view is hugely depressing. Through the swirling fog, I see concrete walls stained shades of black and grey from long exposure to smog, soot and acid rain. The yard is bordered with formidable dormitories, each two stories tall, their grey walls slashed with twin rows of shadowed windows, though some leaks a pale white light. The grounds are covered with tarmac, cracked cement and a few small areas of lawn. There is one small stunted tree. Except for the patches of grass, the stunted tree is the only living thing in view and I stare at it wistfully.

"Get away from that window," bellows a deep angry voice.

I turn around to see a large guard standing outside the grill. He raps the bars with a black truncheon then stalks away. *I am definitely not going to like it here*, the thought echoes repeatedly through my mind. The large inmate I offended is standing in a shadowed corner staring at me.

After being fingerprinted, photographed and strip-searched, they lead three of us down a series of cement corridors to a heavy steel door. The guard inserts a large brass key that all but fills his hand. Shoving the heavy door open, he turns and grins, "Welcome to The Hole, boys."

Jail Unit 1 (J-1) has three tiers of cells stacked inside a rectangular two-and-a-half-story building. It is dumbfounding to see such a huge steel cage squatting inside a concrete structure. The guard leads us up a metal staircase to the second tier. As we walk past the row of cells with their desperate human cargo I try not to stare, but my eyes are drawn to the individual cells, which are about ten feet long, six feet wide and less than eight feet tall. From the cells, adult male eyes stare back. Some of them are fearful or hopeless, but most are fierce and predatory. There is the murmur of voices, angry…threatening. I walk close to the railing avoiding the physical threat secreting from the cell's shadowy interiors. The guard stops at a cell midway down and opens the grill. "Arrington," he barks, "inside."

I step to the door attempting to peer into the dim interior, but the guard shoves me fully into the cell and slams the door closed.

I suck air in through my nostrils. It smells rank and stale like a musky tomb or damp cave. A toilet, its bowl heavily soiled and missing its seat crouches in the far corner. I place a hand against the cement wall to steady myself. The concrete is grimy and my hand comes away slimed by a caking of tobacco smoke that over the decades has turned the cement a greasy nut brown. A dim yellow light recessed into the ceiling behind a dirty grill hardly reaches the lower bunk, which is half-shrouded in shadow. A huge black man lies there. He is naked but for a pair of torn and stained boxers. The man emits a heavy musk that fills the tiny cell. I look at his thick muscular arms, barrel chest and hateful stare. I am instantly terrified but know not to show it. He glares with bloodshot red-rimmed eyes.

"Hello," I say warily, "My name is Steve."

He grunts and shows a meaty fist. "Don't gives a damn what youze name is whitey, stay outta my face or I'll bust youze up."

Feeling threatened, awkward and completely exposed, I quickly climb onto the upper bunk. The dirty cement ceiling looms excessively close, a bit like lying down in a metal coffin and half-closing the lid. There is barely enough room to sit up. I close my eyes and listen to the sounds of the cellblock, which are angry and intense. An argument is well underway spiced with foul words and vile threats from the cell above. I hear the flush of a toilet, the rattle of a cell door slamming closed and the creak of the bedsprings from the bunk beneath me. It is very weird feeling my bed move in sync with the man's ponderous body as he rustles about.

I stare at the dim yellow ceiling light then close my eyes wishing I were anywhere but here. I still see the yellow glow of the bulb against my eyelids as my mind journeys inward to happier times.

It is early December and the first big winter swell is pounding Oahu's northern reefs. I look upwards at the yellow sun to check the angle of light as I adjust the camera then look at the huge waves. Later, it would become known as the biggest surf day in 1979; I, however, would remember it as the day I met Susan. I am standing on the beach taking pictures of some stupendous wipeouts with a long, 650mm telephoto lens. The monstrous waves have closed out most of the North Shore. Only the big breaks like Waimea, Sunset and Pipeline are still barely ride able. The trade winds are holding the four-story waves super critical before they break with the crashing sound of rolling thunder. Just a few brave, or slightly crazy, surfers are out and riding the out-of-control waves. The others, huddled in a small pack, are just trying to survive long enough to make a hopeful dash for the safety of the beach between sets. A half-dozen broken surfboards have already washed up on the beach and the morning is only half over.

I have just shot an excellent sequence of an overly brave, or incredibly stupid, Marine who tried to ride a vicious set wave with his little boogie board. When the massive lip pitched with him deeply imbedded in it, the marine found himself in hydraulic-assisted free fall, heading for an astonishing impact with the bottom. His mangled boogie board is just washing up on the beach when I see two very good-looking blondes walking in my general direction.

I, like most of the guys on the beach, pause to watch them striding across the white sand beach. I just did not expect them to stop right in front of me, but then I abruptly recognize Caroline whom I met several months ago at a beach party.

"What happened to your hair?" Caroline finds my near baldness amusing. "Kind of short isn't it?" I avoid the subject of the naval brig and my recent release as she steps closer to run her fingers through the short spiky stubs. "Feels kind of weird," she quips. Caroline is on the University of Hawaii's varsity swim team. Her figure is sleek as a seal's. She looks ravishing in her white nylon dolphin shorts and red bikini top…however my attention rivets on her companion who is absolutely stunning even while standing next to a fox like Caroline. "This is Susan," volunteers Caroline, "Meet Steve, the porcupine."

Susan is wearing jeans, a simple white cotton blouse and sandals. Her long straight blonde hair falls in a silken cascade half way down her back. She is only a few inches shorter than my six feet. She is not wearing any make-up and seems completely unaware that my heart is flopping in the hot sand at her feet. Susan's grin is open and friendly as she says, "I hope you're not trying to start a fad, your hair looks horrible."

"Mind if we join you?" asks Caroline spreading her towel a few feet from my camera's tripod.

"Be my guest," I grin happily.

Hidden behind my sunglasses I ogle Susan as she slides out of her jeans. I could not help noticing that she has the kind of figure that surfers daydream about while waxing up their surfboards. She checks that her burgundy swimsuit is in place…as did most of the guys on the beach then she lies down on a beach towel. She and Caroline share a bottle of coconut suntan oil that they take turns putting on each other's backs. I take off my sunglasses to wipe away the sweat that is beginning to hinder my vision. Meanwhile I miss shooting some good, double over head, tube rides. My surfer friends are going to be bummed to the max.

The girls are just setting down to bask under the tropical sun when a black Great Dane arrives at a dead run spraying sand everywhere. Caroline glares at the big dog as she brushes at the sand sticking to her oil-covered skin, but Susan doesn't seem to mind. She pushes playfully at the big Dane, "Who are you, you big mutt."

"His name is not Mutt, it's Puu," I answer while ruffling the Dane's ears.

"Is he your dog?" Asks Susan.

Puu is leaning against my legs sopping up the attention, "Sometimes I think I more belong to him," I answer, "he tends to be rather possessive of me and his dog dish." Almost as if recognizing the words dog dish, Puu barks and begins to pull on my baggy swimsuit with his teeth.

"What does he want?" asks Susan.

The Dane is bracing his big paws in the sand and is beginning to tug harder. "He wants to be fed," I laugh, "Want to watch? It's amazing what he can do to a twenty-five pound bag of dog food."

"Sure," Susan's smile is radiant in the morning light.

I disassemble the camera and stuff it in a bag then shoulder the tripod as we head for the parking lot. Caroline elects to work on her tan. I like the idea of being alone with Susan.

"How long have you had Puu?" Susan asks rubbing Puu's ears.

"Just a couple of months."

"Really, you two almost seem like soul mates."

"I know," I answer truthfully, "I hear that a lot. It's because Puu and I have a lot in common. I stole him from a guy who was abusing him something terrible."

"You stole him?"

"Yep, the guy kept him tied to a tree for days at a time, often without food or water. When I took Puu he was covered in sores, lying in his own waste, skinny as a rail and beginning to get mean."

Susan stares at Puu's black shiny coat and muscular body. "He seems to be recovering quickly."

"He's young, getting the best of care and a whole lot of love."

"So have you been abused too?" Susan's eyes are full of innocence as she asks that loaded question.

I look into her deep brown eyes, "Couple of months after I grabbed Puu, I was in the Navy brig in Pearl Harbor because of marijuana. So yeah, I guess I was feeling a little abused too; only my sores are on the inside."

Susan is startled by my frank answer, "When did you get out of the brig?"

I glance at my watch, "just over a week ago."

Susan looks at me, almost like seeing me for the first time. Then she quickly picks up a stick and throws it for Puu. He is off in a burst of speed, snatches up the stick and runs back with it. Just before dropping it at Susan's feet he chomps down half crushing the stick and biting it in half."

"Does he always do that?" Susan is holding the two crushed pieces of stick.

"It's why I usually throw much bigger sticks."

Puu leads the way out to the parking lot where Revelstoke is parked. I unlock one door so Susan can peer inside. "Is this where you live?" she asks.

I snap my fingers at Puu who jumps inside. "It's where we live," I nod at Puu, "He considers it his own mobile dog house, I call it Revelstoke."

"You made this?"

"Yeah, it used to be a Chevy truck until I altered it a bit with a hammer and power saw.

Opening a cabinet under the sink, I pull out a heavy bag of dry dog food and half fill monster dog's dish, which is made from the lower third of a metal trashcan. Susan is watching Puu inhale his mountain of food. "Do you need feeding too?" I ask.

"Yeah," quips Susan, "but I wasn't going to ask by jerking on the back of your swimsuit." After both of us have eaten and Puu has gone back outside to play, Susan and I continue to talk for over an hour, then I suddenly realize that it is a perfect time to ask Susan out; the thought makes me tongue-tied. Susan crosses her long legs, brushes a wisp of hair from her face, looks right, then left, takes several deep breaths and probably wonders why I am not asking her out.

"Are you going to ask me out or not?" She finally asks.

"Ahh…err…I'd love to," I croak.

"You'd love to what?" asks Susan. She is affecting an innocent look.

"I'd love to ask you out," I blurt.

"Well, that's an original idea, why don't you try it?"

"Would you like to go out with me tonight?" I could not believe that there is a distinct quiver in my voice.

"Hmmmmm," she places a finger to her lips as if she is pondering my offer.

"Well?" I ask impatiently.

"I'm thinking about it." There is a mischievous glint to her eyes. Then she nods, "Okay, but you'll have to pick me up at the restaurant where I work. I get off at nine, but if you arrive early, I'll make you dinner."

I grin at her; it is a big sloppy grin that threatens to swallow my whole face.

"I'm glad we finally got that over with," teases Susan, "Dare I ask what we are going to do?"

"Listening to music in Waikiki would be nice." I feel the grin pulling at the flesh around my eyes probably giving me a Quasimodo look.

Later that afternoon we are in the parking lot with Susan standing beside Caroline's car, as they are getting ready to go. Susan gives me another one of her innocent looks then asks, "Would you like to know the address or even the name of the restaurant where I work?"

I feel like such an idiot as she writes the information down on a piece of paper and stuffs it into my T-shirt pocket. "Don't lose that," she quips.

My heart and I stand there watching them drive out of sight. I do a happy little jig about the parking lot. In the middle of a one-legged spin, I notice two of my surfer friends watching me, their surfboards tucked under their arms. Water is dripping from their wet shorts. They are standing in a puddle of their own making, which means they have been standing there for a while…they didn't look happy.

"I hope you're not going to tell us that you haven't been shooting pictures," pleads Jay.

"Ah…"

"Steve, this is the best surf we've had all year. I almost killed myself out there thinking you were getting it all on film.

"Ah…"

"Do you see his dog?" inquires Jay, "I swear I'm going to kill him, but we better not try it in front of that big crazy dog of his."

My shrill whistle brings Puu bounding up a couple of seconds later. He stops at the puddle at the surfers' feet to get a drink before jumping nonchalantly into the truck. "Well, gotta go guys," I smile and make a fast exit.

Parking that evening outside the restaurant where Susan works, I quickly pull on a pair of old jeans and my favorite Hawaiian shirt after giving it the sniff test. I practice my best Tom Selleck smile in front of the mirror, give Puu orders to guard the truck and then step out into the tropical night with my hopeful thoughts.

A small bell attached to the restaurant door tinkles as I walk into the restaurant. I immediately see Susan who steps quickly over to greet me. We stand there for a moment grinning at each other while the little bell jingles cheerfully above us.

Laulima is one of those Hawaiian hippie-type restaurants where customers sit directly on the floor on top of pillows while eating off low Japanese tables. Soft, environmental music drifts from the walls and sandalwood incense wafts lightly on the air. The place is packed, mostly with strange-looking characters—I fit right in.

On Susan's recommendation, I order a bean tostada, then she scurries off to serve the other tables while I try to appear as though I am not watching her every move. She turns to smile in my direction then disappears into the kitchen.

Unbeknownst to me, and despite the protests of the Hawaiian/ Chinese cook, she is busy building a monster bean tostada. She piles on the frijoles until they begin to slop over the side of the plate. Since I am watching the kitchen door as alertly as Puu observes an untended picnic basket, I see Susan as soon as she exits the kitchen. She is carrying a large plate on which squats a respectable bean mountain. I am wondering if it is for the family of four sitting at the next table when she abruptly plops it down in front of me. An ounce of beans slops onto the table. I stare in awe at the size of the bean volcano. "This is a tostada?" I blurt.

"Is there anything wrong with it?" Susan is again affecting her innocent smile.

""No, it looks…fine," I offer lamely, "any chance of trading this spoon in for a shovel?" If my Hawaiian shirt had long sleeves, I would have rolled them up.

Ten minutes later, Susan returns as I am sopping up the last of the beans with a corn tortilla. "You ate the whole thing," Susan is gaping at my empty plate. She runs back into the kitchen and returns dragging the Chinese cook. "Look," she points proudly, "he ate it all."

Instead of listening to music, we decide to walk on the beach in Waikiki under a full moon. We talk about harmless subjects discovering each other with words, while sensual energies lurk subtly beneath our social dialogue.

It is Susan's idea to go back to visit Puu. After romping with him in the parking lot, we go inside Revelstoke where I put some Hawaiian slack key music on the stereo and light a few candles. Above us, the stained-glass skylight admits a soft lunar glow from the full moon. Falling silent, we stare into each other's eyes, then Susan raises a hand to her pony tail, a moment later her golden hair falls in a fan across her upper back and shoulders where it gathers the soft candle light and seems to have a sparkle all its own. I take a silken lock into my hand and lightly place it to my lips. Susan's eyes are very wide and very trusting as I kiss her.

A deep rumbling voice reaches out from the lower bunk sounding like a bad-tempered bear just disturbed in its lair. "The name's Mose." The cavernous voice pauses, "Looks man, since we's be bunkies, we gotta talks some, but it don't be meaning we's friends or nothin. If sumthin goes down, Old Mose is gonna have to waste ya. Nothin personal whitey, just the way things is."

I say nothing.

"Hey whitey," the voice thickens as he snarls, "youze listening to Mose?"

"Yeah, you said you may have to waste me."

"Good," grunts Mose, "so longs as ya understands."

Actually, I do not understand any of this, but for one thought lurking in a corner of my mind, *I did this to myself! It's my fault, now how am I ever going to live with it?*

"Youze gots any cigarettes?" I listen for, but hear not the slightest friendliness in that deep baritone.

"Don't smoke."

"I knows youze don't smoke, white boy," he grumbles, "Youze don't carries da smell."

It is startling to realize that Mose is aware of my odor. It is such a primal thing, one animal smelling another. Does he also scent my fear? My mind takes a step backwards in its humanness. I have to think differently here. It is now all about survival and it strips away everything that has ever brought me comfort. From now on, I am going to have to exist and think on a more primordial level. I have to let the animal inside of me awaken. Here it is not going to be about intelligence, but rather cunning; compassion has to stand aside so a more brutal intensity can assure the survival of the animal abruptly prowling about within me.

"They sells cigarettes in duh commissary store," growls the voice, "smoking makes Old Mose relaxed if youze catches my drift."

I stare at my hands then clinch each into a fist and scrutinize them carefully—they don't look nearly big enough. These are what I am going to have to rely upon to survive in this primal inmate world. I instantly know that I will never resort to making any kind of knife or other weapon. I will survive, I will fight if I have to, but what will happen to me in the process?

The evening passes incredibly slowly. I have no way to measure time. The guard walks the catwalk at irregular intervals. His presence announced before he arrives by the tinkling sound of his heavy key ring and then by the thud of his heavy boots. Mose gets up to relieve himself. The small cell rapidly fills with an overpowering reek of urine. He continues to pee; it takes a long time for him to empty his bladder. There is the rush of flushing water, then the gurgling of the toilet, but the smell lingers.

"Gots anything to eat?"

I roll away from facing the wall. Mose's huge head and shoulders hover at the edge of my mattress. He looks hopeful. "Didn't sees ya carrying anything in, figured youze might have sumthin in youze pockets." One of his huge hands is pawing at my mattress. The scarred knuckles bare a prison house tattoo, "HATE."

I glance at the other hand. It says "LOVE." I anticipated it would say, "KILL."

"Youze don'ts have nuthin in your pockets?" Mose says it almost sadly, a disappointed bear.

I shake my head, "No, I don't have anything."

"So whats good are ya?" he growls and stomps the single pace to the opposite wall, "Whys do I always gets da losers?"

I am amazed. He thinks me a loser...I was thinking that he was the loser.

Mose's head disappears as he leans over then begins rustling about in the locker. "Nuthin," he mutters, slamming the thin metal door closed. He lowers his bulk onto the lower bunk grumbling despondently.

The lights go out abruptly as the guard yells for the inmates to shut down their radios, which only a few possess. I lay in the darkness alone with my thoughts, but for the lingering night sound of a restless cellblock. I listen to the pacing of the guards, the scuff of boots, the grumbling of the inmates and softly, almost beyond the range of my hearing...someone crying.

"Good thing that ain't youze!" snarls Mose. "Can't be standing men crying. Makes me wanna break sumpin." He snickers, "Now that would give em sumpin to cry about."

Doesn't seem to matter that I am not answering; Mose is content to do all the talking in the dark cell.

"Youze ever heard a grown man squeal?"

I feel my heart begin to race. Is he threatening me?

"I's heard em hit the high notes, just likes theys a girl."

Abruptly the blood begins surging through my veins and there is a rushing sound in my head. Is Mose working himself up to something? My fists clinch and unclench as my body readies to defend itself.

"Youze one lucky white boy up there cause Old Mose ain't into none of that," he chuckles, "bets youze real glad to hear that ain'ts ya?"

He punches the bottom of my mattress forcefully. For him it is a playful contact, but I feel the massive power behind that solid contact. "Youze glad that Old Mose ain't gay ain't ya?"

Relief is flooding through me, "Absolutely." I am surprised to hear a small laugh escape my lips.

Mose snorts then echoes my laugh, chuckling deeply. "Bets youze didn't think youzed be giggling on ya first night in da joint."

"No Mose," I smile into the darkness, "I surely did not."

A gentle answer turns away wrath, but a harsh word stirs up
anger. Proverbs 15:1

"Courage is fear that has said its prayers,"
Dorothy Bernard

Chapter 24

TERMINAL ISLAND FEDERAL PRISON,

J-1 (JAIL UNIT 1), OCTOBER 1982

N THOSE first few waking moments before my mind fully engages I hope beyond reason that it is all just a bad dream; that I am not really confined in a Federal prison. Then I hear the rumble and clang of a cell door slamming and the grumbling sound of inmates awakening in the cellblock as the reality of my incarceration rushes back and pounces upon me. There is a sudden ratcheting noise of heavy circuit breakers being thrown in rapid succession then the darkness is swept away first by the dim light in the cell followed immediately by the arch lights over the catwalk. I close my eyes not yet willing to let the chaos of a waking cellblock descend upon me.

This is actually my fourth day of incarceration. Immediately following my arrest, I was taken to the Los Angeles County Jail for interrogation and processing from free man to federal inmate. I refused to give any information until I could talk to a lawyer. Since I did not have one, I would have to rely on the government, which seemed slow in providing a court appointed attorney. I also was not given access to a telephone in that first twenty-four hours, not that I wanted to call anyone. I could not imagine calling my mother, "Hello Mom, it is Stephen, look I am in prison." *Nope. No way was I going to make that call.*

The Marshals took me to court the second day for official reprimanding into custody with a bail of fifty thousand dollars. I had no idea if that was high or low. I also now had a court appointed attorney. He told me that I was in extremely serious trouble and that he was only temporarily assigned to my case. It did not seem like a good idea to talk to him, so I didn't. It was so strange; here I was in the biggest crisis of my life and I could not talk about it except to myself and I was remarkably uninformed there. So, I just sat where they told me to sit and walked when they told me to move. It was a bit like my first day at the U.S. Navy Boot Camp only a whole lot more depressing. At boot camp, I was looking forward to military adventure and seeing the world, which is why I joined the Navy. Sitting in the jail cell, my perspectives were solely about extremely long-term incarceration and I did not even want to speculate about the inmate misadventures that waited for me in the very disturbing future.

The highlight of the day occurred later that evening with the arrival of a very rumpled and upset Morgan. In his confused and self-pitying state, he was not a wealth of information either.

"Have you told them anything?" whispers Morgan urgently.

"No." It is my fourth or fifth word of the day.

"Good, don't talk to anyone. Just follow my lead," urges a thoroughly frightened Morgan. He has every reason to be worried. As the great mastermind behind this criminal venture he has succeeded in ruining his family and aligning himself with the most deadly and bloodthirsty criminal enterprises in the world...the Medellin drug cartel, which has butchered thousands of people in South and North America. The United States Government wants to put him and his colleagues (that being his sons, Stretch and myself) behind bars for a very long time, but the Medellin Cartel is probably already putting out a price tag on our heads. Not only has

Morgan lost millions of dollars worth of cocaine, he is serious leak potential. Which he is proving right now as he calls attention to himself in the form of an urgent need for a telephone. He spends the next hour demanding the right to call his attorney, but is generally ignored by the guards who have already told him that he could not call until the morning.

I listen to Morgan as he paces the cell, which does not fit any of my concepts of a jail cell. Instead of bars the front of the cell and its door are inch-thick plate glass. It does not take a genius to figure out that we are probably being videotaped inside a special cell wired for sound, which is why Morgan did not want to talk to me about the arrest, which is just fine with my intense desire to be left alone. I do not need to hear about his problems, my mind is full of my own. *What am I going to tell my family?*

I could not help but wonder if Morgan is serious about my following his lead. So far his leadership has resulted in the worst seven months of my life and the future only looks to be a whole lot worse. I decide to pretend to be asleep to discourage any more dialogue. Morgan would just lie to me and I am not in the mood for any more of his deceptions or manipulations. Then a sudden thought stands up right in the middle of my consciousness waving its arms for attention. I do not work for Morgan anymore. I don't have to listen to him, obey his instructions or anything. The power he had exercised over me is gone! While analyzing that amazing thought, a third defendant in our case arrives in the adjoining cell

Morgan hears the one of the guards mention the man's first name causing Morgan to leap out of his bunk and rush to the plate glass. After the visible guards leave, he whispers loudly, "John is that you?"

"Who's that?" Answers a harried sounding voice.

"It's me. Morgan Hetrick. So they got you too."

"Yeah, I know."

"Don't say anything," urges Morgan, "I figure these cells are wired."

"No kidding. Look I don't want to talk right now anyway."

"Okay, we'll wait until the morning."

Morgan rushes over to my bunk. "That is John Z. DeLorean," he gushes.

"Who?" I ask.

"John DeLorean, don't you know who John DeLorean is?" Morgan is exasperated.

"No," I shake my head. At the moment, I did not really much care. It is the middle of the night and sleep is my only temporary escape from the madness that my life has become.

"John DeLorean as in the DeLorean sports car," Morgan sounds like he is lecturing a third grader. "As in ex-Vice President of General Motors, multimillionaire jetsetter, cover of Time Magazine kind of guy."

"Oh." Okay, I am impressed, but so what? "What's he doing in the next cell?"

"He is going to be a defendant in our case."

"Why?" I knew I am sounding clueless, which I am. Morgan never confided anything to me until absolutely the last moment, which reduced the chances of my making a rational decision. This is not an excuse, just a reflection on Morgan's manipulations. He did the same thing to the girls he was always after.

Morgan leans in and whispers very quietly into my ear, "The cocaine in your car was for him."

"I don't think I want to know this," I answer heatedly. I cannot believe that Morgan thinks whispering will keep the electronic bugs from hearing him. Anyone who reads spy novels knows you need a background noise like flowing water to mask being overheard. "Look Morgan, I just want to go to sleep and next time you want to whisper something to me flush the toilet first."

Morgan peers over at the toilet bowl, "Hey, good idea. You can do the flushing thing while I talk with DeLorean in the morning."

The idea of me repeatedly flushing a toilet so Morgan can try to manipulate DeLorean, Cover of Time Magazine kind of guy, confirms that I am finished working for this man.

"You just wait until tomorrow morning, when the press gets wind of this," Morgan fans his hand, "it is going to be a real media circus." Morgan suddenly smiles. He is standing right next to my upper bunk with a great big grin plastered on his face. He is looking forward to tomorrow. Talk about an attention hound. I roll over and face the wall. *It would be a real drag for my mom to see my picture in the paper.* It is the last mental event in my thoughts as I drop back off to sleep.

While I am sleeping on my jail bunk, the presses of the nation's newspapers are in overdrive about DeLorean's arrest. My mom did not learn about my arrest from the Los Angeles Times where the three of us had made the front-page dead center. She got to hear it from her television on the morning news; just seconds before her telephone lit up with multiple calls from friends...people who were less than friends looking to gloat...family and the national press.

The following day is everything Morgan is hoping for and daydreaming about; for me it is a media nightmare.

Sitting in a cell in the basement of the Federal Court Building in Los Angeles, I watch the Marshals talking excitedly about all the media attention. They are arguing over who is going to get to escort me. A female Marshal with masculine, close-cropped hair and wearing Ray Ban aviator sunglasses comes up with the simple solution, "Why don't we all go?"

A general nodding of heads lends approval to the idea. "Hey, let's really dress him up in chains," offers a fat Marshal, "make him look like a serious bad guy. The press will love it." The woman Marshal looks me up and down then she grins, obviously, she is terribly amused at the concept of me being a serious bad guy.

She wraps a stainless steel chain tightly around my waist twice then she cuffs and padlocks my hands to the chain. Another Marshal attaches leg irons to my ankles with a two-foot chain leash. In front of the steel exit door, eight Marshals pack tightly about me whispering excitedly to each other. The fat Marshal grabs the door handle then looks expectantly at the others, "Everyone ready?" he asks with a leer. There is a general nodding of heads and giggles of anticipation. Surprisingly it is not the female Marshal doing the giggling.

"Okay," smiles the fat guard, a toothpick peeks out from twin fat cheeks, "then let's rock-and-roll." We hit the lobby going at full speed. My feet are only occasionally in contact with the floor as the Marshals mostly carry me like a trophy. My flying wedge of Marshals plows with glee into the surprised crowd.

People stop to stare excitedly at the chained super-criminal. There are shouted questions and even louder bogus answers. Most figure me to be a serial murderer or human predator. We pass a gentle looking, middle-age woman; she glares at me with hate-filled eyes. I want to shout out that I am not the evil person they suspect, but the chains and heavy Marshal escort nullify my unspoken words.

The Marshals force their way to the elevator bank, seizing the first arriving car. All the people who are already inside are rooted out. A man in an expensive gray suit begins to protest. The woman Marshal jerks him out by the lapels and sends him spinning into the crowd.

After the doors close, the Marshals laugh happily amongst themselves and compare the individual damage they have done in the crowded lobby; obviously, they are having a good time enjoying their role as a posse of bullies.

The elevator doors open at the eighth floor. At the other end of the corridor, a crowd of reporters obstructs the double doors to the courtroom. Seeing the determined approach of the phalanx of Marshals, they quickly clear a path as we jostle our way inside.

Near the back sits my mother and my big brother Jim. We make momentary eye contact; hers are wet from crying, mine are full of guilt. The crowd of Marshals hustles me to a long table where Morgan sits rubbernecking at the sea of press. He has two attorneys sitting next to him.

The woman Marshall takes about thirty seconds to get the waist chain and manacles unlocked. She is so distracted eyeballing the press that she chips a nail. "Damn," she exclaims briefly inspecting the damaged nail, then she grins at me, "This is so exciting. Hope you have a nice long trial."

I just stare at her wondering if she would like to have Morgan's private telephone number, I know he would be into it.

I glance over at the other defendant table. A tall-distinguished man with a lantern chin and silver hair sits between two attorneys. Two or three legal assistants sit in the row of seats behind him.

"Sit down," orders a tall Federal Marshall standing behind me.

"Who's the man at the other table?" I ask even though I know it must be DeLorean.

"Are you kidding?" he laughs, "That is John Z. DeLorean the famous automaker. You should see his wife, now there's a looker." He suddenly gets the look that an original idea is occurring to him. "Hey guys," he whispers excitedly to the other Marshalls who are still crowding the table. "You guys seen DeLorean's wife? Christina Ferrari is a world-class model; talk about a looker. She's on TV all the time. I'm cancelling my vacation next week."

When a person is facing a major life crisis, normal conversations seem so out of proportion and unrealistic. I could not believe that these tough Marshall's are overcome by the media blitz that this case is attracting. Earlier in the morning, I had seen two of these men and the woman with the chipped nail roughing up a Hispanic gang member; now they are media groupies.

As I sit down the fleet of Federal Marshalls abruptly realize that they are standing there with nothing to do. Two of the faster thinking of the group quickly drops their ample behinds in a couple of seats in the row behind me leaving the rest reluctantly to fade back out of the courtroom.

I glance back over at DeLorean's table, it is the first time I have seen the man and suddenly I am beginning to realize what it is going to be like to live in the media shadow of a famous person. First DeLorean's and then Hetrick's bail is set at five million dollars each. Then the prosecutor stands up and asks the judge to raise my bail from fifty to two hundred and fifty thousand dollars. The judge agrees instantly, which I know is not good news.

The John Z. DeLorean case would develop into what has been called the Drug Trial of the Century and it became an international media blitz. The vast media coverage would actually last for several years with feature articles and leading stories in every major network and newspaper in the industrialized world. Playboy Magazine would later run a feature article on the case, which would please Morgan to no end. The most surprising aspect of the media coverage for me is when I read my name along with DeLorean's and Hetrick's in a Doonesbury cartoon strip. It gave the term a media circus a completely new meaning to me in a very personal way. In prison, I would receive many letters from friends I had lost contact with who were eager to hear my thoughts on the trial. I was also about to learn a new term, celebrity inmate...it was not good news.

When the judge finishes with us, my Marshall horde hustles back into the courtroom. They have been waiting eagerly out in the corridor. They wrap the chain back around my waist and clamp the cuffs firmly on my wrists. I cannot help but notice that Hetrick and DeLorean only have two Marshalls each, but then again they have all their attorneys as escorts.

Lying on my bunk back at Terminal Island Federal Prison with my eyes closed refusing to acknowledge that it is morning, I hear Mose roll over and fart. It is not just a simple passing of gas, but rather a major flatulence event; a rumbling, long-winded, passage of gurgling and flapping sounds that is probably leaving another visible trail in Mose's boxers. Then a foul odor like a physical presence ascends from the shadows below filling the jail cell with a nose-hair singeing smell that lingers in the upper levels of the cell where my mattress lies. Just when the air is beginning to return to its normal musky, mildew bouquet, Mose leverages his huge bulk up from the bunk and plops down on the toilet. Not ready at all for what is about to happen next I roll over to face the wall and pull the dirty pillow over my head. Mose is on the toilet for the better part of ten torturous minutes. Half way into it, I am considering asking for a courtesy flush, then decide it would be better to suffer through it.

He finishes up just as breakfast arrives. The guard pushes two plastic trays through a slot in the grill. Mose sets mine down on the locker and then climbs back onto the lower bunk with his tray. I scramble down to look at the tray. There are a couple of unrecognizable items on the tray. One is a flat liver-colored disk somewhat greasy with curled crispy edges. The other is a white pile that appears to be some kind of clumpy cereal. Beside it is a hard-boiled egg, two pieces of burnt white toast, a half-melted pad of butter and a pint-sized, half-crushed, carton of milk.

"Youze sits on the toilet," Mose interrupts my examination of the mystery meat.

I look at the recommended seat questionably, "I do?" This is not good news.

"So we's can talk."

Holding my tray, I cannot help but notice that there are still a few chunky things sticking to the inside of the bowl. Hoping I am not about to commitment a major inmate etiquette fopas, I push and vigorously hold down the handle giving the toilet a through washing out, which does not accomplish all I hoped it would.

I am not sure if I am ready for a social Mose. Then I notice it is not me he is looking at but my tray

"Would youze sits down and stop screwing around," Mose is getting impatient to visit.

"Do you know what this is?" I ask pointing at the thin slab of what appears to be some kind of processed meat that has been dreadfully abused. I sniff at it, but my sense of smell is not functioning so well after Mose's morning activities.

"It's fried baloney, don't ya wants it?"

"No!" I recoil at the thought, "I am a vegetarian."

Mose's hand strikes so fast that I barely see it snatching the fried baloney from my plastic tray. He pops it into his mouth with great relish and chews enthusiastically. "Never met no vegetarian before," he says around the rapidly disappearing baloney. While watching the demise of the fried baloney, I am thinking it would have been a lot better if I could have offered him the fried baloney and then he could have politely accepted and I would have passed it to him with my fork. Only they do not give us forks, rather it is a combination plastic fork and spoon called a Spork.

"So what does youze eats?"

Mose seems genuinely interested and it is an excellent chance to build better relations with him. "We try to only eat what's good for us; vegetables of course, fruits, nuts, and grains. We try to avoid animal products like cheese…"

Mose hand strikes again interrupting me in mid sentence. It is like a black snake striking. One moment my hard-boiled egg is sitting on the tray next to the unidentified white pile and an instant later, it is gone.

"Hey!" the word just kind of leaps out of my mouth.

Mose rolls the egg on his tray fracturing the shell into tiny white pieces. His thick fingers quickly peel most of the shell away and he pops it into his mouth. "Animal product," he mouths.

I watch his giant white teeth mashing my egg about. Then it is gone as he maneuvers his tongue to suck something out from the gap between his two front teeth except one of the teeth is missing; it is a rather large gap and it causes Mose to lisp. Mose eats with his mouth full on wide open. It is kind of like watching a spinning garbage disposal occasionally spitting out a chunk or two. "I was considering eating that egg." I am trying to sound just a bit offended without being too offensive. Sitting opposite Mose with him half in shadow and half lit by the dull yellow bulb above, I see just how massive and muscular he is with biceps the size of my thighs. He is sitting leaning forward, the thickness of his shoulders, layered with corded muscles and a covering of blackheads, is startling. At that moment, if he wanted my whole tray he could have it. Yet, I did not doubt that I needed to exercise my masculinity or he was going to be walking me around on a short leash.

Mose shrugs, "Youze want those grits?"

So, that is what the white pile is. Growing up in California I have never seen grits before. It is just something I read about in books. I quickly plunge my Spork possessively into the grit pile. I am very suspicious that Mose is not looking to be social at all. He just wants me on the toilet so he could raid my tray.

"Youze wants to take a good look at those grits," he says opening his eyes wide, the white around his pupils flash in the shadow of the upper bunk.

"Why?" No way I am going to lose my grits to the human food vacuum.

"Pries it apart and looks for lumps."

"Lumps?" I hesitantly probe the grit pile with my Spork, which is indeed kind of chunky.

"They's snot in it."

"What!"

"Snot," Mose rubs his nose then realizes it needs picking, which he does aggressively with an index finger the size of a large sausage. "Inmates, they's cooks the food. Somes times they blows snot into it…sames with da meatloaf and da oatmeal."

I hold my tray out to Mose who enthusiastically swipes the grits off onto his tray with his thick fingers.

I look at the two pieces of burnt toast, tab of melted butter and half-crushed milk carton and wonder how I have been so quickly conned out of most of my breakfast. Munching on the toast, I see Mose getting eye-lock on the squished milk carton. "Don't even think about it," I grumble.

At eight in the morning, the guard opens all the doors on our tier and yells, "Yard time."

We file out from the dim interior into a cold late October morning. The sea fog is back; it drifts about the narrow J-1 yard, which is a constricted rectangle less than a hundred feet long by about sixty-five feet wide. Tall walls topped with razor-sharp concertina wire closely hem in the narrow cement yard. The razor wire drifts in and out of visibility with the shifting fog. A basketball hoop hangs from the far wall and in a corner, there is a rusted out universal gym. Mose lumbers over towards the universal and sits down his ample buttocks on the bench press. He pushes the pin through the bottom of the weight stack and commences doing repeated bench presses effortlessly. Walking about the yard, I sneak a look and notice from the numbers that he is lifting two hundred and fifty pounds like it is nothing.

"The guy's an animal."

I glance over and notice a lanky white guy walking a step or two behind me. He has long stringy brown hair, acne scars, an Adams Apple that bobs when he talks and a shifty look that seems to be taking in everything and everyone in the yard. He shuffles, shoulders rounded, chest concave, a serious doper. Normally I would avoid a character like this, but glancing around I notice that his type is in the majority for us Caucasians. Fact is I do not see a normal looking person in the whole bunch of us. Everyone either looks mean or is making their very best effort at looking mean. Most of the inmates are either Mexican or African American. Of the forty men in the yard, only ten are Caucasian. Later I would learn that the Latinos inmates were from many different countries including Colombia, Nicaragua, Honduras, Mexico, Costa Rica and the USA.

"Hey new meat," he drawls, "I'm Hank."

"Really?" An image of my good friend leaps to mind. I think of his smile, his strong character and solid moral commitment. In my mind, I see him in uniform at our graduation, standing tall radiating confidence and good will. Then I look at this corrupt Hank, wearing dirty coveralls, slinking at my side. It is obvious that this guy doesn't have both oars in the water. I shake my head sadly. I have forfeited my friendship with the real Hank; instead, this counterfeit Hank is now forced upon me. "My name's Steve."

"Everyone knows what your name is new meat," Hank smiles showing gaps where he is missing a couple of teeth. The others are yellowed and grossly crooked.

"Because I'm the new guy?"

"Nah, you're DeLorean's codefendant, seen your picture in the paper." Hank attempts to nudge me with his elbow, but I step away from the gesture. I absolutely do not want to know this guy.

Hank nods towards the far wall of the J-1 yard. "That's Jail Unit 2. It's where they put DeLorean and Hetrick. It's a lot better than

The Hole."

This is all news to me. I am wondering what other tidbits of interesting information Hank might know, then he drops a bombshell.

"Looks like they got you figured to cooperate."

"What? What are you talking about?"

"Ratting off DeLorean," he shakes his head as if I am clueless,
which is not far from the truth. "Come on, aren't you a little curious
why the Feds stuck you in The Hole while the other two are cruising
in J-2?"

"Hadn't thought much about it." Actually, I hadn't thought about
it at all. Mose had been occupying most of my waking thoughts.

As if he is reading my mind Hank nods towards the universal
where Mose has a two hundred pound black inmate riding the
weight stack so he can do four hundred fifty pound bench presses.
The inch-thick steel lifting bar is slightly bent under the massive
load. "Yeah, well I bet you thought plenty about your cellmate. Ain't
no accident you being in his cell and all."

"What are you talking about?"

"Man, you really are clueless." Hank is looking at me like I am
leading him on. Then he shrugs, "You better smarten up dude or
you ain't gonna last long."

*Smarten up? I have the village idiot looking at me as if I am a couple
of fries short of a Happy Meal. I am getting the feeling that in prison intelligence is not measured by intellect, but rather by brute cunning. Yet maybe
right now the smartest thing I can do is gather information. Just seems
strange soliciting it from the local doper sporting half of a warm six-pack
for an I.Q.*

"The hacks don't normally put new white meat in with the
baddest and meanest black dude in the whole joint." Hank raises
an eyebrow, "understand now?"

"Meanest and baddest?"

"It's what I said. You've heard about the kid who doesn't get
to do recess with the rest of the students because he doesn't play
well with others?" Hank makes his eyes big and round giving him
a strong resemblance to a surprised scarecrow, "Well Mose is not

allowed in general prison population because he doesn't play well with the other inmates."

"So you think they put me into his cell to scare me into cooperating."

"Well duh!" He does a slow grin, look I don't want to be seen talking with you too much."

"Why not?" So now, I am the J-1 leper?

"When you rat out DeLorean it's not going to look too good to have been hanging out with you."

Now that is impressive, Mr. Dirt Bag is worried about his sterling reputation by being seen with me. Prison is really going to mess with my head.

Half an hour later, I am back in the cell with Mose, who's in a slightly better mood having gotten to throw around some heavy iron. "Youze better start hitting the weight pile boy so youze looks less like prey."

I have always considered myself in excellent physical condition, particularly as an ex-Navy frogman. I have run marathons, do push-ups in sets of fifty, pull-ups in sets of sixteen or more and can crank out several hundred sit-ups in a couple of minutes…and Mose thinks I look like a walking victim?

"Youze wants some advice?"

"Sure."

"Wouldn't be talking about your vegetarian thing; makes youze like a rabbit or rodent looking to get swallered up."

"Better if I look like a predator, huh?"

"Youze? A predator?" Mose belly laughs, "Ain't gonna happen veggie man."

I must have looked slightly depressed. Mose smiles showing huge white teeth, "Gots sum more advice. If youze survive being in my cell youze gonna get some kind of respect out in da yard."

"We back to talking about cigarettes again?"

"Na, I ain't much into smoking, it's just expected. But if youze shares your meat, I will keep our secret about youze being a rabbit and all."

"Not a problem for me." I look at Mose more closely. He is

carrying many scars; the physical and emotional ones are visibly present. This man hasn't lived an easy life.

"Why they got you in the Hole?" *Wow, did I just say that? Last thing in the world I needed was to start sounding like Old Mose.*

Mose glares for a moment, his wide nostrils flare, "Cuze I'ze a real man. Don't tolerate those whimps in da population. Everyones acting like theys sumthing...strutting and paradon...talking da jive. Youze opens youze mouth to me youze better be prepared to backs up what youze says. Youze don'ts wants youze mouth over loading whats your muscles canst handle.

"Oh."

> *"Perhaps the most valuable result of all education is the ability to make yourself do the thing you have to do, when it ought to be done, whether you like it or not; it is the first lesson that ought to be learned; and however early a man's training begins, it is probably the last lesson that he learns thoroughly."*
> Thomas H. Huxley 1825-1895

Mose and I were bunkies for the first week of my incarceration at Terminal Island, the most intense seven days of my life. We never became real friends, I had to guard my words carefully. Seldom did we talk...particularly not about anything important to him or to me. He was a man boiling with anger and resentment augmented with an extremely low stress threshold. His rage always lurked just beneath a fiery temperament that needed but the barest excuse to come roaring forth. He lusted to break things. Since our bunk and locker were metal his physical rage was channeled towards other inmates. It was amazing that though we were crammed in that tiny cell over a period of a very long seven days, I did nothing to trigger Mose's wrath...or maybe he just tolerated me for my share of the fried baloney.

When people ask me what it was like to be incarcerated, I often tell them, "Go into your bathroom, invite in two or three of the

scariest and most socially unacceptable people you know, and
then lock the door for a couple of days." Take super-stressed men,
already prone to violence and with maximum brain damage from
drug abuse then force them into narrow confined spaces for long
extended periods with a less than caring staff ensures that there will
be maximum carnage. The Hole was well named.

The morning of my eighth day would reveal a depth of Mose, I
could not have imagined, nor the impact it would have on how I
thought about myself as a brand new inmate.

"Yard time," yells the guard repeatedly as he walks the length of
the cellblock dragging his truncheon across the bars with a loud
rapping sound. Men hurriedly put shoes or sandals on their feet
and stand eagerly at their doors. Twenty cell doors open automatically as forty men step forward, make a right turn and descend
down the metal staircase then out through a side door and file out
into the yard. Mose heads straight for the universal gym where he is
always assured first place on the bench press by right of weight. Two
teams quickly form for a game of basketball...no whites or Latinos
allowed. A few of the older Mexican inmates sit down at a wooden
table to roll cigarettes and enjoy a loudly played game of dominos
where the pieces are slammed down with all the enthusiasm and
vengeance of a knife planted in an opponent's back. Many of the
inmates begin walking in a counterclockwise direction.

I tighten the laces on my running shoes, while noting a couple of
inmates staring at them enviously. Running shoes are rare in prison
and apt to be stolen or just taken under threat of violence. Being
held up for your shoes is a form of inmate extortion that probably
has its roots in elementary schools where bullies learn the tricks of
the trade by assaulting smaller classmates for their milk money or
lunch box candy. In prison, if you surrender your shoes without a
fight the harassment and violence will absolutely not stop with just
losing the leather off your feet.

Before anyone has a chance to say anything to me, I launch off
on a fast-paced counterclockwise run. I could not generate much
of a sustained speed with so many of us in the narrow yard, so I did

short fast sprints with rapid decelerations. As happens in confined places with people moving randomly about, I had a minor collision with a black inmate trying to save the basketball from going out of bounds. Avoiding physical contact with other inmates in prison is an extremely serious matter, particular between the races. He curses me with a foul word though the fault is not mine...well mostly it is not mine; we just happen to be in the same place at the same time. Since I have the most momentum, it moves him back a step or two. As our attention focuses on each other, the game pauses, inmates stand and stare. The man is tall, muscular, sweating and upset. He glances right and left noticing that the other players are watching.

"Sorry," I say lightly. It does not hurt to accept fault. He is still trying to decide what to do so I am offering him an easy out. I watch him trying to make a decision. One of my blessings and great faults is that I have a very fast mind. I am not referring to any kind of special intelligence. If I were that smart, I wouldn't be where I am. I'm only making reference to the speed that this brain processes information. I just seem to get there a lot faster than most people... not that the result is always the best decision or action on my part. The biggest problem with a gift like this is that I often have to wait for others to make their decision and since I also have HADD DE (Hyper Attention Deficit Disorder Deluxe Edition), it means I can get bored waiting for someone to decide to do something. This can be very unsocial and borders on downright rude behavior on my part...or so I have been advised on a numerous occasions.

"Sorry?" he still has not made up his mind where he wants to go with this. As a matter of fact neither have I. They say everyone gets tested in prison, maybe this is my moment. The guard is watching from behind the chain link fence. He should have seen that I did not do anything major to cause the problem. If I am going to have to prove myself doing it in the light of day with even odds and no weapons present has a certain merit.

In my younger days, I might have already clobbered this person. Mose and I were a bit more alike that he might have imagined. In high school, I was the tall skinny kid that was often the target of bullies. I soon learned that bullies like to take a couple of moments to draw everyone's attention as they worked themselves into a confrontation with an apparently easy target. While a bully was going through the slow mind process of getting ready, I would just hit him as many times as possible before he realized the fight was already in progress.

The man tosses the basketball to another inmate and smiles. *Okay playtime* the words thunder through my mind. Without really seeming to, I drop into a defensive stance. Appearance wise it does not seem like I have done much of anything...but I have.

For more than a decade, I had studied various types of martial arts. I hold a black belt in taekwondo and a brown belt in Preying Mantis Gung Fu. It was the Gung Fu that I favored because it lent itself well to my tall frame. Just as the name implies I would adopt the fighting techniques and stance of the Preying Mantis insect. Bending the knees slightly lowers my center of gravity a couple of inches below my belly button giving me a solid stance for blocks, hits and kicks as well as faster lateral movement. I can quickly surge into or away from my attacker. Turning my toes slightly inwards improves my traction and re-enforces the centering of my body. My arms seem to just hang a bit forward, but actually they are instantly ready to block with an upward movement that is the classical mantis arms up, hands (or claws) draped down. The advantage of this hand/arm movement is that it is very relaxed making the reactions extremely fast, fluid and lethal. To block an incoming strike I only have to raise my arm angled into it, brush the oncoming hand or fist to the side just far enough to miss my head or torso. By letting my cupped hand slide over my opponent's wrist I can momentarily capture and redirect his striking fist a bit downward while accelerating his forward momentum. This brings the opponent's head down and forward as I release the wrist and reverse the motion with a back fist strike to his nose which is potentially accelerated into the impact by his off balance forward momentum. The entire movement takes years to learn well, yet can then be delivered in just a heartbeat or two. Over the next couple of seconds, there will be a whole range of other options open for ending the fight depending upon how much damage one wants to do. That question will be determined by whether my opponent is trained in the martial arts or is an experienced street fighter because then it can get real messy for both of us.

The man I am facing is right handed, which he reveals as his right shoulder dips slightly. Okay he is telegraphing a right punch. The heal of my left foot rises slightly into a cat stance as I prepare to pivot into his strike. I will block his strike with my right hand and forearm then rotate my body at the hips to the left redirecting his momentum. This generates a considerable amount of energy mass ratio as his body and head follows the downward direction of his right arm at which point I will reverse direction delivering the aforementioned right-handed back fist to his nose, which should equate to physically lighting this guy up. This fight could well be over with just the one back fist.

"Hey Lewis." Mose hasn't spoken loudly from his seated position at the bench press, but he instantly has the other black's man complete attention. Mose does a shoulder shrug; a *let it go* kind of motion.

The black man looks back at me, snatches the ball from his companion and returns to the game.

After the encounter, I have lost my urge to run so I just wander about the narrow yard occasionally staring through the chain link fence at the general population yard, which is about a hundred times larger than our small confined area. Glancing about me, I wonder about the men who are mostly hanging out in groups of two or three talking softly; bank robbers, murderers, gang bangers, drug dealers and the occasional smuggler like me. *Wow, what have I gotten myself into?* I wonder for the thousandth time.

Back in our cell, I stand watching the barred grill automatically sliding closed in unison with all the other doors on our tier and then turn to climb up onto my bunk. Instead, I find an angry Mose standing right in front of me. Up close, he is so huge, towering over me. His muscles, swollen with blood from his work out, stretch his sweat stained.T-shirt across his massive chest and thick arms. He glares as he takes a deep breath and jabs two thick fingers into my chest. "Youze is one stupid white boy!" he growls.

"What!" The two fingers are shoving me up against the bars...it hurts.

"Shuts up and listens," snarls Moses. "What youze doings runnin alls overs da yard likes youze owns it getting in everyone's business."

"I was just running."

"Don't youze know about respect or nuttin? Everyones be needin their space and youze out theres running through it likes youze got no respect for thems. Most important thing in da yard is respect."

"I didn't know," my response sounds lame, like I am answering to an elementary school teacher for a playground foul up.

"Looks, be drug deals a goin down, gangs jiving bout their private stuff, the queers wanton to talks their loves words and youze rabbiting all bout putting everyones on edge. Thens youze gets a run in with Lewis. Shoulda said sorry and moved on, but no youzes gots to stands there in his face egging em on."

"I wasn't egging him on," I argue.

"Yeah, wasn't that youze I saw getting ready to do some of daht karate dancing?"

How did Mose know about that? I wonder. I did not actually do anything noticeable.

"So what was youze big plan afters you hits him?"

"Plan?"

"Don't plays stupid." Mose is poking harder with his two fingers. "Youze thinks if youze hits him it's all over? Youze knuckles a gang member front of everyones and youze thinks hes gonna just forgets bout it? Youze be dead tonight afore youze even knows it."

"I was going to pop him in the nose." I surrender the information.

"I knows that," Mose turns away from me and sits down on his bunk; a bear with a problem cub. "So did everyones in da yard. Dis place is a jungle, youze survives by being a smarter predator than the rests of da pack. Ain't nos rules in heres. It's alls bout survival. He whosa standing wins. Da sucker laying in a puddle of his own blood dun lost for good. Ain't no rules, ain't no social thing. Just do da dude and disappears afore the hack sees ya."

Moses puts his face in his hands, rubs the stubble of his short hair then looks up at me with a great sadness. "Youze listens to me rabbit, dis place ain't what you thinks it is. You don'ts pays attention for one second and youze winds up with a toe tag or workin as some man's bitch."

Toe tag? He means dead; it is a startling thought. I mentally see an image of me on a gurney. I don't like it.

"Do nots be thinking inwards in here's, youze gots to be thinking outwards all's the time. Youze better be paying attention to thems cuz they's be paying attention to youze." Moze slaps his chest with a meaty hand, "Looks I'ze scared all da time. If Old Mose is scared youze should be sum kinda terrified."

"You're scared," *what does Mose have to be afraid* of I am wondering.

"Youze probably thinking Old Mose is so big and mean I gots nuthin to be afraid of...ain't true. Everyones in here's afraid. I'z afraid all da time. Smallest inmate in da joint tapes a knife to a broomstick and nails ya throughs da bars while youze sleeping. How youze gonna prevents that? Or maybe's theys puts rats poison in yur oatmeal or throws something flammable on ya and sets youze on fire like pork on da barbeque."

"Sorry Mose," I really mean it as a host of unwanted violent images marches through my mind with me on the receiving end of broomstick knives and combustibles.

"Sorry? I'll tell youze what ta be sorry bouts. You done mades an enemy already of Lewis. Since he's a gang member that means youze gots yourself a wholes bunch of new enemies to contends with and theys be talking about youze right now."

"Should I apologize to Lewis?" I ask not liking the thought at all.

"Hell no, just stays out of his face. Act like nuthin happened.

However, I'll tells you what. Next time youze start rabbiting around da yard, I will do youze a favor and knocks your butt down afore someone else with attitude does it for ya."

"Thanks Moses," I smile gratefully, "I also really appreciate your calling off Lewis."

"Did him a favor too. Man didn't knows he was messing with a frisky bunny."

I crawl up onto my bunk wondering how I could have been so stupid. Talk about being clueless. Mose was right. I just wanted to run; burn off some nervous energy. So, I go bolting about the yard…a yard filled with drug deals going down and gangs plotting turf wars and murders. I was the fool dancing in a minefield. Kind of hard to imagine that I almost willingly got into a confrontation with a gang member; I was the naive new guy courting disaster.

Mose shifts and the whole bunk shakes. He tends to get a bit restless when it is nearing lunchtime. I spend a couple of minutes pondering Mose. The crazed tough-guy image he projects makes for one very lonely life. Beneath that mean exterior hides a great big heart that just wants someone to care about him. Amazing, the guards put me in with him to soften me up; instead, Mose is teaching me the ropes. If I had any money, I would buy him a whole carton of cigarettes.

Laying there listening to the disruptive sounds of an active cell-block, I decide to try a mental martial arts technique to soften the auditory impact upon my nerves. I imagine the repetitive sound of waves breaking softly on a beach. Inside my head, I hear the gentle cascading sound of small breakers, followed by the tumbling clatter of little coral rocks and flowing sand as the water rushes back towards the ocean. With my eyes shut, I think about a black Great Dane running out into the water chasing a stick. I will myself to remember this moment in time and for a little while it is almost like I am there as an observer traveling backwards through time.

Susan and I are sitting on a blanket watching the sunset. Puu returns dripping water, he drops the stick onto the blanket then shakes throwing water droplets everywhere. Tropical winter in

Hawaii, the water drops are refreshing. Susan is unpacking a picnic basket full of vegetarian treats. Puu snuffs hopefully then buries his black muzzle into the basket but it holds little interest for him. He snorts then looks expectantly at Susan. She playfully offers Puu a leafy celery top, which he consents to sniff then with a disappointed exhalation, he lays down putting his large blocky head between his big paws and groans. Rubbing the Dane's ears, Susan asks, "Didn't you bring anything for Puu?"

I dig to the bottom of the basket and proudly hold up a large can of Mighty Dog. Susan opens the can and dumps the sixteen-ounce cylinder of meat onto a paper plate, which Puu inhales in a couple of loud gulping mouthfuls. He licks his muzzle clean then contentedly lays his head in her lap. Susan is thrilled as Puu gazes at her with adoring eyes, until he loudly passes gas.

We are sitting in the lee of the Royal Hawaiian Hotel's lanai where a Polynesian show is just beginning. As the red sun slowly disappears into the calm sea, Hawaiian dancers flood the stage moving in rapid sync to the beat of drums. I scoop the remains of our veggie dinner, like so much compost, back into the picnic basket. With a sigh of contentment, Susan leans back into my arms. I stare at her while she listens to the music and watches the exotic dancers through eyes that reflect the flickering light of burning tiki torches. I run my fingers through her long blond hair; it is such a privilege, my touch is gentle, my thoughts intense. The beat of the drums increases as fire dancers leap onto the stage twirling batons tipped with swirling flames. The heavy rhythm of the drums soon matches the beating of my heart...I let my hand slip slowly from Susan's hair.

"Stop that," complains Susan.

I quickly apologize while moving my hand back to safer ground.

"This is just our second date," declares Susan, "last night doesn't mean you can just maul me whenever you want. In fact, I've been thinking about it and maybe we should just be friends."

I find the implication of our just being friends a saddening thought.

"Don't give me that hurt puppy dog look of yours," she says angrily.

"Okay," I hold up my hands, "Let's just sit here and listen to the music." Susan is incredibly pretty, particularly when glaring angrily at me.

"I'll be good," I lie, adopting my most innocent smile.

"She looks at me suspiciously, "You promise?" I nod my head not wanting to lie to her again. Susan smiles and leans against my shoulder after fluffing it like a pillow.

I feel my heart beginning to race with the drum beat again. To keep from getting into any more trouble, I quickly pick Susan up and run down to the water with Puu running alongside barking. "No," yells Susan as I cast us both into the cool tropical water.

She comes up sputtering and laughing. I take her into my arms... then am startled as a deep baritone invades my thoughts. "I smells lunch," blurts Mose. The bunk shakes as Mose's feet hit the floor then he pads three steps to the barred grill to peer hungrily down the catwalk.

After another less than imaginative meal partially shared with Mose, the guard opens our door, "Gather up your stuff Arrington," he orders, "you're moving to J-3."

From the locker I collect my toothpaste and brush. With my only other possession, a comb in my back pocket, I step through the door and take a last look at Mose. He is exactly as I met him, glaring from the shadow of his bunk/cave. I know that the hatred radiating from him is directed at the guard, the prison and the whole system, but not at me.

"See ya Mose," I say softly.

"Youze gonna pay whitey for not buying me those cigarettes," he snarls. It is not a real threat, just Mose staying in character for the guard's edification.

As the corrections officer slams and locks the door, Mose throws himself at it. He rattles the steel bars in his massive grip, "Youze ain't gonna keep old Mose in the Hole forever," he rages. "And don't be sending another white wimp in heres."

The guard, who has taken a couple of protective steps backwards, yells, "Shut up Mose or there'll be no dinner." The guard knows exactly how to get Mose's attention, who snuffs like a bear, slams his palms against the upper bunk, then he snatches the upper pillow and takes it with him as he crawls back into his lower bunk lair.

In that instant, I knew that Mose is already missing me, which is a very surprising thought indeed. In his own way Mose, who is desperate for a friend, has reached out to me in the only way he knows how. His barriers are always up because he has a reputation to maintain as the baddest and meanest black man at Terminal Island Prison. I suddenly knew that if anyone in J-1 had truly intended me harm he would have had to go through Mose first.

"Screw your courage to the sticking place…" Shakespeare

Photo Arrington
Jail Door...the interior cell walls are less than two feet wider than door.

"The keenest sorrow is to recognize ourselves as the sole cause
of all our adversity," Sophocles

Chapter 25

TERMINAL ISLAND FEDERAL PRISON,

J-3, NOVEMBER 1982

ARRIVE IN J-3 wearing handcuffs, a wrinkled orange jump suit and with all my possessions in one back pocket. I am not what you would call a man of substance or in inmate lingo, "I am not having things." While the guard is opening the heavy metal and thick glass door, I watch the inmates eyeballing me from the metal grill on the other side of television room. They must not have been too impressed because once I am inside the guard lets them back into the room and all eyes return to the television screen where a cheesy soap opera is playing. I am about to learn that many inmates are addicted to soap operas in a big way, kind of like their family away from home.

J-3 is a single-level cellblock on the lower wing of the prison hospital. Upstairs is the nut ward. A passageway runs the ninety-foot length of J-3 with a bank of cells on each side. At one end is the television room where the men eat their meals, which I figure is a vast improvement over J-1 sitting on the rim of the broken toilet seat with Mose hungrily eyeing my tray.

The guard leads me to a cell about the same size as the ones in J-1, but instead of an open grill, there is a heavy metal door with a little window in it. "You're in here," he knuckles the door then grunts as he settles his heavy leather belt on his broad hips before wondering down the corridor to his office. I watch him go then pull on the door handle. Somewhat amazingly, the door opens; it is not locked. This is a major event! A prison door, I can actually open and close. I find it intriguing, so I open and close it three or four times.

"Hey idiot," yells a voice, "open it or close it but get it over with."

I step inside to see an older man sitting on the lower bunk reading a book. "What are you staring at?" he asks.

"I just came over from J-1."

"And that explains exactly what?"

"I can actually open and close a door in this place."

"Well ain't that amazing. How long were you there…a couple of decades?"

"No," I shrug realizing I might be sounding a little stupid as I tug on the door again just because it so pleases me. "I was there for a week, well actually eight days."

"A whole eight days? Wow, and you're already into this thing with doors?"

"I am Stephen Arrington," I try changing the conversation.

"Hey! You're the Fall Guy!" The man leaps to his feet to shake my hand. "I'm Morris."

Morris is in his sixties and all of five foot one or two inches tall with a slight frame and a paunch from soft living. Later, he would reveal that he is an Armenian and owns a couple of restaurants or to be more exact he will soon be the ex-owner of the restaurants because of an over enthusiastic tax withholding plan. Morris had been quite creative with his taxes so he would be getting his meals free compliments of the IRS for the next couple of years.

"Why'd you call me, Fall Guy?" I ask.

"Watch and see, you're going to take the fall for DeLorean. It's the little guys, like you and me, who always gets to take the hit. The rich guys get off because they got the big time lawyers."

"So," grins Morris, "Is DeLorean guilty?"

Instantly my guard goes up. Morris could not have been more obvious if he had written the word *snitch* on his forehead with a felt tip marker. So large scary cellmate did not work and now the Feds are resorting to Morris the small friendly Armenian snitch. "I don't have a clue," I answer warily.

"It's okay," Morris has one hand up between us, "I don't have to know and just in case you're thinking it...I'm not a snitch."

I step past him completely convinced that he is indeed a snitch and empty my back pocket into the locker.

"That's all you got?"

"So."

"Just curious," Morris peers over my shoulder for a better look. "That's like nothing; you got to be the poorest inmate I have ever seen."

"I didn't arrive exactly prepared."

"Well I sure did."

I glance at his shelf in the locker. There are a couple of pair of socks, neatly folded T-shirts, bars of soap, shampoo, letter writing materials, some paperbacks and other personal items, but nothing to get excited about. "Yeah, I can see you be having things."

Morris laughs, "Not there," he lifts up his mattress, "here." It looks like a commissary store; there are cartons of cigarettes, candy bars, beef jerky, a half dozen flattened *Cup of Noodles,* salted nuts and other food treats. There was so much that even Old Mose could spend a couple of glutinous days gobbling himself into snack oblivion.

"The *Cup of Noodles* are gonna leak when you add the hot water."

Morris is offended, "I don't eat out of Styrofoam. I heat them in a ceramic cup in the microwave."

"We have a microwave?"

"Of course, in the television room." Morris grabs one of the flat-tened *Cup of Noodles*. "Want one? You can use my cup."

I imagine Mose getting a look at this stash. He would roll Morris up in that mattress and stuff him in the corner then pounce on the goodies with both paws. "How do you protect all this stuff?"

"Why do you think I'm offering you the noodles?" Morris glances at the door. "One of us has to be in sight of this cell all the time."

"What about when we go outside?" I ask.

"The guard locks all the cells when we're in the yard." Morris is still holding the flattened *Cup of Noodles*, "Rather have a candy bar?"

"Na, you keep your stuff, but I could use some sheets."

"No problem," Morris digs behind the locker. "Normally you get your sheets from the guard. The stains can be something awful, but I got a spare set right here." Morris holds them out hopefully. This man is desperate for a friend, but I sure am not going to be his guard.

"Thanks," I take the sheets and begin making the upper bunk. I flip the mattress over unhappily amazed at the depth of the over-lapping stains that are upon even deeper stains and put the least dirty part towards the window...I do a double take...a window? The view would not be very interesting to the average person. The glass on the barred window is glazed to prevent anyone from seeing out. However, someone knocked out a couple of the panes so I have a fine four-inch by six-inch view of a cement walkway. Standing on my tip toes and looking down I can see a plant. I did not know what kind of plant, but it is very green. Moving closer to the window and looking up I could see the sky. I spend five minutes watching a passing cloud.

"What are you looking at?" Morris is trying to peer over my shoulder, but he is too short.

"A cloud."

"What kind of cloud?

"A white one."

"What's so interesting about it?"

"That it is there."

Morris sits back down, "He is amazed by doors and a cloud. Why can't I have a normal cellmate?"

Dinner arrives at 5:00 p.m. and it is quite pleasurable to eat it in the television room. Not that there is any improvement in the quality of the food, but I do get to sit at a table with three other inmates where I quickly learn how to steal a car and get a false driver's license in just a couple of minutes.

After lockdown, Morris and I spend a few hours visiting. He tells me about his case and I share how I went to work for Morgan thinking it was an opportunity for a new beginning. I do not tell Morris any of the critical details, but I do reveal enough to upset my defense attorney...when I get one. I am revealing a little with Morris because I have made an important decision, I will plead guilty because I am guilty. What I did has caused harm to others and there is no excusing that. In the last half-hour before lights out, I begin writing an article for *Surfer Magazine* warning about drug mistakes. The photo editor for the magazine is a friend of mine and he has already gotten approval for the story.

When the lights switch out, I lay down for the first time in an unthreatening cell. I revel in the breath of a wind blowing through the broken panes. The air smells almost fresh despite the cell's obligatory stench of tobacco from the nicotine-slimed walls. There is such an intense feeling of pleasure being in a locked cell with a non-aggressive inmate. I fluff and snuggle the pillow though it smells of old mildew, close my eyes and soon fall asleep.

The next morning, I wake to see sharp-edged shadows of jail bars marching across the cell wall in sync with the rising sun. Upstairs someone flushes a toilet, a rapidly repeating morning event. The metal bunk lightly shakes as Morris, who is snoring on the bunk beneath me, rolls over and farts loudly. I quickly strike a match to mask the foul odor seeping upwards into the still air. It is surprising that such a little guy can expel so much stinky gas. He gave me the matches last night anticipating that I would need them. This qualifies as inmate good manners. I am beginning to believe that the constant farting in a cellblock is from the poor quality of the food combined with a lack of exercise by the men. While watching a wisp of gray smoke curling upward from the burning match, I faintly hear the distant call of a military bugle. I instantly recognize the bugle's first notes, it is the *Call to Colors.* On many military bases across the world and upon a half dozen ships at sea, I have instantly stopped whatever I was doing upon hearing the very first note of *Call to Colors* and come to rigid attention, right hand crisply saluting the flag of the United States of America. I have served that flag in war and in peace; raw emotions surge out of my heart and soul and for the first time I choose not to suppress them.

Two hundred yards from my window, across an unknown number walls and fences, stands a Coast Guard Base at the harbor mouth. I can easily visualize the brilliant red, white and blue colors of the American flag ascending the shiny pole while the bugle call brings the formation of sailors to attention. Memories of me in dress white uniform come vividly to mind, standing proudly at parade saluting the flag as it ripples and snaps in the wind. The image sends my heart spiraling downward into an abyss of terrible sadness and despair.

I burrow deeper under the thin prison blanket. Wetness threatens to spill from my eyes as a shudder stagger-steps across my soul. I never would have allowed myself to cry in Mose's cell in J-1, he just would not have understood…his reaction uncertain, but with a small non-threatening Armenian snoring and passing gas in the bunk below, I let the tears come willingly. I pull the thin cover over my head and cry silently letting the tears wash over the pain in my tortured soul. I cry for a long time careful to make little noise. Finally opening my eyes, I wipe at the moisture that clouds my vision and see that the shadows of those jail bars are a little lower on the wall and that Morris is peering at me from the edge of my mattress. He is standing on his toes, his nose barely reaching the edge of my mattress. "I cried too when I first got here it helps," he offers me some toilet paper.

I wipe at my eyes and blow my nose then sadly tell Morris what the bugle call means to me. How it stirs memories of a prouder past that now lost still lives deep within me. Military training and our code of ethics runs deep in a career sailor, particularly for those of us lucky enough to have served in *Spec War* (Naval Special Warfare Command).

Morris stares kindly, "Steve, you really don't belong here, you don't have a real criminal mentality."

"Thanks Morris, but I'm being emotional because I really do belong here."

"No, it was Morgan's fault; he came into your life when you were the most susceptible. I mean come on, your dad died just two weeks before you went to work for Hetrick."

"It's not that easy, Morris," I look carefully at my new friend with a gentle mid-Eastern accent, "Morgan stepped into my life with his criminal manipulations because he knew my character was flawed. Remember, I am the one who made the marijuana mistake and that's what gave Morgan the idea to capitalize upon it. I'm the one who set me up."

Morris stares, "Never heard anyone argue for their own guilt in here before. Instead of writing that magazine article maybe you should be writing a book about all this. It might help others not to make the same mistakes, and it'll give you something constructive to do...I mean let's face it, we're both going to be here for a very long time." The thought of his own incarceration descends upon Morris like a black cloud, he frowns and sits down on the edge of his bunk.

We both quietly sit in the jail cell pondering our dismal futures until the guard opens the door for breakfast.

In the television room, I try to give my fried baloney to Morris who is offended by the offer, but then trade both his and mine for a small pile of grits. Amazingly, I am developing a taste for it less the suspicious lumps of course. I also manage to trade in my picking-up-a-really-bad-smell orange coveralls for a Navy blue set that actually somewhat fit. I then wait in line for the payphone where I have a very discouraging conversation with my new public defender. After his words of encouragement, which revolves around a plea-bargain that involves somewhere between thirty and forty-five years in prison, I decide to write a few hugely embarrassing letters to friends. Lacking envelopes, stamps or even their addresses it will be awhile before I can mail them. Then I go back to the television room after noon count (confirming that the prison had its full inventory of inmates) for a particularly unappetizing lunch of macaroni and cheese, canned peas, white bread, red *Jell-O* and orange *Kool-Aid* along with inmate conversation on how to cash checks with someone else's name on them. Though the meal lacks nutrition, all the colors certainly make it look entertaining.

"Yard time," yells the guard.

It is in the J-3 yard that my life begins to change from the depths of despair to a quiet simple hope.

We quickly line up at the yard door. I look eagerly about as I step out into the blazing sunshine. The J-3 yard is a bit larger than the J-1 yard and it has a slightly better view of the North Yard through a twelve-foot tall chain link fence. Hanging in the middle of the constricted yard surrounded by three towering cement walls is a torn, but serviceable volleyball net, which I am quite happy to see as I like V-ball a lot. There is a rusted-out, half-functional exercise machine and the standard bent basketball hoop hangs from a pole near the far wall. Surprisingly, the cracked cement deck has a dirt section that is about five feet wide and twenty feet long. I walk over to peer at the dirt while a couple of the inmates begin running the small perimeter in a counter-clockwise direction. I join the joggers eager for exercise, but am extremely careful to stay at an acceptable pace. With each loop, I become more aware of the drabness of my surroundings. I particularly notice the small green lawns in the North Yard and a complete absence of anything living in our yard, but for us corrupt inmates. I also observe from this perspective that there are actually several dwarf trees in the North Yard. Standing under one of the trees, I see a stooped old inmate feeding a flock of pigeons. Every so often, another inmate will walk by and give him a couple of slices of bread smuggled out of the chow hall. The old man nods without looking up, not actually acknowledging who has given him the bread, which he begins to shred as he shuffles amongst the crowding pigeons. His whole attention is upon the birds. When the crumbs are gone, the pigeons circle once or twice, then in a sudden beating of feathered wings, they fly upwards and settle on a second story building's ledge. The stooped old man stops his shuffle and just stands there, head down staring at the grass. I see two more inmates leave the chow hall heading in his direction. They hand him slices of bread, it is like putting tickets into an antique machine as the old inmate begins to shuffle again shedding breadcrumbs. The birds arrive in a flock of activity. They peck and head bob about his feet as he shuffles head down in a small circle.

Half an hour passes and I am still running. Repeatedly passing the dirt section, I have noticed that under a layer of trash and cigarette butts there is a bit of dead brown grass. By the exercise machine, I look at a dented bucket, and then I see two inmates getting a drink from an old faucet on the wall. I stop running and look back towards the dirt section. There is a half-foot tall cement curb surrounding the dirt's perimeter. When they designed this prison, someone intended that grass should grow there. What a thoughtful consideration. An idea begins to form in my mind that will surprisingly change how I think about and value myself.

Fetching the dented bucket, I carry it over to the uppermost corner of the strip of dirt. It is here in a two-foot by three-foot section of dirt that a bit of the dead grass lingers. Though the grass is obviously deceased, I am wondering hopefully about the roots deeper in the soil. Using my fingers, I rake a fair-sized patch of dirt clean carrying the debris away in the bucket. Then I carry the pail to the faucet, which only produces a dribble of water. It takes a full two minutes to fill the bucket, which I then carry over to the cleaned patch of dirt. Kneeling I almost reverently begin to pour the clear water onto the cleaned section of dirt. It feels like an implausible privilege to have this opportunity, it is also surprising that I even thought of it in the first place.

My action is somewhat prompted by an ancient Japanese proverb that I had read while studying the martial arts, *The wonder, I carry water*. Such a simple concept, yet its significance is impressive when one truly ponders it. This five-word proverb implies that there is a water source and that the author is healthy enough to carry it. Because he or she bears the water, it implies that the person is taking it to a home and probably to a family, which equates to love, service and responsibility. The main thought is that the author is sensitive enough to appreciate the wonder of such an immensely simple act. After air, there is nothing more important to maintaining life than water. It sustains us, allows the farming of crops, flows in our blood plasma, cleans our bodies and is essential for motion. With these thoughts flowing through my mind like a mental waterfall, I do my bucket chore every day for two weeks. The other inmates think I am probably going crazy on them or looking for an insanity defense, but I just keep carrying the sloshing bucket and reverently pouring it over my patch of dirt. Interesting how action assumes possession.

It happens on a Monday. I know it was Monday because they served eggs over-easy, fried sausage and baked beans for breakfast. I trade my over-cooked sausage, which looks a lot like something dug out of a dirty litter box, for another inmate's Boston baked beans. It is hard to imagine that he thought he had gotten the better part of the deal. The whole meal has been prepared several hours earlier in the main kitchen. The meals are then loaded into a metal cart and wheeled to J-3, where the rations are microwaved to re-heat and thoroughly rubberize the eggs. After the orderlies clean up the television room, the guard lets us out into the yard. I immediately go over and look at my section of dirt and stare in awe at a couple of dozen tiny green sprouts of grass just beginning to break through the soil.

No farmer could have been happier than I at that moment. I have helped to make something beautiful happen. In this miserable place, something wondrous is actually growing and I have had a hand in it. I quickly fetch my bucket then a few minutes later am slowly letting the water dribble over the fresh sprouts of grass. I watch the clear water slowly cascading from the bucket and think about the proverb, "*The wonder, I carry water.*"

At the faucet again, I cheerfully watch the water slowly dribbling into the old dented bucket. I listen to the change in pitch of the falling water; first, as it spills into the empty bucket's bottom with its hollow high tinny sound, then a brook-like gurgle as the pail begins to fill. I inhale the crispness of the water vapor rising from the bucket and dunk my hand into it and then let the water dribble from my fingertips onto my upraised face. The cool water wets my lips quenching a deep inner need for something good outside the ponderous negative sameness of prison. It feels exciting to be doing something so simple, yet so wondrously good.

I am on my third bucket of water when the guard calls my name, "Arrington, get over here."

I set down my bucket and walk warily over to the guard who looks me up and down, then asks, "What's with this bucket thing?"

"Just trying to grow some grass."

"Why?"

"Not much else to do here...and it feels good."

"Think you're accomplishing something?"

"Yeah." Instinctively, I am aware that my bucket thing is a lot about how I think and feel about myself. I am dirty inside and know it. It is as if I am pouring that bucket over my soul, but I am not about to talk about that to anyone...not even myself...at least not yet.

"Want a job?"

"What kind of job?"

"Cleaning," the guard almost smiles, but then remembers it is not in his nature to smile to an inmate. "The cellblock has two order-lies and I am losing one to general population today. You serve the meals and clean the cellblock."

"Okay," I nod, having noticed something special about the order-lies. Whenever they clean up the television room or the corridor the rest of us have to be locked in our cells until they are done. They are also the first ones out of their cells to prepare the morning meal. Being an orderly equals less time confined in a prison cell. What could be better than that?

"There's something else," he cannot suppress a smile this time, "you get seven cents an hour."

I smile, "A whole seven cents?"

"Don't knock it. If you're here long enough, it can really add up." He chuckles as he walks away.

"Hey Arrington," yells one of the inmates, "get off the man's leg."

"What's that mean?" I ask in a friendly way. My positive response takes him off guard.

"Aren't you over there sucking up to the hack?"

"Nope," I shrug and put a smile on my face even though I would like to pop this worm's head like a zit. "Didn't you see him order me over to the fence? He wants me to be an orderly."

"You gonna to do it?"

"Absolutely, pays seven cents an hour." I walk over towards the volleyball game and join in on the white guy side. Inmate etiquette prevents me from playing on the side of the Latinos unless invited, which just was not going to happen.

When we go back inside, I ask Morris, "What does it mean when someone says get off the man's leg?"

Morris laughs, "Think small dog humping a person's leg."

"Oh."

"It's a pretty heavy inmate slam; means stop sucking up to the guard."

"Everybody here sure wants to know a person's business."

"Sure, they got nothing else to do." Morris smiles, "So what did the guard want?"

"Wants me to be an orderly."

"That means they are going to move you into cell one; the orderly cell."

"I also get seven cents an hour."

"Hey, after your first day you'll have just enough to buy a candy bar."

"Yeah, I guess I'll be having things."

The cell door swings open and the guard is there. "Strip your sheets off, you're moving."

I collect my toothpaste, toothbrush and comb, drop them into the rusty bucket and follow him to the first cell on the same side of the cellblock.

The orderly in the cell is moving his bedding from the top bunk to the lower bunk. "Hope you don't mind if I take the lower bunk, been here longer...earned it."

"Don't mind at all, I am Steve."

"Know who you are Fall Guy," he extends his hand, "I'm Clayton."

Clayton is another short guy, about five-foot-four with long brown hair tied into a ponytail and sporting a friendly smile; good teeth.

"I'm a site scout, work for the movie industry. I look for filming locations. It's a pretty fun job."

"But right now you're an inmate."

"Yep, cocaine."

"Me too."

"Already know that. Sure you don't mind my taking the lower bunk?"

"Absolutely, I far prefer the upper bunk."

"Why's that? It is a lot easier to get into and out of a lower bunk."

"Same can be said for some for someone looking to get into it with you."

"Oh."

While making the upper bunk my minds slips back to Vietnam. I was very lucky in that conflict. Though I made four tours with the fleet, I never got hurt nor did I hurt anyone. Yet, knowing that you are going into combat at any level heightens one's awareness in a global way. Everything is about odds. What are the odds that someone is going to shoot something in your direction and how do you reduce the odds of being there when the bullet arrives? I had already figured out that it would be hard to defend yourself from a lower bunk. An attacker has all the advantages and with the bunk up against the wall, the victim has nowhere to go. The bottom bunk is a trap.

I climb up onto the upper bunk, which is my own personal sanctuary. Sitting cross-legged, I am first to see any one lurking at the door. Score a huge advantage for the upper bunk. I have the advantage of height and I can escape off the foot of the bed or dive right into an attacker (mass and downward velocity verses a standing object at rest). Anyone looking to stick me has to reach up, which means there will be less power in his attack.

I am quite happy about my decision then suddenly I hear a loud gurgling sound. The four-inch pipe directly above my head begins to vibrate and there is an abrupt whooshing, vibrating sound.

"Did I mention that the nut ward's sewer pipe runs right over the upper bunk?" asks Clayton pleasantly.

"The moment one gives close attention to anything, even a blade of grass, it becomes a mysterious, awesome, indescribably magnificent world in itself," Henry Miller

"I always wanted to be a motocross racer. If I ever get out,
I will be around sixty, I guess..." Bill Smith, 17 years-old
serving a life sentence for murder. When asked about his
seventeenth birthday in Houtzdale State Prison, he said,
"Outside I would have had a party. And I would feel like I
was getting a little older. Here you do not notice. I cried a lot.
It is something you have to get used to, I guess."

Chapter 26

TERMINAL ISLAND FEDERAL PRISON,

J-3, NOVEMBER 1982

THE NEXT morning it is still dark outside as I eagerly await the opening of our cell door. I am looking forward to being the first one out in the quiet of the morning. The chow cart comes over between 6:00 and 6:30 am. I hear the guard coming, his big ring of keys chiming gently as they swing with the rhythm of his stride. I listen to the big key sliding metal on metal into the lock then, with a squeaking of the hinges, the door swings outward. The guard is a dark silhouette in the morning dimness behind the glare of a flashlight. Something else is swinging from his hand; it glitters as it swings in and out of the small pool of light...handcuffs.

"Arrington," the deep voice fills the quiet of the cell, "you're wanted in court."

A couple of minutes later, he opens the television room door to the outside where another guard and two cuffed inmates are waiting. I fall in and he marches us past the J-1 yard and into the administration/control building. They put us in the holding cell where our breakfast is waiting; grits, a hard-boiled egg, dry white toast, and a small frosty carton of orange juice that I thoroughly enjoy taking long slow sips..

The guards manacle us to a chain then lead us down the rusty staircase, out through the twin security fences and into a waiting Marshal's van. I stare out the window on the drive up to the court-house watching the City of Los Angeles awaken to a fresh new morning. The sights and sounds are overwhelming. Everything is interesting. Terminal Island Federal Correctional Facility is about drab colors, dirt, grime, rust, mildew, body odor, confined spaces, odd deposits of human waste and the constant threat of severe physical violence on a seriously depraved level. I watch people driving to work, kids waiting for school buses, motorcycles weaving freely through the traffic. I see houses still dark on the outside, but with windows of warm inviting light. All too soon, we exit the freeway and drive down Broadway to the courthouse. There are all sorts of people on the streets, men in business suits and tramps in rags. I see attractive women in skirts that sway as they walk and long red hair blowing in the wind as one woman runs to make a traffic light. We stop for the red light and I see a tall woman on the side-walk peering at the darkened cargo inside the Marshal's van. She abruptly gets a disgusted look on her face and walks briskly away. I look at the inmate sitting behind me with his face pressed against the window grossly licking the glass pane with his tongue and I too am disgusted. How humiliating to be bundled into this cargo of demented criminals.

They take us to the basement-holding cell where we wait for hours. There is nothing to do but sit and stare. Rather than look at the other inmates, I watch the drama outside our cell. Marshals are at their desks or conducting the business of moving inmates. Public defenders come and go. I never thought that an office could be so interesting, particularly one with no windows in the basement of an old building.

Finally, it is my turn upstairs. I walk cuffed with two Marshals. We pass through the lobby and people step cautiously out of our way. Many pause to look, but it is nothing like the last time I was here with my flying wedge of Marshals. We ride up in the elevator alone.

In the courtroom, DeLorean and Hetrick are sitting with their attorneys. My newest court appointed attorney is late so I sit alone. Morgan nods at me from the other side of the table. It is the first time I have seen him since the arrest. Rumor has it that he is going to cooperate, but that is what the jailhouse rumors always say. Morgan still lives in J-2, but DeLorean is free on bail. He looks a lot different from the man I saw last time who had spent the night in a jail cell wearing an expensive but wrinkled suit. Now he is groomed, sitting tall, owns the courtroom. He is the center of attention and knows it.

I glance around at the crowd that is beginning to fill the courtroom. My mother and brother are not present. I particularly notice the ladies until my court appointed attorney arrives in a hustle with a bulging and battered briefcase. "This is just a procedural thing," he says shuffling papers, "DeLorean's and Morgan's defense teams are making discovery motions to find out what evidence the government has."

"What about me?" I ask.

"You and I are just along for the ride."

"You mean we are just going to sit here and do nothing?"

"Yep, better than sitting in a jail cell isn't it?"

I glance about the courtroom at all the normal people, "You got that right."

The court proceedings take all of about fifteen minutes, then the handcuffs go back on. The Marshals lead Morgan and I separately from the courtroom. The two Marshals and I join a young couple in an elevator. I think they are probably law students or legal assistants. She has long blond hair, a striking figure, innocent good looks and is happy. He is obviously thrilled to be with her. They are discussing lunch and which restaurant to patronize. When the elevator reaches the lobby, I watch them heading for the big double open doors. The sunlight halos her hair then my Marshals and I take a left turn towards the staircase that leads down to the basement.

In the holding cell, I trade my baloney on white for a bruised apple. It is another couple of hour wait before the Marshal's van is loaded with its misfit cargo for the return trip to Terminal Island. I notice that Morgan has not returned to one of the three holding cells, which means he is still somewhere upstairs. I do not doubt that he is cutting a deal for himself. I am alone now and prefer it that way. I have my own decisions to make…they won't be easy, but they will be mine.

Back in the cellblock, I have missed dinner so am treated to another sack lunch with baloney on white. I chuck the baloney, but force down the bread. I do not like the taste of the doughy white bread that harbors the salty residue and smell of the baloney, but it fills a hole.

> *"It dawns on me every day; I am going to be here for life,"*
> Scott Walker, 18 years old, serving two life sentences
> for murdering a man in a basketball game.

Awake at 4:00 a.m. with nothing to do and nowhere to go; it is an inmate thing. The Department of Federal Corrections hopes that idle inmates will turn their thoughts towards corrective behavior. My six weeks in prison has not shown any sign of corrective behavior amongst my fellow inmates. They are mostly satisfied using the idle time to do nothing at all except for having an avid curiosity about each other's cases, what is in other inmate's lockers and the usual terrorism reeked on the weaker characters in the cellblock.

So far on the advice of my court appointed lawyer and the

generally unasked for opinions of numerous inmates, I am going to be in here for quite awhile. Currently there is nothing on my agenda except how to survive each day relatively intact. What troubles me is that I can anticipate a relatively large number days in a prison facility. My most fearful thought is how many days... hundreds...thousands? My mind just cannot wrap itself around a number higher than ten thousand, yet according to my grim faced public defender I am looking at forty-five years, which astonishingly equals sixteen thousand four hundred and twenty-five soul-busting days. *How do I cope with an uncertain equation like that?* I ask myself... repeatedly.

A rumbling sound drops out of the thick concrete bottom of the nut ward; it rushes through the adjacent cell then scuttles towards my bunk. The thick iron pipe directly above my head begins to vibrate emitting a gurgling sound that slows and sloshes as the effluent flow hits an obstructing elbow before plunging into the down pipe that runs past Clayton's head on its race to the sewer. There is a final swooshing noise that trickles to a softer dripping sound that lingers for ten or twelve seconds. A drop of condensation from the moist pipe drops onto my pillow. The number of drops on my pillow approximately defines the number of nighttime flushes, which gets me to thinking about inmates who track their days inside the joint with marks on the walls. Looks like I will be keeping track of my days and nights with toilet sounds and water drips.

I stare at the stained cinderblock wall four feet away. It is mostly shaded in darkness but for a patch of dim light in a lower corner from a North Yard security light outside my window. There are shafts of darkness hovering in that soft patch of reflected light; suspended there by the security lights that wash over the window's bars. Inside a prison cell, it is impossible to escape all the reminders that one is truly locked inside a cage. A flash of fury surges through my mind in an emotional roaring flood that momentarily drowns my sensibility, but it passes faster than the gurgle and spurt routine of the sewer pipe. Getting mad and all worked up does not help when confined in small spaces.

So Stephen whatever is going to come of you in here? I wonder for the hundredth time. *More importantly, how am I really going to handle this? Giving up my freedom does not mean I have to forfeit control over who I am on the inside. I am still me. That is something. Being in one piece in a prison cell is a whole lot better than being in the prison hospital riddled with double OO buckshot and hollow-point bullets after my close up and personal encounter with the DEA posse. Instead of a hospital bed, I could just as easily be sleeping the long-forever in a cold dark moist grave. Yuk! Alternatively, I could be a pile of rotting meat and mossy bones in a Colombian jungle after my south of the border adventure; just another unknown victim of the cocaine and on-going cartel war. Therefore, I have some things to be thankful for. I am also no longer in the employ of one Morgan Hetrick and his trigger-happy Colombian friends. That is a huge plus. Kind of amazing to think that I have been freed from a life that was out-of-control by being arrested and locked into a prison cell; I guess freedom really does come in many guises. Oddly, I feel as if I have more freedom in this jail cell than when I was with Morgan living his multimillionaire lifestyle.*

I glance about the darkened cell. *This is freedom?* I ask as though arguing with myself. *Guards tell me when to eat, when to go to and when to leave my cell, when and if I can go outside into a confined yard, when I can and cannot shower and they restrain me with handcuffs and leg irons on occasion, but yes, I am feeling more free than when I was under Morgan's thumb...how incredible.*

I do not like being in this cell, but currently there is not anything I can do about it. Well there is, I could cooperate, cut a deal, but that would mean giving up Sam. I happen to know that he is still running free in San Diego from a couple of collect telephone conversations with friends other than Sam. I did not dare call him as they record all prison telephone calls; knowing Sam, he is prone to saying the absolute wrong thing at the worst possible moment. *Therefore, to protect Sam, I am making a decision that cooperation is not an option.*

Okay Stephen, so you are accepting the decision that you are going to be here for a while, a very long while, so what next? For most of my adult life I have been able to successfully put a positive spin on just about anything that happened to me...that all changed with my marijuana mistake followed by criminal activities with Hetrick and company. I realize that this is an important confession even if I am only making it to myself in the darkness of a prison cell. My life had been pretty terrific; full of military adventure, physical challenges, sporting risks, world travel and surprising awareness and wonder at the intensity and beauty of the human experience on an inordinately unique level...then I blundered into marijuana and the diminished brain activity that it imposes.

I turn and stare at the puddle of light with its repeating shadows of jail bars on the cinderblock wall. A cockroach climbs into the pool of light, changes direction and disappears back downward into the darker shadows. *Confinement is my reality. How do I make the best of it?*

Abruptly, I become aware that I am thinking clearer now than over the past couple of years. My thoughts are more crisp and distinct. It is as if a sharpened focus has returned, a mental curtain rising. *Am I thinking with better definition because I have been freed of the stress of Morgan's manipulations; no longer having to live with lies and threats or the loom of a prison cell? No,* the answer is abrupt; *what is missing is the lingering side effects of marijuana stupefaction.*

I can feel my positive attitude about life in general wanting to reassert itself. *Here, in a prison cell?* I ask. Then I know *it is what is going to save me.* I glance back at the jail bar shadows on the wall... *can I really do this, make something positive out of a really screwed up mess with no expiration date?* I nod to myself. *Yes, I can...because I have to believe I can. There is not anything else for me; failure is not an option, not in here.*

Where do I begin?

Right here...I begin now!

As quietly as possible, I climb down from the upper bunk. It is chilly in just my boxer underwear, but I focus on ignoring the modest discomfort. I bend my knees slightly lowering myself into a cat stance and assume the posture of an alert preying mantis. In extreme slow motion, I go through a series of katas (karate dances or stylized martial arts routines). What would normally take two minutes in a dojo (karate gym or place of training) takes fifteen minutes here as I concentrate on becoming that combative insect in extreme slow motion. I occasionally notice my shadow on the cell's wall and then try to make that shadow more mantis-like by slightly shifting my posture. No cockroach would approach with an alert Mantis in the cell. My blocks and strikes have the slow fluid movement of sap running down a tree. It takes so long to take a breath that by the time I exhale, I am eager for another, yet I will my lungs to fill and empty ever so slowly. Then in segments, the pace quickens. I fling as many fists strikes and snap kicks as I can in thirty counted seconds, then shift to flowing blocks to recover, then repeat the attack and defense routines again.

It is challenging moving about the limited space of the narrow cell. Beside the bunk, I have less than four-feet of width with five-plus-foot of length; the locker takes up the other two feet. The cell's floor space then widens beyond the bunk by the door, but it is also where the toilet/sink combination squats. I use every inch of the floor while the obstacles serve to focus and discipline my move-ments. Snap kicks go over the toilet and locker, back fists, snap punches and thrust hits stop just short of the bunk or the cinder-block walls. I try settling into a very low *horse stance* with my spread legs all but touching the bunk and wall. In this squat position, I am almost shoulder lever with the three-foot tall locker, which is four feet behind me. I am preparing to practice an *Iron Palm Strike*, a devastating thrust hit that is very specifically applied. I block a pretend strike from an imagined opponent in front of me then turn to confront another anticipated opponent behind me. Pivoting on my left foot, I step forward with my right using the momentum to accelerate the strike, augmenting it with a hip thrust and extended shoulder snap. The left side of my torso rotating backwards almost drives the strike as much as my right side's rotation forward. This generates a lot of energy and increased velocity, which I focus into the strike exhaling just before impact to make my body denser while mentally concentrating on driving my palm through the locker door, which is my imagined opponent. I thought I would be about an inch or two short of actual contact…I was not.

The resounding metallic ring just two feet from Clayton's head brings him instantly vertical in his bunk; luckily, he is a short person.

"What are you doing?" he blurts.

"Being an insect"

"Killing an insect?"

"No being one."

"A bug? You think you're a bug?" Clayton has that look reserved for relating with crazy, or drugged out, inmates.

"No, I am imitating the movements of a Preying Mantis," I am eyeballing a hand-sized dent in the locker's stainless steel door. "Sorry about the noise."

"What did you do; kick the locker?"

"No, a palm strike."

Clayton is checking out the door, "That was a palm strike?"

"Well yeah," I start slipping on green coveralls, "Kind of an aggressive one."

"I guess. You really dented the door," he slides his feet to the floor then open and closes the locker to make sure the door still works, then looks at me over his shoulder. "Karate, you were doing karate."

"Actually it was Preying Mantis Gung Fu."

"I thought it was pronounced Kung Fu," Clayton's hair is doing a just-woke-up-vertical-affair, "I have seen the series. It is definitely Kung Fu, you know."

"Actually that was a television series called Kung Fu with an actor named David Carradine pretending to be a Shaolin monk. What he did was mostly special effects. Gung Fu is one of the variations of the martial arts developed by Shaolin monks and modified by martial arts devotees like Bruce Lee. The other difference is if you are speaking Cantonese or Mandarin."

"Bruce Lee did Gung Fu, not Kung Fu?"

"Actually he took Gung Fu and other martial arts and came up with his own style called *Jeet Kune Do,* which mirrored his combat philosophy built around minimum movement to defeat an attacking fist."

"What makes Gung Fu so special?"

"Well it is fast, fluid, and recognized as one of the more lethal of the martial arts."

"Why?"

"Well for one it has the Iron Palm Strike."

"What's that?"

"It can be delivered with more force than a fist strike and a true master can focus the strike to do a specific level of damage."

"What do you mean level of damage?"

"There were Shaolin monks who could hit a stack of wood planks and consistently break only one of the planks. It did not matter if the target plank was on top, in the middle of the stack or on the bottom."

"Can you do that?"

"Absolutely not," I shake my head, "I studied under a little old Chinese guy in Hawaii and he was not into breaking things. It is rough on the bones and connective tissue."

"So how good are you?"

"Not good enough." I shrug knowing that I am telling the truth.

I hear keys softly clacking then the lock on our door opens. "What are you guys doing in here?" asks the guard.

"Nothing," Clayton and I answer.

"Well don't be banging on the furniture." He glances about the cell not noticing the dented door, which was hard to miss except most of the locker doors have dents from frustrated inmates. "It's 6:00 a.m. get the television room ready for breakfast," he orders as he steps back into the semi-dark corridor.

The breakfast cart arrives thirty minutes later and the guard wheels it inside after locking us behind the grill. This morning it is creamed beef on toast, what the inmates call SOS (*S—t on a Shingle*). I am now a bit savvier and have gotten myself onto the vegetarian menu list, which certainly is not anything special. The tray with my name on it (creatively misspelled) has a box of *Rice Krispies*, a small carton of milk and carrot sticks. *Carrot sticks for breakfast?* The cooks, assisted by inmates, are not exactly motivated or creative.

I knock off the Krispies in about thirty seconds then rummage about in the cart for any extras. Score! There is a bunch of bananas along with a jar of jalapeños. This is a Latin American thing. The Colombian inmates, a source of prison wealth and violence, have arranged for a special delivery. I leave the jalapenos untouched, but manage to peel off a banana without leaving any evidence of my theft. *"Wow! It is hard to imagine that I am risking upsetting Colombian hit men over a ripped-off banana, but hunger will do that to you. And to think I am doing the vegetarian thing for my health."* I have to eat the banana clandestinely, there are no guarantees that Clayton will not give me up. Three bites and its gone, only chewing when Clayton is busy at the other end of the television room. I slip the peel into the bottom of the trashcan and straighten up just as Clayton returns to the cart.

"You're not as sneaky as you think you are," Clayton states flatly.
"What?"
"Stealing the banana from the Ochoa brothers."
I am stunned. How did he know?
"Thought you were smart to just take one."
"How'd you know?"
"I was watching your reflection in the window banana breath."
"You can smell the banana?"
"Absolutely and you can bet that the Ochoa brothers will sniff your breath when you deliver their bananas. Come on! These guys live on a different level of evolution; they are much closer to their animal ancestors."

I glance toward the locked grill, which is now beginning to fill up with hungry inmates.

"Here gargle some coffee," Clayton offers me a half-filled Styrofoam cup.

While I am swishing coffee in my mouth Clayton whispers,

"Taking bananas isn't smart because they sometimes know how many bananas are suppose to be in each bunch. That means you get to deliver the bananas to the Ochoa brothers. Also whatever you do keep your paws off the jalapenos…that could get you seriously hurt."

At 7:00 a.m., the guard opens the grill again to let the rest of the inmates into the television room. The Colombians take a table in the corner, gun fighter seats. I nervously walk up to deliver the jalapeños and the raided banana bunch. The older Ochoa brother smiles; he is missing both his front teeth. The jar of Jalapeños disappears under the table. He then tears off a small banana and offers it to me. As I reach to take it, I hear him breathing in, catching my scent.

He smiles, apparently the coffee hides my theft, yet his eyes do not share in the smile; they are cold and flat. I return to the cart and offer the banana to Clayton.

"Don't worry you passed," he grins, "but only offer me half of the banana otherwise it is a bit suspicious. I break the banana in half giving him the smaller piece.

"See you're learning," Clayton wraps a napkin around the banana half and drops it into his chest pocket.

"Aren't you going to eat it?" I ask.

"Trading material."

"For what?"

"You'll find out soon enough."

I peel my banana half and eat it slowly savoring each of two bites. The fruit tastes so fresh and alive. Most of our food comes from bags, boxes or cans and is prepared with little or no imagination except for a bit of creative culinary abuse and demented spicing with various types of living and dead waste.

Glancing back at the Colombian table, I notice that the brothers are staring at me. Hard to imagine that I actually thought I was being cautious.

After cleaning up the television room, Clayton and I are back in our cell for noon count.

"Thanks again for watching out for me." I offer gratefully.

"No problem, we're bunkies so we gotta watch each other's back. You want to survive in the joint forget about trying to be one of the guys. We are animals here living in a crowded jungle; lots of predators, but not nearly enough prey. So, we squabble and fight over everything. Imagine a bunch of gorillas and only one banana... who's going to get it?"

"The biggest and the meanest?"

"Or the smallest, fastest and brightest," smiles Clayton who is only five foot four. He reaches into his pocket and extracts a small cigar.

"So that is what happened to the banana."

"Cost me a hardboiled egg too."

"Where did you get that?"

"Off the veggie plate with your name on it."

"What?"

"Next time be the first one to the cart," Clayton puts the cigar back into his shirt pocket and walks out of the cell.

That evening just before lockdown Clayton slips into the cell carrying something wrapped in an old white towel. "You're going to love this. We're going sailing tonight."

"Sailing?"

"Yep, traded the cigar and a Hershey bar for one night's rent on this baby," Clayton unwraps the towel to reveal a beat-up radio. It is about the size of an average dictionary, scratched black plastic with a two-inch mono speaker. "Ain't much to look at but this fifty cent speaker is our ticket out of here for a couple of hours."

"So turn it on."

"No, we got to wait until lights out. The brother who owns this warned me that the batteries might not last more than another hour or two. You like jazz?"

"Don't know, never really listened to it."

"Well you're about to, nothing like jazz in the dark to carry your soul out of the joint and onto a higher plane."

I spend the next two hours writing a couple of letters to friends,

I have not heard from in years. My letters follow the same script, which first elates then depresses me greatly. I begin each one by writing about my diving adventures as a frogman while living a nomadic life in Hawaii. I describe Revelstoke recapturing what it was like camping on the beaches and up before the sunrise to surf. I share about camping in a mountain valley next to a babbling brook where after breakfast I would hike through a rain forest to a waterfall for my morning bath. Then I would write about the marijuana mistake, the ending of my naval career and how I blundered into the cocaine underworld. I wrote about my arrest and described the jail unit. Each letter begins with happy memories then descends into the horrible inmate life that is now my reality.

I lick the flap of the last envelope sealing the witness of my depression inside. I address the letter then stare at the return address FCI (Federal Correctional Institution) Terminal Island, what a lousy name. I did not like the words Terminal Island, which has such a final sound to it; like my life might end right here one day in the too near or too distant future. A prison named Terminal Island; it is a hope busting kind of name.

With my depression hovering about me, the lights abruptly go out. I hear Clayton switch on the little radio. There is a soft burst of static then he dials in a jazz station. The nighttime cellblock noises fade to the distinct sound of a jazz trumpet. It is amazing the quality of the music coming from that little two-inch speaker. I focus my entire attention upon the swell and ebb of the musical waves. Clayton has the wisdom to say nothing, just letting the music wash over us in the dark cell. I listen to the complexity of the songs appreciating how each musical note blends into the one before and the one after and begin to understand that music truly is a composition; a complex mathematical equation where harmony lives and rules. I listen to a woman's voice lifted in celebration of life, her words cascade off the walls filling the darkness with meaning. I haven't heard a woman's voice lifted in beauty for a month, but it seems like forever. Then a man sings of losing the woman he loves. His words are haunting as my thoughts ride on every one of them.

The music of the night begins to fade on the fifth song and then it skips a beat and is gone.

"Dead batteries," laments Clayton as he switches off the radio.

Surprisingly, I do not mind. The silence in the cell allows me to recapture the echo of the night music. I have never heard harmony so perfectly, nor listened more intently. The music has been a celebration of life defining the undefeatable hope of the human spirit. I immerse myself in the fading memories of the music and then gently fall asleep.

"Awareness is good, but without skills and ability tied to that awareness, all you have is anxiety," Tony Blauer

The next morning I wake up cold. It is early December and an early winter chill is seeping through the old prison walls. Somewhere in the building, there is a boiler for heating the radiator pipes, but it is not working. I am not harboring any repair hopes; just feeling lucky, my incarceration is in Southern California and not snow-bound Montana. Ignoring the chill, I climb down from my bunk to practice my Gung Fu as quietly as possible. At 6:00 a.m., the guard opens the cell door so Clayton and I can organize the television room for breakfast.

I pause just outside the cell door to watch the guard striding away. He is a receding shadow in the long dark corridor. His heavy key makes a sharp metallic sound as he unlocks the far door, walks through it and then locks it behind him. I look up and down the prison corridor insuring that it is truly empty; that no demented soul is lurking in the shadows with mischief on his mind. *This is a really crummy way to get a bit of breakfast,* I silently think to myself. The darkened cellblock is so depressing with its double battery of thick steel doors; but I am wary of allowing any despair to enter my thoughts that could lead to deadening my mental state. I am fully alert... combat mode. In Vietnam, we called it *Locked and Loaded.* Ready! Even supposedly empty the prison corridor exudes a brooding sinister presence that stirs the mind to fearful considerations.

Standing at the door, I am entertaining a mental image of a jack-rabbit at the mouth of its burrow listening, smelling the air, looking for any threatening movement. Alert, quick thinking, fast and agile that is me, the *Energizer Bunny.*

"Can you move now? I am hungry," complains Clayton.

I move so Clayton can step around me.

"Was that one of your Praying Mantis things again?" he asks rubbing sleep from his eyes and blundering down the corridor towards the television room. *Clayton the point man,* in the jungle I would take lead, I have the training; but prison is a different kind of jungle, concrete, steel and lurking weirdoes (singular and in groups) with homemade weapons; walking nightmares with bad attitudes and corrupt violent intents. I let Clayton walk ahead of me, primary prey in the lead. If any lurking weirdo pounces on Clayton, I can leap to his defense…from timid bunny to war rabbit; reminds me that I should read *Watership Down* again.

"Actually it was kind of a rabbit thing." I answer Clayton's question after ensuring the television room is indeed empty.

"Rabbit?" laughs Clayton, "What are you now? The Attack Bunny? Going to thump something with your paws?"

"Na, bunnies cannot defend themselves except against a smaller rodent, they can only run and hide. Either they are more alert than other animals or they wind up inside other animals."

"You weren't really impersonating a bunny were you?"

After casing the television room a second time just to be sure, I turn and nod, "Yep."

"Why couldn't you be a wolf or a really big bad tiger?"

"Because those animals have a different type of behavior; they are predators looking for lunch. An animal not looking to be lunch has an awareness more focused on immediate survival."

"So you mentally become different animals?"

"I just try to mimic their survival techniques."

"How do you know which animal to be?"

"Depends on the situation, I have studied the movements and fighting techniques of the praying mantis, monkey, mongoose, tiger and crane."

"Not bunny?"

"No that is one of my own; seemed more appropriate to a dark prison corridor that is supposed to be empty."

"What about mongoose, isn't that just another rodent?"

"No, a mongoose is an attack rodent; they eat snakes."

"Snakes?"

"They win through superior defense. Bruce Lee based his whole martial art form on the little mongoose. *Jeet Kune Do* means to turn the fist. The mongoose lures the snake to strike, which it avoids then it strikes before the snake can recover. The mongoose is a very worthy warrior; he eats snakes."

"Okay, so ask your question?"

"What question?"

"The one you've been thinking about all night."

"Okay, how do I get my own radio?"

"Knew you wanted to ask me that," he laughs while placing four chairs about a round table. First, you have to fill out a permission slip, which takes over a month for approval, longer if the guards don't like you. Then you submit the slip with an order form to the commissary store."

"How much does a radio cost?"

"Twenty-nine ninety-five," then he adds with a slow smile, "at seven cents an hour it'll take you only four hundred and twenty-eight hours to buy a radio." Clayton sighs, "I already did the math. We work a seven day week and get paid for a six hour day so if you don't buy anything else, that equals seventy-one days of cleaning up after really twisted inmates who love leaving gross messes; then you'll be having things; a man of substance. It'll earn you respect."

"You're kidding."

"Absolutely not, you become a man of having things and people here will react differently to you. Means you can barter and that makes you important."

"I am not looking to be important, I just want to survive…and I would like to have a radio."

"Don't knock having things. It could save your life. Having things means you can do favors like loaning it out for an evening or rent it for something you want. Having things gains you the kind of respect that helps to keep the riffraff away."

"So I want to be having things?"

"Didn't I just say that? Course some bum might stick you in the back one night for your stuff."

I am beginning to realize that prison is like a university on life. I just wish I did not have to attend all of the prerequisite courses.

Thinking about the radio, I do some of my own calculations. Considering I have to buy stamps to mail my letters and a few toiletries I can figure on having that radio in about three months. A quarter of a year wait for something I desperately want right now, if anything, prison is going to be about learning patience and delayed gratification. For a couple of moments, I ponder waiting forty-five years for my release. Maybe by then I will be able to afford a color TV. I sigh, put my hands in my pockets and stare at the darkness outside the yard door waiting for the food cart to arrive.

I hear rolling wheels, gentle clanking noises of trays bouncing then see an inmate pushing our food cart to the North Yard door. I notice he is wearing a hair net as he opens our cart, snakes something out and walks away chewing on it. I start to get angry, then remember that I have a stolen banana prior.

The guard locks us behind the grill to wheel the cart inside. I can smell the oatmeal from behind the bars. Funny, I never noticed before that oatmeal smells so good. As the guard unlocks the grill he whispers, "You guys did a good job cleaning yesterday so I ordered an extra two meals."

It is surprising how excited I am imagining two extra bowls of cold oatmeal.

Unpacking the cart, I find the tray with my name (creatively miss spelt) before Clayton can get his paws on it, then peruse the other trays for a couple of bowls of relatively lump-free oatmeal. Only my vegetarian tray and a Jewish inmate's kosher meal have name labels. Seems to me that having my name on a tray is an invitation for some maniac in the kitchen to put something nasty into my entrée. For a demented inmate, knowing the name of the unfortunate guy getting your body wastes in a bowl might be too alluring so I am taking no chances on snot seasoning...or worst. Whenever they serve us oatmeal or grits, I switch out that part of my plate for someone else's. *No Stephen, this certainly is not YMCA camp.*

While heating the oatmeal in the microwave, I rinse off then munch one of the perpetual carrot sticks that are always a part of my veggie tray. Instead of letting the perpetual carrot sticks get boring; I think of them as entertainment for the rabbit I am pretending to be this morning. I take little bites with my front teeth and paw at my ear for Clayton's and my amusement; if you do not laugh in prison you wind up crying. We eat on the move while continuing to set up the television room. The rest of the inmates will soon be gathering at the grill and it is best if they do not see us orderlies eating while handling their trays; makes them kind of suspicious...

rightfully...that we might be raiding their meals.

"Gate!" yells the guard. The waiting inmates quickly move away from the grill so the guard can unlock it. The television room floods with boisterous hungry inmates and for the next half-hour, Clayton and I are busy serving in a riotous tip-free milieu. Well maybe I should not call it tip-free. So far while serving meals I have learned how to steal a car or an identity, break into houses, score stolen credit cards, make crack cocaine and cook crystal meth from a very dubious recipe that has the potential to blow up the cook and his residence.

After the rest of the inmates are locked back in their cells Clayton and I give the television room a serious cleaning. This is an every meal event, as the men seem to be in a serious competition to see who can make the biggest mess. It is like repressed emotions coming out of frustrated children who resented mom enforcing table manners. It is remarkable what one finds stuck beneath the tables or boot-squished under the chairs. Clayton and I do a good job...after all there is an oatmeal incentive to consider.

Later the guard announces yard time and we line up at the J-3 yard door for our coveted hour of sunshine. I am standing near the front of the line with an old black man staring at me with bulbous eyes. He tries to edge a little closer to the front of the line, but the inmate ahead of him pushes the old man back. The old man glares at me again then sticks out his elbows like a bird defending its territory to make sure I stay behind him. I am highly amused.

When the guard opens the door, the line begins to file out, but as soon as the old man is out the door, he begins a running shuffling gait for my patch of grass. I pretend to chase after him, but he is cackling with happiness at his success of being first. He beats me to the lawn by a couple of steps, unzips his fly and begins to pee upon my grass. It goes on for a rather long time. I believe he saves up for this moment. He is a statue of absolute bliss watching his pee stream. I am sure that he is reliving boyhood memories in the process.

Walking over to the faucet with my bucket, I pause to stare up at the sky unhindered by the distortion of a thick prison windowpane. It is a thick broken overcast, yet the sky has such incredible depth as I peer into the cloudy heights. Far vision is something jail inmates do not regularly get to exercise. From the confined yard, I only see a very narrow piece of the broad sky. Then I walk over to the faucet with my dented bucket and stand there holding open the spigot's rusty spring-loaded knob. The small spout of water driven by inconsistent pressure either coughs ups a weak upward stream or leaks a downward dribble. Since I continuously have to adjust the bucket's height to catch the flow, I turn the chore into a musical event. I carefully listen to the trickle of the water slowly filling the pail; I have come to enjoy this humble waterfall-like sound. The trickle of falling water creates a soft liquid melody. It is surprising how in prison one tends to take pleasure in the smallest of things. The gentle sound of the spilling water delights me. I love how it makes a hollow drumming cadence when the bucket is empty, which becomes a splash fest until the water level reaches an inch or so. By raising, lowering and tilting the bucket I change the pitch and depth of the water music. I do not close my eyes to listen; I want to see the trickling cascade of water. I watch the water level leisurely climb hearing the pitch deepen as the bucket gradually fills. Then it is off to the new grass to watch what is so clean and pure pouring from the rusty bucket onto the young green living sprouts. This is my main recreational moment of the day. I watch the spilling water turn the dry earth beneath the sparse grass a deep wet vibrant brown. What was once litter-strewn dead dirt is now life producing soil. I smell the wet earth scent of the dirt as it sucks up the water. Leaning closer, I see a small bug climbing one of the short green stalks and imagine its world from a bug's perspective. Obviously, it likes the new grass too, which has to be a lot better than a cigarette butt or gum wrapper to climb on even for a bug.

Six buckets later, I set the pail beside the jail unit door then eagerly take off for my morning run. Now that I am familiar with all of the inmates in my cellblock, I know who to avoid as I run at a faster pace than the confined area would normally allow. I inhale deeply the fresh ocean air. I smell kelp from the rocks of the break-water just outside the east prison wall. I hear a seagull complaining about something beyond the walls, but gulls are always complaining about something. It is frustrating to be so close to the ocean that I love, but not being able to see it. Yet I am thankful to be so close to it. Water, I love water. The sound, the taste and the liquid feel of it.

All too soon our short hour outside ends, I take a last glance at the sky then walk reluctantly into the dim corridor. Inside the cellblock, I grab a thin hole-worn towel from our cell and head for the shower room. Hanging the towel from a hook I glance at my distorted reflection in a sheet of stainless steel screwed to the wall over the sink. This piece of metal functions as an inmate-safe mirror. One side of the steel sheet is bent after a frustrated inmate tried to rip it off the wall; he was probably looking to make a weapon. My warped reflection is distorted by the bent metal, yet the image I see is reassuring...I am still me. I look away and step into the shower.

I spin the hot water knob all the way open. There is no threat of being burned by the tepid water, which is never more than luke-warm if that. I stand under the weak stream with both eyes on the open door. I do not need any inmate surprises. Lately a Latin smuggler has been making unwanted advances. I have been hostile in return so I do not know why he continues to harass me...maybe it is the publicity thing. The DeLorean Case is regularly on the front page of the Los Angeles newspapers and is a nightly feature on the television news stations. Some of the guys get off calling me a celebrity inmate; it is an odd word combination. Maybe the Colombian is jealous of the attention or possibly, he wants to make a name for himself. When I am near, he likes to brag about the guys he has forcefully had in other prisons. Physically he is not especially threatening, not more than six feet tall carrying about two hundred pounds. I may have to hurt him if he does not back off. He recently pled to a drug conspiracy charge with intent to distribute cocaine. His sentencing is scheduled for next month, which is when they will release him to the North Yard. Interesting that I would think of being sent to the North Yard as a release, but being locked in this constricted single wing of a building is really getting to me.

Lunch is a real inmate crowd pleaser...hot dogs and stale potato chips with a soap opera blaring from the television. The Latin dude is bragging loudly about another of his supposed reluctant inmate conquests. Apparently, the story is for my benefit as he keeps looking in my direction. I am beginning to feel downright hostile towards him as I drop his tray onto the table from a height of about a half foot.

"Hey, homes," he glares, "careful with the groceries." He glances at his cronies about the table, "Housewives can be so darn moody."

Yep, I am definitely going to have to hurt him. Fighting can land both of us in The Hole and I have no desire to go back to J-1. I should confront him when no one else is around; not an easy challenge in a crowded cellblock where everyone is interested in everyone else's business.

The next morning, I wake up even earlier than normal and spend the time concentrating on my Gung Fu moves. I have added push-ups and sit-ups to my routine with some isometric exercises. Lately, I have been working on increasing the speed of my movements. To attain faster reflexes requires very loose muscles and a calm focused mind; not easily achieved during the intensity of a fistfight. Prison fights are brutal affairs usually involving home-made weapons so my trying to stay relaxed is going to be hugely challenging. I have practiced karate for fourteen years, but never with this level of intensity and earnest commitment.

My opportunity to discourage the Latin predator arrives suddenly. I had no time to consider, only to act. We are lined up in the corridor beside the yard door. I am last in line because of a sudden urge to leave my T-shirt inside my cell. It is surprisingly sunny outside and I want to feel the warmth of the sun on my skin. The shirt will stay fresher on my bunk and there is less chance that an inmate will nick it if I leave it outside on a bench. The laundry cart is still a long two days away. The guard is outside holding the outer door open counting the men as they step out. Once we all file out into the yard, he will walk back inside through the short hallway to lock the inner and then the outer yard doors, then he will exit through the North Yard door and stand just outside the fence to watch us. Currently he cannot see inside the cellblock, which is an automatic inmate opportunity for mischief. Cortez has maneuvered himself to the end of the line just ahead of me. When we are the last two in the corridor, he turns suddenly and leers at me. "Hey housewife, daddy's here," he abruptly grabs my pectoral muscle and squeezes hard.

Feeling his disgusting hand on my bare skin, I react instantly; seemingly without thought, but years of training and conditioning instantly take over. Cortez is about to open his mouth to say some-thing raunchy, but the only sound that comes out is a shriek of intense pain as I lay my hand over his, twist his wrist and violently invert it towards his forearm. Applying pressure at the thumb joint and savagely rotating his palm inward means I own this man. With very little effort, I could shatter his wrist joint. Instead, I slam my forearm into the backside of his elbow making an arm bar for leverage and easily force Cortez to bend over at the waist, in a head down position. Raising his hand and arm upwards forces his head down below his butt…the man is helpless and in serious pain, which is very gratifying. From his initial touch to my achieving this pre-takedown position has taken less than two seconds. I now have many options from dislocating his shoulder to completely taking the joint apart with the added bonus of an accelerated smashing of his face into the floor or a handy cinderblock wall. Instead, I all but effortlessly hold him helpless. I lean close and snarl in this rodent's ear, "If you touch me again, I will break your wrist and tear your shoulder apart." I shove him away and without looking back walk down the short hallway to step out into the sunshine.

"Hey!" the guard yells down the hallway, "who's lingering in there?"

Cortez stumbles out massaging his wrist and rolling his aching shoulder.

"What were you doing?"

"Nothing," he grumbles.

The guard steps inside to lock the doors as Cortez glares at me. I stare back with intense hatred then turn my back on him, which is a huge inmate insult, pick up the bucket and head for the fountain.

Three buckets later, my heart rate still is not normal. Cortez is playing dominos pretending nothing has happened. His defeat is not something he is going to talk about, which would destroy his reputation as a resident bad guy. Because no one knows, Cortez is not honor bond to try to get back at me. My Cortez problems are history, not that I would ever let my guard down around him. However, I now have a lifelong enemy. Instead of the usual six buckets full of water for the lawn, I stop at three. I have too much energy bubbling in my veins to wait for the dribbling fountain to fill the bucket. I start to run the small perimeter, but the pace is too slow for all my energy with a dozen pacing men always in the way. So instead, I jog to the wire fence and start doing pushups or sit-ups. When my arms or stomach tires, I leap up and sprint for the opposite wall. I drop for more pushups/sit-ups…then sprint, repeatedly. I know why I am doing this. It is an animal thing; showing an adversary your strength and endurance; letting him know that it would be a huge mistake to challenge this animal. How primal... how so very appropriate in this inmate jungle. I am enjoying myself immensely. I want to pound my chest and howl. I have passed my first real physical test.

Back inside, I choose not to shower. I want to stink...I am in animal mode. When lunch arrives, I eye the rows of blackened hamburgers in the cart wanting to eat them all. I am in a mood. Instead munching the carrot sticks returns me to sanity. I gobble everything on my veggie tray where the main event is two scoops of white rice with a small pile of peas and a couple of pieces of white Wonder Bread. Unsatisfied I go to my secret hideout. Using a broom handle, I raise a ceiling tile where I have concealed a couple of cereal boxes (individual servings) of raisin bran. Clayton sees me, but it is no big deal, I know where his secret stash is too only he is more into hiding desserts.

The guard opens the grill and the inmates rush for their favorite tables. I spy Cortez at a corner table and drop his tray the usual six inches, but he ignores me pretending incredible interest in what the uneducated jerk next to him is saying. I resist the urge to paw the floor with my sneaker and growl; I am on a primal high.

The rest of the week passes uneventfully, which in prison is pretty darn good. It is noted by the other inmate bullies that Cortez has now chosen to ignore me; even though I occasionally foolishly bait him. Fewer inmates are willing to listen to his stories; he struts less. In our primal society, where almost nothing goes un-noticed, a predator has been defanged. It interests me to watch the pecking order re-shuffle itself. On Friday, Cortez is transferred out to general population. Clayton and I are cleaning the television room after lunch. The rest of the cellblock is in lockdown. The guard locks us behind the grill then the North Yard guard opens the outer door and Cortez steps to the door, turns to stare momentarily at me then turns his back and walks out into the North Yard.

"That guy really hates you," says Clayton.

"Yeah, I know."

"He used to like trying to bullying you."

"Yeah."

"So what did you do to him?" Clayton asks for the twentieth time.

"It's not what I did to him," I answer, "it's what I didn't do to him.

"There are risks and costs to a program of action, but they are far less than the long-range risks and costs of comfortable inaction," John Kennedy

Shot this picture of Susan that 1st day at the Pipeline.

"When you meet someone better than yourself, turn your thoughts to becoming his equal. When you meet someone not as good as you are, look within and examine your own self,"
Confucius

Chapter 27

TERMINAL ISLAND FEDERAL PRISON,

J-3, DECEMBER 1982

WEDNESDAY MORNING is commissary day, the highlight of another drab week. If an inmate has money in his prison account, he can make simple purchases from a short shopping list that includes cigarettes, candy, instant coffee, Lipton tea, Cups of Noodles, toiletries, etc. Many inmates lacking their own funds try to borrow from others or commit assorted acts of extortion on the weaker inmates.

Standing in line waiting for the commissary issue, I glance over my shoulder to see the kindly, old black man, the one who so likes watering my lawn with his urine, disappear into his cell. A homeless man from the back streets of Los Angeles, I know that he has no family or friends to send him money. He is much too proud to consider borrowing from the other inmates. When the commissary cart makes its weekly appearance, he quietly shuffles down the hall and sulks in his cell. As I see his cell door close, I happily think about the surprise I am getting for him.

The old man is a chronic cigar smoker. Yesterday, I watched him hand rolling a homemade cigar from the cheap bulk tobacco issued to the inmates by the prison staff. He begins by wadding up a handful of the loose tobacco into a fat cylinder, which he carefully lays into a brown paper towel. Rolling the paper towel back and forth on a wooden bench, he tamps it into a crude cigar. Then he lightly dampens the thick makeshift cigar with water from the drinking fountain, which caught the attention of Shorty, who has to come over to investigate.

"What ya doing?" asks Shorty leaning over the elderly man's shoulder.

"I'm dampening my cigar," the old man replies patiently.

"Why don't you just lick it?"

"Cause I ain't got that much spit," the old man grumbles.

"Well, how come you gotta wet it anyhow?" Shorty could be very persistent with his questions until he gets what he considers a satisfactory answer.

The old man turns to regard Shorty, the contemptuous look on his stubbly face shows that he does not think Shorty is very bright as he growls, "Because if I don't wet the paper towel first, the fire will run right up the sides of the cigar and fry my face."

"Oh," shrugs Shorty, who interest satisfied, walks away.

Finally, I arrive at the front of the commissary line and receive a brown paper sack with my last name printed on it in crude pencil drawn letters. I take the sack to my cell to open it. It is never wise to let other inmates see your purchases. I set the sack on my bunk and peer anxiously inside. For the barest moment, a childhood memory leaps vividly to mind. I remember being in elementary school and opening my sack lunch in hopeful anticipation of finding peanut butter cookies inside. The memory passes quickly as I reach into the sack and instead of cookies remove two small boxes of cigars. Each paper box holds five cigars. I carry them to the old man's cell and tap lightly on his door. It is never a good idea to enter a prison cell without knocking. You are libel to see some rather disgusting things that can be quite mentally haunting.

"Come in already," grumbles the old man's raspy voice, "I ain't got no key to keep you out no how." I open the door and step inside. The close air in the cell carries the old man's smell like a signature. There is, of course, the lingering odor of his homemade cigar smoke, but also there is the sickness smell common to an aged person who is slowly dying. The staff is bunking the old man in J-3 because they do not have room for him in the prison medical ward upstairs. He has multiple advanced cancers and the staff anticipates that he will probably die in J-3. The old man shares that belief. It is very sad to consider that his life will end in this lonely, uncaring jail. Then again, maybe it is better than dying in an alcoholic stupor in a dark alley hacking out your lungs in the shelter of a dumpster with rats eagerly awaiting your demise. At least here, he is sober and conscious that death is stalking him. Maybe that is why he made a foolish attempt to rob a bank with just a crudely written note. At least here, his last days will be with a full belly and sleeping on a bed out of the weather.

The old man is lying on the half-shadowed lower bunk, his bulbous eyes gleam in the semi-darkness. "What do you want, youngster"" he asks.

I hold up the cigars, "The commissary man made a mistake and put these here cigars in my sack. Rather than return them, I thought you might want them."

The whites of the old man's eyes flash in the shadows, "Don't want no charity boy." He coughs wetly into his stained pillow; it racks his slim frame.

"I got them by mistake," I say softly.

"Saves your money for yourself," he grumbles.

"My brother sent me the money. It doesn't hurt to share his kindness." Taking a step closer, I set the cigars on the edge of his bunk. "You might as well have them. Better than just throwing them out don't you think?"

I turn swiftly and exit the cell. Outside in the corridor I take several deep breaths washing my lungs of the death smell that lingers in that cell. The commissary cigars will not do his lungs any good, but they have to be better than inhaling burning paper towels and thick wads of loose tobacco. I hope that the reduced smoke with its lessened load of debris might help to lighten some of his pain and give him a bit of comfort. Before depression can set in, I quickly return to my own cell and tear open the commissary sack. Inside is the little box radio I have been anxiously awaiting courtesy of my brother's check deposited into my prison account.

Removing the radio from its protective box, I set it on the dented locker. It is just a little mono unit with a single two-inch speaker. Turning it on, I tune the radio to a local 60's station and hear the opening strains of one of my favorite songs from high school. I turn the volume up as the music builds on itself, the happy surfer beat washing in waves into the hollowness of the cell. I close my eyes, giving myself up to the music, amazed that the tiny fifty-cent speaker so fills the small cell, its sound reverberating off the walls and driving away the noise of the jail unit outside my thick metal door. I immerse myself in music and am a much more cheerful soul when an hour later I leave the cell to set up the television room for lunch. Clayton is in court today, I look forward to his surprise when I share the radio with him tonight.

Out in the corridor, I see the old black man shuffling along with a big toothless grin wrapped around one of those store-bought cigars. His eyes look even more bulbous than normal as his jaw industriously works that cigar. As he passes he quietly says, "Thanks, youngster," then goes tramping off down the corridor followed by a dense cloud of cigar smoke.

For the rest of the week, he struts around the yard smoking or just chewing on those cigars. He wastes not a bit of those precious store-bought cigars, when they get down to half-inch stubs he carefully saves them in his pocket to remake into one of his homemade cigars for later. Then on Saturday morning, the guard opens the old man's cell door to find he passed away in his sleep. As they take the thin body away on a stretcher, I know that I will always remember him best seeing his lanky frame poised over the small lawn with the stub of a cigar sticking out of his mouth while he happily peed on my grass.

During the early evening when the cellblock is its loudest, I usually try to immerse myself in a good book. There is little outside stimulus in prison to draw the mind's attention from itself. Since I cannot journey outward, I take long trips within. I follow many paths on the winding course that leads to my inner being. I discover secrets that I have unconsciously hidden even from myself. I have sealed them away under the lock of acute embarrassment. Sometimes I stumble unexpectedly upon one of these uncomfortable memories. I identify them easily by the habitual mental cringe that I experience whenever they come to mind. Mostly they are about stupid little things, petty incidents in my life, mostly childhood blunders and adult humiliations. I find that by re-thinking them, plunging into their essence, I can forgive myself by understanding what I had done wrong thus wiping away the guilt. I heal many old wounds and can soon freely remember them without the habitual cringe. It is a wonderful discovery and it actively encourages me to seek out those dark memories like buried treasure. I rejoice in their detection and the revelations that they teach me, then I sweep them away like unneeded baggage.

That night in my cell, I dwell upon the vitality of life that I am missing, locked within these drab prison walls. At the cell's window there is little for me to see at night. A thirty-foot-tall security wall blocks most of the view and looking up I cannot see the stars for the bright glare of the security lights glaring downward from their tall poles. I think about the old man passing away here. The only things that I know gave him any pleasure were the cigars and peeing on my lawn. I wonder what memories shuffled through his mind while peeing on that grass. Did the lawn help to carry him back to his boyhood memories? I think about the isolation and weathering the old man forced upon his soul. Then I consider what kind of future I have imposed upon myself. Will I grow old inside? Will I die in the joint. Will my death be sudden and unexpected? Does it anticipate my release to general population where the gangs and murderers wait?

Clayton is sleeping below, so I pick up my radio insert the earplug that came with it and quietly listen to music from my child-hood on an oldies station. An image of the old man racing ahead of me for the lawn, one hand fumbling at his zipper, keeps echoing through my mind. It stirs up another memory of my brother Jim and I standing on a green field as children and seeing who could pee further. Back then, I never would have imagined that prison lay in my future. I just wanted to be a diver for Captain Jacques Cousteau. I realize that I was a happy child, with good fantasies and high hopes. Things began to change towards my becoming a teenager. My dad seldom came home until well after dinner. At night, I would hear my parents arguing. He claiming long hours selling houses, she suspecting another woman. Jim turned sixteen, bought a car and with it, he fled the lonely sadness of our home. Our room mostly became just my room. Childhood happiness left our home when I became a teenager; packed its bags and walked right out the front door. My dad and brother disappeared through that door. Made the answer of how I was to live the rest of my child-hood plain and simple…I was suppose to walk through that door too…the sooner, the better…so I did.

Still not ready to sleep, but not wanting to think about my past family struggles anymore, I climb down from the bunk and stand barefoot on the cold concrete floor. Silently opening the locker, I take out a picture of Susan and Puu Bear that Sam mailed me and look at it under the glow of the security lights glaring in through the window. Susan is on the beach about to throw a stick for Puu to fetch. The lens has caught her with one arm over her head, the stick just released from her fingers. Her long blond hair is blowing in the wind and just beyond the two of them, the wave faces are running twenty feet plus. In my mind, a window into the past slowly opens.

I remember I was sitting on my surfboard in the lineup at

Laniakea Beach Park and saw Susan on the beach waving at me. I was instantly stoked. Susan never bothered to watch me surf before and I was in perfect position to catch a set wave that was rushing in from the open ocean. I paddled furiously surging ahead of the other surfers who were after the same wave. At the last instant, I realized that the wave was bigger than anything I had ever tackled at this break before. From the crest of the wave, I had a sudden elevator view of a twenty-foot tall vertical wall of surging water. For a heart-sinking moment, I wanted to back away from the frightening vertical edge, but then I felt my board falling away as I dropped into that long downward plunge screaming my lungs out. Somehow I maintained enough control to make the bottom turn, the board was flashing across the wave face; I was going faster than ever before on this break—but not fast enough.

With a sinking feeling, I saw that the whole wave was pitching as it washed over a shallow inner reef. Then the thick lip came crashing down like a liquid door closing, trapping me inside a spinning fluid barrel that was rapidly collapsing upon itself. Angling the board hard into the wave face, I made a desperate attempt to arrow the board, followed hopefully by my body, though the thick wall of rushing water and I almost made it. Caught inside the vortex of turbulent water, I could see that I was within a foot of the surface as I strained to punch out the backside of the wave. Looking through the shimmering distortion of the backside of the wave, I saw a bird flying in the sky...then the wave pulled me irresistibly backward. It was like being in a high-rise elevator with a broken cable. They call the rapid backward flushing sensation I was experiencing *being sucked over the falls*. As I watched the rapidly receding sky, I knew that I was in for a very serious trashing.

The thick lip, weighted down with many tons of water, slammed its small human luggage into the sandy bottom. I was extremely fortunate not to hit hard jagged reef. The air I had gulped seconds before was hammered out of my lungs by the massive hydraulic impact. All about me, bubbles were swirling distortedly in a wildly spinning turmoil of rolling water. The surfboard leash on my ankle stretched to double its normal length then snapped. Curled into a tiny protective ball, I bounced along the sandy bottom towards a rocky reef wondering if I was about to do the reef-shredded human hamburger, drowning-thing with Susan watching my last moments from the beach.

Desperately, I made it back to the surface just in time to be slammed by another wave. My surfboard had long since departed for the beach as I began my second underwater excursion, which was a lot like being caught inside a giant Maytag washer stuck on the heavy rinse cycle.

I finally arrived back at the beach, picked up my surfboard that was floating in the froth and tottered wearily across the sand with my broken leash dragging behind me.

That is when I saw Susan throwing the stick, which Puu was fetching back to her. Staggering up to her, trying hard not to wobble at the knees, I asked, "Hey Susan, did you see that magnificent wave I caught?"

Susan gave me *the look*...I knew it well. She had a low opinion of girls who sat on the beach watching their boyfriends surf. She was far too active of a girl just to watch her boyfriend play in the water. "No," she answered shrugging her shoulders, "I was playing with Puu. Why?"

Standing there with wet sand filling my ears and stuffing the crotch of my swimsuit, I realized that the throwing motion Susan was making with the stick looked exactly like the waving motion I saw from out in the line-up. She was playing with Puu, not waving at me.

"Oh, no reason," I replied, dragging my thrashed body toward the truck and half a bottle of aspirin.

I had only gone a few steps when Susan caught up with me. "Steve," she said taking my free hand in hers, "You don't have to try to impress me with your surfing, I already love you."

I could feel the surfboard wax melting in the back pocket of my swimsuit.

Stepping close against me, Susan raised her face and smiled in a way that needed immediate attention. As I lowered my face to hers, I saw Susan close her big brown eyes, and then suddenly my sinuses drained their heavy cargo of salt water that the big wave had impacted into them. In shock, Susan's eyes flew open as sinus-slimed water flushed across her shocked face.

In the darkened cell, I cannot help the laughter that explodes from me. A moment later, a flashlight beam probes into the cell through the small security window in the cell door. I see the guard's face; he is probably wondering what this inmate is doing standing in the dark and laughing. The beam of light switches from me to my bunk; the meaning is clear. Climbing onto the bunk, I turn my face to the wall hoping to recapture my memories of Susan and Puu; instead, I fall into a deep undisturbed sleep.

The next morning, I am up early. Clayton is off to court again and I have to prepare and serve breakfast alone. Afterward the guard locks the rest of the inmates out of the television room while I mop the floor. They pace anxiously behind the locked grill waiting for me to finish so they can come in to watch their soap operas. When the floor is dry, the guard opens the grill and the inmates rush to place chairs in front of the boob tube. Again, the guard locks the grill, only now I am on the other side as I begin to mop the corridor. From the television room I hear the men shouting at each other as they argue over what they are going to watch. Shorty wins the argument with support from four Latinos who actually could have cared less...they just liked going against the three black inmates in the room. The guard switches the channel to Shorty's soap opera. Two of the men who wanted to watch cartoons sit angrily at a back table playing cards. The third black man just sits and stares at Shorty with open hostility.

Pushing the mop side to side, I think about the impact that television has on us inmates. For many inmates their only contact with the outside world is through the glaring orb of the television set. From its flat dimensional image, they sample the essence of life beyond prison walls. Television programming can act as an alternate reality through which many convicts blend their own mixed bag of memories and experiences as they try to project themselves into the imagined reality the actors are portraying. Some of the convicts are so starving for stimulus that they almost seem to be feeding as they stare hungrily at the television screen.

From the far end of the corridor, I hear the high-pitched squeal of Shorty. He is not just watching *All of My Children*, he is living it as he sits in front of the tube talking and shouting at the actors as though he is part of the dialog.

After finishing the floor, I retire to my cell to read. As the cell door closes behind me, the noise from the television room thankfully diminishes. Anticipating that I will have an hour or two to read quietly, I recline completely unaware that in the next few minutes I will be thrown into a violent confrontation with another inmate.

As an orderly, I have the collateral duty of changing the channel on the television when the guard is not there to do it. If left to themselves the other inmates will quickly get into fistfights over the television. So, a vote is taken on channel selection, though usually it is still the biggest bicep that makes the actual decision.

I am a couple of pages into the paperback when Shorty opens the door and asks me to change the channel. A moment later standing before the television, I am reaching for the knob when I hear a frightening growl of outrage. Spinning about I am shaken to see a large, muscular black man hurling a chair from his path as he comes at me shrieking, "I'm going to rip your face off."

The paperback falls unnoticed from my hand. I cannot show fear as the enraged man stomps right up to me. We are all but chest-to-chest with fury distorting his face as he growls, "What gives you the right?"

I point at the bulletin board where the television rules hang.

"Don't give a damn," he pulls the offending paper from the wall, wads it up and throws it down then thrusts his face inches from mine, "What gives you the right, inmate?" he snarls.

A mist of spittle sprays my face. His eyes are fierce, lips curled, shoulders hunched as he clenches his hands. I see muscles bulging beneath his white T-shirt and an icicle of fear knifes through me.

This is it screams my mind.

"I'm going to kill you!" he growls as a few of the other inmates move quickly away from us. Shorty is watching intently from one side, for him this is better than any soap opera.

Why, shrieks my mind, *why me?* Yet, I already know the answer, by accepting the orderly job I have taken, from an inmate perspective, a position of authority and privilege. By changing the channel, I have trampled upon his rights...it is a respect issue. In fact, it is worse than that, he probably thinks that I, an inmate, am pretending to be a trustee or inmate-guard-wannabe. The stupidity of it all makes me mad!

Abruptly, like a furnace door swinging open, my own anger blazes to instant fury. I have contained myself too long. This is the last straw as my sanity flees before the fiery winds of a burning rage. Unconscious, my body adopts a karate-fighting stance. Focusing on my adversary, I have suddenly become a primal male animal ready to fight for its survival and territory. The inmates who haven't already moved scatter clearing a fighting area for us. Shorty, bouncing on his toes, yells, "Yeah."

I ready myself to block his attack. When an enemy strikes, he creates an opening. Steve, the mongoose hopes to instinctively block and counter. Fourteen years of martial arts training focuses in an instant sparking a heightened state of combat awareness and concentration. Slitting my eyes enhances depth perception as I carefully watch my opponent's shoulders. It is important not to focus on the eyes of an adversary, as they can be deceptive and misleading. Any strike by my foe will first be precursored by shoulder movement. My hands stay low, cupped downward, just barely raised above waist level. I look unprepared but I am being deceptive. This is a camouflaged fighting stance as I assume the stilled movements of my praying mantis mentor. My Gung Fu master in Hawaii taught me to diligently mimic this warrior insect's long-armed strike because it so fits my lanky frame. His teachings crystallize into a fabric of mind and body coordination that will react without laborious conscious thought on my part or so I hope. Though I am besotted with rage an icy calmness settles upon me as I remember my teachings and consciously will my muscles to relax. A stressed muscle moves far slower than one that is fluid and loose. My opponent is stronger than I am so I will have to be faster and more cunning than him.

There is rage in the man's eyes. I glare back. Hot blood pounds at my temples. Just when I think he is going to attack—he does not. Instead, he hesitates even though he continues to threaten, "I'm going to waste ya, man!"

Instantly, I know it is over. He is not going to attack, from this point on it is all bluster; a bully working on his image. Unexpectedly, I have already won for having stood my ground. In a voice almost calm, I answer his verbal challenge, "A man does what a man has to do." Later I would think how stupid that statement initially sounds. Yet it is not a threat that I am voicing, just a simple commitment. I am ready to fight and he knows it. I am aware that he expected me to cower because of his size and muscular strength. The thought makes me angry again; I really do not like bullies. Yet it is really over as I see the fighting lust draining out of him. He curses and struts about while glowering at me fiercely, but I know he is just blowing off steam. Then he stops right in front of me and in a hardened voice says, "You better be learning things if you're going to survive in prison, boy."

As we continue to glare at each other, I abruptly realize that he is re-evaluating me. I am a surprise for him; there is just maybe a hint of respect in his eyes and a deep knowing primal intelligence. He is a street-smart man who fully understands prison and gang mentality. I nod, acknowledging that the respect is mutual…not that there is any evidence that he respects me at all. Then he turns and sits down greatly diminished from the monster of but a few moments ago.

When the guard heard about what happened he offered to transfer the man, who he considered a troublemaker, into the hole (J-1).

"No way," I quickly replied, "the problem between us is over."

The guard shrugged his shoulders and walked away, probably

thinking about the futility of helping inmates.

I do not have any more problems with the black man though I often catch him watching me through hooded eyes. His presence keeps me on my toes. I find that when I am around him, which is often in our confined cellblock, I am more alert, more keenly aware of what I am doing. I pay greater attention to what I say and keep my body orientated to repel any sudden hostility. I am constantly reminded that I am in the company of a worthy adversary. This is a concept taught to young American Indian warriors who were encouraged to seek out a truly worthy adversary. The tribal elders knew that it was good to have a strong, cunning and talented opponent upon which to sharpen wits and abilities; a forced awareness and on the job learning program with serious survival incentives. I am living in a prison full of extremely aggressive opponents with the continuous threat of real violence a constant companion. I am facing life in prison completely alone, but for just a couple of friends; two of them are short and weak, the other one is massive and strong, but probably wouldn't openly admit to being my friend. Actually, I do not anticipate seeing Mose again considering that he is permanently locked in the hole, yet there is no assurance that I won't wind up back there again. Living in a violent prison society means nothing is certain. Secretly, I wonder what my worthy adversary thinks of me...then again I have not yet come to terms with what I think of myself.

> *"Deep unspeakable suffering may well be called a baptism, a regeneration, the initiation into a new state,"* George Eliot

The lights have been out in the cell for a couple of hours and I cannot sleep. I am deeply troubled and worried that prison might be irresistibly changing me for the worst. I am afraid that I may be on the verge of becoming a more violence prone person.

My mother and brother came for a visit today and something shocking happened. At the table in the visiting room an unexpected raging emotion abruptly surfaced in my mind...I had a sudden urge to punch my mother. I actually saw a mental image of my fist heading for my mother's face. Why did an unbidden thought like that pop into my mind? I have always loved my mother and have never considered hitting any woman; especially not my mother. The thought was too repulsive to consider. Yet I did conjure up the image...why?

I lay there rethinking our conversation, but what would prompt such a violent response? It has to have something to do with my being in prison. Is prison changing me that much already? I know I am more aggressive, but that is because I have to be to survive in here. However, is this violent streak spreading uncontrollably? I can mostly rule out my encounter with the black man, which was defensive on my part. My recent incident with Cortez might seem to be pointing in that direction, yet I had consciously resisted actually damaging him though the urge to break something had been eagerly present. The vivid mental picture of my hitting my mother is still prowling around in my mind and I do not like it lurking there in the darker corners. I am in deep self-evaluation and desperately need someone to help me.

I wrestle with this image that I do not like long into the night and slowly I begin to better, but not fully, understand. I am carrying a deep inner resentment that my mother does not really care that much about me. To be fair to her, she did raise me and nurse young Stephen through his childhood injuries. After the divorce, she had to find a job while saddled with the burden of raising an adolescent son. My brother Jim had moved out right after the divorce then joined the Army and went off to Vietnam. After my dad left, I was mostly on my own, which was not anything new. All four of us Arringtons lived our separate lives. My father had no parental urges.

Over the next three years, I worked a series of after school jobs to pay my own expenses. Neither my mother nor I spent much time in our home; it was where we changed our clothes and slept. We did not eat together and seldom did we visit. I saw my friends' mothers far more than my own.

Two weeks out of high school, I joined the Navy. I did four tours in Vietnam not receiving a single letter or telephone call from her. Returning from my first tour to Vietnam, I hitchhiked to her apartment to surprise her and knocked on the door. A stranger answered. My mother had moved and neither he nor I knew where.

Later, my mother got married for the second time, but her husband and I did not have much in common. I would dutifully visit her, but it was not something I particularly looked forward to, just an obligation.

That is partially what had so upset me in the visiting room. I felt my mother had come to visit because it was what she was supposed to do. However, there was something else. She was just too thrilled at all of the attention my case had generated for her. It was what she was talking about when I had that terrible mental image. How her telephone was just ringing all the time because people wanted to know how she was handling her son's arrest. Our visit was providing her with a wealth of gossip to share with her friends.

In the semidarkness of the cell, I begin to realize that I am still harboring childhood anger over the rejection by both of my parents. It is not a prison thing corrupting my humanness; it is the emotions of a frustrated child inside an immature man, who is not dealing well with incarceration. The only companionship that I have is letters from friends or the occasional collect telephone call I make somewhat reluctantly and my conversations with Clayton or Morris. Later I would learn that Clayton actually was a snitch working for the government. I never told him that I knew because I really needed a friend. I know that he felt the same way because he knew that I knew, but we just did not talk about it.

A week after my move to Clayton's cell his lawyer came to see him. At the end of the J-3 cellblock, just beyond the guard's office, was the attorney visiting room. While pacing the corridor, I had seen him with his attorney and had not thought much about it. When Clayton returned to the cellblock, the guard called my name for an attorney visit. It was a bit surprising because my court appointed lawyer only saw me at the courthouse. I walked into the attorney visiting room and was surprised to see Clayton's lawyer standing there. He claimed to be representing the government with an official offer seeking my cooperation. The man felt slimy, I did not like talking to him. I knew that becoming a snitch meant working for the less ethical side of law enforcement and that they completely take over your life. It would mean being owned again by someone like Morgan. I said, "No," and very sadly returned to my cell.

Clayton asked me how it went and I said, "You don't want to know." After that, we were just content to be friends, the government snitch and the reluctant celebrity inmate who was dealing with mother issues.

Remembering the day I hitchhiked home to discover that my mother had unexpectedly moved called another memory to mind that occurred earlier that day fourteen years ago. I had been dropped off at a freeway exit that did not have an onramp. I had to walk over a mile carrying a heavy sea bag on my shoulder to the next onramp. I was in the process of feeling sorry for myself, when I saw a group of handicapped students on a school playground. One of them sat on the other side of the fence in his wheelchair watching me walk by on the street. I threw him a casual wave, which he enthusiastically returned waving with both arms. It made me ponder what I looked like to him, walking on two strong legs and wearing a sailor's uniform, which spoke of world travel. No doubt that child would have given anything to be carrying that sea bag in my place and wearing a uniform that promised world travel and adventure. I made a promise back then not to feel sorry for myself ever again. I ponder that promise until I fall asleep.

The next afternoon I am sitting in the television room catching the news. It is still surprising to see my arrest being repeatedly played as a clip in news stories about DeLorean.

"Hey Arrington," yells an inmate reading a newspaper in the back of the room, "Guess what?"

I turn in my chair not very interested in anything this dim wit might have to say.

"You made the funny page," he cackles.

"What?"

"Doonesbury, the cartoon strip," he is pointing at the paper, "you're in it."

"Na."

"Yeah, Trudeau is doing a strip on the DeLorean case becoming a movie." Listen to this," he giggles, "one of the cartoon characters is telling a bag lady that you kept your boat berthed next to his in Fort Lauderdale, then he boasts that he even loaned you his deck gun for one of your clandestine operations."

The inmate shakes his head, "That's pretty funny stuff; I'm in prison with a real live cartoon character." He turns to stare at me almost as if he is seeing me for the first time. "Hey," he says, suddenly inspired, "how about autographing this for me?"

The next day a toilet clogs in one of the other cells. The guard admits two inmate plumbers from general population to fix it. This is an extremely rare event. The staff segregates jail unit inmates from general population inmates to prevent hits (murders) from going down during important court cases. The guard watches them working for a while, but then bored he retires into his office, which is at the other end of the cellblock behind a thick security door. From there he cannot monitor the cellblock, which is why the two inmate plumbers chose that moment to walk boldly into my cell.

I am relaxing on my upper bunk idly reading, <u>Lord of the Rings</u>. Completely engrossed in the fantasy story of trolls, dwarfs, wizards and hobbits, I do not realize that I am in danger until I casually look up from the page to see who is coming through my door—my alarm is instantaneous.

The two burly inmates crowding into the cell are bikers. The headbands they wear identify them as members of the Aryan Brotherhood, a white racist gang known for its extreme violence against other inmates. They both have the muscular build of dedicated weight lifters. I immediately realize that they are general population inmates and that a hit is going down—, and that I am it!

The first one through the door has deep set, fanatical eyes that glare from a heavily bearded face. At the corner of his right eye, there are three blue tattooed teardrops. "Are you Arrington?" he demands gruffly.

My eyes fall to his right hand, which grasps a long, heavy-duty screwdriver. Rust covers most of the shank, but for the nicked tip that is deadly shiny from a recent sharpening. I have never visualized a screwdriver as a weapon before, but now the horrible image of being stabbed by that long, rusted shank explodes in my mind. I am literally on the verge of voiding my bowels. I feel them turning watery with fear. I know I may be about to die. It seems so incredibly unfair. I urgently want to flee or at least be able to stand to defend myself, but there is no opening. One biker is at the foot of my bed and the close-eyed one is approaching from the only open side. I am trapped as death crowds against my bunk.

The brute with the screwdriver leans heavily on the edge of the mattress, "Hey," he growls, "I asked you a question." He shifts his weight to his left foot, apparently to give him driving force. I know he will first thrust for my gut. I want to distance myself from him, but the wall presses coldly against my back. The other inmate glances out the door to make sure that the guard is not about, then whispers urgently, "We gotta hurry man."

I want to scream, instead in a weak whisper I hear myself say, "Yeah, I'm Arrington." *Stupid, stupid,* yells my inner voice, *why did you tell them your name?*

The inmate transfers the heavy screwdriver to his left hand; the tip wavers between my gut and groin. I am hoping to block or deflect his strike with one hand and then try to drive the paperback book into his eye. The brute grins through his dark beard showing yellowed and crowded teeth. I watch his right hand disappear into his shirt pocket and extract a piece of crumpled newspaper. "Mind signing this for me?" he asks hopefully.

It is the Trudeau Doonesbury comic strip. I sign my name quickly with the stub of a pencil to mask my trembling fingers.

"Worry gives a small thing a big shadow." Swedish Proverb

Photo Sam
In prison surfing is but memories treasured. Author surfing at Black's Beach in San Diego before moving to the desert.

"I know how men in exile feed of dreams of hope,"
Aeschylus 525 – 456 BC

Chapter 28

TERMINAL ISLAND FEDERAL PRISON,

J-3, DECEMBER 1982

L ATE THE next afternoon, physically and mentally exhausted, I am napping in my cell. Abruptly, I hear inmates shouting and the crash of chairs and tables being thrown against the walls and tumbling across the floor. The guard runs down the corridor furiously yelling, "Lock down, lock down, everyone into your cells now! Move it!" Then I hear him on the radio urgently calling for assistance.

Clayton is in court, so I am alone in the cell wondering who just got beat up in the television room. Inmates from the television room run past my door heading for their cells. Half a minute later, a posse of guards charge down the corridor. One of them takes his ring of keys and starts locking all the cell doors, the rest rush into the television room. Standing at the cell door nose-pressed to the small security window I am surprised to see one of the older inmates, his white shirt splattered with blood, hands cuffed behind his back, being roughly drug down the corridor by two furious guards. The guy is in his late sixties. He is a white-collar crime kind of inmate in for insurance fraud. What would he be fighting about and with whom? Sometimes the old guys can get very cranky if one of them is caught trying to cheat at dominos or cards. With three or four inmates in a card game cheating is a routine event. I see a medical orderly wheeling in a gurney and a couple of minutes later he returns from the television room with a bloody cargo. The shocker is that the victim is a young guy. He is new in the cellblock, nineteen, maybe twenty years old. What would cause an old man to go off on someone more than forty years his junior? Blood-soaked bandages cover most of the young man's head. Whatever happened he lost big time…to an old guy?

Five minutes later the guard opens my cell door, "Arrington out!" he snarls. The man is in a major mood.

I follow him as he stomps into the television room, which is a shambles. Overturned tables are strewn about, some upside down and others lying on their sides, a wide swatch of blood splatters one wall and before it blood pools on the floor. There are multiple boot prints from guards having walked through the still slowly spreading puddle of crimson. "What happened?" I ask stunted.

"Soap opera fight," he answers gruffly, "clean it up." Then he marches down the corridor to his office to begin a very long report.

Alone in the shadow of violence, I stare at the horror of all of the blood. A mop bucket with its attached wringer lies tipped over on its side by the blood-splattered wall. The wringer's metal handle lies on the floor half inside the pool of blood. I right the bucket then pick up the metal handle careful of the dripping blood and drop it into the bucket then roll the mop wringer down to the dip sink room. I rinse off the handle, fill the bucket with warm water and return to the television room. First I mop up the blood on the floor then sponge the blood from the wall all the time thinking about what had just happened and why. The old man's prison profile just got drop kicked to the top of the violent behavior charts. From low-risk white collar prisoner with the modest privileges it implies to violent, high-risk inmate headed for the Hole and some seriously hostile company. Whatever charges he was facing before are modest compared to assault with a weapon in prison. At his age, he has probably just sentenced himself to the rest of his life in prison and it will not be at a low security facility. Nope, he is going to do hard time with the most vicious of inmates. Since he is not particularly large, nor athletic, he is going to be a perpetual victim. All because he felt a need to pick up a pipe from the mop bucket and wallop a younger man with it...over a soap opera.

Few inmates get visitors. Many of the solitary men are so desperate for normal companionship that they often become addicted to soap operas, which in some strange way is an odd substitute for a real family life. The orb of the television seemingly mutates into an imaginary window to the outside world free of concrete, bars, razor wire, frustrated inmates, homemade weapons and perpetually angry guards. Changing the channel on an inmate addicted to soap operas can be a life-threatening mistake. Our newest inmate undoubtedly did not know that and is now paying the price of his ignorance in the prison infirmary with a fractured skull. That is two lives forever altered over a channel surfing dispute. The repercussions for bad choices certainly do not end with arrest and incarceration, rather it is just the beginning of serious suffering and tragedy.

I carefully wheel the sloshing, but not spilling, mop bucket down the dim corridor of repeating steel doors to the deep sink room. The steel bucket is dented and banged-up, it wheels are wobbly and its cargo of crimson liquid ripples as I push it along—unable not to stare into its depths. Though I know it is mostly water, it looks like three or four gallons of blood. At the door to the deep sink room, I pause to flick on the light. The recessed low-watt bulb is protected with a thick-yellowed piece of grimy glass and a rusty wire screen. The dim light falls in a yellow cone directly over the deep sink leaving the rest of the tiny room shadowed. I pick up the heavy bucket and slowly begin to dump the liquid into the deep sink and then I just stare unable to look away. The sink is old, cracked, stained and mildewed with a rusty drain half-clogged with human hair and other filth. I watch the crimson liquid swirling down that dark drain like a giant leech sucking blood and suddenly feel physically ill; it is as if I am seeing my own life swirling down that black hairy hole. *"I am never going to get out of here alive,"* the thought smothers me in the dim confined room, *"I am going to die in this prison,"* screams my mind. I let the bucket fall from my hands. It lands rim down in the sink, leaking rivulets of blood that slowly crawl towards the red stained drain. I back out into the corridor just as the guard arrives.

"Get back into your cell," he commands, "we are on full lock down."

In a daze, I walk into the cell my hands covered with blood as the heavy door locks behind me. I wash at the sink then strip off my splattered T-shirt and soak it in cold water, then wring it out and hang it from the doorknob to dry. It is cold in that cell as I climb up onto my bunk and pull the threadbare blanket around my shoulders. In a deep depression, I stare at the ceiling pipes then close my eyes.

The guard returns at dinnertime to let me out to serve the meal. I push the food cart down the double bank of cells. He unlocks each door so I can hand in two trays and then he slams the door closed. He is still in a major mood over all the reports generated by the fight. The main course is meatloaf; each serving baked with a dollop of red-oven-blackened ketchup on top. There is a scoop of mashed potatoes with congealed brown gravy, canned green peas, two pieces of white bread and a carton of milk. For dessert. there is a small square of yellow Jell-O with some suspicious white streaks embedded in it. Only a fool would eat that Jell-O. I am a robot as we go from cell to cell. Closing the door to the last cell we return to where we started to collect the empty trays. A third of the trays still carry their cargo of contaminated Jell-O, which means most of the inmates are not very observant about what they eat. Score points for the kitchen pervert. I wheel the cart back into the television room then return to my cell and stand there as I watch the door slam closed and hear the heavy key turn in the lock.

I pace the narrow cell, three steps and turn, three steps and turn until Clayton arrives with his brown paper dinner bag. I briefly tell him what happened, then in no mood to visit climb up onto my bunk.

Two in the morning and I am still wide-awake, thoroughly depressed and dead tired. I am pondering how I, just like that old man, have foolishly thrown away my freedom and am now condemned to watching what is left of me fritter away in a jail cell. *There has got to be more than just trying to survive in prison.* My thought is a plea cast out into a very dark void while my imagination struggles with what I have done. I slowly begin to think about salvation and am surprised to realize that I know almost nothing about it. A thought keeps ricocheting around in my mind; a remembered Bible verse, "The blood will set you free." I certainly know about blood, it still feels like I am covered with it. I can smell its reek despite repeated washings at our cell sink. The verse I realize is a promise, not that the blood may set you free, but that it will set you free. *Can it free me in a prison cell?* I need to talk with someone, but am so completely alone.

The thought comes suddenly like a fast rising bubble rushing towards a turbulent surface to burst quietly yet commanding my full attention. *You are alone only because you have chosen to live your life that way.* This thought is so exceedingly powerful that it smashes through my mental defenses leaving me feeling totally exposed.

I have always lived alone. As a child and as a youth, my family moved almost every year. I never built any lasting friendships and soon convinced myself that being a loner was my choice when it truly was not. I had few friends, my relationships were shallow... that is what I got and that is what I gave in return. I had spent a couple of decades actively designing a self-image of myself without truly considering what or who I was becoming. All my choices were pre-determined by my continuous quest for self-fulfillment on my own terms. My relationship with God was also for my convenience. If around Christians, I usually admitted to being one too, but I did not live my life as one. I was completely self-absorbed.

There is no sudden decision, I just find myself climbing down from the bunk in my shorts and getting down on my knees on the cold concrete floor. The last thing I see before closing my eyes are the shadows of the jail bars silhouetted on the lower corner of the cell's wall. It is an aptly visual reminder of how far I had fallen. For a long time, my mind is silent as I am a solitary witness to so many unhappy images from my past. I think about coming home from YMCA camp to find that my already broken family was now shattered; of standing alone at my high school graduation; of my mother dropping me off at the Naval Induction Center, then just driving away…not even a wave goodbye; of serving in Vietnam and of the ones who did not return; of the women I have known and left; of my leaving the Operations Department with my command's back's turned towards me, of my father's funeral; of Morgan and his manipulations; of Stretch and the drug plane; of the Colombians laughing around the gun-laden dinner table; of the car trip with Sam, then of the agents with guns; of shuffling into prison in a chain gang; of meeting Mose and finally of all that blood in the sink and upon my hands…and, Lord help me, upon my soul for all the harm the cocaine caused that I helped to bring into the United States.

I am not sure that I am going to pray until it just happens. *Father, I am so very sorry. I have thrown my life away. My friends have turned their back on me and society has locked me away, but what about You? Are You there for a sinner like me, a felon in a prison cell?* I am not actually expecting an answer, so am completely amazed when I get one. It is not a spoken word heard that touches me, rather it is a single inner word that explodes in my heart and instantly swells filling my heart and soul. The word is *ALWAYS!* In a heartbeat, I am forever changed. Gratitude floods through me. The Word has not taken away my guilt; what it has taken is the tragedy of the moment and in its wake left the joy that God loves even a sinner like me.

The fatigue of only a few moments ago washes away in a flood of emotions. There is no doubt in my mind that God has taken compassion on me in my greatest need and answered my prayer. I am not a wasted person; I have value, the coin of which is that God loves me even though I am a flawed person.

Climbing back onto my bunk, I want to lay awake all night long treasuring this moment. Instead, I instantly fall into a deep and restful sleep.

"Everything has its wonders, even darkness and silence, and
I learn whatever state I am in, there in to be content,"
Helen Keller

The next morning when the guard opens the door, I go immediately to the bookshelf in the television room. There are a dozen paperbacks all rejected by the other inmates and four Bibles. I look for an intact one. Some of them are missing pages. Inmates sometimes use the extra thin pages from Bibles to hand-roll cigarettes and joints.

After breakfast, I return to my cell and with great anticipation open the Bible. I, of course, begin at the beginning. I now realize that this is a living book. I am not just reading; it is more as if I am nourishing my soul and quenching my thirst for understanding. There is a hunger inside of me to know more about God, His creation, His salvation and my place within it. I read about the suffering of His chosen people and the revelations of the prophets. In a prison cell, I slowly being to discover freedom. My life is taking on new meaning and I realize that even being in prison I now have purpose, focus and meaning. The days pass quietly. A temporary peace settles upon the cellblock as the Christmas holidays approach.

A new inmate is in the cellblock. He is only eighteen-years-old—too young to be an accessory to armed bank robbery. A high-school friend encouraged him to drive the get-away car while they were both high on crack cocaine.

The kid is using the corridor pay phone to call home; it seems his parents do not yet know that he is in jail. I am buffing the tile floor so am present to hear the whole conversation; at least his half of it.

"Hello, Dad," the boy's voice trembles on the verge of breaking,

"It's Billy."

Billy pauses while his father shouts into the phone. Though several feet away I hear the anger in his voice, but not the words. "Dad, listen," pleads Billy, "I'm in Jail."

The voice on the phone is furious with anger.

"I...I drove my friend Larry to the bank," sobs Bill, "I swear I didn't know he was going to try to rob it."

"Hello, hello," Billy looks blankly at the handset. "I can't believe it," he says looking at me, "my father hung up on me." For the next couple of hours Billy repeatedly tries calling home, but there is no answer. I am serving dinner when Billy finally gets through on the telephone with a collect call to his brother. I move closer so I can listen in. "Elliot, it's me, Billy, I need..." There is a short pause. "What!" shrieks Billy, "how can he be dead? I was just talking to him this morning!"

Billy's face goes ashen as he listens, "Heart attack? Dad had a heart attack?" Billy leans against the wall for support. "What do you mean it's my fault?" he asks stunned. Billy hangs up the telephone and turns to face us, tears streaming from his eyes. "My dad had a heart attack while I was talking with him this morning. My brother says it's my fault," Billy shutters as uncontrollable sobs rack his thin body. "He doesn't want me to call home anymore." Billy turns and flees into his cell.

Not a week later, the teenager's public defender comes to see him in the attorney counseling rooms. When Billy returns to the cellblock, he is crying again. It is not until later that we learn that his grandmother, grief stricken over the loss of her son (Billy's father) apparently died of a broken heart. Billy's family is blaming him for the double death. Unable to cope with the situation, the young man turns into a walking zombie. Except for meals, he stays mostly in his cell or paces the corridor refusing to talk with anyone.

It is early afternoon and I am reading in my cell when I hear the guard ordering the men behind the grill so he can open the North Yard door. Moments later, the guard raps my cell door with his baton. "Get out here Arrington," he orders.

I step out, but he has gone into the television room so I follow full of curiosity. I find him standing over an old beat-up cardboard box. The cardboard is holed, torn and stained with some green stuff sticking out here and there.

"What is it?" I ask.

"A Christmas tree."

"Really?"

"Put it together," he orders, then walks away with his keys swishing metallically...Santa without his reindeer and lacking a merry attitude.

I lift off what remains of the lid. The plastic tree is in a shambles; looks like it has been run through a wood shredder. I blow off about a decade of dust revealing branches twisted back upon themselves, lots of missing plastic pine needles and amazingly a quarter string of petrified popcorn with a dusting of dead green mold and petrified black rot. There are also a few scratched ornaments and many colorful shards of what used to be ornaments. My mind plays with the concept of *Christmas at Terminal Island Prison*. Okay this is somewhat cool; maybe just what I need, a holiday distraction.

I carry all the parts into the shower and give them a good dousing with warm water. I watch rivulets of grime running down the drain, which does not do a whole lot for my Christmas spirit. Back in the television room, I assemble the assorted parts with varying amounts of force and after a lot of twisting and plucking have something that looks like an evergreen road kill after an encounter with an eighteen-wheeler truck. I hang the few intact ornaments, cracks, chips and scrapes towards the wall, then ponder the heap of ornament scraps. Imagination can take you to some interesting places, for me I went from cell to cell gathering up empty toilet paper rolls. Using toothpaste for cement, I attached the scrapes of plastic to the outside of the toilet paper rolls. Not only did this add color, but also the toothpaste from a distance looked a bit like globs of snow. I accidentally discovered that if I tore a couple of the toilet paper rolls open and fanned one end and folded back the other end, I could cement them into something that looked a bit like angel wings. It went on top of the tree and did not look half-bad though I was only one of the few who thought it resembled an angel. I wrapped one of Clayton's spare sheets around the base to add to the snow effect. The couple of stains that were quite prominent only added to the realism of the great outdoors.

The guard swung by on one of his tours and seemed pleasantly surprised. In any case he was motivated enough to find me a string of colorful lights. I ran another idea by him and soon he had me locked in my cell with a bowl of popcorn from the nut ward upstairs, a handful of thread and a needle. It was because of the needle that I had to be locked alone in my cell. The other guys would love to have that needle so they could mark their bodies up with prison tattoos. With such a poor conception of what constituted art from an inmate perspective, I did not place much value in their critical assessment of my paper roll angel. The only down side to stringing all that popcorn was that someone had salted it. Every time I stuck myself with that needle, I got a salt burn.

As dinnertime approached, the guard locked the guys up in their cells then wheeled in the food cart. Since the guard was being so cooperative, I had made another request. Inside the cart, there was a half roll of tin foil. While Clayton set up for dinner, I made some homemade tinsel and wrapped each light with a reflective aluminum shield. Turning off the overhead lights on the Christmas tree side of the television room set the mood and the guard released the rest of the inmates to a mixed review.

Most of the men are pleased to see the tree, but a Mexican bank robber down for the third time curses, "Christmas is the last thing I want to be reminded of in this joint."

"Ah, Carlos is just sore he didn't get a new bike last Christmas," quips one of the other inmates. The Mexican had been arrested while fleeing his last bank robbery on a stolen bicycle; he is often harassed about it.

Billy is late for chow as usual. When he sees the Christmas tree, he smiles broadly, which warms my heart and makes all the effort I put into the tree worth it. At the dinner table a new inmate, who does not know Billy's tragic story, inadvertently asks, "Hey kid, I bet your family is really missing you it being Christmas and all."

Bill's spoon pauses in mid-air, then his face crumbles as uneaten beans spill from his mouth and tears flow from his eyes, then he flees back to his cell.

The Mexican slams down his spoon, "I'm getting real tired of that sissy."

"Hey Carlos, leave it alone," I caution forgetting to mind my own business.

"What do you mean 'leave it alone?'" rages the Mexican. "I have to share a cell with that cry baby."

"He's going through some tough times," I offer trying to calm the Mexican inmate down.

"I'm going to show that punk what a tough time is all about," yells Carlos making a rude hand gesture.

"Come on, it's Christmas Eve," I am only trying to reason with the idiot to keep him from taking it out on the kid.

Carlos shoves his plate away and stands up, "Well, screw Christmas and screw you too!" He stomps out of the television room

The room has gone completely quiet. No one has anything to say as the men finish their Christmas Eve dinner, then by ones and twos most of the inmates retire to their cells. A few watch a little Christmas programming on the television. I go to my cell and stay there until 9:00 p.m. then come back out unplug the tree and leave the empty room to go quietly to bed.

The following morning, the bugle at the Coast Guard base wakes me up. It is my first Christmas inside the joint. How depressing, I drop down onto the floor and put on my prison jumpsuit. While preparing breakfast I discover that someone ate most of my popcorn string off the Christmas tree and some idiot childishly abused the silver-foiled toilet-paper roll angel. I would spend the next couple of mornings repairing the tree after determined inmate abuse; it was something I felt very good about, restoring Christmas to the cellblock.

After breakfast, the guard delivers a Christmas box to one of the black inmates. We are allowed to receive one Christmas box from our family. Leon is ecstatic as he opens the box to see a bean pie. He has been talking about it for weeks, which has my curiosity aroused. I have never heard of, nor seen, a bean pie before and am standing hopefully nearby eager for a small piece. To my great surprise, Leon jams his fingers into the pie and tears it apart. Gobs of creamed beans splatter onto the floor. Leon grins as he stops poking about in the mashed beans then removes a small plastic bag to the great excitement of his friends. They go shuffling off with their bag of cocaine leaving me alone with the ravaged bean pie. I poke my finger into the goopy mess and lick it. Surprisingly, the pie is quite tasty, kind of like a pumpkin pie. I wrap up what is left of the pie in a piece of aluminum foil left over from the Christmas tree and hide it in my secret spot above the ceiling tiles. If Leon asks about it I can return it, if not I will be in bean pie oblivion tomorrow morning. Old Mose would be proud of me.

After lunch, the guard calls a few of the inmate's names for the visiting room. The rest mope about or spend their time arguing over television programming. I expect no visitors today having told my mother that I preferred she spend the holiday with family. Prison is depressing enough for us inmates, why force it upon our families?

I am in my cell engrossed in the Book of Matthew when I hear someone knock at my door. I look at the small security window and see that it is the guard. A guard knocking? I am intrigued as I open the door and the guard hands me a brown paper bag with a little red ribbon as I step through the door. "What's this?" I ask.

"Merry Christmas," he says pleasantly, which blows my mind. This particular guard hates inmates and is most at ease threatening us. To see him smiling and cheerfully offering me a brown paper bag with a red bow around it is a bit overwhelming.

I accept the bag and smile my thanks. There are a couple of guards in the television room with a cart full of brown paper sacks wrapped with a single strand of Christmas ribbon. It is a completely awkward moment for everyone. The guards are standing on one side of the room attempting to be friendly when they obviously do not feel sociable to the inmates at all. The inmates are suspiciously standing on the other side wanting to be thankful, but leery of guards bearing gifts so they examine the paper sacks instead. Inside are a can of Pepsi and a small box of assorted chocolates. Unfortunately, I know why the guards are probably being so gracious. In prisons, the Christmas holidays have the highest rate of suicide and inmate violence. On average only ten percent of the men get semi-regular visitors. One of the guards shared that in women's prisons only two to three percent of the female inmates get repeat visitors. Lost and alone can be a perpetual state for those of us who have purposefully made bad-choices. I imagine that it must be toughest of all upon juvenile inmates. What a despairing equation for losing a young soul to hopelessness and the anger it usually results in; locked up, all alone, but for some seriously violent gang members for room-mates. What a horrible path for a developing child who may now become more twisted towards the dark side. If they do not know God, whom do they turn to? This is why street gangs promise a youth that they will become their family. That promise must bear a lot of attraction to a child that feels abandoned by his or her family and is locked away by a society that…in the eyes of the youth…does not want them.

Courage is the ladder on which all the other virtues mount,"
Clare Booth Luce

Author's note: the State of California consistently spends four times more on incarceration than on higher education. The 2006 budget for California prisons was $8,500,000,000 compared to $2,000,000,000 for colleges and universities. For the cost to incarcerate one youth (over $80,000 per year) California could fund two to three students through a junior college or university. In 1977 there were less than 20,000 inmates in the California Department of Corrections, in 2007 that figure had grown to 174,000, an increase of almost 900%. One out of every six inmates is doing life in prison (equates to twenty-five years or more), yet the adult crime rate in California *has not fallen. Due to raising health care costs, each older inmate can cost California taxpayers over $70,000 per year. Is this a worthwhile investment of this vast amount of money or could some of the billions be better spent helping non-violent inmates (men, women and children) to put their lives back together to the betterment of society? Due to almost 200% overcrowding in California prison, non-violent men, women and some youths are housed with murderers and human predators. In 2007, California approved adding 53,000 more beds to the prison system at an added cost of $6,500,000,000. The budget for corrections for 2008 has been increased to $9,840,000,000; an increase of 15% in one year. The budged has increased 44% in the last two years and don't forget the special budget of $6,500,000,000 to add new prison beds. It is a crime against society that the California Department of Corrections is allowed to operate in such a financially bloated manner, while allowing so many of their charges to be violently abused and grossly mistreated…thus insuring that corrections will be a growth industry for the foreseeable future.*

*"I know of no more encouraging fact than the unquestioned
ability of a man to elevate his life by conscious endeavor,"*
Henry David Thoreau

Chapter 29

TERMINAL ISLAND FEDERAL PRISON,

J-3, DECEMBER 1982

WITH THE new year rapidly approaching, I am thinking about what I can do to change my life for the better when a startling idea comes to me.

The guard has learned to somewhat trust me. Trust is a rather dubious relationship between guards and their inmate charges. When a guard feels an inmate has earned a small measure of trust he or she may allow them certain modest privileges such as actually talking to them instead of at them. Most guards work double shifts spending sixteen hours or more in the cellblocks, go home to sleep, and are back the next day at 8:00 a.m. for another double or triple shift. Many choose to catch their shuteye in the prison to save the commute. As such, prison guards are in constant association with numerous felons who are looking for dubious ways to take advantage of them. It tends to make them a cynical bunch. So, when a corrections officer becomes comfortable enough to lower his or her guard around an inmate it is a trust not to be foolishly violated. Being friends with a guard has positive and negative implications. A friendly guard will watch out for your safety and possibly head off dangerous situations. However, other inmates heavily frown upon anyone being friends with a guard; they wonder what the hack and his trusted inmate are talking about when no one else is around. Therefore, it is a dangerous path I walk asking favors of the guard.

This morning he has agreed to leave me locked in the cellblock while everyone else goes outside into the yard. From my cell, I watch the last of the inmates walk out through the yard door then the guard looks back at me, "Have a good time."

"Thank you," I answer as I step out into the corridor. It is weird and strangely wonderful to be completely alone in the cellblock; the silence seems strange and enticing. I feel like a child whose parents have finally decided that he can stay at home alone without a sitter. The house takes on a new strangeness that is ever so alluring. I only have one hour so I step back into the cell and quickly strip down to my shorts then pull the bedding from Clayton's and my bunks and drag them out into the hallway. Then I go into the deep sink room and get the roller bucket, fill it with tepid water and wheel it into the cell. Armed with two cans of scouring powder, brushes and sponges, I begin scrubbing the cell top to bottom. The overhead pipes are the worse with thick layers of rust, hardened grime and decades of dust falling on old, but still growing, mildew. I begin throwing around water, lots of water; it drips from the pipes mucky brown at first, then shades of grey. I am a cleaning slob not caring that water is sloshing everywhere; the floor is awash with wet muck. The more water the better; it is like a baptism gone wild. When the dirty water begins to flow out upon the corridor floor, I quickly mop it up and empty the bucket into the deep sink. I feel nothing but good emotions watching the dirty water chasing down the drain. While there, I scrub out the deep sink too. This is an outer and inner cleansing of the deepest kind. I refill the bucket, rinse out the mop and re-attack the cell. I assault the nicotine film thickly coating the walls and discover that our cell is not dull yellow after all, but rather a flat dingy white. I am totally into this chore. Water drips from my body as I sponge, scrub and scrape. I have accumulated a half dozen of the least soiled towels from the laundry cart and wipe down the ceiling pipes and walls. I particularly work hard at cleaning our window watching it get progressively brighter in the little cell with the added sunlight. With my time winding down, I place fresh bedding on the beds and put on a fresh pair of coveralls. I am behind my cell door when the inmates begin to file back in.

Clayton opens the door then stops and stares from the threshold, "Whoa, what happened in here?"

"I have been cleaning."

"Obviously, but why?"

"We needed it."

"Are you implying something?"

"I am not referring to you, it's about me and the cell."

"Tell me I am not living with a nut case."

"I just didn't like living in a dirty cell and decided to do something about it." I glance at the clean walls and window admiring my handy work, "this place really needed cleaning."

Yeah, for about fifty years," Clayton runs a finger down the wall noting that it comes away clean.

I look up at the six-inch sewer pipe above my bunk. It is bone white with clear drops of condensation wetting it. Yes, the cell needed cleaning, but it is so much deeper than just that. Washing the cell felt like I was scrubbing on my soul. No longer will the rusty pipes soil the condensation that falls upon my pillow and sheets. The drops will not have that surprising acid taste in the middle of the night nor will I wake with my pillow stained with rust. The nicotine funk is gone from the cell and the walls are a uniform soul-inspiring flat white, yet what I enjoy the most is the clean sunlight pouring through the window that now brightens the dreary cell. At the moment, life is good for this inmate.

After lunch, the guard arrives with a few more Christmas boxes;

one of them is for me. The staff only allows each inmate to receive one box for the entire year.

A couple of weeks ago I asked a friend of mine to send me a box. I gave him very specific directions on what to put in it. Most important were some pictures of Puu and Susan. I also asked for five pounds of assorted herbal teas and two pounds of hard candy.

I go into my cell to open the box, but unfortunately, more than a few inmates follow me inside. I open the box to discover that my friend has reversed my instructions; there are three pounds of hard candy and only a pound of herbal tea. With the other inmates crowding about me the hard candy goes in about five minutes, while I stand guard over the tea.

That night, just before lock-down, I heat a cup of water in the microwave and drop in a bag of herbal tea. Smelling the fragrant scent of the tea, I use it to recall a memory of Susan and Puu. It took place under an incredibly clear night sky recently washed by a passing tropical rain shower. There was a multitude of stars splashed across the dark tropical heavens. A crescent moon hung low on the horizon closely accompanied by the glowing orb of a planet. The evening was warm with fragrant trade winds blowing lightly through the tall coconut trees, causing the long leaves to rustle softly.

Susan, Puu and I were at an outdoor garden party at the University of Hawaii. I was sipping a cup of tea and watching Susan. Though we had been together for over a month, she kept our relationship a secret from her friends. As such, I was not allowed to touch her in public even though I promised not to be gross about it.

I noticed a couple of guys giving Susan the eye. I was considering how much fun it would be to slam their heads together when I felt Susan tugging on my sleeve. She had been eyeing a happy couple obviously in love, their arms wrapped around each other and looking quite snug about life in general. I guessed that Susan liked what she saw because she turned and looked at me with those incredible liquid brown eyes of hers and shyly said, "If you want you can put your arm around me."

"Does this mean that you're my girl?" I asked hopefully. My heart had entered its flopping-on-the-ground stage again.

"If you're asking if I love you the answer is yes, with all my heart," Susan stared at me unblinking, her eyes burning holes into my heart.

We moved away from the other people and found a broad banyan tree to sit under. I leaned against the thick mossy trunk while Susan settled her head into my lap, her arms wrapped tightly around my waist. Puu lay down beside us under a gardenia plant with white velvety flowers that emitted a potent flowery bouquet. A quiet chomp announced the demise of a gardenia flower, which Puu spit onto the grass, sniffs, then walked away. With Susan's face burrowed into the hollow of my neck, her breath caressing my skin, she said in a little girl voice that has lodged in my mind ever since, "Steve, I love you so much; please don't ever let me go."

The lights go out in the cell. My cup of tea has grown tepid in my hand. I carefully put the picture back into the locker, climb up onto my bunk and stare at the shaft of light coming through the window. I refuse to follow the beam of light to the wall where it paints the perpetual shadow of jail bars. Instead, I inhale the fragrant smell of the tea while trying to recapture the memory of Susan's breath upon my neck and her arms around my waist. A flashlight momentarily burns through the cell door's small window. The guard, who has already pulled down a double shift in J-2, is now covering J-3 for triple overtime pay. He is making great money, but is very sour about it. I am glad that he is on the nightshift because if this were a dayshift he would take it out on us.

> *"Thou shalt not be a victim. Thou shalt not be a perpetrator.*
> *Above all, thou shalt not be a bystander."*
> Holocaust Museum, Washington DC

On New Year's Eve, the problem between Billy and the Mexican comes to a head. At 11:00 a.m., the guard lets us out into the yard even though it is lightly raining. Most of the inmates stand against the cement wall smoking cigarettes and complaining about the weather. Because of the light rain, I left my bucket inside and am working out on the universal machine. Billy is pacing the yard oblivious to the weather. He takes a candy bar from his pocket and begins to unwrap it. As he walks past the inmates lining the wall, a tall, thick-bodied black man suddenly steps into his path. Instead of backing up or trying to walk around the black man, Billy just stands there speechless; the candy bar is poised halfway to his mouth. The black inmate snags the candy from Billy's hand, then very deliberately raises it to his own mouth and bites off half of it. Billy frightened and still unsure what to do, just stands there.

Two more inmates step away from the wall; one of them is Carlos. He stands beside the black man. "What's the matter, punk, too afraid to fight for your candy?"

Billy still has not moved. He looks from Carlos, to the black man and then his eyes lock on what is left of his candy bar. The black inmate passes the half-eaten bar to Carlos who slowly shoves it into his mouth and begins to chew purposefully while staring at Billy.

Finally, Billy begins to step backwards away from the leering Mexican, but Carlos' hand shoots out and grabs Billy's shirt. "Hey punk, if you won't fight for your candy bar, I guess you won't fight for your candy ass either."

Billy has not moved. His shoulders are slumped, chest concave, he slouches in complete surrender. It looks like the spear of Carlos' hand has impaled him.

"Will you..." Carlos pulls Billy a step closer to him, "will you fight me?"

Billy shakes his head, his long wet hair hides his eyes.

I am sorely tempted to get involved, but hesitate because Billy needs to stand up for himself. I also know that nothing is going to happen with the guard watching. Yet, Carlos is weaving an evil web about his victim; it is a spider's dance. Carlos chose his quarry well. Billy is defenseless just like prey in a web. At the universal gym, I wonder what happened in Carlos' life that has made him so mean. He is a mid-sized predator with street cunning. He only goes after smaller, weaker prey that will not fight back.

Carlos looks Billy up and down then with a snort of contempt stalks away.

Later that day, I ask the guard if he could move Billy out of the Mexican's cell. The guard looks at me and shrugs, "This isn't a boy scout camp we're running. Billy has to stand up for himself. Better he learn that lesson here in the jail unit than out in general population where he will be walking gay bait."

That night the winter storm hits with full force. Thunder reverberates through the cellblock and echoes off the prison walls. Rather than go to sleep at my regular time, I decide to stay up until midnight to hail in the New Year. The passing of time is always an event for inmates; it means we are that much closer to our release. For most inmates getting out does not equate to going home... most do not have homes, which is one of the reasons so many come back so quickly.

I stand at the window wrapped in a blanket against the cold watching raindrops pounding against the warped glass. I stick my arm out through a broken pane to feel the cold rain washing over my hand. Bold flashes of lightning intermittently shatter the black of the night. The strobing light flashes upon the scalloped glass casting running shadows of rain rivulets into the cell, the liquid shadows make it look like the cell walls are crying.

I reach under my pillow and remove a picture of Revelstoke parked in a tropical forest above Waimea Falls. In it, I see Puu standing at the open back doors with his floppy ears down. I remember that Susan was inside cooking cookies and could almost hear her ordering Puu, the Nose, out of the kitchen. There was a strong trade wind blowing that evening as I mentally see Puu jump down and walk up to me for some serious ear rubbing and butt scratching.

It is cool outside, but the interior of Revelstoke is warm and inviting with the enticing aroma of cookies right out of the oven; I step inside.

Susan sweeps her long blond hair to one side as she closes the oven and smiles at me. She is wearing a blue silk crop top and black nylon *Dolphin* shorts; it is a runner's outfit and she wears it very well indeed. I collect a hug, two cookies and a kiss, life is very good. Outside I hear the wind playing amongst a bamboo forest. It is elephant bamboo with trunks as thick as a man's hand span. The wind is bending the tall bamboo's leafy tops causing the trunks to clack against each other like a wondrous giant wind chime. The hollow trunk-to-trunk sounds are beating out a primal cadence in sync with the gusting of the tropical wind. I take a cookie to the back door and look out at the tall swaying elephant bamboo. Susan steps up behind me and places her arms around my waist.

"When do you expect to have to leave Hawaii?" she asks.

Susan and I are living on borrowed time. The Navy machine is awaiting my transfer papers from the personnel department. For some odd reason they are slow in coming, which pleases me greatly. After my release from the brig, I reported as ordered back to the command. The Executive Officer had been reluctant to have me back around the rest of the men, so he ordered me to go back out the base gate and to pretend that I was on leave. I was to report in once a week to check on my orders and occasionally to pick up a paycheck. I thought the transfer process would take a couple of weeks, but three months have now passed. Three glorious months of surfing, hiking with Susan and Puu and being totally in love in an island paradise.

Watching Puu running and barking amongst the swaying bamboo with Susan's arms around my waist I am so happy and so very afraid that I will lose her when my orders come. "I don't know why they haven't arrived already," I answer sadly.

Susan rubs her head against my shoulders as a strong gust of wind blows through the elephant bamboo forest and the answering sound is magnificent. The trees thunk and clack loudly and I can feel Susan's heart beating against my chest.

Standing before the prison cell window, I feel the bite of the icy wind blowing through the broken panes as a sudden chill runs though my body causing me to shudder. I see the rain splashing against the window like an ocean of tears. Thick drops run in long rivulets down the panes to puddle on the sill and suddenly I am crying…not crying in self-pity, but rather for the wonderful happiness I have known and so treasure. The images I am recalling are a bandage that caresses my battered soul. Turning away from the window, I see the lightning strobe against the cell wall, for a moment it paints abrupt shadows of the jail bars and a splash of tears and then because the rain dampens the light from the security lights, the cell fades to semi-darkness.

The next morning the guard lets me out of my cell at 6:00 a.m. to begin getting the television room ready for breakfast. The cellblock is cold enough to be almost frosty this first morning of the New Year. The building's antiquated radiator, installed in the early thirties, does little to hold off the winter chill. Rubbing my sides to promote warmth, I go to the cleaning locker for a bucket to wash the tables. Passing the door to cell nine, I hear muffled sobbing. I pause wondering if Billy is okay then shrug off my curiosity; Billy often cries.

I am busy cleaning the television room, when at 6:30 a.m. the North Yard guard opens the door and pushes in the food cart. Opening the cart's doors, I look at the plastic trays stacked one above the other. The twenty-eight meals are identical; bowls of oatmeal, blackened bacon strips, white toast, milk and coffee. Everything is cold to the touch. While stacking the bowls of oatmeal in the microwave, I notice some contain coagulated lumps of floating brown goo. Though I truly enjoy oatmeal, I know I will not be able to eat it because of the suspicious nature of those lumps.

Looking down the corridor to ensure that the guard is still in his office, I climb up onto a table and pushing up one of the ceiling tiles reach into my secret food hoard. There is not much there, a couple pieces of fruit and several small boxes of cereal. While the oatmeal is cooking, I secretly munch a bruised apple then wolf down a box of corn flakes. When I hear the guard unlocking the cell doors, I throw the empty corn flake box into the trashcan as the rest of the inmates begin to flood into the television room. None of them is happy to see the corrupted oatmeal. Leon uses his spoon to dip out one of the larger lumps. "I hope the cooks aren't being creative with the dead rats in the kitchen again," he says optimistically.

Shorty smashes one of the lumps with his Spork and carefully eyes the flatten goopy mess. "It looks like cooked stomped-on rodent innards," he assures the new inmate sitting next to him. The man pales as Shorty picks the flatten glob up and pops it in his mouth as he chews like a connoisseur sampling a rare dessert. "Nope, it's just snot...the guy must chew tobacco to give it that urine-like color."

Carlos swaggers into the television room, sits down at one the tables and begins to spoon the oatmeal into his mouth without comment. The guard surveys the room and notices that one of the chairs is vacant. He marches back down the corridor. "Billy," he shouts, "get out here and eat your breakfast."

At cell nine, he pulls open the door and yells, "Hey, get out of bed, you know the rules."

"Leave me alone," Billy's high-pitched voice carries easily into the television room.

"Get your butt out of that bed."

I see Carlos whispering to his three cronies. They look in unison down the corridor and laugh; it is a cruel snickering sound...evil reveling in foul accomplishment.

Shorty, who is monitoring the hushed conversation, turns to pass the news on to Leon. I am taking four more bowls of lumpy oatmeal to the adjoining table when I hear Shorty say, "The kid gave it up last night." The words stop me in my tracks; "Giving it up," is an inmate slang for saying that someone was raped.

As the news travels from table to table in an excited wave, I turn to stare at the Mexican. Carlos is grinning, pleased to be the focal point of so much attention. Our eyes lock, he smirks then looks away. The noise in the television room slackens as the inmates strain to listen to the argument going on in cell nine.

"I'm not going to play games with you, kid," rages the guard. "Either get out of that bunk or you're going to J-1."

"I don't care," shouts Billy.

"That's it," yells the guard slamming and locking the door. "Pack up your stuff; you're going to the Hole." He stalks down the corridor to lock the grill to the television room and then raises his radio to call for the North Yard guard.

They take Billy out through the back door. He is crying and walking hunched over. The inmates are standing three deep at the grill watching the drama unfold. A tall lanky inmate with acne scars on his face turns to Shorty and says, "Sure be handy having a girlie boy like that right in your own cell."

I am furiously cleaning the tables. My anger boils and froths at the edge of barely restrained hostility. Amongst his small crowd of twisted friends, Carlos is being treated like some kind of pervert hero. They are anxiously asking him for the depraved details. I stare at the group of vile men with unconcealed disgust.

I am finishing loading the trays back into the cart when the guard returns to unlock the grill. "Everyone get ready to go outside."

The inmates crowd the door while the guard counts heads as they pass out into the cold morning light. Carlos and I are near the back of the line. As we pass through the door, he sees me staring angrily at him. He smirks, "Told ya the kid was a punk."

I resist my desire to grab the Mexican by the throat and shake him like a pit bull with a rodent. Watching Carlos step out into the yard and walk arrogantly away, I know that he and I are heading for a serious confrontation. I just did not expect that it would happen so soon, or that it would be resolved with a volleyball.

Carlos joins his friends at the volleyball court. He playfully punches one of them then makes a grinding motion with his hips. The inmates laugh at the crude motion…evil on holiday.

Leon, my black inmate friend is standing on the opposite side of the net. "Hey Arrington," he yells, "come on, the South of the Border Gang wants to challenge us gringos to a game." Leon is standing at the net opposite Carlos. I stride over and lightly push Leon over one position. My heart is hammering as I face Carlos who rises to the challenge.

"In your face, I put the ball in your face," he threatens.

Saying nothing, I settle into a stance and eagerly wait for the ball to be served; I am in combat mode…an ambush eager to be sprung.

The ball bounces from side to side. Then Carlos, who has been yelling for a set gets one. The ball is set high and close to the net. He waits for the ball to descend before jumping. His eyes locked up on the ball as he leaps; he has not noticed that I am already airborne. Carlos is still going up as I reach over the net and slam the descending ball. All the pent up anger inside of me is focused in that downward strike. I actually growl as I spike the ball directly into Carlos' upturned face. The impact slams into his face, knocking his head back, he staggers backwards trying not to fall. For an instant, he is dazed. I am stoked as Leon hoots, "Yeah, great spike."

Carlos shakes his head to clear it, then leaps at the net, "You cheated, you reached over the net."

Leon picks up the ball then looks at Carlos, "We're inmates, you stupid idiot; we don't give a damn about no rules…our serve."

Carlos glares at Leon then grimaces at me, "You're going to pay," he threatens, "you only got that shot because I wasn't expecting it."

Our team serves the ball. When one of the Latin men hits it back, Leon lobs the ball directly to Carlos. It is a slow lob and seems almost intentional. Carlos moves under the ball yelling directions to the short Colombian smuggler standing next to him. Obviously, Carlos is going to pass the ball so he can get a proper set back. With spread fingers, Carlos delicately pops the ball up. He is still under the ascending ball when Leon, who has timed his jump perfectly, leaps high, reaches over the net and sledgehammers the ball straight back down into Carlos' upturned face. Carlos buckles at the knees and slumps heavily to the ground. Leon's shot was more powerful than mine, but he also drove the top of the net downward a couple of feet and his hand was still in contact with the ball when it smashed into Carlos' face. I was jealous of such a magnificent shot.

Carlos comes up cursing then grabbing the ball, he viciously slams it toward Leon. The poorly directed ball flies upward and straight into the anti-personnel wire lining the top of the wall, which instantly punctures it. The ball deflates with a short hiss while hanging obscenely from the wire, then if falls to the ground with a flat plop.

"Carlos, you stupid idiot, I saw that," yells the guard, "get your butt over here."

Leon snickers as Carlos stalks past us at the net, which proves to be more than Carlos' tortured ego can bear. He takes a wild swing at Leon and misses.

"Alright, that's it," yells the guard grabbing Carlos and cuffing his hands behind his back, "you're going to the Hole."

"Come on, I didn't even hit him," complains Carlos.

"It ain't about Leon, fool," rages the guard, "Billy didn't deserve it, you twisted pervert."

The conversation made me wonder, what did the guard mean by didn't deserve it. When would anyone deserve to be raped? I wonder about this because the inmate rumor mill alleges that some guards will sic inmate gangs upon other inmates as punishment.

Watching the guard leading Carlos away, I wonder what will happen to Billy. News of the rape will spread through the prison like a wild fire. Everyone will know that Billy will not fight to defend himself. It means he will be a target for the other inmate homosexuals.

I try to force the thoughts of Billy and Carlos from my mind. I just do not want to deal with the horrible images of what must have happened in cell nine. With the volleyball punctured, I walk over to the lawn and pick a handful of grass then hold it to my nose. I fill my lungs with the rich smell and for a moment lose myself in an explosion of boyhood memories that revolve around mowing neighborhood lawns for a buck. As the sudden memories begin to fade, I breathe deeply trying to maintain contact with my lost youth, but the memories are gone and the reality of prison is back upon me.

That afternoon they moved two new inmates in to take Carlos' and Billy's cell. One of them is Morgan, whom they have moved from J-2. This is a major bummer. I just do not need him in my life and now there will be no escaping him. I wait until he is alone in his new cell, then open the door and go inside. Morgan is unpacking a large cardboard box into his locker. It is full of cartons of cigarettes, candy bars, *Cups of Noodles*, etc.

"What's with the cigarettes?" I ask, "You don't smoke."

Morgan turns and smiles, "Influence and protection."

He extends a hand, which I ignore.

"So how ya doing?" he asks.

"I am doing time, Morgan," I answer hostilely, "how do you think I'm doing?"

Morgan looks me full in the eye, "So cooperate, that's what I am doing."

I knew it was coming. There was no way Morgan was going to do his own time if he could put it off on someone else.

"What kind of a deal did you get?" I ask, my opinion of him hitting a new low.

"Cooperate against Max, tell what I know and I get to go free in four or five years."

"So what are you doing in J-3?"

"They thought I should tell you that this is your last chance to cooperate."

"No thanks."

"Why not?" he offers a counterfeit smile, "you could get off with just a couple of years."

"I'd have to testify against Sam and I just do not see myself as a snitch working for some government agency trying to corral druggies and misfits. I want out of the drug world, not dunked deeper into it."

Morgan shrugs, "Choose your own poison."

"Look," I glare at Morgan. Why did he have to promise me so much, a new life and a second chance, when his real intent was corruption? "Just leave me alone," I say angrily, "I don't like you being in my cellblock."

Morgan laughs grimly then shakes his head, "Your cellblock?

Guess you better get used to it."

Not a week later, they transferred Morgan to a high-security cell in San Diego at a facility that specializes in protecting prison witnesses in high profile cases. Having him out of *my cellblock* pleases me to no end. Yet it is a hollow victory. I cannot shake the realization that he is getting out in only four to five years.

*The wicked strut about on every side. When vileness is exalted
among the sons of man.*
Psalm 12:8

*In considering the following please remember that to become
a prison guard only requires a basic high school education or
GED equivalent. Corrections officers regularly work excessive
overtime because of excessive financial reward. One of the
results is that prison guards have the highest rate of spousal
and child abuse of any government occupation. In 2006,
over fifty prison guards earned in excess of $200,000 and
one, a Lieutenant in the Department of Corrections earned
$254,000. The Governor of California earns $206,000 a
year. How is it possible for a corrections officer to earn four
or five times what is paid a public school teacher with an
advanced college education? Don't forget that California
spends over four times more money on corrections than it does
on higher education.*

"Character cannot be developed in ease and quiet. Only through experience of trial and suffering can the soul be strengthened, ambition inspired, and success achieved,"
Helen Keller

Chapter 30

TERMINAL ISLAND FEDERAL PRISON, J-3, MAY 1983

WINTER IN the cellblock plods by, but finally the weather warms and spring arrives. Both Morris and Clayton have pleaded guilty, been sentenced to a few years and transferred out to general population. According to the guards, I have been in J-3 longer than any other inmate in their memory. Standing at the fence in the J-3 yard, I stare at the men in the North Yard envious of their freedom. It may sound strange yearning for the rights of a sentenced inmate, but such is the fortune of a jail unit inmate. Usually the men serve only a few weeks to a couple of months in a jail unit while processing through the courts. I have been down over eight months without even a trial date being set. Both DeLorean and Hetrick are battling the court process with their regiment of lawyers. Morgan is mostly trying to sweeten his plea bargain. I now have my own attorney, but know that in the end I will plead guilty. I am just waiting for the best opportunity to cut a deal that does not involve my snitching out Sam. I happen to know that he is surfing his brains out in San

Diego, which does nothing to improve my mood.

I have decided to be depressed today. It is spring and I am tired of being inside a cellblock on the ground floor of the single wing of a drab hundred-year-old building. My hour outside, except when it is raining or the guard is not in the mood, just is not enough. I want to know what is beyond the far fence on the southern boundary of the North Yard. In the distance, I see inmates walking down an outside corridor that I have heard leads through a breezeway to the South Yard.

Breezeway, my mind plays with this fascinating word. To walk where there is consistently a breeze. We almost never feel wind in this confined yard with its towering walls. They say that the breezeway parallels the breakwater. When the ocean is raging the froth from the waves soaks anyone walking along the breezeway. That is something jail unit inmates never experience…weather; except through a small broken windowpane. I would love to stand out in the rain or be soaked by wind-driven seawater. Instead, I stand here with my fingers embedded in chain link and just stare.

Beyond the breezeway is the mythical South Yard. It is where they house the honor inmates. Now there is another term for the mind to play with, *honor inmate.* It denotes more than not getting in trouble. It implies that the inmate is taking the right steps towards personal rehabilitation. This means he is working a job, attending counseling classes and enrolling in high school GED or college courses. They do not offer these rehabilitative opportunities to us jail unit guys.

I know that the South Yard has no walls on two sides. One can see outside the prison through a double row of twenty-foot tall chain-link fences topped with razor wire. On one side is the Pacific Ocean, on the other is the channel that leads into the Port of Los Angeles' inner harbor. I desperately want to be a South Yard honor inmate. Being free is not a place my imagination dares to visit. I am willing to be realistic about my future. I did the crime and now I have to face doing the time…but how much time?

With my depression hovering closely, I fetch my rusted bucket and begin carrying water to my lawn. It has grown greatly over the winter and spring. The twenty-foot long by six-foot section that was once just dirt and trash is now a lawn with thriving grass; there are no bare spots. The grass has gotten greedy demanding half my yard time to satisfy its growing thirst. Parts of it are a foot tall. Suddenly getting an idea, I do something strange. I set my bucket down beside the grass, walk to where it is tallest and then lay face down upon it. Turning my head to one side all I can see is grass. I inhale its fragrance and stare at the multiple green blades growing so densely. If I had the time, I would go to sleep here.

"Nature will bear the closest inspection. She invites us to lay our eye level with her smallest leaf and take an insect view of its plain," Henry David Thoreau

"What are you doing Arrington?"

I do not look up not wanting to break the small magic of the moment I have created. I recognize the guard's voice and know I must answer. "Just lying here," I answer.

"You're not losing it, are you?"

"No sir just wanted to look at the grass up close."

"Well do me a favor and stand up. This is just too weird."

So, I stand up, denied a simple escape because I am being too weird. Lock me in a building for the better part of a year and yes, you get weird. Civilians just do not fully realize how much you give up with incarceration. Punishment affects us on many different levels and freedom lost can be a forever event. Now that is a hope-busting concept, yet teenagers who play with guns and hang with those of criminal intent are courting that exact baleful future.

I am tempted to remove my shoes so I can stand barefoot in the grass patch, but the guard is watching me carefully now. He is not ready to deal with a shoeless Arrington. The real tragedy of this situation is that if I act too weird for him he may be tempted to fill out a psycho report on me and I could wind up in the nut ward doing the Thorazine shuffle. Rather than take any more chances with me the guard goes for the easy solution and terminates our yard time early. As we shuffle back inside one of the inmates quips in passing, "Thanks Arrington." As though it was my fault the hack has no imagination.

That afternoon brought witness to something never before seen in the J-3 yard...an inmate gardener with a power lawn mower. I stand at the television room window and watch him wrestle the heavy mower through the double security gate, then he has to lever it up over a cement curb that surrounds the grass patch. He does the pull start thing and a couple of passes later the whole patch is mowed; butchered more like it. Then he begins wrestling the heavy mower back out. I wave to him as he passes and he glances over recognizing me instantly, "You're the idiot who's been watering this grass, aren't you?"

The next morning I collect a cigar box full of the grass cuttings and take them back to my cell. I lift the lid, finger the blades of cut grass then hold them to my nose and inhale deeply the fragrant smell. The grassy bouquet carries me back to Hawaii and the day I met Susan's parents.

Her father is out watering the lawn as we pull up in front of the house. Two minutes later Puu and I are under close parental scrutiny. It does not help our introduction when Puu starts things off by making a deposit on the man's manicured lawn. Her father and I are standing side by side as Puu digs his back paws into the lush, delicate grass making long scratching scars in the perfect green carpet. I am discovering that the man is heavily into oriental gardening, the perfect harmony kind of gardening he fell in love with in Japan. He gapes at the clumps of flying grass. I am just plain speechless and know that our first meeting is not going well.

"Puu, I yell in frustration," the damage already done, "get over here."

Susan's father takes a couple of steps closer to the large offensive steaming pile. He looks somewhat amazed at the size of it then glances sternly at me, "That's an awful big dog you got, Son."

"Yes Sir," I answer lamely, not missing his use of the word awful, "he's even rather large for a Great Dane."

"So I noticed," Mr. Longway looks again at the large offensive pile as if he could not believe it is really squatting on his perfect lawn with the twin three-foot-long deep gouges in the grass. "I guess you would like to borrow my shovel?"

I am carrying the shovel back into the garage with its still steaming cargo when I see Susan and her mother step into the back of Revelstoke. I am so anxious to get back outside to make sure that nothing else goes wrong that I do not notice that the large plastic trashcan I am dumping Puu's load into is actually Mrs. Longway's oversized laundry bin.

Rushing back outside, I see that a neighbor has joined Mr. Longway, who is standing at the back of the truck eyeing the interior of *Revelstoke* suspiciously. I arrive just in time to hear the neighbor quip, "I don't know about you, Walt, but I sure wouldn't let my daughter in the back of that thing."

Walt looks at the neighbor probably wondering what business it is of his.

Undeterred the neighbor takes a second shot, "Heard about these custom vans, on the mainland; they call them *passion wagons.*"

Susan's mom steps out of the truck beaming, "I really like your home, Mr. Arrington, but that bed is a bit tiny isn't it? I mean for a tall guy like you?" she smiles at me...clueless.

To my stunned amazement Susan instantly answers, "Oh no, mom, it folds out into a full double bed, there's loads of room. Want me to show you how it opens?"

Walt tries to look past Susan at the bed under discussion while his neighbor snickers in self-satisfaction. "Well," he gloats, "how do you figure she knows how to do that?"

Before anything else could go wrong, I quickly break in on the dangerous conversation. "Susan, we gotta go, we don't want to keep our friends waiting." We are going hiking in the mountains above Waikiki. Susan steps out of the truck and thankfully closes the backdoor. I whisk her around to the passenger door and hold it open until she is safely inside. Rushing to the driver's side, I quickly jump in and start the engine.

Susan rolls down her window, "Oh mom, will you wash my jeans?

I need them for work tonight."

"Certainly," she answers, "where are they?"

"In the laundry hamper in the garage," replies Susan.

"I'll do them right now," she heads with determination for the open garage door.

Driving away, I see Walt and his neighbor talking animatedly. We are just safely rounding the corner when Susan says, "You forgot something."

"What? What did I forget?" I am exasperated after the disastrous first meeting with Susan's father.

Susan smiles sweetly and says, "Your dog."

"What's with all that snuffing?" The voice interrupts my memories of Susan and Puu.

I am still pressing the fist full of grass to my nose.

"Whatever you're doing up there, get it over with so I can sleep," complains my new bunky.

New inmates came, got sentenced and left. I had a parade of new bunkies, but then with the sweltering days of summer the government offered to deal on a plea bargain. If I plead guilty to two counts, one for conspiracy and the other for smuggling, they would drop possession. There was no offer of minimum sentencing. I was okay with that since the cocaine was never mine in the first place.

The judge accepted my guilty plea then ordered me to be returned to court in two weeks for sentencing. The time delay would allow both sides, the prosecution and the defense, to prepare arguments for final sentencing.

A week goes by and I am in the cellblock doing the corridor promenade circuit. The walking helps to burn off my nervous energy though the view is not much. I am following inmate etiquette of mostly looking at the tiled floor to avoid eye contact with the three other walkers. It is a modest effort at privacy that can get you beat up or stabbed by not observing it. Abruptly, I notice a couple of inmates eagerly gathering at the door that leads to the guard's office and the attorney visiting room. I walk up to the thick window with chicken wire embedded in it and peer over the shoulders of a rapidly growing crowd. I see the guard talking with a stunningly attractive woman in a business suit. She glances at the window, which is full of lust-filled eyes and is about to look away, but then she turns, meets my eyes, smiles and then nods to the guard.

Unreal, here I am avoiding looking people in the eyes and suddenly I have a beautiful woman making direct eye contact with me. It is unsettling and overwhelmingly exciting.

The guard unlocks the door and growls, "Get back you perverts."

The men in front do not move except to shuffle to keep the men behind them from trying to crowd forward.

"Arrington," barks the guard, "in here now."

The rest of the inmates part reluctantly to let me through. One them quips, "Lucky dog," as I step forward. The guard closes the door behind me.

"Hello Mr. Arrington," says the woman offering her hand, "my name is Ginger Hartman. I am a Federal Probation Officer assigned by the court to prepare your pre-sentencing report."

"Hi," I am trying not to stare. Her hand is so soft, yet her grip is firm. It is a woman's hand, in mine, wow! Ginger is tall, athletic, sophisticated and in her mid-thirties. For her visit to our cell-block she is wearing a white silk blouse with the top two buttons undone and a tight black business skirt, the hem of which is cut high enough to complement her long, well-formed legs. She has both the guard's complete attention and mine. "Want me to hang around?" The guard asks hopefully.

"Not necessary," Ginger favors him with a smile, "our conversation is confidential."

The thought of being alone with Ginger is so very appealing that I smile at the guard. He frowns; I will pay later for that smile. He thinks I am gloating that he is being asked to leave—actually, I am just suddenly in the very best of moods.

"Come with me," says Ginger as she steps into the attorney visiting room. I could not think of anything more appealing than following her into that room. I cannot help looking at her long legs. She turns and catches me, but offers a smile anyway. Inside there is a small table with two chairs on opposite sides. "Sit down," says Ginger.

I obediently sit and watch Ginger as she walks around to the other side of the table, picks up her chair and carries it back to my side. I turn my chair to face her as she sits down opposite me and crosses one leg over the other. The smell of perfume wafts lightly past my nose, setting it to quivering. When she speaks, I hardly hear her first words as I try not to stare at her lipstick and slightly pouting mouth. I have not been this close to a woman in so long, I could easily spend hours just looking at her, as could the rest of the cellblock. The inmates are still crowded four deep at the security door though they cannot currently see her.

Ginger gets right to the point, "Mr. Arrington, I'm here to take a statement in your own words as to why you became involved with Morgan Hetrick and John DeLorean."

"How do I rate such a magnificent-looking parole officer?" I ask, trying not to grin all over myself; however, I already suspect that the government hopes to get more information out of me this way.

Ginger laughs. "It's a government plot," she answers smiling with those rouge lips. "You're supposed to tell me everything you know."

Her reference to my talking about the case instantly makes me nervous. "I'll tell you what I did, but I won't snitch on anyone else," I reply seriously.

Ginger almost seems sympathetic as she says, "Actually, with Morgan, his sons, the pilot you flew with and Max all cooperating, I doubt there is anything you can tell us that we don't already know."

They got Max and he's cooperating? Wow! I think to myself, then say, ""I'm pleased to hear that." I glance at Ginger again realizing that this woman probably now knows more about the case than I do. It is surprisingly reassuring. I glance at her eyes, which are probing my own. "Miss Hartman, I am going to be completely honest with you. I am a very foolish person who got caught up in more than I could handle with some very sophisticated criminals. I'm not arguing that it wasn't my own fault, just that I got caught up in something I didn't know how to get out of without being killed."

Ginger leans forward, looks deeply into my eyes and blinks, "So tell me about it."

I completely understand that she is using her attractions on an attention-starved man…and it is working. In prison, you are so very much alone. No one touches you; all stimuli are about being prepared to defend yourself. In this safe room, I can completely relax; I do not have to worry about being overheard or taking a knife in the back. Yet, what I say or don't say will significantly contribute to the judge's evaluation of me as a convicted felon at sentencing. Suddenly it becomes very important for me that Ginger understand my motivations for not snitching. "Look, you should know the reason I am not cooperating. It is because I understand that I deserve to do the time. Snitching would make my incarceration a lot more difficult. I'm trying to find myself again and attempting to put my time off on someone else just doesn't fit with me."

Ginger is surprised, "You're not going to argue for probation?"

I manage a weak smile. "I know my answer sounds square, but I'm going to say it anyway because it's true. I can't completely blame Morgan for what I did. When he told me he was a smuggler, I should have run, but I didn't. I guess I was too greedy. The bottom line is that I am guilty despite the manipulations."

Ginger sweeps a lock of red hair from her green eyes. "So what kind of a sentence should we give you?"

My answer just comes forth, "Five years."

Ginger looks startled. Even I'm surprised at my answer, yet it feels good and right with my soul to have said it. My deepest hope for a doable release date is putting out its first questing root.

I look away from Ginger and stare at the wall, hope is growing in my heart as I glance back at her and say, "A five year sentence would mean I could be out in three years with good behavior. It's enough time for me to learn my lesson, but not so much that prison might change me for the worst."

Ginger sits back in her chair and regards me carefully, "I've already interviewed Morgan. He admits that he twisted your arm, but you're right that you still have to be punished. Yet, I think in the end you'll come out of it okay."

I pause to imagine Morgan's reaction to Ginger. He would have told her everything just to keep her in the same room. Despite his cooperation, I hoped he would serve his full five years. His interview with Ginger would be a perfect punishment as they lock him away until he reaches old age.

After our interview, Ginger stands and offers her hand. As I take it she smiles, I feel her fingers wrap around mine, she does not let go. "Steve, let your positive attitude continue to lead you," she is looking deeply into my eyes, "I see so many inmates come back after such high hopes, but I somehow know I won't see you here again."

"Guard," she calls.

As the guard eagerly steps into the attorney door, Ginger smiles and says, "I hope you get your five years." She picks up her briefcase and walks through the security door to the outside corridor without looking back. A delicate perfume lingers in the close air of the cellblock.

The guard snickers, "How about that, she's hoping you get a five year sentence. What did you do to so upset her?"

"Upset?" I smile at the guard, "I'm hoping for the same thing."

Most pre-sentencing reports total three to five pages. Later that week, I would learn that Ginger submitted a twenty-six page pre-sentencing report to the judge. In it, she recommended that the government's effort to help rehabilitate this particular inmate would best be served by giving him a minimum sentence. The prosecutor wrote an addendum to her report referencing the foolishness of minimum sentencing, particularly for an uncooperative drug smuggler. The President's War on Drugs required that examples be made particularly in high profile cases that were commanding so much public attention.

September second is a cold blustery day. Riding to court in

the Marshals van, I chew my fingernails to the quick. My second winter in prison is approaching, but how many winters will I see from behind bars? Two nervous hours later, I am sitting anxiously in the courtroom watching the prosecutor, James Walsh begin to present his case. He turns and points an accusing finger at me, then says loudly, "The United States of America charges Stephen Arrington..." His words hammer at me like a physical blow.

The prosecutor continues arguing that by not cooperating, I am hindering society's War on drugs. He mentions my prior trouble in the Navy and several times refers to the huge amount of cocaine that I helped to smuggle in from Colombia. Then, surprisingly he runs out of negative things to say. It is as if he does not have anything else bad to say, just that he is asking for a substantial sentence to send his serious message to other criminals. He concludes and moves to sit down.

Before he makes it to his seat, Judge Takasugi abruptly asks a few questions of his own. "Mr. Prosecutor, do you have any evidence that Mr. Arrington knew anything about this drug deal before he took possession of the car or that he was involved in the supposed conspiracy with Hetrick and DeLorean?

"No," answers the prosecutor.

The judge continues, "Do you believe that Mr. Arrington has made any money off of this or any other crime and is there any possibility that he may have hidden any money away?"

The prosecutor looks unhappy. "No, with Mr. Hetrick fully cooperating, we have complete access to all the appropriate bank records.'

"You may sit down," says the judge.

My defense attorney, Richard Barnett, then stands up. He begins by referencing a long list of community service that I have done over the past years. He notes that I have been a CPR and First Aid instructor for the Red Cross for over fifteen years. He talks about my fourteen-year military career during which I made four tours to Vietnam. He tells how I had risked my life as a bomb disposal frogman while engaged in dangerous missions for the Navy, the

Secret Service and the C.I.A. for which he cannot even give specifics in my defense without violating the Secrecy Act because of the clandestine nature of the operations. He points out that I resisted involvement in Morgan's criminal enterprise and that Morgan had to resort to gross manipulations to force my cooperation.

Then, Rick concludes his arguments, "We admit that Mr. Arrington is indeed guilty, but we are talking about two multi-millionaires allegedly involved in a conspiracy and a young man who only had twenty dollars in his pocket when he arrived on the scene. A severe sentence is neither appropriate, nor fair when you consider the level of his involvement and his resistance to participating."

Next, it is my turn to take the stand. The reporters have packed the courtroom as usual. I am ready to admit to my crime, yet I also want my words to have an impact with so much press about to record what I say…a message to others about how things can go completely wrong in life, particularly when drugs are involved. I have to begin twice because my voice cracks with emotion as I try to speak.

"The greatest words I have ever heard were, 'Federal agents, you're under arrest.' Those words freed me from a nightmare. I had been living a life of deceit. I did things I was afraid not to do. When Agent Scotti arrested me, he later said, 'Well, I guess this isn't the best day in your life.' I replied, 'Actually, I think it is.' I knew that my arrest was really a new beginning. I had been rescued from a life that was totally beyond my control."

"From my jail cell, I asked Rick, my attorney, not to request a bail reduction because in prison, I was coming to terms with what I had done. I knew that the earlier I began serving my sentence, the sooner I could again become a productive member of society."

"As a Christian, I now know that good must come of all things. I want to share what I have learned from this situation. As soon as I am able, I would like to speak to high-school students about drug abuse and the realities of prison life. I want to prevent others from falling into the same traps."

I know that my crime calls for punishment, and I am prepared to pay my debt to society. Your Honor, I am sorry for what I have done and am ready for sentencing."

In the next couple of moments, my whole future is going to be determined. I know that the judge's decision will be heavily influenced by my airplane flight to Colombia and by my careless involvement of Sam. Despite the fact that I had actually tried to protect Sam from Morgan's influence, it certainly would not look that way to the court. I cannot tell them that Sam was a willing participant. In their eyes, my involvement of this innocent young man was inexcusable and it totally detracts from my credibility as a victim. Yet, I cannot tell of Sam's eager participation without jeopardizing his freedom. Remaining silent about Sam's guilt even to my mother is not easy.

The clerk's voice is loud and impersonal. "The defendant will stand for sentencing." The judge peers solemnly at me over his glasses then calmly reads the sentence from his notes. I focus on his words, wanting to freeze the moment so I would remember it always.

"Mr. Arrington, for count one, I sentence you to five years." I am unconsciously holding my breath. "For count two, I sentence you to an additional five years."

Ten years? The sentence staggers me. After a pregnant pause, maybe Judge Takasugi is being dramatic for the press, he adds, "Both sentences will run concurrently."

Abruptly, there is a heavy thump directly behind me. Spinning about I am dumbfounded to see that Ginger, apparently moved by the sentence has fallen out of her front row chair on to the floor. She quickly stands then pauses to smooth her skirt, which has every man's attention in the room except for the judge who is still reading from his notes. I know I should be focusing on the judge, but Ginger has a way of capturing my attention. She quickly re-takes her seat as the judge concludes the sentence by awarding me three years special parole.

I tear my eyes from Ginger just in time to see the judge smack his gavel down, "Court dismissed."

The Marshals stand and begin to lead me from the courtroom. I try to give the thumbs up sign to my mother so that she will know that I am okay, but it is difficult to do when wearing handcuffs. It will not be until I call her from the prison that night that I am able to explain that I have gotten five, not ten years. A concurrent sentence is kind of like two punishments for the price of one. I could be out in less than three years because of the eleven months I have already served.

I arrived late back at the cellblock, bologna sandwich on stale white in hand. All the other inmates in J-3 are waiting for me. When I step through the North Yard door in my handcuffs, they cheer. The national news agencies broadcast the details of my sentence on all three major television stations. The inmates feel that I have received a fair sentence as do I. In fact, I have received the exact sentence I told Ginger I felt I deserved, which is probably why she reacted so emotionally to the judge's ruling. I will always remember her as the first government employee in the Justice Department to believe that there was hope for me.

A friend has saved my vegetarian dinner, so at least tonight I do not go hungry. The prison cell's forty-watt bulb snaps off at exactly 10:00 p.m. Lying there in the dark, my eyes wide open because I am too excited to sleep, I feel like my life has taken on a new meaning; the beginning of a something good growing out of the ruins of my life. I can finally reconcile myself to serving a sentence that has a completion date.

I eagerly await the rights and privileges of a sentenced inmate in general population, which may not sound like anything to get excited about, unless you have been locked down in a cellblock for the better part of a year.

"Far away there in the sunshine are my highest aspirations.
I may not reach them, but I can look up and see their beauty,
believe in them and try to follow where they lead,"
Louisa May Alcott

*"If you lose hope, somehow you lose the vitality that keeps
life moving, you lose that courage to be, that quality that
helps you go on in spite of it all. And so today I still have a
dream,"*   Martin Luther King, Jr.

Chapter 31

TERMINAL ISLAND FEDERAL PRISON,

J-3, SEPTEMBER 1983

A WEEK LATER, the North Yard guard comes for me. It takes about
thirty seconds to empty the locker of all my possessions into a
small box that I barely fill. It amazes me how little I own, yet how
much these few articles mean to me as I place them into the box.
My radio, which sings to me at night and overshadows the daily
noise intrusion of the cellblock. The journal upon which I capture
my deepest emotions and where I store my pictures. The Bible that
is my constant companion as well as my teacher and comforter. My
precious supply of tea goes in alongside a change of underwear, two
pair of socks (one pair with heel & toe holes), a comb, a toothbrush
and a half-used tube of toothpaste and a bit of floss. I carry my little
box through the television room where some of the inmates pause
from whatever they are doing to wave me off…though in fact they

could care less. None of them understands my eagerness to join general population. To them, I am just another guy who lost in court, as will ninety-nine percent of them statistically, but they do not know that yet either. Almost all harbor false hopes that they will beat the system. I have not met a single inmate in J-3 who was truly innocent. They are just hoping to get lucky with a legal ploy. For them the jail unit is a place of semi-security compared to the wild stories and lurking threats of general population. It is in general population where most inmate murders and rapes occur...and I am eager to go there—jail has brought me to that.

As I stand at the North Yard door looking out, I am experiencing eager anticipation and a deep sense of dread of facing the very real perceived dangers. It is surprising that anticipation outweighs my sense of dread. I am ready to go forward in life and right now, that path leads into a concrete and steel jungle where inmate logic rules and the worst sort of human predators freely prowl. When going to war as I did in Vietnam, one needs to adopt a survival mind set; to be mentally prepared to adapt to and win...or just to survive. Armed with my Bible and a determination to do only good, I do not doubt that by being honest and fair with others and relying upon my growing relationship with God that I will one-day walk out of general population a free man. I will also continue to practice my Gung Fu. Being a Christian does not mean I should not be prepared to defend myself.

I am carrying a quote in my mind by M.H. McKee, a cerebral blue print on how to model the rest of my life, "*Integrity is one of several paths, it distinguishes itself from the others because it is the right path and the only one upon which you will never get lost.*" Integrity is the path I choose to walk upon as I prepare to journey into general population. I will become that honor inmate and I will do it by earning the respect of my overseers and my peers—as twisted those peers may be. By assigning the guards and prison staff a new mental title, overseers, it recruits them as aids to my progression through prison. To most inmates' way of thinking a guard is an adversary, someone to fight and to plot against. To work my way through the system, to take advantage of its positive opportunities is my mind set; integrity is what will lead me as I prepare to step through that frightening door I stand before.

For a moment, I think of Hank's smile and sense of courage to do what is right, purposefully not choosing or desiring an easier path. I remember how he always supported his friends and grinned at adversity. *Hank, old friend, what you taught me then serves me, the convict, now. I so regret it took me this long to learn that lesson. The hardships I could have avoided, the wonders I should have known.*

I reach out and touch the thick steel door…the cold hard barrier that is about to open to a new beginning. With great anticipation, I looked forward to all the rights and privileges of a sentenced felon.

I stand patiently waiting for over an hour. In prison one learns that things happen at their own plodding pace. Finally, I see the North Yard guard heading for J-3 reaching for his ring of keys. There is the solid clack of the key turning in the lock then the door swings open and I stand there unable to move. Despite the beckoning sunshine and the alluring smell of ocean-fresh air, I am emotionally paralyzed. Every time I have passed through this portal, I have worn handcuffs. Conditioned to orders, I look dubiously at the guard who impatiently says, "So take off, Arrington, you've been here long enough to know the drill."

With the box under one arm and integrity riding like a hopeful passenger on my shoulder, I begin to walk disjointedly across the immensity of the North Yard. Actually, the yard encompasses but a few acres of cement and grass, but my perception of space has changed significantly after living in the restricted space of a jail unit for eleven long months. Walking alone, I feel naked and exposed under the hard uncaring glare of the general population inmates who stop what they are doing to watch *new meat* entering their yard. I glance backwards at J-3 noting how small the building looks from the outside. My only regret is that no one will care for my patch of grass and that it will die under the late summer sun. Prison is like that; it bears no mark of the human beings who pass through it, but for the temporary passage of the graffiti gouged into its walls, crude drawings and raw words...silent pleas and un-shouted anger that will be cemented over to build new cells for America's rapidly growing prison population.

I stop at the edge of the concrete walkway just before the expanse of green lawn then remove my socks and shoes and pad happily onto the grass. A feeling of sudden freedom flushes through me as stress and internal conflict fall away like shedding a heavy cloak after a drenching rain. I wonder at the feeling of intense joy I am experiencing as I make the transition from jail inmate to sentenced felon.

How do I explain the desire to belong somewhere, to have a place I can call my own, even if it is just a bunk inside *chez clink*? Somewhere in the yard, I hope to find a friend, an inmate who is not thinking all the time about plea bargaining or sentencing dates. I have been an island too long, a solitary point of attempted reason in a raging sea of emotions and brutal violence. With high expectations, I put my shoes back on, open the door to A Unit and step cautiously into the dim interior.

From the guard at the front desk, I get my bunk assignment then go to put my few possessions into the locker. I feel like a stranger walking down the hall passing unfamiliar faces that pause to stare, yet offer no comment. The hostile silence that greets me is unnerving. I count bunks in search of my own while hoping that my new bunkies will be at least semi-normal. At number thirty-four, I stop and stare in acute disappointment. The lower bunk is covered with a disgusting array of stains, much of the bed's stuffing is missing; it resembles a filthy rag more than a mattress.

Unfortunately, the bed is the good news when compared with my waiting bunkies. Four of the men are present in the eight-man cubicle. They are a mixed bag of druggies who at midday are already stoned. One of them is lying on my bunk drooling onto the pillow. Another is squatting in a corner with his head nodding back and forth, as he tries to keep loose contact with reality. The other two are a couple of druggies staring at me with sincere hostility.

I instantly know the situation. They will be up most of the night shooting up with heroin or cocaine. Since all their money goes for drugs, they cannot afford to buy commissary items from the prison store, so they will be borrowers and thieves. It means that there will be a lot of fighting and arguing. I badly try to see the positive side to all of this, but sadly realize it just does not exist.

I step pass the two men staring at me. They are a scruffy looking pair with blue bandanas tied low on their foreheads. They are a regular Mutt-and-Jeff combination. One is tall and lanky, the other short and dumpy. They both glare at me, then looks of interest flicker across their faces as they watch me store my few items in the rusted metal locker. "Hey, you got any cigarettes? The dumpy one inquires gruffly.

I turn to look at the misfits. The dumpy one has shaved both sides of his head in a crude Mohican. I cannot imagine that I would ever purposefully have a conversation with either of these idiots, "Don't smoke."

Dumpy takes a deep breath and throws out his chest; he looks like a puffed-up toad. "What about candy? You got any candy?" he asks trying to glare fiercely from under his dirty bandana.

"Why don't you just watch what I put in my locker, then you won't have to ask me any more stupid questions." *They cannot seriously think they are intimidating.*

The stork leans past Mr. Toad to get a better look into the locker. "What's in those little bags?" he asks with hopeful suspicion.

"Herbal tea," I answer, knowing it will weird them out. The stranger I am to their way of thinking will only work to my advantage.

With a look of disgust, Mr. Toad glances at Mr. Stork, "Just what we need, one of those creepy hippie types."

Mr. Toad and Mr. Stork slink down the corridor leaving me alone with the slob drooling onto my mattress and the stoned black youth, who I now notice has vomited recently onto his shirt. I flee the depression of the dim cubicle and head for the beckoning sunlight outside.

I have had a policy for most of my life to try to be a nice person and to do good things for others. It is interesting that while selling marijuana to my friends in Hawaii, I still thought of myself as a good and a nice person. Same goes for my slum time with Morgan. So goes self-deception. Anyway, in J-3, I made it a point to show others respect whether I felt they deserved it or not. Being polite and deferential did not cost me anything and anyway I was absolutely in no position to judge others. However, dealing with this new group of fools is going to be challenging and I am not eager for the difficult lessons it will bare; adversity will only make me stronger…I hope.

As I eagerly stroll towards the breezeway that leads to the South Yard, I notice men turning in my direction and talking; new meat alert. The corridor is fifteen feet wide with high grey walls open to the sky. I feel like an explorer as I round a ninety-degree turn to the left, then fifty feet of narrow concrete corridor to a ninety-degree turn to the right, and then there it is stretching into the distance… the breezeway. Actually, the breezeway is only about three hundred feet long, but to this jailbird distance is relative to the seventy foot long J-3 corridor. The open ocean is suddenly a living presence that stretches outward to infinity. I walk slowly next to the chain link fence staring at the water, listening to the liquid sound of it lapping at the rocks and the occasional squawk of seagulls who are always arguing over something. The ocean has been an unseen presence for nearly a year; it is like shaking hands with a long lost friend.

At the end of the breezeway, I arrive at the South Yard in eager anticipation with all the thrill of a child entering Disneyland for the first time. A wide expanse of green lawn lies spread out before me; an entire football field of lush grass. I could not help but wonder who waters it. There is a small dormitory rumored to have college dorm like rooms that each house only a single occupant. The Honor Dorm, for *new meat* it is an impossible dream. A long old clapboard building houses the weight room. I walk the yard's perimeter twice before hearing the loud speakers announcing 12:00 p.m., count time. I have to hurry back to Animal House to be counted standing beside or lying upon my bunk. I do not look forward to meeting the rest of my new bunkies in the eight-man cubicle. Walking down the dim corridor, I can already hear them cussing and arguing loudly. To get to my bunk, which is now vacant, I have to squeeze past two husky black men, who are doing an extended soul brother handshake. They pause to scowl at me. "What do you want?" demands the larger of the two.

"You are standing in front of my bunk," I answer.

"Ain't your bunk no more," retorts the black man, "you've been moved to the other side. Sanchez was already here and cleared out your stuff." Wondering what is going on and where my few possessions have gone, I wander toward the other end of the dormitory and run into Sanchez.

"Hey, Steve, so they finally let you out of J-3." Sanchez is grinning hugely, as if he swallowed something tasty. He had been one of the more normal men in J-3. He was down for cheating on his taxes and falsifying a government contract. "Check out this bunk," winks Sanchez. "Do you think it is an improvement over number thirty-four and the sleaze patrol that slums there?

I stare where Sanchez's hand is resting. It is a top bunk with a nice thick mattress, clean sheets and an un-holed blanket. The bunk stands against a window with—an ocean view! "For me," I gasp.

"Right on," Sanchez beams, "you just happen to be standing in the celebrity inmate wing of Animal House. Let me introduce you to the guys."

The other men in the cubicle are mostly in their forties and fifties, all of them are in for white-collar crimes. By the wealth of books and expensive clothes, it is apparent that they are men of some influence; *they be having things*. In this relaxed cubicle, I can look forward to quiet evenings of intelligent conversation and quiet companionship. Lying on my new bunk while waiting for the guard to count us, I stare happily out the window. The panes are made of regular glass. There is no warping to the glass surface or steel mesh outside the glass panes to spoil the view, just the ever-present jail bars, a flat cement walk and a chain link fence. Ten yards from the window the Pacific Ocean quietly laps at moss-laced and seaweed-covered rocks. I watch two crabs scurrying amongst the rock's cracks and crevices. The joy I felt earlier surges though me again; it is a body tingling feeling of pleasure. I know I will be happy here; at least as happy as one can be considering that this is after all a prison housing violent criminals. The other bunk would have meant continuous hostility, fighting and maybe a whole lot worse—like a nighttime attack by a group of predator homosexuals or a violent visit while I am sleeping by a paranoid druggie with delusional issues.

One of the harder things to accept about prison is that inmates have no true rights and that simple circumstance can mean the difference between happiness and hate, or friends and enemies. Prison is a place where some people come to die or have their life spun off in a warped direction because an unforeseen event comes crashing down upon them simply for being in the wrong place at the wrong time.

In the next cubicle, I see the eighteen-year-old youth named Billy, who had such a rough time of it in J-3. Now he is living in a harsher environment than the jail unit where he had to contend with a single attacker. In general population there are many sexual predators seeking young men who are not prepared, or willing, to defend themselves. When there are over a thousand inmates pressed into close quarters, they live on a more primordial level where logic has little play; it is all about who is the meanest and most violent. In this hostility-edged atmosphere, if an inmate cannot stand up to the threats of violence and continuous intimidation then he becomes the plaything of the human predators, who in prison usually runs in packs or gangs.

Looking over at Billy, I am saddened to see that he really is a punk now. He is wearing make-up and in his tight pants, he moves in a suggestive way as I see him flirting with a biker inmate. Maybe in some misbegotten way he feels that he deserves this punishment for his crimes. Guilt sometimes makes people think and do the strangest things. Later, they will transfer Billy to another institution where he will take his own life. Suicide, another tragic inmate flees prison for the long forever.

A startling thought leaps to mind. The risk I took confronting Carlos meant nothing regarding the direction that Billy would take in prison. Regarding defending or avenging Billy, it had no impact for the victim. So who did it affect? Well it impacted me, I stood up for what was right, a good thing. It also impacted Carlos, who according to rumor was still in the hole. For a moment, I entertain thoughts of him sharing a cell with Mose, then realize that would be unfair to Mose.

After count, I head for lunch wondering what it is going to be like in the big chow hall when I hear my name called. It is Clayton sporting a beard.

"Hey what's with the beard?" I ask pleased to see him.

"Do you think it makes me look more fierce?" he asks hopefully.

"No." I reconsider as his shoulders slump, "Okay maybe a bit like a ferocious rodent, a macho beaver or a ferret with attitude."

"I like that," laughs Clayton, "a ferret with attitude." He hits my shoulder, "come on let's do lunch."

We step through the double doors into a huge chow hall full of noise. Two long rows of inmates stretch along the walls before twin food lines. Looking at the harden and violent men standing in line, I think that this is the last line someone would consider cutting into, then surprisingly I watch it happen.

"Isn't it dangerous cutting the line?" I voice to Clayton.

"It's a gang thing. No one would do it without a lot of heavy back up. Even then, they have to take a serious look at who's standing in line without getting caught looking. It's a macho issue. After awhile you'll notice that opposing gangs never get into the same line at the same time. It is like they got it timed."

I notice heads turning as a very large black man arrives happily calling out greetings. He is easily six foot six inches tall, weighs in excess of three hundred and fifty pounds and has massive shoulders. He is wearing a shiny pink chest-hugging T-shirt, black nylon shorts with his lower pimpled cheeks exposed and has large colorful plastic curlers in his hair. He sashays right up to the front of the line and takes a tray as two gang members step backwards out of his way.

"What is that?" I say a little too loudly.

"Shush," cautions Clayton, "that is Tiffany."

"Does he belong to the gay gang?"

"Nope, he is a gang. Everyone is afraid of him."

"Actually he looks kind of...friendly?" Tiffany is flirting with everyone around him and they are all being extremely polite in how they respond.

"That is exactly the problem. When Tiffany falls in love, it makes no difference to him if it's just a one-sided attraction. Say the wrong thing and suddenly you've got a new boyfriend whether you like it or not."

"I'll make sure to stay out of his way."

"Don't worry you're not his type."

"That is really terrific news."

"The Tiff likes big guys who think they are bad."

"Excuse me?"

"He is into taking down big macho guys who think they are tough. It is something amazing to see. Some new guy shows up strutting as if he owns the place because he is used to making smaller guys cower in other joints. Then The Tiff starts batting his eyes at him and he thinks it is some kind of joke. Next thing you know he is the one walking around with his tail between his legs because he just got chewed up by a much bigger and meaner dog."

When we reach the serving line most of the food is looking abused and picked over. The salad is wilted lettuce, nothing else. The remaining scalloped potatoes are the hardened kind baked to the bottom of the metal tray. Only the lima beans are hardly touched.

"Whoa, check it out," I blurt happily.

"What?" Clayton glances up and down the food line wondering what has me so excited.

"The lima beans, I love lima beans."

"You know Steve," Clayton shakes his head, "you're pretty weird; hope it doesn't damage my reputation."

After 4:00 p.m. count, I head back down to the South Yard with great anticipation to watch my first sunset of 1983. I walk the yard's inner perimeter stopping under a row of eucalyptus trees that form a windbreak. I inhale the unique scent of the Australian trees then begin filling my front pockets with eucalyptus pods under the watchful stare of the guard in the security tower. He probably wonders what I am up to when actually my whole intent is just that I like the pod's strong scent; I intend to put them into my locker to counteract the smell of my socks. With my front pockets bulging much like a chipmunk's cheeks, I walk over to a palm tree, sit down on the grass and lean my back against the tree's trunk. It feels good to lean against something other than rough cement. Imagine not touching a tree for almost a year...only cold cement or hardened steel. Facing west, I gaze at the sun, while it slowly descends behind the rolling hills of San Pedro. As the day fades to dusk, thousands of tiny lights flicker to life on the darkening hillside. The seaport's winding streets come alive with moving ribbons of vehicular light, flashing yellows, glowing reds and intense glistening whites. Residential and traffic lights blink or flicker to their own rhythm, while for a few minutes the setting sun silhouettes the sloping hillside in a bright red halo. I spend the early evening wandering about the South Yard watching the lights of San Pedro glistening in the darkness when abruptly I begin to hear live music. It is coming from the inner channel that leads into Los Angeles Harbor. I step up to the fence and cock my ear to hear better as the music grows and then I hear laughter and the tinkle of happy voices raised in celebration. Appearing abruptly from behind a large darkened warehouse there are brilliant lights floating upon the dark water, sparkling white lights, merry reds, warm blues and emerald greens as I realize I am looking at a cruise ship going out to sea. I distinctly hear a woman laughing; the sound reaches right down inside of me and shakes my very core. I abruptly realize I have not heard a woman's laughter since before my incarceration. It is such a joyous sound and it stirs my emotions in an intense, welcome way. It is the single most pleasing sound I have ever heard. I mentally store the memory away to be unwrapped like an endlessly giving present for later appreciation. At that instant I long to be free of prison more than at any other moment, yet know that I have a time to serve. It has become an honor issue to me.

Sixteen years ago, I joined the Navy during the Vietnam Crisis to serve my nation. I was proud to be an American and wanted to help others to be free like us. As a youth, I had been fascinated by history and knew that there had never been another nation like the United States. I joined the Navy because I wanted to be a part of that proud history. Drugs corrupted the honor I held so dear within myself; something I treasured that gave value to my life. But in the fog of drugs, I did not realize I was forfeiting my honor and my focus as an American fighting man. What became more important than anything else was my next high; yet I freely and foolishly argued that marijuana was not addictive.

Now in prison my mind is clear. I have new purpose and focus. I am determined to serve my time honorably, to willingly pay my debt to society. It is why I did not cooperate or testify against Sam. The government did not need my cooperation, not with Morgan, his sons and Stretch, the pilot already cooperating. Later, Max would become a key witness against Manual Noriega, the once President of Panama. In the scheme of things I was a very small fish and Sam but a guppy. Therefore, I will shield Sam from the corruption of prison and I will be a spark of principle in this penitentiary of vileness and corruption.

I watch the great white ship slip from my view, then the laughter and the music fades and my eyes return to the lights sparkling on the hills of San Pedro. The quiet moment is broken by a sharp magnified voice, "Count time, count time." I turn away from the multicolored lights and begin walking up the breezeway with the gentle sound of small waves breaking upon the rocks and I know deep in my heart that I am truly a very blessed and lucky inmate.

The next morning I go to meet with the Recreation Officer and request assignment to his department. "Why recreation?" he asks scratching his backside. "We pay the least. In the kitchen you could earn more and you can lift extra food." Spoken like a true prison guard.

"I want to be involved in a department that makes people happy. I can learn to run the movie projector, I can help with the stage and I would really be into watering that football field."

"Yeah, we've all heard about your water thing," he quips. "Okay, so let's go water the football field," he says rising from his desk, "I will show you where to find the hoses and sprinklers." My heart soars as I follow him out the door, *hoses and sprinklers!*

My assignment for the whole day is simply to water the football field; it makes me feel giddy as we head for the hose locker. I set out three whirly bird sprinklers, begin at one end of the field and slowly work my way to the other end in stages. I only abandon the field for lunch and return with four pieces of bread I have smuggled out wrapped in napkins in my socks. Even if caught, I would not get in trouble for the bread; the guards are far more interested in high-ticket items like steaks and hard-boiled eggs. The bread is for the many birds that come throughout the day to bathe in the shallow puddles of water on the grass. I particularly enjoy throwing small pieces of bread in the path of the approaching stream of water from the sprinklers to watch the agile seagulls swoop in like a competitive flying squadron, maneuvering for all their worth to miss the pulsating stream of water yet be the first to the bread crumb.

Dragging the long hoses, watching the whirly birds shooting their long jets, dodging traveling streams of falling water and getting wet, I am completely in my element. I love water; it is why I became a diver. In the afternoon, the sunlight begins painting wandering rainbows in the lively water cascading over the wet green grass. I am like a kid in a water park. I give the whole football field a thorough soaking and revel in a job well done. The grass must be incredibly happy.

At the end of the workday, I shut off the taps, begin coiling the long heavy hoses and carry them back to the Recreation Department

Locker. I sling a coiled hose over each shoulder enjoying the sound of squishing water under my sneakers. I am reminded of my short Japanese poems, "The wonder, I carry water." At first reading, it does not seem to say much until you get your mind around it. I imagine an elderly Japanese farmer with a yoke over his shoulders with twin pottery jugs slung from the ends. I see him treading a dirt path through rice fields to a paper-walled structure with a shingled roof. He removes his sandals before walking inside; maybe he bows because this place is so important to him. His wife greets him with love and if there are children they are happy. Water only brings good things. There will be a sharing time as they drink the water together. Later, maybe the ceremony of a hot bath. Lastly, I think about the writer of these simple words. He or she recognized that intrinsic value of the simple act of putting these five words to paper, "The wonder, I carry water." That is the moment I fully commit myself to writing a book about my misadventures in prison and with Morgan.

Strolling across the wet grass, listening to the gentle surge of the ocean swishing amongst the breakwater, watching seagulls fly in the sky, I think *The wonder, inmate carries water-hoses.*

The Recreation Officer meets me at the locker to lock it. "You really soaked the football field," he says seriously.

"Sure did," I answer proud of my very thorough job.

"But it's Friday."

"Yeah?"

"On Fridays we only give it a light watering. Soaking it means it may not dry out by the weekend when everyone wants to run, play and lay on it. This is not going to make you very popular amongst the rest of the inmates."

> *"You cannot escape the responsibility of tomorrow by evading it today,"* Abraham Lincoln

I am standing near the end of the chow line when someone grabs my arm from behind. I turn expecting to see someone I know because inmates are extremely careful not to touch a stranger. An Arian Brotherhood gang member stands close to me. He is a couple of inches taller than my six feet, has bulging muscles, face and neck tattoos and wild eyes. This is a guy with real attitude problems, probably only loosely attached to reality, and he has a serious grip on my arm. "You're the dude who's writing that book for kids? Warning them about drugs?" he asks gruffly.

I look from his scarred face to the hand gripping my arm. He gets the idea and pulls back his hand. "Yeah, that's me." I answer after he releases his grip.

"Come with me," the grip is back as he begins pulling me towards a corner. I am about to resist when he says, "Got somethin for you, don't want anyone else listening in…it's personal."

I am intrigued, "It's personal but you want me to write about it?"

"Yeah, but the kids won't know who I really am and soon it won't matter no how," his eyes are not wired properly to his brain; there is a missing connection or a detour to another planet in that drug abused brain. One moment he is intensely staring right at me then his eyes are off on an adventure of their own shooting all about the room before finally setting on the ceiling for a couple of seconds then with a jolt, like a circuit reconnecting, his eyes rediscover me. It does not help that he also has a lazy eye, which never quite focuses on where he is looking. It gives the impression that he is talking to someone standing behind me and to my left. "They call me Loco. I'm also kind of gay."

"Oh." I have no idea what my response should be to a gay announcement in prison, but it makes me extremely uncomfortable that he is making this admission to me.

He beams, "That's why I'm talking with ya."

"What?"

"Didn't mean that; everyone knows you're straight."

I am quite pleased to hear that that word is out and circulating within the prison's gay community.

Wild Eyes grabs my arm again, "I want you to write about me."

"Why?"

"Cuss I'm dying, I got the Big A."

"Big A?"

"AIDS man," the eyes take a quick independent turn about the room; it is as if he is seeing everything slightly off kilter; visual stereo without an amplifier to balance out the signal. "Don't be talking bout it or I won't have any kind of love life anymore."

Love? What a corruption of that word. He has a sexually transmitted disease that kills and is perfectly okay with passing it on to people he supposedly cares about. Murder by disease served up by a twisted aficionado.

"I want you to write about my addiction." One eye is staring fiercely at me; the other is more interested in a saltshaker on a nearby table.

"I don't think I care to write about that kind of behavior."

"I'm talking about drugs man. I'm a heroin addict. It's how I got Aids and it's what's killing me."

I look at this very scary man and see fear, deep intense, hope-killing fear.

"I want you to write about what happened just before I got arrested. Me and a buddy were shooting up. He was doing the first load when suddenly he starts shaking, vomits on himself, goes rigid all the sudden, then quivers and bam, the dude dies. I sat there for about ten minutes wondering what to do?"

"You were thinking if you should call 911?"

"Na, he was stone dead; weren't nobody gonna help him." The wild eye is examining the debris on the floor. "I was wondering if I should do a full hit."

"You're kidding."

"Figured he O.D. (overdosed), so I did only half a load. Shot up and passed out. Woke up in the middle of the night lying next to a dead guy. Man, he had one bad funk…really starting to stink you know."

"You used the same needle?"

"Yeah, after I wiped the vomit offa it."

"Your friend dies and you shoot up with the same stuff?"

His good eye blinks, "It's what addiction is."

The wild eyes look up at the ceiling pipes then vacantly across the room, "What do you suppose happened to the junkie when word hit the street that Bobby died shooting his stuff?"

"Someone turned him in?" I hazard.

"Na, dude sold out all his stash after doubling his price. Word was his dope was so good it killed Bobby and he was some kind of hard-core doper. It was a boss recommendation."

"That's nuts!"

"No, that's addiction."

"You want me to write about this?"

"You have to man, it's all I got," there are tears silently running down from those fierce eyes; they glisten as he stares at me then down at the floor. The tears wet one of his neck tattoos…a biker on his machine going away down a desert road. "I'm dying of the Big A and I got nothing to leave cept for that story."

"Martyrdom…is the only way in which a man can become famous without ability," George Bernard Shaw

Photo Arrington
Animal House; top far right window is author's. Beginning of breezeway is on left
between Animal House and industry building at base of guard tower.

But they lie in wait for their own blood; they ambush their own lives. So are the ways of everyone who gains by violence.
Proverbs 1:18-19

Chapter 32

TERMINAL ISLAND FEDERAL PRISON,

A-UNIT, OCTOBER 1983

O VER THE next couple of weeks, I practically live in the South Yard. Each morning I am up early, anxious to go outside. Standing at the security door to Animal Unit eagerly watching for the guard, I feel like a puppy that cannot wait for his owner to let him out. Running alone in the early morning darkness is the closest I can come to actually feeling free. Light of heart, I enjoy racing the sunrise, counting off the laps before the first light, while the rest of the prison slumbers.

On the morning of September 27, I am even more anxious than normal as I stand just inside the door waiting for the guard; it is my thirty-third birthday. At 6:02 a.m., I hear the guard's shoes plodding on the cement path that leads to the door, guards almost never move fast enough for a waiting inmate. Finally, there is the sound of a key turning in the heavy lock. I wait until the guard's footsteps fade away before slowly pushing against the door. To push against an outside door and have it open is probably only amazing to inmates and toddlers. With almost the thrill of a child escaping the house, I bolt for the South Yard.

A dense sea fog lies heavily on the ground and covers the still surface of the ocean. With each lap around the dirt track, I push the pace a little faster, racing against the dim red glow that is slowly growing on the fog-bound horizon. I sprint the last half mile then climb an old set of wooden bleachers to better see the globe of the rising sun, its blood-red light misted by a shroud of white fog.

From a nearby tree, a bird twitters a greeting to the new day. Inhaling deeply the crisp morning air, I feel totally at peace with the world. The fact that it is my birthday lends vitality to my sense of well-being and is a convincing argument to do a little weight lifting before breakfast. I am riding on a natural high as I jog toward the open door of the weight room without the slightest suspicion that I am happily heading towards a terrifying encounter.

A light mist floats in the still cold air inside the long narrow weight room. The few windows that have not been broken out of the old clapboard building are frosted with dew. Iron weights and rusty steel bars lay scattered haphazardly about the wooden floor. I stoop to pick up a long steel bar; it is cold and the dew that covers the chilly metal wets my hands. Turning toward the bench press to rack the heavy bar, I smell the pungent musk of marijuana smoke. That is when I see the two men. They are standing just outside the backdoor in the shadows getting stoned. Their dark silhouettes, shrouded in the white fog, have a disconcerting sinister air about them. Slowly the two men begin to walk towards me. The fog drifts from their bodies in long wispy tendrils that cling to their silhouettes in a smoky embrace. The empty room waxes colder at their stealthy approach. I have the intimidating feeling of being openly stalked.

They are only a few feet away when one of them, a Samoan with a massively thick body raises a blunt finger to his nose, pinching off one nostril, then he snorts forcefully. A thick wad of mucus lands inches from my foot. The other inmate laughs loudly—the high-pitched laughter of a demented maniac. The Maniac, who looks like a Polish mercenary, has a hulking muscular build. His shaved head has a blunt bullet shape; he probably has the same IQ as a twenty-two caliber bullet. The exposed skin on top his head glistens in the mist...I think it is sweat. He opens his mouth revealing a dark gap where two front teeth are missing. The man looks remarkably like a villain from a James Bond movie. He steps closer then leans his meaty hands on the heavy bar, which I have unfortunately set down. I regret not having the bar in my hands; it would have made nice weapon. The Maniac leers maliciously, the gap in his damaged teeth causes him to lisp as he threatens, "You ready for a little pony ride, boy?"

Startled, I straighten up. My happiness of a few moments earlier has already fled before the storm of their ominous approach. Now I desperately try to remain calm, while sudden fear sweeps through me. I have to make an effort to keep my voice even as I answer gruffly, "Well, it's a good thing there's no one down here but us men."

The Maniac cackles his insane laugh then thumps me solidly in the chest with one of his beefy hands. I almost lose my balance from the unexpected impact. The man is fast, very fast. I feel the surge of adrenalin flowing through me, the fight or flight stimulus, but which should I do?

"Acting tough isn't going to save your butt, creampuff." He is chewing what I think is a piece of gum, but then I see it is a couple of cloves of garlic. Smacking his lips loudly he eyes me up and down. I decide to kick him in the groin. This is not an easy decision. Who wants to attack someone so much bigger than yourself, particularly when he has a giant Samoan along for the pony ride? Fierce anger sends hot blood coursing through my arteries. Pony ride, a fun childhood expression horribly corrupted by these two ugly beasts. The only diversion I have to try escaping is to attack first.

Sudden voices pull our attention to the front door. A couple of biker types are just walking in through the open doorway. "Hey,

Bad Bill," yells the Maniac, "look what I got me here."

Obviously, the Maniac had not paid close attention in his third grade English class; I doubt that he made it to middle school.

While the Maniac is momentarily distracted, I glance over my shoulder at one of the broken windows. Maybe I can make my escape by diving through it, I think hopefully, because I know I do not stand a chance against four burly inmates and I am not going to just stand there and wait to see what happens.

The Samoan sees my fugitive look and takes a lumbering step to cover my only apparent escape route. He snickers in anticipation. The Maniac swings his bullet head back toward me grinning in a wicked way. One of his meaty hands sweeps automatically downward shielding his groin.

Okay, no groin shot, I size up his knobby knees. A quick snap kick angled into the knee can dislocate the joint making it impossible for bullet head to stand. After taking out his knee, I am planning another snap kick to his groin or face, whichever is the most exposed. The double snap kick has to happen fast because I am probably going have a charging Samoan coming at me. Either, I will dodge him, my best chance, or I will go for a throat shot. I glance at his tree-trunk legs…a knee shot will not work with him. Terror fills my thoughts, goading me to the edge of fury as I prepare to fight for my life.

"Hey, it's the Fall guy," I freeze. Bad Bill is holding out his hand in my direction. "Hey, remember me?" he asks hopefully? He looks like a sad-eyed hound dog hopeful for attention. He continues, "You autographed the Doonesbury comic strip for me." The memory floods back. He is one of the inmate plumbers who slipped into my cell in J-3.

"Hey Gonzo, this is one right-on dude." While shaking my hand enthusiastically, he smiles brightly, "Gonzo calls me Bad Bill, but my friends call me Sweet William." Bad Bill turns to Gonzo, "Fall Guy refused to rat out DeLorean. My friend here is a celebrity; one newspaper refers to him as Upright Steve."

My status in the weight room instantly goes up several notches as

Sweet William's good buddy.

Gonzo shifts roles in a heartbeat, from attacker to want-to-be-best friends. He insists on helping with my workout. I have loaded the bar on the bench press with one-hundred-sixty-five pounds and have a very enthusiastic Gonzo spotting me. I barely manage to squeeze out ten repetitions.

"Ah, you can do more than that," he lisps. Then he adds a ten-pound plate to each end of the heavy bar. For the next hour, I get to lift *creampuff weight* while helping to spot the heavy iron with Gonzo, Bad Bill and the Samoan, known for some strange reason as *Chick*. Toward the end of the workout, I want to use lighter iron, but Gonzo knuckles me good naturally in the chest and leers, "Ya gotta drive the heavy iron, sugar." Then smiling sweetly, he adds, "If you wanna stay a virgin in here, ya gonna need bigger muscles, cutie."

Later, while walking back up the breezeway with my arms hanging rubbery at my sides, I think about how the joint has a way of inducing inspired workouts. Silently I say a mental thanks to Trudeau; amazing Doonesbury comic strip to the rescue and it does not even have a superhero. Several hours later, I remember that it is my birthday, but I do not feel like celebrating anymore.

"One's dignity may be assaulted, vandalized and cruelly mocked, but cannot be taken away unless it is surrendered,"
Morton Kondrake

Walking down the breezeway, I glance at a large wart growing on my index finger. I tried to get some wart remover from the prison clinic, but they refused. Probably afraid I would try to feed it to another inmate, which in prison is a justifiable concern. I look at the abrasive concrete wall to my right, and then resisting a powerful urge not to do this, place the wart firmly against the wall. For the first six feet or so it doesn't hurt, then it does...I continue to walk. After a couple of dozen feet of serious wart abrading, I look down at my bleeding finger. Yep, the wart is gone.

This is not my first attempt at prison cosmetic surgery. In J-3,

I had a nerve ganglion growing on my wrist. It is a gelatinous sac the size of a large marble that was growing under my skin. In the old days people would strike them with a Bible to rupture the sac. My cellmate used a heavy law book he had checked-out from the prison library. It worked, but it took two firm smacks applied by a very enthusiastic felon.

Arriving at the South Yard, I see the old man in his wheelchair and walk over to him. He is one of the scarier inmates in the prison. He had been arrested in 1948 for hijacking a truckload of cigarettes. In 1952, he killed another inmate, followed by two more in the sixties. Four years ago, he stabbed a guy who had gotten too close to his wheelchair while shouting insults at him. I keep a leery distance as I reach into my sock and take out a napkin-wrapped piece of fried baloney and give it to him. There is an unapproachable prison cat that he likes to feed. Walking away, I wrap the still bleeding finger in the napkin and head for the football field.

Once a month the American Indian inmates are allowed to worship in a homemade sweat lodge on the South Yard lawn. They build a small bonfire in which they place round smooth stones. Smooth stones are less likely to crack or explode from the heat. They light the fire a couple of hours before sunset. After the sun descends behind the foothills of San Pedro, the Indians will dig the hot stones from the red ashes of the fire with a forked stick and carry them into the hut for their sweat bath.

It is a half hour before sunset; I am sitting downwind from the fire and its adjacent small domed hut just to smell the wonderful campfire smell of burning wood. In prison, one learns to take pleasure from the smallest and seeming unimportant things.

Sitting down upon the grass on that chilly late afternoon in early October, I inhale the smoky fragrance of the fire. Closing my eyes, I say a quiet prayer, which as usual involves my safety in prison and a big wish to get out sooner rather than later. As a now practicing Christian, I believe I have learned my lesson and am eager to get on with a new life. I open the Bible, I am carrying to an arbitrary page and casually read a sentence—abruptly the stability of the world about me shifts.

When I sat down, my thoughts were clouded with speculation about my life in prison. I wondered how serving time inside such a callous and dangerous institution is going to make me be a better person.

I stare in amazement at the answer that lies beneath my finger, which is pointing to Romans, chapter five, verse three, "But we also exult in our tribulations, knowing that tribulation brings about perseverance, and perseverance, proven character, and proven character, hope; and hope does not disappoint."

Prison is my tribulation! If my incarceration is viewed as a ordeal in which to temper my moral fiber, then the tribulation that is my daily companion is leading me to growth—growth in spirit and in character. Prison, when viewed as a place of growth for someone who needs it (who more than inmates?), takes on a unique perspective not often found in the tameness of a civilized society. I reach for greater comprehension and am aided in that quest by adversity, which is my guide and teacher.

As I think these thoughts, my eyes wander to the end of the sentence in my Bible, "And hope does not disappoint." There is the anchor that will get me through prison. I know in my heart that God loves me and with His guidance, I can be a good person again. My hope is to one day be recognized again as that good person. Tucking the Bible under my arm, I walk back up the breezeway to A unit at peace with myself.

It is quiet in our cubicle in A Unit as I climb upon my bunk. Still wearing my T-shirt and jeans, I slide under my top sheet and worn blanket for warmth. I fluff the thin pillow and fold it into a wedge then lie on my stomach and peer out the barred window. I am waiting to watch the moonrise. For me it is an important event. Living in Revelstoke I patterned my nightly activities on the rising of the full moon. It is a terrific time for night surfing or a late evening hike. Tonight, I will be a passive observer of the moonrise. In prison, the deviant behavior level takes an uptick during the full moon. My bunk will be an early refuge from the inmate intrigues that are already being planned. I listen to the soft breathing of two men sleeping in the cubicle. They are resting now in anticipation of late night activities. I have no idea what they are planning, nor do I want to know.

Looking out the small window, I mentally prepare for the celestial theater that is about to unfold. The sky begins to darken with the sun setting in the west, which I cannot see from my eastern facing window. I look out across a vast expanse of coastal ocean towards Long Beach Harbor. A crease of red light slowly becomes visible in the fast approaching darkness with the arrival of the harvest moon. It is a fallacy that darkness falls; actually, it rises expanding upwards from the Eastern horizon. The reddish moon rising silhouettes the tall masts of warships in the harbor. It is from there, in the late sixties and seventies that I sailed on naval destroyers to Vietnam. Another time, a prouder place, but I do not pause to consider the implications, tonight is about experiencing the moon and its light. As the bottom of the globe climbs higher, I see its soft crimson light reflected on the still calm ocean water, which is sheltered by a mile long breakwater. I stare at the mirrored surface of the water and then I cannot help myself as the red light dancing on the ocean causes a memory to unfold.

Susan, Puu and I are walking on the beach at Waikiki. I picked her up earlier from her dormitory room at the University of Hawaii. We each have one arm around the other's waist. I am enjoying the soft feel of Susan's silk dress as it slides with each step. I love this woman so much that it hurts deep down inside. I am so fearful of losing her after four incredible months together. I lean a little closer to her and nuzzle my face into her neck and thick mane of blond hair. I smell the fragrance of coconuts and think what it would be like to spend the rest of my life with her and fear settles into my stomach with a sinking feeling.

"Susan," I say softly, "my orders arrived today."

"I know," she glances at me then looks away, "I could tell by how withdrawn you are acting."

We walk a little further then she stops and turns towards me,

"When do you leave?"

A sad wetness to her eyes is ripping my heart apart. "Next week," I say sadly.

Susan just looks at me; it is such a deep penetrating look. No one has ever peered so deeply into my soul; I treasure the moment and feel something awakening. I like having her inside of me and want so desperately to keep her there…I am so afraid that it may only be a memory I will be keeping. Everything depends on her answer to my next question. "Susan," I begin to ask faltering and having to start again, "Susan, would you like to come to California with me?"

Susan smiles, she is radiant, her eyes glow, her voice is full of excitement, "Yes Steve, I will come to California with you."

My joy is like a fire that flushes through my entire being. The fear of losing her instantly evaporates in the furnace of our love.

We sit on the beach eagerly planning our future. Puu is sleeping with his head in my lap. He snores with one paw moving occasionally in pursuit of dog dream adventures. Susan's head lies against my shoulder as she lightly strokes Puu. "Steve," she says softly, "what about Puu?"

"What about Puu?" I rub his ears then scratch his side, which puts the paw into second gear.

"Well," Susan's words come out slowly, "if two of us are going to be living in *Revelstoke* it will be cramped, but with monster dog it will be hugely crowded."

The thought of leaving Puu in Hawaii had not entered my mind.

"You have lots of friends who would love to have Puu." Susan is very nervous and I can tell she is worried about what she is voicing, instantly I want to comfort her. I pull her head into my lap and look at the two individuals I love most in the world. *Yes, Puu is a dog, but he is not just any dog…he is my dog. What will be best for him?* In California, there will be leash laws; he will not be able to run free on the beach as he does here in Hawaii. I am heading into the big unknown. I do not know what I will be doing or where I will be doing it. Eventually, I will probably windup at college, but until then…all is in doubt.

The two most important living parts of my life are with me now and one wants me to leave the other behind...what should I do?

Susan sits up and leans her head on my shoulder, "That couple that watched Puu when you were in the brig, Puu liked it there. They have such a big backyard. They asked me to tell you that they would love to have Puu."

I absolutely do not want to leave my four-legged friend behind, but Revelstoke is cramped quarters for two. With Monster Dog pawing about, well he will always be underfoot. With no yard and unknown responsibilities, where would I keep him? Undoubtedly, my love for Susan clouds my judgment because giving Puu away turns out to be a foolish and a very sad decision that I will have to live with for the rest of my life.

It is overcast as I pull into my friend's driveway. Puu seems to know something is up as he stays quite close to my side. We take Puu into the backyard where I pass over the handle to Puu's leash.

I kneel and ruffle his ears just so he knows that I love him, and then with my heart breaking, I turn and quickly leave, closing the gate behind me so he cannot follow. Puu barks once to let me know that I have forgotten him. I hurry out to Revelstoke and begin driving away refusing to look back. I hear him barking anxiously, tears stream down my face. Rounding a corner the barking gives way to a long drawn-out howl that slowly fades with distance, but keeps echoing inside my heart.

Susan has to work that evening, so I spend a rainy night alone on the North Shore. I miss Puu terribly. I realize how much a part of my life he is and feel empty inside. I am also experiencing a lot of guilt having betrayed my best friend. His favorite towel lies abandoned on the floor. I think about how much fun we have had with that old torn towel. I would use it to dry him off after his daily bath in the ocean, which is when he would fight me for possession of it. I am considering going back to fetch him; Susan and I can work this out.

The next morning, I wake feeling miserable. I feel so desolate not seeing Puu's wagging tail and not having his head crowding my pillow with big sad eyes begging for attention. I go to a pay telephone and call Susan. As soon as I hear her voice, I know something is wrong. Stuttering and crying, her words broken with sobs, she says, "Steve, I'm so sorry."

"Susan, what's wrong?" My heart thumps wildly.

"After you left," she gasps for air, "Puu jumped the fence. He ran out onto the street and was struck by a car. He died."

In the cellblock, I pull the worn prison blanket over my head and silently cry.

"Although the world is full of suffering, it is full also of the overcoming of it," Helen Keller

"Chaos of thought and passion, all confused..."
Alexander Pope

Chapter 33

TERMINAL ISLAND FEDERAL PRISON,

A-UNIT, DECEMBER 1983

DESPITE ALL my best efforts, sometimes it is difficult for me to escape depression. A fit of despair descends upon me with the approach of my second Christmas inside. A mid-December storm echoes my mood, as I lie upon my bunk in the middle of the night unable to sleep. Staring out at the raging ocean, I watch wind and ocean-surge driven waves beating against the rocks at the base of the security fence. The wind is blasting directly into my window hurling sheets of rain and ocean spray against the glass. The bunk's previous tenant broke out a third of the glass panes. Normally, I enjoy the fresh air that blows through the empty panes, but tonight, in a vain attempt to keep the rain out, I first try bending cardboard over the empty panes. However, the wind driven water with its briny taint soon soaks through the heavy brown paper, allowing the cold drenching wind entrance to my bunk. I try stuffing my T-shirt, my socks and towel into the empty panes, but they do not work either, as water causes them to sag and leak wind and rain. My mattress is turning into a sponge. I cannot quietly move the bunk with a two hundred-and-thirty pound man sleeping on the lower bunk. Wearing two pairs of sweats, I borrowed an extra pair, and wrapped tightly in my now half wet prison blanket, I cannot help shivering as I stare out the dark window. Beyond the glow of the security lights, I see seagulls flying desperately against the blustery wind. Finally tiring they land on the turbulent water, until it sweeps them too close the rocks. Then they have to fly again, some of them eventually seek shelter inside the prison walls.

It is a powerful night full of energy and lust for life. I mentally strive against the bars that hold me and wish for the future and its far off promise of freedom. Like a beast in a cage, I rise from my bunk and stalk the dark corridor preying on the electrical flash of lightning and the deep rumble of thunder that reverberates through the dark halls. The fury of the storm fuses with my need for life outside this concrete and steel quarantine that binds me. I rave for my freedom and silently fight against the society that locks me away from it as I stride the corridor angrily; a human fury swirling in the eye of the storm.

The next morning finds me sitting red-eyed in the unit lounge. My fury and passion has washed away with the passing of the storm. A gentle rain is washing the window outside.

I feel a lot better now about the approaching Christmas. I think to myself that there are times when it is best to express the passion of our feelings to help flush away the negative energy that often paws about inside of us.

Standing up, I decide to indulge myself this Christmas by decorating the entire visiting room. After breakfast, I track down the Recreation Officer and get him to allow me access to the basement storerooms where they keep the old Christmas decorations. It is very creepy being in the bowels of the prison alone. Of the three overhead light fixtures only the one furthest away is working. Dust particles float languidly in the still air, old boxes cast dark shadows against the damp cement walls. *What a creepy place to store Christmas ornaments and decorations.*

Rooting around in a dank and moldy corner, I worry about encountering something sinister, such as an old electric chair or something equally creepy. Instead, I dig out a six-foot-tall standard prison-issue, plastic Christmas tree and four dusty cardboard boxes full of chipped Christmas lights and bright but dusty ornaments. There is also an assortment of inmate-crafted ornaments mostly made from painted cardboard or carved wood; most of them are either rat chewed or fed upon by mold and fungus. It is a little depressing looking at the condition of the handmade ornaments, an incarcerated person's Christmas hope stuffed in a moldy box, cloaked in dust, and wrapped in darkness.

Dragging the boxes down the shadowed corridor, raising a trailing cloud of dust, I imagine a woodsman in a frosty forest with a real Christmas tree on a sled. I am about as far as one can get from that happy image as the dust motes in the air send me into a coughing spasm. I deeply regret not having a real tree to decorate. Christmas seems counterfeit and seriously hollow minus the wilderness scent of a Douglas Pine, its bark oozing tiny cascades of honey-brown sap.

Placing the Christmas goods on the recreation department cart that I use to haul the heavy lawn hoses, I tow my squeaky wheeled sleigh to the visiting room. A guard locks me into the large empty space as I begin to go about my task. I string chipped ornaments and faded ribbon from the walls and ceiling then erect the plastic tree in a corner of the room. I spend a couple of hours weaving the lights around the tree and hanging all the handmade ornaments in its branches. I want the past hopes of inmates long gone to have the place of honor on the plastic tree. I plug in the merry lights using them to frame each of the old handcrafted ornaments.

Next, I industriously begin wrapping empty boxes to put under the tree. Some of the Christmas paper is mildewed, which I place facing the floor or cover with a piece of faded ribbon. I am beginning to mentally tire of my labors when I hear a tiny thump against one of the thick windowpanes. I go over to the east bank of windows and am surprised to see by the low light that the sun is already setting. I think how quickly the day has passed as I look out into the fast approaching winter night. I missed lunch.

At first, all I see is the restless ocean beyond the security lights; then a tiny movement on the concrete pad just outside the window attracts my attention. Lying by a spool of razor wire, in a bright pool of light fluttering occasionally, is a small brown sparrow. Apparently blinded by the bright lights, it flew into the thick plate glass.

Had I been home, I would have gone outside and carefully collected the small bird. Even if I could not nurse it back to health, I would have at least given it comfort, like a box filled with warm towels so it could die in peace. Instead, hands pressed to the plate glass, I watch it slowly die in the cold chill of the dark evening under the harsh glare of the security lights. It flutters a bit, then once more frantically before lying still…and with its little life went the last vestige of my wanting to celebrate Christmas at Terminal Island Prison.

Reluctantly, with my spirit dragging behind me, I return to the plastic tree and again begin wrapping the empty boxes. I cannot help the tears that cloud my eyes, the lights of the tree shimmer with wetness; haloed in out-of-focus rainbows I stare at the old inmate ornaments wondering how long they were buried in that basement. I do not know if I am crying for the small bird or for myself, but the silent tears continue to fall freely all the same. They spill upon the fake presents dampening the Christmas paper. The colors begin to soften and run and in the process, make me sadder by the moment.

The chill of the evening is just beginning to make my hands stiff with cold when I finish wrapping the last of the empty boxes to put under the plastic made-in-Korea tree. Staring at the artificial tree with its litter of vacant presents, I wonder if the gay deception does not really make a statement about the spiritual hollowness of Christmas in prison.

I stand against the cold metal door for over an hour longing for my jacket before the guard remembers to come for me. Because he is tardy, or just doesn't care, I have now missed dinner too. Walking across the chilly and blustery North Yard, with my hands deep inside my pockets, feeling miserable and self-pitying, I stop and look upwards into the heavens. In the middle of the yard, there is no bright glow from the security lights because their brightness lines the perimeter walls. I am looking upward into a black halo filled with bright stars. I see the Big Dipper and follow its handle looking to find the North Star, Polaris, the only star that does not move in the night sky. With it, I have always been able to find my way. The North Star speaks to me of travel, adventure and mysteries that lie beyond the next bend in the trail or over the ocean's horizon. However, the dark halo of night sky is just too small and confining to include the North Star. Hands in pockets I walk head down into the breezeway.

"Nothing is so strong as gentleness; nothing so gentle as real strength," Francis de Sales

With the trial behind me, Sam comes for his first visit. Sitting next to the Christmas tree, we enjoy a wonderful, laugh-filled conversation. Sam is happily telling me about the events that happened to him the night I was arrested.

"I went back to the Valley Hilton and caught that science fiction movie I told you about. I fell asleep before it ended and didn't wake up until late the next morning. That's when I began to wonder where you were. I went out to MacDonald's for breakfast and when I got back there was still no message from you.

"McDonald's? You were staying at the Valley Hilton and you go to a fast food joint for breakfast?" I ask.

"Yeah, had a couple of Egg McMuffins. I needed to eat fast and get back to the room in case you called."

"You could have stayed in the room and ordered anything you wanted," I state the obvious, "it was all covered with Morgan's gold American Express."

Sam stares blankly for a couple of seconds, "Man, I could have had some righteous groceries."

"So, what happened next?"

"Except for a couple of more trips to McDonald's, I hung out in the room for the rest of the day watching cable television." Sam pauses dramatically, "Then I decided to catch the evening news and there you were in your *Surfer Magazine* T-shirt wearing handcuffs. It totally blew me away."

"It was quite a shock for me too," I answer laughing.

"Yeah, well my life got really frantic after seeing that," Sam says seriously. "I snuck back down to San Diego using nothing but back streets and stayed well under the speed limit. It took me over six hours to go just over a hundred miles."

"You must have been pretty scared," I realize I had not really considered what Sam must have been going through.

"Scared?" Sam smiles hugely, "Man, I was freaked out! I spent the next couple of days sleeping in my car and hiding out."

"Hiding where?"

"Surfing at La Jolla Shores," Sam visibly shivers as he remembers. "I darn near froze I spent so much time out in the water. I would sit in the lineup for hours keeping an eye on the parking lot. Every time I saw a non-descript car cruising the lot I'd panic."

"Don't you think hiding out at your favorite surf spot was maybe not so smart?"

"La Jolla isn't my favorite spot, Windansea is much better, particularly since a south swell was running. I missed some great waves hanging out at La Jolla, which is why I knew that they wouldn't be looking for me there."

"Do you really think that DEA agents have a surfer mentality and would know which surf spot to check because of the angle of the swell?"

Sam uses undefeatable logic on me. "Yeah? Well they never found me until I went to my mom's house."

"And?"

"Finally got so cold, I went home for a hot shower. I was washing the shampoo out of my hair when mom knocked on the door and said that I had visitors. I asked her to wait, but she said I should come out now seeing as they had badges." Sam rolls his eyes, "They were DEA agents. I thought they were going to take me away for sure, but all they wanted to do was talk."

"Wow," I am really enjoying this conversation. It is incredibly interesting hearing the other side of the most electrifying couple of days of your life.

"I told them I didn't know there was cocaine in the car just like you told me."

"Were they buying it?" I ask.

"No," laughs Sam, "the agent said that if they wanted me, I'd be on my way to prison right then and there."

"They didn't want you?" I am amazed.

"Nah, he said they decided to let me go after I almost got them killed the night of your arrest."

"What?"

"Yeah," Sam grins, "after leaving you at the Marriott Hotel, I immediately got lost in downtown traffic. It was bumper to bumper and I was going the wrong way at a crawl. So I just swung the Baja bug over the center divider and after bouncing off the curb raced in the opposite direction to make up time until I realized that I was going in the right direction after all." Sam is actively using his hands to describe the action, "So I just jumped the divider again, not knowing that I was being followed by two carloads of DEA agents. The agent said the lead car almost got taken out by a bus when they tried to follow me." Sam grins in delight, "Can you imagine, I lost two carloads of special agents and I didn't even know I was being followed."

"Sam, can we go back a couple of steps?" I ask.

"Sure."

"The DEA told you that they weren't interested in you?" I ask trying to keep my voice dead calm.

"Nope, said I would just complicate the case. You see there were people already talking about cooperating."

"Really?"

"Yep, that pilot you flew with and Morgan's sons."

"Did they interview you again afterwards?"

"Nope," Sam smiles, "and they knew Morgan was going to cooperate too."

"Sam, did it ever occur to you why I didn't cooperate?"

"Yeah, I was wondering about that." Sam gives me his serious look, "Why not? You might have gotten less time if you had been more helpful. I mean it's not like you were on Morgan's side on purpose."

"Less time," I echo, "Sam, I didn't cooperate in order to protect you."

"Oh."

For a couple of seconds, I say nothing as I ponder Sam's revelation. If the judge knew that Sam was another victim of Morgan's manipulations, not mine, he might have given me a reduced sentence. If I got three years instead of five, I could be out in two months instead of two-and-a-half more years. I sit there feeling absurdly stupid. How dense could I have been not to have gotten this information sooner. Yet, there had been a good reason why I couldn't openly communicate with Sam. A month after my arrest his car was broken into…the only thing stolen was a couple of letters I had written him. Other friends of mine suspected that their houses had been broken into, then Buzz, Morgan's son, returned home unexpectedly and catches a DEA agent searching his bedroom. The DeLorean case was full of intrigue, complex conspiracies that reached as far as a foreign head of state and a couple of clueless surfers.

Sam breaks into my thoughts, "You know I can't stand pineapple anymore?"

With that statement I realize that there is absolutely no advantage in my getting on Sam's case for not telling me that the DEA wasn't interested in him, but I am going to take a small measure of revenge. "Sam, I need a favor."

He looks at me suspiciously.

"I want to trade sandals."

"What do you mean you want to trade sandals?" he pops his head under the table to eye the decrepit flip-flops I am wearing. "Duct tape, they're duck taped?" He asks, then peers closer, "Is that green stuff growing on them mold?"

Half an hour later, I watch my friend walking awkwardly in my old flip-flops as he leaves the visiting room. It is not easy watching him walk through the door to freedom, to complete independence and to unhindered surf adventures, while I head for the metal security door with the bad-attitude prison guards and psycho inmates waiting for me.

That evening I lay awake pondering Sam's little revelation that the DEA was not interested in him. I had gone to such extremes to protect someone when it was not even needed. Apparently, I could have told my full story and maybe, just maybe, I would already be a free man. This realization is the most powerful argument in my life to always tell the truth, the whole truth and nothing but the truth. It is a lesson that will be hammered home every day for the rest of my incarceration. The only thing that makes it semi-manageable is that the Lord knows I am here. I close my eyes and say a prayer placing my complete trust in Him, "Dear Father, Your will, nothing more, nothing less."

My next visitor is Marjorie, one of my closest friends, though over the years we seldom got to see each other. I needed to talk with someone to whom I could truly open up my soul. I see her as soon as I enter the visiting room, sitting in the sunshine next to the window where the sparrow died. She is trying to ignore the leers from a couple of inmates and one of the guards. Our eyes meet over the crowded room. It takes me a minute to work my way through the press of humanity, some of whom are involved in the worst sorts of semi-clandestine deviant activity. Finally, I stand before Marjorie. She smiles, her eyes all but sparkle, yet she cannot mask the sad look that momentarily, passes across her face as she gazes at her friend with whom she shared so many underwater adventures, who now is an inmate. Then she bravely recaptures her smile and steps into my arms.

For the longest time, we just stand there holding each other. For a few precious moments, I am at peace with the world. Standing in Marjorie's arms, I grasp how much I have missed simple human contact. This is my first hug in well over a year and suddenly I realize how much I have missed human contact. There are so many things that prison deprives you of, yet sometimes you do not realize what is missing until you are abruptly reminded of them by their absence. It is as if an empty hollowness in your life is one day brought to your attention and then you wonder how you could have overlooked that emptiness before.

After the most unforgettable hug of my life, we sit down. Marjorie smiles, her eyes warm in friendship. "How do you cope with this place?" she asks in wonder glancing at some of the stranger characters in the visiting room.

"I just do it," I answer, "it's not like there's a choice. "If you think these guys look weird in here, know that there are dress codes for the visiting room. Inside the prison, they basically wear whatever they want. It is a regular circus in D Unit, also known as Drug and Drag Unit.

"You mean some of the men dress up like women?"

"Not all the gay inmates dress up," I am enjoying shocking her, "but the ones that do go all out. They compete with each other as to who is the best-looking girl in the joint. Others go for just the most outrageous, the strangest or the most deviant."

Marjorie shakes her head, "You can't be serious."

"Oh yeah," I point with my eyes to a slim Colombian in a peach silk shirt talking intimately with a striking Latin woman.

"So what is so strange about him?" she asks, "At least he is sitting with a woman."

"Well," I grin, the girl is his sister and a little while ago, she was the one wearing the silk shirt. She brings Juan all her hand-me-downs including her silk drawers."

"Her underwear?"

"Particularly her underwear, they're in high demand in the joint."

Marjorie's eyes begin to water as she giggles openly, "How do they make the switch?"

"The underwear is stuffed in her purse, but for some of the outfits the other gay inmates will stand blocking the visiting room guard's view. Juanita, that's the guy's prison name, came in wearing a T-shirt and tight nylon pants. She arrives wearing multiple layers. When she leaves, he will be the one wearing the multiple layers with a few pair of silk underwear stuffed in his pockets. He will slip the guard a couple of bills to get through the body search. He wears the clothes for a while to get the other girls' attention, then sells them and shares the profits with his sister. They have a regular boutique going and make several thousand dollars a month."

Her jaw drops, "How can they make that much money inside a prison?"

"Gay inmates tend to have the most cash; you don't want to know how they earn it."

She is stunned, "And the guards let this happen."

"Sure, long as they get their cut."

"This place is an insane asylum."

"We even have a blonde surfer girl inside," I tease, "her name is Marjorie."

"You're kidding me now," she complains.

"No, I'm not. You should have seen the spat she had with Juanita when she wouldn't let Marjorie try on a pair of her black silk running shorts."

My friend holds up her hands in mock defense, "Enough about the boys, I want to know about you."

"So ask?"

"What's the best and worst thing about prison?"

Surprisingly, I am able to answer with a single word, "Discipline, I enjoy the discipline I impose upon myself; it helps to strengthen my character and adds focus to my inward journey as I seek to understand myself better. It is through discipline that I hope daily to turn this prison time into a positive experience."

"Okay, what's the negative side of discipline?"

"I hate the regimented, uncaring discipline of the prison

system. Logic doesn't apply in here. As far as most of the guards are concerned inmates don't have anything coming, but punishment and a hard time from them; like it's their job to brutalize and torture us inmates."

"Wait," interrupts Marjorie, "the guards don't actually torture inmates?"

"Absolutely," I nod my head, "Some of them feel their job is to make sure we suffer and if you really get on the wrong side of a few of these guards they will arrange to have you beat up or gang raped."

"They aren't supposed to do that!"

"What they are supposed to do and not do doesn't particularly fit the reality of cruelty in prison. You've heard the expression that power corrupts and absolute power corrupts absolutely?"

"Sure, but..."

"Marjorie, prison guards basically have absolute authority over inmates. Many of the felons in here behave in the most corrupt ways possible. This gives those with the authority all the implied moral permission that they need to personally justify enforcing their own sadist punishment."

My friend shakes her head, "Okay back to the downside of discipline."

"The other type of discipline is the inmate rules of social behavior, only they're not written down except maybe as graffiti on a wall. If you violate inmate rules, and some of them are pretty twisted, it can get you stuck in the back, raped or poisoned. Trying to balance prison rules and inmate rules is a full-time occupation."

Despite the limited joviality of our short time together I can tell that she is depressed seeing me here in such a hostile environment—come to think of it so am I.

Like all prison visits, ours ends too soon. Marjorie gives me another hug, but this one is about going away; a momentary clinging to something that means so much yet you have to willingly let it go. Then she passes through the visiting room door and out into a world that is alive with change, stimulus and excitement. I, however, am channeled into a narrow dirty-walled room for "Strip and show," where standing naked on a cold cement floor, I must turn before the guard and then bend over while he peers diligently with his flashlight. Sometimes I think the promise of freedom somewhere in the future is the only thing that keeps me going.

The following week I receive a blank journal in the mail from Marjorie. In her flowery script, she encourages me to record my thoughts and feelings. It is a journal that she one day hopes to read. The journal is tall and thin with expensive white bond paper. The cover is bound in fine black cloth. The black outside contrasts with the pure white pages within. The journal of empty pages, like me, is waiting to be filled. In a sense, the blank pages represent a new beginning, a journey waiting to be taken, an opportunity to establish new goals and commitments. The words that I will write on these empty pages will be tracks that lead back to me; the me, I am becoming and the me, I eventually hope to become.

Prison has become my dojo (place of enlightenment). My philosophy is to experience each moment with the fullest of being and awareness. Every action or non-action has meaning and purpose. Joe Hyams expresses it well in his reflection of Zen upon the teachings of karate: "Enlightenment," it has been said, "means to recognize the harmony of ordinary life."

"Nothing is what rocks dream about," Aristotle

My intent is simple perfection of accomplishment, no matter how insignificant the task and total awareness of every act. "The wonder, I carry water," the realistic appreciation of simplicity in life.

I ponder the Eastern teachings that I have learned in my karate classes and from many trips to Asia with the Pacific Fleet and think how often the goal in Eastern philosophy is to achieve perfect awareness and simplicity of life. I find these goals far better answered in the Bible. Enhanced awareness is found in following the teachings of Jesus Christ, the only perfect person who has ever existed or will ever exist on this planet. Every morning when I wake, I pray asking for a closer walk with He who guides me. Being a practicing Christian is a self-correcting lifestyle that leads to heightened awareness as I strive to be a better human being. Zen teachings require that we empty our minds, to try to focus on nothingness, essentially to be nothing...outside caring. Nothing touches you, you touch nothing. I am not looking to become hollow or uncompassionate...I want to be actively involved in the full passion of life. I want to live a life full of meaning and purpose. Christ teaches me to focus on love, the giving and receiving of love. The Bible has a Greek word for it, *agape*, perfect love...God's love for man. If we could but be a reflection of that perfect love. In prison, it is a formidable task. I am not that strong, I am not ready to turn the other cheek...I do not have that kind of perfect courage. One of the magnificent wonders of Christ's life is the patient and gentle courage he always demonstrated. Even His anger was perfectly just when he chased the moneychangers out of God's temple.

I look at the empty journal in my hands, so much to learn. Yet, I have the time, I have the opportunity and I am in a place that forces self-perception and inward growth. In prison, if one does not grow, then he or she is apt to be stepping out of that institution on the wrong side of the scales of life. If there is not growth in prison, then the opposite lessons tends to predominate. Love is replaced with hate, giving becomes taking, compassion is beaten down by aggression and a human being mutates into a sadistic animal. Without love, life truly is hollow, nothingness is achieved because that is a sinful person's reward...nothing, nothing but unhappiness.

Three days before Christmas, I nervously appear before the Parole Board to find out how much of my sentence they are going to require me to serve. The guidelines call for thirty-six to forty-four months. I await their decision all but holding my breath. They are considering the longer sentence. My flight to Colombia and error in involving Sam weigh heavily against me. I lack credibility as an honorable person for exposing an innocent youth (Sam was twenty-one) to the dangers of the criminal underworld. Yet, because of my excellent record at the prison, I am awarded thirty-six months. I am ecstatic; it means that I now have less than twenty months to serve.

To serve is an interesting concept that I have begun to use when thinking of my stretch in prison. To serve implies that I am a co-participant in this rehabilitation project. The Department of Corrections is supposed to be about corrections or correcting behavior, yet sometimes it feels like I am one of the few who actually understands that concept.

Jim, my brother, comes to visit sporting a new winter coat. I note how warm and comfortable it looks then casually mention how cold it gets inside my cubicle at night with the missing windowpanes and the haphazardly working heater system. People visiting inmates should only wear old, worn-out clothes. Out in the yard, I show off my new coat to Clayton. Life in the joint is not always without its humorous side.

Two nights later, it is Christmas Eve as I wander down to the South Yard to watch the Christmas Parade of Boats. Up and down the channel brightly lit yachts all aglow with decorations, pass in a line. Some of them have speaker systems that play Christmas music. I am bewitched by the pageantry. While staring at a particularly festive vessel, a white-hulled sail boat with twinkling red and green lights I realize how lucky I am to be at Terminal Island. I could just as easily be at a more isolated prison in a desolate desert or worse yet in a Colombian prison with unimaginable adversity. In a Colombian prison, inmates are sometimes tortured and American inmates are often targeted by Colombian gangs and cartel soldiers. Sometimes families back home have to pay ransom money to Colombian criminals so that their incarcerated family members are not raped or killed in prison. Likewise, they have to pay off the guards to insure they are fed adequately. Here at Terminal Island, I am somewhat safe as long as I stay alert, avoid trouble areas and am attentive to treating all with respect. Yet there is something almost magical about serving my time at Terminal Island. I left my home-town as a youth to follow my childhood dreams upon the oceans of the world. Now as I serve my sentence in prison, the ocean is here; almost like it is waiting for me...a promise patiently waiting to be fulfilled.

The loud speakers announce count time. I shove my hands into the warm pockets of Jim's new coat, and then walk with a crowd of other inmates back up the breezeway to Animal Unit.

Sitting on my bunk, my legs crossed, I stare through the barred window at the breakwater just beyond the wire fence. The seawater laps at the rocks and swirls about my consciousness. I am still quite amazed at my good fortune to be here, but there is a new hope building in my soul. With a visible release date, I need to begin planning my future, and of course, I want it to be upon the ocean... and here it is waiting for me a dozen feet from my window. Lately some of the inmates have begun referring to me as *the luckiest guy at T.I.* Mostly it is about my naturally buoyant nature, which makes me more acceptable even to the hard-cases. Many of the inmates are amazed that I faired so well in my sentencing particularly considering that I did not cooperate. Though my job is low paying, it is one of the best and most sought after positions in the prison, working in the recreation department and running the movie projector. Men have noticed my top bunk with its second story window that has a view of the sun and moon rise. To them I do not seem to have any problems, which is simply because I don't hang with the gangs, treat all with respect and am not carrying any bad baggage from my arrest; such as angry criminal partners. Morgan and sons will have to fear the Colombian drug cartels for the rest of their lives because of their cooperation.

I fluff my pillow then lay upon my belly to stare at the dark restless ocean beyond the security lights. In the distance, I look at the glow of lights from Long Beach Naval Station and in my mind; I drift back to my last days in the United States Navy.

I arrived at Treasure Island Naval Base in California, on March 15, 1980. Susan and a few friends came to see me off from the airport in Honolulu. Susan will join me in about three weeks. The Navy was not discharging me, rather I was being released on appellate leave while awaiting final disposition on my Bad Conduct Discharge. This was why it has taken the Navy over four and a half months to process my papers and transfer me back to California. My hopes were not very high for a favorable ruling from the military court, which tended to err in favor of a strict interpretation of the Naval Code of Military Conduct.

I spent two lonely weeks at Treasure Island processing through the Navy's methodical paper machine. Fortunately, since I retained my rank as a chief petty officer, they did not assign me to any work details. My time was my own. I spent most of it just walking around San Francisco or just sitting on the beach watching the sun rise and set. It was a time of raw emotions. I hurt desperately from Puu's death. I felt empty and lost. The Navy had been my home for almost fourteen years. I had been so proud to be a frogman and a Vietnam vet and now it was all ending in disgrace. The future was an uncertain dilemma. At the end of each day, I stood alone on the cold San Francisco beach facing toward Hawaii, which happened to lie exactly beyond the sunset and thought of a woman with golden hair—and a sad-eyed Great Dane that was no more.

At the naval base, the personnel department wasn't fully aware of my true situation. My orders had simply read "Process for discharge," but in the service jacket there was a thick manila envelope; stamped on its cover in bold red letters were the words, "TOP SECRET, FOR COMMANDING OFFICER'S EYES ONLY." I assumed it contained the results of my court-martial with orders to initiate my appellate leave. To me it was a frank statement by the command that I was such an embarrassment they did not want just anyone reading the full transcript of my fall from that proud community.

On March 31, I was told that my papers were ready. I thought it might have been more appropriate if they had waited one more day for April Fools.

An anorexic clerk, wearing over-sized wire rimmed glasses smiled as he pushed the papers across the desk for me to sign. I casually looked down at them—instantly time seemed to stand still. I stared dumbfounded at the colorful and ornate document beneath my hands. In bold, capital script, the words "Honorable Discharge," seared themselves into my brain.

"You okay Chief?" asked the skinny clerk.

"Yes, I'm fine," I answered wiping a sudden cold sweat from my brow. Someone, I realized, has made a very big mistake.

"Just sign right here," said the clerk beaming through his thick glasses, which magnified his eyes. He looked like a little helpful mouse with his narrow face and big eyes. My hand shook slightly as I signed the precious document.

The clerk slipped the discharge papers into a manila envelope; then he leafed through the remains of my service jacket. He paused encountering the manila envelope stamped "TOP SECRET." I saw that it was unopened. He flipped it over, glanced at the still secure seal and then shrugged, put it back in my file and closed it. The rest of the papers, including my Honorable Discharge papers, he placed into a manila envelope and slid them across to me.

I snatched up the envelope and got halfway to the door when the clerk yelled out, "Hey chief, hold on."

I seriously considered not answering, just beating feet out of there, but instead reluctantly turned around.

"You can't leave yet, chief," he implored, "your check is still coming over from disbursing."

"Check?" I re-crossed the room and sat down while keeping a firm grip on my envelope. I received my final paycheck the day before, so was curious what this check could be for...a day's pay? The check arrived ten minutes later.

"Just sign here," smiled the helpful clerk. I signed the cashier's form and received a green-colored check with the Department of the Treasury logo stamped across its face. It took a couple of seconds to be sure I was reading the numbers correctly, *For the sum of five hundred and 52 dollars.*

"What's this for?" I asked.

The clerk seemed surprised, "Leave not taken, of course. According to your service record, there are twenty-two days of leave not taken. You get a portion of your base pay back, it's like a bonus.

Is there a problem with the sum?"

I could only sit and stare at the helpful young man. After all the effort the Navy had made to punish me, a couple of clerical errors had wiped much of it away. The twenty-two days the clerk was referring to was the time I spent in the Navy brig.

My elation at being released was soon saddened as I took my uniform off for the last time. Never again would I walk with a military swagger to my step with medals pinned upon my chest. I carefully folded the dress military jacket and put it into a suitcase. I was slowly closing the lid when I saw the EOD insignia flash once in the low light. Then I shut the lid with an audible snap thus ending fourteen important years of my life.

The next morning I wake early; it is Christmas. After an hour of stretching and some yoga, I find myself standing in the lobby waiting for the North Yard guard. He is late. A couple of other inmates complain bitterly about the delay. I lean against the opposite wall, calm and relaxed. Instead of being angry about the wait, I use the time to harmlessly daydream. When the guard finally arrives, the men greet him with petty complaints and foolish anger. The guard frowns as he prepares an angry retort, but then as I pass I wish him a Merry Christmas and mean it. He smiles and waves me out the door.

> *"If you limit your choices only to what seems possible or reasonable, you disconnect yourself from what you truly want, and all that is left is a compromise,"* Robert Fritz

The New Year comes and goes, winter grips the prison and the short days are too long. In the projection booth with my feet propped up on the wall, I watch the movie through the little window high up in the back of the theater. On this Sunday afternoon, I am showing a Mexican western. I have no idea what the actors are saying, so I just sit there staring. My body is in the prison projection booth, but my mind is somewhere else entirely.

For two weeks after my release from the Navy, I am in a perpetual state of worry. I secretly wonder if Susan will really join me. Then her plane lands at the Los Angeles International Airport. Standing eagerly at the arrival's gate, I suddenly see her running down the ramp then she throws herself into my arms. My world brightens like the sun spreading across a high mountain meadow. Holding her tight, feeling her heart beating against mine, I am abruptly alive again.

For the next three months, we are complete nomads traveling little used roads and lonely highways. We begin by driving north to Sequoia National Park in the Sierra Nevada Mountain range. At sunset, we camp in Wolverton, a mountain valley where winter snow still lingers. Wisps of fog drift through the tall redwood trees as I light candles inside of *Revelstoke*. That night it snows heavily though it is early spring. We are warm and toasty inside *Revelstoke* because I have fired up the gas furnace that I installed four years ago, but never used. Susan, an island girl who has never seen snow before spends most of the evening with her nose pressed to the window watching the falling snowflakes.

At first light Susan bounds out of the truck and I am right behind her anxious to share in her joy and a moment later am struck by her first ever snow ball. We build a snowman with pinecone eyes. Behind us, *Revelstoke* is buried to its hubcaps in new snow. We walk amongst towering sequoia trees each mantled in twinkling snow crystals. Hand-in-hand I wander with my tropical girl into a winter wonderland.

Wildly in love, we drive slowly toward the Northern California coast. We wind up in Big Sur where we weather a Pacific storm camped on the sheer cliffs of a rocky promontory overlooking a raging ocean. Surrounding us and helping to break the bite of the storm, is a small grove of wind-swept Monterey Pines, each uniquely sculpted by the blustery weather that buffets the truck through the long night.

In the morning, the ocean has worked itself into a surging froth. Wrapped together in a blanket, we drink hot chocolate and watch the waves surging amongst clumps of floating seaweed and algae-laced rocks. In the afternoon, we wander along an overgrown trail that leads into a small old-growth forest, where we play hide-and-seek amongst the thick barked trees. The cool air is fragrant with a bouquet of earthy smells, old leaves and wet moss. A sea fog lends a mystical quality to our adventure.

Living a gypsy life of continuous quest and discovery, we drift north along the coast on an enchanting journey beyond the common place. We laugh together driving past suburban homes in the evening with windows reflecting immobile people sitting before glaring televisions. Outside we run with the mysteries of the night, questing for adventure under the stars and following the primal lure of the changing phases of the moon. Our lives, patterned by sun, moon, wind and tide, dance in harmony with the rhythms of nature. With the revolution of the planet as our alarm clock, we wake before sunrise to watch the early morning light herald the beginning of each new day. Every dinner comes wrapped in a scenic sunset and with the night comes the intriguing question of whether to camp in the mountains or at the beach; to sleep to the rippling sound of a babbling brook or the rhythmic crash of pounding ocean waves.

The Fourth of July finds us camped in Tuolumne Meadows in the upper Yosemite valley. Patches of snow still cover the ground where the shadows dwelt most of the day. The campground has few facilities, just cold running water and portable chemical toilets. The other campers are shivering in their tents or trying to huddle close to smoking campfires. In Revelstoke, Susan and I are in the lap of nomadic luxury. Susan is cooking banana nut bread in the oven. We are warm and snug inside Revelstoke. I have Hawaiian slack key guitar playing on the fourteen speaker stereo system and am lounging in my own personal hot tub. The bathroom has a large plastic deep sink built into the floor where I hang wetsuits and damp towels to dry. It is just large enough to hold me in a compact sitting position, which conserves water supply. I watch snowflakes drifting pass the window quite happy about life in general.

The next day, after a long day of hiking mountain trails, we bathe in a fast flowing mountain stream. The water is ice-cold snow-run-off. We find a secluded spot, strip down to our swimsuits then run together screaming into the chilly water. Susan stops mid-stream to wash her long legs, looking incredibly beautiful, as I stand watching her with my heart pounding wildly for the words I am about to say. "Susan," I move closer to the woman I love so she will hear me over the water babbling at her feet. "Susan." She pauses and looks up. I think she senses what is coming as she stands very still and gazes at me with a questioning look. I am not sure if it is the icy water or her stunning beauty that takes my breath away. I call her name again, visible wisps of vapor float from my lips, "Susan, will you marry me?"

For a moment, all is still except but for the quiet gurgle of the water flowing over the rocks and the chirping of a bird in an ever-green tree. Then Susan smiles, her face radiant in the late afternoon light, "Oh yes, Stephen," her voice like a song that sings to my heart, "I will."

She shivers in the icy water as I take her in my arms. My happiness is complete, I am ready for the future—not knowing that in a week, we will be separated forever.

 Our last seven days fly by then she must use her airline ticket before it expires to return to Hawaii. Susan is in favor of marrying right away at a courthouse, but I am reluctant without her parent's permission. Driving her to the airport, I am suddenly nervous. I wait with her until the very last moment before she has to turn away to walk down through the boarding gate. I watch her walking backward down the ramp, and then with a wave, she disappears around the corner and from my life forever. Standing alone, staring at the closed ramp door, I suddenly know that I will never see Susan again.

In Hawaii, her parents argue bitterly against our marriage. Friends counsel that she should give it more thought. By not being together, we drift apart. I should have gone to Hawaii, but I had reservations of my own. Marriage is such a daunting proposition when beginning life again from scratch with the scar of having to leave the Navy under a cloud of failure. Then Susan writes that she is seeing someone else. Six months pass then I receive another letter, Susan has married one of my professional surfer friends on the North Shore.

In the projection booth, my despair deepens. When the movie ends, I wait for the Mexican inmates to shuffle out. I dim the lights and sit alone in the dark with my misery in close attendance.

"When one door of happiness closes, another opens; but often we look so long at the closed door that we do not see the one which has been opened for us," Helen Keller

Photo Arrington
South Yard, football/baseball field next to breakwater with G-Unit in background.
Author's room faced trees on south side.

*"Human beings, by changing the inner attitudes of their
minds, can change the outer aspects of their lives,"*
William James 1842-1910

Chapter 34

TERMINAL ISLAND FEDERAL PRISON,

A-UNIT, JANUARY 1984

FOUR MONTHS have passed since my release into the general population and I am pleased to be basically immune to most inmate intrigues. Yes, I have had my close encounters but none of them descended into full physical violence. I avoid the gangs, troublemakers and druggies. I have a few friends, read books and study the Bible. I am attending a computer and an English class, show movies on Friday and Saturday nights in the theater and enjoy watering the football field. One day, while moving some large boxes on the stage at the old prison theater, I discover a full-length mirror leaning against the wall. I pause as I see myself reflected in its dusty image. Picking up a rag, I wipe it clean then step back and stare. I have only seen my reflection poorly in the distortion of prison stainless steel mirrors. Obviously, the guards do not know this mirror is here, which could be broken and made into multiple inmate weapons.

When the mirror is relatively dust free, I step back and look at myself. It is me, the same old me I have always known. There are no stress lines on my face, which is kind of surprising. I am thirty-three years old, fit and healthy. I am wearing 501 jeans, my faded blue Surfer Magazine team rider T-shirt (the same one I wore in Las Vegas), and white sneakers. They are all a little worse for wear as I was wearing them when I was arrested. The Recreation Officer had gotten the T-shirt and jeans out of the Administration Building for me.

It is at that moment that I fully realize that I am going to come out of this okay. That I am an intact human being and far better off than the mental wreck that arrived in a chain gang fifteen months ago. I am still standing on the stage ten minutes later when a guard opens the entrance door at the far end of the long dark building. A shaft of sunlight casts his shadow across the far wall that is three stories tall. His is a towering silhouette, prison guard magnified. "Hey Arrington, you in here?" his voice bounces off the far wall and echoes about the vast empty theater as if it is the tall shadow shouting the question.

I step away from the mirror so he will not see it. "Yes."

"You're wanted up at Animal House." He closes the door returning the vast darkness to a quiet peaceful state. I love this old theater. It is the one place where I can actually lock the door from the inside and enjoy true privacy, which is an otherwise unavailable commodity in prison. In its peaceful solitude, I can completely lower my guard, relax and think deeply without interruption. I enjoy showing the weekly movie. Sometimes I come in here in the middle of the week, splice the film together in the projection room then watch it all by myself serenely surrounded by the vast empty quiet void. I can fully immerse myself in the film as I watch it play out on the huge screen. Previewing the movie to check the splicing sequence is actually part of my job so I do not need permission to do this. Sometimes I preview a particularly good or meaningful film several times.

A little nervous, I head for Animal House to see the Unit Manager.

I worry because when a staff member singles you out for a visit it is usually not good news for the inmate.

Knuckling the door once to announce my presence, I step inside the small dingy office, which is overflowing with the presence of the hugely fat administrator inside. The obese man is fully engrossed in an empty donut box. He is poking about with one blunt finger in the hopeful pursuit of an elusive crumb or two. Each morning, he arrives with a dozen glazed donuts tucked under one arm, which he swiftly polishes off well before the ten o'clock coffee break.

The Slug, his inmate assigned nickname, grunts. It is the kind of grunt that can only be affected by a very fat man. It wafts into the small enclosure and fills the air with a sweet sour scent. I look forlornly at the firmly closed window and wish for a breath of fresh air. Sucking in his huge gut, the Slug is barely able to open his desk drawer enough to pull out half a pack of gum. His fat fingers quickly unwraps the foil, then wadding the multiple sticks of gum together; he pops the resulting ball into his mouth before speaking. In repulsed fascination, I watch his fat lips slowly form a sentence around the thick wad in his mouth, "Pack up your stuff." The Slug only speaks in abrupt sentences. He is so out of shape that sitting up straight causes him to be short of breath.

I am not surprised that they are moving me. Animal Unit serves mostly as a transit dormitory. The staff likes to keep close tabs on new meat until they settle into the system. I do however, wonder where they are going to put me. Each dormitory or unit has its own personality with varying levels of violence. The Slug consults his paperwork and in the process discovers a donut crumb on his desk blotter. A fat finger quickly jabs at the sugarcoated globule of fat and flour then he sticks his treasure-loaded finger between his thick lips. His piggy little eyes squint up in obvious swine-like pleasure as he sucks, then blurts two words, "G Unit."

"G Unit! I'm going to G unit?" I ask excitedly.

The Slug is perturbed; he does not like repeating himself. His pig eyes narrow unhappily, "G Unit."

"Thanks, Mr. Ryan," I answer. I go quickly to my locker to pack my things.

Five minutes later, I exit Animal house happily carrying stacked cardboard boxes. Apparently, persons unknown have noticed my good behavior, because they are moving me very early to the Honor Dormitory. Normally, it takes well over a year just to be considered. I am buoyant as I walk the breezeway with my three small boxes of possessions. I have become a man of substance…*I be having things.*

I step through the main door of the honor dorm, where an inmate clerk is waiting for me. "You're Arrington," he says knowingly then flips through a stack of index cards, "you're in room four. Here's your key."

"My what?"

"Key, it is a small piece of metal one uses to open locks."

"I get to unlock my door?"

"Not only that but you get to lock it too. It is quite an amazing invention," he says sarcastically.

"Na," I am amazed, "I get a key to my room."

"Boy, you new guys," he shakes his head, "here's how it works. You get a key to your room because by the time you reach the honor dorm you're usually having things. Having things leads to stealing; you get your own key."

"Well that is terrific!"

"Don't get too excited, the guard gets the master."

"That's okay, a locked door means privacy."

"Yeah, except for the guy across the hall, he's kind of weird." He looks me up and down, "I think the two of you are going to get along just fine."

Walking down the hallway I notice how clean it is, the main bathroom is tidy and modern. I arrive at room number 4 and insert my key into the door and then with a surge of anticipation push it open. Inside it looks just like a college dorm room. On one wall, there is a wooden hang-up closet, a couple of drawers and a built-in writing desk. Against the other wall there is a twin bed with a tasteful fake oak frame. The mattress is fully six-inches thick, pushing down on it with one hand I groan with satisfaction. Sunlight floods through an open bar-less window. A palm tree stands to the right of the window frame. The tip of one of its broad green leaves hangs just inside the sill. Setting the boxes on the desk, I lift a houseplant from the top cardboard box and place it on the windowsill. It is a small wild fern I found in the shade of a debilitated bleacher on the football field. It is now growing in a colorful ceramic pot that I made in the hobby shop. Another houseplant, a broad leaf unidentified something or other, goes on the desk. I am about to cement a couple of scenic pictures cut from magazines to the wall with toothpaste, when I hear a voice from the open door.

"Don't goop-up the wall with toothpaste; use some of my scotch tape."

I turn to see a man about eight years my junior. He is tall, slim, longhaired and looks normal but for a scar that slashes across both lips. It is the guy from the front desk. "You have scotch tape?" I ask.

"I'm a clerk, of course I have scotch tape."

"So you're the weird bunky across the hall."

"Yep, I am also the one who got you moved to the South Yard."

"Wait a minute, you did it? Not a real clerk? I mean not a prison employee?"

"Most of the prison staff could care less about us. They've been corrupted by being here too long, working those double shifts for the overtime pay. Almost their entire day is spent around inmates who are always either trying to scam them or telling them outrageous lies. Just when they think an inmate is semi-normal, the guy suddenly stresses out and goes ballistic with fists, boots, teeth and maybe a homemade weapon. It is not a real confidence builder in inmate integrity."

"So how did you get me moved?"

"It was your attitude; attitude is everything. Everyone knows you pled guilty, but didn't deal to put your rap off on someone else. The guards respect that, taking responsibility and not complaining."

"So a clean record is everything?"

"You're not listening," he says sitting down on my desk; a man with time on his hands, lots of time. "A gang banger can have a clean record by just not getting caught. It's your attitude the staff watches. If half the idiots in here paid any attention, they would know that is what the judges look for too. It is why you only got five years."

"How come you know so much about me?" I am not hostile, just curious.

"Found out a couple of days ago that the guy living here was transferring to a camp. So, I started looking around. I didn't want a gang banger or weirdo type living across the hall. Knew you were kind of normal and I like what you've done with the football field. By the way the name's Ralph."

"Steve," I put out my hand to shake.

"Already know your name," his hand is cool, grip firm as we shake hands, "I even know your middle name is Lee."

Ralph steps out to fetch the promised scotch tape from the desk in his room and as he returns says, "Bank robber."

"What?"

"You were wondering what I am in for," he has a knowing smile, "I started robbing banks right out of high school."

"You were still just a teen-ager."

"And a drug addict; needed to feed the habit. Started with marijuana when I was twelve and by the time I graduated, I had a three hundred dollar a day crack habit. Couldn't earn or steal enough to support the need so I bought a toy gun and hit three banks in two weeks. Lucky I didn't get shot. I was pretty strung out and heading for suicide by cop."

"How much time did you get?"

"Fifteen years," Ralph glances down, a sad look plays across his face, "done just six."

We spent the next half hour jawing. It was cool hanging with a normal guy who is not into drugs, brewing pruno (homemade alcohol), does not smoke and has no interest in scamming me for something. Our relaxed conversation made me feel like a real person living a normal day, but when someone walks down the hallway we both warily turn putting our backs to the security of the wall. Being in prison is a twenty-four hour a day state of mind. You just don't offer free opportunities like an exposed back too many times and get away with it.

"You cannot dream yourself into a character; you must hammer and forge yourself one,"
James A. Froude 1818-1894

Photo Tim Tyler
Boron Prison Camp

"When you make a mistake, don't look back at it long. Take the reason of the thing into your mind and then look forward. Mistakes are lessons of wisdom. The past cannot be changed. The future is yet in your power," Hugh White 1773-1840

Chapter 35

TERMINAL ISLAND FEDERAL PRISON,

G-UNIT, APRIL 1984

LIVING IN the Honor Dorm for the next three months was as close to contentment in prison as I could get. I enjoyed my job in the Recreation Department and knew whom to avoid in the yard. I had figured out the cruise ship schedule and liked to watch the big festive ships go up and down the harbor at night. I had talked the recreation officer into purchasing some Frisbees and during free time would sail them carefully over the football field. One has to be very aware when throwing things in a prison yard. Imagine accidentally hitting someone like Tiffany in the back of the head. I was a regular in the weight room, but only very early in the morning before the weirdoes hit the weight pile with their caveman mind-set. I would run the South Yard perimeter for hours at a time on weekends. Ralph was into the Bible too and we had meaningful conversations after lockdown. For an inmate life was so good something just had to happen to change it.

At five in the morning, my door slams open. "Arrington, you got ten minutes to pack up your things."

"What?" I ask groggily.

He tosses a small cardboard box at me, "You're leaving. This is for your stuff."

"Leaving? For where?"

"Camp."

"Camp? What camp?"

"Boron, you're going to the high desert."

I look at the small box, "Hey all my stuff won't fit in this little box."

"Tough, leave the rest behind," he shines a bright flashlight right into my eyes, "now you got nine minutes."

I am dressed in two minutes. I pick up the little box. In goes the radio, Bible, diary, my few pictures of Susan and Puu, toiletries and Sam's sandals. I leave my houseplants and the ceramic pots I made in pottery shop on the desk. I glance at my favorite pictures that will stay taped to the walls and my extra prison-issue clothes. I look at the box and see that except for Jim's jacket and Sam's sandals, I am back to what I carried out of J-3. Ralph opens his door as I step out of the room. We shake hands. "Going to miss you," I say in a state of shock to be leaving so suddenly.

"Wish I was going with you."

"To the desert?"

"Any camp has gotta be better than a prison."

I take a last look at my room, glance at a plant on the window-sill in its rusty tin can, my scenic pictures on the walls and smile forlornly at Ralph.

"Move it Arrington," the guard points down the hall with his flashlight.

We walk out into the early morning darkness. The guard is quiet but for the sound of his boots and the metallic swish of his ring of keys. I am glad he is not talking as I pack away memories from my year and a half at Terminal Island. We pass the recreation locker with the hoses and sprinklers, and then walk across the football field; the grass feels good beneath my sneakers. He picks up the pace along the breezeway as I stare out over the ocean, which I will not be seeing again for a very long time. Then we are through the corridor and into the North Yard. I see Animal House to my right with its long two-story bay of dirty windows. Straight ahead of us is J-3. The lights are on in the television room and I see two orderlies going about the business of setting up the room for breakfast. The little J-3 yard is shadowed from the security lights, but I already know the little patch of lawn is gone. It is again a lifeless stretch of dry dirt with a covering of the dead grass and accumulated inmate debris. There is no evidence that I have spent almost a year of my life there, but for my memories. We pass J-1 squatting sinisterly in the dark. The guard opens the door that leads up a flight of stairs to the holding room. Halfway up the stairs we pass the door to the projection booth where I spent so much time splicing films and showing pictures for the inmates on Saturday and Sunday nights. He opens the heavy steel door at the top of the dingy stairs, then after taking my box, he shoves me into the holding cell. He is not being malicious, just a guard thing…expression of authority regularly re-enforced.

I immediately go over to the window where the broken pane remains un-repaired and look out. The view is the same as the first time I peered through this small open pane, but now everything has meaning where good and bad memories reside. I see the bench under the tree where the old man fed the birds. He died months ago; no reason, just died. The pigeons are still present and hopeful, but they are now mostly ignored.

"Get away from that window!" barks the guard.

I turn to look at him wanting to be defiant, but then know it will serve no purpose. So I smile, it is a tolerant smile, the kind one would offer an idiot. The look is not lost on the guard who says something foul followed by the word inmate. It is a hollow victory and I did not just make a friend. Attitude is everything. He looks at my box and smiles ruefully, "This might catch up with you in a couple of weeks." He tosses it onto a desk.

"Sorry officer, I am just stressed out and not thinking."

He stares at me then the hardness around his eyes softens. "Yeah, I'm coming off my third double shift this week, so go look out the stupid window already."

He turns to another guard, "Acting like he is going to miss this place. I tell ya, all inmates are certifiably nuts."

I find myself staring at the bench where the old man fed his flock of birds. No one has taken his place since he died; the birds come and go, but no longer gather at the appointed hour three times a day. There is no evidence that he was ever here, no one cares that he is gone. However, I now carry a vivid mental picture of his mechanical shuffle, and when I get out I will remember to feed the birds for him.

The holding cell fills with half-a-dozen other inmates. I hear two Federal Marshals stomping up the steel stairs from the sally port. One of them glances in the cell, "I only see seven; I have paperwork for eight."

"Yeah, we had a last minute replacement. The guy got caught smoking dope last night so no camp for him," says the Guard in control. "They're bringing over his replacement right now."

The steel door to the yard opens and a harried looking Ralph steps through. We grin at each other as they push him into the holding cell.

Something amazing, maybe only to me, happens on the way to Boron. We get on interstate 10, the same freeway I came in on with all that cocaine, which means we pass within a couple of hundred yards of my mother's house. Sitting in the back of the Marshal's van wearing handcuffs and leg irons I am riding down drug smuggler's memory lane. If I could go back eighteen months in time, I would see myself coming from the other direction. If I only knew then what I know now. I should have stayed in college. Better yet, I should never have done the marijuana. I would still be in the Navy up to my ears in adventure and be less than three years away from earning a monthly retirement check. I decide to let that thought go...it is just far too depressing.

Boron Federal Prison Camp is on the side of a modest hill in the middle of a vast desert valley. In every direction, it is flat with brown and black mountains in the hazy distance. Most of the camp including the dorms, cafeteria, administration buildings and firehouse are on the lower part of the hillside. Towards the top of the hill, which rises about a thousand feet above the desert plain, are the classrooms, wood and metal shop and radar dome. During World War II, this was an Army radar station. All the buildings are one-sided clapboard and well weathered under the unyielding desert sun. The buildings leak sand when the wind blows and the desert wind blows regularly.

They assign me to a four-man cubicle with three strangers. None of them has been inside a real prison. It is somewhat fascinating that these white-collar inmates carry none of the hardened wariness that a high-security prison breeds into its charges. They thought that the camp was tough time. I just smile as I unpack my cardboard box, which takes about thirty seconds. Okay all moved in; time to explore the camp.

Ralph and I meet outside and begin walking up the hill. On our left, opposite the entry gate, is a grass-free baseball field. There are so many small rocks jutting out of the dark hard-packed dirt that when someone hits a grounder you have to be fast on your feet to field or dodge ricochets. The administration building, visiting room and control building are on the right as you enter the camp, followed by six dormitories that are staggered on the hillside. Just above the baseball field is the firehouse, honor dorm and cafeteria. I see something opposite the cafeteria that brings my feet to a sudden stand still.

"Look at that," I blurt.

"What?" Ralph does not see anything of importance.

"Look through the crack under that wooden gate," I say heading in that direction; I am looking at the sparkle of sunlight upon water. "There's water...lots of water!" On the gate is a sign *Swimming Pool*

Hours, Saturday and Sunday only, 10:00 a.m. to 3:30 p.m.

"A swimming pool, Ralph it's a swimming pool." I am ecstatic, "I haven't been immersed in water since Florida."

Ralph outdoes me, "Yeah, well I haven't been swimming since high school." He pauses as he realizes the significance of his statement. He walks a bit more depressed, but there is an added spring to my step as I have thoughts about immersion while we continue up the hill. I keep turning around hoping to get a look at the size of the pool. Midway up the hill, we look down on the employee housing project to our left. It cannot be the most exciting place to live for the staff's families. I decide right then to make an extra effort to cut the guards a lot of slack. I once read in a prison publication that federal and state correctional officers have the highest rate of spousal and child abuse of any occupation and I do not want in any way to contribute to that. Near the top of the hill, the road loops to the right where we pass the government radar dome, wood and metal shops and the classrooms. From the top, we can see at least twenty miles in every direction. Though the landscape is mostly flat and covered with sage, cactus and tumbleweeds, it is fascinating to see so far. J-1 and J-3 have taught me to appreciate vistas in an entirely different way. It is early April and a light dusting of snow lies in thin patches upon the vast desert.

Walking down the loop road, we follow a short branch off to the left (north), which leads to the Chapel on the Hill. From it, we can see Highway 395 in the distance and below us the swimming pool, which looks slightly larger than a postage stamp. It is okay; right now, I would get excited over a bathtub.

Sitting in the shade of the chapel, Ralph and I are still captivated by the desert vista spread out before us. To be on the tallest hill, thought it is only three hundred feet high, almost as far as the eye can see is in an inmate sense incredible. Twice, we watch giant B-52 bombers fly directly over the camp. Later, I would discover that many military jets from Edwards Air Force Base regularly overfly the camp as they vector in on the radar dome above us. Occasionally, we would even hear the unique double sonic boom of the space shutter returning for a landing at Edwards. Boron might not be so boring after all.

We arrive at the cafeteria in time for lunch. There is a total absence of gang bangers, tough guys and drugged out weirdoes. I get kind of stuck at the salad bar.

We arrive at the cafeteria in time for lunch. There is a total absence of gang bangers, tough guys and drugged out weirdoes. I get kind of stuck at the salad bar.

"Steve you're making a pig of yourself," Ralph is shaking his head.

"Look, look," munch, munch, "tomatoes, cucumbers, carrots," munch, "broccoli, cauliflower and even croutons." I am loading my plate and eating on the go; total rodent heaven.

We sit at a square table for four so we can watch each other's back, a Terminal Island habit that does not go away with time.

Stepping outside a very fat cat steps into our path. "Who are you?" I ask gleefully squatting down to rub his ears and ruffle his fur.

"His name is Crackers because he loves them," says a passing inmate, "give him a cracker and he is your friend for life."

Ten minutes later Ralph is getting impatient, "Steve we are going to be late for orientation, enough with the stupid cat."

Crackers is lying spread out on the sidewalk all four paws in the air getting his belly scratched. "Okay, okay." He follows us halfway to the administration building then is distracted by an inmate with a cracker.

After orientation, I get to meet the Unit Manager who will determine our job assignments and counsel us about re-habilitation. The re-habilitation lecture lasts about twenty unmotivated seconds; the man does not like inmates.

"I don't do re-habilitation counseling because it doesn't accomplish anything but waste my time." He is fat, bald but for a fringe of brown hair on the back and sides, with thick saggy skin and speaks like a genuine redneck. "Your record from Terminal Island says you are a model inmate. Just means you weren't caught, you prison inmates are always up to something. However, because your record is clean, I'm going to let you choose your job; you wanna be a plumber or a dishwasher?"

"Actually sir, I would like to be an inmate fireman."

The man glares at me, "Did I say fireman? I said plumber or dishwasher."

I did not expect this to go well, but I had to ask, "I know, I said fireman because I have a lot of qualifications from the Navy and…" He cuts me off with an abrupt wave of his hand.

"Forget fireman," he shouts, "look I am only gonna explain this once. The fireman position is for honor inmates only and you gotta be here eighteen months just to be considered for the program," his finger is tapping on my file, "plumber or dishwasher?"

"If you're asking me what I'd like to do, I gotta say I would like to be a fireman."

"I knew it; you're just another trouble maker."

"But…"

"Shut up, you're a plumber, wise guy; now get out of my office."

Outside his door Ralph is waiting his turn, "What's he like?"

"A bit like a redneck Tiffany going through menopause without medication."

I did not know the Unit Manager has walked to a file cabinet by the door. He moves extremely lightly for a man forty pounds over-weight. "That supposed to be funny?" he snarls.

"I don't know him," Ralph is pointing at me, "we just rode up in the van together."

"Get inside."

Ralph gives me a look as he passes through the door. I have not done either of us any favors.

When he comes out, we walk off together. "How'd it go?" I ask.

"About what one would expect after you did such a great job of upsetting him. He wanted to know who Tiffany was. He was being such an obvious jerk, so I told him."

"Na."

"Yep, the guy's a clod. He had it in for me the moment I walked through the door. Called me a prison inmate as opposed to a camp inmate. The guy's got issues."

"You ask him about a clerking job?"

"No way! I could wind up working for him. I asked for a kitchen job. You see all those groceries behind the serving line?"

While waiting for our job assignments we were stuck for a week building walls by stacking lava rocks; lots of rocks. During my first break, I went down to the firehouse to meet with the Safety Officer who was a surprisingly nice guy.

"Sir, I would be a real benefit to your fire crew," I begin hopefully. "I spent almost fourteen years in the Navy. In damage control parties, I was number one hose man and led the attack on a ship's kitchen fire. I also learned advanced first aid as a hyperbaric chamber supervisor."

"A what?"

"Recompression chamber for treating divers with the bends," I am hopeful; he sounds interested. "My rating was Machinist Mate Chief. I could help maintain the trucks and emergency equipment."

"So why do you want to be a fireman so badly?"

"Well sir, the bottom line is that firemen help people. They might even get to save lives. I am really hoping for a fireman job because it would help give my life value. I was a bomb disposal frogman and trained to make right choices in an emergency. I take instruction well, know how important it is to be reliable, to be a team member and to follow orders."

"Really? Inmates aren't known for doing what they're told."

"Sir, I would be the best fireman you've ever had. I would not cause any trouble at all. I will work long hours with a smile on my face and every job I do will be done to the very best of my ability."

"That is quite a promise."

"Sir, you never met McNair, my instructor at Bomb Disposal School. He did more than train me well, he taught me the value of working as a team member, which is exactly what fire fighting is all about. I understand that firemen go into life threatening situations as a team. You have to think with a cool head, make right decisions the first time and be willing to lay your own life on the line for a victim or even another fireman. I do not have any bad habits, am focused and am very hopeful about this position."

You're informed, I will give you that," he glances at my file, which he brought to our meeting, "your record from Terminal Island looks good, but you realize you're asking me to go over the head of the Unit Manager."

"Sir, I will not let you down. I know I am asking a lot, but I will put my whole heart into this because in the end it is about saving lives and property."

"I will let you know," he closes my file, "you're dismissed."

That night I prayed up a storm. I know that when we pray for something the answer is not particularly going to be what we want to hear. Amongst the staff, I have made a friend and a foe. The foe was of my own making because of my foolish mouth. Now my biggest hope in prison would ride on what these two men would decide. I went back to my prayers, "If it be your will…please."

The next morning, Ralph and I are standing outside the Unit Manager's door. We have been waiting for half an hour when the Unit Manager steps out of his office and posts the work assignment sheet on the bulletin board. He glares at the both of us, I smile back hopefully then he goes back through the door and slams it. Instantly my heart surges with hope.

Ralph leaps for the list, "Plumber, I'm a plumber. I thought he needed dish washers?"

I am trying to peer over Ralph's shoulder, "What about me?"

"Oh man, no it cannot be."

"What, what?"

"I get one word, plumber, you get a whole sentence," he reads in a snide way, "Arrington, firehouse, re-assignment honor dorm, room 3."

"What?"

"Not only do you get to be on the fire crew, they are moving you to the honor dormitory. Everyone else has to wait eighteen months to be eligible for the honor dorm and they're moving you there in less than a week."

I quickly head outside pulling Ralph with me. I want to get away from the Unit Manager's office. "So what did you say to the Safety Officer?" Ralph asks hopefully. "I better write this down. It has got to be some really good stuff."

It takes almost a full minute to pack up my things because I am not sure whether to take or leave my sheets. I decide to leave them; the honor dorm must have a better selection.

My new roommate is Henry, an ex-CIA agent, turned politician... turned bribe taker. He is an easygoing casual kind of guy. "You are one lucky fellow. I have never seen the Safety Officer so fired up to get someone onboard. He and the Unit Manager had one major argument so he went to the Warden, who okayed the deal."

"Hope I haven't caused any bad blood between them."

"Are you kidding, the Safety Officer hates the Unit Manager and vice versa. In fact, everyone hates the Unit Manger including the Warden."

"You think some of the other inmates will be mad that I am in the honor dorm so suddenly?"

"Na, you're a prison inmate. They won't risk setting you off, besides everyone's stoked that you put it to the Unit Manager."

"I did?"

"Yeah, that guy really hates you now."

"Terrific."

After dinner, I wash my jeans, which are getting threadbare. I carefully wring them out and hang them to dry on the window-sill. A dry desert wind is blowing so it will not take long. I am just settling down with a good book when the fire siren wails. I grab the still damp pants and promptly jam my foot straight through the crotch. I have torn the pants from mid seam all the way to the knees. Wearing them is not an option so I drop them to the floor, pull on my sneakers and run down to the firehouse in my T-shirt and boxer shorts.

Each fireman has his turnouts standing ready. Their jackets hang from hooks with their helmets; their pants are accordioned over the boots with the suspenders laced on the outside for quick entry. They only have to step into the boots, pull up their trousers, snap the suspenders over the shoulders, grab their jacket and helmet off a hook and they are ready. I am not. The chief engineer pulls the fire engine, a 1967 Ford, out of the big double bay and waits on the threshold with the engine idling. I grab a pair of trousers from a pile, pull them on and jam my feet into a too large pair of rubber boots. Instantly I notice that one of the suspender straps is broken. I do not have time to change as I am worried that the truck might leave me so one strap will have to do. The trousers feel quite large with a big gap around the waist. Does not matter, the jacket will cover them as I grab one and throw it on.

The Chief Engineer turns on the flashing red lights forcing me to rush to the workbench where I have spied a helmet, and then I run for the truck where Henry is standing on the back bumper waving for me to hurry. I jump aboard with the helmet in one hand and grab a hold of a polished chrome handrail with the other. He hits a buzzer to signal that we are all aboard and the engineer kicks it into gear as we turn hard right and pull out onto the street. The big truck turns toward the gate and accelerates. The gate barrier swings up and we charge out onto the highway. As the truck begins to gain speed, I am ecstatic. The only vehicles I have ridden in for the past year and a half are Marshal vans with their windows sealed and covered with security wire. I am in the open air on the back of a speeding fire truck, red lights flashing, siren wailing...this has all the excitement of a prison break. Wait until Ralph hears about this. Nine days ago, I could not have imagined in my wildest dreams that I would be storming down a desert highway on the back of a fire truck on an emergency response. When we pray the answer is not always yes, but wow did the Lord ever answer my prayer in an astonishing way!

I look at the desert flying by as we accelerate with the siren continuing its long plaintive wail. Glancing at Henry I smile. He grins and punches me in the arm. It is just too wild riding on the back bumper of a fire truck. Because of safety ordinances I am not aware of any fire departments that still have their firemen ride on the back of a fire truck, but we are inmates and safety ordinances aren't a real big a deal to us. The dry hot wind in my face is invigorating; it entices a long surfer hoot from me. This is better than dropping in on a big Hawaiian wave. We are hitting around fifty miles per hour and I have not yet snapped my helmet strap into place, I am holding it on with one hand. I loop the other arm through the handrail then use that hand to try to snap the two ends together. My fingers discover that it is missing one of the snaps, which is why it was lying on the workbench. I have no choice but to hold it on with one hand.

We turn onto Highway 365 southbound. The road is flat and straight as the engineer puts the pedal to the medal; we accelerate to this truck's top speed of sixty-five miles per hour. The wind dramatically increases and has found a foothold in my bagging trousers, which are whipping in the wind like a warning flag. We pass a couple of cars that have pulled over, I want to glance over at them but holding onto the helmet with one hand and the truck with the other is a fulltime occupation. I am thinking about trying to wedge the helmet into the hose bed when a large bug splats into the plastic faceplate. Reluctant to take a big bug in the eye and not seeing any place to jam the helmet, I keep it on. I am completely embarrassed and hoping that Henry does not notice my distress. That is when my trousers start to slip. The suspender straps share a common adjustment buckle in the back. Because one strap is broken, it is feeding its unused webbing to the one over my shoulder, which I can feel getting substantially longer. Fire fighting turnouts are thick and weighty, made with heavy fire retardant materials on the outside and lots of insulation on the inside. With there being so much extra material bagging around my thighs the wind has found ample purchase and is beginning to pants me. My drawers are drooping, I am not wearing my jeans and unfortunately, there is nothing I can do about it. I am careful not to make eye contact with Henry; whom I can plainly hear giggling.

Fortunately, we hit a long uphill grade, which dramatically slows the truck reducing the wind, but it is too late for my trousers, which are now down around my knees. Henry is laughing himself silly. I see him push the buzzer on the intercom and speak loudly into it. I might die of humiliation and figure it could not get much worse, but then I hear a horn and what sounds like a couple of women hooting. I risk a glance over my shoulder and see the lights of a car about thirty feet behind us. The high beams flick on. My boxers are flapping in the hot desert wind and I have no doubt that Ralph is going to hear all about it.

Thankfully, we finally arrive at the scene of the fire. It is a Volkswagen bug completely involved with the fire burning throughout the entire vehicle. Flames are going twenty feet into the air. The car's driver is standing beside a highway patrol car. I do not know it, but the chief engineer has already determined that the car is totaled. Also the police officer radioed him that the gas tank had ruptured ten minutes ago spilling its flaming cargo. Since there is no threat of the fire spreading to anything else this would be a good time to test the new guy. As we come to a screeching stop, I gratefully step off the back of the truck and pull up my trousers. There is no time to mess with the straps as Henry hands me the nozzle to an inch-and-a-half attack hose and shoves me in the direction of the fire. Another fireman leaps from the front of the truck deploying a second attack hose and hits the front of the Volkswagen with a jet of water. I feel my hose charge as it swells in my hand like a thick black python. I open the nozzle and a solid stream washes up the backside of the bug. The water rapidly douses the flames as we close in and move from the exterior fire to the flames inside. I scuttle forward; my trousers are dragging again. Back splash from my steam and overspray from the other hose has thoroughly wetted my turnouts. The added weight is causing my pants to drag at the ankles. I maneuver to the driver's side of the VW bug just in time to take a solid blast of water from the other attack hose. It goes right through the open windows and hits me in the chest and face driving me backwards; with my feet hobbled, I lose my balance and fall onto my backside. I leap back up, scuttle to the side of the oncoming stream and continue pressing my attack until the fire is completely out.

I feel my hose losing pressure as the high-pressure jet dwindles to a dribble. I am standing there under the fire truck's twin spotlights with my boxers dripping in the front and muddy on the backside with my helmet askew and my heavy wet trousers at my ankles. The VW Bug's driver and the highway patrolman are staring. The other firemen are a total loss with uncontrolled laughter. Thoroughly soaked, my boots sloshing as I help to store the hose, I feel my own laughter rising up uncontrollably and so goes my initiation into Boron Inmate Engine Company 52.

> *"Only actions give life strength; only moderation gives it a charm,"* Jean Paul Richter 1763-1825

The next morning, I enter the firehouse wearing prison khaki trousers and hear Henry telling everyone that I am now a fully baptized inmate fireman. The Safety Officer smiles and shows me where the spare turnouts are stored.

I dig through the turnout locker noting that this is very old gear. "Where do we get this stuff," I ask, "the Salvation Army?"

The chief engineer grins, "Inmate fire departments are at the absolute bottom of the list for gear issue. We're still using some of the same turnouts issued to the Army during World War II, which is when this base was built. Last night we should have used a foam depressant, but all we got is a couple of rusty five gallon cans of fire retardant made from animal blood. The stuff is outdated, but I am saving it for a real emergency."

"At least the trucks look good," I offer.

"The Ford fire truck was given to us because it has a bent frame from getting rear-ended. The back end has a tendency to drift at high speeds, which it only achieves going downhill. Our Mac fire truck was built in fifty-four, the engine's only running on half its original compression."

"Stoked to be a fireman huh?"

"You bet. This is the best inmate job in the entire Federal Department of Corrections," he stands a little taller. "There ain't another inmate fire crew like us in the whole United States. Most inmate fire crews fight forest or brush fires and that's a highly dangerous job, but we're the only inmates that's got a firehouse with its own engines and an area of sole responsibility. We are the initial fire response crew for a twenty-five mile radius of this camp. That's serious responsibility. Civilians and their families are depending on us."

He pats the bonnet of the old Mac, "Come on, I'll teach you about the trucks."

First, he shows me what is in the various lockers on the trucks, which is mostly older Army equipment. I am familiar with most of it because the Navy uses the same kind of equipment, just a more updated version. It is while he is showing me the pump and pipe lay out on the 67 Ford that my military training kicks into gear. "This pump is real temperamental," he cautions, "it's gotta be primed just right or she'll get air-bound and won't take a suction." He works a hand primer a couple of times to show how it works. I slip under the truck to look at the pump casing. "Here's your problem," I spy it instantly, "your gland sealing fiber is worn, leaks air in and water out. I can try tightening it down, but I bet we can order some."

"They don't like spending too much money on our equipment," he laments, "got us on a non-existent budget."

"Replacement fiber will cost just a couple of bucks."

"I think they might go for that."

"What did you do in the Navy anyway?"

"I was a bomb disposal frogman, but my rating was Machinist Mate Chief," I slide out from under the truck, "I can fix just about anything on both of these trucks."

"Have at it," he waves as he walks away, "I'm going to fix a pot of coffee."

Over the next couple of weeks, I thoroughly go through both of the big trucks and a smaller pumper pickup truck. I tighten up gears, fix wiring, replace seals and pretty much get everything in decent working order. These are emergency vehicles and the work I am doing could save someone's life, maybe even an inmate fireman's life.

The total cost in parts was under two hundred dollars; the Safety Officer was thrilled. I did not tell him that I swapped out a couple of the spark plug wires in his Government Issue pickup to replace the worn ones on the 54 Mac.

Once everything is working properly, I get out a hose and wash the Old Mac. It is great fun washing a fire truck; a kid kind of project. The wet tarnished red paint and dull chrome and steel have a lack luster gleam under the bright desert sun. I order a couple of cans of car polish from the supply clerk and am quite excited when they arrive. I plan to start right after breakfast before the heat of the day sets in with a vengeance. It is mid-spring and I can only imagine the intense summer heat waiting to descend upon the camp.

Walking into the shade of the firehouse, I look with satisfaction upon the antique fire truck. Memories of the scouring of my prison cell are echoing through my mind. There are certain times when doing a particularly good job at something has the unique ability to change a person from within. For me growing a lawn in a vacant prison yard and scrubbing a prison cell are two of them. Polishing up this lifesaving machine bodes great promise. Cracking the first can of polish, I determine to save the bonnet for last. I intend to thoroughly savor this project. I begin at the top polishing the roof and the chrome trim around the rotating red light. The fire truck has many layers of good quality red enamel paint. Rubbing away the tarnish, I see the paint acquire a soft mirror like depth. There are fine cracks around the edges, but they become more subtle with each coat of wax.

Around 10:00 a.m., a couple of the firemen join me, but for them it is just work, not a labor of love. By lunch, each has found an excuse that lures them away. On the third day, my fingers are sore from all the work, but my heart glows with satisfaction. I finish the last section of hood, do a final buffing on the chrome siren that rides on the left fender and on the chrome bulldog that Mac trucks have made famous. I step back to eye my work. The truck looks magnificent…well the fire hoses could use a good washing.

Cleaning out the hose bed is an education. I go inside to talk with the Safety Officer.

"Sir, when was the last time someone rotated the two-and-half-inch fire hoses on the Mac?"

"Why?" he asks cautiously.

"Well, I am going to wash the hoses, but some of them look kind of rotted."

"Let me see, I have been here three years," he has a pencil to his lips, "yep, the answer is nope."

"Nope?"

"They've never been rotated."

"That's what I thought," I am doing a very good job of not appearing judgmental, "mind if I do it?"

"Not at all, but you should know so far we have only responded to car fires. The one-and-a-half-inch attack hoses are all we really need. The two-and-a-half-inch hoses are for house and building fires and we'll have plenty of assistance if that ever happens." He returns to his newspaper as he distractedly waves one dismissing hand.

I wind up throwing out one third of our lengths of two-and-a-half-inch hose. A hose break in the middle of fighting a fire could be disastrous.

When "Do no evil" has been understood, then learn the harder, braver rule, "Do good." Arthur Guiteman

Chapter 36
BORON PRISON CAMP, JUNE 1984

A T 6:00 a.m. the next morning, I am standing just inside the entry door of the honor dorm waiting for the guard to unlock it so I can go for my morning run. I hear the crunch of his boots on the sand and gravel outside. His flashlight plays over the double glass panes on the doors, and then I see the metallic ring of keys as he inserts one into the lock. I wait until he is a comfortable distance from the door before stepping out and taking a deep breath of the cold air so I do not alarm him. I take a couple of running steps, leap over a tumbleweed and hit the road that leads uphill. I have not been able to lure Ralph out for an early morning jog so I run in solitude. It is how I prefer it anyway. I will run until well after the sunrise.

In the predawn twilight, I eagerly start up the hill. I can antici- pate surprising several jack rabbits, various desert mice and a few birds. Entering the loop around the hill and beginning to accel- erate I feel my lungs fill and expel more rapidly. The desert air is clean and crisp. Stars are fading from a sky that is beginning to pale. I am halfway up the hillside when the first jack startles from sagebrush almost at my feet. It zigzags ahead of me as I put on a burst of speed trying, but failing, to keep up. This is how I do my unanticipated wind sprints, chasing desert bunnies.

Rounding the top of the hill, I see headlights off in the distance on Highway 395. People going places while I run in circles at the prison camp. The motorists are probably bored with the long haul down a straight and empty desert highway. I am on high bunny alert thinking about my future. I am about at the halfway point of my prison sentence. I do not know the exact date of my release, which will be determined by the parole board and a camp staff review board headed up by my buddy, the Unit Manager. Guess I will be here for a fair while.

Starting my second leg around the hill, I again accelerate the pace as I head up the road. I reckon that I am in the best condition of my life. My routine is to work out with weights on even days and run on odd days. It is probably only in prison that a person can maintain such a strict unchanging, mind-numbing, schedule. I am six feet tall and weigh a hundred and sixty-five pounds. I am not carrying any fat and would like to get up to a hundred and seventy-five pounds, but it is hard to do on a strict vegetarian diet in prison.

Unexpectedly, a whooshing sound comes rushing out of the vast desert quiet. Looking towards the sound, I see a dark shape rushing towards the prison camp hill. It is no more than a couple of hundred feet above the flat desert floor. I am near the top of the hill as the large military jet passes to the lower right of the radar dome. I stare in amazement at a ground-hugging B-1 bomber in supersonic configuration as it flashes by at nearly five hundred miles per hour. The roar and wind of its engines is a momentary visible presence as the desert shrubbery bends to its swift passage. I stare after it, a rapidly diminishing silhouette that quickly disappears beneath a twilight sky into the shadows of the desert floor.

I have stopped running and stand staring at the dark horizon and think about my past life as an EOD Technician. In the Navy, part of my job was to work with advanced military aircraft and its

sophisticated weaponry. Sometimes, I helped to coordinate operation support of ground forces with flight resources. I have called-in
ground strikes by F-4 Phantom fighters in fleet operations that
required training drops of live five-hundred pound bombs. I have
participated in jungle operations and once our team was lent to the
CIA.

Standing alone, in the near dark, on a desert hillside, I think
of the vastness of the Pacific Ocean. Upon its swell I have raced in
a small rubber boat under a descending ballistic warhead; it's fall
retarded by three parachutes. As we swoosh alongside, my task is to
leap into the water to attach a lifting bridle before it can sink. This
was the very missile that defined to the soviets under the Regan
Presidency that we had the capability of successfully targeting an
incoming ballistic missile…thus effectively ending the Cold War. A
nearly bankrupt Soviet Regime could no longer afford the high-tech
arms race. Again, under the command of Frontier Control, I find
myself in another racing rubber boat…this time under a descending
launch platform from a Minuteman III missile. The platform had
contained the huge missile, which had been loaded into the massive
bay of an Air Force C-5 jumbo cargo jet. This enabled the missile to
be deployed from anywhere in the world to its target with very little
advanced warning. To launch the multi-warhead missile, the tail
ramp of the aircraft is lowered and a pilot chute deploys three larger
parachutes that instantly drag the launch platform and missile out
of back of the C-5 jumbo jet. As the missile begins to fall the drag
of the parachutes bring it to a swinging vertical orientation. The
payload continues to swing under the canopies in diminishing arcs
until it is in a stabile launch position. The missile fires and goes
down range while the launch platform continues its descent to fall
into the ocean. My job is not to recover the massive platform, but
to sink it. I have to be careful because there are wires, parachute
cords and a stabilizing harness floating about the platform. The key
is to cut away the flotation so the platform can sink without getting
tangled in any of the debris, which would mean an express trip to
the seabed over three thousand feet below.

As the desert wind softly blows, I stand under the desert twilight sky and think about that day I stood outside the Commanding Officers door after informing him of my decision to end my military career. Then, it wasn't too late for me to step back inside and sincerely apologize…I could have continued my quest for adventure, gone to Australia and a year later realize my dream of becoming a naval officer. Instead, I glance downward at the prison camp and reluctantly return to my dorm room.

The days and weeks pass as I work out, run and maintain the firefighting equipment. The only change in my daily routine is watching the weather.

Outside my dormitory window, I watch a late spring sandstorm raging. The spring winds can blow intensely cold in the high plains of the Mojave Desert. The abrasive fury of the seasonal sandstorms adds such dimension to desert weather. Across the compound, I see an inmate struggling to open a dormitory door held shut by the gusting wind, which momentarily shifts. The door swings abruptly open with a loud crack, casting the inmate down the steps where he falls heavily onto the ground. It takes him a few moments to rise unsteadily to his feet, then leaning into the blowing sand, he sets off for the chow hall with his head down, which is why he does not see the hurling plastic trash can that takes him out at chest level several seconds later.

Judging by the fury of the storm, I decide it just is not worth going to chow on a day like this, particularly when the Sunday brunch special is creamed beef on white toast, grits, stewed prunes and yellow Kool-aid; actually, I would have enjoyed the stewed prunes.

Inside the room, I lie shivering upon my bunk all but cocooned in two threadbare blankets. A thin, gray cloud of dust particles hangs suspended in the room, while more dust, with its baggage of frigid air, continues to seep in through the weathered frame of the windowsill. From a lower corner of the window, a tiny cascade of sand leaks in a steady stream onto the floor where it is busily building itself into a small mound. The falling grains remind me of the slow relentless passage of prison time. I want to flee back into the Vietnam paperback I have been reading, but my cold and stiff fingers are currently jammed knuckle deep into the reluctant warmth of my armpits.

I figure nothing could lure me out of the room on a day like this—then over the mournful howl of the wind, I hear the wail of the fire siren and bolt from the room.

Sprinting into the fury of the windstorm, I see the chief engineer driving the Ford fire truck out of the huge, double doors of the firehouse followed closely by the red Mac. The older truck's headlamps, dimmed yellow by the blowing sand, resemble two enormous, angry eyes. For an instant, the red fire truck with the side aluminum ladders resembling wings looks like a raging dragon furiously exiting its lair.

Rapidly donning yellow turnouts, I leap onto the back carriage of the old Mac. We speed away with the rear of the truck fishtailing into a high-speed turn. Our mechanical beast flies into the storm, the roar of its siren a primal scream that clears lesser vehicles from its path.

Clinging to the back of the truck, I revel in the excitement of the moment as the sand-laden wind whips past my face shield at fifty miles an hour. The wild ride after weeks of institutional boredom rivals the thrill of a prison escape. My life inside prison walls has been slow and much too dreary; the prison sentence seems to drag. My spirit yearns for new vistas, outside adventure, passion and excitement.

We climb the grade to the south leaving most of the blowing sand behind, then top the hill and arrive at the scene of a terrible accident; a head-on collision between a small pickup truck and a heavy delivery van. The driver of the van is hurt, but his injuries are relatively minor. It is a very different situation in the wreckage that now hardly resembles a pickup truck; the young driver inside is dying. I stand at the front of the severely crumbled vehicle with a charged fire hose in the event of fire. Most of the shattered windshield is lying inside on what remains of the truck's dash. I have an unhindered view of the young man's last moments. After prying off the jammed driver's door, the other firemen are trying desperately to keep him alive. The steering wheel is pinning him to the seat. Some of the engine is in the driver's compartment. There are massive cuts in his face, which hardly bleed a sure sign that we are losing him. I watch his eyes go out of focus, his head fall to one side and then his body slumps as life rushes out of him.

We gently lay the body on the desert ground beside a mesquite bush. I watch tentacles of blood weep from the body and soak slowly into the brown sand and dry dirt. While we wait for the coroner to come and collect the body, I think about this young man's life so abruptly cut off. There is nothing fair or unfair about life…it simply is. Each human existence is a mystery waiting to be played out. Our best chance for a quality, meaningful life is to be truly aware, to strive for excellence, to do good things, to hold truth dear, to love and to be loved. If we are careful in our choices, stay active and eat healthy, we should enjoy a superior existence. Yet, for our lives to have meaning and purpose, we must reach beyond our personal needs and human desires. It is the human capacity for love that adds so much depth and value to life. Jesus defined it perfectly, "The two most important commandments of all are to love God with all your heart and soul and to love your fellow man as you would love yourself. All the laws and the prophets are based on these."

When the coroner arrives, we help him to bag the body and place it in the back of his vehicle. Then I walk back to where we had laid him upon the ground. I lift up the fire hose and just barely opening the nozzle spray water upon the spots of blood washing them into the ground.

That night, after the winds have subsided, the stars stand out clearly in the dark sky. Staring into the black void of the desert night sky, I listen to two Mexican inmates playing guitars while singing outside on the dormitory steps. Their melancholy melodies lead me down paths of love and tragedy. I think about the vibrancy of life and how quickly it can be extinguished.

In my hand, I hold a ripe peach. It is my first peach in almost two years. I bought it several days ago at the camp store and have been eagerly waiting for it to ripen. Turning the peach in my hand, I inhale its fragrance and look at the soft subtle colors of the fuzz-covered skin. I have never so closely observed a peach. I realize how perfect a creation a peach is as I sink my teeth into its succulent flesh. As this sorrowful day draws to an end, it feels good to be alive; the peach's flesh tastes uncommonly delicious.

I think that life is expressed well in a peach. When it is ripe, we harvest the fruit and eat of the flesh. A peach fulfills its purpose when it is eaten, if the seed is spit upon the ground from it a tree may grow. I wonder if it is somewhat the same with Man. Death is always stalking us, hovering closely even as we frantically pursue our industrious lives. Through our individual experiences of love and tragedy, we grow and ripen with knowledge and understanding. Then one day we surely wither and die, unless like the young man, our lives are cut short. I wonder if when the Lord calls us to judgment…will He savor the fruits of our brief, yet intense lives?

Spring slides into early summer. Despite all my working out and running, I still weigh one hundred and sixty-five pounds. This morning my day begins with an eight-mile run. On the final leg of my last loop, I slow to a walk and look down towards the firehouse a quarter mile away. It is such a profound blessing to be an inmate fireman with such serious responsibilities. The Lord has given me an astonishing gift. The regular inmate condition is an almost continuous feeling of despair, a serious lack of self worth and an unending wait to maybe, just maybe, find purpose in life again. To be a felon is to carry a curse, to be seen as a flawed human being. It is like wearing your corruption on the outside for all to see…a prison jacket that labels you a sleaze. Many guards continually re-enforce this negative imprinting upon their charges. Inmates are very aware that fully eighty percent of them will be re-incarcerated, twenty-five percent will be back inside within thirty days of their release and few will know limited freedom for more than a year or two. So fear is our constant companion, we are stalked by it day and night. In the incessant turbulence of prison, it is the physical fear of being attacked. According to some government estimates, approximately 65,000 rapes occur daily in men's prisons in the United States. The violence is far worse in the youth lock-ups. This hugely violent atmosphere breeds mental corruption often twisting already damaged souls towards the path of the criminally bent thus leading to a type of immoral insanity.

Upon his release, an inmate constantly worries that he will accidentally do something that might violate his parole. It can even be an almost non-event, somebody falsely accusing him because of his inmate past, getting into a fight that he did not start or being a slave to drug addiction. Approximately eighty percent of all people arrested in the United States are at the time under the influence of a drug. It is not easy to readjust back into society when fear hovers over your shoulder and past corruption clings like a leech to your soul. The climate of a prison is a general absence of love and caring balanced by an over abundance of hate and fear.

So why am I thriving in prison? It is simply because of the love of Jesus Christ and His teachings. That perfect love gives me unquenchable hope. It helps knowing that I am here for the purpose of character development as I read in Romans 5:3-5, that we rejoice in our tribulations. I am learning that by doing good for others then that goodness is reflected back at me.

After showering and eating breakfast, I walk into the shaded firehouse. All the men in the bay are looking quite sober and then I remember that this is the chief engineer's last day. The review board recommended a three-month stay in a half-way house; he is getting out early and is not quite sure if he is happy about it or not. It is the biggest problem facing a short-time inmate, the lurking question of an uncertain future. Prison is about regimen; everything is planned and determined by the staff and its regulations. You do not have to worry about finding a place to sleep, laundry is done regularly, food is served three times a day and medical care is provided, but real life on the outside is full of uncertainties. He shakes each of our hands, seems to look into my eyes a bit longer than necessary and then without another word walks with his shoulders back, head tall, down to the administration building.

We watch our departing friend silently until he passes through the security door down by the gate. I turn and glance at the rest of the fire crew; they have a suspicious look like they are up to something.

"Are we in agreement?" asks the senior crewman. There is a general nodding of heads then they look purposefully at me. It is a serious moment; I am trying to remember if I have done anything wrong. The senior man walks over to the chief engineer's turnouts and removes the red helmet from the hook. Then he walks to the end of the row of turnouts hanging from the wall where as junior man my fire fighting gear hangs. He removes the yellow helmet from my hook, glances at me and then hangs the chief engineer's red helmet under my name. I am stunned. The senior fireman should be advanced next, not me the newest member of the team. Yet as I see him looking at me, a smile creases his face, he nods his approval and then the team files quietly into the office. As the last one steps through the door, I hear him say, "That is the first time I have ever seen Arrington speechless."

I go up to the helmet and touch it. My heart thuds in my chest with emotion. I have not felt like this since my graduation from bomb disposal school over eight years ago. I am a part of something special. We may be incarcerated, but we are not just inmates. We belong to a much bigger fraternity of firefighters, men and women who by their profession may be called upon to lay down their life for another. It is good that no one else is in the fire bay for as I turn to look at the fire trucks my vision clouds with barely held-back tears. I spend the next fifteen minutes walking around the Ford truck, touching its emergency equipment and running my hands over the paint. I open the cab of the big Ford and touch the keys that hang in the ignition. I say a quiet prayer of thanks and ask that I be found worthy and that none of these men get hurt or are lost under my leadership. Then I start the engine and drive out of the firehouse.

Every morning the job of the chief engineer is to drive the fire trucks around the loop of the hill to make sure everything is working. The last vehicle I drove was on the wrong side of the law; I was a felon at the wheel of a car full of millions of dollars worth of cocaine. This time I am driving a giant piece of life-saving machinery and I am in the custody of the law, yet I can now truly consider myself one of the good guys again. How cool is that? I motor out onto the road and turn uphill. There are men walking on the tarmac that are slow to get out of the way. I drive slowly not minding that the walkers linger on the road; the longer this short drive takes the better.

Rounding the top of the hill, I drive out to the Chapel on the Hill, our little inmate church. I switch on the radio and listen to the radio traffic for San Bernardino Command. At anytime they could be calling Engine Company 52 and we would be ready.

After lunch, I walk back to the firehouse and see the men waxing the big Ford. They will not let me share in the work so I go into the Safety Officer's office.

"Morning, Mr. Lambert." He is reading the local newspaper, I have never actually seen him doing any work, which is okay with me.

"Hey chief," he replies.

Those two words stop me in my tracks.

"Is it something I said?" he asks.

So, I tell him about my marijuana mistake in the Navy and how the last time I was addressed as chief was in a surf shop. "I never thought I would be called chief again," I say wonder in my voice.

"So chief, did the boys surprise you?"

"You bet."

"Just so you know, I didn't have anything to do with that decision although I think they made a good one. I figure it is better to let them pick their own leader." He leans forward, "They can ask you to step down too. It's all about trust."

"I will not let them down. I take this far too seriously."

"Figured that," he snaps open his newspaper ready to end the conversation.

"I need a favor."

"So ask."

"Think you could call San Bernardino Command and see if we can get some free training?"

"No one's ever done that before," he frowns; prison guard considering doing something beyond his normal profile.

"So?"

"Okay, I'll make the call. Can't hurt to try."

"Thanks," as I turn to walk out the door, he re-opens his newspaper getting back to the business of the day.

A week later, Ralph and I are sitting on a bench outside the honor dorm watching the sun going down and talking. "You know Steve," he says, "it's kind of eerie just how lucky you are for an inmate. The judge could have nailed you at sentencing, yet he let you off pretty easy."

"True," I answer.

"At Terminal Island all kinds of good things happened to you; including my getting you into the honor dorm earlier than any other inmate I ever heard about."

"Yep, though there were a few tough moments where I could have gotten killed." "I don't think you were under any real threat. It's like God likes you or something."

"Go on," I urge. I am very interested in Ralph's thoughts on this subject, which is very close to my heart. I have spent many long hours pondering exactly what he is expressing.

"Then we come here and you not only score the best job in the whole Federal Prison System, you move into the honor dorm in less than a week. That kind of stuff just doesn't happen by accident."

I am nodding my head and motioning with my hand for him to continue.

"Now what's it been, three months and you're in-charge of the fire department. You are totally high energy all the time, yet for an inmate, you're the most relaxed guy I know. Why are you so lucky?"

"In your first question you used the word lucky and you referred to it again in your last question as well, but it is the wrong word. I am not lucky, I am blessed. I agree with you that God likes me, however, a better choice of words is the perfect love that God has for each and every one of us. Jesus said if we but have the faith of a mustard seed, we could move mountains. Did you know that the mustard seed is one of the very smallest of the seeds in the Middle East? I fully believe that God is watching over me, just like He watches over each and every one of us. Yet, to have a truly loving relationship with Him we must believe that He is there actively working in our lives."

"I believe," answers Ralph quickly.

"Believing is one step, what about surrendering?"

"What do you mean surrendering? I believe, isn't that enough?"

"No, absolutely not. Surrendering is about offering yourself to His service. Ralph there's a mighty struggle going on…good against evil. To be an effective Christian warrior a person has to realize that they are in a war, take a side and fight to the very best of his or her ability. I don't think most people are aware that this war is happening all around us; it's a global event."

I pause then say, "Let me ask you a couple of questions? Do you believe in God, Jesus and the Holy Spirit?"

"Yes."

"Who is the Holy Spirit?"

"I don't know some kind of good ghost."

"At the Pentecost Jesus called the Holy Spirit the Great Comforter. Jesus said He had to leave in order to let the Great Comforter do His work. When we surrender to God, we open ourselves to be empowered by the Holy Spirit. Please understand that I am not the best one to be trying to explain this."

"No problem."

"Well then, when I pray I thank the Lord for His perfect love and ask forgiveness for my sins."

"Yeah, I do that too."

"Then I thank Jesus Christ for His sacrifice and teachings. Someone once wrote, 'I asked Jesus how much He loved me. Jesus said I love you this much, and then He spread His arms open wide and died.' Jesus loves us that much. I try to remember that when I pray."

"That is pretty heavy."

"It is the greatest love man has ever known or ever will know."

I look at Ralph wishing I could say it better. My friend needs to know that being a true Christian means being fully committed, something he is not yet and something I am still learning. "Our walk with Christ is about always learning, always growing, but it is a never fully getting there kind of project."

"What do you mean never fully getting there? Isn't believing in God enough?"

"We are not perfect and never will be while we are walking on this planet and believing is a part, but not the whole part of our relationship with God. When asked, Jesus said that the two most important commandments of all were to love God with all our heart and soul and to love our fellowman as we would love ourselves. To me that means we have to want to do good in this world. Underline want to."

"That's it?"

"No, it is just part of it."

"This is getting complicated."

"No, actually it is quite simple. The third and final part of my prayer is to the Holy Spirit. I ask Him to come inside of me. To help wash out what is wrong with me and to fill me with His goodness and power to do good works for others."

"The Holy Spirit?"

"Yes, I am asking for the gift of the Holy Spirit in my life; He empowers us just like He gave the apostles their abilities to heal and do real miracles."

"I thought it was Jesus who taught the apostles to heal," Ralph counters.

"At the Pentecost, Jesus said He must leave in order that someone greater than He can come, then He went up to each apostle and breathed the Holy Spirit into him. After that the apostles were able to do great miracles in His name."

"I had no idea."

"Remember, I am not explaining it very well. Do you believe in Satan? That he exists?"

"Sure."

"What about evil spirits and demons?"

"No," Ralph laughs.

"If you believe in angels then why don't you believe in demons? They are mentioned in the Bible. What do you think happened to the fallen angels that were thrown out of heaven with Satan?"

"Angels fell to earth with Satan?"

"Actually fell is a relative word, the Bible says they fell like a lightning bolt; that is some pretty serious acceleration. God threw them out."

"That's heavy."

"Actually it is war. An all-out "take no prisoners" war. But because it is a spiritual war we only see the effects of it, not the major players themselves."

"What does that mean?"

"Well I have not seen God, nor his angels and thankfully I have not seen Satan or his demons, but I see the effects that Satan and his demons have on people all the time. A lot of his recruits were living in Terminal Island and there's more than a few of them here at the camp."

"I haven't seen any Devil worshipers."

"It's not that simple." I pause to think, "How do you feel when you do something good?"

"That's easy, I feel good," laughs Ralph.

"Okay, how do you feel when you do something bad?"

Ralph frowns, "Well I guess I feel bad."

"Please be more specific, you guess you feel bad or you do feel bad?"

"Okay, I always feel bad when I do something wrong."

"Then why do you do the bad things? I mean if you know that doing wrong is going to make you feel bad, why do you do it?"

"I don't know."

"Satan is the great what?"

"Deceiver."

"So who does he use to do the deceiving?"

"Demons?

"Yeah, when it gets serious, but in daily life he uses people."

"What kind of people?"

"People who are slipping into his control, friends, family, even ourselves."

"Ourselves?"

"When someone lies who do they have to lie to first?" Ralph is taking too long to answer so I do it for him, "They lie to themselves. They have to convince themselves that it is okay to tell or live the lie."

Ralph nods so I go on. "Think back to when you were robbing banks. Did you in your own mind find some justification for what you were doing?"

"Hey, I was all drugged out!"

"Fine, did that help you justify going into a bank with a toy gun, which they thought was real, threaten innocent people and take the bank's money?" I hold my hands up innocently, "Just asking."

"I was robbing the bank, not the employees," Ralph argues angrily.

"So Ralph, my friend, you have not quite let go of the lie yet. The bank is owned by people. You weren't robbing a thing, you were robbing people. You were using force and scaring people to take what was not yours."

Ralph doesn't like what I am saying; my friend is getting madder as he glares at me.

"Before you go over the top, please remember you're not talking to a saint. I am an ex-drug smuggler and I know that cocaine hurt a lot of people so, my friend, we were both in the same felonious boat."

"Yeah," laughs Ralph instantly relaxing.

"People who are busy making bad choices are continuous liars. They are working full time to convince themselves and others that the wrong they are doing is actually mostly okay. What they don't realize is that they are doing their balancing act on a bolt of lightning aimed straight into oblivion."

"Just for lying?"

"Lying is just part of it because we use lies to try to cover up what we are doing wrong. Truth is one of the words Jesus used most in the Bible. Try counting them; it's there a lot. The Bible even refers to the Sword of Truth, which cuts through lies and deceit."

I stare out over the desert gathering my thoughts, then say, "A Christian tries to live a truthful life. It does not mean it always happens because we are human and we still try to justify all that we do in life, but there is one absolute that every Christian knows and that is we cannot lie to God. We fear Him."

Ralph pounces, "I thought we were supposed to love God, not fear him?"

"Wrong, God tells us to fear him. He is a jealous God."

"What happened to free choice?"

"We are always free to choose, but fear and love are two powerful motivators. You can love God and fear Him at the same time. Actually that is a standard parent child relationship."

"So this war we are in, Satan recruits with lies and God recruits with truth?"

"Absolutely and every day I pray that the Lord will use me to fight for Him. Ralph, I fully believe that my time here in prison is a lot like being a sword in a furnace. He is tempering me, preparing me for what is to come."

Ralph interrupts my solemn moment, "Instead of a sword in stone, you're more like a shank in prison concrete."

"This is not something for you to make fun of Ralph. I am being absolutely honest with you. The sword refers to truth, it cuts through lies and deceit."

Ralph shakes his head, "Well, I still think you're lucky."

" I am not lucky, I am blessed; I am blessed because I am working to surrender so I can serve. This same miracle is waiting for each and every one of us if we are willing to serve Him."

"Hold it! In order to win you have to surrender. Who ever heard of surrendering to win a war?"

"Satan," I pause to let the thought have impact. "It is what Satan fears most from man. If he can appeal to our ego, our wants, lusts and our desires, he has a chance to corrupt and pull someone to his side. But when a person surrenders fully to God then that person becomes a great warrior of truth and Satan cannot fight that."

"So you think you're a Christian warrior?"

"It is what I am trying to become. It means being truly focused towards what is good, to be loving and forgiving, it is about self discipline, being truthful, studying the Bible to learn, having companionship with other Christians and working towards a real relationship with God, Jesus and the Holy Spirit."

"Do you believe it is really going to happen, this Christian warrior thing?"

"Actually I believe it is happening with all my heart," I put my hand on Ralph's shoulder, "remember the faith of a mustard seed? Well I believe all of the good things that are happening to me here in prison are to help build my faith and to teach me commitment. I believe that I will have far greater tests and work to do in the future. This is just the beginning. I am still doing the sword in the kiln thing."

"Then you believe that God thinks you're special."

"No, I believe that God sees the potential in all of us and wants to shower each of us with gifts to do His work, but most of us do not even ask for these gifts."

"What gifts?"

The sudden wail of the fire siren shatters the still of the desert night. I erupt from the bench and hit the ground running. Over my shoulder I yell, "Here's a gift happening right now," but I doubt Ralph heard me.

In the firehouse, I run to the racks of turns-outs. Last week I carefully folded my trousers over the tall rubber boots so all I have to do is step into the boots, pull the trousers up to my waist and snap the suspenders over my shoulders; a three second procedure.

I see a very excited reflection of myself in the polished mirror of the door as I pull it open slide onto the seat and hit the ignition. My jacket and helmet are already lying on the seat where I placed them last week. The helmet's visor has been cleaned to a glossy sheen and de-fogged. I am so ready for this moment; like a sixteen-year-old with a new driver's license and his car freshly polished and ready for that first driving adventure. I pull the big truck out onto the threshold to keep from asphyxiating the other arriving firemen and switch on the radios.

"San Bernardino command this is engine Company 52 standing by," I say excitedly into the microphone.

"52 respond code three (red light and siren), single car accident involving injuries, Route three-ninety-five, six miles south of four corners."

"Roger, 52 responding code three," I am so excited that I have a sudden urge to pee, but with a couple of deep breathes the moment passes.

I lean my head out the driver's window and yell, "Single vehicle accident, no fire, we're responding only with this truck."

Henry slides into the passenger seat followed by an escort officer. A buzzer in the cab announces that the last fireman is aboard which is the moment I have been waiting for. I floor the accelerator. The spinning back tires leave twin smoking skid marks as the truck leaps out onto the road. Rounding the corner, I see the gate swing up and jam the gearshift into third. We fly down the road, emergency lights strobing the desert landscape brilliant red, the siren like a primal scream challenging the night. I glance over at Henry and the guard, they are both grinning at me fully caught up in the excitement of the moment. I send a loud surfer hoot sailing out the window and go for fourth gear. I am ecstatic. In my excitement, my right foot begins to tremble from keeping the gas pedal jammed against the floorboard. If I could, I would stuff my rubber boot into the carburetor. Even the guard is fully into it judging by the look of anticipation on his face. The moment gives me an amazing thought, his expression is something I have never seen before on the face of a guard. I have seen guards angry, bored, disgusted, sometimes rarely smiling, but never excited. He and I are sharing a real human moment. It is not a guard and his charge…it is a couple of guys in a fire truck on a red light and siren adventure.

Eleven miles down the highway we come upon a white station wagon with its front end embedded in a sand bank fifty feet from the pavement. A weaving broken path of torn desert brush and deep tire marks in the brown sand tells of a speeding car out of control. It had blown a tire and the elderly gentleman driving it had almost rolled the vehicle. His wife sits beside the car with an injured leg. The rest of the crew quickly renders first aid while I confirm that the ambulance is only a short distance away.

As an emergency response, this is a relatively tame situation. We provide basic first aid for their minor cuts and lend comfort to the elderly couple. Other than that, there is not much for us to do, but wait for the ambulance. After it departs with the couple, we turn the scene over to a highway patrolman and drive slowly back towards the camp. I have the window down to enjoy the warm desert wind blowing into the cab. There is just something special about driving a fire truck, particularly during the magic of night with all the chrome gauges glowing softly against a red dashboard.

At Four Corners, the guard asks us to stop and treats us to a cup of gas station coffee, which is about five times better than what they serve us at the prison. It is the best cup of coffee I have ever had.

After parking the truck and securing the firehouse, the five of us firemen walk together up to the honor dorm. The inmates in the television room are watching a police series. I listen to a siren coming from the television and think about the chrome siren on the fire truck that had been wailing about four feet from my head an hour ago. I just had the most amazing bout with excitement, real adventure and I am wired from the coffee. I would love to continue my discussion about gifts with Ralph, but he is now locked in his dorm.

In Malachi 3:10, the Lord promises that if we freely pay our tithe that He will open the flood gates of Heaven so richly will He bless us. Well, that is how I feel about the Lord's gifts. As we use our gifts to the best of our ability to do His work, He will flood us with more gifts. I think of a story I once read. In this story, a man dies and goes to Heaven where an angel shows him around. On their heavenly tour, they come upon a large warehouse. "What's this huge building?" asks the man.

"It is where the Lord stores gifts not given," answers the angel.

"Do I have any gifts in there?" asks the man.

"Yes you do," the angel answers politely.

The man quickly rushes inside though the angel tries to call him back, "Wait, wait," but it is too late. Inside, the man sees many shelves with row upon row of beautifully wrapped presents. Only there are no nametags, he has no idea, which one was meant for him.

He goes back outside and asks the angel, "There are no nametags. How do I know which present the Lord meant for me?"

The angel compassionately replies, "They were all meant for you, but you never asked."

Although it is but a story, I believe that the Lord wants to shower us with blessings, but we do not ask or our purpose is not for the greater good of others. When we pray and ask the Lord for help, I believe He always answers, but our own fixed misconceptions often get in the way. He is not a servant to our desires or needs. Our Lord is the sovereign King of the Universe. Absolutely, He knows what is best for us, but His answer may not be what we expect or desire, and therefore we may not understand that our prayer was received, considered and acted upon. I actively pray for forgiveness and know that I have it, yet I still must serve my period of incarceration. This is a huge mental leap forward for me as a Christian…my incarceration serves me. Without this time in prison, what would I have learned or gained from my criminal mistakes?

My incarceration is about character development, learning to trust God, believing in my own self worth and discovering that hope in God does not disappoint.

Like the chief engineer before me, I have a fear of the future not knowing what is waiting for me upon my release. Only unlike him, I plan to go forward with confidence because I am not alone. Believing that the Lord has a mission for me, then He will pave the way towards its completion if I will but have the faith to follow willingly.

After saying my prayers, I tuck into my covers and wonder what awaits me after my release.

A week after our official request, a real-life fire captain arrives at the camp. He runs us through some drills, which rather puts him in a state-of-shock. Next, he checks over our equipment barely able to hold back his mirth and then he has some serious discussions with me and the Safety Officer. He makes three trips to the camp in a week running us through numerous extensive drills then invites us to join a countywide training evolution. I elect to take the antique Mac figuring the professional firemen would enjoy seeing the old fire truck.

We arrive early in the morning at an old desert motel in the middle of nowhere that is to be leveled for a newer facility. Each of the motel rooms is a separate little structure, which will be set on fire one at a time. Once the unit is fully involved each of the participating fire crews is going to be evaluated on how well and how quickly they put out the fire.

In the parking lot, we are the surprise hit of the day. None of the other fire departments has worked with Engine Company 52. They are thrilled to see the old Mac and find our antique uniforms and equipment equally amusing. Some of them eagerly pose with us for pictures and give us some of the Polaroid shots.

I happily look at the photo given to me of the entire crew standing beside a fire truck. I will treasure it greatly; it is one of only two pictures taken of me in prison. I glance about, there are twenty county firemen visiting with our crew. The other inmate firemen are happy, in a festive mood, yet relaxed, easily enjoying the camaraderie of being with other firemen. I realize that we are participating in a rare civilian moment. In prison and in a prison camp, inmates are always on guard, there is no such thing as fully relaxing. It is unthinkable that an inmate would casually stand in a large group of men so exposed, not even concerned about watching his back.

A loud siren interrupts our social moment with the fire crews and then the brigade commander orders us to our trucks. He instructs the first truck's crew to drive down the block, make a U-turn and stop at two yellow traffic cones while the inspection staff sets one of the units on fire. When it is fully involved, the commander radios the truck, "Engine Company 24, respond code three, simulating two alarm fire with possible victims inside."

We inmates are very impressed by what we see. Team after team professionally and quickly knocks down the flames, vents the building and then rushes inside with their air packs to carry out the two rescue dummies. No team takes longer than four minutes from start to finish.

Our fire captain stands with us evaluating each response and giving us hints on how to get the best performance out of our equipment.

Finally, it is our turn for the last standing motel unit. As I start the fire truck one of the inspectors says, "You guys don't have any civilians to rescue."

"Why not?" I ask.

"You don't have air packs," he has the look that he is stating the obvious, "can't risk any of you inhaling too much smoke."

"What do you expect us to do when we have real victims in a real fire?" asks Henry.

"I expect you'll vent the building, go in low behind a wide jet of water to push away the smoke and drag them out like any other fireman would, but here you're limited by your equipment and safely regulations always comes first."

I am as nervous as a long-tailed cat in a room full of grand-mothers in rocking chairs, as I tap my fingers on the steering wheel while the truck idles before the two traffic cones then the radio blurts, "Engine Company 52, respond code three, simulated two alarm fire, negative victims."

I rev the engine; pop the clutch and key the radio, "52

responding." I accelerate two hundred yards down the road and come to a screeching stop at the hydrant to drop one man with a five-inch supply hose and a spanner. He runs ten feet, takes a wrap around the hydrant with the hose and leans away from it as I accelerate another fifty yards down the road. This is a forward lay and a professional team can drop the hydrant man by just slowing down the truck. We are not of that caliber yet and earlier we had seen a hydrant man drug behind a truck when the hose snagged and failed to play out of the hose bed. Our hydrant man was a short timer and did not see any reason to risk being hurt this late in his sentence. Since I was the one who laid out the five-inch hose in the truck's bed, I was quick to agree with him. If it snagged and he got drug it would be my fault.

We are twenty-five yards upwind of the burning building so the smoke is blowing away from us. My number one hose man runs out the one-and-half-inch attack hose, while I prime the water pump then engage it and rev the engine from the control board. We have water on the fire in less than one-and-a-quarter minutes from when we rolled. The first hose man is our second most experienced fire fighter. He has his nozzle on wide spray to keep heat away, crabs right up to a window slamming the heavy brass nozzle into the glass shattering it. Flames begin to pour out around him, but he pushes them back with a fan spray and then goes to a solid stream to attack the hot spots.

Meanwhile my other two firemen are running out a two-and-a-half-inch diameter hose. Rather than charge the full three hundred feet, we save water and time by breaking loose the hose connection at the third length and spin it onto the truck's coupling. When Henry, the lead hose man, nods that they are ready, I charge the hose as they lean forward into it. The surge of water is so great it would fling them about if they were not fully focused on controlling the thick jet of water. Meanwhile the hydrant man is standing by to charge the supply hose. Earlier we decided to use our manpower to get the water on the fire first using the truck's main tank. Only now do I hook up the hydrant hose. The other crews had used axes and pry bars to open the door and break out the windows to vent the building and get water on the fire. The inmates with the two-and-a-half-inch hose uses the big bore stream of water to blast the door off its hinges then they press the attack inside taking the fire down almost instantly. Ours was the third best time by enough of a margin that we would have been able to evacuate the rescue dummies given a chance and still keep third place.

The lead inspector walks up to us as we are coiling our hoses. "Great time, but you broke the rules by going inside without air packs," he cautions.

"Of course we broke the rules," quips Henry, "we're inmates; it's kind of expected of us."

"Sorry sir," I try to mediate, "just doing what you said, the best we can that our limited equipment will allow."

He laughs, "Actually I like how you blew the door off its hinges." He runs a hand over the chrome siren on the fender of the old Mac. "Cool truck."

"The most beautiful thing we can experience is the mysterious.
It is the source of all true art and science," Albert Einstein

*Engine Co 52 at San Bernardino training event, author center, other inmate
Firemens' faces purposefully blurred.*

"I live in company with a body, a silent companion, exacting and eternal," Eugene Delacroix 1798-1863

Chapter 37

BORON PRISON CAMP, JULY 1984

THE CAMP boils under the hot desert summer sun with no relief. Not only is it smoking hot in the dormitories, but also I have an issue with the flagpole a couple of hundred feet from my window. If the guards do not tie the hoisting rope tight enough its metal clamps bang against the metal pole relentlessly night and day. They padlock the shackle so when it bangs and clangs in a stiff wind there is nothing I can do but try to ignore the loud metallic sound, which is basically impossible.

At breakfast, I have established a working relationship with one of the inmate cooks. He makes me regular bowls of oatmeal sweetened with raisins and I bribe him with avocados from the camp store. As a fireman, I now earn a walloping twenty-two cents an hour. I am scooping up a big spoonful of oatmeal as Ralph arrives at my table with a loaded tray.

"How can you choke down all of that oatmeal?" he asks lifting a piece of greasy bacon to his lips.

"My hope is to die healthy," I counter.

"What?"

"You heard me," I am eyeing his tray, "I want to die healthy."

"Isn't that a contradiction in terms?"

"No, by eating the right foods, exercising, sleeping well, keeping stress down, running in the sunshine and drinking plenty of water I intend to be as healthy as possible right up until the moment I die."

"Oatmeal is boring. I'd rather indulge, live my life fully and die early than eat mush."

"Actually from what's on your tray you certainly will not live life fully, but you probably will die early."

"Hey, don't knock the All American Breakfast," he scoops in a mouthful of fried eggs with a chunk of hash browns. "This is absolutely my favorite inmate chow."

"Ever notice the average All American physique?" I ask in a charming way, "fat and getting fatter."

"My body thrives on greasy food."

"What do you think the Roman Gladiators ate?"

"Meat, lots of red meat." Ralph demonstrates ripping a piece of greasy bacon with his teeth, "Probably ate it raw."

"Actually they were on a rather strict diet of grouts and beans. They were mostly vegetarians."

"You're nuts."

"No I'm not, though they ate those too. Their diet is documented in old Roman records. They wanted their gladiators to be strong, have dense bones and a layer of protective fat to protect them from sword cuts."

"You're not having fun with me?" The bacon strip hangs in his hand, like a wilted lie faced with the flame of truth.

"Nope, the body needs complex carbohydrates, the type of fats that are beneficial (high density fat lipoids), a lot less protein than most people assume, plus absorbable minerals, micro nutrients and antioxidants almost all of which are in my bowl right now."

"That's just oatmeal and raisins in there. You don't even have any milk so where's the protein and calcium?"

"Protein and calcium from plants are in the easiest form for the body to absorb. If you recall from the Book of Genesis the Lord intended man to be a strict vegetarian in the beginning. Meat has all kinds of negative chemicals, think toxic wastes that are dumped into the meat eater's body. As for the calcium in cow's milk we are not calves; it was designed for bovines not for people."

"Wasn't designed for us?"

"Remember the Book of Genesis? According to a lot of research cow's milk is not particularly good for children and it's not very good for you either."

"But I like milk."

"Yeah and you also wolf down a lot of cheese and ice cream."

"So what are anti-oxidants?" asks Ralph trying to change the subject away from his favorite foods.

"Oxidants are oxidized molecules that in the process have been stripped of an electron. To become stable again they need to gain or share an electron. Inside your body, they accomplish that mission by stripping or combining with those electrons from molecules in living tissue. It is believed that the result is accelerated aging, disease and death. Anti-oxidants provide that sacrificial electron thus preventing your molecules from being raided and damaged or destroyed."

"You're kidding?"

Oxidation happens to everything even metal, which rusts. Leave a piece of steel laying about in the environment long enough and it will rust away to nothing."

"Are you saying that it is like we are rusting on the inside?"

"Yeah, but it is an outside process too, antioxidants react to all our tissues; that includes skin, hair and eyes."

"So I'm rusting."

"Ever watch a slice of banana or apple turn brown?"

"Sure."

"It happens pretty quick when exposed to air, doesn't it?"

"Yeah," Ralph is sneaking another bite of bacon."

"That is the oxidation process at work. If you squeeze lemon onto the banana or apple it will slow down the process because lemon juice is full of anti-oxidants that it forfeits to the oxidants in the place of the apple's or banana's molecules."

"Then why aren't you eating any lemons for breakfast?"

"Because raisins and prunes have more antioxidants than lemons or just about anything else you can name."

"Look I'm an inmate, I don't get much pleasure in here so let me eat my bacon, eggs and fried potatoes in peace."

"Okay."

"So how's your morning going?"

"Well I was up at three, did my stretching, yoga, karate and hit the weight pile."

"You're trying to bum me out, aren't you?"

"No, I am simply trying to share knowledge that would benefit you greatly for the rest of your life. The body is a biological engine that has the ability to grow and rebuild itself. The cleaner the fuel you put into your biological engine the better it is going to do its job and the longer it will run. Clean fuel saves the body energy. So what do you think is the best food for you on your plate?"

"The hash browns?"

"Potatoes are a terrific food; unfortunately they peeled away the skin which is where most of the minerals and a lot of the complex beneficial enzymes are found. Then your hash brown patty was deep-fried in a vat of oil. In restaurants and commercial kitchens, the oil for deep-frying is seldom changed on a regular basis. That oil is a densely loaded oxidant factory, plus it is loaded with trans fats."

"Trans fats?" Ralph frames the question as if he is saying the name of a foul disease, which is not far from the truth.

Trans fats are saturated oils that clog arteries, add fat to the body and promote the production of low-density fat lipoids. Pry your hash brown patty apart and see how deeply it has soaked up all that oil."

Sam's patty is so hard he has to

cut it with a knife, which still winds up being a mostly crunchy affair as it comes apart. "Kind of like a thick potato chip."

"Perfect," I leap on his analogy, "How long does it take to eat a regular-sized bag of potato chips or a cylinder of *Pringles*?"

"If I am really hungry about five minutes or less," Sam has a wistful look on his face, as we don't often get potato chips.

"Well the calorie content of that potato chip bag or cylinder of *Pringles* is about nine hundred calories; that's almost half your daily calorie allotment or the equivalent of eating nine to eleven potatoes depending upon their size, which would take me about two days."

"Well, eggs are good for you, aren't they?" he asks hopefully.

"Personally, after honey, I think eggs are one of the best animal products you can eat."

"Good," Ralph digs in.

"Just not those eggs."

"Oh come on, what's wrong with these eggs?"

"Well they are fried, they'd be better poached or boiled but that is only part of it. Chickens are born with wings. It's an animal that God designed to fly. The egg industry keeps its commercial egg laying chickens in small cages. As a chick, it never knew the hen, its mother, and never got to know what being a real chicken is all about; it's just a small egg-laying factory. Often they even shorten the chick's beaks so they don't hurt the financial bottom line by damaging another chick. It walks on wire its whole life and the eggs fall through a chute to a collection point. It doesn't get to scratch on the ground and eat bugs, nuts, seeds and pebbles, which are essential to being a healthy happy bird. Instead it eats commercial feed meant to maximize profits that are also loaded with antibiotics to prevent mass chicken die offs from disease. You don't even want to know what they have been known to put into commercial animal feed."

"Actually I do." Sam is pouring a ton of catsup over his hash browns.

"Well for one thing, animals that die and cannot be considered safe for human consumption are sent to rendering plants where they are ground up and mixed into commercial feeds. So in the end what is considered unlawful to sell for human consumption winds up inside us anyway."

"That sucks!"

I think I am reaching him. "Commercial chickens are under a lot of stress from their crowded and confined environment and a diet which causes them to produce their own non-natural chemicals, which goes into their eggs and their tissues and guess what happens to the commercial chicken when it dies?"

"Goes into the animal feed bag?"

"Yep, next stop the old rendering plant."

Ralph has the most unhappy look on his face, "And the bacon."

"Well we are back to the animal feed issues, a bit better living conditions, but now there are a few more chemicals involved sometimes including growth hormone for rapid weight gain. They do get to nurse off their sow so they have a much better idea that they are pigs. But boy oh boy when piggy goes through the slaughtering plant that is one stressed out animal and the curing process for bacon is a major chemical bummer for your body."

Ralph is staring at his plate, "So it's the catsup?"

"Yep, it's the healthiest thing on your plate. Tomatoes are loaded with Lycopene, which is one of nature's most powerful antioxidants, is found in abundance in tomatoes and it helps to fight cancer."

"Great," smiles Ralph, "because I like catsup a lot."

"Well, it does have its downside."

Ralph glares at me.

"Read the label."

Ralph picks up the catsup container, "Tomato paste, corn syrup, water, vinegar and salt."

"Corn syrup, that's liquid sugar with a unique downside. Beside all the calories it's packing, corn syrup doesn't shut down the bodies' cravings, which means your appetite is not satisfied."

"What are you talking about?"

"If you consume a cola drink it doesn't satisfy your hunger because the right chemical signals are not being sent to the brain. Therefore, someone can chug twenty or even thirty ounces of cola and still be hungry, even though they've just taken in one-third or more of the calories the body will use in an entire day. So the body stores those extra calories, as in fat and getting fatter."

Ralph laughs and nods towards a hugely fat corrections officer sitting on a stool by the exit door. He is there to ensure we inmates do not attempt to smuggle food out of the cafeteria. The man has an insatiable appetite and regularly waddles into the kitchen for snacks. His inmate nickname is Box of Rocks referring to the lack of intellectual ability he exhibits. Whenever Box of Rocks is on chow patrol, the food smuggling rate goes up enormously. We only have to wait until he waddles into the kitchen to sneak the groceries out the door. I have many priors taking crackers out to the camp cat. Anyway, Ralph has noticed that Box of Rocks is sucking on a can of soda and he has another waiting next to his ample backside.

"He's a heart attack looking for a place to happen," I quip. "He can't respect himself, which makes it hard for him to respect anyone else."

"Tell me about it, he's always giving me a hard time."

"It's because he's not happy. He's dealing with an addiction and losing."

"By the way there's another down side to corn syrup. It is often accompanied by citric acid, particularly in fruit drinks and sodas."

"I thought citric acid was good for you?"

"It's the combination that's bad. Citric acid strips the protective film off your teeth, allowing the corn syrup direct contact with the enamel, which promotes the growth of organisms that cause tooth decay and gum disease."

"I've only had a couple of cavities," Ralph says in his defense.

"That's really good, but no cavities at all would be better," I smile ruthlessly, "don't you think?"

"You've never had a cavity?"

"Nope."

"You know there just might be something to this health food thing." Ralph reluctantly puts down his fork, "If I go get a bowl of oatmeal, will you promise not to say anything when I pour milk on it?"

"Deal," I'm ecstatic. Have I actually won over a new health convert?

"One last question," he stands and turns towards me, "if you're so well informed what are you doing in here?"

> *"The unexamined life is not worth living,"*
> Socrates 469-399 BC

Ralph's question cuts straight to the bone. I am a reasonably intelligent person with a fundamental desire to do good work and believe in doing what is right…so what am I doing in prison? Greed comes to mind though I do so try to deny it. I am also rather quick to tell people that the threat of guns had a lot to do with it. Yet, why did I really allow myself to slide into the criminal underworld? I do not like people who behave wrongly on a regular basis. I decide to follow my errant steps back to the beginning of my wayward behavior. It is time to understand what went so dreadfully wrong with my morals, values and right focus. All I have to do is see where my feet changed course from the bright path of integrity to the dark alley of corruption. For a moment, I wonder how far back into my life I will have to go, but then realize it really does not matter, as an inmate I have all the time that the trip will require.

I elect to go back just over a decade to my first shore-based assignment at Naval Air Station, Point Mugu. I was assigned to the EOD Detachment as a support diver. One night I was at a party trying to pick up an attractive nurse when she invited me into the backyard to smoke a joint. Remembering my negative introduction to dope in Vietnam a few years earlier, I was going to refuse, but being that I was well into a six pack of beer I shrugged and decided why the heck not?

Though I continued to prefer beer to marijuana, my occasional use of dope would now begin to have a growing impact upon my life. It certainly made me more susceptible to using it in Hawaii where the marijuana was significantly more potent as well as socially addictive as it was so immersed into the island surfer lifestyle that I would later embrace.

Besides my support diver duties, I was also the base scuba diving instructor at NAS Point Mugu. That is how I met Morgan Hetrick; who hired me to give him private scuba lessons. Afterwards, we sometimes dove together off his yacht around the Channel Islands. Morgan was going through a divorce and was very keen on trying to capture the attention of young women with his yacht, private jet and pockets full of money. Back then, he was a legitimate businessman making after-factory upgrades to Cessna Citation Jets and converting French military training jets into commercial aircraft at his hanger in Ventura, California. I quickly saw that his moral standards were not very high, yet we got along.

So if I was willing to tolerate his low moral standards what did that say about my moral standards?

Anyway, he would put some money in my pocket for teaching his girlfriends to scuba dive or for driving his luxury motor home up to Reno so he could fly in and impress his date. It surprised me that Morgan never stayed in his motor home; he just wanted it there for his date to see. I knew I was part of Morgan's pickup scheme. Having a friend a couple of decades younger than him made it easier for Morgan to score with youthful women. I guess I was kind of a bird dog helping to point out his prey...not that I was taking any responsibility for my role. I do remember having to work at justifying my association with Morgan to some of my friends, yet it was not something that kept me up at night.

One thing I always noticed about the women Morgan picked up. They certainly were not after him for his looks...it was all about the money and the lifestyle. If I had thought about it, I was tagging along for exactly the same reasons.

Therefore, in a sense I was prostituting myself too. It is amazing that I actually maintained a very high opinion of myself back then because my perspective was coming from some awfully low places.

I do admit to liking Morgan during my Point Mugu period. He was a bit of a rogue, but in a sort of enjoyable way. He had a way of laughing that the girls thought cute. He was quick to help someone in financial trouble and he took good care of his parents.

So doing something right does not lend justification for doing something wrong. This thought borders on serious inmate argument material. For a career felon doing a little good basically justifies doing something bad; it is like they think their modest contribution to helping one person validates ripping off someone else.

It was the likeable side of Morgan that I was remembering when he offered me that job in San Diego as his right-hand man. It seemed like such an excellent opportunity; escaping the surfer drug culture for an exciting career in commercial aviation. I was not going to work for a stranger, Morgan had been my friend, in fact, I had a bit of a father thing going on about him. He encouraged it by saying he wished he had a son like me. Only now did I realize how much he was into manipulating me. This was made easier because my real father died two weeks before Morgan offered me the job.

My father was living near Big Bear Lake in the mountains above San Bernardino with his second wife. She was only six or seven years older than me and my father seemed as happy as he had ever been, which isn't saying much as I had seldom seen him smile or heard him laugh during my childhood. Then the doctor told him that he had ALS (Amyotrophic Lateral Sclerosis). I visited him once a month, then he abruptly died at the age of Fifty-Two.

Losing my father got me to thinking about my own life in a big way. I was thirty-two years old and going nowhere. Sure, I was enrolled in college, but I was not degree oriented. I was just passing time while trying to figure out what to do with the rest of my life. Living in a truck in La Jolla, working in a surf shop and spending most of my time stoned was not exactly a long-range life-enhancing career plan. I was going nowhere and knew it. Losing my dad was like a jolt from an electric cattle prod. Therefore, Morgan calling with an incredible career opportunity in aviation seemed like the perfect answer to my problems. My dad had been a pilot and I was sure he would have been proud of me getting into the world of commercial aviation.

Sitting in the dark of my room in the honor dorm, I remember the friendly eager look on Morgan's face when he began his list of promised bonuses; a commercial, multi-engine instrument license, my own plane, a fat salary and one-day Executive Vice-President of Morgan Aviation Incorporated. Such big promises to recruit a sales person out of a minimum wage job at a surf shop. Did he really have to make the dreams seem so big when his real motivation was to recruit a pilot to fly drugs from South America?

After Morgan revealed his true intentions for me, he softened his attitude and shared how he slipped into the smuggler's world. Maybe he was trying to justify what he was about to do to me.. After his divorce settlement, he lost control of his multimillion-dollar aviation company. The expensive toys went back to the bank and the playboy millionaire wound up broke. Angry at life and not willing to try to build it all over again from scratch, he began smuggling tropical fish and lobsters out of Central America into the United States. Soon he discovered bigger profits smuggling exotic South American animals, which he sold to zoos, wild animal parks and to private hunting clubs. Flying drugs was just the final step of the smuggler's dance for Morgan. He had found the solution to his financial problem, but now needed pilots to get into the big money. He began with two of his sons, followed by Stretch and then me. He was building an empire of immoral fools.

Yet what actually set me up for Morgan's manipulations in San Diego in the first place? Well I was broke with no other viable opportunities, which was specifically because of my addiction to marijuana.

Therefore, my drug dependence superseded my previously constant desire to succeed in life. Whoa, that is heavy! I think to myself. *My need for regular marijuana stupefaction had been actively determining my direction and focus in life. I was hanging out with losers, which in an odd way justified my daily goal to get high. In our demented world, getting stoned was okay, which meant they were okay, therefore I was okay and drugs were okay. Weird! I was really messed up.*

It is somewhat amazing to be pondering my period of marijuana addiction with a now clear mind that truly wants to understand why I had allowed all of this to happen to me. I did not just become a doper; I fully embraced it.

I think of my EOD career that I loved yet threw away and wonder how I could have been so foolish. There was a prime motivator working against me back then, the anger I felt at my failure to earn a commission as a naval officer. Yet now that I think about it, I truly did not deserve that commission. My Commanding Officer was right; I was very immature living in my truck with a constant surf priority and my marijuana use fully disqualified me from holding any position of authority. This is particularly true in a profession where lives were on the line and my men had to rely upon me to make sensible decisions regarding their welfare. It is hard to imagine that I was getting stoned when I could be called upon at any time, night or day, to disarm a bomb or even safe a nuclear weapon. Oh how foolish I was and yes, my court martial was fully deserved.

From the men about me in prison, I have learned that addiction cuts across all social, educational and age levels. It can bring anyone down who thinks it is okay to experiment with addictive chemicals. Which brings in another reason why I am here, the word ego keeps stomping through my mind.

Throughout most of my teenage and early adult life, I have had a heavy dose of confidence that has prompted me to think that I was right even when I was completely wrong. I could always find an excuse to defend my erroneous position. When I went to prison all of my excuses dried up...reality check in a big way.

There was another motivation I had not really faced yet and it was high time to do so—greed. I hooked up with Morgan because I wanted the easy buck. Why work for it when all I had to do was suppress my moral character in favor of Morgan's manipulations? That was completely my own fault made more palatable because of my marijuana addiction. Therefore, Stephen, you sold yourself. Yuck! I had prostituted all that was good in me for money. How had I gotten so shallow? Again it comes full circle right back to drugs. In the midst of my drug addiction, I would always contend that I was fully in-control. I was fighting with myself, arguing against moral limitations and in the end I lost.

I now understand that there are many kinds of addiction. The person on their deathbed with lung cancer begging for just one more cigarette. The alcoholic whose unquenchable thirst leaves them sleeping in alleys. The obese person who cannot satisfy their hunger as food becomes their constant obsession. The sexually addicted who prostitute their bodies, yet never find love or satisfaction. The workaholic who over strives to provide for their family but leaves them bankrupt in the coin of love. The person whose ego demands that they have the very best of everything even when their debt is untenable. The thin individual who sees a fat person in the mirror so purposefully throws-up the nourishment that would sustain them. Yet we wonder why the suicide rate is so very high in the United States, particularly amongst the young. Child and spousal abuse have soared alongside the astronomic increase of drug use in America. Is there any wonder that over half of all marriages in the USA, the land of dreams, wind up in separation and divorce?

So what is the answer? Jesus says it straight, pure and simple, "Drink of my water and you will never thirst again." With Jesus, I have found peace, love, understanding, forgiveness and an answer for my addictions. Some argue that it cannot be that simple, yet it is...though the striving towards Christian values and morals part is a never-ending task. Yes, I judge myself every morning and every evening and always, I am found short, yet I am also still loved. So each day I try a little harder, three steps forward and two steps back, but all that truly counts is that my eyes are upon Him as I constantly renew my daily effort to be better than the day before.

With time, we find that not only can we help ourselves, but we can begin to help others. That meaningful purpose gives us the added strength to go on; three steps forward...two steps back. The human condition of trial and error imposed upon us ever since the admission of original sin.

In my room, I turn on the light chasing away the darkness and open the Bible as I prepare for rest. I think that this is a good evening to read Ecclesiastes. I enjoy reading the words of King Solomon, the richest and most intelligent king of all Israel. What advice does he give us after he sampled all the pleasures of the known world? That all of our efforts are like striving after the wind, that at the end of the day what gives pleasure is to know that we have done a good job and to take satisfaction in the pleasure of it.

If I consider prison as an important, necessary step along the path of my development then it becomes an opportunity for growth instead of merely the punishment for which it was designed. Perspective is everything. If I can accept my incarceration as a necessity, could I then take an even bigger leap of faith and believe that it could in fact be a gift of no small magnitude? Prison has already taught me that all problems in life come wrapped in a blessing. Hardship can drive us to our knees, yet it is difficult to stumble once you are on your knees. To be humbled prepares the heart and soul to be more accepting and more forgiving. To forgive un-hardens the heart and frees us from negative emotional baggage.

So whose fault is it that I am here? It is my own fault, not Morgan's. He did not corrupt me...I was an eager participant in his manipulations because I was already corrupt. Honestly knowing what is wrong with me, I can now ask God to take away my sins and for the Holy Spirit to wash away the corruption I have harbored for so long inside me through self-deceit and finally I can ask Jesus to give me a heart of love instead one of stone. Before I can be freed of a sin, I must first take ownership; acknowledging that the sin is mine, that I have foolishly allowed it into my life and only by the grace of God can it be taken away. I did not earn that grace and there is nothing I can do to amend the wrong, but to ask for forgiveness. Thus is the perfect love of God for His flawed creations (the flaws self-imposed).

I close the Bible, reach up and turn off the light, quietly say a short prayer and then thinking of myself as a traveler in the way station of prison, I wonder where the outbound bus will take me.

"The Bible is alive, it speaks to me; it has feet, it runs after me; it has hands, it lays hold of me," Martin Luther

Photo Greetz Kristof
B-1 Bomber in supersonic configuration

"Courage is the ladder on which all the other virtues mount,"
Clare Booth Luce

Chapter 38

BORON PRISON CAMP, AUGUST 29, 1984

ND OF August and it is blazing hot in the high desert. Luckily, this afternoon we are attending a first aid class in the education building which at least has a working swamp cooler. We have lost one of our veteran inmates to an early release and are breaking in a new guy. The class is on the verge of getting seriously boring when abruptly the guard's radio squawks loudly, "Fire crew, respond code three, a large jet aircraft has crashed approximately six miles east of the camp:" We run for our vehicles.

Climbing up into the cab of the Ford fire truck, I pause for an instant to stare at a towering cloud of thick black smoke billowing into the pale blue sky on the Eastern horizon. I am hoping it is not one of the giant B-52 flying fortresses. The massive bomber carries a multitude of explosive hazards including ejection seats with explosive bolts and small rocket motors, shape charges to blow away emergency hatches and sometimes the B-52's carry cruise missiles under their wings. Even the aircraft's sophisticated metal parts can be a serious hazard; some metal alloys when burning emit highly toxic gases and if we put water on the flaming metal, it could violently explode raining molten metal on the unwary.

There is no doubt in my mind that we are about to face an extremely dangerous situation that would tax the abilities of a highly trained and well-equipped fire department. We are just an inmate fire crew, completely ignorant of the sophisticated techniques employed on high-tech military aircraft. Our fire truck are cast-offs from other departments and we are outfitted with mostly worn-out vintage equipment. "Yet, we are highly motivated and willing to take a higher level of risk," I think to myself reaching for the ignition key. The big engine roars to life, I rev the engine to two thousand RPM; switch on the radios then hit the red light and siren. The high low wail of the siren precedes the fire truck out of the parking lot. Double clutching I jam the shift lever into second even as a tracer of doubt flashes through my mind. I realize that if we are not really careful an inmate fireman could die today. I think about the new guy and realize that I better keep a tight rein on the men...ignorance combined with over enthusiasm could put the whole crew into a seriously tight spot. I momentarily think of McNair's brutal but firm teaching techniques and mentally thank him.

The firehouse pickup truck with a small water pumper in its back bed leads the way down the narrow road at forty miles an hour. I am right on its tail with the big fire truck, which is a mistake as I realize the pickup has lured me to go too fast. I see the dormitories whipping past my window and a group of inmates quickly stepping back from the roadway then they stare in alarm. I pump the brakes in anticipation of downshifting. Ahead the pickup slows and turns sharply by the chow hall. I try to downshift, but cannot get the transmission to drop into a lower gear. I pump the brakes harder nervous that they might lockup and throw the big rig into a skid. The heavy fire truck sways right then left, the turn is going to be a near thing. The firemen on the back lean outward and to the right in worried anticipation of a high-speed turn that could flip the fire truck. At the last moment, I give up on the turn and plow straight ahead onto a curving driveway that leads to the control-building parking lot and a bank of inmate telephones. On the narrow tarmac surprised inmates scatter from the path of the hurling truck, this is usually a walkway with only an occasional camp vehicle on it patrolling at slow speed. I ride the brakes slowing the heavy machine as the control building begins to fill the windshield. I desperately pull back on the shift lever and finally feel it slip into second gear then quickly pop the clutch while stomping harder on the brakes. The engine roars as it takes the load, but it is enough as the heavy truck's bumper comes to a stop ten feet from the large pane glass window of the control building—much to the relief of the wide-eyed guard inside. Backing the truck rapidly, running over two metal trashcans in the process, I turn toward the open gate and floor the gas pedal; gravel flies from the back tires spraying several inmates who have taken shelter behind the bank of telephones. I will hear about it later from one of them in the chow hall. The guard in the control building wasn't thrilled either. I drive over a curb onto the main road and pass under the raised gate. The pickup truck is a quarter of a mile down the road and accelerating. In the rear view mirror, I see a four-wheel drive carryall fall in behind us. Pegging the rpm in third gear, I shift to fourth, only then do I have a free hand to radio the San Bernardino Command Center to advise them that we are rolling, "Command, this is Engine Company 52 responding code three to a downed aircraft of unknown origin. Be advised we are heading for a thick column of black smoke rising into the sky six miles east of Boron Prison Camp in open desert terrain. Engine Company 52 urgently requests multiple engine and helicopter backup."

"Roger 52 advise possible size and type of aircraft."

Downshifting for a stop sign and moderately braking before accelerating onto the main highway forces me to speak in a rapid stutter. "The smoke column has reached one thousand feet and it is still climbing. Judging by the size of the cloud that has already formed I believe it has to be a very large military aircraft, potentially a B-52 bomber with possible explosives and weapons on board."

"52 did you say B-52 bomber?" asks a stunned voice.

"Roger, but we don't actually know what we're responding to, but it is big, real big. Call Edward's Air Force Base and see if they are missing anything large and if so if there are weapons aboard."

"Roger, Engine Company 52 keep us closely posted on your progress."

On the Boron radio, I hear that our prison camp ambulance is rolling which is a first.

The squelch on the radio hisses loudly as the call goes out, "All engine companies, all engine companies, we have a major situation involving a possible downed military aircraft potentially with explosives and military weapons involvement, this is a three alarm response, companies 24 and 18 respond with all engines to assist 52 currently northbound on highway 395 in the vicinity of Boron Prison Camp. I repeat that a possible large military aircraft is down that explosives and weapons hazards may be involved. San Bernardino Aviation Unit, scramble rescue chopper 3 and put 4 in standby. All other engine companies are ordered to standby."

In the cab, my heart races with the intensity of action that the radio call is demanding. This is huge. I imagine the other firehouses, boots running, men yelling, fire trucks rolling out of bays, sirens wailing and we inmates are the very leading edge of this massive response. We will be first on the scene; I press the gas pedal down and pray.

A mile down the desert highway I see a dust cloud where the pickup truck has turned onto a dirt firebreak. I take my foot off the gas pedal, downshift to third and then shift down to second gear before accelerating into the turn. The back of the fire truck fishtails wildly before it regains traction throwing a broad swath of dirt and gravel. I hear the men on the back holler in excitement. Back there it must be like riding a bucking bronco. I shift into third but keep the rpm down. The firebreak is not well maintained. There are cuts and potholes in the narrow dirt track. I am weaving continuously trying to avoid the bigger holes. The carryall is riding in the thick dust cloud trailing my fire truck, which is probably why he does not see a large deep hole in the middle of the firebreak. The carryall hits the hole solidly. In my side mirror, I see it weaving sharply from side to side then it slows to a stop. It will not be until later that I learn the battery broke free and slammed against the hot engine breaking the radiator fan. I follow the spreading dust cloud of the pickup truck ahead of me. The two men I have left behind are prison staff who has never rolled with us before so I do not feel that they will be missed by us now. We have our obligatory staff escort as the Safety Officer is riding in the pickup truck.

I am continuously changing gears, downshifting for shallow ravines and accelerating up small hills. The guys on the back are really having a rough time of it. Through the side mirror, I see one of the side compartments spring open and all its contents are dumping on to the dirt road. A fire extinguisher goes bouncing off into the desert scrubs leaving little clouds of dust with each of its multiple impacts. I do not like losing any of our equipment but do not dare stop for fear of getting stuck or losing valuable time. While driving, I am operating two radios, one to direct other emergency vehicles to the scene and on the other keeping the camp advised of our progress and location.

Three miles into the firebreak the pickup truck swings left into the open desert terrain following a more direct line toward the towering smoke column, which is definitely getting much bigger. I follow employing skills learned in the Navy operating four-wheel drive vehicles on sand beaches and on rough jungle roads. I keep remembering that this big truck was meant for highways, not off-road conditions. Ahead of us, the pickup mows down a large sagebrush, which hid a sharp angled berg. The truck launches off the berm, the right-side tires partially leave the ground. It crashes heavily back onto its right side then slams into a thick clump of desert shrubbery. It continues fifty feet plowing up plants and knocking over cactus before rolling slowly to a stop in a cloud of dust. Two rattled firemen and the Safety Officer climb awkwardly out of the cab and jump onto the big Ford as I slow to pick them up. The heavy fire truck is now crowded with bodies.

In the near distance, I see a jet fighter circling the huge black plume of smoke. *We have to make it,* I think to myself and now it is all riding on this last vehicle. Lives could be lost if we fail to get to the accident site quickly. I am praying that I will not fail by getting stuck in the soft sand or in one of the shallow ravines. When the rough terrain gets even worse, I send Henry running ahead to help pick a clear path. Having a running fireman looking for obstacles means I have a couple of extra seconds warning to pick the best path through the rough terrain. I am using our heavy bumper to knock down taller shrubs so I can see a little further ahead. Soon Henry is visibly lagging in his heavy fire fighter trousers and heavy steel-toed rubber boots. I honk my horn and beckon him to jump back onto the truck as I drive past. Another fireman strips off his heavy jacket and leaps off the back of the truck to take his place, running against time, running to save the lives that might hang in the balance of our timely arrival.

We come to a flat area and I hit the horn to call the running fireman back aboard. I pick up speed and go for third then abruptly see the gully. It is a wide drop off and there is no way around it. I can see that the other side is a soft upward slope about two to three feet tall. I glance left and then quickly right. The gully runs too far to attempt going around it. I am committed to a split second decision. "Just go for it," urges the Safety Officer.

I have already downshifted to second, I let the rpm drop off as the front tires go over the edge. The front tires collapse the gully's rim then the front of the truck noses down a couple of feet. I feel the fire truck's under carriage scooping more dirt from the rim then the rear twin tires drop down, spinning for a moment in the soft sand before our forward momentum carries us onward. I keep the front tires as straight as possible, but we still slide side to side depending on the traction under the rear twin tires. The gully is only about fifty feet wide and I still have momentum as the front tires hit the opposite rim. I give her just a little gas not wanting the rear tires to spin out. We are down to about three mph as we slowly climb up and over the rim then I increase the throttle, but keep the speed down as we weave between two boulders, ease up over a slight

rise and suddenly the accident site is spread out before us. When we
are only five or six hundred yards from the burning wreckage when
two Air Force helicopters suddenly pass directly over us. We had no
clue they were coming until they are right on top of us, the heavy
thump of their rotors are clearly audible inside the cab. Through
the dusty windshield, I see a large fiercely burning fire with thick
rolling clouds of black smoke to our left; just ahead, there is a glint
of reflected light splashing off a shiny silver capsule. The main fire is
spreading outwards in all directions, but it is moving fastest towards
the silver capsule driven by a light wind...I accelerate the last fifty
yards then break and turn left arriving parallel to the door of the
capsule spraying a fan of dirt and sand. The helicopters circle once
to check the site then quickly settle to the ground creating twin
clouds of swirling dust about fifty yards to our right. From close up
the capsule is rather large considering what it is. I recognize it; it is
an ejection pod from America's most advanced stealth airplane. I
read about this unique ejection pod in a flying magazine. There is
only one aircraft in the world where the whole crew of three ejects
in a single pod—the B-1 Bomber. This is just the second proto-type
of this futuristic stealth design. An inmate fire crew, the absolute
bottom of the drawer for emergency response teams, is first on the
scene at the crash site of America's newest super-secret weapon...
the stealth bomber. This is way beyond my wildest expectations. I
can only imagine what high-tech hazards face us and I have spent
years on aircraft carriers walking under the wings of state-of-the-art
military aircraft checking their ordnance loads. *Well,* I think to
myself, *right now it is just a bunch of burning high-tech wreckage and our
job is to save lives.*

The capsule has come down about three to four hundred feet
from the actual crash site. The spreading fire is right on the verge
of engulfing the escape pod. The desert brush at one end of the
capsule is burning loudly radiating waves of intense heat fanned by
the wind. Two parachutes, one lying in the dirt the other draped
over the side of the pod, are beginning to smolder. The men inside
could be roasted alive by the wind-driven surging heat preceding

the wall of fire. I yell at Henry to get water on the leading edge of the fire then send our new guy to help him with a shovel. Our limited water must be used sparingly. The Safety Officer and our other firemen pry open the hatch along with the Air Force crewmen who are arriving from the helicopters. Three bodies are pulled from the ejection pod. Unfortunately, the pilot is already dead, but two other badly injured air crewmen are quickly carried to safety.

Later we would learn that the plane had been transferring fuel at very low altitude, about three hundred feet above the ground. The fuel transfer and low speed put it into an abrupt stall. They ejected so low that one of the three canopies did not have time to open, the pod's nose crashed sharply into the ground. The pilot was immediately killed from crush injury.

I leave the Safety Officer and one fireman to help attend to the injured men. There is a major fire raging where what remains of this super high-tech aircraft. An area the size of a football field is burning fiercely. The blackened metal wings of the aircraft are a crumpled mass of broken and semi-molten metal awash in angry red flames that are erupting forty feet into the air fed by tons of jet fuel. The aircraft's huge tires are burning furiously, spewing heavy clouds of thick undulating black smoke. We quickly suppress the worst of the flames with foam, but there is no way we are going to be able to put this fire out. We only have the one five gallon can of fifties vintage foam and a limited amount of water. We stay downwind (East) of the burning metal alloys only long enough to increase the width of our fire line so it cannot again threaten the escape pod or helicopters where the injured crew is being treated. We are fortunate that the sparse desert shrubbery makes the fire more manageable. I send all but one fireman to the North side of the crash site with shovels to contain the fire from that front, then, carefully rationing our water, drown out the hot spots on the South side. The wind blowing from the West is keeping the fire from extending in that direction. Once the fire consumes the remainder of the jet fuel and flammable parts it will mostly burn itself out. I do not doubt that the Air Force would like this fire out as soon as possible, but there is nothing more that we can do.

When it is obvious that we have the main fire under control and the last of the brush fire is burning itself out, I climb up into the cab and pick up the microphone, "San Bernardino Command, this is Engine 52, the aircraft fire is under control, I repeat the fire is under control. I have one dead air crewman on the scene and two major traumas being evacuated by military helicopters."

Multiple dust clouds are erupting all around us as more and more military helicopters settle to the ground amidst spreading clouds of swirling dust. Counting the two that already arrived there are at least a dozen choppers on this small piece of desert. The accident site is beginning to look like a Vietnam airhead as several security teams, running with rifles at the ready, dash from the landing choppers to set up a protective perimeter at the outskirts of the crash site.

"Engine 52," the radio blares, "advise aircraft type."

I hesitated momentarily holding back this piece of key information then say, "Aircraft type B-1 bomber."

There is a pregnant pause, and then in plain English I hear the radioman's excited voice, "Did you say it is the B-1 bomber?"

"Roger, some of it is still burning, but the fire is contained."

"Command acknowledges aircraft type B-1. Be advised that Engines 24 and 18 are thirty minutes ETA (Estimated Time of Arrival) your location. Do you still require backup and air support?"

Through the windshield of the fire truck, I see dust clouds from many land vehicles heading for the scene. A big yellow crash truck comes in from downwind and begins to spray a heavy stream of white foam onto the smoldering wreckage with its top-mounted water cannon.

"That is a negative command," relief is flooding through me... we did it. Our job is done, "Be advised that multiple Air Force emergency vehicles are arriving on the scene and that the fire is now out. Cancel 52's request for air support and backup."

The inmate firemen, carrying their shovels over their shoulders, return in ones and twos to the sparse shade of the fire truck, their blackened faces are creased with white smiles of satisfaction. I look at the tank's water gauge, which is a tick below empty. I shut down the temperamental pump while Eric winds in the rubber attack hose and Henry re-lays the two-and-a-half-inch hose in its bed on the back of the truck. Another chopper settles about sixty feet away. The blast from its rotors blows stinging sand into our faces. As I rub sand from my eyes, I see a man step down from the skids. He is an Air Force officer wearing a forty-five automatic on his hip as he walks self-importantly up to our fire truck. He stops to look at the fire truck's door insignia. His lips move as he reads out loud, "Boron Prison Camp, Engine Company 52." Stunned he looks at me, "You guys are inmates!"

"That's right, "I answer proudly, "Engine Company 52 at your service."

His hand rests on his pistol. It is something an inmate would not miss. "This site is classified top secret," he orders, "inmates can't be here."

"If we inmates weren't here you'd still have a nasty fire to deal with, sir, and maybe a few burned crewmen from your B-1," I say stating the obvious.

"What makes you think it is the B-1?" the young officer is alarmed.

Are we playing guessing games? I wonder, "Come on, it's the only plane that has an ejection pod."

"Well pretend you don't know that it's the B-1 okay? This is to be kept totally under wraps and that is directly from the White house and the Joint Chief of Staff as of," he glances at his watch, "fifteen minutes ago."

I had forgotten how precise the military likes to be. *Well I have got something he can throw into his report.* "Ah…I am afraid it's not exactly under wraps anymore," I hold up the microphone. "San Bernardino Command requested aircraft type…I told them B-1 Bomber. It is critical information for our fire response, total potential victim analysis and unit coordination."

"Well this is not a civilian operation," he barks

"Not anymore," I agree. I realize that he is not going to thank us. This is amazing. Inmates are used to not having anything coming, but this is huge. We just helped save the lives of two of their men, but are any of these military types paying attention? I look at my guys who have mixed expressions. They are waiting for someone to say something in recognition of a job well done.

The officer snarls, "It is a good thing you're already inmates or your careers would be over."

"Careers? What careers?" Henry heatedly joins the conversation, "we're inmates, this is not exactly our livelihood."

"What do you want us to do?" I ask cutting to the chase.

"I want you out of here," he looks around at all the activity then removes his hat wiping sweat from his brow, and then putting his hand back onto to his pistol adds, "like now."

"Okay 52, load up." I shake my head so just maybe the Air Force officer will realize he is being a complete jerk, but he is too caught up into his John Wayne thing.

For a moment no one moves.

"Hey guys," I smile, "great job, let's take it home."

Following our tracks back out I am surprised at the number of Air Force vehicles that had accidents of their own while rushing to the crash site. The desert is littered with a half dozen vehicles some of them skewed into ditches, others with their tires dug into the soft sand. Actually, I am not surprised after all, we lost three of our four responding vehicles. It was a rough trip. The sides of the gully have been flattened out by numerous large tires. I expect that over the next couple of days our rough route will become a well-used road.

When we hit the paved highway, I see that both sides of the tarmac are lined with numerous press vehicles. I learn later that they had monitored my radio calls. Within minutes of which San Bernardino command was receiving inquiries, some from as far away as New York City, asking them to confirm that it was indeed a B-1 Bomber that had crashed in the desert.

Back at the camp the word quickly spreads that not only were we inmates the first ones on the scene, but that we also broke the news story. We found ourselves very popular with the inmates, but unfortunately, the prison staff did not see us as quite the popular heroes. It did not help that I talked with a reporter on the telephone who contacted me through my attorney. I was kind of hoping that the reporter might want to write something good about us, but he was not interested in inmate good deeds and I would not give up any details on the crash. I wanted to talk about the wild ride across open desert and share how inmate firemen were regularly risking their lives in the desert to help others. The reporter wanted to know what was now classified information so after a couple of minutes of non-communication I hung up the phone. Barely ten minutes after leaving the telephone bank I was called to the Unit Manager's office. All inmate telephone calls are monitored and recorded.

I knock at the Unit Manager's door then warily step inside.

"Why were you talking with the press idiot?" he asks with grim satisfaction.

Instantly, I realize the magnitude of my mistake, which has placed me squarely back under the control of the Unit Manager. There is not anything I can say that is going to make a difference with this man, not that he gives me a chance. "Well I got news for you inmate you're off the fire crew."

"But..."

"Shut up!" He yells leaping up from behind his desk. He stomps right up to me then poking a very irritating finger into my chest yells, "Get your butt up the hill and report to the plumbing shop supervisor now!" I feel his spittle spraying into my face. I want to hit him; instead, I turn my back to the man and walk out the door.

Walking angrily up the hill, I feel my emotions turn to burning frustration. I have not broken any rules, nor did I give out any classified information...not that I had any obligation not to do so... but I did give someone who hates me the leverage he needed for personal revenge. My frustration centers on my not thinking the situation through better in the first place. I can be angry at the Unit Manager, but the fault is my own; I should have known better. Being in a prison camp with its somewhat more relaxed atmosphere has taken some of the edge off of my inmate survival instinct.

The plumbing shop is just below the top of the hill. Apparently, to make sure he knows right where I am at the Unit Manager has me assigned to the tool bin. The inmate I am replacing is ecstatic. "You're going to hate this job," he states happily. "It really sucks." On the wall of the tool bin there is a sign listing the rules for issuing tools. Someone has crudely lettered their own set of rules on the bottom: *#1 Inmates have nothing coming. #2 For all other situations refer to rule one.*

There is something I intend to share with young people when I get out of prison regarding choices. No one likes to be told what to do, particularly not teenagers and young adults. Yet when one forfeits his or her freedom because of bad choices they are sentencing themselves to continuous detailed instruction from motivated, but not particularly well educated prison staff. They will be told when to eat and when to sleep. They will be ordered to stand with their face to the wall for long periods and to walk within painted lines. They will have to learn to tolerate shouted abuse and not respond when insulted, demeaned, hit or clubbed. When you forfeit your freedom, you sacrifice a lot more than the average young person ever takes into consideration when pondering unlawful behavior. This point had been particularly well proven during my early days in Jail Unit 3. I will never forget that night almost two years ago.

It is dark outside my cell window as I lie hopefully upon my bunk in J-3. My cellmate was transferred out to general population this morning and now its evening without a replacement. If I am lucky, they will not assign another inmate to my cell until tomorrow morning. An evening alone in the cell would be incredibly good. I have not been actually alone since my arrest. It gets to you, being constantly surrounded by criminal nut cases who are avidly interested in your every move—like if they did not pay close attention, they might miss an opportunity at harassment or exploitation.

It is a half hour before lockdown when the guard opens the cell door, "Hey Arrington, I got a new bunky for you." He is laughing, yet his posture shows that he is wary of who is standing just out of sight. Instantly attentive, I sit up on the bunk wondering who or what is going to come through that door.

"Inside," the guard orders the unseen person. I notice he has one hand wrapped around his nightstick. This is not good. His fingers are white from clutching the stick so firmly—the hack is scared. I hold my breath. A criminal is about to walk through that heavy metal door and this felon is going to heavily influence my peace or lack of it for the unforeseen future. *Terrific,* I think to myself, *I just hope he is not a gang banger.* Gang bangers attract trouble like rotten food attracts flies and maggots. The inmate who is going to share my cell turns out to be my worst nightmare.

A brute of a man stalks into the cell. The visibly relieved guard instantly slams and locks the door. It is startling to hear the lock thump home. Lockdown is not for another half hour; the guard is definitely scared of this man—and now so am I!

The huge thug dwarfs the cell; he is like a rhino looking for trouble. He sniffs at the stuffy air, snorts his dissatisfaction then notices me and glares. "Swore I'd never wind up in a damn prison cell," he curses, "never should have let them take Bruno alive." He tramps over to the metal locker throws open its door banging it loudly against the wall. He glances at me over his hairy shoulder as if daring me to say something. I set down the letter I have been writing; all thoughts of home, family and friends evaporating in the flush of icy fear that envelopes my heart.

Bruno jams his few possessions into the locker then kicks the door closed. He turns aggressively, an angry rhino looking to trample and maul something. "They set me up with that stupid lie detector test," he rages. "Wasn't my fault the old lady died. The jerks acted like I killed her on purpose." Bruno abruptly growls and swings a meaty fist into the concrete wall. He hits it twice in rapid succession. Suddenly there is not enough air in the cell to fill my lungs, "You killed a woman?"

Bruno turns away from the wall, glares at me and shrugs his massive shoulders, "Yeah, some old broad who had been flirting with me. I wouldn't have been interested but I was drunk and she was asking for it." He stomps two steps to my bunk and leans heavily on it, his foul breath washes over me as he grumbles, "Was on a cruise ship where I worked as a mechanic and that makes it a bloody federal offense."

"But why did you kill her?" I am working hard to contain the panic that wants to rise up from my gut, trying to hide my fear, which desperately wants to dance out of reach of this maniac.

Bruno's anger flares as he begins passionately arguing for his self-supposed innocence, "Damn it man the old broad was asking for it, wasn't my fault. Hell, I was so drunk I didn't even know I was pounding dead meat!"

Pounding dead meat? His words explode in my mind. *What was he doing to her?* Listening to him telling his macabre story and hearing the way he absolves himself of any blame, or of even simple compassion, convinces me that Bruno is a full-blown lunatic. I feel the hair on the back of my neck standing on end. *I am locked in a cell with a homicidal maniac.*

Bruno's face reddens as his anger abruptly peaks, his eyes widen and his nostrils flare. He is about to go off. I am getting ready to leap from the bunk, but then he suddenly spins around and slams a meaty fist into the wall again—once, twice, three times! It happens so fast. He stops and stares at the torn flesh on his thick knuckles then licks at the blood. He spits red saliva onto the floor then growls and slams the wall three more times, a left jab, right cross and then steps in with a left hook swinging his chunky hip into it. I recognize the technique it is a basic boxing combination. I am locked in a cell with a massive mad man and he is a trained fighter!

"I am going to get them," Bruno the boxer rages, "I am going to waste somebody."

I stare at the downward spreading red stain where his fist impacted against the cider block wall. The blood is vivid red against the white wall I had cleaned months earlier. Finally, he sits down on the lower bunk and grumbles. It is a deep rumbling sound coming out of his massive chest, a rabid rhino wanting to rip something apart. I am absolutely silent and unmoving upon my bunk. I have no idea who "them" was that Bruno is going to get, but knew there is not a chance of my falling asleep tonight with Bruno, the insane murderer, in my cell. Sitting upright on my mattress, I am so glad to have chosen an upper bunk.

All night long Bruno tosses and turns on his mattress occasionally talking in his sleep. It is the first time I have heard someone cursing in their sleep. I listen to him snoring loudly becoming instantly ill at ease every time the snoring stops afraid that he might awaken. I pass a very long night locked in a small cell with the most violent person I have ever encountered.

The next morning when the guard opens the door, I am immediately out of that cell. "There's no way I am going back in there with that lunatic, he is nuts."

"No problem," the guard, who came on last shift, casually grins, "you're right about him being a lunatic. He is supposed to be upstairs in the nut ward doing the Thorazine shuffle, but the watch commander accidentally routed him to J-3. It was just a mistake."

"Just a mistake!" I am livid, "That mistake could have gotten me killed!"

The guard laughs grimly, "Count yourself lucky that big guy didn't take a fancy to you."

I do not appreciate his joke. "It is not funny," I snarl.

The guard's attitude changes in an instant...inmate conditioning. "Hey shut up," he yells in his thick Bronx accent.

"Shut up?" I shout back feeling confrontational. I did not really mean to say it that way, it just slipped out.

"Yeah, that's what I said, shut up!" He bellows taking a step closer to me with one hand slipping down to his nightstick.

I glare at him trying to make a conscious effort to swallow my anger because I am heading for big trouble and know it. This is not the man who locked Bruno into my cell. I am just so stressed out having been up all night listening to the monster on the bunk below panting.

"One more word, inmate, and I will throw you in the hole," he shoves me against the wall, "you got that, dirt wad?"

I nod…that is all he is going to get, but I know I am being foolish; inmates do not win ego contests with hacks.

"Get in the cell." It is such a short, demeaning order and the guard revels in my submission as I stalk angrily across the threshold. He slams the heavy door shut purposefully waking Bruno. From the other side of the metal door he shouts, "You can explain to your bunky why breakfast is going to be a little late for you guys."

"What's the hack shouting about?" growls Bruno. Great, he wakes up in a foul mood.

"I was arguing with the hack." I did not know what else to say and it is the first thing that comes to mind.

"Yeah, give em hell." Apparently, Bruno approves. "Wake me if that breakfast thing changes," he rolls over and faces the wall apparently going right back to sleep.

Two guards come for Bruno before the watch change at 8:00 a.m. Breakfast is not an option for him. Apparently, the staff does not want an upset Bruno around the rest of the inmates where there might be the risk of violence…a one-man stampede more like it.

I try to clean the blood smears from the cinderblock wall, but they will not completely wash away. The stain of Bruno is persistent on the wall and in my mind, where it leaves another type of scar that would last much longer than any simple stain. *Yeah, when you sacrifice your freedom you forfeit a lot more than one would ever suspect.*

In the Boron plumbing shop, the days seem longer while I whittle away the hours in my dusty cage. The tool bin is a wire cage inside a steel building that gets roasting hot under the desert sun. The rusty wire mesh cage is about the same size as a prison cell only not as tall. The low wire ceiling is hugely depressing. The wire mesh top is only a foot above my head. Motivation is hard to find as I stare at the old tools about me. The worst part is occasionally hearing the fire siren wail and being locked in this stupid pen. My frustration is made worse because the Unit Manager has replaced most of the crew. The official reason for removing me is that I am a too high profile inmate, the celebrity thing working against me again. He also pulls our cardiovascular surgeon because he felt there is too much liability having an inmate doctor helping people. Henry has been released to a halfway house. The new chief engineer is not picked by the crew. The Unit Manager assigns his inmate clerk to that position. Someone writes *I Spy* on his helmet. Morale is low amongst the fire crew and training is non-existent.

The next few months seem to crawl by; time passes ever so slowly in my cage. Fortunately, I am still living in the honor dorm because I have not broken any rules. The last two veteran firemen are desperate to have me back. The new chief engineer is not mechanically inclined and cannot seem to figure out how to prime the pump even though he has been shown repeatedly by the Safety Officer. During an emergency, he tends to panic. Without effective leadership, the crew is falling apart. After all they are an inmate crew… it is not like they are training for a career as firemen. The biggest concern of the men is not advancement in a fire department—it is about getting out of this prison as soon as possible.

My main contribution to the team was my enthusiasm and intense desire to do a good job. The men knew they could rely on the equipment because I maintained everything to the best of my abilities. This meant they could push a fire attack with confidence. On their second fire response, the crew lost a motor home because they were too late getting water on the fire. The new chief engineer had difficulty priming the temperamental water pump.

My third Christmas comes and goes uneventfully. I continue my early morning runs and weight routines. Working in the tool bin is my re-enforcement not to get mentally lazy. This may be a camp, but it is still part of the prison system where anything can happen. It is unfortunate for all concerned that inmates are mostly just lumped together. Putting non-violent inmates with extremely violent felons assures severely damaged people…both physically and mentally… upon their release. Merry Christmas America your criminals are coming back, they are going to be leaving prison far angrier than when they went in and now they've got a chip on their shoulder against society.

It is dark thirty as I suddenly wake up on New Year's Eve

morning. My frogman training has conditioned me to fully awake and immediately rise from bed. I hope one day to get over it, but not until prison is in my past. I slip quietly out of the room. The other inmates think I am nuts to always rise so early, yet in prison to be considered mentally off balanced can only work in your favor as people tend to keep a greater distance from you. I am regularly in bed between 7:00 and 8:00 p.m. My early to bed routine means I escape the mindless chatter of the television, which is echoed by the equally monotonous babble of most inmate conversation.

I quietly slip out of the small two-man room carrying a blanket and a mug with a tea bag in it. Like Terminal Island at Boron, we are allowed one five-pound Christmas box and as usual, mine is loaded with tea, which drives the guards nuts. All those dried leaves arouse their suspicions. They are rather disappointed that they just find tea leaves. I only get the one chance at a year's supply so must ration it carefully. Stopping at an old banged-up drinking fountain, I place the mug under the hot water spigot and push down on the bent rusty handle. For several seconds it coughs and gurgles then sputters before finally spitting up a weak trickle of tepid water. I enjoy listening to the old fountain going through its liquid labors and the tepid water is far better than no warm water at all. A wire-covered night light is about fifteen feet away; by its dim glow, I admire the cup in my hand. I made it in the camp pottery shop. I have a whole collection of them. Each is hand-painted; this one has an underwater scene. A sunken sailing ship lies on a submerged reef, its tattered sails flutter in the current while long-leafed seaweed drifts about the hull. There are sharks and fish along with a deep-sea diver stomping across the bottom with a treasure box in his arms. His air hose weaves up amongst the ship's broken rigging. I put many hours into each of my cups, something pleasing to remember my quieter times in prison.

I find a clear area to lie down my blanket and then between sips of tea go through my stretching routine. I adopt several yoga postures mentally following the paths of muscles and structure of bones consciously aligning my skeleton while taking the joints through their full range of motion. Throughout I imagine a skyhook connected to a thread pulling at the top of my head. I pretend it is lifting my head upward forcing a stretching and aligning of the spine.

From yoga, I drift to Tai Chi, slow sustained movements seeking the perfect form that allows four ounces of effort to defeat a couple of hundred pounds of aggression. Truly only a Tai Chi master could achieve such a magnificent defense. I would settle for one hundred-sixty-five pounds defeats or outruns enraged inmate. My transition to Gung Fu is purposeful as it begins with a solemn bow of respect to my old Chinese master in honor of what he has taught me. Each karate move must conform to what precedes and to what follows; harmony and physics equally applied seeking perfect balance. I am far from perfect, yet contentedly so. I enjoy moving nearly silently about the large room, the stepping around of chairs and of tables is woven into my improvised kata. Imagined attackers dance with me as I go through my various routines, *Sifu Mui Fa Lock* (plum flowers descending), *buck yuen Tow Toe* (white ape steals the peach), and *Fay an jang* (flying goose palm) a potentially fatal strike. There are many who believe that the Gung Fu iron palm strike is the most powerful focused hand strike in the art of karate.

At 6:00 a.m., I am standing at the outside door wearing a T-shirt, two sweatshirts and a pair of old jeans. It is cold outside, a high desert winter cold that chills to the bone. I hold old leatherwork gloves in one hand and a second half-empty mug of semi-warm tea in the other. It being New Year's Day, I am feeling indulgent... besides it looks really cold out there. Frost covers the upper and lower corners of the door's glass pane. I sip my tepid weak tea and wait for the guard to open the door so I can go lift weights. The weight pile is tucked against a barren hillside behind a dormitory so it should be mostly shielded from the ten-mile per hour wind blowing relentlessly outside, which at the moment looks like it is gusting to fifteen or even twenty mph.

I see a sudden gleam upon the glass, which brightens as the corrections officer approaches. The guard's flashlight swings in pace with his rapid step. The brightness upon the frosted glass comes and goes like the sweeping beacon of brilliance from a light-house. Even in the desert thoughts of the sea often accompany me. As the guard nears the door, the light steadies. The ice crystals gather the concentrated cone of light and scatter it into thousands of mini-specks of radiant color like tiny jewels. I hear the heavy key go into the lock, the snap of the dead bolt unlocking, then the light sweeps away as he heads for the next dormitory.

I step out into the crisp desert darkness filling my lungs deeply. But for the retreating form of the guard, I am alone; gloriously and completely alone and I revel in it. I walk with confidence in the dark knowing the location of the various obstacles, bushes and large rocks until I am blindsided by a bouncing tumbleweed hurling out of the dark.

The weight pile is mostly in darkness but for a dim glow from a security light under the roofline of the nearby dormitory. A thin coat of frost covers the flat-back bench, which I sweep away with my gloved hand. The falling ice crystals tumble downward in a gently glowing ivory arch. I load up the barbell with a couple of wheel weights then lie down on the bench and lift off the heavy bar. The metal is ice cold through the thin worn leather of my gloves, even colder at the palms of my hands where the gloves have two large holes. I have owned the gloves since my last Christmas package at Terminal Island. I try to ignore the cold as part of my mental disci-plining. Quietly I go through my morning routine wondering if indeed I am slightly crazy to be doing this in the bone chilling cold. My first set is a warm up routine as I stare upwards at the vast dark heavens glistening with starlight. It reminds me how incredibly small I am and how unimportant my problems in the vast scheme of life on this planet. I listen to birds rustling and chirping in the bushes as they begin to voice their readiness for the new day. I too am ready and curious for what the day will hold. For the vast majority of inmates, prison is about intense stifling boredom. They complain about it always, yet it is a condition of their own mostly repeating creation. To a man, they want the time to pass more quickly, while

I hope to stretch out every moment. Life beyond circumstance is what we make of it. Our existence is a dynamic, hugely eventful, ever changing, yet consistent repeating series of patterns. We, the choice maker, are the variable, self-determining, always in motion, and learning with each passing day. God blesses us with freedom of choice, yet too often this independence of thought and action is of little use to the average inmate or indeed to many people in general. I recently read an intriguing sentence, "Some people make things happen and some people watch things happen, but most people do not know anything happened at all."

My being on the weight pile in the cold darkness is me expressing my will on my own terms. I am completely in-charge of this moment...lacking the presence of a prison guard or a gang of demented inmates lusting for primal diversion. As the camp slowly awakens, I will lose a portion of this freedom. I will have to sacrifice it to the demands of the prison staff and to the sometimes bizarre social needs of the other inmates about me. Living with criminals puts such a sharp perception upon how the human mind thinks, adapts and tries to enforce its will upon others through various manipulations on many different levels. Criminals are all about self-satisfaction...what will benefit them the most and how to get it with the least possible effort. Sometimes it is almost like there is a greater inmate satisfaction in taking something by force or deception than simply asking to see if it might be willingly shared. A primordial way of thinking, *I take therefore I am better than you.* Inmates relate well to the image of the romantically inclined cave man dragging his club in the dirt in search of a love object. Physical relationships with the criminally bent can only be destructive to all concerned, particularly the children.

On their hopeful path to self-discovery many inquiring men have gone to the ends of the earth...I have come to prison. What amazes me is the recent realization that I am exactly where I need to be to further my own quest of self-discovery. Old Stephen Lee has issues to deal with that involve his character, morals, ego, perceptions and discipline. The discipline is proving to be the easiest of all because mostly it revolves around the physical; for all the others I have to delve deeper inside myself and I do not always like what I find, which led me to a fascinating discovery back in J-3.

During my inward journeys, I sometimes still find myself stumbling upon a purposefully hidden memory, something from my past that I am ashamed of that causes an immediate inward cringe upon its discovery. Thrilled at the discovery of another awkward humiliation, I pursue the thread of that recollection, following it as it weaves the mental fabric of its wrongness so that I can mend what is wrong by better understanding its original cause. In a sense, I am learning to live better with me, the often-blundering human being. By making changes on the inside, I am becoming more likable on the outside. If we do not think well of ourselves then that negativity is going to contaminate all of our other relationships. This is one of the reasons why so many inmates have social troubles.

So here in prison, I am making a big effort to spend more time with myself. Getting to know why I am the way I am.

As I go through my weightlifting routine, I focus on non-injury exercise. In prison, an injured inmate is an enticing target. For most men weightlifting is a testosterone thing. Who can lift the most while grunting like animals and slamming the weights down in an ape challenging goad. Good weightlifting simply requires that the weight be controlled at all times, that form never be broken and that all of the muscles of the body be trained in harmony.

On the flat-back bench, I push the weight up slowly two seconds, stopping just before the arms lock out. When a joint is fully extended or locked the initial load at the beginning of the next repetition is partially placed on the connective tissues, small fibers and tendons, which only serve to loosen the joint promoting tears and injury. I then take four careful seconds lowering the weight, again fully controlling it and stopping a fist width above my chest. Bouncing the weight off the chest stresses joints as does lowering the heavy bar too far. The shoulders are the most complex heavy-load bearing joint of the body. There is a range of motion that benefits the shoulder girdle and lowering a heavy bar to the chest exceeds that beneficial range. To exercise the chest and its core supporting muscles properly, I do semi-wide and narrow grip benches while varying the angle of the lift to stress the whole muscle group. I follow this pattern with all my exercises remembering to work equally on doing pulling routines. A balanced weightlifter can pull the same amount they can lift. Most guys tend to focus on building the muscles they can most easily see in a mirror, I go after the hidden ones, which are our core muscles. This particularly includes the ones found under weightlifter's belts, which is a deceptive tool that provides support while allowing core lower back muscles to remain weak. What good are massive biceps when the lower back is prone to failure?

I sometimes wonder why people do not take better care of their bodies. I have come to think of my body as adventure machine. Of course, I did not do it any good smoking the marijuana, but that is behind me now. When I get out this body is going to be the vehicle I rely upon for all my future challenges and adventures. It only makes sense to get in the best possible shape then commit the time and effort to stay that way. Living an active, physical life is so much more fulfilling. Being a disciplined person means taking charge. A healthy body gets sick less often and is more prone to allowing a person to do the things that make life adventurous and worth living. How would one prefer to walk, with a spring to their step eyes looking for opportunity or plodding with their head down following old habits?

"Obesity is a mental state, a disease brought on by boredom and disappointment," Cyrill Connolly

"The disappearance of a sense of responsibility is the most far-reaching consequence of submission to authority,"
Stanley Milgram

Chapter 39
BORON PRISON CAMP, JANUARY 1985

IN LATE January, I am in my cage working out with some of the tools. I have a whole routine. Right now I have a heavy pipe wrench tied to a toilet plunger with a four-foot long piece of rope. I am repeatedly raising and lowering the heavy pipe wrench by rolling the rope up and down with the toilet plunger.

"Arrington, stop playing with the tools," yells the shop manager unlocking my cage door. "You're wanted in the Unit Manager's office."

I step out wondering what mischief the Unit Manager is planning for me now.

"Move it Arrington," growls the guard, "he said immediately."

The door is open so I walk cautiously into the Unit Manager's office. There are four staff members sitting around a long table. The Unit Manager, my enemy, sits at one end of the table. He stares sternly in my direction. The Unit Counselor opens the conversation with a surprise statement, "The Warden called a half hour ago and wanted us to do an immediate evaluation of your file for your bi-annual counseling."

I am not due for evaluation for two more months. Something is up and I am as wary of this meeting as a minnow being eyed by four big fish. This cannot be good news. All my inmate-attuned alarms are firing on full voltage.

The counselor has my file open in front of him, "Mr. Arrington, because of your good conduct and service on the fire crew we are going to send you to a halfway house a little early."

"Early?" a sudden grin slops over my face, "how early?"

"Well," he pauses then smiles, "how does five months early sound to you?"

I am astonished. It means I will be leaving Camp Boring Boron in less than four months. "Thank you," I stand eager to tell Ralph the news.

"Ah, Mr. Arrington, there's something else." The counselor looks at the Unit Manager who is still glaring angrily at me. The Unit Counselor nods encouraging my enemy to speak. The Unit Manager wipes his mouth as if removing a bad taste then reluctantly says, "How would you feel about going back onto the fire crew?"

"What!"

"We need you back on the fire crew," he is extremely unhappy to be saying this.

The Safety Officer comes to his rescue, "Mr. Arrington, we had a rather embarrassing event happen this morning. There are a couple of congressmen visiting the camp and it seems that they have heard wonderful things about our inmate fire crew...it's the B-1 Bomber thing. Anyway, they wanted to see the fire crew in action. I set a forty-four gallon trashcan on fire in my driveway over at staff housing. The truck arrived red lights flashing and siren wailing which attracted all the kids in the staff reservation. Only the fire burned itself out while your replacement was still trying to prime the pump."

I look at the Unit Manager and grin...I cannot help myself; the tool bin was a tough punishment.

"The Warden is a bit upset."

"Upset?" the counselor echoes, "he was standing right there with the congressmen and all those kids were laughing. The fireman just stood here with his empty hose hanging until one of the other guys thought to grab a fire extinguisher. But by then it was too late the fire had already burned itself out."

"Yeah, the only thing burning then was the Warden's temper... he was smoking."

The Safety Officer looks at me then turns towards the Unit Manager and smiles, "The Warden called this impromptu meeting to have you re-instated back onto the fire crew effective immediately. Your job is to re-train the fire crew and to get a new chief engineer up to speed before you leave in four months."

I look at the Unit Manager and smile knowing there is nothing he can do to me. My enemy slams his notebook closed and stalks angrily from the room. I kind of like being in his office without him in it. So, I take advantage of the situation.

Ten minutes later, I rush into the plumbing shop, after running up the hill and breathlessly tell Ralph the news.

"So why didn't you ask to have me put onto the fire crew too?" he asks unhappily.

I grin at my friend, "I did."

"What?"

"Yeah, you're coming with me."

In Ralph's hand is a wet plunger. He hasn't been doing anything foul with it; he just finds that the staff tends to leave him alone when he is carrying it around dripping suspicious fluids onto the floor. With a double overhand stab, he sticks the wet plunger to the tool bin sign.

I look at the plunger with surprise, "Did you do that on purpose?"

"Do what?"

"Look at the sign," the two middle words of *Rule #2 Inmates have nothing coming* have been blotted out by the wet plunger.

Ralph reads out loud, "*Inmates coming.* Hey I like that."

The other item I negotiated in the Unit Manager's office was to have his clerk replaced. The man was real bad for moral. The replacement I requested is a very eager orthopedic surgeon. We had four physicians at Boron, mostly in for insurance and Medicare fraud, and like me they were eager to put their skills to work; a purpose driven life far exceeds the alternative.

At the firehouse, I take the fire crew through each and every piece of equipment. I show them that priming the pump is all about the sequential opening of valves and timing. We go through drills and together lay out fire attacks for all the buildings in the prison camp.

On the night of the full moon, the fire siren abruptly wails. Joyously I run for the firehouse and pull down on the chain that raises the big bay door. The fire truck's paint glistens in the shaded light as I open the door and climb inside. Every morning I have awakened with the hopeful anticipation that the fire siren would sing its dramatic song immediately ending whatever I am doing and calling 52 to action. It is the most incredible gift being an inmate who gets to save lives in the desert. I say a silent prayer as I turn the ignition key. The engine cranks once and catches immediately; I rev the engine then pull out onto the pad and switch on the radios and grab a microphone; my voice quivers with excitement, "San Bernardino Command this is Engine Company 52 standing by."

"Roger 52," comes the immediate static-filled reply, "respond code three, two vehicle accident involving injuries, Route 395 eight miles south of Four Corners, ambulance dispatched."

"Roger Command 52 responding code three," I replace the microphone as the buzzer sounds that everyone's aboard. I flip on the rotating red light and key the prison camp microphone, "Control, 52 requesting correctional officer escort." The Safety Officer has the day off so one of the guards will have to take his place on the passenger seat.

I half floor the pedal as the big truck surges out onto the road. At control, I stop for a very fat guard who lumbers from the control building.

"Oh no," exclaims Ralph who is sitting next to me, "It's Box of Rocks, the staff idiot."

He opens the passenger door and slowly levers his ponderous bulk up grunting loudly as he pulls himself inside. I am eager to roll and anxious at how long it is taking him to get settled. Finally, I floor the pedal before he fully closes the door.

"Hey, slow it down," he barks.

I look over at the lazy fool wondering if he cares that we are an emergency vehicle responding to an accident with injuries and that lives might hang in the balance of our timely arrival at the scene. How could such an important thought have difficulty percolating down into his self-indulging mind set? "We have been directed to respond code three!" I growl double clutching into second, "That means red lights and siren and we are legal to speed responsibly and I haven't even hit twenty miles per hour yet."

He grunts his response flicking one hand like it is not really that important.

"The guy's a slob," whispers Ralph who is crushed up against me. "Reminds me of The Slug at Terminal Island. He stinks like a pig. Are you catching the body odor action? I hope he doesn't fart, I swear I will gag if he unloads a big one in these close quarters."

I switch on the siren though we are alone on the access road, I do not want the guard to overhear my friend's negative comments. It never benefits an inmate to demean a guard, though the urge at times can be irresistible. The Department of Corrections does not exactly always get the sharpest tools in the shed, particularly at its more remote prisons and camps. Box of Rocks is a few fries short of a Happy Meal and I do not want him hindering our emergency procedures, which means keeping him unperturbed, uninformed and uninvolved. I shift into third and then fourth gear accelerating all the time. It is a little hard grabbing the floor shift because the guard's bulk has forced Ralph half on top of it. The desert is flying past my window, as I check the side mirrors to make sure that all the compartments are closed and that the three men standing on the back bumper are okay. Through the windshield, I look at the pale orb of the moon, which is still low on the horizon. From looking at the pale light of the moon I stare at the flicker of the road's white strips disappearing beneath the grill of the fire truck then glance sideways at the arid landscape as the rotating emergency light strobes the desert with flickering waves of red brilliance like a broad-beamed laser. I can feel my heart pounding as my foot jams the gas pedal to the floorboards. I absolutely love this job. I suddenly realize that I suffer when not part of a team, then another thought superimposes itself on my consciousness. I am at my best when leading a team; it is what I have trained for all of my adult life. My time at Boron is short and when I get out the only team I can anticipate leading is likely a broom, dustpan, mop and maybe a bucket. I morbidly entertain a mental picture of myself in a set of coveralls, maybe with a nice janitorial logo. I adjust the mirror to distract myself from these gloomy thoughts of the probable future racing at me.

Approaching Highway 395, I slow, down-shift to second gear using engine compression to break the heavy vehicle, then swing the wheel hard right...the rear of the truck slides into the turn where there's a bit of gravel on the road. The inmates hanging on the back lean into the skidding turn then one of them keys the buzzer and yells into the intercom, "Go gettem Steve." I recognize the voice of the orthopedic surgeon who is normally used to a high excitement lifestyle. I bet he is really digging riding on the back of this fire truck. For the past six months, he has been washing dishes. Such a waste of talent, yet that is a key factor of incarceration. Punishment always takes priority; for some staff management the more perversely administered the better.

I overtake a couple of vehicles, which slow and move slightly to the right, but do not actually pull over. I have to move into the opposite lane to pass. Box of Rocks furiously rolls down his window and begins barking profanities with repeated hand gestures at the drivers. I slow for the stop sign at Four Corners then accelerate through the intersection once the opposing traffic stops. The road ascends a steep grade bleeding off the heavy truck's speed. It is frustrating crawling at twenty miles per hour with the lights and siren going, but we are almost to the top of the hill. The cars we passed earlier easily catch up with us and one goes for the pass. It is one of the drivers who refused to pull over for us earlier. We top the grade and I go for third gear accelerating rapidly. I quickly catch up with the car ahead of us and crowd his bumper—in frustration, I switch the siren to a higher pitch and I lay onto the horn, but again he refuses to pull over. It takes a couple of minutes before I can safely pass. Only an idiot would purposefully hinder a fire truck in full emergency response. Someone could die because this fool wants to play road games. Box of Rocks is into full road rage as we pass, if he had a gun he would probably be shooting bullets. Instead, he is spraying spittle into the prison camp microphone demanding that the control officer call the highway patrol to pull the guy over.

I forget about the thoughtless driver behind us and the angry fat guard going into testosterone overload in the passenger seat as I see two sets of flashing red lights up ahead. An ambulance and a Highway Patrol cruiser are pulled to the side of the road half-shielding a large, older model car with an accordioned front end. Twenty feet into the desert a crumpled sedan is upside-down with its roof half-caved in. A hysterical woman with a baby in her arms is being tended by a medic at the back of the ambulance. As I step down from the cab, the highway patrolman runs up to me. "The driver's pinned, there is not much holding his foot on, the other medic is inside the car."

Two of the firemen run forward with pry bars and cutters, the third, our orthopedic surgeon, carries the first aid kit. I watch our doc drop down onto his belly onto the dirt then quickly slithers into the wreck through the broken passenger window. That's going to be one surprised accident victim when he finds out an orthopedic surgeon is crawling into his upside-down car to make a house call.

Ralph does not wait for the fat guard to lumber out the passenger door. He follows me out the driver's side door and quickly unrolls the black rubber attack hose then runs to the front of the vehicle. I charge the hose and then switch on our dual heavy-duty spotlights flooding the accident site with bright cones of yellow light.

Box of Rock daintily lowers his fat bulk to the ground, the high step was a bit of a challenge for him as that side of the road slants away and then he proceeds at a high-speed waddle over to the highway patrol officer. "Get in your car, I want the driver of that red Chevy that just passed us arrested," he bellows.

The highway patrol officer gapes at the fat prison guard, but then decides to ignore him as he keys his radio and gives directions to the accident site to an evacuation helicopter. I climb up onto the top of the fire truck for a better view and spy a clearing big enough for the chopper. I yell at the highway patrol man to put his headlights on the clearing then I check the direction of the wind, which is blowing about ten miles per hour out of the west. Knowing the chopper will land into the wind, I swing one of our twin spots to light up a set of obstructing power lines.

Two minutes later the flashing lights of the chopper come in low and fast over the dark horizon. It does a hard banking turn to check the landing site as the cone of my spotlight momentarily gleams on the broad spinning blades then he straightens out and settles into a brown cloud of swirling dust that the wind fans into a billowing cloud.

I look over at the accident scene and see the firemen lowering the injured driver onto a gurney. His lower leg is splinted and heavily bandaged with bloodstained dressings. The three firemen and the medic run for the helicopter with the gurney and slide it into the side door as it opens. The medic leaps inside, one of the firemen slams the sliding door shut and the chopper immediately lifts off.

The heavy thumping sound of the long-bladed rotors biting into the air paints memories of Vietnam in my mind then the chopper rises thirty feet into the air, lowers its nose and accelerates passing right over the fire truck. I know it is more than a dozen feet above me, yet it feels like I could reach up and touch the chopper's belly. I see metal seams and rivets in the under carriage highlighted by the revolving belly strobe, I feel a hot blast of wind from the rotors and hear the roar of the twin turbines increasing speed. I watch the flashing lights climbing over the highway then it levels off at three hundred feet and accelerates away into the vast desert night sky.

From the heightened perspective on the hose bed, I look at the patches of bright light that pool upon the accident site that now seems a bit vacant, like a movie set after the cameras have stopped rolling and the main actors have left the stage. I leave the twin spots on while the guys store the equipment. The ambulance takes the woman with her baby to the hospital. The highway patrol man waits patiently for a tow truck having studiously ignored Box of Rocks who is now sulking in the passenger seat of the fire truck. Then I shut down the spots and still standing on top of the fire truck stare upwards into the heavens. The stars are radiant across a velvet black canvas. The full moon is now high into the night sky. I sense a feeling welling up from deep down inside of me. It surprises me, yet it does not, as I realize that, I am happy, so very happy and so very right with the world.

Driving the fire truck back towards camp at a much slower pace, I explore the intense feeling of pleasure that I am experiencing. It goes deeper than the rush of helping someone else in great need. I am reliving an emotion I had thought lost forever. Something I have missed greatly without fully realizing that it was gone, but feeling so very vacant without it. It is that intense feeling of camaraderie of being part of a team after successfully completing a dangerous mission. I have spent most of my adult life as a Navy diver and bomb disposal frogman. The training I went through was so very exciting, the missions intensely challenging and extremely adventurous. I am only thirty-four years old, still young, a whole new life waits for me. Yet, I cannot suppress the staggering realization of all that I have thrown away as it flickers through my thoughts.

Going into the theater of my mind, I replay the big screen image of the most embarrassing moment of my life. It is my last day with the EOD teams in Hawaii. I am being transferred to Treasure Island in San Francisco, California for final processing out of the Navy. Inside the Quonset hut, which is the Operations Department for Explosive Ordnance Disposal Group One, Lualualei Weapons Station, Hawaii, I pick up my orders from the clerk who refuses to look me in the eye. I glance about the room, which is empty but for the two of us, everyone else is conveniently absent or outside at morning quarters. I shoulder my heavy sea bag and for a moment consider slipping out the backdoor. I can hear the Command Master Chief detailing the morning's assignments. It would be much easier for everyone if I silently disappear out the backdoor. Instead, I walk to the front door, grab the knob and firmly open it.

Stepping out into the bright tropical sunshine, I pause on the raised front steps and look at the men in formation. There are twenty plus frogmen in two ranks standing at parade rest facing the Master Chief who is reading loudly from a clipboard. In the ranks, every head swivels towards me. These men are my friends, but much more than that, we are a fraternity of blood brothers, men who have gone into extreme danger relying one upon the other. The Master Chief looks up from his notes and sees that the men are distracted. His head swivels on his broad shoulders as he looks in the direction of the distraction. For the barest moment our eyes lock, his face instantly hardens then he turns away and in a stern voice barks, "Command, come to attention." The men, who are dressed in UDT's (Underwater Demolition Team swim shorts), green utility shirts and green CB hats, come to rigid attention. "About face," he orders. Both ranks instantly turn as a unit facing away from me. It is absolutely silent as I walk in my dress whites down the steps and cross the deep green lawn in the direction of the quarterdeck. I keep my back ramrod straight thankful that no one is looking because twin tears are running down my face.

Oh marijuana, you treacherous weed, what I so foolishly allowed you steal from me.

I glance at the two other men in the dark cab. What a strange trio we make. Ralph is here for his greed of drugs and money, which has stolen the last days of his childhood. Box of Rocks is a slave to his insatiable appetite; the incredible amount of fat he carries is an enormous burden that continuously weight him down and he works at a job that he hates with charges he despises. Finally, there is me; well I am the imbecile who had the idiotic desire to chemically tamper with his brain and therefore forfeited a life full of challenge and military adventure. Which of us is the greater fool? *It is me, it is me,* my mind shouts. All that I am and all that I will ever be is dependent upon my mental abilities and I put it all on the line just to get stoned. The guard may have never known the joys of being healthy and athletic, so his may be a fault of ignorance uncorrected. Eating may be his only enjoyment in life. Ralph is also a victim of drug use, but I suspect there are other family factors he hasn't revealed yet. Therefore, it is I who am without excuse for I had it all. I had the best teachers, a wonderfully adventurous career, a free lifestyle and an active, inquisitive intellect that was perpetually challenged by a stimulus rich environment seasoned with spasms of intense danger…and I tossed it.

Surprisingly my self-recrimination does not spoil my buoyant mood. It is just a startling realization of how far I have progressed towards looking at myself in an open and honest way. I glance at the fuel gauge then look at Box of Rocks and am surprised to realize I do not know his real name. To hide that fact, I tap the fuel gauge to draw his attention, "Need to stop to top off the tank."

"Good idea," he grunts.

We have an account at the gas station at Four Corners. I pull the truck up to the pumps. The station is well lit. I get out, remove the fuel cap and pull the hose from the gasoline pump as the men on back step off to stretch and talk excitedly about the accident. I notice Box of Rocks is waddling into the station mini-mart no doubt in pursuit of low-grade nourishment.

A mini-van pulls up to the opposing pump. The kids inside are excited to be so close to a fire truck with the men standing about in their turnouts. The driver steps out and smiles at me, as he is about to head inside to pay for the gasoline before pumping. I see him stutter step as he reads the seal on the driver's door, *Boron Prison Camp, Engine Company 52.* He suddenly looks at us from a whole different perspective, instantly in his mind we go from trusted firemen, hero-types, to a gang of murderous leering inmates. He spins about, hurries back into the mini-van and drives rapidly away with his wife yelling at him. I offer a friendly wave to his rear view mirror, which he does not return...but his children do enthusiastically. If I had been quicker, I might have touched off the siren for them, which would have probably given Box of Rocks a fatal heart attack.

The man in question is stepping through the mini-mart's double doors, a real convenience for the hugely fat man. "Who are you waving at?" he asks bluntly.

"Kids, they liked the fire truck."

Box of Rocks frowns, is he thinking he shouldn't have left us alone? Then I realize that he is facing a much more immediate dilemma. In his hands, he is carrying a box with a dozen chocolate covered donuts. Box of Rocks is wider around the waist than he is tall. In fact, he is quite short with fat stubby legs and he is looking unhappily at that first tall step into the truck's cab. He cannot manage that much height with only one supporting hand. I can see his reluctance to ask for any help because then he would be obliged to share part of his donut horde. So he goes through a very labored process of first setting the donut box down on the floor mat and then he uses both hands to lever himself up onto the running board. Next, he lifts the box of donuts to the seat and raises a ponderous leg onto the cab's floor, then placing one large ham onto the seat; he uses his hugely broad butt to push the box of donuts over, but quickly grabs it before it can invitingly touch Ralph. Finally, he gently lays the donuts onto his lap. Now he is free to settle into the seat and close the door. It would be impossible for him to snap the seatbelt. The whole procedure takes about twenty seconds. Ralph and I are watching the process intently. Box of Rocks smiles at us; it is a smile of accomplishment in solving a problem with the bonus of donut denial for the inmates. Fat man made it into the truck without having to ask for help and therefore does not have to share his donuts with people beneath his station. It is his first and last smile of the evening. I guess we all measure accomplishment in our own way.

During the final six-mile drive to the camp, he gobbles all dozen donuts. Rather than watch Box of Rocks' heavy jowls working the chocolate pastries I think about helping that young family tonight.

I turn onto the government road that leads up to the prison camp. My excitement bubbles over as I radio control to raise the gate. We pull through the barrier, and then stop to let Box of Rocks out of the truck. He says nothing, not good job or it was a pleasure, just nothing but grunts and heavy breathing noises as he lowers his ponderous bulk to the tarmac spilling donut crumbs and then he waddles into the control building. I watch his massive frame silhouetted by the dim light inside the doorway. He hitches up his pants and turns sideways to pass through the opening then steps out of view as the door automatically closes. I wonder at his hollow life then decide I am being too judgmental…and over something that does not really concern me. I would be glad to talk with the guard. Maybe I could influence how he thinks about others or how he thinks about himself. *Hey, have you heard the good news? God loves you! In fact, he loves correctional officers and inmates equally. Did you know that? We are equals before the King. Isn't it astounding!*

In my room, I ponder my future, a thought that shuffles regularly through my mind with its limited possibilities. What kind of a first job will I have to suffer through? I will need to find work immediately and having Boron Prison Camp, as my last residence is not going to look good on a resume. That means I am probably going to be saddled with one of those mop and broom occupations until I can invest serious time to find something respectable. I pause and mentally laugh at my selection of words, *respectable?* Though I have been so blessed in prison, civilians never see recently released inmates in the terms of respectable. Usually employers view fresh parolees with active suspicion. Maybe I will be lucky to get a janitorial job, instead I could be heading for a pick and shovel opportunity. At least as a ditch digger, like a diver, I get to start at the top and work my way down.

Early the next morning a very surprised Inmate Arrington stands before the Unit Manager's desk. "Who said you could leave the base without my authorization?" he yells in a loud blaring voice.

"What authorization are you talking about?" I ask genuinely confused.

"I put you back on the crew to train them," he rages, "nobody said anything about you leaving the prison camp."

"What is the point of my being the chief engineer if I don't lead the crew on fire responses?" I ask, thinking it a fair question.

"Listen inmate," he snarls, "I don't give a damn about fighting fires outside this camp. You go through that gate again and you're going to have me to contend with…you got that?"

The next time the fire siren wails, despite the threats of the Unit Manager, I do not even consider not going. Each attack I lead is an opportunity to teach the new men from real experience. This is my seventieth, and probably last, response. I have only two more months to serve. I climb up into the cab knowing it is for the last time. It is a strange hollow feeling, yet I am making a choice knowing the ramifications. I am not breaking a prison camp rule as I have already checked that out with the Safety Officer, who advised me that I should make my own decision. I am the designated chief engineer and with that assignment, I accept certain responsibilities that I personally feel obligated to fulfill.

Not far from the camp, a Toyota pickup truck has collided head-on with an 18-wheeler at a combined speed of over 130 mph. The driver of the big commercial rig has a broken arm, but the driver of the pickup is dead and mutilated.

The red Toyota is a flattened, scrunched up mess. The steaming engine, driven inwards and upwards with tremendous force, is half in the cab impaling the driver on the broken steering shaft. We spend over an hour just cutting the ravaged body out of the mass of rubble and torn metal. The force of the horrendous impact has disemboweled him and his legs are half-torn from the mangled body. A stream of blood mixed in a horrible collage with oil and gasoline runs in a broad slick across the hot black tarmac. It is a horribly depressing sight; I flush the wet mess from the road with a fire hose. The high-pressure jet chases the hideous collage of body and engine fluids into a swirling maze glistening with dark-hued rainbows of gruesome color.

Seeing the highway patrol trooper walking up towards me, I shut off the hose.

"Hey inmate," he says in a friendly way, "remember me, I saw you standing on top of the fire truck when that helicopter flew right over it."

"Yeah, that was me." I offer my hand, "Steve, Steve Arrington."

"Hugh," he takes my hand, "You're the chief engineer of these guys?"

"Yep, best darn inmate fire crew in the United States."

"I believe it; you guys got a professional way of handling things. I liked how you lit up the power lines for the chopper pilot...he's a friend of mine."

"Seemed the right thing to do," I am enjoying being an inmate visiting with an officer of the law.

"What are you in for?"

"Smuggling cocaine, I shouldn't have done it...wish I didn't."

"You're a Christian, aren't you?"

"Discovered Him in a prison cell," I laugh. "How could you tell?"

"The way you told me what you did, that you knew it was wrong and took responsibility for it all in a short sentence."

"Well I'm in trouble again," I say, suddenly wondering why I am volunteering that information.

He glances out into the desert then his eyes slice back to me, an officer of the law about to hear about trouble.

"One of the staff at the prison didn't want me leading the crew off base anymore," I shrug, "it's a personal thing between him and me."

"So why did you do it?"

I spill my guts to a stranger in uniform. Well actually, he is not a complete stranger; he is a Christian, which makes us brothers in a manner of speaking. We just happen to be on opposite sides of the law, but I am trying to get over to his side the best I could.

"You know he's going to pull you off the fire crew?"

"No doubt about it." I shrug.

"But you went anyway."

"Had to." I kick at a clump of sand, frustration expressing itself.

"I understand."

"You do?"

"Yeah, I wear a uniform and with it come responsibility. You're wearing a uniform too and these men are your team. You owe that uniform, those men and the family of that body over there in that bag the best you got. A man in a uniform can't resist doing what they're trained to do. So when you go back and see that man you've got a problem with you stand straight and tall...make that fireman's uniform look good."

I pause to take a better look at this trooper, "Thank you," I say quietly, we shake hands and I turn to go.

"Hey, Steve."

I stop and turn around. He has his ticket book out and a pen in his hand. "What's the name of the unit manager?"

Driving the truck through the gate, we pass the Unit Manager's office and I see him glaring at me through the window.

While the men store the gear in the firehouse, I calmly walk over to the Unit Manager's office and knock on his door.

"Enter," comes the gruff voice.

I step inside. "Figured you wanted to see me," I say politely remembering to stand tall.

"Damn right," he snarls, "you disobeyed me and you broke camp regulations."

"I am truly sorry, but I felt an obligation to lead the men," I am being respectful. "It is what a chief engineer is supposed to do."

"You know I could severely punish you." It is a statement not a question. However, I think he is wrong about my breaking a camp regulation, I actually followed my job profile, but it is a losing argument nonetheless so I keep it bottled inside of me.

I pause before I answer, taking a deep breath, suddenly eager to defuse the situation. There is no benefit in our fighting, not for him and certainly not for me. "Sir," he looks up surprised at my willingness to use that word so respectfully, "I take this assignment seriously. When I walked in this door almost a year ago, I told you I wanted to be a fireman more than anything. That is still true. I did not lead the team out of the camp to make you angry; I did it because I felt it was my duty to do so."

"Well I have a duty to do also. You've had a couple of months to train the crew and let's hope they are ready because you're off the fire crew effective immediately."

"Yes sir, I expected that," I shrug.

"I have already cleared it with the warden so don't get your hopes up in that direction."

"I won't."

Did he just smile? It was not a very big smile, but it was there for a moment before he sent it away.

"Plumber or dishwasher?" he asks. I realize he is politely giving me a choice.

"Well actually sir, except for being a fireman I would really like to be a teacher."

"What?"

"Can I maybe go to work in the Education Department?"

"Why?"

"Because I can teach, I have a California Teaching Credential in Marine and Related Technologies."

"You want to teach Marine Biology to inmates…in the desert?"

"No sir, I just like teaching. I'm sure there are some things I can share with the guys. Also I am writing a book about my time in prison."

"What does that have to do with anything?"

"They have a typewriter up there."

"Oh."

"I can write nice things about you and this conversation," I offer hopefully.

"What did you teach again?"

"Scuba diving, Ventura City College gave me a limited services teaching credential to run a scuba program for them. They needed to give it an official sounding name so I suggested Marine and Related Technologies."

The smile is there again, it is not huge or radiant, yet it lingers and he is amused. "Okay, get your butt up the hill to the Education Department." He makes a note in my file and closes it.

"Thank you, sir." I turn to leave.

"Hey inmate."

I stop at the door and turn to face him.

"When you came in here I was going to rip your butt apart and throw you back in that cage in the plumbing department. What just happened?"

"We got off to a bad start at the beginning and we never corrected it. You just realized that I am actually a nice guy."

"You're an inmate...a prison inmate."

"True, but I'm a likeable prison inmate."

"Make me a promise."

"What's that, Sir?"

"When you get out...I don't ever want to see you back here again."

On my walk up the hill to the Education Building in the hot afternoon sun, I am relaxed and at peace. I have made a character building choice over playing it safe or the inmate way of avoiding responsibility. When I stepped into the Unit Manager's office, I was prepared to face my punishment and surprisingly I was also willing to forgive him regarding his normally poor attitude towards me. That put me in a calm, friendly mode that allowed him to treat me as a real person and listen to my explanation...not excuses, but a real explanation of why I did what I did. And he accepted it at face value. Surprisingly the situation, which could have gone very bad, has turned out pretty darn good.

I glance up towards the top of the hill at the Education Department Building. I am looking forward to spending some serious time writing my book. I want to capture the intensity of prison. Originally, I had intended to write a book that might scare young people into not making bad choices. Surprisingly it has become a book about hope. I also have a fascinating new challenge, teaching inmates to read.

As the days and weeks pass, I do not really have much to complain about in these final days at Boron. I have most of the day to myself since I only teach night classes. It is a peaceful time, an opportunity to think deep thoughts, to take inward journeys and to dream about the future that is rushing at me.

"Forgiveness is the fragrance the violet sheds on the heel that crushed it," Mark Twain

I awaken slowly in the darkness then my mind suddenly rushes to full consciousness. I grab my digital watch on the nightstand. I eagerly push the little button that backlights the tiny numbers. It is 2:00 a.m. and this is my last day in prison! I pad silently across the floor to my sweats then slip out of the room carrying one of my hand-painted cups and a tea bag. I have been sharing the tea and am now down to my last one. I fill the cup with warm water at *old gurgle and spit* then continue into the television room. I quietly clear a small circle, deposit a few pieces of trash in a waste bin and then sit down on the old wood floor. I sip my tepid drink; it is the best cup of tea of my life. I inhale the fragrance of Jasmine, which reminds me of my more peaceful times in Asia during the Vietnam Conflict. I am anticipating that this will be my last truly tranquil moment for some time. Life is about to descend upon me with all of its time schedules, bills, chores and duties. As I prepare to start my life from scratch, I mentally count my possessions. The government has released Revelstoke, which is waiting for me at Sam's house. I also have two surfboards and a wetsuit also in Sam's care. That is it; I do not have anything else, except for a three thousand dollar student loan—making the two hundred dollars in my prison account seem very small indeed. I also have a six-point-five-million dollar tax lien the government is holding against me voiding any chances of my getting a small loan.

I have a picture that Sam sent me of himself. He has promised

that he will keep Revelstoke safely parked in front of his mother's
house. The picture does not give me any confidence in his word. In
it, Sam is standing at the backdoor of Revelstoke, which is parked at
the beach. Not only has he taken my only real possession on a road
trip, but he is also wearing my shirt. I suspect that my supposed
best friend is also exploiting my surfboards and my wetsuit. I do
not doubt that he is driving Revelstoke around without insurance.
Sam lives his life according to his own imaginative rules; the first
of which is there are no rules if they inconvenience him. He just
does not acknowledge responsibility. I have written him about how
important Revelstoke is to me, yet in the world according to Sam,
he will find justification for whatever he wants to do. The only true
restriction hampering him is his constant lack of money; a condition
related to his lack of neither work discipline nor any serious type of
higher education. I have taped Sam's picture on the wall above my
bed. It is a constant reminder that I will live my life according to a
simple law...discipline rules.

For all of my time with Morgan, seven plus disastrous months,
and the thirty-one-plus months I have served in prison, I have been
without true control of my life. If I go back further to my marijuana days in the Navy and my college doper experience, I must
honestly give up another two years. Amazingly had I stayed in the
Navy only one and a half more years from this moment I would be
eligible for retirement. Instead I am about to start my life over, with
a student loan to pay off, a huge tax lien, a felonious record and
only two hundred dollars in my pocket. Yet I have a certain confidence because I am no longer alone. I have the Lord in my life and
the promise He gave me in a prison cell, a single word that means
everything...*always.*

I slowly and quietly go through my Gung Fu routines. I do sit-ups
and push-ups on the wooden floor and pull-ups from a doorsill.

A few minutes before six, I lace up my running shoes then wait
patiently at the door. When the guard unlocks the door, I step
outside into the predawn darkness. The guard is walking heavily
away, but he stops and turns, the beam from his flashlight washes

over me, "Good luck, Arrington."

"Thank you Sir," I respond. Amazing, I still do not know *Box of Rocks* real name.

The desert wilderness just before sunrise has a lonely beauty that washes away the mindless chatter of my mind while encouraging a certain purity of inspirational thought. I am eager as I run up the hill contemplating the freedom that is rushing at me. I set a fast pace. On the dark road ahead, I hear the patter of small paws in the darkness. It is still too dark to see the young rabbits that flee my approach. The small cottontails and jackrabbits are of an age to have left their den and their mother and are now learning their survival skills as they scurry off the road for the dubious safety of the desert shrubs. I often see rattlesnakes and rarely coyotes and sometimes owls on the security light poles; living in the wild is not easy on young rabbits. Running the loop, I watch the rising sun, its brilliant red light spreading over the vast desert floor, while listening to the rhythm of my feet pounding on the road; the cadence is like the ticking of a clock counting off time. Each step carrying me quickly closer to 8:00 a.m., my scheduled release time.

Returning to Dorm 7, I see Ralph waiting for me leaning against the door. He has one hand out with a huge smile on his face. I remove my running shoes and hand them to him along with my sweat socks, which are still warm from my feet. He has not been so bold as to ask for the socks, but I know he wants them. It is just one of those inmate things. A good pair of un-holed sweat socks is almost worth their weight in cigarettes (inmate money). He follows me silently to my room, yet I sense his eagerness for what I am going to give him tempered with the reluctance of losing a best friend. The loss of a best friend is a terribly significant event in the solitude of prison. It is more than your closest confidant leaving; it is having to stay back alone, while one goes forward the other stays behind. Opening a drawer, I take out my treasured radio and place it in his hands. It looks good perched on top of the socks and running shoes. Its plastic box is scarred and scratched, yet Ralph is as excited as I was when I first took the little black box from its plastic wrapper in J-3. His smile is huge as I glance back down at the radio. For a moment, I see the radio from a civilian perspective. It is a cheap little mono box radio with a fifty-cent speaker. I can buy a much more sophisticated model with my first paycheck. I look at the inexpensive radio with real heartfelt fondness knowing that no entertainment system will ever have more value to me than this little scarred box radio resting on a pair of old running shoes and a pair of sweaty socks.

After a cool shower, I put on worn-out jeans, a holed T-shirt and a pair of frayed tennis shoes. I pick up a small cardboard box, of the size that I carried from J-3. Inside is my Bible, black journal, my pictures, a half-dozen hand-painted coffee cups and a few toiletries. I take a last look at my room, then close the door and wander casually down towards Control to pick up my release papers. Walking past the firehouse, I look at the fire trucks in their shaded bays. Who would have ever thought that I would have such exciting memories from prison? I walk up to the big Ford and run a hand over its fender. I see my reflection in the brightly polished paint. I press my thumb firmly onto the shiny surface leaving a fingerprint; Stephen Arrington was here.

The fire crew is still at breakfast so I cannot say goodbye to each of them, yet I do not mind; I want my leaving prison to be a private moment.

Walking down to Control, I stop at the barrier and look at the camp one last time. I have learned so many things about myself, here and at Terminal Island, yet I will not miss prison at all.

After collecting my papers, I walk to the freedom side of the barrier and stare down the long, straight highway. Time passes, my brother is late. How amazing, my freedom waits so tantalizingly close, beckoning to me, yet I can go nowhere. I am not free of the prison camp, or its guards, until I sit down in that car, close the door and Jim drives me away. Until that moment actually happens, I am not free. Though I hold release papers in reality, I am still an inmate at prison's doorstep...and my brother is late. An hour passes, then two. I stand in the sun too nervous to sit and just stare down that long black tarmac road.

Finally, three long hours later I see my brother's car approaching. Jim stops alongside me and reaches across to open the door. "I got lost."

"No kidding," I answer, "did it have to be today?"

I am about to sit down on that passenger seat, when suddenly I hear the distinctive wail of the Ford's siren. The fire truck is coming rapidly across the dirt baseball field trailing a spreading cloud of rolling dust with its red lights flashing. The truck comes to an abrupt halt on the baseball field; a dust cloud settles about it. The fire crew is hanging off the back and sides. They wave vigorously. Then standing at the back rail of the truck I see Ralph, the friend I so desperately needed and found in general population so long ago. Ralph waves happily and suddenly I realize that the crew has been patiently waiting to see my ride arrive, before driving out onto the field. A sad smile begins to play across Sam's face, but then he visibly brightens and signals happily with two thumbs up. Today it is my turn; his release waits in the not so distant future.

My brother Jim smiles knowingly from the driver's seat. Understanding that this is a special moment between parting friends, he reaches out and touches my arm. I climb into the freedom car with tears clouding my eyes. As Jim begins to drive down that long straight road, I turn in the seat to stare at the fire truck and the waving inmates until distance and a dip in the road drops them from my sight.

When we reach the main highway, I stick my head out the open window and feel the wonder of freedom rushing past all around me. It blows through the open window playing with my hair, causing me to blink in its intensity, carrying within it fresh scents remembered and the sounds of life unhindered. Looking back, I see the prison camp hill with its radar station on top slowly fading with distance and suddenly I am a civilian again…well almost.

As we climb the long grade going south, I look back and to the east where the B-1 Bomber crashed. Soon we pass where the Volkswagen burned, my first fire response, then where the young man died and

I washed his blood into the dirt and sand. Ten minutes later, I see the spot where I stood on top of the fire truck when the helicopter flew right over my head. I glance at Jim, who is just driving; for him this is just empty desert.

An hour later, as we leave the high desert and drive through San Bernardino County, I stare at all the vibrant colors. Prison at its normal is so drab, grey and colorless. I just wish Jim had not been so late picking me up.

The halfway house is only two miles from Disneyland. We pass within sight of Fantasyland en route to the halfway house. Jim and I had planned to stop for lunch, but his being late means I have to report in directly; being late is strictly forbidden. Jim and I shake hands curbside, my family was never very big into hugs, then I walk into the facility's office carrying my inmate file in a sealed envelope and my small cardboard box. I smile realizing that my moving box has gotten smaller and smaller ever since my leaving Animal House (A-Unit).

A bored clerk gives me a towel, a pillow, a set of sheets, two blankets, a long list of rules to read and a key to a small apartment that I will be sharing with three other men. The facility is actually an old apartment complex with locking security gates front and back. It houses forty something men. I find the apartment and unlock the door. The front room is tiny with a couch leaking its stuffing. A small kitchenette has a refrigerator and electric stove. There is no kitchen table, so I assume we eat on the couch, which would partially explain the mass of stains covering the cushions. I open the refrigerator door. There is not much in there; the few items have names written on them. There are a number of patches of mold growing on the inside walls and on the shelves.

Surprisingly my empty bed is right next to a window. I am thrilled, but wonder why the other person in the room would choose the bed against the closet. I make up the bed thus staking my claim should anyone decide to change their mind. They say that possession is nine-tenths of the law. For inmates it is kind of like peeing on your territory to keep other predators out of your space. I sit down on the newly made bed to read the rules with great anticipation. I am already aware of all the things I cannot do; after all, it is a facility under the control of the Department of Corrections, what I want to know is what I can do. I skim quickly down to the part about when I actually have to be here. *Hmmm? Report in after work no later than 8:00 p.m. then in the room for count 9:00 p.m. Then free to leave the facility at 6:00 a.m. to go to work. Weekends I am free to leave the facility at 6:00 a.m., but must return by 9:00 p.m. Violation will result in immediate re-incarceration.* I look at my digital watch, 3:00 p.m.

At 3:01 p.m., I am back at the curb heading north at a rapid pace. I have a map in my back pocket with directions to the nearest supermarket. Ten minutes later, I step through the market's automatically opening doors. It is the first auto opening doors I have encountered since the elevator doors at the courthouse. I step through twice because it pleases me. I grab a cart then stop to orient myself and devise a plan. In my wallet, which has sat in a government locker for two-and-a-half years, I only have two hundred dollars. This has to last me until my first paycheck and that will not happen until approximately two weeks after I find a job. I am under no illusions that writing my name on an item and putting it in the refrigerator will keep convicted felons from eating my stuff. I walk every isle because this is an event for someone use to stuffing napkin-wrapped wads of peanut butter into his socks. Half an hour later, I leave carefully carrying a double paper bag containing a loaf of whole wheat bread, a jar of peanut butter and another of strawberry jelly (the cheapest type of jelly), a dozen eggs, four apples, a bunch of bananas, a roll of plastic wrap and a bar of soap. I have spent twelve dollars and fifty-seven cents or about six point three percent of my total funds. I figure I have about three day's grub in my paper sack. I actually spent about five minutes debating buying a box of tea but decided I could not afford that luxury yet.

It is evening and I am in bed staring at the dark window in my bedroom. The other three guys, whom I have met, but have no desire to know, are in the front room gambling their wages. I listen to them arguing and cursing over the slap of the cards. Trying to close my ears to the abusive noise, I am about to begin a prayer asking for guidance and hope. Abruptly a flash of multi-colored light splashes across the window's dark glass followed by the modest thunder of small explosions. *Fireworks!* Kneeling on the bed, I stare excitedly out the window at a barrage of fireworks in the near distance. It is the middle of May and almost the end of spring. School groups are having their end-of-the-school-year parties at Disneyland. The theme park is celebrating the beginning of the seasonal crowds. The evening fireworks display is why my roommate did not want the window with a view.

Following the firing of the last rocket, I snuggle back into my covers. After The Flood to seal His Covenant with man, God sent a rainbow. For the end of my incarceration, I get Disneyland fireworks.

"The dream was always running ahead of me. To catch up,
to live for a moment in unison with it, that was the miracle,"
Anais Nin

The author checking a commercial diving student at the College of Oceaneering.

"Courage and perseverance have a magical talisman, before which difficulties disappear and obstacles vanish into air,"
John Quincy Adams

Chapter 40

ANAHEIM, CALIFORNIA, MAY 1985

S ITTING QUIETLY on a cement bench, I stare at my reflection in the curved warp of a sheet of stainless steel that is wrapped around a thick cement column. Memories of a prison mirror echo through my mind. My image, like the huge and empty parking lot that surrounds me, is ill defined and oddly distorted in the bent reflection. I look exceedingly small and very alone in the vast emptiness of black tarmac and concrete that fills the metal mirror's curved horizon.

I think that the malformed reflection aptly mimics what I am feeling inside, which is a bit lost and quite out of place in a world grown uncertain. It is my first day out and about in a free world, but the future is clouded and full of self-doubt. I have not at all lost any confidence in God, just troubled about where Stephen Arrington is heading and when is he going to get there...wherever there happens to be.

I am returning from my first visit with a parole officer, which unfortunately took me all the way to Long Beach on three separate city buses. The round trip costs me six dollars and eighty cents; that is another three point four percent of my total finances. *I have already gone though ten percent of my funds,* I think unhappily. Between buses, I await the connection that will take me back to the halfway house. I have no idea what the future holds for me, nor what kind of job I hope to find. I plan to commence the search for employment tomorrow.

A grossly distorted white, black and yellow bus appears in the warp of the metal mirror, passing from left to right as the image accordions outward, then squishes in at the center before lengthening again as it stops with an ear piercing screech of brakes directly behind my bench. A slim black youth in a shabby army jacket steps off the bus to the sharp hiss of the sliding pneumatic door opening and closing. With a loud grinding of gears the bus drives noisily away trailing a cloud of thick black smoke that lingers acidly in the air long after its departure.

Reaching into a wrinkled paper bag on the bench beside me, I take out a hardboiled egg and crack its white shell on the cement bench. I hardboiled all dozen eggs and hid them in my drawer. No way was I going to trust the refrigerator. Of course, they could steal them from my drawer, but it may appear to be a bigger risk. An egg out of the refrigerator could be explained as an accident. Pawing about in my drawer would be a no-excuse outright theft. The black youth standing at the edge of the mirror's reflection turns at the sound of my peeling the shell and appears to be eyeing my egg enviously. The distortion of the warped mirror makes his eyes look unusually large, like a starving child. I reach back into the wrinkled sack and taking out a second egg and hold it up wordlessly. The youth quickly joins me on the bench.

We peel our eggs in silence.

Out of the corner of my eye, I notice that he has chewed his fingernails to the quick and that they are black with grime. They sharply contrast the clean white flesh of the egg. "So, where are you coming from?" The youth asks politely while munching hungrily on half his egg.

"Today from my parole officer…yesterday, from prison," I reply unemotionally. "Would you like some salt?"

Salting the remaining half of his egg he somewhat nervously asks, "What were you in for?"

"Poisoning people," I answer flatly.

White chunks of egg and bits of yellow yoke splatter the curved sheet of stainless steel as the youth spews the half-chewed egg. "What!" he chokes.

"Just kidding," I laugh, morbidly pleased that my sense of humor has apparently survived the prison experience intact. Looking at my young temporary companion, I cannot help but feel bad about my little joke. He is quite shaken. A small piece of egg dribbles from his lower lip onto his pants leg. He dusts it off looking quite forlorn about wasting half the egg.

"Would a peanut butter and jelly sandwich make you feel any better about spewing your egg all over the parking lot?" I ask. He brightens visibly.

We both look at the crinkled brown paper sack that sits between us with it promise of more food. I remove both of the peanut butter and jelly sandwiches I made earlier that morning. Chunky peanut butter and thick strawberry jelly leaks grossly from between the semi-flattened slices of brown bread. I offer him the least damaged one, which he opens and eyes suspiciously. He clamps the gooey mess back together then waits until I have bitten into mine before he risks a tentative bite himself.

I cough and pretend to choke. He just looks at me tolerantly then takes a big bite and mumbles around a thick mouthful of sandwich, "So what does it feel like your first day out of prison?"

"It is wonderful to be out. Yet it's hard to explain how I feel. It's like I am on the outside trying to find my way back while not sure that I am wanted or even belong here anymore.

The youth looks down at his dirty clothes, "Yeah, I know what you mean." He wipes a glob of peanut butter from his cheek with the frayed sleeve of the olive-drab jacket. "But if you've served your sentence haven't you paid your debt to society and all?"

"It's not that simple to shed an inmate mentality," I reply throwing in a shrug to make light of what bothers me so intensely. "Institutional conditioning runs too deeply; prison and all its experiences are still inside me fighting with my emotions. I think it is something that I will have to live with for the rest of my life." An ugly vision of Bruno pounding the cell wall flashes through my mind as if to prove that his memory is still stalking me.

A moment later, the squeal of hot brakes announces that my bus has arrived. I wad the now empty paper bag into a ball and toss it into the trashcan before stepping onto the nearly empty bus. The youth waves in an unsure manner as the bus drives away then he shuffles toward the trash can to inspect the paper bag. I have no idea what clues it might hold for him.

Selecting a seat near the back, far away from the other three people on the bus, I sit down and close my eyes to shut out an insecure world that lacks the luster I dreamed about from prison. Being around people makes me feel as skittish as an abused puppy in the city pound. The halfway house is just another part of the institutional system that still unconditionally owns my body. When one is reprimanded into custody, he becomes a straightforward property issue.

The following day I board another bus. I am on my way to the College of Oceaneering in Los Angeles Harbor, where they teach commercial deep-sea diving. Actually, this is not exactly my idea. The probation officer had told me to go to the College of Oceaneering. I figured maybe that he knew something I did not. In any case, they might have a lead on where an ex-con diver could find a job. My hopes are not very high. I am just hopeful I will not have to start out pumping gasoline at some out-of-the-way service station or sweeping floors at a mini-market. I am certainly not expecting any employers to get wildly excited about hiring an ex-felon. Even in my mind the tag "drug smuggler," has an ugly ring to it.

I catch a bus to the industrial harbor town of Wilmington, which is another twelve miles beyond Long Beach. While walking a half mile to the school I do the mental math, eight dollars sixty cents round trip. That is another four point-three percent of my prison savings. Remembering that I only earned twenty-two cents an hour at Terminal Island and then I got a modest raise at Boron; being an inmate fireman brought in a whole quarter an hour. The bus fare today represents a full week's salary at Boron. Therefore, the money I am spending really has a lot of meaning for me. I am carrying a paper sack containing three sandwiches (the last of the loaf), an apple, two bananas and three eggs; it is going to be a long day and I don't want to be hungry on the bus. I will have to buy more bread and another dozen eggs when I get back this evening. At the entrance to the school, I mentally tuck my tail between my legs and go inside. Five minutes later, I am standing at the air diving supervisor's door. Tom Mix stands as I knock and enter. "Are you here to sign up for a class?" he asks hopefully.

"Actually I am looking for a diving job," I answer a lot more hopefully.

Tom Mix sighs, "We're not looking for anyone right now but you might as well tell me about your qualifications." He puts his legs up on the desk, a man who has time to burn.

"Well, I am an ex-Navy diver and an ex-felon. I just got out of prison the day before yesterday."

Tom is so startled that he spills coffee into his lap. He leaps to his feet, but it is too late; his pants are thoroughly soaked at the crotch and one thigh. "You sure know how to surprise a fellow don't you," he says wiping ineffectually at the wet spot.

"Sorry," I offer looking at the mess I have caused, "I just didn't want to waste your time and thought it would be better if you knew right off."

Tom pauses for a moment before saying thoughtfully, "I think I need some more coffee. Would you like a cup?"

"Do you have tea?"

"Tea?" he asks like it is a wimpy kind of thing. I can almost see the gears turning in his head. Then he seems to remember that I am an ex-felon; therefore, I cannot be too wimpy.

"Coffee would be fine," I quickly correct.

He goes over to a coffee pot and pours two cups, "I don't have any cream or sugar."

"Black is okay," I answer. I hate black coffee, but it seems important to prove that I am not the least bit wimpy. I hold the cup chest high trying to make my bicep look bigger adding to my non-wimp look. The last time I applied for a job was at the surf shop and before that, I had my extended naval career. I am not very experienced in job hunting.

So what qualifications do you have as a diver that would make you a good teacher here?" he asks.

"I started my diving career as a deep-sea hardhat diver then switched over to Explosive Ordnance Disposal diver. I am not just an air breather, I'm mixed gas qualified." *Air breather* is an insult; mixed-gas divers like to label divers who are only compressed air certified. Abruptly, I remember that Tom is the Air Diving Supervisor. *Did I just insult him? Well this job is history,* I think unhappily.

Tom interrupts, "That's all well and good, but this is a civilian commercial diving school. We don't have any need for military-orientated training."

"Okay," this is not going well, "I am also a NAUI and PADI scuba diving instructor and have taught on a master instructor level. In the Navy, I was a hyperbaric chamber supervisor (recompression chamber) and an EMTD (Emergency Medical Technician Diver) so I can teach the treatment of diving maladies. I am also a certified Red Cross Instructor for teaching CPR (cardio pulmonary resuscitation) and first aid."

"You've been busy."

"I've always believed that an individual should know all that they can about their chosen profession, so I also picked up a Water Safety Instructor Card and..." *dare I say it?* "a California Community Services Teaching Credential for Marine and Related Technologies."

"What's that?"

"Ventura City College needed a scuba instructor. If you have seven years experience in a profession you can teach that subject at a junior college level."

"What's in the paper bag?"

"My lunch."

"Really? Peanut butter and jelly?"

"I am on a bit of a budget."

Tom continues to ask me questions about my background.

"As an ex-machinist mate chief, I can repair almost any kind of diving or boating equipment. I have studied expository writing so I can help draft teaching lessons."

His interview is complex and I discover just how deeply I have prepared for a diving career. Two cups of coffee and a very full bladder later, I finally have to ask, "So do you know of a diving job that an ex-felon might qualify for or know somewhere I might apply?"

"Sure do," he answers off-handedly, "you're going to work for me as a CORE instructor. Come on we'll get you a set of keys and I will give you a tour of the school."

I am bewildered, "I got the job?"

"Sure you did...hope you don't think I have that much time to waste just sitting around jawing."

"But I thought you said you weren't looking for anybody right now."

Tom laughs, "I was funning you. I actually needed a core block instructor." Tom happily punches me in the shoulder; he is enjoying himself. "Yesterday, Jim Joiner, the President and owner of the College of Oceaneering told me that you'd be dropping in and that I was to hire you right off." Tom grins at the look of surprise on my face, "I knew since yesterday that I would be hiring you which meant I wasn't looking for anyone. Get it?"

"I guess, but why me?"

"Jim got a call from a Highway Patrolman up in the Mojave Desert last week. He even sent down a couple of reference letters. Want to see them?"

"Absolutely."

Tom hands over a thin folder. Inside are three letters of

recommendation, one from the highway patrolman at the suicide site, one from the Safety Officer and amazingly one from the Unit Manager, who referred to me as a model inmate with an excellent record and a cooperative disposition.

"Want that tour of the school?"

As we walk the school's hallways together, Tom casually says, "There are a lot of ex-felons working in the diving industry. You guys seem to fair well working in isolated conditions such as on offshore oilrigs. You'll have two ex-felons in your physics class."

"So I'm the new core block instructor?" I am assuming these are the basic pre-dive classes; physics, diving physiology, decompression tables, history of diving, etc.

"Yeah, but we'll move you into all the aspects of the basic commercial diver class including rigging, equipment repair, tank and barge diving, project evaluation and you've got a collateral duty."

"What's that?"

"School medic."

"Really?"

"Yep, you've got more qualifications in that department than any of my other instructors. Remember we are a commercial diving college and most of my staff is your basic commercial diver types who have gotten too old to handle the hard physical labor. I am actually quite pleased to be hiring you. I have needed a good core instructor who knows first aid."

Tom leads me into the instructor lounge and knuckles a small wooden locker, "This is yours and so are these." He drops a ring of keys into my hand. "Go see the receptionist. She has your employment papers to fill out. Other than that I will see you tomorrow morning at seven thirty."

Half an hour later, a very amazed Stephen Arrington walks out the front door of the College of Oceaneering. For months, I have worried about trying to find work as an ex-felon. My Christian friends told me to put my faith in Jesus and things will work out according to His will as long as I did my very best. The rest of the felons promised me that I would have great difficulty just getting a job that did not involve a close relationship with a broom or a shovel. At the camp, my faith had been high, yet I also had the security of three meals and a place to sleep. Yet as soon as I was released, though I had a bed and enough money to ensure three meals a day for several weeks, self-doubt began to seep in. With all my Christian commitment, I had just demonstrated that I did not even have the faith of a mustard seed. *Wow, so much to learn.*

At the bus stop, I only have to wait a couple of minutes then board a bus heading east. I grab a bus schedule and begin to study it occasionally looking out the window to orient myself to the town of my employment. I reach into my pocket and finger the ring of keys. How surprising…to start the morning with such low hopes and now in the early afternoon to become a responsible person with a ring of keys. I reach deeper into my pocket for the room key and add it to the others. I settle into the bus seat totally enjoying an overpowering sense of belonging. On the ride out, I was simply an ex-felon, right out of prison, casting about, but not belonging. Now I am going to be a teacher at a junior college. Tomorrow they will issue me books and study guides. I will meet students whose only knowledge of me is that I am their new instructor.

Back at the halfway house, I unpack a bag of groceries. I am in a celebratory mood though it is sobering to have spent nine dollars and eighty-five cents. That is another five percent of my money gone, which means I have already spent one quarter of my funds. Thankfully, I now know that my first paycheck is just eleven days away. That is eight workdays meaning I have to allocate eight dollars and sixty cents per day for the bus. That equals thirty-four point-four percent of my total funds, counting the twenty-four percent I have already spent equals half of my money. Not springing for the box of tea was a good choice.

That night I am early to bed wanting to be fresh and bright for my first day at work. At 9:00 p.m., I watch the fireworks streaking into the sky over Disneyland. The brilliant colors rocketing across the dark sky are like a seal of approval on a promise fulfilled. I settle deeper into my blankets, smile at the world and fall asleep.

The first few days at the college are very hectic as I learn my schedule and get to know the students. On Saturday, the clerk at the halfway house rings the room that I have a visitor. Our telephone can only receive incoming calls. I rush to the office to see Sam standing at the curb with Revelstoke looming over his shoulder. The truck is looking older and a bit worse for wear, yet so many wonderful memories reside in its wood and metal chassis. Sam and I visit about old times and all too soon, it is time for him to head back for San Diego. "So give me a lift to the Grey Hound Station." He says.

"I don't have insurance," I respond, "but come on I will walk you to the bus stop; it's just down the street."

"You're kidding," Sam is shocked. "You're not going to give me a ride?"

"Sam, driving in California without insurance is against the law."

"So?"

"So if I break the law they can send me directly back to jail, do not pass go, do not collect two hundred dollars."

"That's not going to happen," laughs Sam, "come on I've been driving for six months without insurance and it didn't hurt me none."

I realize that it is time to share a few truths with my friend. "Sam if you had gotten into an accident, I am the one who would have gotten hurt...Revelstoke is all I have and you've been driving it without insurance."

"You're really not going to give me a lift?"

Is it not sinking in? I wonder hopelessly. "Sam, that clerk sitting in there monitors everything I do. If he sees me driving a car without providing him with a copy of my insurance card, then I am in violation of my parole."

"Okay," he grumbles, "how much is the bus fair?"

"Seventy-five cents."

"Okay, make it a buck, plus the twenty dollars I spent on gas getting up here and the Greyhound ticket is eighteen more, so round it off to an even forty dollars you owe me."

I give Sam the money then walk him to the bus stop as promised. Walking back towards the halfway house I do the mental math and no matter how I figure it I am going to run out of money before payday. Outside the halfway house, I step up to Revelstoke's back-door, unlock it and step inside its cool dim interior. It is like coming home from a very long trip away or a near fatal sickness. One of my surfboards is stowed in the shower. It is more dinged that I remember. My wetsuit, which was almost new is now sun-faded and worn at the knees. I go through the cupboards, which are bare but for a few boxes of three-year old spices. I switch on the ignition and am not surprised to see the gas needle just above empty. I then step to my closet, which is also empty but for a pair of worn out sandals and then pull open a couple of drawers that only hold a few torn T-shirts and a pair of frayed shorts. I sit down on the bed and glance about Revelstoke's wooden interior and I am happy. This old truck means so very much to me and I am very lucky that the government was willing to release it back into my care. I open the oven and see a stainless steel pot with a dented lid, which gives me an idea.

Half an hour later, I am back from the supermarket having spent a mere five bucks. I have a two-pound bag of brown rice, a sack of beans and a cylinder of oatmeal, which was on sale. Though I am staying in the halfway house, I will prepare and eat all my meals in Revelstoke. Tonight and for the next six nights I will eat rice and beans, I will take a container of cooked rice and beans to school for lunch and for breakfast, oatmeal…no honey, no milk. The simple meals I will spice with the acute pleasure that I am eating them in my own home. I cannot charge Revelstoke's batteries, but have found a couple of candles in the back of a drawer and run the radio on low volume for only an hour each evening.

The following Friday is payday. I have a total of three dollars left in my wallet. Opening the pay envelope, I see a check for eight hundred, fifty-three dollars and thirty-five cents. It seems like all the money in the world. I make a deposit on auto insurance, re-register Revelstoke, fill its gas tank, top off the propane cylinder and fill the refrigerator and cupboards with food including three boxes of tea. I get a haircut then buy a new pair of jeans, a pair of white high-top sneakers and a pair of swim trunks...life is good.

The next two months passes quickly. On the diving barge, which is moored in Los Angeles Harbor, I have been assigned to teach the night diving classes. It gives the students a feel for diving in a working harbor at night, which can be very disorienting and dangerous. We start at sunset and wrap up the class by 10:00 p.m. I have had to get special permission with a letter of explanation from the college to arrive late back at the halfway house.

Standing on the wet rusty deck of the diving barge, I stare out over the dark water at the lights of the harbor. Surprisingly the College of Oceaneering is only about a mile from Terminal Island Prison. We are just a little further up water and on the same side of the harbor; the sights and smells are so very much like what I saw through the prison fence. I am deeply disturbed by the prison's foreboding presence, which lurks far too close to where I am standing. Sometimes school business takes me dangerously near the institution's gray walls, which always causes me to tremble deep down inside. The guard towers, with their dark mirrored windows, have a sinister air about them that is quite intimidating even when viewed from outside the prison walls.

Beyond the lights of the dive barge, I look at the dark hills of San Pedro. The view recalls far too many prison memories of the South Yard. I can see the same city lights on the hills and hear the prison's siren call and know it is seeking to pull me back into its walls.

Shadowy inmate reflections linger about me and haunt my sleep. I do not rest well at night as phantom DEA agents, prison guards, and inmates stalk my dreams. Often I wake up in a cold sweat. In the deep dark of night, it sometimes feels like I am living a desolate nightmarish reality, like I am dreaming my freedom. I live daily with the secret terror that I might accidentally be dragged back inside prison because of a simple parole violation, like missing daily count at the halfway house or accidentally getting into a fight with one of the other halfway house clients, some of whom are super stressed and on a knife-edge of losing it.

On the dive barge, we run a little long securing the equipment on a lightly raining night and then I hit heavy traffic caused by an accident driving back to the halfway house. I am later than I should be as I walk through the office door to sign in—then stop in my tracks when I see a horrifying sight. Sitting upon the clerk's desk is a cardboard box stuffed with my few possessions. They have emptied my room. *Are they sending me back, just for being a little late?* Screams my mind, *surely they should understand…I was working late!* I stand there in a total loss and in complete dismay. My heart collapses into itself as I vividly remember the cold and dank Terminal Island holding cell, which is where they would take me for a parole violation; it is the closest Federal prison.

"About time you got here, Arrington," grumbles the clerk shuffling about the papers on his desk. "Here, sign these discharge papers."

"Discharge papers?" I echo weakly wondering if I heard him correctly.

"Yeah, they arrived with today's mail. The judge has commuted your sentence from five to three years."

Grabbing the papers, I quickly scan the pages and see that Judge Takasugi has ruled on an appeal I submitted over two years ago. *Who would have ever thought he would rule on my appeal after my release from prison?*

"You know you can't spend the night here tonight," the clerk says wearily breaking into my thoughts.

"What?" I ask looking up from the court orders.

"This means you've served your sentence and therefore the halfway house cannot be responsible for your safety around the inmates."

He said the inmates, I think gleefully, *not other inmates. I am no longer an inmate; I am now a parolee!*

"Don't expect any arguments from me, "I quip happily. I quickly sign the discharge papers, tuck the little box under one arm and dash though the door.

I drive Revelstoke to Huntington Beach and park it in an approved camping slot after paying the five-dollar camping fee. Too excited and full of energy to sleep, I walk along the water's edge staring out to sea. The rain earlier in the evening has washed the Los Angeles smog from the sky. It is amazing to so unexpectedly step across this new threshold. I am no longer on probation, my sentence is officially stamped time served. However, I still have three years of Special Parole to do. I am now a parolee, which means monthly visits to the parole officer. A parole violation will still hurl me, like a lightning bolt, straight back into prison, but I am no longer Inmate Arrington…*just call me Steve.*

I watch the shadowy waves rolling irrepressibly in from the vast dark ocean and wonder if my fear of going back to prison will ever leave me. That fear means I am always wound up, there is no simple release, no letting go; I am now a free man, but living in near constant fear of re-incarceration.

The next day after school, I begin the search for a place to live. I am so blessed to have Revelstoke, but need a place to park it on a long-term basis and cannot afford a trailer park. I end up renting half of a Mexican family's driveway on the poorer side of Los Angeles harbor for forty bucks a month. Across the street, an oil well dips and pulls with an endless reciprocating squeal twenty-four hours a day. It is like the heartbeat of this tough Mexican neighborhood, where police cars prefer to patrol with backup close at hand.

Revelstoke becomes the one anchor that I completely latch onto. It is a refuge of good memories and I use it as a place to hide. I am fleeing the social life that I fear for my own self-induced cage. I cannot help but think that the interior of the Stoker is almost as small as my J-3 jail cell (two foot wider and four foot longer). I feel terribly exposed living in a driveway. I hear people walking and talking outside Revelstoke at night, either going to and from the house or passing by on the sidewalk. Fortunately, I installed Revelstoke's side windows rather high up (seven feet to the bottom of the sill), so it is difficult for passersby to see inside. The months pass ever so slowly as I try to cope with my mental scarring.

On some Sundays, I attend church. It is a large warehouse affair with thousands of people in attendance at each service. Yet, I am lost in the crowd. At the beginning of each service, they ask us to say hello to someone and shake hands, but nothing comes of it. I arrive alone and leave alone. My life outside of the college is hollow and uneventful. I would like to talk with young people about choices. I know a bit about those now, but my drug felony makes it difficult to approach a public school principal with this idea. Inmate conditioning prevents me from looking someone respectable in the eyes. It is more than a fear of a stranger's judgment; it is an inmate thing. In prison, eye contact is a violation of privacy and personal space. Public school teachers are by nature suspicious of any stranger wanting to talk with their students. I am just too mentally fragile to stand that kind of moral scrutiny.

In the dark of the night when I cannot sleep, I listen to the mechanical whisper of the oil dredge across the narrow street and silently pray asking the Lord to show me a way out of this family's far too public driveway and back into a semi-normal life where I can talk with youth about choices. The Lord answers my prayer on a cold grey December day in the strangest, yet most powerful way.

I am teaching a core subject in a warm classroom, thankful that I am not out on the cold diving barge when a student explodes through the door yelling, "Mr. Arrington, they need you down at the harbor—hurry, Chris is drowning!"

I grab my first aid kit and run after the frantic student.

On the diving barge, semi-controlled panic rules as a team of divers quickly gear up. A short while ago the victim screamed into the radio-telephone that he was pinned, that the project he was working on had fallen on top of him and that he could not leave the bottom. Then from the surface speaker came the dreadful gurgling sound of water filling his helmet—just before the line went dead. They immediately jumped the stand-by diver, but it was not going well.

From the deck speaker, I hear the standby diver, who is in near darkness forty-five feet down on the muddy bottom of the working harbor, "Chris is badly fouled. A heavy metal cylinder is lying across his back. I can't get it off of him."

"What about his helmet?" The instructor yells frantically into the radiotelephone.

"It's off—he looks dead," static punctuates the tragic reply.

Suddenly there is a loud stomping of booted feet as the set of just suited up rescue divers tramp quickly across the metal deck and leap into the water. Twin huge splashes soak their tenders then the seawater spills across the deck and swirls around my boots before draining down through a gap in a cracked weld. The rescuers grab Chris's umbilical (air hose, wire communication and safety wire) and use it as a descent-line to get to the accident site.

Glancing at the log keeper, I shout anxiously, "How long has it been since you heard water flooding into his helmet?" I know that after four minutes without oxygen irreversible brain damage begins to occur.

The shaken student looks at his log then the clock," Coming up on seven minutes," his voice breaks as he begins to stutter, "Mr. Arrington...is Chris going to die?"

I turn away not wanting to echo what he has guessed. Seven minutes is just too long. I feel helpless while a young life is ebbing away in the cold dark mud at the bottom of the harbor. Standing at the edge of the diving barge, I peer anxiously at the mass of bursting bubbles that surface in a large foreboding boil from the divers working desperately below.

"We got him." The words erupt from the surface speaker, "We're coming up."

The diameter of the bursting bubbles increases rapidly like a pot of water left boiling too long on a hot stove. It is a sign that the divers are nearing the surface. Chris's head breaks the surface surrounded by the rescue divers wearing Kirby-Morgan helmets with reflective faceplates. Each of the hard-shelled helmets is a different solid color: red, yellow and blue with pieces of shiny brass and chrome. The men look huge in their black wetsuits and working harnesses. There is a lather of splashing water as they work to lift Chris up high enough for us to grab him. His head flops lifelessly, his wide-open eyes staring sightlessly from a froth of white water. Kneeling at the edge of the barge, I reach down and grab Chris's chest harness. My face is just inches from those lifeless eyes as I instantly remember the exact same look in the eyes of the teenage driver that we lost in the desert when I was with the fire crew. *Not this time,* I promise myself. Getting a firm grip on the harness straps, I begin to haul the limp body upward. Other hands grab supportingly at my clothing from behind and then upon Chris as we drag the flaccid student onto the unyielding metal deck. I know that we are rapidly losing a desperate race against time. Chris's skin is a ghastly shade of deep purple from a complete lack of oxygen and an excessive amount of carbon dioxide. The black pupils of his eyes are dilated, fixed and staring—as if he has already passed from this world.

Ignoring what those terrible eyes foretell, I place one hand under Chris's neck and the other firmly on his forehead then quickly tilt his head back to establish an open airway. Chris's mud smeared skin is cold and clammy under my hands; like touching a refrigerated cadaver. Taking a deep breath, I seal my mouth around his icy blackened lips and forcefully blow air into his lungs. I see his chest under the black wetsuit rise while in my mind I ask the Lord for His help, *"Father, let us not be too late. Let it be your breath not mine."*

With the first breath, seawater gushes out of Chris's mouth from his grossly distended stomach. I roll him towards me to keep the water from flowing back into his lungs. I give him three more rapid breathes then quickly unzip his wetsuit zipper to relieve pressure on the chest before locking my hands over his sternum and beginning full cardiopulmonary resuscitation (CPR).

It is surprising how easy it is to do CPR on a real person. I have actively taught CPR for over fifteen years. After all of those seemingly boring late night classes working with plastic mannequins, I am suddenly doing CPR for real. I see his chest convulse inward a full two inches under the driving force of my clenched hands. Though his dark purplish skin slowly waxes to a deathly pale shade of white, I know his chances of recovery are not good if not non-existent. He has been down far too long. I continue with the efforts to revive him despite being convinced that he is already gone. In my mind, I see Chris the vibrant young student, who just hours earlier wished me an enthusiastic, "Good morning," as he hurried to the diving locker. I continue the compressions on his chest while another instructor kneels to help with the breathing.

It is a full twenty minutes before the fire department arrives on the scene. They immediate hook Christ to a portable EKG machine that measures the body's vital functions. They order us to pause the CPR while they check the meter, which reflects a total flat line indicating clinical death. I quickly begin the CPR again as one of the medics readies an Ambu Bag with an oxygen reserve, which he uses to take the place of the other instructor doing mouth-to-mouth resuscitation. The lead medic kneels opposite me, "Okay, we got him now," he says through clenched teeth as his hands take the place of mine on Chris's chest. I surrender my position, stand awkwardly and then step back uncomfortable at being demoted to mere concerned observer.

"Where's this guy's wallet," yells one of the firemen. The CPR on Chris is interrupted while they lift him onto a rolling gurney. From the barge's locker room, a student comes running holding up Chris's wallet. A fireman takes it and flips the wallet open checking the driver's license. "Got an organ donor," he yells.

The firemen rush the gurney up the barge ramp to the pier. They shove the body through the back of the ambulance then the doors slam shut and the emergency vehicle speeds away siren wailing. As the siren slowly fades, I stare at a pool of rusty water where Chris's body had lain on the barge deck. I remember the blood stained desert sand in the Mojave after the coroner took away that poor teenager's body and a deep sadness begins to settle upon me. I step to the railing and stare down into the water.

"They got a heart beat!" yells a fireman on the pier holding up his radio.

Everyone stops what they are doing and we all stare.

"Spontaneous breathing," he yells, the radio now pressed

under his helmet to one ear. We crowd around him full of hope as he listens. "Okay, they're diverting to a chopper pad for evacuation to Northridge Hospital." There they would treat Chris in an ultra-modern hyperbaric facility inside a high-pressure oxygen environment (recompression chamber).

At the end of the workday in the instructor's lounge, we are all still very sober; no one's hopes are very high. The odds are that irreversible brain damage has already occurred. Word from the hospital is that Chris is in a deep coma...as expected.

The following day we hear that they moved Chris to intensive care; his condition is considered extremely critical. His mother had sat weeping at the side of his bed throughout most of the night. The situation looked completely hopeless. The doctors warned her to expect the worst. If his heart stopped again, they would have to be ready to harvest his organs.

It is mid-morning when Tom Mix barges through the door of my physics classroom. "Chris is going to live," he yells, "He woke up and he's talking."

I stare open-mouth with a piece of chalk halfway to the board where I have been diagramming the volume pressure relationship of a cylinder at a depth of sixty-six feet.

"No sign yet of brain damage," the words are spewing forth, "the doc thinks it's a real life miracle. He doesn't know of anyone who's fully recovered after over eight minutes without oxygen. Chris woke up with his mom sitting right there; he asked her what was going on."

"I thought you couldn't live that long without oxygen?" blurts one of the students.

"They think it was because of the cold water slowing down his metabolism and the high partial pressure of oxygen in his body from being at almost fifty foot of water depth," explains Tom, who smiles at me and says, "Good job."

I say a silent prayer of thanks.

The next day Tom calls me to his office. "Come in, Steve," he says standing up coffee cup in hand. "Do me a favor and sit in my chair."

"What?"

"I just want to see something," he is pulling me around the desk, "come on, sit down."

I drop into the chair as Tom goes around to the other side of the desk and looks at me. He raises his hands forming them into a rectangle and peers through the opening like a cameraman framing a shot. "Perfect. It works."

"What works?"

"My desk fits you."

"It does?"

"Yep, as of right now you're the new Air Diving Supervisor."

"Huh?"

"Yep, I am leaving for the Philippines. Got a job with a treasure diving outfit."

"Treasure?" I ask intrigued.

"Can't tell you a thing," he picks up a duffle bag and begins randomly stuffing items into it, "just that I'm leaving and Jim Joiner has authorized your promotion." Tom drops the duffle and leans both his hands upon the desk, "Everyone thinks you did an incredible job taking charge of Chris's CPR. Don't worry; you've got what it takes and the students like you."

"Wait a minute," I stand up, "when are you leaving?"

Tom looks at his wristwatch, "In about five minutes."

"You're leaving now?"

"Yeah, your promotion is immediate. You're getting a fifty percent pay raise effective today." Tom looks around the office, shoves a couple of more items carelessly into the duffle then shrugs his shoulders and glances at his watch, "What do you know? My five minutes are up." With those parting words, he steps through the door disappearing from my view.

Still completely surprised I glance around at my new office… amazing.

Early the next month, Chris returns to the College of Oceaneering with no apparent brain damage and joins a class that is just beginning practical harbor diving. It is startling to see him walking the hallways, I too vividly remember him looking very dead. The morning he is assigned to dive the mud monster, I arrange the schedule so I will be running the dive operation. I am like a mother hen, checking and re-checking everything.

I walk over to check Chris's harness while the tenders are suiting him up. "You okay?" I ask.

"Yes instructor," he laughs though his smile seems a little strained. It is understandable the mud monsters almost killed him last time.

"You know," Chris has a momentary faraway look in his eye, "I remember drowning."

"All of it?" I lean in and place a comforting hand on his shoulder.

"Yeah, pretty much," Chris's deep brown eyes look directly at me. It is a little disquieting seeing those eyes so full of life. "I was cheating on the project."

"Really?" I smile encouraging him to tell me all of it. I sense that this sudden admission is part of his healing process.

The mud monster is an advanced underwater project. It is a heavy device partially buried in the soft mud on the floor of the harbor. It is a thick iron cylinder about five feet tall and two and a half feet wide. It is bolted at its base to a cement footing. The diver's task is to attach a webbed bridle with a lifting bladder to the top of the cylinder. Next, he must unbolt the mud monster's feet and using an air hose fill the bladder with air. The bladder is of a size to make the cylinder lighter, but not big enough to lift it from the bottom. It is a planned safety feature as teaching commercial diving realistically is a dangerous occupation. The diver's job is to lever the cylinder up, freeing it from the suction of the mud, and then move it to another footing and bolt it back down and remove the lifting bladder. The project normally takes about an hour; it is a timed grade.

"What I did," Chris is looking down at the deck, "is remove the footing bolts, but instead of attaching the lifting bridle I removed the cylinder's inspection port and inserted my nemo (air hose used for determining depth by the resistant water pressure).”

“So you were going to save time by using the air from the nemo to displace the water inside the cylinder to lighten it.”

“Yeah, but it got away from me,” nods Chris, “the darn thing started to lift up off the bottom. I was afraid it would shoot to the surface and that I would be dropped from the school for cheating.”

“That would have been a possibility,” I admit, “rather dangerous just for a better time.” Echoes of my reprimand from Instructor McNair bounce about in my head for my cheating on the deep-sea diver race for a better time at the Indianhead pool.

“So I grabbed it with both arms. I actually hugged the stupid thing so I could roll the inspection port up to dump out the air.”

“At which point it became extremely negative.”

“About three hundred pounds negative, a great big iron casket. It tumbled toward me knocking down me to the harbor floor and then rolled onto my back. As more air dumped out it got heavier driving me deeper and deeper facedown into the mud. I knew I was going to die and panicked…so I removed my helmet. Like that was going to help.”

Chris is staring at me with those incredibly innocent eyes wide open. “I remember how stupid I felt as the water and mud closed around my face. It was so dark and so very cold and then I tried to scream, but couldn’t underwater. It’s the last thing I remember.”

“Chris,” I say carefully, “you don’t have to make this dive today.”

Chris straightens up on the diving stool, “Yes I do.”

For the next fifty minutes I anxiously pace the old barge’s deck then hear Chris’s triumphant voice over the radio-microphone, “Project complete; stop the clock, diver coming up.”

When he surfaces, I help Chris remove his mud-smeared helmet. He looks at me and smiles, “It’s smaller than how I remembered it.’

Because so much time had elapsed while he had been trapped underwater, the Los Angeles Fire Department and the Red Cross credits me with saving Chris’s life. The Red Cross arranged an award ceremony to present me with their highest award for lifesaving, The Certificate of Merit. In the audience sits James Walsh, the prosecutor in my case. I invited Mr. Walsh personally wanting him to see that an ex-felon could turn his life around. He now seems almost like an old friend. When they hand me the award I look down at the signature upon it in wonder. The Director of the Red Cross had already told me that Ronald Reagan, President of the United States was very serious about signing these awards personally. Looking at that remarkable signature, I remember hearing President Reagan announcing his war on drugs while I was driving that drug-laden car in Florida.

The Red Cross Director takes out a small gold and white award and pins it to my jacket. I finger the small piece of shiny metal and remember the terrible sadness I felt when I removed my naval uniform for the last time. I think about my tragic state six years ago when I placed my military medals and chief's insignia into a little wooden box and sadly closed the lid. Receiving this honor for lifesaving washes away all that old sadness, yet more importantly, it makes me realize that I really can step into a new future and put prison and its awful memories behind me.

Saving Chris's life becomes the turning point for getting my life back to into focus. I truly feel good about myself again and can deal with people knowing my criminal past. It also gives me the courage to approach school principals with my passionate desire to speak with students about drugs, crime and prison—one so often follows the other. Now not only can I be openly honest about my past, I can use it to help others.

The world has indeed taken on the golden glow that I had envisioned from my prison cell. There is however, one more thing I have to do before I can truly put my past behind me. It is time to sell Revelstoke.

After ten years, the Stoker is getting old and I am so ready for a more secure home. I give notice to the friendly old Mexican lady, who is sorry to see me leave. Not only will she lose the driveway rent money, but I also carried her trashcan to and from the curb. The *For*

Sale is not on the old truck very long before I get a buyer. Surprisingly it is an older man living alone. He wants to retire to Mexico and build a house alongside a river. He figures that Revelstoke can be his temporary home while he builds a more permanent structure. The day he drives it away is terribly sad and yet charged with positive energy at the same time. I watch Revelstoke driven down the street by a stranger. Slowing at an intersection it makes a right turn and disappears down the corridors of my mind where my memories of Susan and Puu reside.

Listen, my son, accept what I say, and the years of your life will be many. I guide you in the way of wisdom and lead you along straight paths. When you walk, your steps will not be hampered; when you run, you will not stumble.
Proverbs 3:4-5

Photo Arrington
Cynthia Elizabeth Arrington, sky and scuba diver, mountain climber, skier
and adventure person extraordinaire.

*"The world has its own fate and we are part of it. Of course,
it is partly our business to modify the fate of the world. So if
we are just spectators, we are acting just like a dead weight.
We must be active actors, because the greatest adventure of the
universe is the human adventure,"*
Jacques Yves Cousteau

Chapter 41

COLLEGE OF OCEANEERING,

WILMINGTON, CALIFORNIA, MAY 1987

I HAVE BEEN working at the College of Oceaneering for almost two years. I enjoy my job but yearn for the adventure I had known in the Navy. I lust for travel to exotic places and chafe to get back into an active diving career. However, my special parole will not run out for over another year, so until then I am stuck in Los Angeles County—or so I thought. Global travel and a wealth of world-class adventures are racing toward me...which is unexpectedly linked to a potted houseplant growing by leaps and bounds directly behind my desk. I purchased the broad-leafed plant on a whim at a small mom and pop Mexican market along with a frozen pizza. Someone knocked the little plant off of a shelf and ran it over with a cart. I felt sorry for it lying on the tiled floor with other market debris; its split plastic pot spilling out most of its dirt. Barely a foot tall with a bent stem, exposed roots and a two-dollar price tag its future did not look good. The clerk would only accept twenty-five cents for the abused piece of vegetation. I first planted it in a small pot and placed it under the skylight in Revelstoke, but it quickly grew too big for those cramped quarters. So I took it to my office and put it in a dented steel bucket with a holed rusty bottom that was lying under a pier. The other instructors wondered why I would use such a trashed and rusty piece of metal as a decorative pot, but I kept my J-3 Yard memories to myself. Every couple of days while pouring water over the dirt, I would run my hands over the old pail's sides. The wonder, I carry water.

The plant thrived. More and more vines climbed out of the pot and went off in different directions in search of anchors and a sunbeam or two. The vines draped over picture frames, hung themselves from shelves, swirled around electrical cords and essentially became a serious presence on the wall. If I left the window open too long questing appendages would have to be lured back inside. A few months ago one of the other instructors had asked, "What are you going to do when that thing reaches the ceiling?"

After a moment's consideration, I carelessly replied, "Move on to another job."

Now as I sit at my desk admiring the morning light coming through the office window with the gargantuan plant looming behind me, it likes sunshine too, I hear Doug quip in an innocent voice, "So tell me about your new job."

Confused, I ask, "What are you talking about?"

"Your plant," Doug points to the giant vegetative growth behind me, "it just reached the ceiling."

Spinning about in my chair, I see that the plant has indeed sprouted yet another leaf. It is on the verge of opening. The slightly bent green tip is brushing lightly against the white ceiling tile with the movement of a gentle breeze blowing through the open window. "Maybe I spoke a little too carelessly," I answer disappointed to be going nowhere in the foreseeable future.

I pour the rest of my coffee, which has grown cold, into monster plant's pot. I think it likes the caffeine maybe that is why it is growing so rapidly. Collecting the diving log for my class, I head for the door. I have scheduled myself to teach in the harbor this morning. Letting the door swing shut behind me, I can still hear Doug laughing good naturedly as I walk down the hall.

Outside it is one of those beautifully clear spring days in early May. The bright morning sunshine is dancing in a sparkling tapestry upon the smooth seawater that laps ever so gently against the barnacle-encrusted wooden pilings of the inner harbor.

Down at the barge, I wipe black oil from my hands with a red cloth. I am teaching the students how to hand-crank start the diesel air compressor without hitting their head with the detachable metal crank. Over the heavy pant of the diesel engine, I faintly hear the pier phone ringing. It is a distance away and I just barely catch it on the sixth ring. While trying to blot out the heavy pant of the diesel engine, which rumbles loudly in the background, I hear the voice of Don Santee, expedition leader and chief diver for The Cousteau Society. Don enjoys going for shock value so he opens the conversation with eleven mind-jarring words, "Steve how would you like to come and work for us?"

Earlier in the year, Don had sat in on my diving medicine class just to brush up on any new changes that had occurred in treating diver's maladies. Like almost every other diver that Don met, I offered him my services should he ever need a diver. I sincerely meant it when I made the offer, but I never actually expected him to call. I was just giving voice to a childhood dream; a dream that I thought was too incredible to come true. Particularly since I was an ex-felon and did not even speak French.

Listening to Don on the phone, I cannot believe that my childhood dream is suddenly settling down roots. "Don, it would be my absolute pleasure to come to work for you," I answer enthusiastically.

"Great! You had better give notice to the college right away. I need you as soon as possible."

"Oh, one more thing," Don adds casually, as if it is just an after-thought, "your title is going to be chief diver. I have more expedition work than I can handle and my wife is going to kill me if I don't start spending a little more time at home." Don laughs…well actually he cackles…then the line goes dead.

Chief diver? For The Cousteau Society? My mind is having trouble wrapping itself around this momentous news because Jean-Michel Cousteau knows that I am an ex-felon and that I do not speak French. Don could not make this offer without Jean-Michel's approval. One of Jean-Michel's best friends is also very close to me. Marjorie had introduced us and I had had occasion to have dinner with them on two occasions. My happiness is barely containable as I begin to hoot and holler while dancing about the barge's rusty old deck. Meanwhile the students are staring from the top of the pier wondering if their instructor has just lost his marbles.

Finishing a flying spin with a two-footed stomp that lands my work boots in the middle of a puddle of rusty water, I leap from the barge and bolt up the pier scattering the confused students from my path. At the top of the walkway, I pause to yell back at them to finish setting up the dive stations, but not to get into the water until I return. Dive students are a shifty lot and apt to pull embarrassing tricks on their instructors and each other if not watched carefully. A couple of days earlier I had asked one of them to run up the dive flag. The young student had promptly raided one of the female student's lockers and run her bra up along with the blue and white dive flag. The young lady had retaliated by flying his boxer shorts from the same pole the next morning, but only after rubbing the backside with harbor mud and soaking the front with lemonade to make it look like he had a continence problem.

I find Doug in the recompression chamber room where he is conducting oxygen tolerance tests on a junior class. I dance about him waving my arms shrieking, "Guess what? Guess what?"

"Whoa…slow down," implores Doug, "you look like a hovering helicopter trying to take off with a heavy free-swinging load."

"I just got a job offer over the pier telephone," I gasp between pants. "Shake hands with the newest chief diver for The Cousteau Society."

"Nah," laughs Doug trying to free his hand from my grasp, "you're kidding me."

"Really? Watch how fast I give two weeks' notice," I yell over my shoulder as I race out the double doors.

On the day I leave the College of Oceaneering, I bring Doug a potted plant and leave it on his desk with a note: *When this plant reaches the ceiling, you're out of here.*

It was a miniature cactus. Much later, he told me that in its first year the small cactus had grown less than a quarter inch—despite over-fertilization by Doug. Then he had gotten a kitten that took a swing at the little cactus batting it across the room. It took the resulting sting from a thorn personally and promptly swatted it out the window.

> *"Whether we are filled with confidence or fear depends on the kind of thoughts that habitually occupy our minds,"*
> John Orterg

I went to see my parole officer regarding my three-year special parole, which could hamper my leaving the country. Considering that I am going to work for The Cousteau Society my parole officer promptly signs the paperwork immediately ending my parole obligations. With his signature and the slamming down of a big ink stamp, I again become a free citizen of the United States sixteen months early.

Several months pass as I learn the ins and outs of the Cousteau expedition office in West Hollywood and then Jean-Michel Cousteau sends me to Costa Rica in Central America on my first expedition. My excitement knows no bounds as I anxiously meet the French dive team for the first time. Fortunately, all of the French men speak English. With a basic French language book tucked under one arm, I eagerly board an eighty-five-foot long Swedish schooner named Victoria, which The Cousteau Society has chartered for this expedition.

At sunrise on the following day, we hoist Victoria's tall sails and with the outgoing tide leave the small port town of Punta Arenas on the west coast of Costa Rica. Our destination is the solitary island of Cocos in the warm Pacific waters three hundred miles due west. This beautiful volcanic island, lush in tropical foliage and sheathed in spectacular waterfalls is also known as Treasure Island. Fable and historical records points to tiny Cocos as the hiding place for vast amounts of lost pirate treasure. In my cabin at night during the three-day passage, I lie on my bunk feeling the gentle rocking of the schooner and dream of treasure chests filled with gold doubloons, pieces-of-eight, pearl necklaces and jewel-encrusted cutlasses.

At sunset on the third day of our voyage, I find myself at the plunging bow of Victoria watching dolphins riding the bow wave. The setting sun paints beautiful iridescent patterns of passionate color on the dolphin's slick backs. I am taking pictures of a couple of the French divers who have climbed out on the bowsprit and are now hanging upside down beneath it trying to touch the wet backs of the dolphins. I glance towards the horizon off the bow and surprisingly see the sharp volcanic tip of Treasure Island caught in the blood-red sphere of the setting sun. For a few moments, the red globe silhouettes the island's jagged features. Looking at the mysterious island, I can only wonder what adventures await us in this tropical paradise.

Over the next couple of weeks, we make numerous dives in the virgin splendor of Cocos. We swim with large schools of thousands of jacks and barracuda that part before us as if they are a living metallic curtain, flashing in the submarine light like burnished silver as we venture into their midst. There are schools of hammer-head sharks, some of them over twelve feet long. From the relative safety of the seabed, one hundred fifty feet down, we watch the large sharks swimming overhead like a ghostly squadron of death raiders.

At the end of each day, with our skins taunt from long exposure to the tropical sun and sea salt, we bathe under the spilling coolness of a waterfall that cascades thirty vertical feet directly into the sea. It requires a bit of finesse to nudge the inflatable boat's bow against the moss-slick rocks at the base of the waterfall then hold it gently in place with the engine at low rpm while we soap up. It gets even more challenging to keep the small boat from slipping away with the waterfall pouring heavily into the Zodiac as the surging ocean waves sweep us back and forth. It is a time of buoyant amusement as our soap slick bodies find little purchase on the Zodiac's smooth rubber pontoons. Towels are not necessary. After the shower, we speed rapidly across the protected bay with the zodiac just skimming the surface while the wind quickly dries our hair and skin.

Back aboard Victoria, in the warmth of the tropical night, we dine topside at a large communal table under the broad rope-wrapped sails. Laughter leads us into the night. We toast the glorious sunsets and listen to the music of the trade wind as it rustles through the furled sails and sings lightly in the rope rigging. The old wooden hull creaks and groans in its own dance with the rolling swell of the ocean inside our protective bay.

At the end of the expedition, three of us descend in tight formation with underwater scooters. Mimicking acrobatic pilots, we do synchronized loops and rolls for the underwater cameras then dive down to a depth of one hundred and thirty feet to pass through an awesome underwater cavern. Trailing buoyant steams of iridescent bubbles we fly through the spacious underwater grotto, its walls draped with vibrant living corals. Suspended in the cavern are numerous schools of fish, each patterned differently in bright colors that part before our passage like successive shimmering veils as we traverse the length of the two hundred-foot-long submarine passage before exiting into the clear blue water on the other side.

Returning to West Hollywood, I spend a frantic month readying the equipment for our next expedition. We are going to Hawaii to film Humpback whales in Maui and molten lava flowing underwater on the Big Island.

As a chief diver and now expedition leader, it is my responsibility to make sure that the small mountain of gear we are taking on expedition is working properly before our departure. In many ways, it is a lot like when I was with the EOD teams in the Navy. Diving equipment has to be checked and repaired. The portable generators and compressors need to be run under load to ensure that they do not fail at the worst possible moment. However, unlike the frogman teams we are taking cameras, sound equipment and underwater lights instead of guns, ammunition and explosives. Ours are expeditions of discovery. I love every aspect of our work. As explorers, our fare is incredible adventure spiced with the knowledge that we are actively helping to protect marine wildlife and improving the quality of life for all of us and for the generations of people who will follow. Jacques Cousteau once told me that people protect what they love. I remember when the Cousteau Documentaries first brought whales, dolphins and sharks into our front rooms in the 1950's and am astounded at my incredible fortune just two years out of prison.

While working late on a Sunday night, I think about our upcoming expedition scheduled to depart for Hawaii in three weeks. I cannot wait to return to the Hawaiian Islands where so many of my favorite memories reside. A memory of Susan is rummaging around in my mind as I hear unexpected voices upstairs. A moment later two sets of legs descend the circular staircase into the basement. The second pair is long, feminine and very interesting; they have my complete attention as all thoughts of Susan flee before Cindy's friendly smile.

Bruce Hamren, one of our researchers and a diver, eyes me suspiciously while introducing me to his younger sister. I guess I look a little too enthusiastic about meeting Cindy. She has a captivating smile and an open easy manner that is very refreshing. We talk about diving and other harmless subjects while Bruce hovers worriedly at her side. It seems that Bruce only brought his sister by this late because he did not want her to meet any of the overly friendly Cousteau divers.

He is right to worry; for me it is love at first sight. I soon become lost in Cindy's playful hazel eyes, which are almost on a level with my own. She stands a shade less than six feet tall. Bruce looks unhappily from her smiling face to mine, then back to Cindy's. Reluctantly he leaves us alone only long enough to pack a dive bag. However, the way he is rapidly stuffing his gear into it I will only have a few seconds alone with Cindy. "Would you like to go out with me next weekend?" I blurt.

Cindy's eyes crinkle as she smiles, "Sure, but do you know that I live in Northern California?" Bruce is having problems jamming his wetsuit into the large dive bag as he glances anxiously in our direction.

I make up my mind in an instant, "I'll buy you an airline ticket."

"Okay," giggles Cindy.

"Okay?" Bruce does not like the implication of that word as he arrives abruptly, "Okay what?"

"Just okay, alright?" Cindy glares at her brother, "Can't I even talk with a guy without your overbearing protectiveness?"

"He is not just a guy," Bruce argues lamely, "he's a diver."

The following Friday, I arrive at the airport almost an hour early. I am carrying a hundred and one long-stem red roses. I am hoping to make a good impression. I do not intend to tell Cindy that I got the flowers on sale.

Cindy is easy to spot as she walks off the plane. She is taller than most everyone about her. I am not sure if I should shake her hand, hug her or chance a kiss, so instead I present the flowers.

"You shouldn't have," she says in a voice that ensures that I should have, "they must have cost you a fortune."

"Nah," I say with a sweeping gesture, "I got them on sale."

"You're not supposed to tell me that," she laughs.

While Cindy has her face buried to the nose in the roses, I take the opportunity to have a closer look at the lady who will become my wife. She is wearing a short khaki jacket with a long matching skirt, which accents her light brown hair. She looks very outdoorsy. According to Bruce, Cindy is into skydiving, mountain climbing and biking, whitewater kayaking, snow and water skiing, scuba diving, and long distance running. Bruce also warned me that she packs quite a punch when she is upset. Cindy certainly does not look violent as she smiles at me over the roses.

Our first stop is a French restaurant where I soon discover that mountain women have big appetites, particularly in reference to rich chocolate desserts. It is a busy weekend full of hiking, outdoor adventure and mutual discovery.

On our third date, I flew Cindy to Maui to join the Cousteau team diving with Humpback whales. We spend an incredible ten days together. Before Cindy arrived the expedition had been full of adventure and excitement, but her presence lends a sense of wonder and playfulness that convinced me that I wanted to spend the rest of my life with this exciting woman. While ashore one afternoon, I met a marine artist who had sculpted a golden ring, a dolphin chasing its tail. I presented it to Cindy that night as a friendship ring, not knowing that it would become her wedding ring.

For our fourth date, I fly north with another big bunch of long stem roses to Sacramento where Cindy picks me up at the airport. Then we drive to the quaint mountain town of Paradise where she lives with her parents. The ride up is very exciting since she drives her Toyota MR2 sports car in a very aggressive way with a total disregard for my frequent white-knuckle complaints. She affectionately refers to the little speeding machine as her pocket rocket. Cindy considers every turn a challenge and by the time we pull into her parents' driveway I am a nervous wreck.

We do not spend very much time in the house before Cindy leads me outside and innocently asks if I would like to go for a hike in the canyon.

Her parent's house stands at the top of a high ridge, which quickly drops away into a deep gorge. Pine trees line both sides of the gorge for as far as the eye can see. The west branch of the Feather River snakes a windy course along the bottom. I gladly accept her offer, having no idea that I am about to undergo a test that has become a family tradition much to the amusement of everyone involved. As a young girl, Cindy determined that she would not be stuck with any guy who could not keep up with her in the canyon. A few minutes later, while lacing up my hiking shoes, I wonder why the rest of Cindy's family has come outside to see us off. "Ready?" asks Cindy smiling innocently.

"Sure," I reply not knowing that the family is now seeing me as the sacrificial lamb. No guy has yet even come close to passing Cindy's canyon test.

Cindy is off in an instant, her long legs literally flying down the steep rocky path. Having expected a hike, I am quite surprised to see her running over the sharp-edge lava cap that plunges down at a steeper angle than I would ever consider rational for rapid walking let alone running. My greatest fear in the world is falling from a steep place that involves rocks. Therefore, I am a little slow getting up to speed and Cindy is rapidly pulling away. I am just trying to keep the fleeing figure in sight. She looks over her shoulder and yells playfully, "Keep up slow poke."

After descending three hundred vertical feet, the steep trail abruptly levels off at a cement flume that is carrying water from further up the canyon. Cindy runs lightly along a pathway beside the flume, but then jumps up onto the top edge of the flume's cement wall. It is a narrow edge, maybe an inch and a quarter wide and she is balancing along it walking towards the other end rather rapidly. What makes the feat impressive is that she is walking backwards with her hands deep inside her front pockets and she is whistling. Luckily, it has slowed her down allowing me almost to catch up. I jump up onto the narrow edge as she drops off at the other end and begins running again. I glance down at the water flowing beneath my boots and do not get six feet before losing my balance. I barely avoid falling into the water by dropping back down to the pathway and charge after Cindy who is just disappearing down a narrow trail that leads into a thick Manzanita forest. The trail is more like an animal path with low overhanging branches that weave sharply downward. Later Cindy would tell me that her family calls it the Magic Manzanita Forest. I run bent over to avoid the low hanging branches as it weaves its way downward, which is surprisingly fun.

The animal path breaks out of the Manzanita forest and I find myself on slippery rock and loose shale, which abruptly reminds me of my serious fear of falling. Cindy is now running down a particularly steep stretch, she jumps over a rock ledge landing on one leg and lowers her body in a one-legged squat as she begins sliding downward rapidly. She is on a sheer dirt hillside covered with leaves and moss which reduces the friction of her passage. Her other leg is straight out in front of her and Cindy's arms are outstretched for balance like a big bird. I do not exactly leap over the rock ledge, but I am soon sliding down on one leg rapidly catching up with Cindy. The difference is she is graceful almost like a downhill skier while I am wind milling my arms totally out of control and picking up speed. Cindy glances over her shoulder and sees that I am rapidly gaining on her, but my prolonged scream is not one of triumph. She comes to an abrupt halt just before some dense bushes. I slide by leaving a wake of tumbling rocks and swirling leaves. As I pass her Cindy shouts, "You do know that's poison oak don't you?" I plow full speed into the thick poison oak patch.

Cindy easily beats me to the river. I am actually suspicious that she is holding back to keep me from falling too far behind. She is standing on a big rock looking at her watch as I arrive at her side huffing and puffing, scratched, bruised, beat up and soon to have poison oak issues.

"Rats," she exclaims, "we are running a little slow."

"Slow?" I exclaim. "What do you mean slow? We just ran down the side of a thousand foot mountain.

"That is not a mountain silly it is just my backyard."

"Well, we'll just have to make up the time on the way back up." I think she is kidding—she is not. As I chase her back up the steep slope of the gorge, I know that this is one challenge I dare not lose.

I am a little lightheaded when we break out of the brush at the base of her parent's house. We are almost side-by-side when her stepfather yells from the back porch, "How did he do?"

Cindy looks up into the bright afternoon sunlight and announces, "I think I am going to keep this one."

So I commend the enjoyment of life, because nothing is better for a man under the sun than to eat and drink and be glad. Then joy will accompany him in his work all the days of the life God has given him under the sun. Ecclesiastes 8:15

Author's note: for years, I assumed that I had passed the canyon test, but when I decided to write about it Cindy gently revealed that I had in fact failed.

"Really, I failed?" I asked surprised and disappointed.

"Miserably," confirmed Cindy.

"Oh," said I.

Illustration by Marjory Spielman
RV Alcyone at anchor, Dangerous Reef, Australia. Note metal tubular sails.

"Life is a pretty precious and wonderful thing. You cannot sit down and let it lap around you. You have to plunge into it; you have to dive through it!" Kyle Crighton

Chapter 42

DANGEROUS REEF, AUSTRALIA, JANUARY 1989

FOR OVER a year I have been leading back-to-back expeditions about the Pacific and now I am in Southern Australia and it is hot, really hot. The Alcyone's deck simmers under the blazing Australian sun. In my silver wetsuit, I feel a lot like a foil–wrapped baked potato. Rivulets of sweat run down my legs adding to the substantial puddles already inside my rubber boots. I stare anxiously at the cool ocean water as I strap on a heavy lead weight belt, then buckle on a second one for added underwater stability. I will not be wearing fins for this dive, nor will I be doing any swimming. That is unless something goes terribly wrong. Swimming in shark-infested water is not generally a good idea, particularly when the predators in question are large, hungry, great white sharks.

Shouldering a silver scuba pack, I begin moving ponderously toward the stern of The Cousteau Society's wind ship. The open hatch of a floating shark cage bobs lightly in the calm water. Sunlight on the glassy surface ripples and sparkles in open invitation.

"Can't you waddle any faster?" urges Capkin, our newest and

youngest diver. The tall, lean Australian is anxious to go below to the dining salon. His nose flares as he sniffs at lunchtime smells wafting through the open door of the bridge. Capkin's first concern always centers on his stomach.

"I don't know how you can get so excited about fish head soup," I reply, spitting into my dive mask to keep it from fogging up in the cold water.

"Only real men eat fish head soup," grins Capkin pounding his ample chest for added emphasis. Despite his ravenous appetite, he has a slim swimmer's waist. He is sporting the beginning of a new beard. His white teeth gleam brightly from the shadow of dark stubble.

The soup in question has been simmering on the stove all morning. At first light, I had mistakenly lifted the lid in hopeful pursuit of oatmeal and looked inside. I still could not shake the memory of those dead fish eyes staring back from a slimly yellow, bubbling broth.

"Would you mind making me a peanut butter and jelly sandwich on whole wheat?" I ask hopefully.

"Bruno is not going to be impressed." Our French chef has a low opinion of peanut butter, catsup, corn flakes, Pepsi and other such American staples. I often bait him by adding assorted condiments to my peanut butter sandwiches, such as: potato chips, bananas, figs, raisins, honey and an occasional cucumber.

"Throw in a pickle," I grin, "that ought to fire him up."

Picking up a Nikonos underwater camera, I suddenly remember the last sandwich Capkin made for me. "Hey Capkin, this time could you check the cutting board for fish slime and scales before making my sandwich?"

Abruptly, a large gray fin surfaces and knifes through the water just a few feet from the swim step.

"Speaking of fish scales," observes Capkin, "Murf is back."

The great white shark's head lifts out of the water and glares in our direction. No light reflects from its dark pupil. The stare is cold and predatory. I watch the fifteen-foot-long super predator glide silently beneath the stern of the wind ship.

Despite the muggy heat of the day, a chill of anticipation runs down my spine.

"You know my dad always said it is better to eat the fish than to be eaten by the fish," confides Capkin leering over my shoulder.

"That is reassuring," I answer wondering if Murf has brought any toothy friends. "Mind pulling the cage a little closer?"

A couple of seconds later I jump through the open hatch of the floating shark cage. Cold water immediately floods my wetsuit, but I hardly notice as I see Murf swimming eagerly in my direction. Apparently, the shark thinks it is his lunchtime too. Thankfully, there are some high-quality steel wire mesh between the oncoming eating machine and me. Murf impacts the cage nose first, which cannot feel very good even for a great white shark. He hits the solid steel bars a second time, then shakes his muzzle like a boxer trying to recover from a head blow. Obviously, Murf is not a very bright shark.

A moment later, Capkin's size-extra-large foot pushes against the top of the cage shoving it out into the tidal current. While waiting for the cage to drift to the full length of its twenty-foot tether, I find it momentarily amusing that this little experiment is my own idea.

Like most fish, great white sharks actually tend to be rather shy around people. The chances of a person being attacked by a shark are only about one-in-fourteen million. However, hanging out with great white sharks in South Australian waters does increase my odds a bit. Particularly as we have been chumming the water with fish parts and gallons of animal blood, which tends to get the sharks rather excited, also known as a feeding frenzy. Couple this with the name of our location, Dangerous Reef, and this should be a happening spot for a serious shark encounter.

So far, we have seen only a few great whites and they have mostly kept their distance. Murf tends to be shy and is not exciting to film. So I figure by being the only one in the water, and with no one on the deck of the *Alcyone* to distract them, I might actually be able to lure the sharks in closer. Capkin calls my unique idea the human bait approach. I optimistically wave a dead tuna at Murf, but he just swims away. In the realm of great white sharks, Murf is rather timid.

Abruptly, the cage jars and a heavy shutter vibrates up through my feet. Looking downwards, I see a huge great white shark chewing on the heavy steel mesh at the bottom of the cage. The shark's large teeth are only inches from my rubber booted feet. It takes me several heartbeats to realize that this aggressive behavior does not fit Murf's laid-back personality. No, the seventeen-and-a-half-foot-long shark industriously going after my toes is Amy. She is a three-thousand-pound great white with a very bad attitude. I quickly swing the underwater camera into action. I see my rubber boots in the frame as Amy torpedoes into the bottom of the cage a second time. The camera catches the shark with her teeth embedded in the steel mesh. Just inches away my rubber-clad feet are pleased to be a part of the image, but not a part of her lunch.

Speaking of lunch, Capkin delivers mine half-an-hour later via balloon. It is a rather strange sight, seeing a yellow balloon floating on the wind towards you with an odd-looking cargo floating on the water beside it. Wrapped inside a clear plastic bag is a very weird sandwich indeed. Snagging the balloon with its unusual baggage, I open the top hatch of the shark cage and climb up into the sunshine to investigate this strange sandwich. I see a bun with a big kosher pickle stuck inside. It looks a lot like a seasick hot dog. Globs of peanut butter, strawberry jelly, mustard and chopped onion leak thickly from the bun.

Capkin and Bruno are grinning at me from the stern of the boat. They look quite happy with their little joke. Yet, I find the sandwich intriguing, so I take a mighty bite, which sets Bruno to choking.

"You are a barbarian," our chef shouts.

"Anyone who makes fish-head soup at breakfast time has no room to talk," I reply while still chewing. My taste buds find the sharp, contrasting flavors a jolting experience.

"You don't deserve any of my dessert you weird American." Bruno is holding up a pink balloon with a white ribbon tied to it.

Hanging beneath it is a paper party plate inside an inflated plastic bag. He gently places it on the water and pushes it in my direction. The little colorful convoy drifts slowly down current towards me.

"What is it?" I ask in eager anticipation.

"It is peanut butter and chocolate cheesecake with raspberry swirls and a topping of Dutch chocolate and heavy whipping cream." Bruno is obviously proud of his creation, "Though you do not desire it after the pickle and the peanut butter sandwich."

Fascinated, I watch the bobbing pink balloon with its dessert baggage. I mentally wipe the drool from lips, when Capkin casually asks, "Seen any more sharks?"

Without warning, a two-foot wide mouth erupts from the water. Massive teeth chomp down bursting the pink balloon. A giant tail thrashes wildly throwing water and pink shredded balloon into the air. Then, the shark...and my dessert...plunge beneath the surface.

"That wasn't Murf was it?" Water drips from Capkin's nose. Bruno's waterlogged chef's hat droops to one side. He is speechless.

"No, it's Amy, and she just ate my cheesecake." I quickly duck underwater to see the shark swimming off with a shredded sliver of the pink balloon floating in her wake. Through the sparkling reflection of the surface water, I see Capkin and Bruno rushing off to alert the rest of the crew that we now have a very active shark at the stern of the boat. For a moment, I am a little disappointed to lose my dessert. Yet I know that there will be other fabulous desserts from the extraordinary Bruno, yet this is already sizing up to be my most exciting expedition with The Cousteau Society. I check my camera then peer anxiously into the deep blue water with great anticipation.

"Security is mostly a superstition. It does not exist in nature...life is either daring adventure or nothing,"
Helen Keller

Two months later we are still diving with the great white sharks. It is a blustery morning at Dangerous Reef. The wind is beginning to turn cool with the approach of fall Down Under. I am quite comfortable in my jeans and a warm sweatshirt, while leaning against an idle shark cage on *Alcyone's* stern. In my hand I hold a steaming cup of hot chocolate, which is tainted by a pungent reek of rotting fish floating in the air. It is wafting up from a rusty bait bucket a few feet away. The foul odor permeates the whole ship. The horrible smell is necessary for attracting great white sharks. The stink of decaying fish is a delicious bouquet to sharks. Using the wind and tide, we are spreading an odor corridor miles long. Any shark that stumbles into that corridor will eagerly follow the tempting stench to its source.

Peering hopefully over the side, I look to see if we have any morning visitors, and that is when I see a dark shape rising rapidly to the surface just a few feet away. My heart leaps in anticipation as the creature surfaces...then barks at me. Hoping for a shark, I instead look at a large pair of inquisitive brown eyes peering in a friendly way from the choppy water. The fur seal pup lifts its whiskered muzzle into the air and sniffs loudly.

Apparently, fur seals also find the disgusting aroma of rotting fish enticing. Reaching into the revolting bait bucket, I carefully lift out a decomposing mackerel. The slimy fish feels squishy in my hand as I quickly flip it underhand towards the fur seal, which swims forward eagerly. Absent-mindedly lifting the steaming cocoa for another sip...my nose is instantly overwhelmed by the close-up smell of decomposing fish slime clinging to my hand. The horrible odor corrupts the chocolate flavor into something that could be found lurking on the bottom of a garbage can.

Lowering the cup, I notice the fur seal pup behaving strangely. It stops short of the fish and peers straight down into the water; abruptly it flees in alarm towards dangerous reef.

Beneath the floating mackerel, I see a dark shadow torpedoing upwards. An eighteen-foot-long great white shark lunges out of the water. Its gapping maul swallows the fish as white teeth glistening in the morning light, clash loudly together. I momentarily see a lifeless orb staring in my direction, then the massive tail throws a broad slash of foaming white water. Quickly jumping back, I am too late. The ice-cold saltwater splashes across the stern drenching my sweats and jeans.

Rushing for the bridge door, I throw it open and eagerly ring the ship's bell, while shouting, "Shark! Shark! All hands on deck."

Below deck, there is instant pandemonium as the crew spills from staterooms. Some of the men are still pulling on clothes, a few are carrying cameras as they run up the narrow corridor. At the lead is Bob Talbot, who is world famous for his creative photographs of whales and dolphins. Passing me, he notices that I am soaked head to foot. I can tell he is powerfully curious about why I am wet, but then the great white surfaces and begins vigorously biting *Alcyone's* aluminum hull. The shark is in a feeding frenzy and looking for the source of the blood leaking into the water. Since the blood is coming from the metal ship, it apparently fits shark logic to bite it.

Bob runs past me and jumps down on the swim step. The small platform is only eight-inches above the water, and just several feet from the ship-chewing shark. Bob likes extreme, close-up, super-dramatic photography. The shark helps by crashing mouth-first into the side of the swim step.

Soon the aggressive shark is joined by several toothy equally aggressive friends. Bob and the rest of us could not be happier. There are now three people crowding the small platform. Capkin attaches a line to a baitfish and uses it to lure the sharks directly to the swim step. Bob is leaning outwards with a very wide-angle lens shooting a seventeen-foot-long great white as it lunges for the baitfish. Missing, the shark slams back into the water, then it quickly dives beneath the swim step, passing directly under Bob's feet. It is a very exciting moment—then, without warning, it becomes terrifying.

Bob abruptly loses his balance. His arms waving in panic, I see him falling helplessly into the water. Incredibly, he lands right on the back of the descending great white shark. He bounces off the dorsal fin and slides into the water, where he is struck by the shark's tail. The super predator, not expecting a hundred and fifty pound man to drop on to its back, bolts in surprise. A great white shark can turn around in its own length...and Bob is still thrashing in the water. Anxious hands quickly reach down to help, but he is slipping beneath the ship as it rises and falls with the swell. There are at least three great white sharks off the stern; we have to get him out fast. Finally, Bob reaches the surface gasping, and waving his hands frantically. One of those hands is still clutching his camera. Capkin and Thierry grab hold of him and lift so hard that Bob all but flies out of the water, literally landing upright on his feet.

Talbot is in a state of shock. He looks at his soaking wet camera, then peers over the side at a passing great white in pursuit of another shark.

"That was a really close call," offers Thierry.

"How did you fall in?" asks Capkin.

"I don't know," Bob looks confused. "I guess I just fell."

Close to where they are standing, a large bait fish dangles three feet above the water's surface from our crane. It is to encourage the great whites to lunge out of the water to get it. Abruptly, one does. It is the same shark that Bob fell on top of only moments ago. Its monstrous jaws rip the forty-pound tuna in half in a single body-mangling bite, then the shark falls back into the water and disappears in a gigantic splash. The shark-generated wave splashes the already soaked divers on the swim step.

Bob stares, slack-jawed at the mangled half of the tuna still dangling from the crane. "How did I fall in?" he asks no one in particular. Carrying his ruined camera, Bob goes below deck to change—leaving me with a very real dilemma.

Apparently, I am the only one who really saw what happened. Well, actually, someone else knows too, but so far, he is not prepared to talk about it.

When Bob was leaning over the water shooting pictures of the great white shark just beneath his feet, I was twelve feet away preparing to shoot a picture of him. I thought it would be a great action shot, and had pre-focused a hundred millimeter lens on the crowded swim step. I clearly saw the third person on that platform (name withheld). He was behind the others, shooting with his amateur video camera. He had one eye open to look through the video viewfinder and the other eye closed to eliminate visual distractions. When the shark swam under the swim step, he had taken a step forward for a better view. With the one-eye closed, he blindly placed his free hand out to steady himself. That hand landed on Bob's shoulder, accidentally shoving him into the water.

That person is now standing in the background of the rest of the activity. I know I am going to have to confront him. Bob needs to know that it was not his own fault. As a wildlife photographer, his is a very dangerous job. He must have complete confidence in his physical abilities and awareness or his future performance might suffer. I wait until the other man is alone.

"I saw that it was an accident," I offer.

"Yeah, he just fell in," the other man says lamely.

I shake my head, "No, you did it accidentally when you were trying to keep your own balance."

"No way!" the man argues.

"Look, you didn't do it on purpose, Bob will understand that," I reply, putting a hand on his shoulder, "but you've got to tell him."

The man shakes off my hand. "I didn't do it," he rages, then storms below slamming the metal door.

Looking unhappily at the closed door, I now have an even bigger dilemma. This is turning into an ugly situation and there is only one solution.

"The truth does not hurt unless it ought to," B.C. Forbes

In life, sometimes people argue for not telling the truth when it might possibly hurt themselves or another person. To varying degrees, these falsehoods are referred to as *white lies.* We lie to someone supposedly to protect them or ourselves…from the truth? Honesty is always the best solution. Lies inevitably wind up hurting, or diminishing, everyone involved.

Going below myself, I find Bob in his cabin, and quietly tell him what really happened. Though he is rightfully angry that the man did not take responsibility for his actions, Talbot also realizes it really was just an unfortunate accident. Yet more importantly, Bob realizes it was not his own fault.

Half an hour later, he is again standing on the swim step taking extreme close-up pictures of sharks. Capkin and Thierry are there to help lure in the great whites, but no one is standing behind Bob. Something I see Talbot confirming for himself with regular glances over his shoulder.

I see the man I confronted standing alone by the bridge. He is looking rather sheepish and unsettled. Right now, the open knowledge of his mistake is making him uncomfortable, but it is a feeling that will pass probably in just a day or two. However, had he kept the lie, it would have burdened him far into the future—maybe even for the rest of his life. That is one of life's simple lessons that sometimes seems a bit hard to learn, lies enslave us, while the truth sets us free.

Kings take pleasure in honest lips; they value a man who speaks the truth. Proverbs 16:13

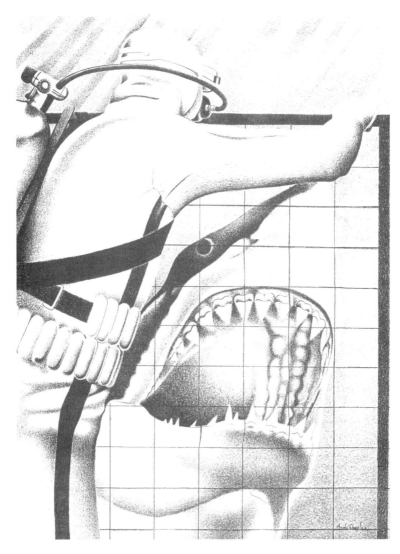

Illustration by Andy Charles
Shark cage door under assault while author holds it closed.

*"The grand essentials to happiness in this life are something
to do, something to love, and something to hope for,"*
Joseph Addison

Chapter 43

CHURCH OF THE RECESSIONAL,

GLENDALE, CALIFORNIA, APRIL 1, 1989

I AM STANDING nervously next to an altar covered with wild flowers;
it is the most exciting day of my life. At my side, Jean-Michel
Cousteau is very handsome in his black tuxedo. He places a hand
on my shoulder and quietly confides, "Not too late to send you
dashing off on an expedition to some remote location."

I grin at him, too full of emotion to say anything witty in return.
The piano begins to play *Canon in D* as the rest of the wedding party
starts their slow march down the aisle. I see my friend Sam walking
at the lead. At his side, walks Cindy's best friend, Dagmar. In three
years, she will give birth to a son, but her joy will be cut short when
cancer takes her two years later. Next comes, Marjorie Spielman,
an artist who has been my friend the longest and introduced me
to Jean-Michel Cousteau. With her proudly walks my big brother,
Jim. I would lose him five years later in the summer of 1994 to

a sudden and tragic suicide. I usually remember him best during happy moments because our laughs are identical. It is when my laughter comes out loud and uncontrollable that I hear echoes of Jim coming from within me. Then, the happiness of the moment is usually shattered. Yet, at this time, I do not know the tragedies that lurk in the near future. Instead, I see Cindy in her flowing gown, and can hardly believe this beautiful woman, my best friend, is about to become my wife. At the altar, we link hands and just before the ceremony begins, we pause to look at all our guests gathered in the small church. I see our families, a wealth of friends and many expedition companions from The Cousteau Society. Then, I turn to face Cindy. In her smiling eyes, I see a future yet to be, made of dreams, hopes and youthful aspirations. Yet, we will also reap a full measure of tragedy and sadness. All of this is simply the recipe of human existence. In this moment in time, Cindy and I link hands and become life-long companions. Whatever the future bears, we will face it together. I will be at her side for the birth of our three children and, only yesterday, I stood with her, as the doctor who delivered Cindy was laid to rest.

If there is anything I have learned about life, it is that all of us will face wonder and tragedy; we will know love and hate, success and failure. Life is a relentless cascade of positives and negatives. To have the strength and courage to face all that is hurling at us takes the fortitude of family and friends. None of us can stand alone, which leads to the most important decision one can make…simply to invite the best friend of all human kind, Jesus Christ, into our lives.

For our honeymoon Cindy and I spend a glorious week discovering coastal California from Big Sur to the giant redwoods of the North Coast. Upon our return to Southern California Jean-Michel asks both of us to come to his office.

"I have a dilemma," he begins cheerfully looking the whole time at Cindy as if I was not even there. "I need to send Steve back to Australia again to dive with the great white sharks."

I already anticipated that I would be going back to Australia.

Jean-Michel found the great white sharks extremely fascinating and was conjuring up some very weird science projects that included a mechanical great white shark and the world's first all plastic shark cage. *Author's note: to read about the mechanical shark see my High On Adventure Series.*

Jean-Michel tents his fingers as he continues, "My dilemma is that we have never had women Cousteau divers and I have a filming sequence I would like to do in the Bahamas. I need three very fit women, who can hold their breath for long periods of time, to free dive with a pod of friendly dolphins."

"I'll go," grins Cindy.

"How long can you hold your breath?"

"I don't know, never timed myself."

Jean-Michel ponders her answer as he strokes his short beard, "Two minutes, at the very least."

Cindy grins, it is her accepting a challenge grin, "I can hold my breath for over two and one-half minutes." She looks Jean-Michel in the eye, "Or I will be able to by the time we leave."

Jean-Michel claps his hands together, "Good, because my other chief diver, Don Santee will pool test you and Marjorie in two weeks."

"What about me?" I ask foolishly.

Jean-Michel turns his head in my direction, as if noticing my presence for the first time. "Why you're leaving immediately, of course."

"I am?"

"See my secretary on your way out," Jean-Michel leans happily backwards in his chair, "she has your tickets."

"I'm leaving tonight?" I ask unhappily.

"Steve," He spreads his hands, "I am not that cruel. You have just got back from your honeymoon. You don't leave until tomorrow. Go look at your tickets; I even got you a red-eye."

"Humor is the great thing, the saving thing. The minute it crops up, all our irritations and resentments slip away and a sunny spirit takes their place, " Mark Twain

Sunrise in the Great Australian Bight watching the bright golden orb of the rising daystar glistening on the ocean's rippling surface. Standing on the stern of the *Alcyone*, I place my hand against a gigantic plastic cylinder. It is ten-feet-tall and five-feet-in-diameter... and feels a little flimsy and somewhat wobbly. *This is not reassuring at all,* I think to myself as I knock experimentally on the thin plastic wall, then peer at my semi-transparent reflection on its shiny warped surface. I notice that the slightly distorted image of me looks a little concerned, maybe even a bit worried. Over the plastic's distortion, beyond my shoulder, I see Jean-Michel Cousteau walk out of the bridge door carrying a white porcelain cup of steaming tea. His reflection joins mine on the cylinder's plastic wall.

"So what do you think of the world's first all plastic shark cage?" he asks proudly.

"I wish it was a bit thicker," I respond knuckling it again...more for Jean-Michel's benefit than mine.

He leans over and gives the cylinder a solid wallop. The thin plastic wobbles causing our reflections to shimmer and dance. "This is not just plastic, it is super-tough *Lexan*," Jean-Michel says proudly, "three-eighths-of-an-inch-thick *Lexan* has been known to stop a thirty-eight bullet."

"But this *Lexan* cage is only half that thick and a thirty-eight bullet weighs only an ounce," I answer nervously. "I want to know if this thing will stop a three thousand pound super-predator."

"Don't forget that the bullet has a lot more velocity than a great white shark," laughs Jean-Michel, "besides I am planning on giving it a tuna test."

"Tuna test?" I am not sure I heard him correctly.

Jean-Michel grins and takes a loud slurp of his tea, "Yeah, tuna test."

Two hours later, Michel DeLoire and I jump from the stern of the wind ship into the open hatch of a steel shark cage floating on the surface. Peaches, an eighteen-foot-long great white shark, immediately comes over to investigate. She peers through the foot-tall open viewing slots in the upper sides of the cage, then chomps down on one corner and gives the steel bars a vigorous shaking. It is startling to see the massive great white's body flex and jerk as she shakes our cage about like a child's rattle. Keeping one's balance inside a shark cage that is bobbing with each passing ocean swell is challenging, particularly when wearing slick rubber boots on a smooth metal grate. Having an almost three thousand-pound shark knocking the cage about looking for a snack makes standing in one place basically impossible. Currently, Michel DeLoire and I are both attempting to stay in the center of the cage...the furthest point from those large clashing teeth. Fortunately, for Michel, he is doing a better job of it and he is catching some exciting, but unfortunately unstable, footage. I stumble and almost fall, then bounce off two of the cage's wire mesh walls half-flooding my dive mask in the process. I urgently want to clear the water out of the mask, but that requires the use of my hands, which are currently protecting the underwater camera I am holding. Peering myopically through the distortion of the saltwater, I see teeth the size of my thumb industriously shredding paint chips from the cage inches from my face. I snap a couple of shots, which when processed are out of focus because the jaws are too close to the lens.

The shark worries a few more feet of the sturdy steel bars like *the-ever-hungry* Capkin going after a corncob, then she turns away and heads downward. Its massive tail slams against the cage as the super-predator charges after another great white shark. Two staggering steps later, I regain my balance, quickly clear my mask, then realize that beside a rational level of fear, I am also feeling a bit seasick. The water visibility is not very good as I feel my stomach rumble in protest at the constant movement of the floating cage. I can see only about thirty feet into the gloomy water as I watch the two great white sharks swim in and out of view with one usually in pursuit of the other. Michel looks at me and grins. As always in dangerous situations, he is having an extraordinarily good time. I try to steady myself inside the still bobbing cage and make a conscious attempt to suppress the nauseous feeling of my growing seasickness. Instead, I burp and taste an unpleasant acid tang inside my regulator and then I abruptly heave-up my breakfast. Blowing chow underwater must be done with the regulator clinched firmly between the teeth, otherwise when you do the spontaneous-gasping-inhalation-part you could drown. The key to vomiting into your mouthpiece is to try to blow out a bit of air to clear the chunks just before that big inhalation. I go through the heave, blow and gasp routine a couple of times. Through my faceplate, I see an expanding multi-colored cloud with floating chunks drifting about my head. A gang of Leatherback fish charge into the cloud going after a bit of their own breakfast. These small fish are always in close attendance with the cage, which provides some protection from the bigger preda-tory fish and they get to gobble fish chunks from the bait stream coming off the stern of *Alcyone*. Fortunately, there is a slight current as I watch the rather disgusting cloud slowly drifting away from me. Then I notice Michel DeLoire staring at the approaching cloud; he is down current and there is nothing he can do to get out of the way. The vomit cloud with its attendant horde of swarming Leatherbacks descends upon Michel.

After pawing at himself with his hands to clear away the debris from his body, Michel shoves me into the down current side of the cage and glares at me. He is yelling something into his regulator; fortunately his words are distorted by the water and I do not under-stand French, particularly that kind of French.

I hate being seasick, but always feel much better after heaving. I offer Michel a smile, but he just glares at me. Looking up through the shimmering surface, I see the crew beginning to lower the plastic cylinder into the water, which immediately commands Peaches' attention. She swims around it twice, eyeing the nearly transparent cylinder suspiciously. The huge shark nudges it once sharply with her snout, but the life-less plastic cage does not seem to hold much interest for her. That is until Jean-Michel drops a forty-pound half-frozen tuna into it. That is when things begin to get positively exciting.

Peaches behavior changes dramatically as she gets the aroma of that tuna. She swims repeated through the odor corridor (down current) of the big fish as it quickly defrosts sending shark tantalizing fish blood and tuna oil into the surrounding water. The giant shark begins swimming enthusiastically around the cylinder looking for a way to get at that enticing fish. The tuna's arrival brings in two more great white sharks charging in from down current. Seeing all the abrupt shark activity, Michel DeLoire decides it is a good time to film with the front door of the cage wide-open. Having the cage door fully open, means Michel can get unrestricted shark footage. This type of cinematography is critical if our films are to be dramatic and exciting for our viewers. Since Michel needs both hands to operate the movie camera it falls on me to hold the door open for him, which requires that I lean outward through the narrow opening and tilt my body to one side. This allows Michel to position his camera over my shoulder. Glancing nervously behind me, I notice that the large bulk of the underwater camera, it is thirty-two-inches-long and a fourteen-inches-in-diameter, will be an interesting obstacle in reference to my getting fully back inside the cage in an emergency. That realization contributes significantly to my heart rate. Feeling the blood pounding under the snug hood of my wetsuit, I silently hope that things do not get more exciting than they already are.

Abruptly, a fourth shark begins swimming rapidly upward from beneath our cage. Michel cannot see the oncoming super predator because he is peering over the camera at another great white shark torpedoing in out of the gloom. I want to yell a warning, but there is that small problem of not being able to talk underwater, except for grunting...or the occasional scream. With my faceplate beyond Michel's camera lens, I cannot turn to look at him. All my attention is riveted on the ascending shark. My concern revolves around the shark teeth in the upper jaw of a great white, which it can dislocate and extend outward from the shark's formidable mouth. The cage bottom's grid is wide enough that a biting shark can extend its teeth a bit, or several toes worth, into the cage. Two loud grunts into my regulator do not get Michel's attention, so I resort to the scream with a bit of head nodding in a downward direction. My antics instantly gains Michel's attention. Apparently, I am causing his camera to vibrate ruining his shot of the shark swimming beside the cage, so he lightly whacks me alongside my head with the camera to get me to settle down. Fortunately, my scream, which underwater sounds more like a weak squeak, apparently frightens the shark beneath us. In complete panic, it reverses directions and plunges back down into the dark depths below. I breathe a deep sigh of relief, which elicits another crack on the head from Michel's camera. He is using my shoulder as a camera rest so he wants me to hold absolutely still.

Trying to breathe softly without moving is beginning to cause my faceplate to fog up. Through the mask's reduced visibility, I see Peaches patrolling in a tight circle around the lightweight plastic cylinder. I would like to take a couple of pictures with the under-water still camera hanging from my right hand...instead I get to be a camera rest for Michel. After panning right, left, up and down, I notice that Peaches is beginning to get upset. Frustrated at not being able to get at that tormenting tuna, she whacks the plastic cage with her snout. The impact rocks the plastic cylinder causing the tuna inside to bounce about enticingly. The swaying fish is too much of a temptation for a fourteen-foot-long great white cruising below our cage. It makes a sudden rush for the dancing tuna. Peaches charges downward to head-off the smaller intruder, who quickly turns away and flees back towards the bottom. Boldly another shark, a fifteen-foot-long male, rockets out of the gloomy water straight at the cylinder. Peaches instantly reverses direction and charges the fifteen-foot-long shark—which immediately turns away and bolts straight towards our open door. When leaning out into open water with a large movie camera resting on your shoulder and a underwater still camera hanging from one of your hands, it is an amazing sensation to see a huge great white shark hurling straight at you. I let the camera tumble into the cage and desperately reach for the door.

From a diver's perspective, things always take a little longer underwater. Michel is backing up as fast as he can, yet the resistance of the standing water and the bulky camera is slowing him down. To get an idea how difficult this is take a rock into a swimming pool. Stand on the bottom and lean forward with the rock in your hands, then see how long it takes before you can reverse your lean and push off in the opposite direction. Meanwhile, I am urgently grabbing at the door and pulling it...against water resistance...over a full arch of one-hundred-eighty degrees, with my faceplate rapidly filling with a jaws-wide-open, charging, super predator. A bare instant after the door slams closed, I see it is about to be squarely impacted by the charging shark. Staring anxiously through the wire mesh, I see the shark's eyes roll back as he extends his jaws and then crashes into the door. My faceplate is only inches from the shark's snout. The thin lightweight steel shudders and bends under the massive collision. The gigantic tail swishes from side to side as the shark bites down on the wire mesh barrier and then shakes it ferociously. At that moment, what is bothering me the most is that I have not yet latched the door. This means I cannot let go of the steel mesh, otherwise the shark might jerk the door open and rip it off its hinges. Barely two inches from my fingers are some startlingly large serrated teeth about the business of industrious chewing. I watch the teeth grinding off several layers of paint and then the shark rattles the whole cage like a hobo with a tin cup looking for a handout. Finally, the enraged shark releases its toothy grip, but it is only so he can get a better bite. I quickly let go of the door while he prepares to reset his dental work a little more aggressively in my direction. I see the upper jaw dislocate in anticipation of the bigger bite. The serrated teeth flash in the gloomy light as he chomps down into the wire mesh again. His jaws are now a little further from the latch. I Quickly grab the outer edge of the door with one hand, and am reaching urgently for the latch—when Peaches crashes into the opposite side of the cage. I guess Peaches thought she was missing out on something. Almost by accident, the jarring of the cage helps as I feel the latch's quarter inch bolt slide into its slot. Retreating backwards towards the center of the cage on my knees, I feel Michel's camera sliding back over my shoulder, then he grips my arm with his now free hand as a signal to remain absolutely still. Kneeling, with my heart pounding wildly, I watch the shark before me finally abandon its attack and abruptly depart in favor of circling the defrosted and now decomposing tuna. Taking a deep breath out of my regulator, I turn to look at Michel and see that he is laughing.

I find his good mood a little irritating and motion with my thumb that we should open the top hatch of the floating cage so I can talk with him about it. Dripping water, we emerge from the slightly battered cage. Michel is in high spirits, "You looked quite busy trying to hold that door closed with the shark chewing on it."

"Why didn't you help me?" I ask indulging my exasperation. "I couldn't close the latch."

"I was catching it all on film," grins Michel, "that's my job."

"What if he had gotten the door open?" I respond.

"Well, I guess I would have gotten that on film too," he laughs, "I was using a wide-angle lens so it would have been a great close-up."

I look at the mirth in his eyes and cannot help laughing with him. "Did you see the size of those teeth? I could feel the steel vibrating as he ripped and tore at the wire mesh."

Beside us a shark's dorsal fin cuts through the water, we both turn to stare at it. The shark is only three or four feet away. *How amazing*, I think in wonder, *to be floating in a steel cage surrounded by great white sharks and to be idly having a conversation.*

"Hey!" Jean-Michel ends our discussion. "If you two don't mind, we are supposed to be conducting an experiment to see how a great white reacts to an apparently cage-less diver."

"What about the tuna test?" I ask skeptically. "Don't you think we should leave it in the cage for just a little longer?"

"Na, look at all the sharks; this is a great day," Jean-Michel is anxious to begin his experiment. "I think we are ready for the human bait."

In building the world's first all plastic shark cage, it is understandable that there might be a few flaws in the design. The cylinder's height, ten feet, prevents me from being able to climb in through the hatch, which is on top while it is onboard *Alcyone*. The thin plastic cage also cannot withstand a sharp blow against the side of the research vessel's metal hull. That means we must lower it quickly into the water, well beneath the threat of the metal stern. That leaves only one way for me to get into the cylinder. I have to jump into the water from the stern of *ALYCONE* and swim down to it.

A few minutes later, standing at the back of the wind ship, staring down into what I distinctly know is seriously shark-infested water, I momentarily consider the wisdom of what I am about to do. I do not intend to jump in when the great whites are present in the up-close and personal sense. Underwater, Michel and the other divers are watching the circling great white sharks. A single hand protruding from the top of a steel cage motions with a thumbs-up gesture that it is okay for me to jump. Yet I still hesitate. The thumb, it happens to be attached to Capkin, who really likes giving me a hard time, signals again—*jump!*

Realizing I am not being paid enough for this job, I take a deep breath from my regulator and leap outwards. It is less than a yard down to the water, so I arrive faster than I would like. An instant later, I find myself surrounded by a cloud of bubbles from my entry and a whole host of imagined sharks. Desperately, with my mask half-full of water from the rushed entry, I look for and see the top of my near-transparent cage. Kicking frantically downwards, I lunge for the hatch cover, throw it open and pull myself urgently down into the dubious protection of the plastic cylinder. Inside the cage, I immediately feel better even though I am still upside-down. It takes a couple of clumsy moments to right myself and then I peer anxiously about looking for the sharks I imagined were all about me. Instead, all I see is empty water, except for the ever-present

Leatherbacks; one of which is chewing on the bottom of my rubber boot. Off to one side I notice Capkin and Michel in their steel cage. Capkin is pantomiming my panicked entry and Michel is pretending to be a great white shark hiding behind him. I put my hands on my hips and give them *the look*, which probably loses some of its impact through a dive mask, but then I notice something really interesting through the faceplate—the ballistic arrival of Peaches.

The massive shark arrows straight up from the depths. She is only feet away when she apparently notices that I am not the forty-pound tuna. The disappointment brings her to an abrupt halt just inches away from the side of the cylinder. Hovering, she peers intently at me, possibly wondering if this is not some kind of nasty trick. But, there is no doubt about it. I am not a dead, rotting fish. She makes one pass behind the cylinder. Maybe to make sure I am not hiding the tuna behind my back. Then with a complete lack of interest, she swims away, and so ends our human-bait experiment for the day.

Chilled from a long day in the cold water, I signal an end to the day's diving. Removing the scuba regulator from my mouth, I use it to pump air into the floatation tanks from which my plastic cage hangs. The air bubbles displace the water inside the floatation tanks creating buoyancy, which lifts the cylinder to the surface. Opening the top hatch, I pull myself up and remove my dive mask. A large boil of bubbles rising to the surface to the right of me is followed an instant later by the buoyant arrival of the steel cage. The top hatch is thrown open as Michel and Capkin emerge laughing and pointing in my general direction. Capkin is in his best form as he shouts, "How does it feel to be less interesting that a rotting fish?"

"That was the most boring shark encounter I have ever seen," chimes in Michel. "Couldn't you at least try to look a little more interesting for the shark?"

"Hold it!" I am not going to let my tormentors get away with this. "Jumping into shark-infested water was not interesting?"

"Maybe you should try moving your flippers in a more inviting way?" offers Capkin.

The conversation might have gone in many interesting directions from there, but Bruno, the chef, steps out on deck and rings the dinner bell. There is instant eager activity as everyone works extra fast to get the gear stowed. I, however, will have to wait in the cold water for a while longer. First, the steel cage has to be emptied of equipment and divers before being lifted onto the deck with the stern crane and lashed in place. It will be around fifteen minutes before the crane is available to pull out my cylinder. So, I re-don my dive mask and slip back below the chilly water.

Cold and alone, but for a couple of leatherback fish nibbling on various parts of my wetsuit, I pause to think about how lucky I am to have this wonderful opportunity to be live bait for great white sharks in Dangerous Reef, Australia. At this moment, Cindy is halfway around the planet free diving with dolphins. Inside my plastic cage, I think about the glass jail cell I shared with Morgan at the Los Angeles County Jail. I recall the fear, the feeling of complete loss and frustration over my nearly fatal criminal errors. To imagine all that has happened since that night just over six years ago. In the cell with Morgan, I remember that I was finally free of his manipulations; in a sense it was like a new beginning. It is hard to imagine that my new beginning began with a well-deserved sojourn in prison. Accepting my punishment was a first step on my path back to rehabilitation. A key thought for anyone undergoing any type of rehabilitation, whether it be from incarceration, drugs, alcohol, whatever; rehabilitation is not an easy process, there is nothing fun about it. However, on the other side of rehabilitation waits all that is rewarding in life, happiness, love, positive adventures and accomplishment. Without the hardship of rehabilitation, there can be no personal growth, no change of character, only a long backward slide down into the depths of despair.

I glance at a trail of blood dripping from the automatic baiter at *Alcyone's* stern. It is this underwater column of blood, ground fish parts and tuna oil that is luring in the great white sharks. The red cloud drifts past the plastic cylinder in sync with the surge and tide. It wafts around the smooth plastic barrier of my cage. That drifting red cloud, it is a vivid reminder of the blood of Christ that finally set me free in prison. Momentarily, I remember the blood of the youth swirling down that prison drain and am so thankful for how far I have come since that tragic incident. It has been quite a journey. First to accept that the fault was my own, then to know that I was terribly flawed and in great need of repairing and cleansing. It took years to grow into the new me and the work is far from finished. But, I am a completely different person now. My life has meaning and purpose…and I am in love with a woman free diving with dolphins half a world away.

Glancing upwards, I see that the team is now ready for me. I open the top plastic hatch and hand-up my twin scuba tanks. Lowering myself back down I do a quick three hundred-sixty degree turn to insure that there are no great white sharks lurking about hoping for a fast food hit and then I extend my arms over my head and kick with my flippers as eager hands grab a hold and lift me onto the stern of *Alcyone.*

Obstacles are what you see when you take your eyes off your goal. Anonymous

It is just before sunrise on another stormy day. It is now late fall on the underside of the planet. I am standing at the stern of *Alcyone,* staring at the stars, and just finishing the 2:00 a.m. to 5:00 a.m. watch. The wind is howling across Dangerous Reef causing *Alcyone* to swing like a pendulum at her anchorage. I am trying not to breathe through my nose. Riding the wind from Dangerous Reef, is a horrible cargo of pungent odors. The tiny spit of rock is a seabird rookery and fur seal whelping sanctuary. The reef smells worse than an over-stuffed diaper pail.

I know there is not a chance of launching the shark cages today, yet part of my watch requires that I continue the chum corridor drifting behind the wind ship. Scooping up a bucket of fish offal, tuna oil and dried blood, I lean over the stern and pour it into the dark water. I am trying to keep the awful stuff from splashing onto my pants, so I'm pouring it slowly. Apparently, this gives the great white shark in the dark water all the time it needs to zero in on the source, because Amy erupts at my feet biting viciously at the chum steam. Leaping wildly out of the way, I inadvertently spill fish offal on to my jeans.

Desperate to change my pants, I instead wipe off the grosser chunks, and then rush into the bridge to grab my camera. Quickly loading it with high-speed film, I dash back outside. I am tying a rotting mackerel to a piece of rope with a yellow balloon on it, when Capkin arrives along with the sunrise.

"Wow! That's some smell out here," Capkin states the obvious as he steps through the bridge door. He takes several very deep breaths through his nose, then snorts loudly.

"Don't tell me you like that foul odor?" I ask.

"Not at all," Capkin states cheerfully, "by overloading the nose all at once, I get used to it sooner. The smell practically goes away."

"Really?" I answer, hazarding several deeper breathes myself. I feel my nose wrinkling in protest. My legs are also not very happy with the slimy feeling of the chum clinging to my jeans.

"Why are you tying that decaying fish to a balloon? Making a party favor for someone?" Capkin's good mood is a direct result of his having just left the galley after having made himself a pre-breakfast snack.

"It's an experiment," I grin in a friendly way, mostly because I am looking for a second set of hands, "want to help?"

"Sure, just as long as I don't have to touch your stinky fish." Capkin is the most enthusiastic person I know, which also explains why he usually has more fun than the rest of the crew.

I excitedly tell him that I have an idea on how to re-create the poster from the movie *Jaws*. The poster is actually a painting, depicting a great white shark leaping right at you with its massive jaws wide-open. Only I am intent on doing it with a real shark. Amy's morning leap has given me the unique idea of dangling a fish from the wind ship's crane, which is why I need Capkin's help.

I thread the rope through the tip of the crane then lower the fish into the still dark water. The floating yellow balloon will keep the fish near the surface. When the great white lunges after the bait, Capkin must quickly pull the dangling fish straight up. To get the fish, Amy is going to have to leap for it.

"I like it," Capkin enthusiastically takes hold of the rope, "where will you stand to take the picture?"

"The swim step," I answer, jumping down onto the small platform, which is just eight inches above the water and two-and-one-half-horizontal-feet from the dangling fish…depending upon the angle of the swell. The movement of the *Alcyone* on the restless water has the dangling fish swinging towards and away from me, something I had not reckoned into my plan.

"This should be real interesting," Capkin deadpans, "what happens if the leaping shark lands jaws first onto the swim step?"

"I imagine I'll be getting off it rather rapidly," I respond peering down a mere eight inches at the still rather dark water from which had recently leaped an eighteen-foot-long shark.

Watching the rotting fish floating just beneath the water under the yellow balloon, I try taking several more deep breathes through my nose, but each time the foul stench remains just as horribly offensive. "Are you sure this breathing deeply through the nose reduces the smell's impact?" I ask, my olfactory receptors in complete rebellion.

"Doesn't work at all," Capkin replies cheerfully, "I just wanted to see if you'd be naive enough to try it."

I'm about to say something in reply, but the great white shark erupts from the water at my feet, thus ending our conversation. Amy lunges for the dead fish, which completely surprises her by flying straight up and out of the water. The astonished shark tries to pursue with her rapidly beating tail, but lacking momentum, instead she falls back into the water. Amy makes five more unsuccessful lunges for the fish, before her bad disposition sends the now, thoroughly angry shark into a biting frenzy. Shark scientists refer to this activity as display behavior. Amy is swimming in circles furiously biting the empty water repeatedly. I watch her working out her frustrations on the water from the swim step. It is some kind of amazing watching, from only a few feet away, a furious super predator keen to bite something and I haven't even had my morning cup of tea yet.

"Looks like Amy is getting a mite stirred-up." Capkin tugs lightly on the line making the baitfish wiggle invitingly.

The enraged shark circles the floating balloon with its dancing fish baggage, then reverses direction, and rapidly swims straight down. "Uh oh," I caution Capkin, "I think this might be it. She's going deep."

Seconds later, I see the dark shape of the shark torpedoing vertically upward like a ballistic missile. As Capkin jerks the fish rapidly upwards, the ton-and-a-half shark explodes from the water, its massive mouth wide-open, and giant teeth gashing in the sunlight. Her tail drives furiously propelling her fully five feet out of the shark-thrashed water. Quickly, leaning outwards with my camera, I shoot a full-frame picture of the fierce predator from less than three feet away. Seeing the enraged shark filling the viewfinder, I release the shutter. I am about to shout with glee, when the balloon and bait fish lands with a solid plop onto the swim step. Caught up in all the excitement, Capkin has accidentally let go of the rope.

"*Uh oh,*" I think to myself. The shark, still in aerial pursuit, is looking in my direction, which is a bit un-nerving. She slams back into the water right next to the little platform. The shark's belly-splash instantly flushes me head-to-toe with freezing salt water. For a moment, I am completely stunned, which sends Capkin into a fit of laughter.

I look at him and grin, then abruptly, hear a loud grinding sound on the swim platform to my rear. Quickly, spinning around, I see the shark right behind me. Amy is angrily chewing on the aluminum swim step. The teeth, gashing repeatedly on metal, are only a foot from my bare toes. Instinctively, I leap backwards...and land on the inflated balloon. The sharp sound of the bursting balloon startles me and I almost leap again, but suddenly remember the shark chomping away at the swim step.

"Hurry, get a picture," shouts Capkin.

I had forgotten about the camera in my hand. I quickly raise it and push the shutter release, but nothing happens. The shark bites the swim step a final time, leaving foot long scrapes in the white paint, then disappears beneath the stern with an angry flick of its tail hitting me with a second fan of water.

I take a long breath to slow my beating heart, I am no longer aware of the foul scent in the air. Excitement always captures the whole mind's attention. Next, I take a closer look at the camera. It is soaking wet.

"That's the second camera you've flooded this year," says Jean-Michel gravely as he steps out of the *Alcyone's* bridge. I soaked another camera on a previous expedition when I got too close to a breaching Humpback whale.

"I can fix the camera," I say hopefully then realize it looks doubtful. I quickly rewind the film then pop open the back. The film canister looks fine. "Wait until you see this shot."

Jean-Michel nudges Capkin, "Do you see what is oozing up around his feet?"

Glancing down, I see that I am standing barefoot on the now smashed rotting mackerel. Some of the squished fish is grossly seeping up between my toes.

"Don't you have anything better to do than play with the bait?" complains Jean-Michel.

Thoroughly washing my jeans and feet does not eliminate the smell of decaying fish. It is the reason why the rest of the crew bans me from eating in the salon at lunch.

Sitting alone in the Captain's chair on the bridge, with a large salad propped between my knees, I think about real life choices. Most of us want adventure and challenge in our lives; yet, few people actually take the time and effort to do something constructive about it.

"Creative man lives many lives; some men are so dull they do not live even once," Dagobert D. Runes.

There are two very real conditions to discovering challenge and adventure in life. They require an active lifestyle and an inquisitive mind. Captain Cousteau once said that the primary motivator in his life is curiosity. The world, right outside each of our front doors, is full of wonder, mystery and potential adventure. The challenge is merely to step outside, to look for the unexpected, then to get involved with it.

My morning adventure with Amy would not have happened, had I not been actively looking for a new way to shoot dramatic pictures of great white sharks. Instead of being inquisitive, I could have just sat on the stern and done nothing...and, of course, nothing would have been my appropriate reward. Boredom is self-inflicted.

"Activity is the only medicine I take. It's very efficient,"
Captain Jacques-Yves Cousteau

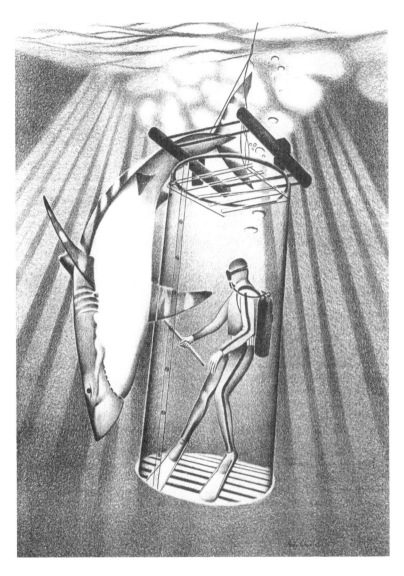

Illustration by Andy Charles
Author inside world's first all plastic shark cage.

"If one advances confidently in the direction of their dreams, and endeavors to lead a life which they have imagined, they will meet with a success unexpected in common hours,"
Henry David Thoreau

Chapter 44

DANGEROUS REEF, AUSTRALIA, NOV 1991

WE HAVE been diving with the great white sharks of South Australia for over two years. During part of that time the wind ship was in dry dock for repairs, while I led another expedition to Hawaii. Now I am back aboard Alcyone watching a seventeen-foot-long great white shark silently glide by just beneath the shimmering water. A small tag beneath her dorsal fin identifies this shark as Amy. This is not good news as Amy tends to get rather aggressive. I decide to wait a few moments before jumping into the water. It is the only way for me to get down to my cage, which I can just barely see six feet beneath the surface. The cage is nearly invisible, which is not very reassuring from a subconscious perspective. The more primal part of my brain is having difficulty with the idea of jumping into seriously shark-infested water then swimming down to a barely visible cage, which both it and my modern-educated mind know is flimsy and wobbly on the surface. Usually diving down six feet to the plastic cylinder is not that big a deal, but this morning Amy seems to be showing abnormally high interest in my short journey. Is she devising a plan to catch me at the halfway point I wonder? Watching the great white shark circling aggressively beneath my flippers, I have the distinct feeling that I am about to find out.

Many people do not give great white sharks much credit for being very smart, yet most people have not gotten to know a white pointer up close and personal. Amy and I are getting to know each other a bit too well for my liking. She is what we refer to as a resident shark. Her marine home is Dangerous Reef, an appropriately named location for Jean-Michel Cousteau to conduct his little experiment. The reef is also a favorite whelping location for fur seals. The fur seal pups are why the great white sharks are hanging out here.

Seeing a shark's dorsal fin knifing through the smooth water fifty yards from the stern, I decide to make a quick jump for the cage. Just as my flippers clear the stern, I abruptly hear our chef shout, "SHARK!"

Looking down, it is alarming see a large dark-torpedo shape slipping out from under *Alcyone*. Abruptly, I realize that the shark in the distance is not Amy. The crafty predator has been hiding under the wind ship's stern and we are now on a collision course. This is the shark I have been training to leap for its dinner. My point of impact is exactly where Capkin and I like to dangle the fish bait. An instinctive fluttering of my flippers does not prevent me from splashing into the chilly water an instant later. My mask half floods with water. A froth of bubbles from my entry further obscures my vision. I barely see the shark at first because of all the bubbles drifting about from my entry, but as they begin to clear away, like a silver curtain rising, I have an unmistakable close-up view of a seventeen-foot great white shark swimming towards me. I do not have time to look again as I turn my back on the huge predator and bolt for the *Lexan* cage. It is very disconcerting having my back exposed to the giant shark, but I know my only hope is to get into the plastic cylinder as quickly as possible. A couple of heart-fluttering seconds later, I reach for the double top hatches of the plastic cylinder and pull myself vigorously downward. I am inside in an instant. Granted

I am upside down in the plastic cage with a half-flooded dive mask, but at least I am inside. The primal guy inside my head wants to come out of its lair and beat up on my conscious mind for being so stupid. Glancing upward while clearing my dive mask, I see the great white shark passing silently overhead, its black orb regarding me with the same hungry look that Cindy affects when in the close proximity of a box of assorted chocolates. My heart is still beating frantically from the frightening encounter.

The great white is not long in coming back. I watch her ascending out of the gloom. The water visibility is only about thirty feet. She must weigh close to three thousand pounds. The massive head swings side-to-side as she approaches until she nudges the bottom of my plastic cylinder with her snout. The black, seeming pupil-less eye regards me coldly from inches away. Confused by the invisible barrier the shark keeps returning, though not actually attacking. That is until she is joined by a second shark, and then by a third. I have apparently rung the shark's dinner bell with my frantic entry into the cage.

The sharks grow more bold and confident in their numbers. They begin to circle my plastic cage aggressively. I am beginning to wonder if they are able to sense my fear, when abruptly a fifteen-footer attacks. Its snout thumps the side of the Lexan cylinder solidly. I am so intent on watching the fifteen-foot pointer that I do not notice that the seventeen-footer has returned; that is until I see a large streamlined shadow passing over me. Turning toward the shadow, I am stunned to see the huge shark hovering vertically alongside my cage. Its pectoral fins are hugging the five foot diameter plastic cylinder as it seeks to get as close to me as possible. Just the three-sixteenths-inch wall of the clear Lexan separates us. Her belly rubs against the *Lexan* as she seeks a way inside. Twisting her head, which is inches from my own, I feel the alarm of real fear staring into that cold, dark orb that is only inches away. She gashes her teeth against the thin plastic scoring it. Then she heads back downwards towards the seabed. I start to breathe a premature sign of relief, but then the huge shark reverses direction and begins swimming rapidly upward. *Uh ho,* the thought comes suddenly; *this is the shark that has spent the most time investigating the plastic cage.* She is coming up like a speeding torpedo, straight toward the bottom of my cage, which is its weakest point. Just a single layer of hollow two-inch tubes with sides less than a quarter-of-an-inch thick lines the bottom of the plastic cylinder. I instinctively raise my feet off the bottom of the cage just an instant before she rams the thin cylinders. The collision drives the cage upwards two feet. I watch wide-eyed as the *Lexan* tubes bend several inches apart admitting her thick snout. Then with brute force, she thrusts her massive head forward, biting furiously at the thin *Lexan* tubes. Fortunately, her mouth is not far enough into the cage so that she can actually bite down on the far too frail tubes. After some industrious chewing, she tries swinging her head, which shakes the bottom of the cage. Earlier I had placed two twenty-five pound lead weights in the bottom of the cage. These two lead clumps are necessary to hold the cage vertical in a modest current. One of them slides across the hollow tubes and smacks her in the snout. Amy instantly withdraws, glares at the lead weight then swims off into the gloom of deep water without a backward glance.

Having had all the excitement I need for a seriously longtime, I signal an end to the morning's dives.

At the lunch table everyone is excited about the filming, which has gone extremely well. Michel DeLoire, the chief of cinematography says in accented English, "Steve, it is very exciting jumping into the open water with a great white shark present, yes?"

I look up from the fish head soup I am eating, which is surprisingly good if you wind up with the bowl minus the gross head.

"Yes, Michel, it's very exciting it scared the heck out of me."

Good," exclaims Michel, he reaches across the table to pour me a half-glass of red wine, which he knows is my limit on diving days. I participate to be polite, after all, it is French wine and the men are very proud of their country's most famous export. "Because," continues Michel, "I would like to film it."

The spoon of fish head soup I am raising to my mouth pauses in mid-air. I look at Michel who is smiling. The Frenchmen are such good practical jokers. "Right, Michel," I chuckle.

"So you will do this for me?" he asks pleasantly. I realize he is not kidding. This is the guy who swam with saltwater crocodiles.

Two hours later, I am standing on the swim step peering anxiously over the side. There are now four great white sharks in attendance. Sometimes they swim leisurely pass the stern, at other times they rocket by in pursuit of bait or each other.

Michel is in his steel cage floating just beneath the surface. Capkin is inside the cage holding his hand up through the bars. The hand signals one. Three is to be my indication to jump. I nervously watch a white pointer swimming in and know that Michel is filming it. The hand flashes two as the white shark passes directly beneath me; fortunately, it is at least six feet down. The hand suddenly shows three fingers. The primal guy in my head is at the mouth of his cave with serious issues about what I am about to do. Taking a deep breath, I reluctantly jump.

Hearing my splash as I break the surface the shark arrows for the bottom, while I rocket for my cage. Seconds later safely behind the plastic barrier, I see the seventeen-foot white pointer returning. Amy swims in to investigate my arrival. She nudges the side of my cage and then appearing disinterested she swims off.

Michel signals from the steel cage that he got the shot. I am pleased to have helped out my friend wondering if I was slightly insane to honor his request. I do not know it yet, but Michel is formulating a second plan. He waits until my guard is down.

The Frenchmen are at the salon table that evening eating steak tartare. It is a fancy name for a pile of raw hamburger with a raw egg floating in its scoped out center; like a small red volcano with a raw egg yolk surprise. To me it looks like a seriously infectious bacterial hit waiting to erupt inside the intestines. My primal guy is actually quite interested. Fortunately, the chef has kindly made me an omelet and quite surprising, he even put a plastic bottle of catsup next to my plate. Normally, the mere sight of catsup insults the chef. He has been known to pound the cutting board with a heavy meat cleaver as he snarls, "Why do you want to ruin my fine French cuisine with American catsup?"

"That was very exciting this afternoon, Steve," grins Michel.

"I guess," I answer. The omelet is delicious. I add more catsup while keeping my head down; I do not want to see the revolting dish that the Frenchmen are eating.

"I only wish the shark hadn't been quite so far down," Michel says wistfully.

Pausing with a bit of omelet halfway to my mouth, I foolishly ask, "What do you mean?"

"How do you say it in American?" he asks, pretending to be searching for the correct words, "Take two."

The following morning finds me standing on the swim step peering anxiously over the side for sharks. There are seven of them today. The water immediately at the stern is beginning to look like the carpool express lane for large predators. The silver wetsuit-covered hand extending from the steel cage that I wished I were in has already struck one. Looking just beyond my flippers, I see that there is no doubt that this shark is much shallower. It is just beneath the surface with the top of its dorsal fin cutting through the water like a knife. Another shark is just disappearing under *Alcyone*, which means I will not know exactly where it is lurking when I hit the water. It is not a comforting thought, playing hide and see with Jaws, particularly when Jaws is present in the plural sense. Primal guy is looking at me and smacking a knobby club against his hand in anticipation of interfering with any more modern choices.

Two…the hand has already flashed two…and the shark is right beneath me. Paul, the engineer peers over the side and says with a shrug, "It's okay Steve, she's only a small one."'"

The shark is fifteen feet long and weighs at least ten times more than I do. The hand suddenly has three fingers in the air. *They're not paying me enough*, I think, taking a deep breath and leaping into the cold water. I am only moments reaching my cage. I open the double hatches and attempt to pull myself quickly downward, but halfway in my tank valve hits the side of the hatch and sticks. My whole lower torso is hanging outside the top of the cage. For an instant, I panic and swim harder, but I still do not go anywhere. I can easily imagine my frantically fluttering fins attracting the attention of the sharks. I push myself backwards, freeing my tank valve and then am able to drop rapidly into the cage. Looking quickly about, I am glad to see that there are not any sharks in close attendance.

That afternoon at lunch, Michel smiles and offers to pour me a half-glass of wine, "No, Michel," I say quickly.

"What, you don't want any wine? But this is French wine." He is affecting a hurt look—he does it quite well.

"Is that all you're asking me?" I am not in a trusting mood.

"Why, yes," grins Michel pouring my glass a little less than half-full.

That afternoon we return to our normal dive operations, which is investigative science as we prepare to conduct non-obtrusive experiments with the great whites.

Staring into the blue, clean water, I remember the shadows of the past and compare them to my life today. The guilt and the self-incrimination, which used to be my daily companions, are almost gone, mostly erased by the forgiveness found through a significant relationship with a caring God. I have come to learn that life should be an odyssey of adventure. To be happy is our true birthright for living in a free society. We should always strive to be better, to reach higher and to set goals that challenge our abilities. Each of us is a treasure to be polished until it shines, but always remembering that the true luster comes from within.

Standing at the stern of the wind ship, I stare at the nimbus clouds from a recent rain as they pass overhead; one stacked above the other from the horizon to lofty heights thousands of feet above the wind ship. In the near distance, I see a double rainbow painted against a vast cobalt horizon. Stepping to the edge of the deck, I prepare to jump into the water, but then out of the corner of my eye I see a large mirror leaning against an idle shark cage. We are using the mirror to see how a great white shark reacts to its own image. I stare at my reflection. The shiny metallic silver of the

Cousteau wetsuit is radiant in the bright sunlight. Behind me, the French tricolor ripples proudly in the wind against a background of cloud-filled sky. The twin rainbows stand out clearly in the upper right corner. I am reminded of the Lord's promise that when we see a rainbow, we are to remember His covenant with us. I pause to think about that incredible word He gave me in the darkness of a prison cell, *Always*, which gives me such unshakeable faith that He is always with each of us. Taking a deep breath from the regulator, I step from the stern of the wind ship.

For an instant, my splash disturbs the calm smooth water. Then an iridescent stream of bubbles rises to the surface where they merrily gurgle and burst before they are gone.

"Fantasies and Reality often overlap," Walt Disney

Illustration by Marjory Spielman
Pondering life amongst sharks

"God gives every bird its worm, but he does not throw it into the nest," P.D. James

Chapter 45
DANGEROUS REEF, AUSTRALIA, DECEMBER 1991

A T SUNSET, we finish securing the shark cages on the deck of *Alcyone*. The captain, a naval officer on loan from the French Navy, orders the anchor raised and the bow of the wind ship turns towards Australia's southern coast. It is the successful end of another adventurous expedition. I listen to the fur seal pups barking on the sharp-edged rocks of Dangerous Reef then walk over to the plastic shark cage, now lying on its side lashed to the deck. It is headed for a Cousteau museum while I will go home to prepare for the next expedition for our Rediscovery of the World series. I go to the bow and sit down on the fairing for the gear housing that turns Alcyone's metal sail's into the wind. I lean my back against the outward curved sail to watch the sunset fade to twilight and then slowly to nautical twilight, which finally fades to full darkness (nautical twilight is the time after sunset that the horizon is still visible for star navigation.).

I am staring up at the stars when Capkin walks up quietly and sits down beside me. The twinkling starlight glistens against the deep black abyss of outer space. With the rolling motion of the wind ship at her top speed of thirteen knots, I watch the heavens tilt and slide back and forth-in pace with the restless sea surging under our keel.

"Want to know what I am thinking?" Capkin's mood sounds buoyant.

"Is this a trick question about food?" I ask knowing that Capkin is often thinking about his stomach and it is getting towards dinner-time, which is running late this evening, as it will be a bit of a celebration for the end of a two-and-a-half-year expedition circum-navigating Australia and Tasmania.

"No, I'm thinking about how much I really like this job," he leans back against the railing. "I love how we never know what adventure we're headed for next or who's going to be there when we get there...wherever there happens to be."

I laugh out-loud. Capkin's awkward explanation exactly defines the typical Cousteau expedition. The world is immense with so much to film and document, that we are never sure where we are going next. While *Alcyone* will remain idle in Australia for an extended repair period in a shipyard, Captain and Jean-Michel Cousteau are planning several expeditions. Some of us will be temporarily assigned to *Calypso* while others will join a flying team which could be sent anywhere on the globe. We never know when a volcano is going to erupt or where a global environmental event will occur, but in the very near future, a Cousteau team will come together—most likely at one of the further extreme ends of this vast planet.

"So," continues Capkin, "do you know the answer to who, what and where...particularly in relation to me?"

"As a matter of fact I do," I answer reaching into the back pocket of my jeans for a telex from the Los Angeles office and flick on a pencil flashlight. "Let me see," I'm drawing out the moment as I pretend to read what I already know is there under the soft glow of the tiny beam. "*Alcyone* will remain in Australia for an extended period of repairs in a shipyard. Meanwhile you get to go home for a six week vacation."

"Um," mumbles Capkin as he immediately begins considering

his upcoming vacation plans, then asks, "so where are you going for your vacation?"

"I'm not," I answer, "Jean-Michel wants me to put together a team to fly to the Turks and Caicos Islands in the Caribbean to dive with Jojo."

"Who's Jojo?" asks Capkin.

"Well Jojo is not exactly a who, it's more like what is Jojo," I answer playfully.

"Huh?

"Jojo is a bottlenose dolphin who chooses to live and play at a dive resort in the Caribbean," I answer, "seems he likes people so much, he would rather hang out with us than with other dolphins."

"Wait a minute!" Capkin leans his six-foot-five-inch-frame toward me, "You're going to a dive resort in the Caribbean to swim with a friendly dolphin? That sounds more like a vacation than work to me."

I find Capkin's words a bit troubling, because I know this is exactly the same argument that Cindy is going to clobber me with when she finds out I am leaving on another adventure so soon. Rather than think about an upset Cindy, I think about dolphin memories.

"You know Capkin," I say quietly, "two times when my life was about to change drastically dolphins were present."

Capkin sits up, attentive, prodding me to continue with his silence.

"It was almost like dolphins were bookends to the most tragic part of my life." For an instant, I feel a shudder racing down my spine as I recapture the mixed emotional memories of incredible wonder and great personal anguish that blend and run together into the individual threads that make up this piece of fabric from my life.

"My first true personal dolphin encounter occurred just as my life was unexpectedly changing for the worst." I pause, and then have to reconsider, "Well actually my life was already on a serious downward slide, but now my bad choices were shoving me towards a dark chasm. I was on the verge of falling into a living nightmare."

On the bow of *Alcyone*, the wind blows a little colder out of the darkness. I cannot see Capkin sitting right next to me. The story just pours forth. Capkin is completely silent, I could have been talking to myself...maybe in a sense I was.

"They were bottlenose dolphins and they came upon me suddenly. At the time, I thought my life had finally taken a wonderful turn for the better, actually a nightmare was lurking in my near future..."

The thought pictures I capture from the recesses of my mind are distinct and crisp, like it all happened just yesterday, when actually the two events cover a period of almost three years. Sam and I are surfing at Blacks Beach, just north of San Diego in Southern California. It is a cold winter day. The breakers are thick and powerful with a brisk offshore wind forcing the thundering waves nearly vertical before they pitch into long curling tubes of crystal-clear water. Surfing in almost perfect conditions, I am regretful that I am preparing to leave the ocean I love to go live in the bleakness of the Mojave Desert. Rather than become depressed about it, I paddle closer to Sam and pour cold water down the back of his wetsuit.

Sam and I are having an intense water fight, when we notice a big swell rushing in on the horizon. We both quickly jockey for position. Sam sets up for the first wave and paddling furiously drops into an excellent left. I let the next two waves pass in favor of the set wave rushing toward the shoreline. As usual, this break is crowded with surfers, but a long shore current places me in the most favorable position. The swell of the wave thickens forming itself into a classic California breaker. The wave crests as it begins to pitch at the center with me lining up for a fast barreling left. I feel the breaker going critical as my board begins the long drop, sliding forward, rapidly gathering speed. One more stroke will launch me into the wave, when abruptly two dolphins surface on each side of the board. I am astounded. My arm plunging down for the water freezes in mid-air. Had I completed the stroke my hand would have come down on the wet glistening back of a dolphin close to its blowhole. Since I am prone, caught in middle paddle, on a surfboard, I look at the slick gray skin just inches from my face and see the dolphin's eager look as it surges forward down the pitching wave face. Captivated by the magic of the moment, time seems to slow down then I notice that my surfboard has stalled at the leading edge of the breaker... not good news. Yet, I cannot tear my eyes from the dolphin as it races downward cutting a graceful arch in the cascading wall of water. It catches up with its companion who is riding inside the wave, just beneath its shimmering surface and then the curl hits me in the back of the head and slams into my shoulders. An avalanche of water sledgehammers me from the board as I fall two vertical stories towards a mighty impact with the swirling water below.

When I finally surface choking and spitting water, I hear Sam guffawing uproariously. Caught on the inside, I decide it is time to head for the beach. Sam, riding the froth of a tiny inshore wave, joins me and we laugh together as we carry our boards up onto the white sandy beach.

"Doesn't sound like much of a nightmare to me," Capkin injects from the darkness.

"Except for a short morning on some small Florida waves, I wouldn't surf again for almost three years," I reply sadly. "I left that afternoon for the high desert to work for a man called Morgan Hetrick. I once looked up to him like a father figure. He hired me as a pilot and I was very excited about the adventure of flying for a living. Then I realized that Morgan had changed from the man I knew; there was corruptness hovering about him now." I feel an inner quiver as my mind recalls the exact moment that I slid over the edge into that nightmare. "Despite the corruption, I still chose to work for him. It was a really bad choice because he had secretly become a drug smuggler. I unexpectedly got caught up in something that was way over my head...something really evil."

Do not envy wicked men, do not desire their company; for their hearts plot violence, and their lips talk about making trouble. Proverbs 24:1

"What happened?" urges Capkin.

"Five months later, I was saved by being arrested," my shrug goes un-noticed in the dark that surrounds us. "I served over two-and-a-half years in prison. The worst part is it was my own fault," I look toward my friend shrouded in the night. "It wasn't so much that I was manipulated by someone who once was a friend, the important part was he knew he could manipulate me before he tried. I now know that life is always about choices; good choices lift us up and bad choices pull us down."

I can sense Capkin mulling over my words. He, like everyone else on the *Alcyone*, knows that I served time in a federal prison for that mistake. "You said that dolphins were bookend to this part of your life," Capkin asks seeking the rest of the story.

"I served the last part of my sentence at a prison camp in the Mojave Desert," As I continue it's almost as if I am reliving the memory. "It was late winter, February of eighty-five. I was waiting at the camp barrier for Sam. I was about to go out on my first furlough."

"What!" Capkin's words leap out of the darkness, "you got to go on a furlough from prison?"

"Yeah, the program is reserved for low-risk, non-violent offenders. It helps inmates to readjust back into society. Anyway I was pretty excited; Sam and I were going to go surfing."

I can tell that Capkin wants to ask more questions; instead, he waits as I feel myself drifting back, rummaging around in memories half a decade old.

Standing in the cold desert air, I stare anxiously at the distant highway. I look at my watch for the fiftieth time in probably ten minutes—then I see him coming. Sam's Baja bug is speeding up the highway with two surfboards strapped to the roof. The off-road-modified Volkswagen soon pulls into the camp parking lot. Sam gets out and waves, then heads for the control booth to sign me out. I feel like a puppy in a pet store anxiously awaiting its release from captivity. If I had to wait any longer, I would be chasing my tail out in the parking lot. After a few agonizing minutes, the guard motions me through the barrier.

Climbing into the Volkswagen with Sam, I intently watch him as he looks over and grins and then he casually asks, "Ready to go surfing?"

Such a simple statement, yet the meaning is incredibly momentous. It reflects the huge gulf that exists in our individual realities. Sam's life is about freedom, mine is about confinement. He gets to be himself; I live the bizarre reality of an inmate, which requires donning a constant disguise to mask my personal thoughts and deeper emotions from the other felons. Yet, for the next thirty-six hours, I will get a short chance to taste freedom again and for a little while just be me. Though I desperately want to leave the inmate portion of me behind, it tags along because it is a living part of who I am. As the Volkswagen speeds towards the ocean over four hours away, I look at my young friend and the surrounding world that is not a part of my inmate existence. He occasionally glances out the window and sees mostly barren desert. I see changing scenery, a feast of new sights as we get further and further away from Camp Boron. In prison, I mostly see the same thing, day-in and day-out. There are few colors to capture your attention in a prison camp. Most inmates and guards wear drab clothes. Inmate excitement usually consists of a small change to a normally never changing weekly meal menu or the season opener for a housewife soap opera.

The Baja bug climbs a ridge and leaves the high desert to drop down into a wide rural valley. I feel freedom like a living wild thing that rushes through the open window with the wind of our passage. I now know that being free is a dynamic force that motivates and drives the gears of vitality making life exciting, challenging and adventurous. Later, when we get caught in downtown traffic, Sam quickly becomes bored, but I am vitally alive. Everywhere I look everything is interesting, dynamic and changing.

When we arrive at the beach, I am thrilled to see the ocean that I love and have missed so dearly. Quickly pulling on wetsuits and waxing up our surfboards, we run across the sand and dash out into the water. It is incredible to feel the ocean in motion, surf lapping at my feet and pulling me out into the frigid water. As we paddle out into the surf, I revel in the first roller that washes over me. In the line-up, I quickly paddle for a medium-sized wave, feeling the exciting downward rush of the surfboard, then as I leap to my feet the wonder of riding a tumbling cascade of falling water. I catch wave after wave, the clean sparkling water washing away the emotional pain and pent-up prison stress from my mind and soul. I surf to the point of near physical exhaustion. Cold, worn-out, I am reluctant to let this moment end. Finally, teeth chattering and thinking I can stay no longer, a magical moment begins to unfold. A pod of bottlenose dolphins swims in to share the waves. Taking a deep breath of air, I dive off the board to swim underwater. I barely see the passing dolphins rushing by me in the low visibility water. The permanent smile they wear faintly registers in my mind. I hear their cheerful clicks and whistles like playground children's happy chatter, and then they disappear into the low visibility gloom. Cold, holding my breath, I fight to stay underwater, listening for the slightest hint that the dolphins are near or are coming back, but they are gone. Underwater, feeling the surge of the passing waves, the magic moment finally surrenders itself to sudden truth that I will too soon be back in my prison reality. I am an inmate living a false fantasy. Prison waits to fold its icy arms around me and these short moments away are like a rapidly ending dream. Alone, I feel very lost...adrift on a relentless tide that I know will return me far too soon to a prison in the high desert.

> *"When you get into the gutter, you get covered with trash, because   that is where the trash flows. On the mountain tops is where the sky and birds are...and you can take yourself there,"* J. California Cooper

"Then what happened?" implores Capkin.

"After the most incredible thirty-six hours of my life I had to go back to the prison camp. Sam couldn't take me so I rode a bus. I remember the terrible forlornness that seemed to capture me. I was descending into a deep depression the closer the bus got to Boron Prison Camp. In the late afternoon, the bus dropped me off on the desert highway. Then I began to walk about a mile up the camp's access road. I felt so doomed going back to that horrible reality."

"It must have been really hard to return to prison," Capkin says softly.

"Yeah, but walking up that road, I knew that all of it was a result of my own bad choices. Looking at the remnants of the sunset in the desert beyond the camp, I realized that my prison stay was almost over. In the not too distant future, the sun would rise with me finally walking out that prison gate for good."

"Locked away for so long," Capkin stands and paces to the rail, "how did you get through it without going absolutely crazy?"

"It wasn't easy, but prison taught me the wonder of freedom, the importance of making good choices and that the Lord was with me."

"What goes on around you... compares little with what goes on inside you," Ralph Waldo Emerson

Capkin abruptly sniffs loudly, "Um, I smell something."

Uh oh, I think to myself, *Capkin mind shift.* "Something capture your attention Capkin?"

He is like a bloodhound on the scent of an unattended steak sandwich. His nose is leading him in the direction of the dining salon. "Where you going?" I ask cheerfully.

"Are you kidding?" laughs Capkin, "It's dinnertime. Come on, I want to know more about this Jojo character."

"In a little while," I settle back against the metal sail, "I want to enjoy this night a little more."

An abrupt *ouch* tells me that Capkin has found something to stumble over in the darkness, then I see a pale red glow from the bridge instruments as he disappears though the side door of the pilothouse. Alone again in the night, I settle back against the turbo sail in close company with my thoughts and the soft throbbing vibrations of the wind ship's twin engines. Except for the rushing sound of water along the knife-edge keel of *Alcyone*, and the soft flutter of the French flag rustling in the wind, the night is silent. I am enjoying the evening solitude. It is always a very satisfying feeling successfully completing an expedition and this one has been exceedingly long, two-and-a-half years encompassing three separate expeditions of diving with great white sharks. Yet my mind is still swirling with memories of dolphins and surprisingly this leads me to thoughts of an elderly lady.

I met Esther in her modest apartment on the windward side of the island of Maui in Hawaii. I had called to make an appointment and promptly arrived at her door with my tape recorder in hand. She could not see very well through her thick glasses, nor was her hearing up to par despite the amplification of her hearing aid, but her mind was sharp and like most older widows, she was glad for a visitor.

"Come in, come in," she bubbles in delight, "sit anywhere." She uses her cane to chase a fluffy cat from a thick upholstered chair. I correctly assume that this is where she wants me to sit. So I do, instantly inheriting her fat furry cat who leaps into my lap. I do not mind the feline companion, but its fluffy tail plays havoc with my notepad and I narrowly miss snapping the tape recorder's lid down on it. I watch Esther settle into a chair, but she is not there very long. This energetic great-grandmother has much to show me and I am very curious indeed.

Esther arrived in Hawaii just before the turn of the century, the daughter of a missionary. As a child, she was fortunate to be a schoolmate of the last queen of Hawaii. While playing alongside the future Hawaiian monarch, this now grand old lady, shared in an education tailored for a royal. Esther learned ancient Hawaiian traditions and historical songs from master storytellers. The ancient Hawaiians did not have a written language, so their history was passed down through songs, dances and stories. Esther was a treasure trove of Hawaiian historical riches that unfortunately would fade away with her passing.

For several hours, and many cups of tea, I heard a multitude of stories about Hawaiian court intrigues, but when she began to speak about dolphin legends, I was all ears. She told me their story in a song that was also a dance. As she sang, her hands wove pictures in the air telling their own share of the ancient tale. Despite her great age, Esther moved gracefully and for a few minutes, I am transported from a small modest apartment into a royal garden as this elderly woman sang and danced the story of the whale, the dolphin and the shark.

Esther sang in old Hawaiian, but she laced the ancient words with English without losing any of the magic of the song. Her flowing hands wove in their own images reflecting the dignity of the giant whale, the playfulness of the dolphin and the jagged intensity of the shark. She told how the Humpback whales came to Hawaiian waters to mate and deliver their young. It was also here that the whales came to find their closest friends and protectors...the dolphins.

Sitting back, forgetting about my notepad, I immerse myself in Esther's song as I watch her gracefully paint the underwater ballet of a whale cow swimming powerfully with a protective bull escort at her side. Before them, swimming playfully, are the much smaller dolphins, their tiny protectors. Though the dolphins seem frivolous with their play, they are alert warriors watching for their enemy, the never sleeping, always hunting shark. The dolphins know that the Humpback cow is near her time. The huge bull hovers closer as the wonder of whale birth begins. The dolphins form a protective circle and acoustically probe the depths to make sure their enemy is not there, but they know he will come—the shark will not be able to resist. As the newborn calf emerges, it carries with it the scent of the mother's womb, which is a scrumptious olfactory lure for sharks.

A shark can detect less than one part of blood in a billion parts of water, and apparently, whale blood sends a unique message of its own to these ocean hunters. Blood in the water indicates that an animal may be in trouble or has died. This powerful lure will immediately bring in the sharks, but often the meal they seek is consumed before they get there. Whale blood, however, announces that there may be a huge feast waiting, so it brings many sharks rushing in from long distances. Sharks will charge up an ocean odor corridor that carries the scent of whale blood arriving in a frenzy to bite, rip and feed. I imagine that it would be difficult for the huge Humpback cow with her bull escort to fend off the much smaller, agile and very aggressive sharks.

Esther's hand movements are humped, sharp and jagged like the attack pattern of a shark. The sharks, she portrays with her hands are in a frenzy of one-minded fury to get at the defenseless newborn calf, but before them arrayed for battle are the dolphin protectors. The flashing teeth of the sharks are kept at bay by the swift and agile dolphins. Though there may be many sharks, they attack independently, while the wiser dolphins work together. They drive off the sharks smashing into them with their blunt noses. These powerful impacts can kill a shark and even in their frenzy, the sharks are leery of such keen underwater warriors.

At the center of the protective circle, the cow gently nudges the new born to the surface for its first breath. Then with the dolphins on all sides, the mighty whale family seeks out the protection of the whale pod (herd). The sharks return to the dark depths—hungry, ever waiting.

Weary from her dance, yet eyes vitally alive behind the thick coke-bottle glasses, Esther settles back into her chair.

Later that evening, I arrive back at the hotel where the Cousteau team is staying. One of the younger French divers enters the room a few minutes after me and wonders where I have been. He is completely astonished that I would spend several hours interviewing an elderly widow lady about ancient Hawaiian songs. "Why spend your time visiting a grandmother about old songs?" he laughs, "you are single and Hawaii is full of young beautiful women."

"But Antoine," I answer, "I'm dating someone." After our third date, Cindy flew back to the mainland two weeks ago.

"So what?" Antoine looks at me like I've got a screw loose, which is actually how I often think about him pursuing an endless line of one-night-stands.

"Antoine, I'm in love with Cindy."

"You're nuts," Antoine shakes his head, my morals are being judged by a flamboyant French bachelor. I find it highly amusing. "They're only relationships until one of them gets a ring on your finger, yet even then the ring is not through the nose," argues Antoine, "I would never be happily married to just one woman."

"On that we can agree," I chuckle.

Antoine slaps on some cologne then heads for the door. "Hey Antoine," I say buoyantly. He pauses with one hand on the door-knob. "If you catch anything tonight, remember I'm the ship's medic."

Antoine laughs then steps through the door. I walk out to the Lanai and stare at the ocean, but in my mind, I again see Esther dancing the song of the whale, the dolphin and the shark. I think what an incredible person she is with her vast treasure of ancient Hawaiian memories. I imagine how lucky a child would be to befriend someone like Esther. Before there was radio or television a child would learn much from the stories of their grandparents. In our modern society grandparents are often perceived as burdens; many unfortunately windup living lonely, idle lives in senior citizen centers where the sound of child's laughter and of small running feet is seldom heard. It is they and the children who suffer. When the grandchildren grow up their adulthood will be more hollow for the lack of sage wisdom and patient love...instead they will carry their stories from what they learned from television programs, movies and the fad music of their childhood. For the majority their fathers will leave their homes making the children's life vacant of a father's love and education. Like my friend Antoine, many fathers are not content to make a true commitment, not to their spouse, nor their children and particularly not to themselves. Then we wonder why children today seem so disconnected from true family values. The answer is we let them slip away or shoved them out of sight and out of mind into a convenient solution.

*Is not wisdom found among the aged? Does not long life
bring understanding?* Job 12:12

Under the dim glittering light of the vast heavens, *Alcyone* rides
the night swell. Through the deck, I softly hear the rest of the crew
in the dining salon. There is the subtle tinkle of glasses and the
sound of muffled laughter. The forward salon windows glow warmly
from flickering candle light within luring me toward the camaraderie below, yet I am not yet willing to leave the quiet solitude of the
wind ship's bow. I know that one day in the not too distant future
all of this will be but a fond and precious memory. I want to capture
the wonder of these times with the Cousteau expedition teams and
to treasure them always.

Staring at the twinkling heavens, I think about the ancient
Polynesians who made star maps with dried stems from coconut
fronds to navigate the vast open ocean. With nothing more than
that and their intense awareness of ocean currents, the ancient mari-
ners discovered the Hawaiian Islands. Then they made repeated
trips thousands of miles back to Polynesia to bring their families
to Hawaii, which are the most remote islands on this planet. My
mind paints a picture of these early sailors paddling their large
expedition canoes with woven palm frond sails. I imagine the men
and women singing songs and beating out a rhythm on hollow
wooden instruments to coordinate and ease their labors. I recall
the heavy drum beat of a Polynesian sailing song and imagine I
feel its cadence pounding out the paddling tempo. Memories of
Hawaii begin calling to me and faintly, over the flowing sound of
the rushing night wind, I mentally hear dolphins approaching as
the remembrance wraps around my consciousness and carries me
away.

It is a bright sunny day off the coast of the island paradise called
Maui. Fifty yards from the stern of our *Zodiac* a gust of water shoots
high into the air, followed immediately by a deep inhalation as
a massive Humpback tail disappears beneath the rolling swells.
Floating on the surface, I hear high-pitched squeals and rapid clicks

of approaching dolphins. Michel DeLoire grins at me through the glass of his faceplate then nods. We take deep breaths together, and then plunge downwards into the path of an approaching Humpback pod. Holding our breath, we descend quickly to a depth of thirty feet. The water is especially clear. We can see a hundred feet or more and the bright morning light is excellent for filming. The restless ocean surface throws wandering sunbeams of shimmering radiance into the deep blue water. About us, the ocean is full of crisp sea mammal sounds. Nearby a bull Humpback whale bellows out its love song. In the silent world beneath the waves, there are no unwanted noises to distract from the mighty leviathan melody that echoes through the air pockets of our bodies. Immersed in the deep tide of whale music, I hear on a softer scale the chirps, clicks and twitters of excited dolphins . One cannot come closer than this to actually floating on a wave of living music. A melody of nature lightly suspended in the rapture of the deep ocean. Peering anxiously into the broad vista of light and water we wait with eager anticipation, then abruptly the marine mammal pod is upon us. Playful dolphins lead the way. There are a half-dozen of them riding the bow wave of the first whale. It is an amazing sight. I knew that dolphins rode the bow wave of ships and boats, which for them is like surfing. Yet this is surfing underwater thirty feet beneath the rippling surface. It makes me wonder if dolphins ride the bow wave of submerged submarines—does anyone even know the answer. There are no windows on the fast submarines for anyone to see. A nuclear submarine can reach speeds greater than fifty miles an hour. If a dolphin could latch onto that underwater bow wave and ride it, would it be faster than any dolphin has ever gone before?

Watching the dolphins leading the way, I instantaneously think of Esther's song of the whale, the dolphin and the shark. *Are the dolphins here to surf, to have fun?* I wonder, *or are they here as protectors?* The bottlenose dolphins are so small compared to the huge whale that swims directly behind them. Michel and I separate, he closes in to film the oncoming whales, but I am captivated by the dolphins. Two bottlenose break away from the lead pack and rush in my direction. Sunbeams play across their slick bodies as the dolphins gracefully wheel about me. They circle so tightly I could almost reach out and touch them. When the angle of the light is perfect, I aim my camera and release the shutter. I do not know it then, but I have just shot my first Cousteau poster. I am smiling at the wise eyes regarding me. They cannot see the smile because of the snorkel grasped between my teeth, but maybe they can see it in my eyes or in the friendly way I wave and gurgle happily underwater. *Author's note: to see this and other images from these true stories, please visit www. drugsbite.com.*

Having checked me out the dolphins race back to join the lead whale, the massive marine mammal, like a silent locomotive, is passing a dozen yards away. Another smaller whale trails the right pectoral fin of the first. This teenage Humpback seems to startle at our presence and rises slightly above us. For a moment, I am slightly concerned to have a whale between the surface and me. I am still holding my breath and would like to go up for another breath of air. I think maybe fifty seconds have gone by, so decide to wait until the whale passes, then I will angle up slowly to shoot a few downward pictures as the rest of the pod slips beneath me. As the giant tail passes only a few feet above me, I snap off another frame, then turn to see a huge whale cow swimming into view. Then to one side and slightly above her, I see a newborn Humpback calf. *So, my underwater friends are here for more than just play,* I say to myself, *the dolphins are here as protectors.* The tiny whale, though still huge by human standards, would normally shy away from the unknown creature in its path. Instead, the baby whale alters its course to swim straight at me. Thinking that Michel may be just over my shoulder, I begin swimming backwards so as not to get in the way of his cinema camera. The little whale keeps coming and seeing me swimming backwards becomes bolder. My lungs are laboring for air, yet I continue to shoot pictures as fast as I can crank the rewind lever on the camera. The baby Humpback seems to be not much longer than a dolphin, yet it has a lot more mass, nearly a ton of wide-eyed innocence. I see the tiny eye regarding me. Just beyond the calf, the gigantic cow swims in close parental attendance. As the small Humpback comes right alongside, only three or four feet way, it more than fills the sports action finder on my underwater camera. I quickly release the shutter, and then begin swimming desperately for the surface. I have been down for probably a minute-and-a-half of intensive swimming and am becoming lightheaded from lack of oxygen. Yet as I rocket upwards, I see the calf's tail beating strongly as it follows me up. A foot beneath the rippling surface the unfiltered sunlight intensifies. I shoot a final picture, capturing the baby Humpback in a halo of light then we both rise into the world of air. From the *Zodiac*, Jean-Michel sees twin plumes of water and air shot upwards, a large one from the baby Humpback and a much smaller one from me. As the little whale tail disappears beneath the shimmering water, I lay on the surface gasping through my snorkel.

In my five years with The Cousteau Society, only three of my pictures would be made into official Cousteau posters. Two of them were captured in this one magical moment; one at the beginning and the other at the end of this single breath-hold dive. I shot over a dozen pictures in that short time capturing a treasury of memories in a mere ninety seconds.

Michel DeLoire's snorkel surfaces a few feet away, yet his head remains underwater. He is still filming with his cinema camera as the rest of the Humpback pod passes slowly below us. I am too tired to do anything but rest and pant. Another pair of dolphins swims by, which is encouraging because it means that mister shark isn't present.

To my right I see Jean-Michel Cousteau in the waiting *Zodiac*, he starts the outboard and slowly motors in our direction. I wait for Michel DeLoire to hand up his heavy underwater cinematic camera then pass up my still camera. I watch Michel effortlessly pull himself into the inflatable, then with a couple of swift kicks of my fins, I follow him aboard. For a moment, I lay on the metal deck gasping as Michel sits up eagerly staring after the whale pod.

"My, Stephen, getting a little out of shape are we?" Jean-Michel asks playfully.

I pull off my flippers and just grin at my almost always-happy boss. I am just too winded to think of anything witty to say.

"Are we having trouble keeping up with Michel DeLoire?" prods Jean-Michel. "After all he is sixty-one years old."

I glance over at Michel DeLoire who is chuckling. He is in tremendous physical condition. I happen to know he is a grandfather several times over. Yet here he is swimming with dolphins and whales holding his breath for long periods, while the whole time pushing around a bulky cinema camera. I know many kids who would not have a hope of keeping up with this energetic grandparent.

I can do everything through him who gives me strength.
Philippians 4:13

"Better catch your breath quickly," laughs Jean-Michel as he pulls the rope start on the outboard, "I see another whale pod heading in our direction."

Less than five minutes later, Michel and I roll back out of the *Zodiac*. We take several deep breathes, then I follow this amazing grandfather, who is pushing a camera much bigger than mine against the resistance of the water, downward into crystal blue water full of whale songs and incredible adventures.

Back in Australia, on the bow of *Alcyone*, I inhale deeply the crisp night air. It feels good to feel my chest expanding against the sweatshirt I am wearing. Catching a scent of the dinner smells, I rub my belly in anticipation of joining the guys in the salon. Then I become aware that I am rubbing a bit more of a tummy than I am use to feeling. For the past several months, I have been mostly hanging underwater in the plastic shark cylinder, instead of swimming. Long exposure to the cold water of the Great Australian Bight has increased my appetite. The result is an extra five pounds...OK... make it eight pounds of added fat insulation. *No wonder the great white sharks were after me,* I think to myself, *all this blubber must make me look like a tempting walrus.* When we hit port, I promise myself a morning run and when I go below tonight maybe I'll just have a simple salad. Not an easy task with Bruno, the chef, at work below.

I am pleased that early in my life, I had the importance of good physical conditioning forced upon me. The mind is the essence of a human being, however for actual physical adventure, we are dependent upon the abilities of our bodies. No one knows this better than someone who suffers the limitations of being handicapped. To be physically challenged limits one's freedom. Yet, for the vast majority of young people their physical condition and liberty of movement, or lack of, is self-determined. We can choose a physical state of fitness that allows us endless opportunities, like Michel DeLoire, or we can impose self-indulgent limitations through laziness and lack of discipline. A couch potato not only restricts their real adventure quota, they are inhibiting their personal freedom as well.

At this point, it is critical to realize that God has given each of us a body that is truly a wondrous biological machine. Unlike man-made machines, the human body can repair itself, fight off disease, recover from illness, and is quite capable at adapting to a wide variety of intense physical demands. The effectiveness of these abilities, however, is directly influenced by the attitude of our mind set. If we believe ourselves to be sick, the body may actually comply by making us more susceptible to diseases. Likewise good health is to a great extent self determined.

When it comes to the health and fitness of our bodies, we cannot under estimate the importance of a positive attitude. For a moment, imagine the pleasure and wonder of having the finely tuned body of an Olympic athletic. Consider all the things you could do with that body such as run long distances and not easily tire, climb mountains with or without a rope, kayak raging rivers, swim the English channel...the possibilities are endless. Can we imagine that body being content to slouch on a couch watching mindless television programs and eating junk food?

A cheerful look brings joy to the heart, and good news gives health to the bones. Proverbs 15:30

A healthy body likes to do things. The proof is in little children who have way too much energy to sit still for very long. When not actually resting to rebuild itself, the human body has to be trained, or forced, to remain idle. Fortunately, the human physique is so adaptable, that even a totally-out-of-shape body can be re-conditioned into a trim, adventure-hungry machine.

In every human being, there are infinite possibilities, all of which are conditional upon our attitude, actual physical limitations and our commitment to self-discipline. We must not only want to change, we must determine that through discipline we are going to make those changes happen.

> *"Imprisoned in every fat man, a thin one is wildly signaling to be let out,"* Cyril Connolly

Physical improvement begins with exercise...period! Conditioning does not come from a pill or a magic lotion...ever! Depending on a person's current state of physical fitness it is best to start out slow to keep from burning out too soon. It helps to begin with an activity that is fun, such as swimming, bicycle riding, walking, hiking or jogging. Personally, I like to mix all five activities because exercise should be enjoyable and diverse to maintain our interest and continued enthusiasm.. Surprisingly initial improvement always comes quickly.

As our conditioning improves, we need to pick up the pace a bit and begin increasing the duration of our exercise program. Recruiting a friend or a family member to exercise with lends companionship, turns work into fun and adds spirited competition. Shame them into it if necessary. Begin to experiment with new activities such as weight lifting, gymnastics and martial arts or join an exercise club.

Weight lifting is one of the best and fastest ways to serious physical conditioning. As such, I would like to share a common sense approach to practical weight training. First, disregard most of the wives-tales being told about weight training. This is an exercise and training program that is ideal for both men and women; young and old alike; however, it is not generally recommended for pre- or early-teens. The American Medical Association conducted a long-term study on weight lifting and determined that the best, long lasting results are achieved through injury free workouts. This means never lifting more weight than a person can effectively control through a total of eight to ten repetitions. The movements should be done slowly without breaking form. The instant a person breaks form, such as overly arching their back, they are risking a serious injury, which could potentially become a lifelong debilitation. No one should ever lift more weight than he or she can manage alone. Having someone *spot you* (help lift some of the weight) greatly increases the possibility of injury. Ideally count off two seconds during a lift and allow four seconds to lower the weight. This prevents joint, connective tissue and tendon injury while greatly reducing the amount of weight lifted, which is far better than blowing out a hernia from trying to lift a massive load.

Repetitions are done in sets with a short rest period in between. Each muscle group should be worked through two to three sets of various exercise then move on to a new group. The idea is to leave the gym feeling good, not totally worn out. Work the major muscle groups first: chest, back, stomach and buttocks, then move on to shoulders, arms and legs. Don't overlook the pull-exercises to keep the body in developmental balance. For more information, consult your library for books on weight training. Be very leery of advice from self-supposed, weight lifting experts. In a gym, many weight lifters are trying to impress each other with how much iron they can do in a single lift. This is where many injuries happen. So remember, *it is not the amount of the weight, it is the amount of the work.*

The martial arts are another form of exercise that I have found to be especially beneficial for coordination, strength and flexibility. Karate and judo should not be viewed as an opportunity to learn to fight; rather these art forms teach one how to avoid fighting. A person who knows how to defend themselves is less likely to be lured into a conflict. One of the major advantages of the martial arts is mastering how a body moves (i.e., stability, balance, range of motion, etc.). The martial arts also develop confidence and self-esteem.

There are many different styles of martial arts, karate and judo. A local YMCA or junior college usually offers excellent family programs. Unfortunately, the martial arts are also loaded with more than their share of weirdoes with their own distorted concept of what this sport is about. The result can be rather strange personal philosophies being dumped onto their students. It is wise to sit in as a visitor and watch a training session at a local dojo (karate training center). Also, pay particular attention as to whether the people are enjoying themselves. If it isn't fun why do it?

Depending on a person's commitment and discipline, their body with time will develop into an exciting human engine capable of carrying them into incredible adventures. In the action world of real life adventures there are no real limits except for brief moments of intense justifiable fear.

Getting in good physical condition has tremendous impact on the quality of our lives. When we feel good about ourselves, we are happier and learn to trust in our abilities, which always lead to getting involved in more adventures and fun physical activities. Exercise is a major contributor to general good health, longevity and happiness.

Despite my sweatshirt and thick jacket, I am becoming cold as I stand and stretch at the bow of the wind ship. The laughter from the dining salon, and the captivating smell of dinner, lures me below. Opening the bridge door, I go inside. Joining my shipmates at the dinner table, we celebrate the end of a long wonderful expedition and avidly discuss the promise of an adventurous future.

"The quality of a person's life is in direct proportion to their commitment to excellence, regardless of their chosen field of endeavor," Vince Lombardi, Notre Dame Coach

Illustration by Andy Charles
The day dolphins took the drop and the Author's wave at Black's Beach.

"Practice being excited," Bill Foster

Chapter 46

PALOS VERDES PENINSULA, CA, JANUARY 1992

❝ LET ME get this straight! You're going to a tropical resort in the Caribbean to dive with a friendly dolphin," Cindy is in a mood, "and you call that work?"

"Well, it's not exactly like I'm going on a vacation to lie in the sun. I'm simply going to work." My answer sounds a bit lame even to my own ears.

"Not a vacation! Look out the window and tell me what do you see?" Cindy throws the curtains wide-open in our small coastal apartment.

There are broad rivulets of rain coursing down the window. Beyond the glass the afternoon sky is dark and dismal. Long walking shadows stalk the nearly sunless horizon under a low ceiling of densely packed clouds. Over the raging ocean, there is a thick wall of thunderclouds tramping shoreward. Huge waves pound the rocky beach, while trees bend and sway wildly to the thrusts of a gusting onshore wind. Strewn on the ground outside our apartment large broken branches attest to the storm's fury. A triple bolt of lightning stabs down from the clouds strobing the dark landscape with harsh electric light. Seconds later the rolling roar of thunder rattles the glass pane before me. I turn and look at Cindy, then cautiously say, "I see a storm."

"It's a major storm!" Protests Cindy, who is bundled in several layers of warm clothes. An electric heater in the corner glows ruby red, but its heat barely warms our tiny apartment. "Stephen, you're heading off for a Caribbean vacation on white sand, sun-baked beaches to swim in warm tropical water with a dolphin buddy." Cindy glares at me, "It isn't fair, diver boy."

I lower my head, acknowledging that I am truly a rascal, then carefully put my arms around the woman I love. Though Cindy is tall and slim, she feels bulky wrapped in so many garments. "I'm sorry I have such a terrific job, Cindy," I apologize while stroking her long hair.

Cindy fakes a sniffle working my emotions a bit harder, "I have to stay home alone in this freezing apartment and study for my finals, while you get to have all the fun."

"Uh, Cindy," I hazard cautiously, "didn't you go out to the Caribbean on a Cousteau dolphin expedition of your own?"

Cindy steps back and pretends a surprised look, "So."

"Weren't you swimming in warm tropical waters with dozens of dolphins cavorting about you?" I push my case relentlessly.

"Well, sometimes there were only a half-dozen or so dolphins... and one day it rained and we couldn't even lay out in the sun," answers Cindy in a small wounded voice.

"And while you were basking in the warm tropics, I was diving in cold frigid water off the southern coast of Australia?" I'm being ruthless, but it is the only way to win with Cindy.

"Okay!" Cindy concedes, "You can go swim with your lousy dolphin."

Immediately, I sense trouble, Cindy never gives in that easy.

Cindy snuggles against my chest and asks, "Did you know that a storm on the coast means fun in the mountains?"

"No, I've never heard that before."

"Of course not," laughs Cindy, "I just made it up, however, I do want to go snow skiing." Cindy begins pulling ski boots and poles out of her sports closet. Where most women have clothes and dress shoes in their closets, Cindy reserves half of hers for sporting equipment. Not counting the stuff crammed in the back out of view, I can see mountain climbing ropes, a parachute, scuba equipment, a high performance water ski and a mountain tent. In our bedroom over the dresser, four bicycles are hanging upside down from the rafters, two mountain bikes and two road bikes. Draped from the sides of the rafters are downhill and cross-country snow skies and two surfboards. Lacking any more room, her windsurfer is tied outside to the railing of our second story patio. Did I mention that she runs with the varsity men's track team at the California State University Los Angeles? No, she doesn't get to compete with them; she just enjoys the dedicated competition.

"But what about your finals?" I ask.

"Silly," laughs Cindy, "I'm a straight *A* student at Cal. State. Besides, if I have to be cold, I might as well enjoy it."

At that moment, it is easy to see why I married Cindy. She is the most fun person I know. While helping her to gather our ski clothes, I realize that I am going to have to work harder at involving her in my adventures.

"Work hard, play harder," Cynthia Elizabeth Arrington

We arrive at the Turks and Caicos Islands at midday after stopping overnight in Miami, Florida. It takes only a few minutes to clear customs at the small island airport because they are expecting us. I have always found that things go faster when following a well thought-out plan. I have been corresponding with the customs department for several weeks so there are no unexpected hitches or delays over our small mountain of diving, photographic and sound equipment.

A very old and weathered black man with sparse gray hair and wearing a faded ball cap is waiting for us in the airport parking lot, compliments of the captain of our charter boat. The elderly man has glasses so thick that he stares for several seconds before he realizes what he is looking at. However, the real surprise is the condition of the debilitated flatbed truck he is leaning against. My eyes rivet on the old truck's shadow at his feet. The bright morning sun is directly above this rusty old bucket of bolts. Patches of dazzling light riddle the decrepit vehicle's shadow from fist-sized rust holes to inch-wide running cracks. On the ground beneath the ancient truck lie bits of rust debris. The rust is the only thing holding this old antique together. I gingerly jump up onto the wooden flatbed and promptly put one foot through a patch of wood rot, which catches the attention of our elderly chauffeur. "Hey there boy, be careful with Old Betsy. She ain't the spry girl she use to be."

"*C'est vrai*," agrees Michel DeLoire in French.

"What did he say?" Henry, the driver, is eyeing Michel suspiciously.

"Michel was just agreeing with you," I say hastily, "*C'est vrai* means "it is true" in French."

"Don't have much use for words that got no meaning for me," complains the old man as he glares at Michel.

"*Pardonne-moi*," Michel offers a short bow, "*le camion est le perte.*"

"What'd he say now?" Henry is getting huffy.

"He asked you to excuse him and he said your truck is perky," I offer in Michel's defense.

Only somewhat mollified, Henry hitches up his pants, then leans against the truck and puts a possessive hand on the dented bonnet. "Better get your gear loaded...and be more careful with my gal."

As we cautiously load our equipment under Henry's watchful rheumy eyes, Michel leans toward me and quietly says, "*Perte* in French means to waste away, I said his truck is wasting away."

I glance over at Henry who is wiping a small opening in a very dusty windshield.

"You want to ride up front?" I ask Michel.

"No way, I want to be able to jump free before the accident!"

After all the gear is loaded, the whole team opts to ride on the back of the truck for safety reasons. The engine coughs, chokes, and then labors to start with a loud rumbling grumble. An acid cloud of black smoke spews from the broken muffler to rise thickly around us through the holes in the flatbed. Henry leans out of the cab to ask if we're ready, then loudly grinds the gears, and with a lurch and a backfire, we're off on another expedition.

The ride through the small town of Providenciales is memorable only in that it is seen through a dense smoke screen. There is only one stop light on Main Street, which is fortunate as we are nearly smothered in a hovering cloud of diesel smoke waiting for it to turn green.

Twenty minutes later, we thankfully arrive at a white sand beach with patches of scrub and grass growing on small dunes. The sand is actually tiny bits of broken coral. Our feet sink several inches into the soft coral bits as we carry load after load of bulky equipment out to the water's edge. A hundred yards from shore the charter boat, *Island Diver* awaits our arrival. I see a man at the stern endlessly trying to pull start an outboard engine, which finally stutters into a reluctant idle with a bad hacking cough. It sounds like the engine is running on only one of two cylinders. The man in a sorry looking inflatable slowly motors in our direction. At first, I think his slow speed is because of the poor condition of the outboard, but I am wrong. It is the pitiful state of the rubber pontoons of his *Zodiac* that so limits his passage through the water. There are no floorboards so the little inflatable awkwardly accordions over each wave.

Mostly under its own power, but assisted by a small wave, the inflatable lands on the beach with a wet sounding plop. The man leaps out of the misshapen *Zodiac*, with its thick covering of repair patches of various shapes and colors, then he happily shakes my hand. "Captain Bill Rattey at your service." For a horrible moment, I actually thought he might salute.

With a sense of dread, I look at the slim man standing before me. He is wearing frayed cut-off jeans with a T-shirt sporting a multitude of holes and rust stains. It looks like he cuts his own hair with lawn shears. Just then, the debilitated truck backfires drawing my attention to it. I glance down at the broken down inflatable, then look in horror at the charter boat a hundred yards from shore. The boat is of a design that went out of popularity around thirty years ago. In my mind, I remember his colorful brochure and lively description of the charter boat's amenities. Jean-Michel's other chief diver, Don Santee took care of the boat charter for me. I can almost hear him snickering in the basement of The Cousteau Society office, which is where Jean-Michel kept his dive teams.

"Captain Rattey," I ask carefully, "Do you get many charters?"

"First one this year," he grins, "really needed the money too, got a few repairs I've needed to make."

I prod the inflatable hull, only half-full of air, it is soft and squishy. "The hull leaks a little," confides Rattey, "we just have to pump her up between trips. Been meaning to fix it, but I put all my time and money into maintaining the *Island Diver*. Ain't any other boat like her."

"I don't doubt it," mumbles Michel, then, I hear him whisper to Marc and Clay, the other two members of our team, "did he really say his name is Rattey?"

Captain Rattey is a good dozen feet away, but he hears the comment. "It's true," he answers, "The local kids sometimes make fun of my name. It's a shame because I could take them out on the water for some fun with the dolphin. But it's kind of hard to be friendly with people who are making fun and laughing at you."

Soon we are chugging out to the charter boat. As I look at the floating wreck awaiting us, I am reminded of the debilitated river-boat from the old black and white movie The African Queen with Humphrey Bogart. As the beat-up inflatable accordions over the waves leaving a froth of leaking air bubbles in its wake, I get a better look at our barely floating home for the next three weeks.

"Now don't judge *Island* Diver by her looks, I don't waste money on new paint and cosmetics if it ain't needed," confides Captain, "that's just make-up anyway. It's the old gal's heart that I am worrying about."

"Worrying about," I echo, "is it the engines we're talking about?"

"Well parts aren't easy to come by," he complains, "and the

tropical salt air isn't too good for her complexion."

Michel DeLoire whispers into my ear, "What is he talking about?"

"Rust," I whisper back.

We arrive alongside

"*Incroyable*," Michel says dryly in French.

"What's that mean?" Asks Captain Rattey.

"Incredible," answers Michel.

The captain beams at what he accepts as a compliment, "She is incredible, I built her myself in my backyard back stateside."

"Really," Michel looks at the boat's blocky lines, "out of plywood no less."

"Yep, finished her fifteen years ago," the captain says proudly, "been at sea ever since."

Pulling alongside the barge-like boat, I grab a handrail to stop our forward motion and it promptly comes off in my hand. "Don't worry, just a little bit of wood rot," Captain Rattey takes the piece of rail and tosses it into a box of other items awaiting repair.

Climbing onto the main deck of *Island Diver*, I cannot help thinking that Captain Rattey's first plan might have been to build a mobile home, and then halfway through the project decided he would rather have a boat. Square and blocky is a good term to describe this mutant floating shipwreck. The vessel, I hesitate to call it a ship, is wide and stout at the main deck with a plywood covered upper area that sags here and there depending upon the lack of application of varnish. The team is not enthusiastic as we spend most of the afternoon storing equipment.

When Captain Rattey announces that he is going to start the engines and shift our anchorage, the team begins making bets in French as to whether the engines will start or drop out of the bottom of the boat. After a full minute of serious cranking, one engine after the other belches smoke and wheezes into an asthmatic rumble. The whole boat vibrates as he engages the enthusiastically out-of-sync engines.

While *Island Diver* chugs laboriously to her new anchorage,

Michel voices what the rest of the team is thinking, "Why are we chartering this horrible boat?"

"We are aboard for the best of reasons," I whisper back.

"We are saving money maybe?" hazards Michel. "Is Jean-Michel having financial problems?"

"No," I reply softly, "it seems Jojo really likes this boat and is very fond of its skipper."

"Really?" My answer startles Michel.

"It's true," responds Captain Rattey who is a good twenty feet away. The man must have radar ears to have heard us particularly over the chug of the decrepit engines. "Jojo spends more time with *Island Diver* and me, than with anyone else."

Almost to add authority to his words, the rogue dolphin in question arrives several seconds later. However, instead of heading for the prow like most dolphins to surf the bow wave, which is rather small a pathetic due to our extreme slow speed, Jojo instead disappears under the stern of the boat. "Where did he go?" asks Michel DeLoire.

"He's down fussing with my props," laughs Captain Rattey.

"He's what?" Michel is not sure he heard right.

"Jojo loves to play chicken with my propellers," Captain Rattey glances at the gauges that indicate the engines' RPM. "This is *Island Diver's* best speed for Jojo. The propellers are turning just fast enough to be thrilling, but slow enough for him to get real close."

"Close?" I echo, "how close does he get?"

"Inches, mate. Right now Jojo is dancing just inches from those big mean props. I think Jojo likes *Island Diver* because she has the biggest propellers of any local boat in these waters," Captain Rattey says with great pride then holds out a dive mask, "take a look for yourself."

While Captain Rattey ties a thick rope to a railing, which I carefully pull on to make sure it will take my weight then I don a pair of fins, grab the end of the rope and slip over the side. *Island Diver* is doing about three knots as I slide into the flowing water. On the surface, I take a quick breath through my snorkel and descend. The current shoves me closer towards the mossy hull of *Island Diver*. I see longhaired moss and sharp-edged barnacles passing inches from my face then I am below the hull and dropping back towards the stern. At first, all I see is a mass of swirling froth and bubbles, and then the big three-foot diameter brass propellers come spinning into view. They are huge, encrusted with barnacles and discolored with age. The blades are jagged-edged and laced with wicked nicks from encounters with unexpected reefs and rocks. The twin propellers with their triple blades are revolving at about a hundred-fifty RPM. Beyond the dangerous twirling propellers, I notice a sleek shape in rapid motion. Sliding further down the rope, I see Jojo dancing precariously close to the brass blades. He moves swiftly from one propeller to the other, swimming forward until his snout is only inches from the wicked swirling blades, then he drops back a few inches and rushes to the other propeller. This is very odd and dangerous behavior, yet the dolphin seems to be enjoying himself immensely.

The propellers begin to slow then stop as Captain Rattey arrives at our anchorage. Looking disappointed, not that I would know how a dolphin's face could show disappointment, Jojo swims to the surface for a breath of air. Noticing me apparently for the first time, Jojo rushes in my direction, stopping at the last instant only a foot away.

I have gotten to swim with many wild dolphins, but the encounters have always been short and the dolphins did not normally get so close. Jojo swims right up to my face and stares. He peers into my mask with one eye then shifts his head to peer with the other. I am under serious dolphin scrutiny and am wondering what he is thinking. Being so close, with a real opportunity to look intimately at this dolphin, to stare right back at those curious eyes regarding me, it is almost like meeting a new kid on the neighborhood block. Jojo bounces a few clicks off me to get my measure as I enthusiastically squeak back like an excited mouse. Imagine two individuals knowing they are about to become good friends though they do not speak the same language.

Later, Captain Rattey would confide that Jojo sometimes just instantly accepts a person and is willing to be their friend. I could not believe that I am to be this fortunate. Maybe Jojo could sense in that moment of our first contact that I am the kind of person who would be a good friend for a dolphin. Maybe it is because I am so excited to be meeting him. It is often like that for dogs and cats who immediately befriend a complete stranger. All I do know is that I am on the verge of a dolphin/person friendship that could lead to three weeks of incredible wonder and interaction with a very intelligent marine mammal.

Jojo and I play tag for the better part of an hour where I am always *it*—despite my temporary advantage of using an underwater scooter. Finally, as the scooter's propeller slowly stops turning from lack of battery power, Jojo decides to swim off. He bounces a few more clicks in my direction then disappears into the depths. The water feels lonely without my new dolphin friend.

Climbing out of the warm tropical water, Captain Rattey is waiting for me with a towel. "Amazing isn't he?" he says with a knowing smile.

"I can't believe we swam together for so long," I reply, then notice that the towel has a musty smell and a covering of some very suspicious stains with a half-dusting of mold. Opting to air dry, I drape the offending piece of cloth downwind on a railing.

"Actually that was quite surprising," Captain Rattey says wistfully, "Jojo doesn't normally play so much with someone the first time... excepting of course for the dog."

"The dog?"

"Yeah, there's a mutt on the next island in the chain, he and Jojo are buddies. They race each other through shallow surf. The dog tries to playfully nip the dolphin's tail and Jojo tries his best to get under the dog."

"Why would Jojo want to get under a dog?" I am intrigued.

"To toss it into the air, of course, flicks him with his tail...ain't much of a dog, just a little thing." Captain Rattey pulls a frayed wallet out of his back pocket and digs out a worn picture, which he hands me. "I carry this around because most people don't believe it."

The picture is yellowed and a bit out of focus, but plainly there is a small-sized dog flying upside down though the air with a dolphin in the water just beneath it. I think about all our camera equipment and hope that we will get the opportunity to capture Jojo and his doggy toy at play. "Think we could motor over to that island?" I ask hopefully.

"Wouldn't be too good an idea to take *Island Diver* that far from the local hardware store," confides Captain Rattey, "if you get my drift."

Disappointed, I again look at the debilitated condition of the boat.

"Did you get it?" asks Rattey expectantly, "Drift, as in adrift."

"Oh," I laugh politely, then watch him head off to attend to a few chores, before joining the rest of the team storing our gear. It is late in the afternoon when the last piece of equipment is un-boxed and placed in a handy location. I stretch feeling a couple of reassuring pops in my spine from all the bending over, then lean against the railing. I am at peace with the world as I watch the sun slowly begin to sink into the ocean. Abruptly, there is a loud squeal of static, then *Canon in D*, blasts from a broadside of suspended speakers. They are in all shapes and sizes, not one matching the other. Captain Rattey flies up the ladder and with a lop-sided grin and asks, "How about this speaker system, huh?"

"None of them match," I offer warily.

"Bought them all used at the swap meet...even dug a couple of them out of the trash. It's amazing what some people will throw away." Captain Rattey stares proudly at his massive stereo system, "Figured if I couldn't buy the best I would settle for the most. Every sunset, I put on this album and spin the volume knob to max."

"Every sunset?" I ask in dread.

"Yep, and watch this," Captain throws a switch turning on a string of lights that are faded plastic fruits. *Island Diver's* antique generator pants and intermittently surges to deliver the extra voltage demand of it. "Pretty classy, huh?" he says proudly then adds, "I figure the people at the resort will hear the music and see the lights and maybe want to come out for a dinner cruise."

I look shoreward at an expensive Club Med Resort and wonder what the management must think of this mad sailor with his floating clunker, blaring static-laced music and faded glowing fruit lights. "You do this how often?" I am already suspecting the answer.

"Every night for the last three years." It is the expected answer.

"Persistent aren't you."

"You bet," Rattey rubs the stubble on his chin, "just hasn't worked yet...then again I don't give up easy. Hey, speaking of dinner, you guys ready for some chow?"

"You're the cook?" This is not the best of news. "What are you going to make?"

"Doesn't much matter, I'll just throw something together out of the refrigerator."

I watch him go dashing off below, followed closely by Clay Wilcox, one of our American divers. Clay stands six-foot-two-inches-tall and has the kind of build that highly interests most young ladies. Like all of the Cousteau divers, Clay is a man with a diversity of talents; however, his main skill is cooking. Clay is a very talented chef. I decide to follow, anticipating that I might be helpful. It winds up being one of my better decisions.

In the galley (term used loosely), Clay is ready to throttle Rattey. "Opening a can of chili and beans, then dumping it into a pot doesn't constitute cooking," he rages then Clay glances into the pot in question. "Did you forget to wash this?" he growls.

"It just doesn't get much cleaner than that," Captain Rattey answers defensively, "beside my water maker has been acting up. I don't like to waste too much fresh water."

"But it's crusty," argues Clay, he opens the cupboard under the sink in pursuit of cleanser and surprises a large colony of cockroaches. The many-legged bugs rush for the darker recesses of the damp moldy enclosure.

"I'll get them," yells Captain Rattey, attacking with a spray can of

Raid, a spreading cloud of insecticide spills across the range where the beans are cooking. The flames surge higher under the blackened pot.

Clay is outraged. "Out!" he orders, "go do your captain thing, but from now on I am in-charge of this galley."

That night we dine on cold sandwiches, but no one complains. Clay spends the whole evening thoroughly cleaning a galley that has never before seen the business end of a scouring pad. Clay separates the foodstuffs from the various insecticides, roach hotels and rattraps. Deciding that the refrigerator is some sort of weird marine biological experiment, he empties the rusty trays and slime-coated shelves directly into a trash can. Clay reluctantly saves a stick of butter, a carton of milk, a box of *Cheerios* and a loaf of only slightly moldy bread and that is only because we need something for breakfast.

The next morning I wake up on a lumpy mattress that smells of old mildew like an aged-cheese. Michel and Marc are still fast asleep, but Clay's bunk is empty. Then I notice that despite the bunk's rumpled look, he has not slept in it. Pulling on a T-shirt and a swimsuit (standard attire in the tropics), I pad barefoot out into the corridor and go in search of my friend. I find Clay sleeping in the salon—a salon that has been transformed. Everything has been cleaned top to bottom. Nothing shines because the surfaces are worn and not of the best of materials in the first place. There is still a lingering odor of mildew, but it is mostly masked with the strong aroma of disinfectant. In the corner, where Clay is sleeping there is a pile of full plastic trash bags.

Stepping outside I am feeling slightly guilty for not staying up late with Clay to help him clean. Yet in a way, I sense this is a personal thing with him. Sometimes it is good to tackle a big job alone, solely for the challenge and satisfaction of accomplishment. Then again, maybe I am only making excuses for myself for not helping. The word *jerk* slips through my mind and lingers pointing a finger at me. I choose to ignore it.

I am a morning person. Somewhere between nine and ten o'clock at night I usually run out of energy. Like this morning, I am up way before first light to take advantage of the quiet solitude. Climbing the ladder to the upper deck, I spend fifteen minutes stretching and then slowly go through some basic karate exercises to limber up. I begin with a series of katas and am halfway through *Buck Yuen Tow Toe* stance (white ape steals the peach), when a warm flash of bright light begins to spread across the horizon. Holding perfectly still, I watch the chrome yellow light wash across the Caribbean waters, then I hear the first stirring of voices from below decks. Captain Rattey has discovered the wonder of a clean galley. He is so excited, I hear him waking Clay to offer him a job, which elicits a response from Clay that promises hazardous repercussions to Captain Rattey's health. Probably noting Clay's height and commitment to physical fitness, I hear the good captain decide to address activities in the engine room. Slowly, I begin the kata in super slow motion, *white ape stealing peach* becomes *sup bat sou* (eighteen old scholars).

> *"It is not the years in your life but the life in your years that count, "* Adlai Stevenson

After breakfast, I grab a broom and give the galley floor a quick sweeping. Clay smiles at me, which makes me feel a lot better about not helping him last night. I feel so good I go looking for a mop and find one with half of its string head missing then give the floor a through swabbing. Clay rewards me with a cookie as we head topside.

Jojo arrives two hours after dawn. Captain Rattey raises the anchor and takes *Island Diver* a couple of miles offshore to the Princess Alexandra Underwater Park where the water visibility will be clearer. On deck, we begin preparing our underwater scooters and cinema cameras, while the dolphin swims happily in the wake of the propellers. Arriving at the park, we hastily tie-up to a mooring buoy, which is there to keep dive boats from dragging their anchors across the fragile reef.

Captain Rattey has already explained that Jojo is pretty much like any other teenager. If something is fun and exciting he wants to share in it, but if the dolphin gets the least bit bored his presence is history. Therefore, the team wastes no time getting into the water— less their jealous chief diver. Jean-Michel chose Clay Wilcox and Marc Blessington as the subjects for this documentary. Since Jojo moves so rapidly, there is no room in the water for an underwater still photographer, who might get in the way of Michel's cinema camera.

Standing at the stern of *Island Diver*, I watch the team's flippers disappearing downwards into a froth of swirling bubbles headed for serious underwater dolphin games. Occasionally, Jojo surfaces for a quick breath or two of air before briskly disappearing back beneath the water. I feel like the extra kid on the sidelines of a base-ball game. I watch as several times Jojo excitedly leaps completely out of the water before plunging back into the fun activity below. Obviously, everyone is having a great time as I stare longingly at the streams of buoyant bubbles popping gaily on the surface.

"Looks like they're having a lot of fun," observes Captain Rattey over my shoulder, which does not add anything constructive to my mood. Then he says, "We've got company."

I see a red catamaran approaching from starboard. The fast sail-boat has only one keel in the water as it swoops alongside *Island Diver* like a predatory bird, barely slowing before it quickly departs leaving a tall athletic woman in a blue one-piece swimsuit in its watery wake. She swims a few feet to the stern of *Island Diver.* "Good morning," she says in a musical voice.

"Steve, meet Rebecca," Captain Rattey offers introductions, "Rebecca this is Steve. I invited Rebecca out because she's Jojo's girlfriend."

"I'm not his girlfriend," objects Rebecca laughing as she shakes salt water from her long red hair, "we just like each other a lot." Since I cannot see Rebecca's legs or feet, which are still in the water, I am easily imagining that this young lady could be Ariel, the Little Mermaid from the Disney series. They share the same laugh.

"The dolphin is madly in love with her," argues Rattey. As if to prove his words true, Jojo surfaces next to this beautiful mermaid and chirps happily.

Rebecca nuzzles the dolphin then pushes him away. "Go play with your new friends Jojo." The playful dolphin just grins at her. "Go on," she encourages, "I know you love their new toys." She is referring to the underwater scooters. As mentioned Jojo has an obsession for propellers. Michel and the rest of the team surfaces so Michel can reload his camera and the scooters need re-charging. As Michel and I attend to our chores, Clay and Marc are completely distracted by the attractive presence of Rebecca. Young single people should never be left alone, particularly with a dolphin present that requires constant attention. As previously mentioned, Jojo does not deal well with boredom and the divers who are supposed to be entertaining him are instead sitting on the swim step flirting with Rebecca.

"Where's Jojo?" I ask anxiously peering into the empty water at the stern of *Island Diver*.

"Oh no," laments Rebecca, "it's my fault."

"It's no one's fault," offers Michel, "let's just find him."

Captain Rattey gets on the radio to see if anyone has seen Jojo. A few minutes go by before we get an answering call from the Club Med resort. "He's just south of our pier," comes the static laden reply, "playing with the water skiers."

"Oh no," Rebecca says despondently, "we'll never get him back now."

"Why not?" I ask.

"Because Jojo loves water skiers," replies Rebecca.

"Yeah," chimes in Rattey, "he loves to knock them over."

"What?" Michel is surprised.

"Jojo sneaks up behind them. He looks for someone on two skies going slow and wobbly then he whacks one of their skis out from under them," laughs Rattey.

"Jojo likes watching people do a face plant at twenty miles an hour," giggles Rebecca, then more soberly adds, "that's why we'll never get him away. He's like a pirate who silently sneaks up his quarries wake and then attacks without warning."

"We'll have to offer him live bait," throws in Captain Rattey.

"Live bait?" Questions Michel.

"The only thing more fun for Jojo than knocking over water skiers, is playing with people being towed underwater. I volunteer to be towed bait," offers Rebecca.

"It's going to be a long tow. I think we need two live baits to double our chances of capturing and holding Jojo's attention," says Rattey looking at me in a speculative way. Michel puts an arm over my shoulder and smiles. It is a look I know too well.

"Sure, I volunteer too," I state the obvious before it becomes mandatory.

Half an hour later, at the water skiing circuit, we locate our wayward dolphin. Jojo is at first nowhere in sight, then abruptly a young girl skier loses it in a wide turn on flat water. She does a towed face plant at roughly twenty miles per hour. A rooster tail of water flies from between her pigtails as she drags face-first for a short distance before letting go of the ski rope.

"Got him!" Yells Rebecca.

A fin silently slips below the surface in the wake of the water skiing causality.

"Into the water you two," shouts Rattey.

Rebecca and I quickly jump into the warm tropical water holding flat hydroplanes. These are wing-like devices with twin handholds on the lower foil; the nose is attached to a long towrope. Captain Rattey jams *Island Diver's* shift knobs forward causing a loud dual clunking noise as the transmissions bashes themselves into gear, then the old boat accelerates to a stately three knots. Angling the hydroplanes downward, we descend in the wake of the ski boat passing closely to the girl's recent impact zone, yet fail to lure out the dolphin culprit. Rattey decides on a high-speed pass and increases the throttles to five knots, which is the absolute limit for human towing speed. At this velocity my dive mask is vibrating against my face, which is nothing compared to the problems Rebecca is having with her one-piece swimsuit. It is bulging in the oddest places with water rushing down the neck of the rapidly expanding garment. Then, beyond Rebecca's inflated *Speedo,* I see Jojo coming in swiftly.

The dolphin does a close pass on Rebecca to checkout her blimp *Speedo,* then continues in my direction. I am thinking Jojo will stop a few feet away, but he doesn't. The playful dolphin flips upside down and slides in right beneath me. We are nose to snout only inches apart. I grin and hum to Jojo a few notes from the Disney Mickey Mouse theme song, which sounds rather good underwater when accompanied with bubble noises. It is exciting to peer so closely into the frisky eyes of such an intelligent creature who is seeking us out simply for fun and games. He squeaks back a short dolphin melody of his own. Then as Captain Rattey swings *Island Diver* back out towards the distant reef, I run out of air. Angling up towards the surface, I see Jojo watching my departure then he begins to swim off. *Does he think I am shunning him?* I wonder to myself. Lingering only long enough for a quick breath or two, I quickly descend and hum shrilly in my best Mickey Mouse voice for the departing dolphin.

The dolphin is almost out of sight when he sees that I am back underwater. Jojo swims in gaily, flips upside down and peers happily into my faceplate from two inches away. As long as I am underwater, Jojo is content to follow us upside down, but every time I surface for air, I cannot linger because he becomes distracted and threatens to leave. My arms are becoming rubbery from exhaustion, yet Rebecca is gamely hanging on, which is quite a feat considering the drag her blimpish *Speedo* is creating. Finally, we arrive at the shallow reef. As *Island Diver* slows, I see Marc and Clay leap into the water with their scooters followed closely by Michel with his underwater cinema camera. As Jojo descends to play with his machine-propelled friends, Rebecca and I wearily surface to rest on the stern of the boat.

An hour later, Marc and Clay have exhausted their underwater scooters' battery charge and Michel is again out of film. Jojo has once more slipped off, only he has not gone very far. We find the dolphin several hundred yards away playing with a small submarine, a two person semi-wet sub. The pilot and his passenger sit in a tiny compartment half-full of water. Compressed air inside the cockpit keeps their upper torsos dry. Jojo is closely inspecting the wet sub's port side propeller. Rebecca and I make repeated free dives down to the little submarine, which is at a depth of about forty feet to shoot pictures. I am almost out of film, when Jojo suddenly stops all activity and appears to be listening. Zeroing in on a sound only he can hear, the dolphin abruptly streaks off in the direction of *Island Diver.*

Rebecca and I follow at a much slower human-speed to find Jojo with Captain Rattey. The scruffy skipper is in the water at the stern of the old dive boat. He is laboriously turning one of the big propellers by hand. Jojo hovers over his shoulder loudly encouraging Captain Rattey with squeaks and squeals as he barely manages a quarter-turn of the big props with each effort. Yet, Jojo is thrilled with the smallest of results. Both of them are eccentric by the standards of their peers. Jojo behaves like no dolphin normally would and finds himself a loner in his underwater habitat. Captain Rattey, strange by the simplest of standards, is a man quite happy and content to be doing exactly what his heart desires. *Who am I to judge what is normal or right,* I think to myself, *when both of these individuals are obviously content with their own chosen place in the world.* The dolphin and the man have made a choice and created a world for themselves that fits their own simple expectations. Captain Rattey is actually living the dream he built for himself; the captain without a crew, skippering a boat assembled from warped plywood and spare parts, yet he has squeezed so much meaning out of this meagerness. Jojo is a rare and unique dolphin living a solitary life mostly away from his own kind in favor of humans and their alluring toys that spin and swirl in the most appealing way. Both of these individuals, the man and the dolphin, are happy with the simple pleasures they have built into their solitary lives.

A man who has a watch knows what time it is; a man with two watches isn't so sure. Anonymous

In a moment of acute personal awareness, I realize that I do not have that kind of courage. I am completely dependent upon the fellowship of others. With this fraternity comes social judgment, of which I am a constant and willing participant. All of us are impacted by peer pressure and to break away from that social bond takes a unique kind of self-awareness. Eccentric people can add a diversity and unique richness to our lives when we look beyond their strangeness to the motivations that inspire them.

I press the shutter to take a final picture of these two happy characters, but the last frame is already used. So, I look intently at the subjects of my attention and quietly imprint them upon my mind; a dolphin chirping happily and a man laboriously turning a huge rusty propeller by hand while he whistles silently underwater.

"If we did all the things we are capable of doing, we would literally astonish ourselves," Thomas Edison

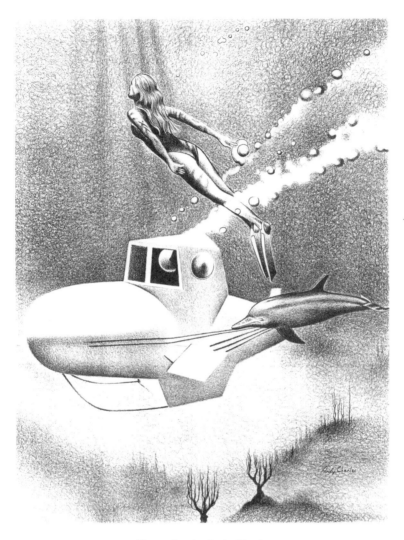

Illustration by Andy Charles
Jojo the dolphin with his friend Rebecca and mini-sub

"When you enter the ocean you enter the food chain, and you do not necessarily enter at the top," Jacques Yves Cousteau

Chapter 47

TURKS AND CAICOS ISLANDS, FEBRUARY 92

EISURELY KICKING my fins under a cloud-filled sky, I watch the red sun slowly sinking into the blue water of the Caribbean then take a deep breath and slip silently beneath the surface. Listening to the soft cascading sound of air bubbles escaping upwards from my snorkel, I think to myself that twilight underwater is such a lonely time. In the shallow depths below, I see the vibrant living colors of the reef fading as the gloom of evening begins to settle upon the shadowy ocean floor. Beneath my flippers, reef creatures and tropical fish probe the nooks and crevices of a coral ridge; some are seeking a place to hide as the curtain of darkness falls, others are eagerly preparing to hunt their supper. Inside the deeper recesses of the coral ledges, night creatures awaken in their lairs. Anticipating a cloak of darkness, they prepare to explore the reef on long spindly legs or with soft slithering bodies stalking unwary or sleeping prey. However, this evening the night shadows will not totally shroud the reef. The underwater nighttime mysteries are going to play out their intrigues under the velvet light of a full moon. Glancing upwards through the distortion of the restless surface, I see the first glimmer of moonlight

741

washing the underbelly of the distant clouds. Soon a pale lunar glow starts to dance lightly on the shimmering surface. The undulating ceiling above captures wavering beams of diffused light that begins to probe the dark depths softening the twilight's deeper shadows.

Fifteen feet above the seabed and only ten feet from the surface, I see a large silent shape emerging from the gloom beyond the weak glow from our boat's stern light. It passes slowly a fathom beneath me as it slips into the deeper darkness of the boat's shadow. Leisurely kicking my long-bladed fins, I pursue the creature, which is much heavier than my one-hundred eighty pounds. Passing through the animal's wake, I feel cool water swirling along my body from the pulse of its powerful tail. Kicking faster, I descend to swim alongside my underwater friend. Jojo is in his sleep mode. He is idly swimming circles around *Island Diver*.

Dolphins rest in a unique way—with only half of their brain asleep at a time. These graceful marine mammals must swim to the surface to breathe and have to be continuously alert for sharks and other ocean predators. For dolphins, breathing is always a conscious act. Therefore, they have to sleep with one eye open. Half of their brain rests while the other half, though somewhat drowsy, remains alert. In the group protection of a dolphin pod, they can watch out for each other. Jojo however, has forsaken the social life of the pod so he can be around people whose company he so enjoys. Lacking the protective comradery of other dolphins Jojo seeks out people and more importantly their boats for safe haven while he sleeps. I watch my marine friend as he idly circles *Island Diver* while keeping a watchful eye out for sharks. In about forty minutes, Jojo will reverse direction and swim the opposite way around our boat so the other half of his brain can rest.

As Jojo ascends for an unhurried breath of air, I surface alongside him. His wet skin catches the soft lunar glow in thousands of reflective droplets of gently sparkling light like flowing liquid silver. I softly voice a few subtle clicks of reassurance so he will know I am alert and watchful. In response, the dolphin emits a soft squeak, like a child turning in its sleep, and then he glides downward brushing lightly against my leg as he plunges back into the dark depths. I revel in the dolphin's light caress his skin soft and warm like liquid velvet over a rubbery skin. Jojo's delicate touch is a deliberate physical contact; a reassuring herd statement of awareness of one another. I imagine it is the type of personal contact normally reserved for other dolphins. I briefly wonder if Jojo is treating me as he would another dolphin. It is a fun thought that I give life to by locking my finned feet together and then swim in an undulating way like a dolphin. Jojo does not seem to notice or is unimpressed so I angle upwards for a breath of air. On the surface, I linger inhaling deeply the warm tropical air.

Swimming slowly with my faceplate half-in and half-out of the water I stare at two completely separate worlds. To the west above the lapping water, I see a vast ocean-hugging horizon of fading sunset colors weeping into darkness. The heavens seem so much closer when viewed from the low perspective of the ocean's surface. It is like being caught between two boundless dark worlds, the vast heavens above and the ocean's incredible depths below. A momentary shudder runs down my spine. I wonder if it is a tracer of fear of that unknown something with sharp teeth and powerful jaws that might be lurking somewhere below my flippers or is it from the chill of being in the tepid water for so long? Regretfully I realize I should have put on a wetsuit before jumping into the tropical water. Instead, I am only wearing a swimsuit with my fins, mask, snorkel and weight belt. Twin two-pound lead weights at my hips are making it easier for me to stay down as I take a deep breath and plunge downward to follow Jojo through the ever-darkening submarine world. The negative buoyancy of the weights allows me to take and hold deeper than normal breaths. Instead of swimming, it feels like I am slowly drifting weightlessly through a twilight submarine atmosphere. Jojo is nowhere in sight so I turn and swim in the direction of the moonrise. The rising lunar orb reflects upside down on the underside of the ocean's shifting surface. I stare at the shimmering sphere seeking confidence in its soft light while acutely aware of the gentle thudding presence of my heartbeat captured in a tiny air bubble lodged within my ear.

The evenings are Jojo's most lonely times. At night, few people are willing to venture into the dark water. It is also when the dolphin's dangers are greatest. Sharks prowl more aggressively in the extended shadows of the night. The dark hours are their feeding time. Every night Jojo must face the many dangers of the dark underwater world alone. So, for at least part of this night, I am making a silent commitment to swim with Jojo. Tomorrow we are wrapping up this expedition of discovery and going home. Before I leave, I want to share a small part of Jojo's private world. I guess I am seeking a greater understanding, or a deeper awareness, of this unique dolphin. Much of my adult life has been spent around marine mammals, but I have never had one of them for a friend before and after tonight, I cannot anticipate that I will ever get to see Jojo again. My evening underwater excursion with Jojo is a private going away ceremony. Of course, Jojo cannot know that we are parting company, but I think he must be used to it. At this tropical island, most people only come for a short holiday.

Beginning to feel a bit chilled, I kick a little faster. I tell myself a quicker beat might make me feel a little warmer, but secretly I am trying to out swim the fears lurking in the darker recess of my thoughts. It does not work. My subconscious mind conjures up images of sharks hunting just beyond the limited vision of my faceplate in the water's deeper gloom. I want to believe that it is only my overly active imagination, but the trouble is that somewhere beyond the barrier of my terra-conditioned senses real nighttime marine predators not only exist they are actively searching for something to eat. Something large enough to tackle a four hundred-pound dolphin might be willing to settle instead for a defenseless hundred and eighty-pound human snack.

My quickened pace brings Jojo back into view. He is continuing his sleep patrol around our boat but now in the opposite direction. I adjust the lead weights at my hips and follow him while thinking about this solitary dolphin that recognizes only a few humans as his true friends. Jojo likes to play with people, but he tends to keep his distance particularly from strangers ever since that terrible day a young man hurt him.

The local people tell a story about a tourist boy who dropped a burning cigarette into Jojo's blowhole. Jojo's relationship with us is now a bit of a push/pull situation. He wants to be with people, but does not trust strangers to touch him anymore. Dolphins and people are creatures that like to touch and to be touched. Physical contact is critical to our wellbeing. Humans, and I would imagine dolphins, suffer a powerful loneliness when deprived of the touch of others of their kind. I know because I suffered through thirty-one long months of almost no physical human contact. The memories of my incarceration still haunt my sleep. Living in a crowd of misfits my sojourn in prison was the loneliest time in my life. I accepted my punishment because the fault and the mistakes were my own, yet the loneliness took a severe toll.

As the dolphin surfaces for a misty breath, I cannot help thinking that the cigarette burn has sentenced this dolphin into a unique kind of prison of wanting to be with humans, but not trusting people in general. What a horrible shock for Jojo, to expect a caress and instead to get a burning object jammed down his airway. Fire is completely alien to marine mammals. All Jojo can now know is that the touch of a human can be unexpectedly painful, yet he still chooses to play in our company.

For a few moments, Jojo rests on the surface. We are near the bow of *Island Diver*. I see someone's distorted shadow pass through the dim yellow light of the pilothouse while I listen to the restless ocean sound of water lapping against the boat's wooden hull. Pushing my dive mask up onto my forehead, I peer into Jojo's one open eye and wonder what is the awake-half part of his brain thinking right now? Reaching out I allow my hand to brush lightly along the underside of Jojo's pectoral fin. The dolphin only welcomes my touch when he is resting. The soft skin beneath my fingertips is warm and smooth. Amazingly, a dolphin sheds its outer layer of skin cells every couple of hours. Lightly I hug him as he passes keeping my touch gentle knowing it can be too possessive of a contact for the wild dolphin to tolerate. Jojo takes a deep breath then silently glides from my arms to slip back beneath the still water. I watch the surface ripples from his disappearing tail then adjust the weights at my hips as I prepare to follow him down. Inhaling deeply I listen to the cool night air barreling down the snorkel, then plunge after the descending dolphin.

Forty more minutes pass slowly then a fully awake Jojo surfaces a few feet away and exhales loudly. I quickly avoid the vapor cloud with its hidden baggage of fish smells. Refreshed from his long nap the dolphin is ready to attend to other nighttime activities. He flicks his tail probably an invitation for a game of tag however, I am far too cold to spend any more time in the water. My fins flutter as I scurry for the stern ladder where I find Captain Rattey waiting on deck with a not-so-recently-laundered towel.

"So how was your nighttime swim with Jojo?" he asks.

"Cold," I answer using the slightly stiff towel to dry my legs. The towel is frayed at the edges with a lingering odor of mildew. Holding it at arm's length, I voice my dissatisfaction with the towel, "Ever consider washing this rag with real soap and water?"

Captain Rattey shrugs off the comment in his normal buoyant way. "Don't need to be wasting time and money taking sheets and towels to some shore side laundry mat. I just tie the laundry bag to a rope and toss it over the side for an hour or so when *Island Diver* is underway. The wake scrubs the stuff clean enough for me."

"I am going to miss you and old *Island Diver*," I reply honestly. Captain Rattey is completely content to be himself without any false sounding pretenses. His dive boat may more closely resemble a rusty old barge, yet it allows him to live in a tropical paradise with a good share of free time to enjoy each day. Almost as if to punctuate that thought, Jojo leaps from the water. For a moment, the dolphin's wet skin shimmers softly in the moonlight, then he disappears back beneath the dark sparkling water.

"Jojo just proved my point," observes Captain Rattey with obvious satisfaction. "If I had been ashore at the laundry mat, I would have missed seeing that dolphin's leap with the light of the moon glistening on his skin. Clean laundry is just something you put into a drawer. A memory of a leaping dolphin lit by a full moon is some-thing you can take with fondness to your grave."

That kind of logic tolerates no argument. Each of our lives has to be experienced from the perspective of the person who is doing the living. There is no greater expert on this than ourselves. We just have to be prepared to deal with the consequences of our actions. Captain Rattey is content to live aboard a less than clean vessel with a repair program that only kicks in when something malfunctions from lack of maintenance. Personally, I am never satisfied unless everything is working under a strict code of efficiency and cleanliness. Then again, that is a direct result of my military training and my efforts as an inmate fireman. A sudden thought tumbles through my mind; I remember sitting outside the honor dorm at Boron watching a moonrise and apprehensively wondering what my future would hold, completely clueless that my childhood dream was patiently waiting for me.

Happiness is in wanting what you have, not having what you want. Anonymous

Hot sand is seeping up between my toes as I stand on the beach on the last day of our expedition to the Turks and Caicos Islands. *Island Diver* is anchored just offshore and we are busy on the beach transferring our equipment from Captain Rattey's old Zodiac to the elderly black man's broken-down flatbed truck for transport back to the airport. Captain Rattey is trying to keep from getting emotional about our departure. Wiping at his nose with a crusty grease-smeared rag he asks us to come visit him and Jojo again one day and then walks to his old frayed Zodiac. I help him push it out into the small waves, then while the rest of the team continues carrying our equip-ment across the hot sand to the waiting truck, I pause to watch Bill Rattey motoring away from the beach. With its continuous leaks and low air pressure his tired old Zodiac accordions over each wave. The out-of-tune engine sputters and coughs as he heads out, then I see a fin in the wake of the Zodiac. Jojo is following the outboard's dented propeller. Arriving at *Island Diver* Captain Rattey quickly ties off the bowline, then leaps into the water to play with Jojo. Watching them surface and dive together, I wonder at the perfection of their relationship. Because of Jojo's presence, Captain Rattey's low-level of boat maintenance has a surprising reward. Bill Rattey is satisfied with keeping his old boat close to shore so he can be with his dolphin buddy. If he strays too far from the resort with *Island Diver* the continuous engine problems could leave him adrift on the high seas. Staying by the shore makes it easy for Jojo to stay in close contact with *Island Diver.*

> *"Let us be grateful to people who make us happy; they are the charming gardeners who make our souls blossom,"* Marcel
> Proust

For the rest of my life, in my thoughts, Jojo and Captain Ratty will be forever linked. I cannot think of one without fond memories of the other. It is a fortunate person who gets to know the life enriching experience of having a friend like Captain Ratty even for a short time. All of us are different, each in our own way. Human differences are what make us unique and it is a condition that revolves around the daily commitments and choices we make. Our actions define our character. Our character determines the direction and focus of our existence. I appreciate Captain Rattey, yet I prefer to spend the time and constant effort to make sure that all the equipment within my care is in good working order. I like things…and people who work for me… to be totally reliable, but that is because my life fortunately revolves around fast-paced adventure and ongoing challenge. Where we wind up in life is a direct result of our daily personal decisions. There is a well-known expression, *To be or not to be.* A lazy person should not anticipate much in the way of challenging opportunities or quests for dangerous adventures. Theirs is simply a self-limiting condition brought on by conscious determination *not to be.*

> *"Do, or do not. There is no try,"* Yoda

"Within my sensitivity lies my strength," Lauren, age 16

Chapter 48

WEST HOLLYWOOD, CALIFORNIA, JULY 1992

IN THE basement of The Cousteau Society office in West Hollywood, I am busy unpacking a small pile of equipment from another flying team expedition when Jean-Michel plows through the door that leads from our small parking lot. As usual, he is in a tremendous hurry having just arrived from Paris. "Bonjour Steve, I've got good news and bad news," he exclaims as he opens his briefcase and begins rummaging inside. Holding a snorkel and a pair of flippers in my hands, I am instantly attentive.

"The good news is my father likes your idea of our going to Vietnam. In six months we'll field an expedition to Vietnam and Cambodia to explore the Mekong River." Jean-Michel pulls a small file from his briefcase. "Here," he exclaims handing me a piece of paper, "This is a list of potential filming subjects. We need to research them immediately."

"Yahoo!" I am ecstatic and instantly eager to go back to Vietnam. As a young Navy frogman, I had entertained wild daydreams about going up the Mekong River on the Calypso. Back then, I did not believe that I would actually join The Cousteau Society let alone get the opportunity to lead a Cousteau expedition up that famous river.

Several months ago I had suggested to Jean-Michel the possibility of fielding an expedition to Vietnam and now it was about to become a reality.

"Where's Don Santee?" asks Jean-Michel.

Chief diver Don Santee is my counterpart and very likeable boss.

"He's upstairs," I answer.

"Well call him down here," urges Jean-Michel glancing at his watch, "I have a telephone radio interview in fifteen minutes."

I quickly step to the base of the circular staircase. "Don!" I shout upwards, "Jean-Michel needs you down here right away."

"I didn't mean for you to shout for him." Jean-Michel is giving me *the look*. I get *the look* a lot—sometimes from complete strangers. Many people have what I consider an unnatural social need to suppress their inherent childlike qualities. They want to act grownup all the time. Personally, the happiest and most fun times in my life revolve around when I was a child or when I am in the process of acting like one. I do not view the child within me as being passive in any sort of way at all. An open childlike perspective in life trusts in simple truths. A child accepts people in general as an opportunity to make a new friend. Little children are not inhibited by a person's appearance, looks or ethnic background. Prejudice is something we learn on our way to adulthood. Setting the child within me free on a regular basis is simply my expressing my true inner nature. I enjoy being happy, am strongly motivated towards pursuing fun and I like to share good things with others. Jean-Michel sometimes lets his childlike qualities shine through, which usually is when he is also having the most fun. Too often, the stress of his command position in The Cousteau Society smothers his youthful attitude, but never for very long. I particularly like Jesus Christ's attitude about children.

> *"I tell you the truth, unless you change and become like
> little children, you will never enter the kingdom of heaven."*
> Matthew 18:3

That's a pretty heavy thing for the Lord to say to his disciples. Jesus is not cautioning us to act frivolous or without responsibility. He is saying something much bigger about how we should live our lives. Only someone who is not hindered with guilt, malice, hate, prejudice, petty jealousies, etc., can truly behave with the carefree abandon of a happy, well-adjusted child. That is me...the happy well-adjusted kid with adult responsibilities.

I believe there is a second childlike quality that Jesus desires of us. He wants our faith in Him to be as strong and untarnished as a child's. As a youngster learns about Jesus Christ, their faith in Him grows unhindered by any doubts or lack of commitment. Little children are very free with their friendship and love...though they do tend to be rather possessive of their parents and of their toys.

As a chief diver and expedition leader it is expected that I will behave in a very responsible way, particularly in emergencies and when conducting complex diving operations. Yet, I enjoy being likeable, I prefer to see the people around me smiling and to hear them laugh or chuckle. I do not act the fool, but do enjoy laughing the loudest at myself. It helps keep my ego in its proper perspective.

"It's okay," I flash a disarming smile at Jean-Michel and see *the look* disappear from his face, "I knew that Don was working at the desk near the top of the staircase." Earlier I had heard Don spelling my last name over the telephone and wondered what he was up to.

Jean-Michel pulls a crumpled map from his briefcase and spreads it across the workbench as Don Santee quickly hustles down the circular staircase.

"Uh oh," Don eyes the map suspiciously, "whenever you open a map it usually means I'm going to one of the more remote places on this planet."

"That's right," cackles Jean-Michel, "you just won an all expenses-paid trip to the People's Republic of Vietnam."

Don glares at me. "So you had to get him all fired up about Vietnam?"

I try affecting an innocent look, but it does not work. Don is still glaring at me as Jean-Michel continues, "Steve had the idea but we're going to improve upon it."

"If it was his idea he should go. Why pick on me?" Don's complaint is more than fair. He favored hiring me because his expedition scheduling was getting out of hand. Don was spending far too much time away from his wife and young son. To reduce his time away he and Jean-Michel hired me as a second chief diver to share the expedition load. However, with two chief divers, Jean-Michel realized he could run twice as many expeditions. From Don's perspective, I didn't help our already heavy workload by suggesting yet another expedition.

Jean-Michel smiles fondly at Don. "Actually you're both going. One of you can lead a flying team on the upper part of the Mekong while the other will join Calypso to explore the delta and the lower part of the river. I've marked points of interest on this map and here is the list of research subjects." As Don groans, Jean-Michel snaps his briefcase closed sealing our future then dashes for the circular staircase. "You two can figure out the details of who's going where."

"Jean-Michel," I shout after him, "you forgot to tell me about the bad news."

Jean-Michel does not even slow down as he rushes upstairs, "Ask Don, he already knows because I called him from the airport. He's probably been eagerly awaiting my arrival so he could spring it on you."

"What bad news?" I ask Don anxiously.

"Been promising my wife that I would stay at home more," he grumbles, "instead I'm off on your bird brained idea of going to Vietnam. Look at this," Don is fingering a side tributary of the Mekong River, "jungle, jungle and more jungle."

"Sorry Don," I offer lamely, "but what's the bad news?"

Don affects his first grin of the morning. "Jean-Michel wants to field a quick expedition to Alaska."

I have an instant bad feeling about this, "Quick as in short or quick as in leaving immediately?"

Don pulls a sheet of paper from his back pocket. "Quick as in leaving immediately. That's what I was doing upstairs; making your airline reservations."

"You did that upstairs?" I ask, "why didn't you just do it down here at our desk?"

"Because you would hear and start asking all kinds of stupid questions just like you're getting ready to do right now."

"Ah Don," now it's my turn to complain, "I just got back from Hawaii." *My*, I think to myself that *sounded lame; like going to Hawaii or Alaska is a chore. It is hard to believe that I am getting so accustomed to incredible adventure in the best parts of our planet that I just want some time at home.*

Don leers at me, "Look at the bright side, it means you don't have to worry about unpacking anymore of this equipment because you can take most of it as is to Alaska. That gives you an extra day with Cindy."

"An extra day?" This sounds ominous.

"Yeah, one plus one makes two," Don is holding up just two fingers.

"Two days! That's it? That's all the time I get at home after being gone for a whole month? In Hawaii? Cindy will be furious!"

"Of course she will," Don is quite casual about the verbal storm waiting on my immediate horizon. "Get used to it." He continues to grumble mostly to himself as he checks the map. "Got any ideas about the tropical diseases lurking in this nasty looking jungle?"

During the Vietnam Conflict, I did four tours off the coast of Vietnam with the Navy helping to rescue downed pilots. I did not have any real in-country experiences during the war so I too am curious about Vietnam's diseases. My memory flickers over some seriously bad remembrances of some heavy warnings about mosquito-born plagues and dangers. I quickly decide not to mention anything about it to Don while he is in *a mood.*

Don stalks over to his desk to consult his Center for Tropical Diseases Booklet. "Oh man!" he laments, "listen to this. Malaria, some strains known to be resistant to most standard medical procedures, Cholera, Typhoid fever...I'm going to look like a pin cushion when the doctor gets done vaccinating me." Don continues reading the long list, "Japanese Encephalitis...oh great this one has a special medical alert tagged to it."

Don has my complete attention. I step closer to look over his shoulder as he madly flips pages. He suddenly stops at a page written mostly in red with a lot of underlining and capital letters for added emphasis.

Don starts to read in a flat monotone, but then his voice pickups up a couple of octaves, "A third of the people who contract Japanese Encephalitis die, one-third have extensive brain damage and the final third mostly recovers with some symptoms of remedial nerve damage."

"What do you think they mean by mostly recovers?" I wonder out loud.

"Probably means you walk around drooling for the rest of your life. My wife would probably find that particularly attractive."

"Read the red underlined part," I urge.

"Na, it's not fair," Don slams the book closed, and then glares at me. It says that the vaccinations to prevent Japanese Encephalitis have resulted in several deaths. So the vaccine is banned for use in the United States."

With all the sincerity I can muster, I say, "I'm really sorry to have gotten you into this."

"You're going to be sorrier than you think, pal," replies Don.

"I am?"

"That's right buddy boy," he cackles, "I'd love to be there when you try to explain to Cindy that my sending you to Alaska is a punishment."

"She'll never believe me," I complain. Cindy refers to my expedition work as going on vacation.

"That's right!" Don's mood is obviously improving. Abruptly, he begins tossing papers into his briefcase, snaps it closed and then heads for the parking lot door.

"Where are you going?" I direct my question at his rapidly departing back.

"Heading home early," quips Don, "I need to pick up some flowers and make a dinner reservation at a fancy restaurant because my wife is going to hit the roof when she hears I'm going to Vietnam and will probably come back a drooling idiot."

The sun is going down as I drive my K-5 Blazer up to our little apartment overlooking the California coast in Rancho Palos Verdes. I stopped on the way home to pick up some wildflowers and a box of chocolates to help soothe Cindy's temper. She is not going to like the bad news of my almost immediate departure for Alaska. I have been trying to think of the exact right words to dampen the impact and have not come up with anything very believable yet. I decide to sit in the truck and do a little more thinking about a quality excuse.

"What are you doing sitting in your truck?" inquires Cindy. She is standing beside the driver's door with a basket full of clean laundry. Our carport is adjacent to the downstairs laundry room.

"Nothing," I blurt leaping from the car with my wildflowers and chocolates.

"Flowers and chocolates too!" exclaims Cindy, but then she gets kind of squinty-eyed. "You're up to something aren't you?"

"Me?" Trying to look innocent does not work under that all knowing glare.

"Yes, you," Cindy augments her words by threatening to bash me with the wildflower bouquet.

I cave-in, "I have to go to Alaska in two days." I hunker my head down to ward off the expected wildflower assault as I lamely add, "I'll probably be gone for three weeks."

"Now you're supposed to ask me out to dinner," Cindy says sternly as she hands me the laundry to carry. Taking the laundry basket, I smile happily looking at the bulge of Cindy's stomach. She is into the second trimester of her pregnancy. I am absolutely ecstatic that we are going to be parents.

"I want to go somewhere expensive," she says nibbling at one of the chocolates. She always takes a tiny bite from the bottom of the chocolate to check the filling. If she does not like it, the chocolate goes back into the box to be discovered later by her kind unsuspecting husband.

"Wait a minute," I am confused, "aren't you upset?"

"Of course, I am, but it's not going to do either of us any good to fight over it," Cindy snickers as she returns a nibbled chocolate to the box, then heads up the stairs towards our apartment.

"You're supposed to be upset," I quickly follow her dropping and picking up pieces of clean laundry along the way. "You're always upset when I'm going off on an adventure and you have to stay at home."

"I'm not upset."

"Well, why not?"

"Because I knew you were going to Alaska before you did," Cindy opens the door, "change into something nice dear because we're going to the Lighthouse Restaurant for dinner."

"Jean-Michel told you?" It is more of a statement than a question.

"Steve," she laughs, "I've got good news and bad news for you."

"He did! He told you!"

"Of course he told me. He has a perfectly good reason to send you off." Cindy stops halfway up the stairs, "But understand this buddy boy, I'm not going to buy your running off all the time and not sharing the fun and adventure with me."

"So that's why you're not upset," I am instantly relieved.

"Don't you want to know about the good news and the bad news?" Asks Cindy innocently.

My relief is short lived, "I thought I had already gotten the good news and the bad news."

"No there's more. The good news is Jean-Michel, Don Santee and his wife are joining us for dinner. The bad news is you're buying."

"I am?" Suddenly I realize that Don also called me buddy boy earlier today. So, he had been talking to Cindy too. "The Lighthouse is awful expensive," I say desperately.

"I know, I suggested it because Don wants to take his wife some-where really nice and it's your fault anyway. He also said something strange about a drooling idiot. Was he referring to you, dear?"

That evening I am sitting next to Cindy unhappily eyeing the high cost of meals on the menu at the Lighthouse Restaurant. Jean-Michel is showing an interest in the *Catch of the Day*, which I suspect is a restaurant ploy for overpricing a fish fillet. Don is teasing me about the wallet-emptying properties of ordering lobster for himself and Hillary, his wife, while Cindy and I consider the advantages of the all-you-can-eat salad bar.

"Just salad?" exclaims Don, "I bring you to a nice restaurant and all you're going to have is rabbit food?"

"Don, I drove myself here and besides we like salad," I answer.

"At least get some chicken," urges Don.

"I'm a vegetarian except for fish."

"Perfect," grins Jean-Michel, "this is a seafood restaurant." He turns to the waitress and orders lobster for Don and Hillary, and the catch of the day for him, Cindy and me. "You're buying, right Steve?"

"Absolutely," I grumble.

"You can use the Gold American Express card in your wallet," he urges, while smiling with his eyes.

"I can?" Jean-Michel has just made my day.

"You didn't tell me that we have a gold American Express card," complains Cindy.

"We don't," I grin at her, "it's Jean-Michel's."

Jean-Michel smiles at Cindy, "Both of my chief divers carry copies of my credit cards."

"You trust them?"

"Of Course," smiles Jean-Michel.

"Even though Steve's an ex-felon?"

Jean-Michel's smile broadens, "If I trust Steve with the lives of my men, then it is a much smaller thing to trust him with my credit cards."

"Dreams pass into the reality of action. From the actions stem the dream again; and this interdependence produces the highest form of living," Anais Nin

"Your vision will become clear only when you look into your heart. Who looks outside, dreams. Who looks inside, awakens," Carl Jung

Chapter 49

SITKA, ALASKA, JULY 1992

I AM SITTING in a window seat aboard a United Airlines flight en route to Sitka, Alaska watching the sunrise from forty thousand-feet. We are flying high to avoid turbulence from the jet stream, which is delivering another storm to Cindy in California. From this altitude, the world seems to stretch forever as the plane flies above a scattered layer of calumnious clouds. I watch the early morning light streak across the dark sky bathing the mountainous landscape in brilliant hues of red hinting of the coming day. For a moment, I consider the unknown challenges waiting for our little team just beyond the horizon as we prepare to begin a new adventure. I think how lucky I am to have a job that encourages me to walk boldly into the unknown, to tackle adventure with enthusiasm and to be able to witness so many of the wonders of the world. Yet what I have is open to all who are willing to work for it. It is through their daily choices that youths chart their adult futures.

Is not the child father to the man? Anonymous

Sitting in the seat ahead of me, a grossly fat man coughs wetly. His smoker's chronic hacking cough tells of smoke- and debris-ravaged lungs laboring through congestive mucus for air. I listen to his overweight body struggling to breathe as he complains to the woman next to him. "They should have a smoking section," he argues bitterly, "I can't even smoke in the stupid bathroom."

Earlier he had also complained about the small size of his dinner. So, his wife forfeited half of her meal to him, yet still he had not been satisfied. For most of this midnight flight to Alaska, he has complained about most everything including his job, relatives, friends and life in general.

His wife leans past him to look at the startling beautiful sunrise. "Look dear, the sun is so red." There is wonder in her voice. He glares out the window, then pushes down the plastic shutter locking away the beckoning beauty from both of them. "I don't care about the lousy sunrise," he grumbles, "get some sleep, will ya?"

"Oh Henry," she complains wearily.

"Leave it alone," he warns. Slouching down he is soon snoring loudly in his sleep. She sighs, then opens a book and begins to read.

> *"Life is too long not to do it right, not to participate—we end up dying before we live,"* Louis L'Amour

A quiet witness in the row behind them, I continue to watch the sunlight spilling across the spectacular Alaskan landscape. Though the woman still feebly tries, I wonder when did these two people give up their childhood dreams? Was it before they married that they forfeited childlike wonder and curiosity of the world? Was their marital union a consignment to accept boredom and unhappiness together? The man looks to be about my age, but physically he is much older. He lives within the mental boundaries of a limited imagination and the corporal barriers of extremely poor physical conditioning. I do not doubt that his best days are now only dim memories far in the past, while I consider my best days still somewhere in the distant future. Well maybe not that distant, Cindy and I are going to be parents in the near future.

Watching the couple ahead of me, I wonder about my own promise to Cindy and about a father's promise to a soon to be born child? When I left for the Turks and Caicos Islands to dive with Jojo, I was constantly aware that Cindy had to remain home alone. The dolphin adventure would have been so much more pleasurable if Cindy could have swum with Jojo too. I keep promising to share my adventures with her, but too often, my promises are weak and feeble because I am not in control of what my employer decides even though he is one of my best friends. I have a terrific job, yet I am a slave to the conditions of my employment, which far too often exclude Cindy. In the first year of my marriage to Cindy, I was away from her on expeditions across various parts of the world for eight-and-a-half-months. No wonder three years later, she is tiring of my frequent departures.

The solution to our dilemma is sitting on my knees. I stare at it fondly, then lift its lid and turn on the laptop computer. I am writing a book about how to put together a diving expedition (*The Expedition and Diving Operations Handbook*, by Best Publishing).

When I first began my attempt at writing a book aboard the Cousteau research vessel *Alcyone,* most of the crewmembers taunted me. They were quite sure that I did not have the ability to write a book, not that they were alone in their skepticism. While enrolled in college in 1981, my English Composition 201 instructor wondered out loud why I was in his class since my major did not require his course. When I told him that I would one day like to try my hand at being a writer he laughed loudly in front of the whole class and said, "Mr. Arrington trust me. I have graded your homework. Don't waste your time. You'll never be a writer." I could not help chuckling as I remembered his words because my first book, *Journey Into Darkness* hit the bookstores six months ago. My professor may have had a good understanding of the technical aspects of the English language, but he lacked the speculative imagination that forges dreams into reality. Maybe my professor was also an aspiring writer, but instead of recognizing our kinship and helping me, he preferred to discourage my efforts. No, it was worse. He was willing to ridicule my efforts and make fun of one of his students before the whole class. It made me angry.

"Why should I trust you?" I asked angrily.

"I know good and bad writing when I see it." The teacher replied gruffly, "That is my job, evaluating writing."

"I am sorry," I answered, "I thought your job was to teach and to encourage students."

The professor became leery, he shuffled the papers in his hand and then carefully said, "Then I encourage you not to waste your time trying to become a writer." To head off any further reply from me, he quickly changed subjects to next week's homework assignment.

Sitting in the airplane, I begin to chuckle as I decide to send the professor a copy of my book.

"What are you chuckling about?"

The question startles me out of my thoughts. Sitting next to me is David Brown one of our diver/lecturers and another one of Don's instant recruits for the Alaska expedition. He is in his mid-twenties, has dark hair and a slim athletic build.

"Just remembering something someone said of no real importance," I answer.

"Writing another book already?" Asks David peering at the computer screen.

"Yeah, I have an expedition book half-done, but I am also about to begin a series I am going to call *High On Adventure*."

"Wait a minute," David is startled, "you want to write two books at the same time? Why?"

"Well, one is technical, so I am going to balance it with a motivational series for young people which will be more fun to write."

"But why all the writing all of a sudden?" asks David.

"David, I am this busy writing because I cannot support a family on just a book or two," I answer knowing he is about to ask the obvious next question. I am putting off the full answer because I am still coming to the conclusion about it myself.

I began writing my first book, an autobiography, in a prison cell. I wanted to capture the intensity of the lockup as a warning to youths about the dangers of bad choices. In that prison cell, I never would have believed that I would finish *Journey Into Darkness* in Captain Cousteau's sea cabin aboard the research vessel *Alcyone*. As the chief diver, Jean-Michel and Jacques Cousteau would allow me to use their cabin when they were not onboard. The surprising part was that in writing a book for others it was actually changing my own life. A commitment to help young people was building within me in its own uncontrollable way. In my spare time at home, I sometimes spoke at public schools encouraging youths to go for their dreams. I had to cancel a scheduled presentation at my own high school because of the need to film an unexpected erupting volcano in Hawaii. It put me in a dilemma that Cindy and I had been discussing for some time. I was considering starting a lay youth ministry as a writer and motivational speaker. Watching the couple in the next row had convinced me that the decision to take a new direction in my life was about to be spoken out loud.

"So ask Jean-Michel for a raise," offers David.

"David," I say carefully, "I am not considering asking Jean-Michel for a raise, I'm going to resign my position."

"What!" David's mouth drops open. "Quit! You have one of the best possible jobs in the whole world...and you're going to quit? To try to write books! Are you nuts?"

"Well actually I want to start a youth ministry," I respond, "and I want to spend more time at home with Cindy and our soon to be born baby."

David looks at me. His mouth opens and closes but no words come out. He strokes his chin thinking. "It is a good idea," he says finally.

Now it is my turn to be surprised, "You agree with my quitting?"

"I agree that family time is important and that a youth ministry is a good idea for you. As an ex-felon, you've put the bad choices behind and gone on to realize your childhood dreams. I think you have a very valuable message to share. A message that is more important than the work you're doing now. It's tough to be a kid today with all the adult-sized decisions being thrown at them." David grins at me, "So when are you giving notice?"

"Not immediately. I'll let Jean-Michel know I am thinking about it. But first I need to do some more writing and I'd like to go on that expedition to Vietnam."

"Good for you," David pats the lid of my computer, "good luck."

David goes back to the paperback that he is reading. I look at the laptop and then glance at the sleeping fat man in the row ahead of me. He could not know that he has so strongly influenced my future life. Within the sleeping obese man slumbers a slender child with long-lost dreams of adventure, challenge and wonder. The potential of that incredible child within is smothered by the fat man's gross self-indulgences and lack of will or determination. The man still has the ability to re-awaken the sleeping child within, but it obviously just doesn't matter enough. Instead, the youth living inside the man will continue to slip into thoughtless oblivion and with that child goes the dreams and vitality of the man's forgotten youth. For a couple of seconds the overweight man jerks in his sleep struggling against something only imagined. His wife places a comforting hand on his shoulder settling him back to restless slumber.

> As when a hungry man dreams that he is eating, but he awakens, and his hunger remains; as when a thirsty man dreams that he is drinking, but he awakens faint, with his thirst unquenched. Isaiah 29:8-11?

While the portly man snores, I have the sudden realization that I must not only write my adventure series for youths; I need to write for the lost children captured within adults who live daily with so little hope and unfulfilled ambitions. Surely, they could not be more lost than I was in my dark and dreary prison cell...seemingly alone. Then I discovered that I had never been alone at all for Jesus Christ had been softly knocking at the jail door quietly asking entrance. With Him came an incredible light that instantly washed away the shadows in my mind where I had been painting myself as a bad and worthless person. In that prison cell, haunted for so long by a darkness of my own creation, I abruptly found freedom from the burden of my sins. I would serve almost three long years in prison, but from discovering Christ onward my life had found purpose again. My Sojourn in a prison cell became an opportunity for growth of character and a closer walk with my Maker. Later His guiding light would lead me to spilling waterfalls in tropical islands, to extraordinary underwater adventures with marine animals and to unhindered physical freedom. The vitality of freedom can be more fully appreciated by someone who has lived without it.

I glance out my window at the full strength of the sunrise. I see the morning light glittering on snow-capped peaks and spilling down on to sheer icy glaciers in the mountain's deep valleys, and I know that the time is near to give back what I have been given. Lifting the lid of my laptop, my heart content with a decision made, I begin to type watching the words appearing on the softly backlit screen *High On Adventure*, Chapter One.

Learn to do right! Seek justice, encourage the oppressed.
Defend the cause of the fatherless, plead the case of the widow.
Isaiah 1:17

Walking down a long wooden pier, I happily stare about me at a vast array of nature's wonders crowding the small Alaskan harbor town of Cordova. In the misty distance, a towering mountain range wears a sheathing of ice and snow. The white capped mountain range with its skirting of green forests makes me think of Christmas. The snow and ice covered mountain tops sparkle magnificently under wandering shafts of brilliant sunlight. It is early in the Alaskan summer, yet the sky is shrouded with thick gray clouds. High-altitude winds stir the cloud blanket tearing open short-lived small patches of cobalt blue sky. The overcast can be so persistent in coastal Alaska that the locals refer to these infrequent patches of sky as blue clouds. Through these small celestial windows, pour bright shafts of late morning light from the northern sun. I watch a particularly bright sunbeam striding across the sheer walls of the surrounding mountain range highlighting a jagged ridgeline, then washing over a mountain summit before plunging down into a high glacial valley. Each point of beauty quickly fades as another equally as stunning replaces it. If I did not know better I could almost think that a giant heavenly flashlight was showing off the majestic wonders of this Alaskan mountain range.

In the little harbor, a gentle, yet persistent rain falls from a resident low-hovering gray sky that appears contained within the body of water. It paints the fishing fleet with a wet sheen that brings out each boat's bold and distinctive colors. The air is amazingly fresh and clean. I breathe in the woodsy fragrance of wet pines and cedar trees along with a spray of salty ocean smells. I slow my pace to better watch raindrops dancing on the harbor water and across shallow puddles on the wooden pier. The wetness brings out the softer wooden hues of the thick timber planks beneath my feet and washes dark streaks of reddish mud from my boots. On a beat-up trashcan twenty feet away two large Alaskan seagulls pause in a savage fight over an empty pizza box to glower at my approach. At the last moment, they take to wing screeching angrily from above, then as I pass they quickly settle back onto the trashcan to resume their squabbling. I continue further down the pier eagerly looking for a specific boat...well actually my quest involves the name of a boat.

I know nothing about the vessel Don Santee chartered for this expedition except for its name *Orca*. It is a name that conjures up images of a fast sleek vessel probably with a black knife-edge hull and a graceful white pilothouse with shiny brass portholes. The only problem with my mental image is the nagging memory of Don's laughter whenever I asked for details of our expedition vessel. Turning a corner onto a narrow finger wharf, I abruptly understand Don's mirth at my repeated questioning.

Orca sways gently to the constant lap of the sea at the very end of the wooden finger pier. Closest to the breakwater it is as if the tiny vessel wishes to be at sea. I read the name on her stern carefully to assure myself this is not a bad mistake, then think again of Don's laughter every time I had mentioned the words *expedition vessel*. Glancing around I quickly confirm that there is no other boat like her in the harbor, which is to be expected. *Orca* is far from her home waters of narrow Dutch canals and sea dikes. She is a motorsailer, thirty-eight feet long with rounded wooden sides sloping to a blunted bow and stern; kind of like a fat domesticated Viking ship with a cabin amidships instead of war shields and a band of fierce Vikings. It is a design made popular in Europe during the nineteen twenties and thirties for family expeditions close to home waters. The main cabin is built low and hugs the narrow deck. The pilot-house windows are wood trimmed with thick coats of forest green paint. Slap a couple of wooden wheels on either side of the hull and the little boat could be mistaken for a gypsy wagon from the medieval days of Transylvania. A soot-covered tin chimney spews a column of black smoke. I watch the dark fumes drifting upwards through the boat's rope rigging and around a frayed rainbow flag before the wind blows it out across the restless water.

I am wondering what Don has gotten me into when the soft sound of wood sliding on wood attracts my attention to the stern. A hatch slides open and out steps the skipper of the tiny vessel for our next expedition of discovery. It is quite surprising to see a mountain man emerge from a small Dutch canal boat. He is very tall and lanky in his movements with a long ponytail that would have been quite striking on most horses. He ties his ponytail with a tan leather strap that also sports a tiny silver bell (fairy ball). The little bell jingles softly as he crosses the deck. The mountain man is wearing frayed 501 jeans, a red flannel shirt rolled up at the sleeves and a big-toothy smile. I am about to meet a grown-up version of Huck Finn as he jumps barefoot down onto the wooden pier.

"Steve Arrington, I presume?" the mountain man extends a large hairy hand. The fairy ball tinkles gaily matching the festive mood of his lop-sided smile lurking beneath a bushy mustache.

I am quite amused to take the offered hand knowing it is pulling me back into the hippie era of the nineteen sixties. "Captain Grimes?" I ask.

"David to my friends. Come on aboard."

David's large hairy feet leave wet footprints on the worn wood steps as I follow him down through *Orca's* open stern hatch. Wafting up from inside the boat, is the rich fragrance of sandalwood incense, the damp odor of wet leather and a yet unidentifiable animal musk. It is not the smell of a single animal, but rather that of a mixed herd of diverse species lurking in the dimness below. Stepping beneath *Orca's* decks is like descending into an accidental collision between a boat, the aforementioned gypsy wagon and an Indian teepee or trapper's mountain cabin. I notice that there are a large number of stuffed road kills draped about the dim interior. A gray squirrel hangs upside down from an overhead rafter with a nut clenched in one tiny paw. Two robins on a hatch-cover table are poised for take-off from an egg-filled nest wedged into a Manzanita branch. A large black crow glares from the head (marine toilet) with a big dried beetle in its beak and there is a rather large flattened rattlesnake nailed to the wall. Various colorful feathers, seashells, beadwork and dyed-leather items hang from the walls of the cramped cabin. I am wondering if Don Santee is purposefully messing with me. It is Don who arranged the charter with *Island Diver*, the plywood boat that looked to have begun life as motorhome and now Don has found me an even weirder vessel with one of Mark Twain's characters for a skipper.

Glancing at David as he moves deeper into the boat's cabin, I recognize a kinship with him that goes far deeper than either of us would expect. Though we do not look, nor dress alike…he with his long ponytail while I with my close-cropped hair have been mistaken for an off duty policeman…yet I see an echo of who I am standing before myself. The vessel David has turned into his seaborne residence is sister to another unique mobile residence. The interior of Orca is reminiscent of Revelstoke that to my knowledge is now somewhere in the mountains of Mexico. David has tailored the boat's interior to reflect and compliment the whims of his personality. His creation is the apparent blending of an American Indian teepee and a gypsy wagon. For me Revelstoke was the realization of a childhood dream fabricated within a large truck resembling a sailing captain's sea cabin on wheels. Sitting down by the robins and their eggs, I look about the cabin and quietly surrender myself to the vivid memories the interior of Orca is rapidly awakening in one of the happier recesses of my mind.

A tropical storm is drenching Oahu. It is early evening, the night sky is cast in a shroud of darkness with a low hovering layer of thick rain clouds. I am parked down the street from Laulima waiting for Susan to finish her work shift. I light four candles with a wooden match then listen to the heavy rain beating a cadence upon Revelstoke's metal roof. The thunderous sound is only somewhat softened by the cedar planks that cover the ceiling. The aromatic cedar smells alive, the heavy tropical moisture is awakening the wood's inner scent filling Revelstoke with its forestry fragrance. I step to the oval porthole that looks out over the truck's cab. Across the street, I see the plate glass window of the vegetarian restaurant and Susan standing as she serves a family of four. A small oil lantern is burning on the table, its warm light washes over Susan's long hair bringing out its sun-bleached blond highlights. She sweeps a strand of hair behind her ear and then laughs as she serves one of the children. I am so deeply in love, so very happy and incredibly eager for her shift to end.

The narrow street is a black rippling wetness under the heavy tropical rain. The surrounding buildings are mostly dark except for the neon lights of the restaurant and an old-time streetlight partly shadowed by a very leafy tree. A three-foot wide stream of dark gushing water scuttles along the gutters, the surface of the flowing water shimmers with colorful light; reflecting the green, red and blue hues of the Laulima's vibrant neon sign. A car passes, its headlights haloed by the rain and then the spinning tires throw an arch of water that splashes across the sidewalk. I glance at my watch then look out a side window that reflects some of the glow from the streetlight. Water drops are running down the glass, but some are captured in the window's screen. The droplets suspended in the screen's wire are refracting the glow of the streetlight into tiny rainbows. In the screen, there is a spider web I hadn't noticed before; it is a descending highway for the droplets and their marching rain bowed hues. Then I see the wooden door of Laulima swing open as Susan steps out. She pauses under the door's overhang, a low-watt bulb washes her with softened yellow light. She is wearing jeans, a white button-down shirt and sandals. She holds a newspaper over her head as she dashes towards Revelstoke and leaps the flowing stream rushing along the gutter. I see small splashes as she runs through the water shimmering with light then she is at the back-door, pulling it open and stepping inside. Instantly, the interior of Revelstoke comes alive with excitement. Puu, who has been watching her run across the street from the driver's seat barks once happily and then jumps down and edging me aside rushes to meet her with his long wagging tail. The huge Great Dane's tail beats a happy cadence against the stove as Susan rubs Puu's ears, then she collects a lick from him and a kiss from me; somehow, I feel that Puu got the better end of the deal.

"I love this rain," says Susan shaking water from her long hair. "Let's go up into the mountains so we can really enjoy it."

Twenty minutes later, I pull Revelstoke into the very top of the Pali Highway overlook. I park illegally with the rear tires up on the sidewalk and with the back of the truck right up against a low protective rock wall. No one will care, we are the only vehicle in the parking lot and the view is stupendous. I swing the double backdoors wide open. Just a few feet away the sheer cliff drops vertically thousands of feet to the broad undulating valley below. We are among the low hanging clouds. Standing just inside the backdoors we can see the whole Kaneohe basin spread out before us. A raging ocean is pounding the shoreline. Palm trees and native plants sway to the surging wind and lightning shatters the dark sky. Below us and to our right and left there are numerous cascading waterfalls brought to life by the massive downpour. Arms around each other we are sheltered from the turbulent weather. Inside Revelstoke, the candles flicker as Susan and I watch the night drama of wind, lightning, thunder and rain. Puu barks at the weather; life is wonderful; I am young, in love and so vitally alive.

Thinking about the wonder of that night my thoughts drift from Susan and Puu to Cindy and our yet to be born daughter. My love for Cindy is far greater for having known Susan and Puu. The passion for life I shared with Susan and my crazy Great Dane in Hawaii has helped to define and remake the man that I am today. Something I had not fully realized about myself is that I had grown up with a limited ability to love. I never had that feeling of deep caring from my parents or from my extended family as a child. To protect my inner feelings, I built mental walls that not only kept others out, they kept me and my deeper emotions locked inside as well. Because my childhood lacked parental love, I was hesitant to accept love from others. The love I thought I was experiencing was a weak corruption of true, uninhibited love. Susan and Puu knocked down the walls that I built as a child, and continued to maintain and live with as an adult, freeing me from my self-imposed misconceptions. After losing them both, I suffered through the extreme loneliness of my incarceration with nowhere to hide my emotionally damaged soul. Prison and my great sense of loss further stripped away the psychological camouflage behind which I was unconsciously trying to hide. Finally, in J-3, I hit rock bottom, which was an essential step in freeing me to give my *self-considered* worthless life to Jesus Christ. My love for God and Jesus taught me to be more accepting of myself and of others, yet I still left prison an emotionally devastated man. Throughout most of my incarceration and during the early days (thirty-two months) of my initial freedom, I had been busily preparing myself to meet the woman that I hoped to one day marry. In the beginning of our relationship, Cindy was quite aware that I was still dealing with rejection issues from my childhood. With great patience, at the workbench of life, we began to build our lives

EXTREME

together. Now she is carrying our child. We are bound together for life in the deepest possible way. It is because of my love for them that I realize my final days with the Cousteau teams is hurtling at me...and I am becoming eager to step across that threshold to a new future, full of mystery, promise and mutual commitment.

> *"We find that great things are made of little things, and little*
> *things go lessening until at last comes God behind them,"*
> Robert Browning

The open-fanged mouth of a rattlesnake two feet from my face startles me from my thoughts. I might have been more alarmed, but for the rusted nail in its head and a couple of dust balls in its nostrils.

"Your snake needs dusting," I say to David who is busy gathering dirty laundry strewn about the cabin and jamming it into an already over-stuffed drawer.

Using a dirty sock to brush dust off the flattened snake's snout David laughs as he quips, "Got kind of lonely being out on the water by myself so I started collecting animal buddies."

"Highway road kills?" I ask.

"Actually I did accidently run over the snake."

The snake's head has an odd backward dent to it, kind of like it was astonished by something just before it died. "What did you do? Club him to death?"

David shakes his head stirring up a couple of musical notes from the fairy ball in his hair. "No way, I don't kill animals except for the fish, but that is just to make a living and for my dinner. The snake was slithering across the highway as I came around a sharp turn. I couldn't miss him completely so I angled my VW camper to go right over the top of the snake hoping the wheels wouldn't hit it. The snake probably would have been okay, but at the last second it reared up into a striking position." The tinkling of David's fairy ball embeds itself into the story and into my memory forever. "Anyway VW buses have real low bumpers."

David seems saddened by his story. So I distract him with a question, "What about the birds?"

"These little guys?" David stares fondly at the robins, which could also use a good dusting and are missing more than a few feathers. "Had them since I was a kid. It was my first attempt at animal stuffing."

There are more stuffed creatures too numerous to describe lurking in the shadows of the cabin's nooks and crannies. The boat is so full of his childhood treasures I begin to wonder where we will store all of our filming equipment. That is when I remember the rest of our little team waiting at the head of the pier with the rental truck full of our gear. I couldn't wait to introduce them to David; the hippie mountain man and his floating road kill cafe.

The next morning, I wake and stretch in the snugness of my sleeping quarters. There are four bunks stacked two high on each side of the narrow cabin. Getting out of the bed is a trial because the tiny corridor between the bunks is an improvised luggage locker stacked waist high with expedition boxes. I haul two boxes up onto the bunk to make room for my feet on the deck then clamber over a couple of bulky dive bags to get to the head. I have good reason not to linger in the small outhouse-sized bathroom. Flushing the chemical toilet is a hand pumping process requiring me to lean directly over the bowl to work the pump, which stirs up an earthy bouquet of overly ripe smells. Reversing direction, I pass a frosty porthole, but cannot see anything through it because of a thick interior fogging on the glass. Sniffing cautiously I confirm it is more than just moisture floating in the still air. The volatile human body odors in the cabin could singe nose hairs.

Before getting Orca underway, I made a stop at the local grocery store, as I am also the self-designated cook for this expedition. The French seldom use beans in their meals and lately I have been feeling bean deprived. Yesterday afternoon, I half-filled a shopping cart with seven large bags of different types of beans. Last night's dinner of pinto beans with whole cloves of garlic, onion halves, chopped chili peppers, assorted spices, jalapenos and Tabasco sauce is an all but visible vapor hovering in the humid air. The human-processed gases are probably mostly responsible for the mist on the porthole. The associated fragrance quickly propels me outside through the back hatch.

Emerging at the stern of the Dutch canal boat, I see swirling fog drifting on semi-dark water. The just rising morning sun is a soft reddish orb behind a curtain of drifting white mist. Pulling up the hood of my jacket to ward off the cold wind from our passage, I stare into the fog seeing momentary clear patches that reveal we are passing up a narrow channel with wilderness shoreline on either side of Orca. Dense forests of evergreen trees crowd narrow rocky beaches where smooth-sided stones glisten with morning dew. The piney scent of the trees floats delicately in the air. This should be a pristine morning of wilderness beauty, but the moment is soiled by another smell lurking in the crisp air. It is an underlying chemical odor leeching up from the rocky beaches. The top layer of wet stones are shades of brown and light tan, but beneath that layer lurks a blackness that weeps into the water with the lapping action of small breaking waves washing up on the shore. Here and there, I see patches of thick black oil floating on the water. The bow swell of the *Orca* spills some of the patches of oil back onto the beach with the slow rush of our passage.

Sadly shaking my head, I acknowledge the purpose for our visit to Alaska. We are entering Prince William Sound. This wondrously beautiful wilderness is ground zero for the worse oil spill in American history.

On March 24, 1989, a supertanker, the *Exxon Valdez*, hit a submerged reef ripping a massive gash in her hull. The huge ship spilt a fifth of her cargo, eleven million gallons of black oil spread in a thick life-smothering blanket across Prince William Sound polluting over three-hundred-fifty-miles of some of the most-pristine wilderness coastline on earth. The oil company was far too slow in their oil spill response as were all the various government agencies. The enormous oil spill ran with the winds and tides over the passing weeks slowly spreading to over twelve hundred miles of virgin wilderness shoreline. In comparison, imagine the entire shoreline of the East Coast between Miami and New York City fouled with a coat of thick crude oil several inches thick.

Passing a rocky point, I see two deer emerging out of the mist, a doe and her fawn. With a soft wind blowing in our direction, they are unaware of our presence. Then the soft chug of *Orca's* small diesel engine catches their attention. They stare in alarm before dashing off into the shelter of the trees.

Staring into the fog aboard the slow moving *Orca*, McNair's two favorite words echoes in my mind, *alert* and *aware*, those two words could have kept the *Exxon Valdez* from running aground.

I am imagining the circumstances leading up to the massive oil spill. A supertanker over half-a-mile off course is heading for Blight Reef, a submerged obstacle whose exact location is indicated on the ship's chart. There are people standing watch on the bridge of the supertanker with state of the art navigational aids including radar, sonar and radio locators linked with satellite and shore-based stations. A supertanker does not get that far off course in dangerously restricted waters unless the ship's watch is not alert or paying attention to their duties.

After the accident, almost everyone in America knew the name of the *Exxon Valdez's* captain, at the time of the accident he was in his cabin when he should have been on the bridge. Almost no one knows the name of the person who was standing watch when the accident occurred. This was the individual personally responsible for being so far off course. There was possibly another person who could have helped avert this accident. A shore radar station is supposed to keep electronic watch on the position of all major ships in The Sound. Had the radar watch been paying close attention to the electronic scope he or she might have been able to sound the alarm over the radio and prevent an environmental catastrophe. I have to wonder were all these people daydreaming, reading books, watching television or otherwise distracted from their sworn duties?

In real life, emergencies often occur with little or no warning.

The impact that a sudden crisis will have on our lives and upon the lives of others is dependent upon our general alertness and our independent ability to react in a focused and effective way when panic is trying to rule. For the *Exxon Valdez* the people at watch, or on guard if you will, allowed themselves to be lulled into boredom. In the simplest of terms, they were criminally negligent. Their lack of attention caused the deaths of hundreds of thousands of animals. Sea lions and otters with oil-matted fur would freeze to death, birds coated in clinging sludge were slowly poisoned and untold millions of fish swimming in chemically toxic water would suffocate leaving untold carcasses on the once pristine beaches and seabeds.

Every single moment in a person's life is something wondrous that will not be repeated again. To tread the present with vigilance unlocks a world of dynamic possibilities and lays a pathway to challenge and wonder. Lack of focus or commitment linked with inattentiveness equates to a dull life spiced with sudden moments of loss and tragedy.

Recently, I read in a small town paper about a teenage girl celebrating her sixteenth birthday. I can easily imagine her excitement waking up to such an important milestone in her young life. That evening her friends and family gathers to celebrate while her mother lights the candles on her birthday cake. After the opening of the presents, a final person steps forward, but their gift stays hidden from the others and is given clandestinely; an evil secret gift lurking under the guise of friendship. The person whispers and beckons opening their hand to reveal a little white pill called ecstasy. It is an illegal drug masquerading behind a name that implies pleasure, but this is a dark gift indeed. The girl swallows the pill probably trusting that this supposed friend would not do anything to hurt her…on purpose. Criminals manufacture designer drugs—those four words should send alarm bells ringing in any sane person's mind. These under-educated felons have limited or no knowledge of chemistry or of the vast complexities of human physiology. The chemicals they use undergo no quality control or testing and come from the most questionable of sources. The girl had also been covertly drinking beer, probably another secret gift from another supposed friend. The alcohol and chemicals from the ecstasy pill lacked only one more ingredient to become a potentially lethal cocktail. The final component was found in the seemingly harmless antihistamine she took earlier for a minor cold. Her sixteenth birthday party was the girl's last living memory. She spent the next two years in a debilitating comma. The deadly chemical combination had killed her brain. The girl lay unmoving day after day, month after month, seasons passing unseen, with machines maintaining her basic body functions. The family forfeited all of their savings and much of what they owned to fight a legal system that would not let them unplug the thumping and whirling machines. Many people in the community verbally abused the mother and father for wanting what they felt would be a compassionate release for their precious daughter. When the machines were finally turned-off, and the young girl put to rest, the tragic family moved to a different state to live out the hollowness of their lives without their daughter. The unwarranted loss of a loved one would haunt the family for the rest of their lives. Few families survive the lost of a child intact. Divorce is rampant for couples that suffer the loss of a child; guilt replaces love and tragedy marches on.

Staring out on the fog-covered water, I think about my own thirty-one month sojourn in prison because of a grossly stupid drug mistake. Some of the inmates at Terminal Island prison were there for manufacturing illegal drugs. I remember that every single one of those drug manufacturers had visible signs of mental damage from exposure to caustic drugs and to the various solvents and acids used in the manufacture of illegal drugs. Simply put these individuals had great difficulty putting together a simple sentence without a fair amount of stuttering, memory loss, attention lapses or drooling. Yet to a person their first commitment upon release from prison was to manufacture more illicit drugs. I would not trust these men to make me a peanut butter and jelly sandwich, yet their caustic wares are available in almost every school and classroom in America.

Thinking of those mentally damaged, criminal individuals and how their lives were tragically laced with an innocent young girl's sixteenth birthday, I take a last look at the swirling fog, then open the door to the pilothouse and step inside.

In the dark, men break into houses, but by day they shut themselves in; they want nothing to do with the light. For all of them, deep darkness is their morning; they make friends with the terrors of darkness. Job 24:16-17

A blanket of warm air greets me as I step into the narrow pilothouse. David stands at the helm humming softly. He flashes me a broad smile then quickly spins the wheel to starboard. *Orca* swings quickly as the bow disappears into a dense wall of fog. David shifts his gaze from the bridge window, checks the compass, then stares intently at a radar screen. We are navigating the narrow channel between Harkins and Hinchinbrook Islands. I look at our plotted course on a chart and then glance at the luminous screen of the radar, which is painting each island's shoreline in glowing red and green bands of soft light.

"Do you smell the reek of the oil in the air?" asks David. He is wearing the same jeans and flannel shirt from yesterday and remains barefooted.

I nod not ready to talk as thoughts of the disastrous birthday girl continue to echo through my mind. Looking at David's weathered face, I see another tragedy playing out. This man loves the wilderness. The Prince William Sound is his refuge for a simpler life. Instead, the wild beauty about him has been ravaged. Simply put we are sailing in the wake of corporate greed and government ineptitude. Though most of us blame the oil company for the spill the real problem lays with *We the people*. The laws of economics determine that it is the consumers of oil and the payers of taxes that will ultimately pay for the cleanup. Therefore, it is with *We the people* where the final responsibility must lay. In a democracy, citizens cannot allow themselves to be ignorant, uncaring, unaware and uninvolved. The immediate cost to us is reckoned financially, yet what of the heritage left for our children and what of the needless suffering and death of a multitude of animals? Some may wonder can a sole individual make much of a difference?

In the late 1980's, Captain Jacques Yves Cousteau led an initiative to ban all nations from drilling for oil and from mining for minerals in Antarctica. He spent years gathering signatures and meeting with the heads of states of various nations. Very much because of Captain Cousteau's efforts, the United Nations adopted a ten-year moratorium on any mineral or oil exploitation of Antarctica. With that major success under his belt Captain Cousteau went on to try to protect what he believes is the world's most important resource of all—children. In the early 1990's he began gathering what would become millions of signatures proposing that the United Nations adopt a *Bill of Rights for Future Generations.* The essence of the bill, which was adopted and ratified into constitutional law, is that the unborn generations to come have the absolute right to inherit a planet relatively unspoiled by the generations before. Captain Cousteau liked to say that, *"People protect what they love."* Through his films and books, Captain Cousteau brought the mysteries and wonders of the underwater world into our homes. In the comfort of our front rooms, we learned about dolphins and whales and we fell in love with these dynamic marine mammals. What sprang from this is a worldwide call to protect marine mammals and the ocean environment.

Jesus Christ told us that the two most important commandments of all were to love God with all our heart and soul and to love our fellowman as we would love ourselves. Our Lord has also entrusted us to love and care for all of His creations.

> *Then God said, "Let us make man in our image, in our like-ness, and let them rule over the fish of the sea and the birds of the air, over the livestock, over all the earth, and over all the creatures that move along the ground."* Genesis 1:26

With those thoughts echoing through my mind, I look out *Orca's* moisture-laden windows. The fog is thinning rapidly as we begin to enter the open water of the Prince William Sound. In the misty distance, I see a wilderness tapestry of glacier-cut fjords and rocky beaches. The lush forest hugs the coastline in a dense fabric of evergreen hues that drape across the contours of the mountainous land, jagged islands and rocky shoreline. The seawater is a vibrant blue teeming with marine life. I see flocks of sea birds flying low over the water as they wheel and dive pursuing fish. Not fifty feet from Orca, I see a playful sea otter tumbling on a floating bed of kelp. Droplets of water drip from its long frisky whiskers as it peers back at me munching a silver and red fish. The otter scratches its cheeks and then quickly dives from view. Beneath the ocean's restless surface, I imagine whales, dolphins, sea lions and the otter hunting the silver glinting fish. Closely rounding the point off Hinchinbrook Island, we pass a colony of sea lions lying amongst slick moss-laced rocks. A large bull barks a warning as the sleek shapes, many of them small pups, some covered with patches of black crude oil, slide gracefully into the choppy water. I open a porthole to watch a few of the braver animals swimming alongside and in *Orca's* wake barking their curiosity.

"The islands only look pristine above the waterline," David states flatly, his voice laced with sadness like someone grieving at a best friend's funeral. "Crude oil still pools beneath the rocky beaches at the tidal levels. The islands are super-saturated with oil. Each tidal change leaches more of that oil back out into the sound."

"Didn't the oil company announce that they cleaned these beaches?" I respond.

"That is what they claim," David says grimly. He nods towards a sheath of papers on the chart table. "I laid out their report certifying these islands as cleaned. Yet, it is a year since the spill and you still see wakes of oil trailing down current from each island."

An hour later, we arrive at our destination. It is a picturesque cove on a small island swarming with people in orange coveralls. Lining the shore are barges and other industrial vessels all involved in cleaning up oil from the spill. Armed with cameras and sound recorders our team goes ashore to document the clean-up effort. On the beach, teams of workers are using steam nozzles to wash oil off the rocky beach and down to the water where other workers are skimming floating oil patches. Following the steam nozzles are more workers whose job it is to pick up each individual rock and wipe off any remaining oil. It is a slow laborious process, which I decide to investigate more closely. I find a young man sitting on an empty plastic bucket leisurely wiping a two-pound rock with a paper towel.

"How's it going?" I ask presenting a broad friendly smile.

"Slow, really slow," he replies in a bored way.

"Yeah, I can see that," I answer glancing about, "looks like there are a lot of rocks yet to go."

"Don't matter much," shrugs the youth, "get paid by the hour, not by the rock."

"Well it must make you feel pretty good getting the oil off," I hazard hoping for a conversation on a deeper level.

"The only thing I feel good about is getting my check at the end of the week." The youth tosses the rock over his shoulder and picks up another one.

"Doesn't it give you any satisfaction cleaning up the oil?" I ask startled by his indifference.

In return, I get another bored look, "Why don't you dig down a bit where I have already cleaned."

Standing up, I walk to an apparently clean area only a few feet away and dig down a couple of handfuls of rocks to find a layer of oil pooling beneath the surface. "Looks like you guys may have missed a few thousand gallons of oil here."

"Course we have," the youth tosses another rock over his shoulder without looking. It lands on the edge of my hole, and then tumbles to the bottom picking up a fresh coat of oil on its bottom side. Pondering the rock in its oil bath, I hear him say, "We only go down about a foot or less. Otherwise this clean up would take forever."

"But if you only go down a foot then the beach is not really clean," I answer.

"So?" offers the youth unenthusiastically grabbing another rock.

I shuffle off glancing here and there to confirm that none of the workers at this site appears concerned about doing a serious job of cleaning the beach. *This crew is apparently content doing the absolute minimum of what they've been told to do,* I think to myself, *it is not the satisfaction of a work to save the wilderness or its wildlife, it is only the paycheck that manners. Yet, I have to hope that there are other crews more fully committed to their work. I happen to know that the volunteers helping the wildlife are fully committed; with or without a paycheck.* I look back at the young man as he tosses another rock into the hole I dug. The rock clacks as it hits the bottom spewing a small fountain of oil. The young man could care less, which is a character statement or the lack thereof. He is a willing participant of fraud and deception made right in his own mind with an hourly wage.

On our last day before heading back to the boat harbor at Cordova, I had the opportunity to ask a mid-level manager of the cleanup effort what he thought about the oil that was purposefully being left behind. The man looked at me for a moment, as if he was weighing my intelligence, or maybe my character, and then asked, "Do you want a serious answer?"

I nodded thinking I was about to hear a company secret. Instead, he told me a simple truth. "Many people in the United States don't really much care about this oil spill." Before I could argue the point, he added a surprising statistic. "Every year, Joe Citizen purposefully pours more oil, acid, paint and other hazardous chemicals down street drains, onto the side of the road and into their trash cans than all the oil spilt by the Exxon Valdez."

I am shocked, "More than the eleven million gallons spilt from the Valdez?"

"Lots more," says the manager. "Something else, all those chemical wastes that people are purposefully tossing into sewers, street drains and trash dumps probably kill as many animals if not more on an ongoing basis than our accidental spill here in the Sound.

Remember this was an accident."

He pauses, and then looks right into my eyes, "you ever flush out your car radiator?"

"Yeah," I nod knowing I am not going to like what I am about to hear.

"Did you let the old radiator fluid just drain out into the street gutter?"

I nod, remembering doing exactly that. I was sixteen years old. Just opened the petcock and stuck a hose into the top of the radiator. Let the water run until it comes out of the petcock clean, just like my grandfather who owned a garage and gas station taught me.

"There are lots of people like you that don't even think twice about draining anti-freeze from their car radiators into the street. Dogs, cats, birds and wildlife drink the stuff because it tastes sweet to them. Anti-freeze is a type of sugar solution that happens to be very toxic to living creatures. Sometimes the stuff even kills kids." The manager shrugs, "Na, I don't think most people care a whole lot about what happens here or anywhere else unless it is in their own backyard."

I watch the manager walking away with his words echoing though my mind. Now years later those words still echo true. I say this as I look at a front-page story in the USA Newspaper. It is a report about the number of wild animals that have recently died at the new Disney World Wild Animal Park in Florida. A litter of four cheetah cubs was accidentally poisoned when they drank from a puddle of anti-freeze. This was a very avoidable accident. Whoever spilt the anti-freeze should have cleaned it up. Maybe, like me when I was sixteen, they were ignorant of the toxic properties of anti-freeze. Maybe their focus in life is inward...a selfish dull contentment with minimal performance. There are many excuses for poor work habits, however none of them will bring back those four cheetah kittens. I pause to wonder if my willful anti-freeze spill killed any animals...maybe, I did not want to know.

One who is slack in his work is brother to one who destroys. Proverbs 18:9

Jean-Michel joins us for the last half of the expedition. I wait for my chance to talk with him privately then he invites me out onto the small-restricted stern of *Orca*. I stand at the edge on a wide flat rail. Our vessel is at anchor in a beautiful wilderness bay at a salmon farm.

"Steve, I have some not so good news," he says quietly. "Because of financial concerns my father has decided to shut down the Los Angeles office."

His words are completely unexpected.

"We'll finish up the Vietnam expedition, but afterwards we are going to move key personnel to the Virginia headquarters. The captain wants you and Cindy to move there."

I instantly know Cindy's attitude about moving so far away from her family, particularly with me so often away on expedition. I run my hand along the Orca's deckhouse roof; the exposed wood is slippery from the continuous moist weather and I wonder if my future is sliding into a new direction much faster than I thought or allowed for.

Jean-Michel continues, "We have to push up the schedule for the Mekong Delta team. They're leaving in early August and that means you can't go."

"What, I'm not going to Vietnam?" I blurt.

"Of course not, that's when you're becoming a father."

"Oh yeah," I feel like an idiot and remove one hand from the stern hatch to swat myself in the forehead in a physical demonstration of my brief stupidity—which turns out to be a really dumb stunt as I lose my balance on the deck's slick railing and fall overboard. The water is icy cold instantly chilling my whole body. My sudden dunking is terribly embarrassing, yet I cannot help but sense that this is a sudden wakeup call. A new life is rushing at me with surprising velocity and it is carrying me rapidly towards a decision.

Jean-Michel leans down and offers me a hand. "You are such a character," he chuckles.

"Don is doing Vietnam without me?" I ask unhappily climbing onto the deck with squishy shoes and clammy pants.

"He's not real excited about it either, Steve. While he is in Vietnam, I have some short trips planned for you to Hawaii, but we're going to be cutting back on personnel and on the expedition schedule."

With water dripping from my nose and cold wet clothes clinging to my body, I realize that Jean-Michel is offering me the perfect opportunity to share my intention to leave The Cousteau Society. "Jean-Michel," I shudder, such an important thing to say, my future is altering and these are the type of words that cannot be taken back, "I can't go to Virginia."

"I know," replies an unsurprised Jean-Michel.

"You do?"

"Absolutely," he shrugs his shoulders, "you're going to leave to go work with kids, right?"

"How did you know?" I am astounded.

"Wasn't hard to guess and I've been expecting it for some time. Who else in the Society asks me for time to speak at churches and public schools whenever he gets a little free time?" Besides, Cindy has given me a few hints too.

"Well, is it okay?"

"Of course it's okay," he starts to put a hand on my shoulder, frowns at my soaked shirt and takes his hand back. "Look, my dad and I have had extensive talks about what to do about the people who are leaving. We figured you would probably see this as an opportunity to go off on your ministry to help kids."

I listen to his surprising words in a semi-state of shock.

"So when you're ready to go we'll add four months full pay and benefits to your two weeks of separation pay."

"Really?" I have been worried about making enough money to support my growing family while starting a youth ministry from scratch and suddenly a huge gift is being given to Cindy and I by two of the most important men in our lives. Yet, I thought they had no idea of my private plans.

"Just promise me that you will stay until we close the office," continues Jean-Michel, "I really need your help to get equipment moved and to wrap up our current expedition schedule."

"I'll be pleased to help Jean-Michel, thank you."

"One more thing, change the menu. I don't know what you're feeding the crew, but it stinks like a sewer below deck."

Late that afternoon, we got underway into stormy weather. The round-sided canal boat rocked and rolled so bad that I spent half the night at the stern heaving my guts out in celebration that my days of getting seasick would soon be over. Kind of amazing to spend my youth daydreaming about adventures on the ocean and not knowing that I was so prone to seasickness. There was another hidden bonus to leaving The Cousteau Society…I could finally stop studying French, a language that to this day still eludes me.

"With a favoring wind and a flowing tide,
A quiet sea and a star to guide,
From the isles of fortune beyond the blue,
May your ship come home
And your dreams come true."
Julianne Ellix, Age 19, Tasmania, Australia

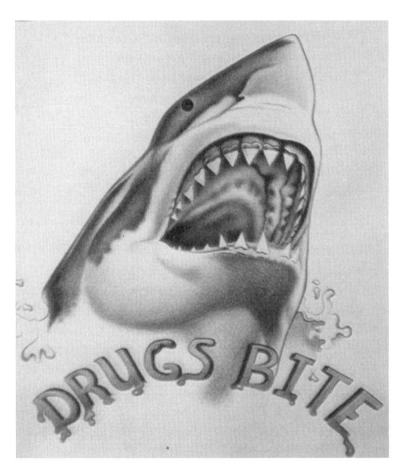

Illustration by Andy Charles
Drugs Bite Logo taken from actual photo shot
by author of the great white shark named Amy

"You cannot dream yourself into a character;
you must hammer and forge yourself one,"
James A. Froude 1818-1894

Chapter 50

SANTA MONICA COUSTEAU EXPEDITION OFFICE,

CALIFORNIA, JANUARY 1993

I AM ALONE in the basement of The Cousteau Society Office thinking what an important day this is and that there is no one here
to share it with me. A squeak from the floor reminds me that I am
not actually alone. I look fondly at the portable playpen beside my
desk. Stetcyn, my four-month-old daughter is awake from her nap.
She gurgles at me so I reach down, pick up my baby girl and offer
her a bottle of warm soymilk. While she works the rubber nipple,
I wonder if the rest of the employees of the Cousteau office are
enjoying their farewell party. Over the past month, the various departments of our expedition office have been departing. The last to
leave is the publications department, all of whom are currently at a
farewell lunch with Jean-Michel. Like me, this is their last day.

Down in the basement, I am feeling forgotten, maybe even a bit
abandoned. Did they accidentally overlook me? Had they known I

was in the basement would someone have invited me to the farewell party? Technically, I am not a part of the publications department; it is their party not mine. Yet we are leaving on the same day. Doesn't that count? Except for Don Santee, who is on vacation, I am the last remaining member of the expedition team in the LA office and to my knowledge, there hasn't been a going away party for the expedition people mainly because none of them are leaving…that is except for me. I am working hard on convincing myself that my absence from the party is just an oversight. But, for the gurgling bundle in the crib I am feeling excluded.

I look at my watch for the tenth or fifteen time in an hour. The Los Angeles rush hour traffic will be starting in half an hour. If I do not leave soon I will be late picking up Cindy, which certainly will not improve either of our moods. Knowing Cousteau parties, I suspect that the farewell lunch may continue for hours. With the sadness of a put-off-decision-made, I place Stetcyn into her car seat on my desk and tuck a fuzzy blanket about her. Then I fold up her portable crib and carry it out to my Ford Explorer. I have already packed my personal items, mostly remembrances from the various expeditions. I return to the basement office to pick up my now cooing daughter and carry her out to the car. The basement door closes and automatically locks behind me. I stare blankly at it for several seconds then get into the car and slowly drive away.

I stop for a street light. The light's red glow is soft around the edges as I realize I am about to cry. After five-and-a-half wonderful years, I am leaving. Just as the tears are on the verge of flowing Stetcyn gurgles happily at me. It is a merry sound, she is staring at me with her eyes full of wonder and instantly I remember that I am voluntarily leaving The Cousteau Society. I have chosen a new path to walk. I want to be a full-time husband to Cindy and a father who is there for our daughter. I have a promise to honor to Judge Takasugi to talk with youths about choices and a commitment to God to do His work.

What I did not suspect as I smile down at my daughter is that I would find far greater adventure and wonder as a lay youth minister than I had known as an expedition leader for The Cousteau Society diving with whales, dolphins and sharks.

"Have I not commanded you? Be strong and courageous. Do not be terrified; do not be discouraged, for the LORD your God will be with you wherever you go." Joshua 1:9

Yesterday, I left The Cousteau Society office and this cold winter evening, I am standing on the diving barge at the College of Oceaneering overseeing nighttime diving operations. It is a part-time job to allow me to earn a little extra money as I prepare to begin my youth ministry. I am not aware of any books that tell how to begin a youth ministry. I figure it is just something that you do and the how part will fall into place. Lacking a concrete plan is not exactly a good strategy for beginning a ministry or a business from scratch, yet I am about His business and fully anticipate that He will step in where and when needed. I am not without some experience, nor do I lack expectations of success. During my limited free time with The Cousteau Society, I have done a good number of public school and Christian youth programs. Many of the teachers and staff at these presentations encouraged me to become a full-time speaker—they felt I could help make a difference by sharing the intensity of what went so wrong and then so incredibly right with my life.

Standing on the barge with my hands in my jacket pockets, I am wrestling with some very serious emotions. I feel like I have stepped backwards in time. I glance over at the old barge's telephone. Five-and-a-half years ago Don Santee called me on that telephone to offer me the dream job with The Cousteau Society. I am very aware of being right back where I was hoping to leave from and am determined not to be here for long. I left The Society to work with youths, not to teach commercial diving. There is just this hovering need to pay the rent and to buy baby food.

The class diving supervisor calls me over to inspect a student diver before he enters the water. I check his harness, diving helmet, bail out cylinder (scuba tank) and the lay of his umbilical before patting him on the shoulder and nodding my approval. The students are wondering about me. They are impressed that their instructor was a chief diver and expedition leader for Cousteau, but they are also wondering what I am doing back here...in a way so am I.

Seeing a puddle of rusty water, I go stand in it. I am near the edge of the barge at dive station three. This is where I kneeled to do CPR on Chris. To date my life has been filled with incredible adventure, flashing red lights and wailing sirens, but what quests wait for me now? I guess the title chief is now truly a part of my past and I cannot yet lay claim to being a youth minister. Therefore, I am the-in-between-man, waiting to see where the Lord will lead me and wondering what paths He will urge me to walk. Mentally I cannot help looking over my shoulder at what I am leaving behind, world travel, underwater adventures and making a difference for the marine environment.

I stare at the dark harbor water where a boil of bubbles is bursting above a student diver working on a project fifty feet down in the absolute blackness of the debris-covered harbor bottom. I imagine him kneeling in the ice-cold, clammy mud working only with his sense of touch with bolts, nuts, flanges, pipes and wrenches, probably wondering where his diving career will take him. For all of us on the diving barge this is a point of transition, a temporary way station on life's long journey. Looking upward from the dark water, I stare at the glistening lights of San Pedro with echoes of Terminal Island Prison fluttering through my mind and in that instant absolutely know that I have made the right decision. My life has been an astonishing adventure and now I will share it, the good and the bad. I have a problem with the message being pounded into youths to, "Just say no." Important choices should not be trivialized and life is very complicated...particularly for teenagers. I think the best message actively involves youthful commitment to aspire towards accomplishment and realization of dreams. It is not a matter of *Just saying no*, it is a determination of *wanting to say no*—no to choices that lead towards corruption of mind, spirit and body and yes to youthful aspirations through discipline, focus, courage, endurance and resolve. My message will be simple, how do you feel when you do something good compared to how do you feel when you do something bad. Just as dolphins are social creatures so are we. When someone is doing something good they always try to share it with their friends; just so when someone is doing something wrong they also try to involve their friends.

I am fortunate that my active interest in photography means that I have a visual documentation of the highlights I have lived. I will begin by showing slides from my training at bomb disposal school, then parachuting out of airplanes and diving down to sunken wrecks from World War II. I will show them surfing in Hawaii, living in Revelstoke with Puu and the adventures of being a bomb disposal frogman working with the Secret Service, the CIA and NASA. I want to illustrate how I had military adventure, travel to exotic places and challenging operations, but foolishly threw it away because of marijuana. I will share how that drug led to smuggling cocaine and then to prison. I particularly want to talk about all that prison takes from you. I will discuss the need for right choices and how doing good for others leads to wonder in your own life. Case in point, how an ex-felon got the dream job of a lifetime leading Cousteau expeditions. I know the youth will find it surprising that I left that dream job to become a full-time lay youth minister, yet I feel deep down inside that a whole new set of adventures are waiting for me. Yes, leaving the Cousteaus to do the Lord's work is a good choice. I feel so good about it I go over and cheerfully chew out a student who is about to enter the water with a twisted dive harness.

"He who learns must suffer, and, even in our sleep, pain that cannot forget falls drop by drop upon the heart, and in our despair, against our will, comes wisdom to us by the awful grace of God," Aeschylus 525-556 BC

*"We make a living by what we get, we make a life
by what we give,"* Abraham Lincoln

Chapter 51

FIJI 1988 AND NEW HAMPSHIRE, OCTOBER 1994

THE BOW of the Zodiac lifts dramatically as a wave rolls over the shallow reef. At the inflatable's bow, twin anchor lines go taut as they resist the swiftly surging water. The submerged reef is only four feet beneath the bottom of the rubber Zodiac. We are at the edge of a vertical underwater wall that plunges straight down hundreds of feet. The waves strike us suddenly as they dramatically change from open water swell to crashing breaker in just a dozen linear feet. Except for *Alcyone* drifting in the near distance, as far as the eye can see there is only empty ocean. There are no landmarks to identify this submerged reef in Fiji's northern outer islands, which is fortunate because we are about to make a very dangerous dive. Deep below us, there is an underwater cave that has taken the lives of some very talented divers. It is best if its location remains a secret.

Donning my mask, I make a last check to ensure the Zodiacs are securely anchored and will not be washed back onto the reef. I nod to the other Cousteau divers, and then silently slip over the side right after a large foaming wave. The rolling water surges with bubbles as I rapidly kick downwards and grab onto a coral pinnacle to stabilize myself against the strong undertow. When the entire team of five is present, we swim to the edge of the shelf, and then quickly descend plunging down a perpendicular wall of multicolored coral. The vertical reef is a hanging marine garden that plunges hundreds of feet straight down to the ocean floor far below. We pass close to a large orange sea fan folding and unfolding in the current with a black gorgonian (brittle starfish) clinging tenaciously to its swaying branches. At sixty feet, we swim by a yellow-banded clown fish nuzzling against an electric blue sea anemone that is its protector and home. Deeper and deeper we descend where the reef's passionate colors quickly dull and their rich hues mutate from vibrant reds and brilliant yellows to dark greens and deep blues.

At a hundred feet, the water turns sharply colder, yet we hardly notice as we race downward plunging into the twilight of deep blue water. This will be a very deep dive and our bottom time will be severely limited. The pressure compresses our wetsuits reducing our buoyancy thus increasing the speed of our descent. At one hundred forty feet, I see the dark opening of the cave lurking below–instantly I feel a chill of dread and anticipation. At one hundred sixty-five feet, we reach the cave's craggy mouth and, as we swim hesitantly inside, we are immediately swallowed by a foreboding darkness.

One after another, the divers switch on their lights. Bright beams of pale light play haphazardly on the cave's narrowing walls throwing sharp-edged shadows that drift with our inward passage. There are no signs of life on the bare rock, but for the dark smear of algae patches and the occasional lobster sentinel with waving antenna peering from dark crevices. The cave's sides constrict to a small throat—it is here that we encounter the first whale skull.

No one knows why this family of four pilot whales died here, or even when, because all we see are the bare bones that are the only witnesses of the wreckage of their lives. Yet, the empty sockets staring from the bleached skull still depict the tragedy and loss that occurred in this dark underwater grave. This, the largest skull, is the bull; a mute guard to what waits within. I wonder if the family of whales fled inside the cave, while the father or protector (escort whale) turned to face a fierce predator such as an orca or great white shark.

Slowly we continue our dark journey inward several hundred feet. The walls continue to close-in as the cave now leads slowly upwards into a small cavern. The second skull appears suddenly resting on a bed of white sand. A flicker of movement inside the staring skull startles me, but then I realize it is just a tiny red fish fleeing our lights.

This is where the cow died. She had enough room to turn around, and like her mate, could have swum out...but apparently chose not to. The answer, I believe, waits above us...through a narrow stone chimney. Carefully I swim upwards into the constricted passage weaving my way though the tight confining rock. My air tanks catch several times and I feel my wetsuit snag and tear. A splash of cold water rushes into my suit, yet I do not know if the chill is from the cold water or the fear of apprehension for what I am about to see. I reach the top of the chimney that opens into a small chamber; the cave's dead-end. I am two-hundred-fifty feet into the foundation of the reef. Here, inside a tiny crypt, are two small skulls lying amongst a clutter of bones on a slender ledge. The skulls are side by side, as if still seeking mutual security—this is where the two young whales died.

Staring at the ghostly remains, I am sure that no threatening predator drove this family into the cave. Rather I believe it was the curiosity of the two young whales at play. Discovering the cave's broad mouth, they probably swam inside to investigate a potential mystery. Yet, as the cave's walls began to constrict they could only swim forward. Darkness would shroud their entry the further they progressed until there was a complete absence of light. With their acoustic abilities to see with sound they could continue, but at what level of impending panic? Behind them, their tails dislodge silt from the ceiling and numerous small particles from the cave's rocky floor. A swirling cloud of sediment would further obscure their way out, probably interfering with their acoustical ability to see. At the small inner chamber, they encounter the cramped shaft of the chimney that beacons upwards. Their instincts would shout that up leads to the ocean's surface and to life sustaining air. Fighting their way through the tight stone passage, they arrive at a dead end where there was not enough room for a whale to turn around, not even enough space for two small calves.

The bull and the cow probably could not refuse following the calves into the dark trap. The bull's bulk may have stopped him just inside the entrance, whereas the cow managed to squeeze all the way into the inner chamber. Though the adult pilot whales should have been able to swim out, I think they chose not to. Listening to the fading cries of the calves, they decided to stay...and that I think is how the family of four whales died.

As we live our lives, pursuing our hopes, dreams, goals and aspirations, we must bear in mind that death is always stalking us as well as the ones we love. Life cannot be lived frivolously. Tragedy potentially lurks around every corner. Yet, future tribulations also bear a special gift of encouragement; a stimulus of love that animates us to live as intensely as possible, to always try to seek out the newness and wonder of our existence.

There is another lesson here, which lies in the powerful love of family and for close friends. We need to cherish and nourish love. Love and only love makes each of us uniquely special and meaningful. Since life is so fragile, we cannot allow the clouding of love with needless anger and petty jealousies. We must always look to support our friends and loved ones, to be careful to part with feelings of goodwill, because none of us knows when or where tragedy will next take its dreadful toll.

I loved my big brother Jim. When I was a child, he was always there to protect me. I remember how I worried when he went off to Vietnam, then a year later it was his turn to worry as I went off to serve my country in that distant conflict. Between us, we made six tours to that war torn land, yet we came home physically unharmed. The personal fears we shared bound us closer than most brothers. Each of us married and started families of our own. Responsibilities often kept us apart, which made our times together that much more cherished. We always parted with a hug...and that is how I will always remember Jim, smiling as we stood arms around each other's shoulders.

Early in my new youth ministry, I was in New Hampshire, speaking to a hundred youth at a Pathfinder Camporee (a weekend camping event for Christian youth). Cindy and I had little money to spare for long distance telephone calls. Whenever I was on an extended East Coast tour, she knew that I would try to call her on Wednesday night and early Saturday afternoon. Right after doing a Saturday morning program for the youth, I went to a payphone and called Cindy.

"Hi Cindy," I say buoyantly as I hear her answer on the first ring.

"Stephen!" she shouts into the telephone, "I have been desperately waiting for you to call."

"Cindy, what has happened?" I clench the phone hard.

"Steve, I have something horrible to say. It's your brother Jim; he shot himself."

I collapse against the wooden wall where the payphone hangs.

"He did it with a handgun in his bedroom. He's dead!"

"Cindy," my voice breaks with a flood of emotion, "I can't talk... I'll call you back."

With shaking hands I hang up the telephone...I am feeling an overpowering sense of loss and very alone with a terrible tragedy riding heavily on my soul. The youth are still in their meetings as I flee into the woods and am there for several hours. I pray, cry and pray some more and then it comes upon me that I need to stay with the youth. Walking back towards the campground a payphone begins to ring. It is on a bathroom wall—it is not the telephone I used to call Cindy. I have no intention of answering that payphone, but I cannot help myself.

"Hello?" I say into the hand-piece still confused why I am answering a stranger's call at a horrible moment like this.

"Is Stephen Arrington there?" asks a familiar voice.

"This is Steve," I answer startled.

"Steve, it's Pastor White."

I am astonished. How did he get this number and what made him call as I was walking past? Charlie White is my pastor at the Paradise Seventh-day Adventist Church. He is calling to comfort me. I stand there listening to his soft reassuring voice, close my eyes and then begin to cry without inhibition. I slowly realize that there are people about me, youths and adults from the campground. They place supportive hands upon me and suddenly I am no longer alone. Then I realize that the children and their families are ministering to the youth minister. Is this why I feel that the Lord means for me to stay here?

Later, I call Cindy and get details for the funeral, which will not be for four more days. It means I can speak at a church tomorrow night to a different group of youth and also at a Christian academy on Monday. It is at the Sunday night church program that the reason for my delayed trip home takes on a whole new purpose and tragic meaning.

I am standing in a dark corridor, while the congregation watches a video I am presenting on whales. It is difficult to do my program with rampant emotions so burdening my soul and competing for my attention.

"Excuse me, Mr. Arrington," the voice coming out of the darkness is soft, not wanting to disturb.

I turn towards the child who has quietly come to stand next to me. She looks to be about fourteen years old. "I am sorry about your brother."

"Thank you," I do not know what else to say.

"They told us not to talk to you about it, but everybody knows."

"It's okay," I answer.

"The pastor's son killed himself," she says abruptly; the gentle voice is full of dread and great inner sadness. In the dark her eyes glisten, there are tears running down her cheeks. "It's why the pastor isn't here tonight. Sammy killed himself last week. We had the funeral on Friday." She is starting to cry, "He was my best friend."

"I am so sorry," I offer. I want to take her in my arms, but hesitate knowing that a man holding such a young girl in the darkness could be frowned upon. I look about for help. There are some ladies close by in the last row.

"Yesterday, I tried to kill myself too," she is sobbing loudly now, "I don't know why I am telling you this; I haven't told anyone else. Maybe it's because of you just losing your brother, only you can understand the pain."

Two of the lady's heads turn at the sound of a child in grief.

The young girl steps into my arms and places her head against my chest, "I just don't have the courage to kill myself...what should I do?" I feel her tears wetting my shirt.

"Ladies," I plea, "help."

The women rush to gather about her, one woman holds the weeping child in her arms and the other begins to rub her shoulders. More and more of her church family rushes to lend comfort; in seconds, I can no longer see her for the small crowd of adults. She stands now where I stood yesterday, in the arms of her church family. I step back and look with amazement. This is why the Lord impressed me to stay. Everyone knew about my grief and the grief of the pastor and his family, but what about the boy's closest friends? Apparently, no one knew how deeply the girl is grieving...and she is trying to face that anguish alone. With no one to counsel her, she was considering suicide, a way to chase after her lost friend.

So is my word that goes out from my mouth: It will not return to me empty, but will accomplish what I desire and achieve the purpose for which I sent it. Isaiah 55:11

A week after my brother's funeral, I seek out Pastor Charles White in his office.

"Pastor White," I ask, "how did you get the number for that payphone in New Hampshire?"

He looks at me full of compassion, "I don't know."

"Pastor White, this is important," I urge. "My brother killed himself on a Thursday night. I didn't call Cindy until Saturday noon. When she told me Jim was dead, I couldn't talk and hung up the telephone. I didn't tell her that I was at a campground in New Hampshire."

Charlie stares at me compassionately and then gently says, "Steve, I have absolutely no memory of how I got that telephone number," he pauses, "but I do know a divine appointment when one happens."

In my heart, and in my future, there is a huge emptiness where a great loss now resides. Fortunately, I am at peace with my memories of Jim. Our love is a cement that keeps us together always. It is a love unclouded by regrets. It allows me to go on with my life while Jim now sleeps in the arms of the Lord.

Knowing true peace in life is not an easy task. It takes constant toil and real awareness to make the most of our brief existence on this planet. We must treasure our lives and the lives of those around us. For no one knows what the future holds. Life is a mystery and security is easily wiped away.

"Although the world is full of suffering, it is full also of the overcoming of it, " Helen Keller

Author with Captain Jacques Cousteau

*"One can never consent to creep when one feels
an impulse to soar,"* Helen Keller

Chapter 52

PARADISE, CALIFORNIA, JUNE 25, 1997

S OMEONE ONCE said that the forties are the old age of childhood. The
realization that in the fall, I will begin my fourth decade laps at
my consciousness like an approaching ocean tide. Yet the thought
is a pleasing one. It seems amazing that I have made it this far—
let alone that I am not missing any limbs or showing visible scars.
Often I look back over the years and wonder at all the adventures
crammed into a thus far very busy life, yet now my thoughts are for
the future. I want my soon-to-be middle-aged years...now that is
a strange thought for me to be considering...to be as full of challenge and adventure as my youth. All my life I have tried to achieve
one hundred percent commitment in my endeavors. Anything less
is a conscious forfeiting of otherwise realizable opportunities. It is a
principle that follows me still and leads towards a promising future.
Certainly, I run a little slower and not quite as far, but my mind remains quick and agile. Growing older is something I look forward
to with great anticipation. With age comes the intellectual gift of
wisdom tempered with the vibrant spirit of the human experience.
Many people claim that life is too short. I believe that a fully lived

life is long and rewarding. With age, the focus of a person shifts to a higher plane of thought and to a deeper expression of love. Yes, I will embrace age, but I will also strive to keep my body agile and athletic.

Wisdom is supreme; therefore get wisdom. Though it cost all you have, get understanding. Proverbs 3:7

Glancing at a mirror in the weight room where I am working out, I notice a young man laboring with a thought. He is standing before the dumbbell rack trying to decide which weights to pick-up…heavy or heavier. I am at the other end of the rack where the lighter weights rest. Something he noticed earlier with a smirk as he checked-out his biceps in the mirror. I guess he finds my lighter weights amusing. Using thirty-five pound dumbbells, I am doing three-fifths. It is a basic shoulder exercise, a standing over-head military press with palms facing forward and slightly above my shoulders. I slowly press the weights upwards until my arms are almost fully extended. It takes about two seconds for the lift and then I lower them even more slowly stopping slightly above my shoulders before repeating the slow-paced exercise. The key is to limit the exercise to the middle three-fifths of the military dumb-bell press. Doing the movement slowly works the muscles harder and allows me to focus on correct posture throughout each repetition. Lighter weight ensures that I do not break form and over-tax my lower back muscles, which is how injuries often occur.

The youth, he is in his early twenties, makes his selection. It is interesting that he chooses seventy-pound dumbbells. Exactly twice the weight I am lifting. It gets even more amusing when he decides to mimic my shoulder exercise. His technique assures maximum attention from everyone else in the gym. This is because he grunts loudly as he uses his whole body to drive the weights upwards before smashing them together at the top of the movement and then quickly lets them drop towards his shoulders so he can use the momentum to drive the dumbbells upwards again for another ear-shattering *clack*. He powers out a set of three repetitions really getting his lower back and legs into the last upward movement and then slams the dumbbells back into the rack. He grins at himself in the mirror and casts a sideward glance at me before shuffling over to the squat rack. I am watching him industriously piling forty-five-pound-wheel-weights onto the heavy bar when my thoughts are echoed by Jack who is standing off to one side, "We won't be seeing much of him in the gym for long."

Jack is in his late sixties, a retired cinematographer, who rides a Harley-Davidson motorcycle and is a gym regular. Jack shakes his head again, "That kid is a disaster looking for a place to happen."

I smile and nod while focusing on my last two repetitions of another set of three-fifths. The youth is carrying about thirty extra pounds in his gut and is wearing sports braces on both of his knees. He is an obvious candidate for the debilitating symptoms of an early old age, which is already beginning to wear on him. He just doesn't know it yet. The large gut puts added strain on his lower back so he wears a weightlifter's belt to support his underdeveloped lumbar and erectus muscles. For every extra pound of body weight he carries it places the equivalent of four added pounds of stress on his already damaged knees when he walks downhill or runs. His posture is poor, his stride heavy and ponderous. I do not doubt that Jack can out run and out swim him for speed and distance. Yet Jack is three times the youth's age. The young man in question notices us watching him so he makes a big deal of his squat routine. The heavy bar resting on his shoulders lacks a foam cover so the metal bar is grinding directly on his fragile neck bones. "No," I answer Jack, "I don't think he will be here very long either."

The way a person moves is an autobiography of their life.
Anonymous

It would be nice to offer the young man a little serious advice, but from his obvious attitude, it would not be well received. There are many ways to be destructive with one's body. Improper exercise,

junk food and consuming other hollow calories, a bad attitude, laziness, a lack of clean air and water, a poor self-image, bad hygiene
habits, etc., all contribute to destroying the quality of a person's
past, present and future life. The past plays a role in who we are
today and who we are today determines what we will most be like in
the future. Personally, I want to be an active senior citizen, a state
of mind that is still somewhere out in the distant future no matter
what statistics said about my age. I want to write books, produce
videos, and visit exotic lands as well as paddle canoes, swim down
rivers with mask and fins, hike up mountains, do off-terrain biking,
surf, snow ski, and indulge in a multitude of other sports. I want
adventure, challenge and a variety of personal quests to be an inte-
gral part of my entire lifespan. With three young children growing
up in our household, my wife Cindy and I are assured that we will
do all of these activities at warp speed. With these lofty goals in
mind, I make a daily commitment to do everything to the very best
of my ability. Childhood dreams are the foundation for adult realities even for senior citizens. Meanwhile I am content to see myself
as a grown-up youth facing the old age of childhood.

Driving home from the gym in my wife's jeep, I am thinking
that life is pretty darn terrific. Rolling down the window to take
advantage of a cool morning breeze, I smell the fresh scent of
redwoods and pine trees. I live in a little mountain town called
Paradise. Our small community sprawls across a broad ridge in
the Northern California woods. Resting near the foot of the Sierra
Nevada Mountain Range we get just enough snow in the winter to
build a snowman or two, but it usually it does not last more than a
couple of days. Right now, I am not even thinking about snow, this
is the third day of summer, it is 7:00 a.m. and it is promising to be
a glorious day. I see puffy white clouds drifting in a deep blue sky.
The towering redwoods and evergreen pines are laced with dew
that captures and reflects the morning light. Rounding a bend in
the narrow road, I slow to allow a frisky gray squirrel the right-of-
away. With its tail held high the squirrel races across the blacktop,
then charges up a dogwood tree. From the safety of a low branch, it

pauses to chatter at the jeep.

I am already looking forward to my next gym workout. Turning on the radio, I anticipate music instead, I hear a newscaster solemnly announcing that Captain Jacques Yves Cousteau died of pneumonia this morning in France. Instantly my buoyant mood crashes. My boyhood hero and friend for over five years is abruptly gone. Captain Cousteau has had such a vibrant impact upon my life and I am already missing him deeply. In our few private conversations, he revealed some very simple truths to me that I will always hold very dear. One of them is that he was never bored. He felt that activity was the best tonic available and that the world was miraculous. He said that when he looked at a rock he did not see a simple stone, but rather the product of a volcano or of heaven. What a masterful way of thinking.

In a daze, I continue driving with a wealth of memories flashing through my mind. Surprisingly, I begin to think about my father… the man I knew so little about. My father and mother became parents at the very young age of sixteen. I now know that my father did not want children. Maybe he felt that my older brother and I had stolen his own childhood. In our house when I was growing up my father strictly enforced his golden rule. When he came home from work, which was usually after dinner, my brother and I were not to be seen or heard. We would seek refuge in our room or simply go outside and play. I desperately wanted a father who cared, someone who would occasionally hug me and teach me how to throw a knuckleball. Without his guidance or direction in my life, I grew up on my own and would later make many avoidable mistakes. Without the love of family, youths and young adults are far more subject to error. In prison, I wanted to become a good person again. I knew that one day I would walk out that prison gate and I did not want all my time behind bars to be wasted. I also knew that somewhere out in the future the woman I would marry was waiting. In prison, I began to polish the metal of myself. Less than three years after leaving prison, I met and fell instantly in love with Cindy.

Cindy's and my fourth date was a moment not to be forgotten.

She was taking me to meet her parents. As we stepped through the front door, I saw something in their living room that boggled my mind a small trampoline. In this house, children were encouraged to play inside. Cindy had grown up with love and caring nourishment. I have to confess that I did not just fall in love with Cindy, I fell in love with her whole family. When we were married a year later, it was her stepfather, a retired missionary pastor, who performed the service. In our family, when it rains we allow our children to ride their bikes inside the house. It's okay, it is an old house that we are slowly remodeling. They're little bikes, one with training wheels and the smallest is actually a tricycle. Going from the kitchen, into the front room, then down the hall to the master bedroom, through the bathroom and back up the hall is a perfect figure eight. On the door jams, low down, there are scratches from the training wheels. Ours is a happy household usually in a state of noisy semi-disarray. It is at the opposite end of the parental discipline that I grew up under…and I love it.

Driving Cindy's jeep down our street, I see Walt, my father-in-law, who is turning eighty, mowing his front lawn. Ruthie, my mother-in-law, is tending her flowers. Cindy and I live next door. As I pull into our driveway, I pause to watch Cindy chasing our three children in a game of tag. Everyone is laughing. Stetcyn Leigh our oldest daughter, almost five years old, runs to the fence and yells, "Come on daddy chase me." So, I do.

Author's note: our oldest daughter's name is a combination of Stephen-loves-Cynthia; Ste + cyn.

"Children are gleeful barbarians," Joseph Morgenstern

Illustration by Andy Charles
Logo for the Dream Machine Foundation

When a man's ways are pleasing to the Lord, he makes even his enemies to be at peace with him. Proverbs 16:17

Chapter 53

PARADISE, CALIFORNIA, JUNE 25, 2007

WHEN WE invite Jesus Christ into our life, we begin a dramatic inward journey of transformation. We walk a path that leads to spiritual growth, understanding and enlightenment. Along the way we will encounter other paths, but the one upon which we should journey is discerned by its landmarks, which are truth, love and forgiveness. On this path, life's complex questions are resolved with simple, yet life expanding, answers. Though the answers are straightforwardly determined when weighed against the benchmark of Christ's teachings, they are not always easy to follow. When confronted with life-wilting personal tragedies it may be terribly difficult to see God's hand reaching out in love, yet I cannot imagine trying to face personal tragedy alone without His perfect love.

Five years ago, I was confronted with a life-altering event… maybe I should say an almost life-ending event. It happened at a birthday party, my son's birthday party. I was sick, very sick and had been for a week. I was in bed feeling miserable, losing fluids in all directions and not feeling particularly social, when Cindy walked into the bedroom.

"I need your help," urges Cindy.

"I'm sick," I groan.

"It's Chase's sixth birthday party, get out of bed." Cindy places her hand on my forehead, her palm and fingers feel cool and comforting. "You're still running a fever, are you drinking enough water?"

"Yes," I answer wearily not knowing that I am wrong...dead wrong.

"Look, just go blowup the balloons then you can come back to bed."

"Okay," I groan pulling back the sheets and slowly raise my weary carcass. I stand in one place for a few seconds waiting for a wave of dizziness to pass. On my way into the front room, I make a necessary stop in the bathroom—it is not pretty and you do not want to know the details.

Fifteen minutes later, I am again feeling dizzy as I glance at the growing number of gaily-colored balloons all about me. When Cindy arrives with a cup of hot tea to restore my spirits she finds me on the floor.

A neighbor, the wife of my physician, took me to the emergency room. I did not know it then, but her husband, Dr. Thorpe was on duty at the hospital. She called ahead on her cell phone to advise him that we were on our way and that it was a dire emergency. Cindy was stuck at home with a growing horde of five and six year-old children with no available adults to oversee the party. She was trying to call in re-enforcements when the business telephone line rang. Cindy grabbed it hoping that she might recruit a volunteer...instead, she heard Doctor Thorpe urgently say, "Cindy, get up here now, I'm losing him."

In the ER, laying on a gurney, it is a startling thing to hear a doctor say something like that. He is talking about me...that he is losing me! My mind is not working very well. I had gotten the names of all three of my children right, but could not remember their ages. I glance over at the two male nurses trying repeatedly to get an IV started. I am so dehydrated that my veins are collapsing.

They are on their seventeenth attempt.

"Let me try," says Doctor Thorpe.

Another doctor has entered the emergency room and leans over me. I glance up at him. My vision is blurred, but I recognize this man as my mind begins to wrestle with a powerful thought. In our little town of Paradise, I get along with everyone I know. I'm an amiable kind of guy. There is just one exception…and he is leaning over me. I am imagining what it would be like if the last person I see on this planet is someone I dislike. It is not a happy thought and later it would become a powerful argument for my being more aware and forgiving regarding out feelings and attitudes about other people.

"Got it," yells Doctor Thorpe. He turns to one of the nurses, "Full drip, get the whole bag of saline into him as fast as possible. I'm going to try to get another IV started in the other arm."

I glance down at my arm, then up at the bag of saline, and see the fluid dripping life into my veins. I look again for the ER Doctor, but he is gone now leaving me with a deeper understanding of what it means to be a Christian. Cindy arrives a few minutes later; she is all eyes and full of worry.

I spent three days recovering in the hospital. I had contracted viral meningitis. The general consensus was West Nile virus probably delivered by a low-flying mosquito in Indiana. At one point, my cerebral pressure was almost double normal. As I lay in the hospital bed recovering, I spent a lot of time in deep prayer. I was thanking God. Thanking him that I was not still sitting in a prison cell for my past criminal foolishness. Had I gotten the full forty-five year prison sentence the prosecutor wanted, I could still be inside a jail cell. Instead, the Lord has blessed me with multiple ministries, a life full of adventure and a wonderful family. Having people care so much about you gives value and incredible meaning to life.

I read and re-read the Book of Matthew, specifically chapter 18, which is known to many as a call to youth ministry. In Matthew 18:3, Jesus tells us that unless we are like little children we will not enter the Kingdom of Heaven. Little children give their love and faith completely, unhindered with complete sincerity and devotion. It is a lesson that we adults struggle with that is best taught by children.

In Matthew 18:6, we are told that anyone who places a stumbling block in the path of a child it is better that that person have a millstone hung around their neck and that they be cast in the depths of the sea. In our modern society, this is a tough time to be a child. They are facing life-changing choices and the messages they are getting are very mixed up; particularly regarding sex, drugs, alcohol and social responsibility. More than one third of school children do not graduate from high school, in some communities the dropout rate is as high as sixty percent, and only sixteen percent of public school students go on to college. Four out of five children will spend part of their childhood in a single parent household. Since 1957, violent crime has increased four-fold and it is getting worse on the streets and in our neighborhoods.

In Matthew 18:12 Jesus says if you have a hundred sheep and one goes missing that you must go look for the one that is lost. With so many children dropping out of school, I wonder who is mentoring them? Youth daytime crime is on the upswing. Children join gangs because the gang members promise to be their family; to give them the love and the respect they crave. Suicide is now the number two killer of teenagers and young adults in America and the fastest growing rate of suicide per capita is amongst children between the ages of ten and fourteen.

In Matthew 25:31-46, Jesus tells us that when we help others that we are helping Him and there will be a special placed reserved for us in Heaven. He also says that if we as Christians fail this trust that the fate for us is far worse than the millstone hung around the neck. Christians have a sacred trust and a God-given responsibility to help others. It is this and our love for Jesus Christ that gives our life its true meaning and purpose. Without direction, we are lost in a world awash in sin and corruption. With the Cousteau Society, my life was full of adventure and it was an important stepping-stone on my path to helping others. However, as a youth minister my life has taken on true meaning and purpose; it gives extraordinary value to each day. In my hospital bed, I continued to pray and gave thanks that through Jesus, I live with unending hope. "And hope does not disappoint..."

At our church, I sought out the ER doctor that I disliked, told him my feelings and said that I had forgiven him for the wrong that had so troubled me. I also asked him for permission to write about my feelings regarding him.

> *"I know of no more encouraging fact than the unquestioned*
> *ability of a man to elevate his life by conscious endeavor,"*
> Henry David Thoreau

What has happened and is happening to me is completely surprising, particularly when one remembers that I am an ex-felon...a convicted drug smuggler. What follows is a continuing story of real-life miracles, unchained adventure and the joy of witnessing God's love in action.

For years, Cindy and I have shared a dream to open a youth camp where we could teach young people to scuba dive. We particularly want to introduce physically challenged children to the weightless wonders of the underwater world. Imagine a young person who has never walked or run like other children. Now see that handicapped youth temporarily freed from the burdens of gravity, braces and wheelchairs as he or she floats or flies in slow motion above a tropical reef swarming with colorful fish that pulsate with ocean surge and tide. That is a multi-life changing event that we want to be a part of and it is on the verge of becoming a reality.

In February of 1998, I went to Fiji to begin a modest medical missionary work. My plan was quite simple. Many people have asked Cindy and I to take them diving in one of the better underwater locations in the world. I immediately thought of Fiji where the people are so friendly and because Jean-Michel Cousteau has a four-star diving resort there. I figured that we would go diving in the morning when the ocean is its calmest, and then in the afternoon, we could volunteer our services at the local government hospital. While at the Cousteau resort, I heard about a Christian academy about fifty miles away that was having financial difficulties. I was told that to help pay off their debt they were interested in starting a youth camp. *A Christian youth camp only fifty miles from Jean-Michel's resort?* Intrigued, I went to investigate.

Unknown to me on that very day the Fiji Mission was taking a vote to sell the academy to eliminate the school's debt. Rumors reached Vatuvonu School that a multi-millionaire American was en route to save the school. An elder from Vatuvonu went to the Fiji Mission to ask them to delay the vote. Imagine their disappointment when instead of a multi-millionaire all they got was a self-supporting, lay youth minister on a shoestring budget.

The Fijian pastor looked at me in my shorts, slightly torn T-shirt and flip-flops. I watched hope drain from his eyes as he sadly said, "We are standing on air and need a miracle to save our school."

So, we prayed together, a Fijian bush pastor and an ex-felon standing on a dirt road in a remote corner of a rural island in the South Pacific. I then asked him to gather the students while I set up my video camera. My plan was to ask the children to sing a song to help save their school, which I hoped to show at churches in America.

As the children gather, grades K through eight, I look at their excited faces, then I say, much to my surprise, "Children, I need you to sing a song that will change the world."

My words catch me by complete off guard. These children live in the rural part of a remote island near the end of a dirt road without electricity or telephones. How are they going to change the world? I look at the children whispering eagerly amongst themselves in Fijian. They are enthusiastically discussing something one of the younger girls has said. She offers me a beautiful eight-year-old smile as I press the record button on the video camera. The children's voices are loud and clear as they begin to sing the most astonishing words in English, "Jesus is a winner man, a winner man, a winner man, Jesus is a winner man, He wins all the time…"

I stare at the singing children in amazement. On the day their school, which has been a Christian academy since the 1930's, is going up for sale, they have the faith to sing that Jesus is a winner man and that He wins all the time.

I have now had the pleasure of showing that video clip to millions of people worldwide on Satellite television and in hundreds of churches. The faith of those barefoot children singing near the end of a dirt road on a rural island in the South Pacific is actually helping to change the world through hope.

Author's note: at the same time that this book is being released, Cindy and I our starting a weekly half-hour television program "High on Adventure" to air worldwide on satellite and cable television (also available on the web at LLBN.TV). Those Fijian children signing "Jesus is a Winner Man," has now aired on various Christian networks over fifty times.

Several days later at the Fiji Mission, I asked for permission to try to save the school. The president first considered me just another meddlesome foreign white man interfering with his mission's financial struggles. "Mr. Arrington," he said warily, "we actually tried to close that school four years ago; we just can't carry their debt. Volunteers have been keeping it going and that means the debt keeps growing. I don't want to close that school, but we just don't have a choice."

I continue to press my hopeful arguments as I notice his gaze drifting beyond me. I think I have lost him—actually, he is reading his own handwritten sign on the wall behind me. It says, "Ours is a Big God." The sign moves his heart. "Okay, Mr. Arrington," he sighs, "I'll give you a simple test."

I lean forward eagerly; I like tests of faith.

"You've got one month to raise fifteen hundred Fijian dollars and send it to the mission. That is ten percent of the school's current yearly debt. You do that and I'll trust you to raise the rest over the next year."

Arriving back stateside, I did an evening program at a church in Chico, California, attended by about thirty adults and twenty or so children. I talked about the faith of those island children then showed the video of them singing *Jesus is a Winner Man*. We raised eight hundred and fifty-six dollars. The significance of that amount did not click in my mind until I did the conversion rate; we had raised just over fifteen hundred Fijian dollars. The next day I bought a postal order at the post office. The cost of the postal order and the international postage left just a little change. I fingered the few remaining coins in my pocket from the offering amazed how the Lord concerns Himself with the details.

Cindy and I started a non-profit interdenominational Christian foundation (Dream Machine Foundation) to save the school. It took less than a year to pay off the school's debt. In that same year, over three hundred missionaries came from North America to Vatuvonu School to help rebuild the old debilitated structures. We also began to build a medical clinic and treated over three thousand patients before we even opened the clinic doors. *To see our new clinic opening in March 2008 visit www.dreammachinefoundation.com.*

For the official grand opening of the clinic, over a thousand Fijians led by six local chiefs came to attend the ceremony. The pastor and head elder at the school came to see me privately just before the activities were to begin.

"Mr. Arrington, we know you don't want to be personally acknowledged regarding the opening of the clinic," states the head elder.

I nod, my suspicions winding up. There had been talk of naming it the Arrington Clinic, which Cindy and I firmly opposed. We will name it the Buca Bay Clinic, I insisted. Naming the clinic after its location meant everyone would know where to find it; a sensible choice.

"The chiefs are unanimous in this," he cautions, "to refuse would be to dishonor them."

"To refuse what?"

"They are going to make you an honorary chief."

"What?"

"The clinic, it means so much to the whole community," the elder smiles, his big white teeth are bright against his dark skin, "it is a lifelong commitment being an honorary chief, it means you will always be tied to our families and to the future of Buca Bay."

I nod my understanding and am quietly amazed at how God so often shows us that all is possible through Him. No one is going to be calling me chief, nor would I allow it. Yet, to think something lost because of my failure, then to have it independently reappear three times after I entered His service is a little miracle on a personal scale.

Two of the children that arrived at our clinic during the opening celebration were suffering from life-threatening heart problems. Two hospitals in California, Loma Linda University Medical Center and the St. Mary's Regional Medical Center in Victorville, California, volunteered to provide free surgeries for both of the children. Jean-Michel Cousteau helped to arrange free airfare for them aboard Air Pacific Airlines. With the ushering in of the new millennium, I watched two young people, a five-year-old girl and a fifteen-year-old boy running with other children. Instead of contending with a bleak medical condition, these two youngsters now have a bright shining future.

The Dream Machine Foundation would sponsor six Fijians to the United States for life and limb saving surgeries over the next eight years. My favorite is a ten-year-old boy who had fallen out of a mango tree. He broke his left leg leaving parts of the bone protruding from the skin. His parents could not afford regular bus trips to the government hospital. After five months, aseptic bone necrosis had set in...the doctor at the government hospital said the leg had to come off to save the boy's life. Instead his cousin brought him to our little bush clinic. What are the chances that the child would arrive at the clinic when we had the only visiting orthopedic surgeon there that year? He did two emergency surgeries in Fiji with a follow-up procedure in Indiana. One year later, I gave the now twelve-year-old boy a twenty-yard head start then sent the whole school racing after him...he outran them all.

These wonders are happening because people love Jesus Christ and they want to do good work for Him and for their fellowman. The Dream Machine Foundation has acquired one hundred acres next to the school where we are now building a Swiss Family Robinson type of youth camp and mission facility. There are towering hardwoods in which we will build bamboo tree houses. On our property is a bamboo forest with some trunks six inches thick. Adjoining our camp is a seven hundred-fifty acre property where our partner, the Natuvu Creek Foundation, is building a state-of-the-art eye and dental clinic to replace our aging facility. I am writing these words at Los Angeles International Airport waiting for my flight to Fiji to film the final construtcion of this new medical facility, which will eventually become a hospital. Currently we are having discussions with three California state universities to put in a marine research facility. Jean-Michel Cousteau has agreed to be the director of our physically challenged youth-diving program. Ten miles from our camp is the *White Wall,* part of Rainbow Reef, one of the top ten dive sites in the world. In eight years, the Dream Machine Foundation has sponsored over seventeen hundred missionaries to Fiji. At the youth camp we will offer scuba diving, snorkeling, sailing, horseback riding, river rafting and we will teach survival skills with Fijian guides; all accessible to physically-challenged, as well as to your average enthusiastic youths. As I reflect on what I am writing, it suddenly occurs to me that Captain Jacques Yves Cousteau died ten years ago today. I am sure that he would be pleased at the direction my life has taken since leaving his employ.

In my writings, I have constantly referred to the fact that childhood dreams are the foundations for adult realities. As a child growing up watching the fantasy world of Walt Disney, I often daydreamed about having my own tree house in the South Pacific. As an adult about to enter my sixties, I am seeing that dream come true and my children are going to help to build it.

> *"If you want someone to care, capture their minds and their hearts,"* Roy O. Disney (brother of Walt Disney)

When Jesus preached the Sermon on the Mount, He spoke about blessings using the Greek word *Makarios,* which also means righteous living, which for me equates to happiness. I now understand that Jesus wants us to be happy and to enjoy a blessed life, which is best achieved by being of service to others. I remember the tormented soul that I harbored in a prison cell. Now as I think of all the blessings that the Lord has given me, one thought comes leaping to mind…to share what He has so freely given. It is why I write and travel across North America talking with youths at churches and public schools. No matter how big a problem seems we never have to face it alone when we have Christ in our hearts.

People constantly tell me that I have lived quite the adventurous life. I politely correct them…*I am living quite the adventurous life.* My past has better prepared me to live today with fullness and intensity, it is laying the path for tomorrow where adventures lurk and challenging quests await their discovery. My step is eager as I follow where the Lord is leading me next. I am happily striding into the future with Cindy, Stetcyn Leigh, Cheyenne Summer and Chase Greystoke Arrington and along with a little white Jack Russell Terrier named Sparky, but that is another story.

THE BEGINNING

"Try not to become a man of success, but rather try to become a man of value," Albert Einstein

To learn more about our work in Fiji or volunteer your services, please visit our web site at <u>www.dreammachinefoundation.com</u>. For inquires about Stephen Arrington's work with youth in churches and at public schools visit <u>www.drugsbite.com</u>.

EPILOGUE

WHERE ARE THEY NOW

1. Susan is happily married, has four boys and is now living in New Zealand.
2. Sam lives in San Diego, where he drives a city bus. He is still single and continues to surf every opportunity he gets. I repeatedly tell him that he needs a good wife to straighten him out and give meaning to his life.
3. Morgan Hetrick, after serving almost five years in prison, retired to Texas, where he later died in a private airplane accident. His funeral was attended by over five hundred people.
4. Gerald Scotti, resigned from the DEA and is now a criminal defense attorney.
5. James Walsh, the District Attorney who argued that I deserved a substantial sentence, thirty years, is now a friend and wrote the introduction to this book.
6. Judge Robert Takasugi is helping to sponsor my application for a Presidential Pardon.
7. Max Memerstein was arrested in 1986 because of incriminating evidence delivered by Morgan Hetrick and his sons. Because Max cooperated, he only severed twenty-five months before disappearing with his family into the witness protection system with a check from the United

States Government for seven hundred thousand dollars for his cooperation. The Medellin Cartel put a three million dollar bounty on his head. A book has been written on his story titled <u>The Man Who Made it Snow</u>. He testified on behalf of the government of the United States against Manuel Noriega, the ex-President of Panama, who is currently serving a life sentence in a Federal prison.

8. Scar Face was killed in Colombia in the ongoing drug war.

9. Twelve-year-old Pedro disappeared into the criminal underworld.

10. Ralph was released after spending six years in prison.

11. John Z. DeLorean, served a total of eight days in prison, was acquitted of all charges, lost his wife in a divorce and died in 2005 In New Jersey.

12. The author currently lives in Paradise, California with his wife Cindy and their three children. He continues to speak in public schools and at churches, while writing books and magazine articles and producing videos to encourage young people to strive for their dreams. Regarding having Stephen Arrington speak at your school or church visit <u>www.drugsbite.com</u>.

Drugs Bite

P.O. Box 3234
Paradise, **CA 95967**
Fax 530 876-9123
Web Site www.drugsbite.com
Email steve@drugsbite.com.

Item Description	Price	#	Total
#101 Extreme (Autobiography)	$24.00	___	$_____
#201 High On Adventure I (youth series)	$10.00	___	$_____
#202 High On Adventure II (youth series)	Sold out until Dec 08		
#203 High On Adventure III (youth series)	$10.00	___	$_____
#301 Out of the Night 3 Gold Medal DVD	$18.00	___	$_____
#302 Journey Into Darkness Silver Medal DVD	$18.00	___	$_____
#303 Treasures of the Undersea DVD	$18.00	___	$_____
#304 Treasures of the Universe DVD	$18.00	___	$_____
#305 Treasures of the African Savannah DVD	$18.00	___	$_____
#306 Talbot's Whale & Dolphin DVD	$18.00	___	$_____
#307 Project Fiji DVD	$18.00	___	$_____

S & H within the USA and Canada, media rate $4.00 Priority $8.00
International orders must go to www.drugsbite.com

Californians add 7.75% tax		$_____
	Total	$_____

Name and address:_____

_____

_____

Visa, MC or AE #_____

Exp _____Telephone #_____

Signature_____

Orders can also be placed on line at www.drugsbite.com
Discount available for wholesale orders.
Drugs Bite P.O. Box 3234, Paradise, CA 95967
Tel Orders & Fax 530 876-9123, Email steve@drugsbite.com